Lecture Notes in Computer Science 16514

Founding Editors

Gerhard Goos
Juris Hartmanis

Editorial Board Members

Elisa Bertino, *Purdue University, West Lafayette, IN, USA*
Wen Gao, *Peking University, Beijing, China*
Bernhard Steffen, *TU Dortmund University, Dortmund, Germany*
Moti Yung, *Columbia University, New York, NY, USA*

The series Lecture Notes in Computer Science (LNCS), including its subseries Lecture
Notes in Artificial Intelligence (LNAI) and Lecture Notes in Bioinformatics (LNBI),
has established itself as a medium for the publication of new developments in computer
science and information technology research, teaching, and education.

LNCS enjoys close cooperation with the computer science R & D community, the
series counts many renowned academics among its volume editors and paper authors, and
collaborates with prestigious societies. Its mission is to serve this international community by providing an invaluable service, mainly focused on the publication of conference
and workshop proceedings and postproceedings. LNCS commenced publication in 1973.

Gianluca Leone · Andrés Otero · Paola Busia ·
Paolo Meloni

Editors

Applied Reconfigurable Computing

Architectures, Tools, and Applications

22nd International Symposium, ARC 2026
Cagliari, Sardinia, Italy, April 8–10, 2026
Proceedings

 Springer

Editors
Gianluca Leone
Università degli Studi di Cagliari
Cagliari, Italy

Paola Busia
Università degli Studi di Cagliari
Cagliari, Italy

Andrés Otero
Universidad Politécnica de Madrid
Madrid, Spain

Paolo Meloni
Università degli Studi di Cagliari
Cagliari, Italy

ISSN 0302-9743   ISSN 1611-3349 (electronic)
Lecture Notes in Computer Science
ISBN 978-3-032-29364-0   ISBN 978-3-032-29365-7 (eBook)
https://doi.org/10.1007/978-3-032-29365-7

This Springer imprint is published by the registered company Springer Nature Switzerland AG
The registered company address is: Gewerbestrasse 11, 6330 Cham, Switzerland

If disposing of this product, please recycle the paper.

Preface

The 22nd International Symposium on Applied Reconfigurable Computing (ARC 2026) was held at Università degli Studi di Cagliari from April 8th to 10th, 2026. The 2026 edition of the symposium aimed to bring together researchers and practitioners in Applied Reconfigurable Computing, a cross-cutting field spanning several research and technology domains, including artificial intelligence, high-performance computing, digital signal processing, communications, control, and hardware security.

This year's technical program included 19 regular papers and 1 short paper, selected from 33 high-quality paper submissions originating from 14 countries worldwide. The accepted contributions investigate solutions for systems requiring enhanced computational efficiency, reduced latency, and adaptive hardware capability. The selection process was both competitive and rigorous: each submission received three to four double-blind expert reviews, with an average of 3.1 reviews per paper. The symposium also featured two special sessions, devoted to *Accelerating Physical AI with Event-Driven Reconfigurable Hardware for Neuromorphic Perception* and to *Collaborative Projects*, highlighting emerging architectures and applications in reconfigurable computing. The contributions presented during the special sessions are included as invited papers in these proceedings.

We sincerely thank all authors for their submissions, as well as the members of the Program Committee and the additional external reviewers, whose expertise and thoughtful feedback ensured the high quality of the technical program. We extend special thanks to Diana Göhringer (TU Dresden, Germany) and Dirk Koch (Heidelberg University, Germany) for their inspiring keynote presentations. We extend our gratitude to the Organizing Committee and the Steering Committee for their collective effort in making the symposium a success, and to the Dipartimento di Ingegneria Elettrica ed Elettronica for its generous sponsorship.

We hope that ARC 2026 fostered inspiring discussions contributing to future advancements in the field of reconfigurable computing.

Thank you for being part of ARC 2026.

April 2026

Gianluca Leone
Andrés Otero
Paola Busia
Paolo Meloni

Organization

General Chair

Paolo Meloni   University of Cagliari, Italy

Program Committee Chairs

Gianluca Leone   University of Cagliari, Italy
Andrés Otero   Universidad Politécnica de Madrid, Spain

Proceedings Chair

Paola Busia   University of Cagliari, Italy

Special Session Chairs

Collaborative Projects

Francesca Palumbo   University of Cagliari, Italy
Claudio Rubattu   University of Sassari, Italy

Workshop on Accelerating Physical AI with Event-Driven Reconfigurable Hardware for Neuromorphic Perception

Xabier Iturbe   IKERLAN, Spain

Program Committee

Hideharu Amano   Keio University, Japan
Nikolaos Bellas   University of Thessaly, Greece
João Bispo   University of Porto, Portugal
Vanderlei Bonato   University of São Paulo, Brazil
João Cardoso   University of Porto, Portugal

Luigi Carro	Universidade Federal do Rio Grande do Sul, Brazil
Ray Cheung	City University of Hong Kong, China
Daniel Chillet	University of Rennes, France
Roberto Giorgi	University of Siena, Italy
Diana Göhringer	TU Dresden, Germany
Frank Hannig	Friedrich-Alexander-Universität Erlangen-Nürnberg, Germany
Christian Hochberger	TU Darmstadt, Germany
Michael Huebner	Brandenburg University of Technology Cottbus, Germany
Xabier Iturbe	IKERLAN, Spain
Krzysztof Kepa	GE Global Research, USA
Georgios Keramidas	Aristotle University of Thessaloniki, Greece
Paris Kitsos	University of the Peloponnese, Greece
Tomasz Kryjak	AGH University of Science and Technology, Poland
Gianluca Leone	University of Cagliari, Italy
Francesco Leporati	University of Pavia, Italy
Paolo Meloni	University of Cagliari, Italy
Antonio Miele	Politecnico di Milano, Italy
Horacio Neto	INESC-ID/IST/Universidade de Lisboa, Portugal
Andrés Otero	Universidad Politécnica de Madrid, Spain
Francesca Palumbo	University of Cagliari, Italy
Nuno Paulino	INESC TEC, Portugal
Marco Platzner	University of Paderborn, Germany
Francesco Regazzoni	University of Amsterdam, the Netherlands, and Università della Svizzera italiana, Switzerland
Martin Rönnbäck	Frontgrade Gaisler, Sweden
Claudio Rubattu	University of Sassari, Italy
Marco Domenico Santambrogio	Politecnico di Milano, Italy
Matteo Antonio Scrugli	University of Cagliari, Italy
Ioannis Sourdis	Chalmers University of Technology, Sweden
George Theodoridis	University of Patras, Greece

Additional Reviewers

Eduardo Honorato	Tiago Santos
Piotr Korycki	Luís Sousa
Muhammad Tahir Rafiq	Emanuele Torti

NimbleAI: Enabling Europe's Strategic Sovereignty through Neuromorphic Technology

Xabier Iturbe

IKERLAN, Arrasate-Mondragón, Spain
`xiturbe@ikerlan.es`

Abstract. Neuromorphic technology enables ultra-efficient event-driven perception inspired by biological senses, unlocking major advantages for low-power and real-time edge and physical AI. The NimbleAI Horizon Europe project advances this paradigm while reinforcing EU strategic autonomy, delivering a European neuromorphic silicon stack of innovative sensors and processors. Integrated with scalable in-memory computing engines, NimbleAI achieves high computational efficiency and adaptability across diverse applications. This paper highlights the main technology components produced in NimbleAI and outlines opportunities for transitioning from research to real-world impact, fostering adoption by industry and the scientific community.

Keywords: Dynamic Vision Sensing (DVS) · Spiking Neural Networks (SNNs) · Physical AI · EU technology sovereignty.

1 Neuromorphic Technology

Neuromorphic technology, inspired by the architecture and event-driven dynamics of the human brain, represents a fundamental shift in computing [1]. By combining sensing, memory and compute in a single architecture and leveraging sparse event-based processing, neuromorphic systems achieve significantly higher energy efficiency, adaptive learning, and real-time responsiveness than traditional von Neumann processors. Unlike conventional architectures, which rely on continuous and brute-force computation, exemplified by GPUs, neuromorphic systems process data only when events occur, enabling more targeted, efficient and intelligent computation. These unique capabilities position neuromorphic technology as a critical enabler for edge and physical AI, offering substantial commercial and strategic opportunities [2].

Europe is rapidly emerging as a hub for neuromorphic innovation. Companies such as Prophesee, Innatera, SpiNNcloud, Neuronova and Neuromorphyx are translating neuromorphic principles into commercial products, from event-based vision sensors to scalable processing architectures. These efforts are supported by major EU funding programs, including Horizon Europe, EIC instruments and EIB investments, enabling startups and consortia to bridge the gap from research to market-ready solutions. Building on this strong European technology base, strategic support in neuromorphic computing is crucial to ensure technological sovereignty, reduce dependence on non-EU infrastructure and safeguard the EU's economic and security interests.

The NimbleAI project (https://doi.org/10.3030/101070679) exemplifies this strategic approach. With €10 million in EU funding and 19 partners across eight countries, NimbleAI is developing integrated neuromorphic sensing and processing architectures optimized for edge deployment. By leveraging CMOS-compatible designs and bringing together leading European technology companies and research centers, NimbleA seeks a rapid pathway from lab to market.

2 Main Results and Impact of NimbleAI

The NimbleAI project strengthens Europe's strategic autonomy by pioneering a new generation of neuromorphic sensors and processors, integrated as standalone components within a prototyping and development platform that enables deployment in real-world applications [3].

At the sensing level, NimbleAI has developed two breakthrough types of event-based Dynamic Vision Sensors (DVS):

- **Foveated DVS**: emulates human retinal processing by dynamically allocating high-resolution sensing to selected regions of interest (ROIs) while simultaneously capturing the full field of view in low-resolution. Designed by CSIC in 180-nm technology, the chip integrates 384×304 physical pixels, which are grouped into low-resolution macro-pixels by default and selectively ungrouped on demand to capture ROIs in high resolution, reducing the generated data volume. The digital foveation controller, designed by Ikerlan and implemented on an FPGA, receives ROI positions, dynamically adjusts pixel grouping on the sensor, and outputs time-stamped events as separate low- and high-resolution streams.
- **Light-field DVS**: inspired by insect compound vision, enables instantaneous depth perception without the computational burden of traditional stereo or LiDAR systems. The current prototype builds on the commercial Prophesee IMX636 DVS combined with a Raytrix microlens array to generate light-field data in an event-based format: *event-fields*. Specialized event-driven stereo-matching engines have been designed and implemented on an FPGA by Ikerlan, creating the world's first monocular passive event-based 3D sensor. This sensor delivers 3D perceptual insights with microsecond latency, minimal data rates, and robust performance across challenging lighting conditions, paving the way for compact, low-power and high-speed 3D perception suitable for energy-constrained neuromorphic robotic platforms.

These sensors are complemented by two specialized event-driven processors, designed to efficiently process DVS sparse event streams with ultra-low latency and power consumption.

- **SENeCA**: is a multi-core neuromorphic processor designed by Imec in 12-nm technology to run event-driven Spiking Neural Networks (SNNs). Operating at up to 500

MHz, the chip combines multiple processing cores integrating RISC-V controllers and neurosynaptic units. It delivers 164 GOPS of compute, 784 TB/s internal memory bandwidth and 30 GB/s inter-core bandwidth, enabling efficient execution of small and sparse AI models at under 1 W, making it well-suited for energy-constrained neuromorphic robotic platforms.

– **Selective attention processor**: Implements a software-defined SNN in silicon to process the low-resolution event stream from the foveated DVS and identify ROIs. This tapeout-ready design performs saliency-based detection using a two-layer SNN with a winner-take-all output, identifying ROIs within milliseconds.

To further enhance flexibility and compatibility with mainstream AI frameworks, NimbleAI integrates a heterogeneous processing engine combining multiple EU technologies: Codasip RISC-V cores for general-purpose control, Menta eFPGA fabric for reconfigurable acceleration, and CEA in-memory computing blocks for reduction of data-movement. This hybrid design has been prototyped on an FPGA running real-world eye-tracking and autonomous driving workloads.

NimbleAI's sensing and processing components are planned for integration into a 3D-stacked silicon architecture. Currently, they are implemented as standalone chips on an FPGA-powered PCB prototype that emulates high-bandwidth through-silicon via interconnections of the future 3D stack, albeit at reduced speed and limited parallelism. This prototype, supported by Linux-based software, enables evaluation of NimbleAI technology in real-world applications. The project has also explored efficient allocation of the sensing and processing components within a 3D-stacked chip using Monozoukuri's 3D EDA Genio tool.

Acknowledgments. NimbleAI has received funding from the EU's Horizon Europe Research and Innovation programme (Grant Agreement 101070679), and by the UK Research and Innovation (UKRI) under the UK government's Horizon Europe funding guarantee (Grant Agreement 10039070).

References

1. Kudithipudi, D., et al.: Neuromorphic computing at scale. Nature **637**, 801–812 (2025). https://doi.org/10.1038/s41586-024-08253-8
2. Yole Group: Neuromorphic Computing. Memory and Sensing (2024). https://www.yolegroup.com/product/report/neuromorphic-computing-memory-and-sensing-2024/, last accessed 2026/03/23.
3. Iturbe, X., et al.: Neuromorphic vision modalities in the NimbleAI 3D chip. In: Proceedings of the 61st ACM/IEEE Design Automation Conference (2024)

Contents

Architectures and Accelerators

Softcores and Optimization

Neural Networks and Artificial Intelligence

Design Tools

Applications

**Accelerating Physical AI with Event-driven Reconfigurable Hardware
for Neuromorphic Perception**

Collaborative Projects

Architectures and Accelerators

Fit for the Edge: Resource and Power-Efficient Multi-stream Anomaly Detection on FPGAs

Dragos Lazea[1(✉)], Tudor Ticudean[1], Tudor Coroian[1], Anca Hangan[1], and Zsolt István[2]

[1] Computer Science Department, TU Cluj-Napoca, Cluj-Napoca, Romania
{dragos.lazea,tudor.coroian,anca.hangan}@cs.utcluj.ro
[2] Systems Group, TU Darmstadt, Darmstadt, Germany
zsolt.istvan@tu-darmstadt.de

Abstract. Modern sensors and IoT devices enable exciting applications but they also face challenges, especially due to data movement bottlenecks to the Cloud. Pushing down processing to the sensors or the Edge can help alleviate these bottlenecks, but it is an open question what types of processing elements are best for this purpose. As many related works show, FPGAs are a promising option due to their predictable behavior, streaming execution semantics, and energy efficiency. However, placing accelerators such as datacenter-grade FPGAs or GPUs right next to sensors, that are often battery operated, or at power-constrained Edge nodes is not practical. Instead, in this work we show that, using the right design approach, it is feasible to implement anomaly detection algorithms with small FPGAs suitable for energy-limited deployments – and this creates exciting new opportunities in using FPGAs for data pre-processing at the Edge.

Keywords: Edge Computing · Anomaly Detection · Multi-Stream Design · Energy Efficiency

1 Introduction

Networked sensors and IoT devices, deployed in large numbers, are generating unprecedented amounts of data, resulting in significant network traffic and increasing Cloud storage and computational requirements. Many IoT applications need data to be processed as soon as it was generated, in a streaming fashion [8,10]. In the setting where all processing happens in the Cloud, delivering predictable results in real-time becomes challenging [2]. Processing or pre-processing data closer to the source (sensors or IoT devices) can be a way of reducing both the bandwidth usage towards the Cloud and the latency of decision taking, and it has been studied in many related works [8,18]. In terms of actual deployment, this additional computation could take place either at the sensors or in Edge servers that aggregate data sources before sending them to

G. Leone et al. (Eds.): ARC 2026, LNCS 16514, pp. 3–15, 2026.
https://doi.org/10.1007/978-3-032-29365-7_1

the Cloud (see Fig. 1). Energy efficiency is crucial in both deployment options: in the former, devices are often battery operated, and in the latter, even though there is reliable power supply, many Edge nodes operate at a fraction of the power budget of a typical Cloud node. This means that, in most cases, placing power-hungry GPUs and other accelerators designed for the data center in the networking infrastructure at the Edge is not an option. For this reason, there is an increasing interest in using specialized hardware, such as Field Programmable Gate Arrays (FPGAs), for energy efficient pre-processing at the Edge [20].

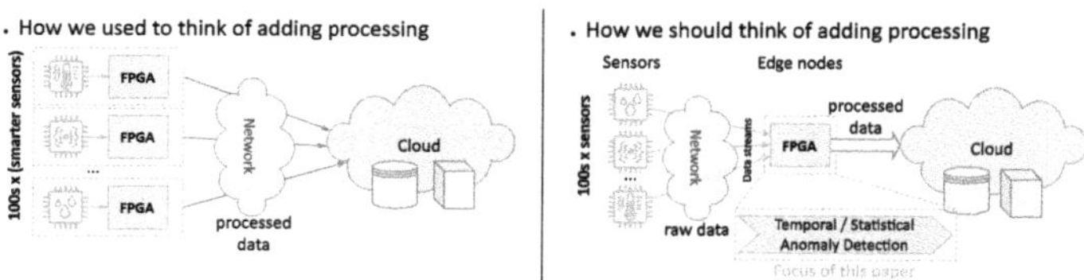

Fig. 1. One can deploy processing (e.g., FPGAs) at the Edge in different ways. By handling data from many sensors, deployments are more economical.

Many related works implement compute-intensive data analytics operations on FPGAs [16,19], using Edge use-cases as motivation, but designed for datacenter-grade FPGAs. In practice, FPGA-based implementations that compete with GPUs or multi-core server CPUs are simply too power-hungry for many Edge nodes. We argue that smaller FPGAs can be still practical for lightweight filtering, aggregation, and anomaly detection at the Edge if two major conditions are satisfied: first, FPGAs cannot be "one trick ponies" and have to perform multiple operations for the data streams arriving at the Edge node, while efficiently using their logical resources. Second, FPGAs have to ensure predictable high throughput and low latency, not to be a bottleneck.

In this paper, we show how anomaly detection can be implemented on small FPGAs in a way that satisfies the above two conditions. We implemented two anomaly detection modules, one based on temporal anomalies and one based on anomalies given by the data-distribution, both using a "multi-stream methodology": the modules work on data belonging to different streams and can share resources across them. In this way, they amortize the cost of multi-stream design across hundreds of concurrent streams. Also, both operate at high troughput and have predictable latency, regardless of the stream contents or the number of anomalies detected. This is in contrast to microcontroller-based implementations of the same algorithms, where constant performance cannot be guaranteed.

To summarize, our contributions are as follows:

– We challenge the common way of thinking of FPGAs at the Edge as lower power GPUs and instead treat them as higher performance microcontrollers (MCUs). This has important implications on the types of pre-processing that is feasible to offload to them.

– Using two specific anomaly detection examples, we explain how to achieve resource-efficient multi-stream processing in FPGAs. These techniques are not yet commonly used in Edge processing.
– We compare our multi-stream FPGA modules to MCU-based implementations and show that they can deliver energy efficient, high bandwidth, and low latency processing at the Edge.

2 Background and Related Work

In IoT systems, anomaly detection identifies unusual values or patterns in time series data [22]. It often involves high-volume, multi-source data and must meet strict accuracy, latency, scalability, and energy demands at the Edge [7,11,13]. As we aim to deploy such tasks on FPGAs, at the Edge, we analysed related work from different perspectives, from the relevance of deploying FPGAs at the Edge, to the type of data processing tasks offloaded, their hardware implementation, and support for multiple data streams.

The suitability of deploying FPGAs at the Edge was addressed in multiple research papers [4,20,24]. The authors of [4] run extensive experiments with compute-intensive applications to show that FPGAs have an advantage over GPUs, as they provide predictable, workload-insensitive execution and better adaptability to both spatial and temporal fine-grained parallelism while using less energy. In [24] it is shown that the use of FPGAs at the Edge can reduce the response time and energy consumption for interactive mobile applications. A different approach is presented in [20], where it is argued that an embedded FPGA coupled with an MCU can increase the flexibility of low-power SoC used as IoT end node by enabling the implementation of non-standard I/O interfaces as well as the acceleration of near-sensor data processing tasks.

Given the advantages of FPGAs for real-time data processing near sensors, there are many related works that implement accelerators for data stream analysis [6,11,12,15,25]. Pipelining and parallel execution are widely used to handle complex data analysis tasks and large/high-frequency inputs while reducing execution time (and making it predictable). Such solutions are used for anomaly detection in hyperspectral images [12], multi-sensor time series [6], and high-frequency single-sensor data [25].

Besides low latency and high throughput, Edge FPGA processing must also handle multiple parallel data streams while efficiently using resources [18,21]. For FPGA-based designs, a common solution to process multiple data streams in parallel is to replicate the processing elements used for a single stream [14, 25]. However, as we also show in this paper, this approach can raise scalability issues, since the design will quickly use up the available resources on the FPGA device. Related work in [9,23] shows that it is possible to share the computational resources of a single-pipeline hardware design between the workloads of multiple tenants. Based on these findings, this work aims to achieve resource-efficiency by sharing the computing resources needed by a single stream between multiple streams of data, while maintaining a low per-stream latency.

While prior work shows FPGAs can support real-time sensor data analysis in Edge-Cloud systems, most place the FPGA near sensors or in the Cloud and focus on single-stream processing. Our work is inspired by state-of-the-art in Edge computing research and considers a more practical way of deploying data processing for multi-stream workloads, while addressing resource-efficiency and execution predictability.

3   Processing at the Edge System Model

The way we assume FPGAs will be deployed at the Edge is different from what most related work on signal processing on FPGAs [12,20,25] considers. That is, we assume that the FPGAs are not deployed together with the sensors, as shown in the left part of Fig. 1, but instead are used to process data from many sensors at an Edge node (right part of Fig. 1). This approach avoids modifications to sensors, supports more practical heterogeneous deployments, and aligns with recent Edge Computing related work that positions computation close to, but not directly at, the sensors [8,13].

In this paper we focus on the design and implementation of processing performed at the Edge, abstracting away from actual network communication. We assume that hundreds of sensors send their data, at a high frequency (e.g., 20 Hz or higher) to an FPGA-based Edge node that aggregates the streams, pre-processes them, and sends the resulting data to the Cloud. We assume that this Edge computing element has to filter out anomalous readings before sending data to the Cloud by performing anomaly detection inside each stream. We implement two variants of an anomaly detection module. The first uses a temporal approach with two-sided cumulative sums [3] to detect sensor readings that "jump" significantly compared to the preceding value of the same sensor. The second module detects when a sensor returns a reading that is statistically different from the previous values in a larger window [5]. Data consumed by each of the two compute elements is transmitted in a single stream that contains both the value measured by a sensor or IoT device, and metadata. The metadata includes, initially, the device identifier and, as they pass through the compute elements, a flag corresponding to detected anomalies.

As follows, we will describe the algorithms for anomaly detection and the design of the modules for FPGAs. What makes our implementation interesting is that we employ a multi-stream design on the FPGA that allows for efficient use of hardware resources, sharing them between many streams.

3.1   Algorithms Description

We chose the algorithms as representative examples of Edge data pre-processing. Our results would generalize for other similar anomaly detection methods.

CUSUM. This anomaly detection technique is a slightly modified version of the *Two-Sided Cumulative Sums* algorithm [3], which allows considering differences between consecutive values as reference points. This method identifies anomalies based on positive and negative differences between the values measured by the same sensor at consecutive points in time. Suppose that $(x_n)_{n \geq 0}$ is a finite subsequence of a data stream generated by the same source, for each x_t, $t \in \{1, 2, ..., n-1\}$, the algorithm computes the difference $S_t = x_t - x_{t-1}$, and then the cumulative sums of positive and negative changes, $g_t^+ = \max(g_{t-1}^+ + S_t - drift, 0)$ and $g_t^- = \max(g_{t-1}^- - S_t - drift, 0)$. If any of the two sums is larger than a given *threshold*, the current value is labeled as an anomaly. To reduce false positives, the *drift* is subtracted from both g_t^+ and g_t^-. The *drift* and *threshold* depend on the use case, monitored phenomenon, and sampling rate. Typically, *threshold* reflects the maximum allowed change between readings, while *drift* represents the expected average change between readings per sampling interval.

Z-Score. In addition to the CUSUM approach, we implemented a Z-Score-based anomaly detection method [5], which identifies anomalous inputs that differ significantly from the expected range in a normally distributed data stream. Supposing that $(x_n)_{n \geq 0}$ is a finite subsequence of a data stream generated by the same source, the algorithm computes the mean, standard deviation, and finally the Z-score over a window of N most recent values, in real time. At each new observation (input), the window is updated by removing the oldest observation and replacing it with the most recent, and the mean μ and standard deviation σ are recalculated. The Z score of the current observation x_t is then computed as: $Z = \frac{x_t - \mu}{\sigma}$. A value is classified as anomalous if $|Z|$ exceeds a fixed threshold, which we set to 3, corresponding to a 99.7% confidence interval under the assumption of normality. The choice of N affects the sensitivity of the method, which influences its ability to detect anomalies.

3.2   Designing for Multi-Streaming

A naive approach of processing multiple data streams in parallel replicates the single-stream architecture per input stream, achieving high throughput but wasting resources and increasing power consumption, and also limiting scalability. Instead, we aim for scalable CUSUM and Z-Score designs that share hardware across streams while maintaining constant throughput.

CUSUM. As shown in Fig. 2a, to define a module that can handle multiple data streams, we expand a simple "single stream" CUSUM anomaly detector by adding logic that feeds the computational elements with input and intermediate data depending on the stream identifier (ID). To discriminate between values belonging to different streams, we augment the actual data with a unique stream ID. Furthermore, we include additional registers to store the cumulative sums computed in the previous step for each stream, as required by the algorithm described in Sect. 3.1. When a previously computed sum is needed or when a newly computed one is available, the registers to be read or written are selected based on the ID of the stream, using multiplexers and demultiplexers. The components that perform arithmetic operations in a pipeline fashion and the FIFO buffers that store intermediate computation results are shared between the streams. All components implement a data flow control mechanism that regularizes the variable data flow traffic.

The multi-stream CUSUM anomaly detector takes as input a pair of values representing the current and previous samples from the same input stream. Since we assume that data from different streams can arrive at the FPGA in an arbitrary interleaved order, we designed a stream selector that stores the previous values of each data stream and, based on the stream ID of the incoming value, outputs a pair consisting of the current and previous value belonging to that stream. The multi-stream CUSUM design in Fig. 2a was implemented in two versions, one supporting integer arithmetic (`Int`) and the other supporting floating point arithmetic (`Float`).

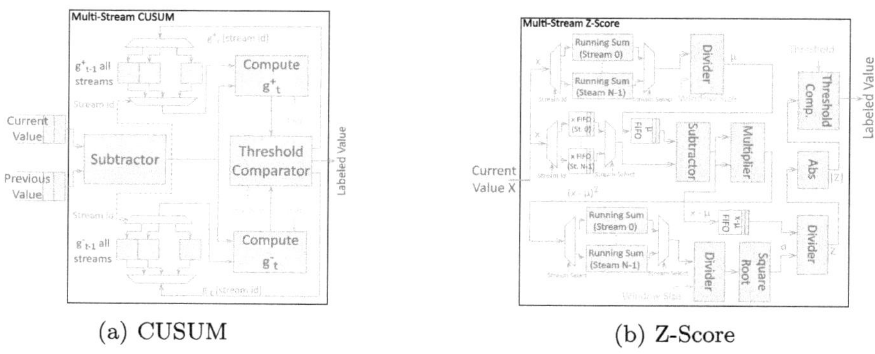

(a) CUSUM   (b) Z-Score

Fig. 2. The multi-stream design of the CUSUM and Z-Score anomaly detectors.

The scalability of our multi-stream design with the number of input streams is ensured since each additional input stream requires only three additional registers for the latest value and cumulative sums. All other resources are time-multiplexed among the data streams. Therefore, the overhead introduced by increasing the number of input data streams is considerably lower than the overhead created by deploying an additional single-stream CUSUM detector for each input data stream.

Z-Score. We follow a similar approach when designing a Z-Score module capable of operating on multiple streams. However, in contrast to the CUSUM module, which operates using only the two most recent values, the Z-Score anomaly detection technique requires maintaining and processing a full window of recent samples to compute the mean and standard deviation, making it significantly more memory- and computation-intensive. Furthermore, the Z-Score module can only operate on floating point arithmetic as it involves operations such as division and square root. This increases resource demands and per-value processing latency compared to the CUSUM module.

We extend the single-stream Z-Score detector by adding logic to route input and intermediate data through shared computational units based on stream IDs. Like CUSUM, Z-Score uses flow control to handle traffic variations. Since pipelining alone doesn't ensure high throughput due to complex floating-point operations, we also employ parallelism (Fig. 2b) to boost performance while keeping resource usage moderate. The first step of the pipeline involves computing the means over the stream-specific windows of most recent values. Considering that the input data can arrive at a considerably higher rate than the achievable throughput of the floating-point arithmetic components shared across streams, we compute the running sums corresponding to individual streams in parallel. For this, we implement a custom running sum module using an accumulator capable of performing both addition (to add the most recent sample to the sum) and subtraction (to remove the oldest sample from the window). We then replicate this running sum module for each individual stream. Furthermore, we use the same module in parallel for computing the sum of squared deviations $(x_t - \mu)^2$ in a sliding window fashion for every data stream.

Since input values are needed when computing both the windowed mean μ and the windowed sum of squared deviations $\sum_{t=1}^{n}(x_t - \mu)^2$, where n is the number of samples in the window, input values have to be buffered. To remove the need for ID buffering and management, we use individual buffers for separate streams and implement a Round Robin scheduler as a counter which sequentially selects the accumulated sums of the windowed data and the corresponding sums of squared deviations to be fed into the shared dividers. Thus, by matching the counter value to the stream ID, the corresponding sums are selected for processing, ensuring that values belonging to different streams are not mismatched.

4 Feasibility and Performance Evaluation

Setup and Devices. We evaluate the scalability, performance, and power efficiency of our hardware designs on two FPGA platforms: a resource-constrained, energy-efficient Basys 3 Artix 7 (referred to as `FPGA tiny`) and a high-performance, but more power-hungry Zynq UltraScale+ ZCU104 (`FPGA large` in what follows). For all further described experiments, both CUSUM and Z-Score designs were clocked at the highest frequency allowing successful timing closure on both hardware platforms: 150 MHz on `FPGA tiny` and 300 MHz on `FPGA large`. These maximum operating frequencies were determined following the AMD methodology for assessing F_{MAX} [1]. We also compare these multi-stream implementations of CUSUM and Z-Score against a naive multi-stream approach, where a single-stream module is replicated for each data stream. In addition, we benchmark these designs against baseline implementations running on two MCUs: an RP2040 chip at 125 MHz (`MCU-R`) and an ESP32 chip operating at 240 MHz (`MCU-E`). In our evaluation, we use the dataset from [17], which contains link quality measurements from 20 fixed wireless nodes, and consider each node-pair series as a separate data stream.

Scalability. Scalability experiments were conducted based on the hardware resources available the `FPGA tiny` and `FPGA large` devices. Measurements in Fig. 3 show the maximum number of input streams which are supported by `Int` and `Float` implementations of multi-stream CUSUM and `Float` implementation of Z-Score compared to the naive solution, also highlighting the hardware resource which runs out first in each particular design. As depicted in Fig. 3a, the multi-stream CUSUM `Int` implementation shows the best scalability, supporting up to 231 streams on `FPGA tiny` and 1268 streams on `FPGA large`. Compared to the naive approach, the multi-stream design achieves an improvement of approximately 10× on `FPGA tiny` and 3× on `FPGA large` for the CUSUM `Int`. Similarly, the multi-stream CUSUM `Float` design scales significantly better than the naive approach, achieving gains of approximately 2× on `FPGA tiny` and 3× on `FPGA large`. On `FPGA tiny`, this improvement results from the constant Digital Signal Processor (DSP) utilization of the multi-stream design, which remains independent of the number of streams, whereas in the naive implementation the DSP usage grows linearly with the stream count. Regarding the multi-stream Z-Score module, the scalability improvements result from the fact that most floating-point arithmetic operations are implemented as components shared across all streams, aside from the running sums, handled by per-stream dedicated units. Therefore, the Z-Score design supports approximately 2× more streams on `FPGA tiny` and 4× more streams on `FPGA large` compared to the naive approach. Although this gain is smaller than in multi-stream CUSUM, the improvement is promising given the computational demands Z-Score.

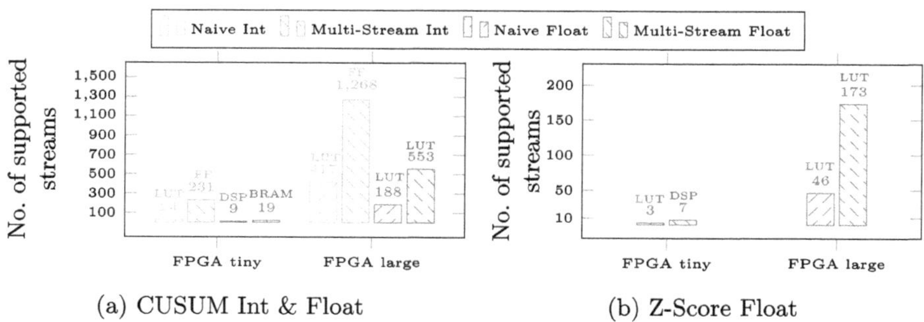

(a) CUSUM Int & Float   (b) Z-Score Float

Fig. 3. The scalability of the CUSUM Int and Float and Z-Score Float implementations in both naive and multi-stream scenarios on the FPGA.

Performance. To evaluate the performance of the hardware multi-stream designs and motivate the use of FPGAs at the Edge to detect outliers in sensor data, we compare the throughput and latency of our solutions against equivalent software implementations running on MCU-R and MCU-E. As shown in Fig. 4a, the aggregated throughput of the multi-stream CUSUM Int module increases with the number of streams up to 7 and then saturates under a Round-Robin scheduling scheme due to the pipelined computation of running sums. However, while the aggregated throughput scales, the per-stream throughput decreases as additional streams introduce extra latency. In contrast, the MCU implementations exhibit significantly lower aggregated throughput despite comparable clock frequencies, as they lack parallel execution. For S streams, the per-stream latency of the CUSUM hardware design is $t_{FPGA} = \max\{14, 2 \cdot S\}$ clock cycles, whereas the MCU-R and MCU-E implementations require an average of $t_{MCU-R} = 582 \cdot S$ and $t_{MCU-E} = 201 \cdot S$ clock cycles, respectively, before processing a new sample from the same stream.

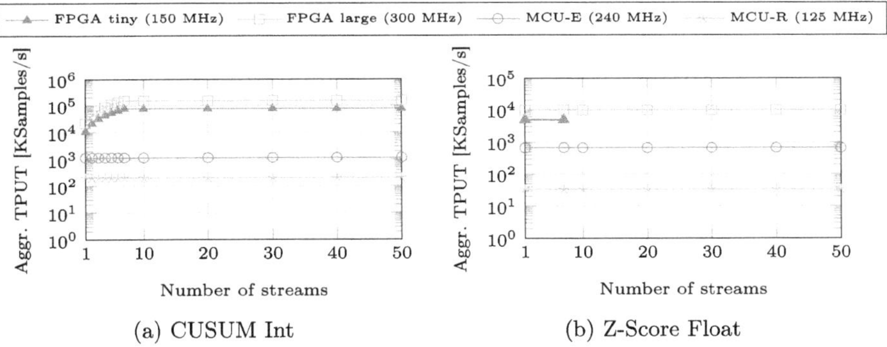

Fig. 4. Aggregated throughput of multi-stream implementations on FPGA vs. Microncontroller Units (MCUs).

Similarly, for the Z-Score module, pipelining and parallel execution on the FPGA lead to a substantial improvement in aggregated throughput. The FPGA implementation produces a new output every 31 clock cycles, regardless of the stream. As with the CUSUM module, the per-stream throughput decreases when additional streams are added, since each stream introduces other 31 clock cycles, resulting in a per-stream latency of $t_{FPGA} = 8080 + 31 \cdot (S - 1)$ cycles when processing S streams. The software implementations on MCU-R and MCU-E require significantly more time per computation, despite operating at clock frequencies comparable to the FPGAs. The MCU-R achieves an average per-stream latency of $t_{MCU-R} = 3948 \cdot S$ cycles, while the MCU-E reaches a per-stream latency of $t_{MCU-E} = 359 \cdot S$ cycles on average–still far below the aggregated throughput of the FPGA implementations.

Power Consumption. When assessing the energy efficiency of our designs, we compare the multi-stream FPGA designs (*multi*) on both FPGA tiny and

`FPGA large` devices against two baseline deployments: a *naive* FPGA with one device per sensor and an MCU-based deployment where each sensor is integrated with an individual MCU. The total measured power (P) considers both computational (P_c) and transmission (P_t). We estimate P_c using the post-implementation Vivado Power Report tool for FPGA implementations and measure it experimentally for MCU using a Power Profiler Kit II (PPK2). P_t is measured under a WiFi communication setup using the PPK2 and the `MCU-E` (3.3 V, 240 MHz), drawing 125 mA during transmission (TX) and reception (RX) and 65 mA when idle (I). Assuming a duty cycle of 40% TX, 40% RX, and 20% I, the resulting transmission power is $P_t = 372.9$ mW, assumed constant across all evaluated configurations. For S streams, we then compute the total power as $P^{multi} = P_t + P_c$ for the multi-stream FPGA since a single device is used to process multiple streams and as $P^{naive} = (P_t + P_c) \cdot S$ and $P^{MCU} = (P_t + P_c) \cdot S$ for the other scenarios, as a dedicated device is used for each individual data stream.

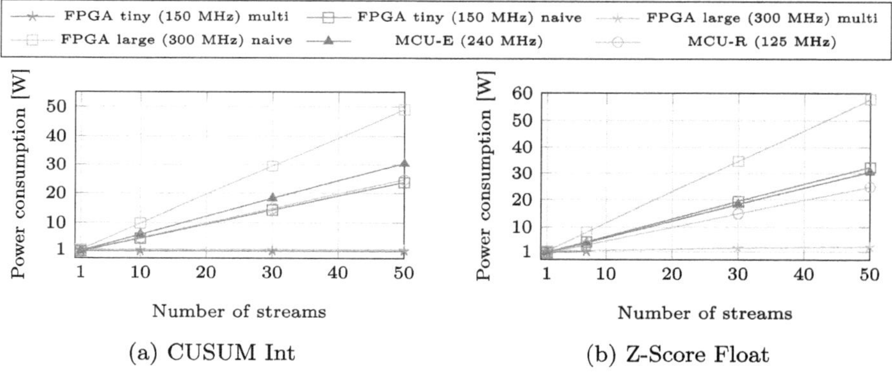

(a) CUSUM Int   (b) Z-Score Float

Fig. 5. Measured power consumption for CUSUM and Z-Score modules on FPGA across varying numbers of streams.

The results in Fig. 5 show the improved energy efficiency of the multi-stream (*multi*) FPGA design. For both CUSUM and Z-Score modules, the power consumption of the multi-stream configuration grows linearly with the number of streams but at a much slower rate compared to the naive FPGA and MCU-based implementations. For instance, at 50 streams, the multi-stream design of CUSUM `Int` consumes around 0.48 W on `FPGA tiny` at 150 MHz and 1.02 W on `FPGA large` at 300 MHz, while the corresponding naive FPGA designs consume $\approx 50\times$ more power. The MCU implementations are even more power-hungry: deploying either $50\times$ `MCU-E` or $50\times$ `MCU-R` devices, each running a single-stream CUSUM `Int` implementation, consumes more power even than using $50\times$ `FPGA tiny` boards in the naive configuration, as shown in Fig. 5a. This highlights the advantage of the multi-stream FPGA design in efficiently processing multiple streams in parallel. A similar trend is observed for the Z-Score `Float` module.

With 50 streams, the multi-stream design consumes ≈ 2.84 W on `FPGA large`, whereas the naive approach of deploying $50\times$ `FPGA large` results in a power consumption of about 58 W and the corresponding `MCU-E` solution requires ≈ 31 W. Furthermore, given power budgets of 1.02 W for CUSUM `Int` and 2.84 W for Z-Score `Float` in the multi-stream configuration with 50 streams on `FPGA large`, the same budgets would allow deploying up to $1\times$ `FPGA large` or $2\times$ `FPGA tiny` for CUSUM `Int`, and up to $2\times$ `FPGA large` or $4\times$ `FPGA tiny` for Z-Score `Float` in the naive scenario, without exceeding the power limits. Similarly, for the MCU-based implementations, where each data stream requires a dedicated MCU, the power budget permits deploying up to only $1\times$ `MCU-E` or $2\times$ `MCU-R` for CUSUM `Int`, and up to $4\times$ `MCU-E` or $5\times$ `MCU-R` for Z-Score `Float`, while remaining within the available power budget. This clearly demonstrates that our multi-streaming approach allows processing many more data streams while maintaining a reduced power footprint.

5   Conclusion

In this work, we investigate the feasibility of using FPGAs at the Edge for data pre-processing. We show that smaller FPGAs, that fit well with the modest energy footprint of an Edge node, can provide high speed processing of many concurrent data streams. This is due to our multi-stream design that saves on resources. We compare our FPGA-based pre-processing modules to two MCUs and demonstrate higher overall performance and energy efficiency – these results pave the way for more adoption of FPGAs at the Edge.

Acknowledgments. This work was co-funded by the Romanian Ministry of Research, Innovation and Digitalization under the project "SENTHICOM - UTCN", contract no. 10.PI/I4/C9, within Romania's National Recovery and Resilience Plan (PNRR) – Pillar III, Component C9, Investment I4 and by the LOEWE initiative (Hesse, Germany) within the emergenCITY center [LOEWE/1/12/519/03/05.001(0016)/72].

References

1. AMD: Assessing the Maximum Frequency of the Design. https://docs.amd.com/ r/en-US/ug949-vivado-design-methodology/Assessing-the-Maximum-Frequency-of-the-Design
2. Andreoli, R., Cucinotta, T.: Towards a holistic cloud system with end-to-end performance guarantees. In: IEEE International Conference on Cloud Engineering (IC2E), pp. 236–238. IEEE (2023)
3. Basseville, M., Nikiforov, I.V., et al.: Detection of Abrupt Changes: Theory and Application, vol. 104. Prentice hall (1993)
4. Biookaghazadeh, S., Zhao, M., Ren, F.: Are {FPGAs} suitable for edge computing? In: USENIX HotEdge 18 (2018)
5. Chandola, V., Banerjee, A., Kumar, V.: Anomaly detection: a survey. ACM Comput. Surv. **41**(3) (2009)

6. Da Silva, L.M., Coutinho, M.G., et al.: Hardware architecture proposal for teda algorithm to data streaming anomaly detection. IEEE Access **9**, 103141–103152 (2021)
7. Giannoni, F., Mancini, M., Marinelli, F.: Anomaly detection models for IoT time series data. ArXiv arxiv:1812.00890 (2018)
8. Goudarzi, Mo.and Palaniswami, M., Buyya, R.: Scheduling IoT applications in edge and fog computing environments: a taxonomy and future directions. ACM Comp. Surv. **55**(7), 1–41 (2022)
9. István, Z., Alonso, G., Singla, A.: Providing multi-tenant services with fpgas: case study on a key-value store. In: Proceedings of FPL'18, pp. 119–1195. IEEE (2018)
10. Khelifati, A., Khayati, M., Dignös, A., Difallah, D., Cudré-Mauroux, P.: TSM-bench: benchmarking time series database systems for monitoring applications. Proc. VLDB Endow. **16**(11), 3363–3376 (2023)
11. Lee, D., Lee, S., Oh, S., Park, D.: Energy-efficient FPGA accelerator with fidelity-controllable sliding-region signal processing unit for abnormal ECG diagnosis on IoT edge devices. IEEE Access (2021)
12. Lei, J., Yang, G., Xie, W., Li, Y., Jia, X.: A low-complexity hyperspectral anomaly detection algorithm and its FPGA implementation. IEEE J. Sel. Topics Appl. Earth Obs. Remote Sens. **14** (2020)
13. Li, Y., Zhou, Z., Xue, X., Zhao, D., Hung, P.C.: Accurate anomaly detection with energy-efficiency in IoT-edge-cloud collaborative networks. IEEE IoT J. (2023)
14. Lou, B., Boland, D., Leong, P.: FSEAD: a composable FPGA-based streaming ensemble anomaly detection library. ACM Trans. Reconfig. Technol. Syst. **16**(3), 1–27 (2023)
15. Meloni, P., Busia, P., Leone, G., Martis, L., Scrugli, M.A.: Exploiting FPGAs and spiking neural networks at the micro-edge: the edgeAI approach. In: International Symposium on Applied Reconfigurable Computing, pp. 296–302. Springer, Heidelberg (2024). https://doi.org/10.1007/978-3-031-55673-9_21
16. Mira, J.L., et al.: High performance connected components accelerator for image processing in the edge. In: International Symposium on Applied Reconfigurable Computing, pp. 210–221. Springer, Heidelberg (2024). https://doi.org/10.1007/978-3-031-55673-9_15
17. Mottola, L., Picco, G., Ceriotti, M., Gună, C., Murphy, A.L.: Not all wireless sensor networks are created equal: a comparative study on tunnels. ACM Trans. Sen. Netw. **7**(2), 1–33 (2010)
18. Ntumba, P., Georgantas, N., Christophides, V.: Scheduling continuous operators for IoT edge analytics with time constraints. In: SMARTCOMP, pp. 78–85. IEEE (2022)
19. Rognlien, M., Que, Z., Coutinho, J.G., Luk, W.: Hardware-aware optimizations for deep learning inference on edge devices. In: International Symposium on Applied Reconfigurable Computing, pp. 118–133. Springer, Heidelberg (2022). https://doi.org/10.1007/978-3-031-19983-7_9
20. Schiavone, P.D., Rossi, D., Di Mauro, A., et al.: Arnold: an eFPGA-augmented RISC-V SoC for flexible and low-power IoT end nodes. IEEE Trans. VLSI Syst. **29**(4), 677–690 (2021)
21. Şenel, B.C., Mouchet, M., Cappos, J., Fourmaux, O., Friedman, T., McGeer, R.: Edgenet: a multi-tenant and multi-provider edge cloud. In: Proceedings of 4th International Workshop Edge Systems and Analysis Networks, pp. 49–54 (2021)
22. Sgueglia, A., Di Sorbo, A., Visaggio, C.A., Canfora, G.: A systematic literature review of IoT time series anomaly detection solutions. Future Gener. Comp. Syst. **134**, 170–186 (2022)

23. Wenzel, L.: Multi-tenancy for FPGA accelorator designs. Proc. HPI Res. Sch. Serv.- Oriented Syst. Eng. 2020 Fall Retreat. 83 (2023)
24. Xu, C., et al.: The case for FPGA-based edge computing. IEEE Trans. Mob. Comput. **21**(7), 2610–2619 (2020)
25. Żabiński, T., Hajduk, Z., Kluska, J., Gniewek, L.: FPGA-embedded anomaly detection system for milling process. IEEE Access **9**, 124059–124069 (2021)

High Performance Convolutional Neural Network Acceleration on Versal AI Edge Devices for Real Time DC Series Arc Fault Detection

Yu Li[1]($\boxtimes$) , Yufei Mao[2,3] , Roland Weiss[2] , and Mario Porrmann[1]

[1] Osnabrück University, 49074 Osnabrück, Germany
{yu.li,mario.porrmann}@uni-osnabrueck.de
[2] Siemens AG, 91058 Erlangen, Germany
yufei.mao@uni-bielefeld.de, rolandweiss@siemens.com
[3] Bielefeld University, 33615 Bielefeld, Germany

Abstract. Direct current (DC) series arc fault detection is a critical task in electrical safety systems, demanding high detection accuracy, low inference latency, and energy efficiency. Convolutional neural networks (CNNs) have shown strong potential for identifying arc fault patterns. However, their efficient deployment on embedded hardware platforms remains an open research challenge. The AI Engine–Machine Learning (AIE-ML), an ML-optimized variant of the AI Engine array in Versal adaptive SoCs, is well suited to these requirements, offering a programmable, vector-centric compute fabric tailored to the constraints of edge devices. To fully exploit this architecture, we develop STANN-AIEML, an open-source hardware–software co-design workflow that enables efficient inference of deep learning models on the Versal AI Edge platforms. The proposed framework streamlines the mapping and optimization of neural networks onto AIE-ML-based architectures, facilitating high-performance and rapid deployments in resource-constrained environments.

This study presents a CNN-based approach for efficient DC series arc fault detection, accelerated on an AMD Versal VE2302 device. By leveraging the STANN-AIEML library, we address key challenges in deploying CNN models on Versal AI Edge devices. The proposed CNN model is fine-tuned to achieve high detection accuracy while maintaining low inference latency. Furthermore, a comprehensive analysis and comparison with state-of-the-art implementations on FPGA and GPU platforms demonstrate the performance advantages of the proposed AIE-ML–accelerated solution. This work advances real-time, low-latency arc fault detection and contributes toward safer and more reliable DC electrical systems across a wide range of industrial applications.

Keywords: Convolutional Neural Networks · Versal AI Engine · Hardware Acceleration · DC Arc Fault Detection

Fig. 1. A DC series arc generated under laboratory conditions.

1   Introduction

Detecting DC series arc faults remains a significant challenge due to the limited research on DC systems compared to alternating current (AC) systems. These faults are often difficult to distinguish from normal DC signals because of electrical noise [19] or the influence of complex loads [20]. Figure 1 illustrates a DC series arc generated under laboratory conditions. Traditional detection methods, which rely on fixed rules and stable patterns, are increasingly insufficient as DC systems grow in scale and complexity. Therefore, research has shifted toward more adaptive machine learning (ML) approaches, capable of identifying arc faults under diverse operating conditions by leveraging data from multiple sources [20]. Effective ML solutions, however, demand high detection accuracy, low latency, and energy efficiency, making embedded platforms with dedicated hardware acceleration particularly suitable for deployment.

With the Versal architecture, Xilinx introduced an embedded platform that combines programmable AI Engine (AIE) arrays with a field programmable gate array (FPGA) fabric in heterogeneous system on chips (SoCs), complementing the graphics processing unit (GPU)- and FPGA-based architectures [12]. An AIE tile combines a Very Long Instruction Word (VLIW) vector processor with Single Instruction, Multiple Data (SIMD) capabilities, local program and data memory. Multiple tiles are interconnected via a high-bandwidth Network on Chip (NoC) to support streaming data movement [3].

To bridge the gap between high-level ML design frameworks and efficient deployment on Versal AI Edge devices, we introduce STANN-AIEML[1] a hardware-software co-design framework that extends the original STANN (Synthesis Templates for Artificial Neural Networks) library [22]. STANN-AIEML is a scalable C++ template-based framework targeting the AI Engine-ML array,

---

[1] Source code available at: https://github.com/ce-uos/STANN-AIEML.

enabling low-latency and low-power inference by exploiting the architectural features of Versal AI Edge devices, including vectorized AIE-ML cores, high compute density, and low-latency on-chip interconnects. STANN-AIEML translates trained neural network models into AIE-ML dataflow implementations and automates their mapping onto AI Engine tiles, providing a complete hardware-software workflow. Through configurable templates, parameters such as processing elements allocation, vectorization, and data precision in STANN-AIEML allow systematic trade-offs among latency, throughput, and power consumption, facilitating efficient deployment under diverse performance and energy constraints.

This paper builds on the work of [16] and provides a detailed comparative analysis highlighting key features, including a scalable C++ template library for implementing diverse neural network architectures for arc detection on AIE-ML with flexible data type support, as well as an end-to-end hardware–software co-design workflow for Versal AI Edge devices. The structure of the paper is as follows: Sect. 2 summarizes the related work in DC series arc fault detection and hardware acceleration, followed by a discussion of the detection system and the STANN-AIEML implementations with key features in Sect. 3. In Sect. 4, STANN-AIEML is evaluated based on the collected dataset. The resource usage, performance, and energy efficiency of hardware accelerators for classification using one-dimensional CNNs (1D-CNNs) on the Trenz TE0950 AMD Versal AI Edge evaluation board are analyzed and compared with different hardware platforms. Finally, Sect. 5 concludes the paper and proposes future work.

2   Related Work

Accurate detection is crucial for DC series arc fault detection to prevent unnecessary shutdowns caused by misjudgments. Meanwhile, the system must react as quickly as possible to minimize the risk of fire and equipment damage. In addition, different neural network architectures can exhibit significantly different performance depending on the characteristics of the data and the application scenario [20]. Dang, H.L. et al. [7] evaluate different models across datasets, with SVM delivers an accuracy of 99.38%. Lu et al. [18] achieved a peak accuracy of 99.72% in a 20 ms window deploying a 2D-CNN model on an NI-CompactRIO9030 system. In [27], Yan et al. tested temporal convolutional networks (TCN) with high sampling rate time series data, reaching 99.88% accuracy with a 150 ms detection time on an Nvidia Jetson GPU. Mao, Y. et al. [21] have demonstrated the effectiveness of fully connected neural networks (FCNNs) with an accuracy of 99.07% in 60 µs detection time on an Avnet Ultra96-V2 FPGA platform. [16] has shown that CNNs are particularly promising for DC series arc fault detection, achieving high detection accuracy of 99.87% even under low sampling rate conditions in 87 µs. CNNs are especially well-suited for time-series signal analysis, as their convolutional structure enables effective extraction of local temporal patterns that are critical for distinguishing arc fault signatures. Compared with FCNN models, CNNs typically achieve higher accuracy with fewer trainable parameters, resulting in more compact models without sacrificing detection performance [16].

The practical implementation of such ML models in real-time environments relies on efficient neural network acceleration deployment on specialized hardware platforms. Focusing on reconfigurable systems, the architectures can be broadly divided into two groups: (1) monolithic intellectual property (IP)-core accelerators with fixed architectures and (2) acceleration libraries enabling flexible accelerator design. These frameworks allow flexible trade-offs among latency, power, and resource usage, and simplify deployment across application domains. IP-core accelerators such as Xilinx Deep Learning Processing (DPU) [1] provide standardized designs with limited configurability, which reduces design and verification effort but limits adaptability.

In contrast to monolithic IPs offering standardized solutions, acceleration libraries and frameworks expose architectural parameters and reusable building blocks, enabling closer alignment between hardware and model characteristics for improved performance and efficiency. FINN [5,24] focuses on quantized neural networks (QNNs), hls4ml [10] provides automated conversion from ML frameworks such as Keras and PyTorch to High-Level Synthesis (HLS)-based implementations. STANN [17,22] translates high-level neural network models into configurable hardware implementations supporting various precisions.

Building on these developments, the Versal ACAP architecture with AI Engine-ML arrays in AI Edge devices provides advantages over traditional FPGA-only platforms [11]. The combination of programmable logic, scalar processors, and vectorized AI engines delivers high compute density, predictable latency, and energy efficiency for signal processing and deep learning [26]. Recent research focuses on AIE-based accelerators [13], acceleration library [8], and a toolchain that supports automatic code generation [23]. In [9], an analytical approach is proposed to maximize the efficiency of deep learning on the Versal AI Engine fabric while considering compute and memory constraints.

To enable high-precision DC arc detection in resource-constrained embedded systems, we develop STANN-AIEML, a hardware–software co-design framework implemented as a C++ template-based library for the AI Engine-ML array on Versal AI Edge devices. STANN-AIEML bridges high-level neural network descriptions and low-level hardware constraints, enabling rapid deployment of performant AIE-ML implementations. By adjusting reconfigurable parameters such as parallelism, vectorization, and data types, designers can explicitly trade off latency, throughput, and power consumption to meet the timing and energy requirements of edge applications.

3   Implementation

This section provides the technical background for the DC series arc fault detection system and the algorithm used for hardware acceleration. Subsequently, the architecture of Versal AIE-ML and various neural network implementations in STANN-AIEML are described. Finally, the hardware acceleration based on STANN-AIEML is detailed.

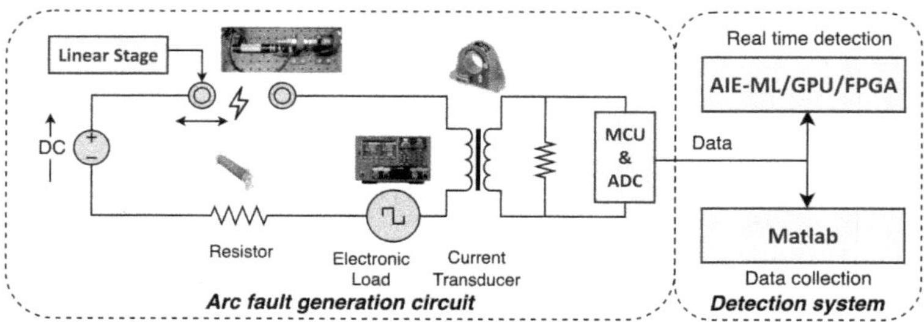

Fig. 2. The DC series arc fault testbench.

3.1   DC Series Arc Fault Detection System

A testbench based on the UL1699B [25] standard, shown in Fig. 2, is used to generate DC series arc faults for data collection and real-time detection. The setup includes a DC power supply, passive loads, and a programmable electronic load to create different operating conditions. The cost-effective detection system, illustrated on the right side of the figure, uses the current signal and consists of a current sensor, a microcontroller unit (MCU) with an analog-to-digital converter (ADC), and a hardware accelerator for deep learning (DL) model execution. Although there is no strict rule for detection time, UL1699B recommends a shorter detection time at higher voltages. Therefore, hardware inference must be fast enough to meet different system requirements [20]. In this system, operating at a 16 kHz sampling rate, the MCU continuously transfers ADC data to the detection system. The data are either collected for training or directly processed by the detection algorithm running on AIE-ML, GPU, or FPGA platforms.

The detection algorithm is first trained and evaluated using data generated from the testbench in PyTorch. As shown in Fig. 3, the method includes two stages: data pre-processing and CNN-based classification. The received time-series signals are initially transformed using a Fast Fourier Transform (FFT) to extract frequency-domain features, improving accuracy and robustness, followed by an L1 normalization kernel [15]. The 256-point raw samples are similarly normalized and concatenated with their FFT outputs to form a 512-point input vector. The network contains two consecutive 1D convolutional layers with identical settings (kernel size $= 3$, stride $= 1$, padding $= 1$, ReLU activation), each followed by batch normalization. A one-dimensional max pooling layer (kernel size $= 2$, stride $= 2$, ReLU activation) is then applied. Afterward, a fully connected layer with 128 neurons and ReLU activation processes the extracted features, followed by batch normalization. The final layer is another fully connected layer with a single neuron and Sigmoid activation, generating binary outputs (1 for arc detection and 0 for no arc). The model is optimized to achieve minimal complexity while preserving high accuracy across datasets obtained under various load conditions.

3.2   Algorithm for DC Series Arc Detection and Dataset

The dataset consists of 73,350 time-series samples, each containing 256 data points. Among the samples, 80 % are allocated for training and the remaining

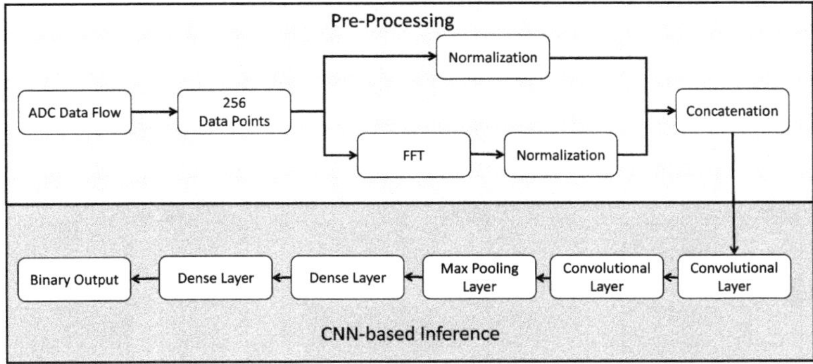

Fig. 3. Simplified DC series arc fault detection algorithm.

20 % for testing. The dataset labels are imbalanced, with an "arc" to "no arc" ratio of 1:3.7. To evaluate the performance of the DC series arc fault detection system, the algorithm is tested using the data collected from the testbench rather than a live ADC stream. During evaluation, the model is executed repeatedly over the 14,670 test samples, and the average inference time per sample is reported [15].

In DC arc detection, misclassification costs are highly asymmetric: false negatives (missed faults) pose serious safety hazards, while false positives (false alarms) lead to unnecessary system shutdowns and economic losses. To reflect these asymmetric costs, we report the confusion matrix, precision, recall, F1-score, and overall accuracy. The algorithm is evaluated on a desktop CPU using PyTorch across 14,670 test samples. The corresponding confusion matrix is

$$\textbf{Confusion Matrix} = \begin{bmatrix} 11586 & 10 \\ 9 & 3065 \end{bmatrix}. \tag{1}$$

Here, the rows correspond to the true classes (no arc fault, arc fault) and the columns correspond to the predicted classes (no arc fault, arc fault), which explicitly presents the distribution of predictions for normal and fault samples: among all test samples, 10 normal samples are misclassified as faults (false positives) and 9 fault samples are misclassified as no arc (false negatives). The overall test accuracy is 99.87%. For the arc class, the model achieves a precision of 99.67%, a recall of 99.71%, and an F1-score of 99.69%, demonstrating excellent detection capability. The false positive rate is only 0.086%, while the false negative rate remains as low as 0.29%, indicating that both misclassifications are effectively suppressed under the evaluated test conditions.

3.3 Versal AIE-ML Architecture

The Versal AIE-ML architecture is illustrated in Fig. 4, consisting of a two-dimensional array of AIE-ML tiles that integrate compute, memory, and interconnect resources. Tiles are connected horizontally and vertically through inter-

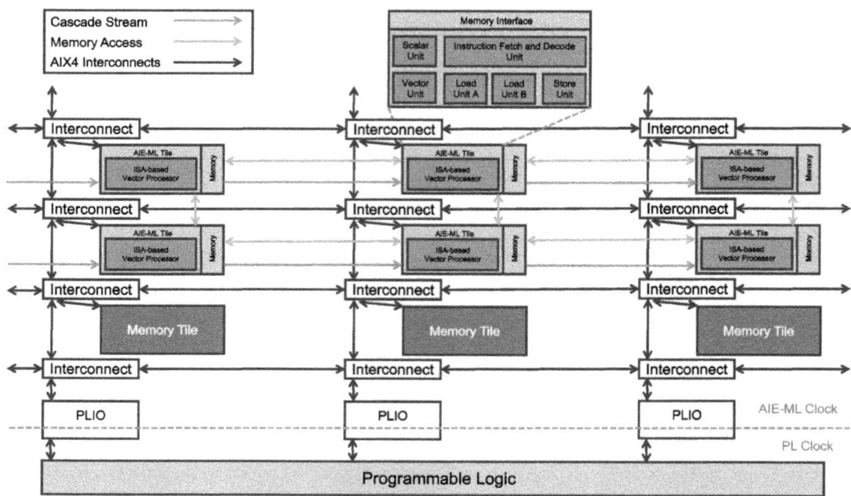

Fig. 4. Versal AIE-ML Architecture.

connects supporting AXI4 data movement and cascade streams, enabling low-latency and data exchange between neighboring tiles. At the array boundary, programmable logic input and output (PLIO) interfaces provide high-bandwidth communication between the AIE-ML fabric and the programmable logic (PL), allowing efficient integration with external logic and peripherals.

An AIE-ML tile combines SIMD and VLIW architectures with support for fixed- and floating-point precision. As shown in Fig. 4, a tile integrates scalar and vector units, load and store units, instruction fetch and decode logic, and a memory interface. Each tile contains 64 KB of local data memory organized into multiple banks and 16 KB of program memory, enabling parallel memory access and efficient data reuse. This tightly coupled compute–memory organization allows high throughput while maintaining predictable latency. The AIE-ML interconnect is central to scalable data movement across the array. Cascade streams connect tiles in a chain to directly forward 512-bit accumulator values with minimal buffering overhead. Local data memories support efficient ping-pong buffering between adjacent tiles, while dedicated memory tiles provide up to 512 KB of on-chip storage each to buffer data streams between the PL and the AIE-ML array, significantly reducing dependence on off-chip DDR accesses. For non-neighbor communication, an AXI4-Stream DMA network enables flexible multi-tile routing. Configurable AXI-Stream PLIOs (32/64/128-bit) further bridge the PL and the higher-frequency AIE-ML array, enabling bandwidth optimization across clock domains and keeping data on-chip to minimize latency [3].

3.4 Data Types and One-Dimensional Layers

In this work, two numerical formats supported by the STANN-AIEML library are evaluated: standard 32-bit floating-point (float) and brain floating-point (bfloat16). The bfloat16 format provides lower precision while preserving the same dynamic range as float, using 1 sign bit, 8 exponent bits, and 7 fraction bits. This design enhances computational efficiency and lowers memory usage [6], ensuring numerical stability without the need for the loss-scaling techniques typically used in half-precision (half) [14]. The AIE-ML architecture provides inherent hardware support for bfloat16 through dedicated vector processing units optimized for arithmetic operations [3].

Based on these two numerical formats, the library implements a collection of one-dimensional layers. The implementations of the 1D convolution, 1D max pooling, and the dense layers are described in the following subsections. In addition, the library supports padding layers and batch normalization layers, which are discussed here due to their straightforward implementation and minor impact on performance. During the padding computation, the input sequence is first stored in local data memory, after which a configurable number of paddings with adjustable values is applied according to application requirements. The padded sequence is then forwarded to the next processing stage. The batch normalization layer performs element-wise normalization by subtracting a precomputed mean and dividing by the square root of the variance plus a small constant, followed by a linear transformation using learned scale and bias parameters. During inference, batch normalization can be merged into preceding convolutional or dense layers by incorporating its parameters into the corresponding weights and biases [28]. This eliminates the need for a separate normalization layer and reduces runtime overhead. Therefore, folded batch normalization is adopted in this work.

3.5   Implementation of Convolutional Layers

Convolutional layers can be realized using several methods, such as direct convolution, the Winograd algorithm [2], and im2col-based techniques [4]. Among these, im2col-based methods are particularly notable because they reformulate convolution operations as matrix multiplications, which are well-suited for scalable and efficient hardware execution. Two algorithms from this class are widely used: im2row and kn2row.

The im2row transformation converts the temporal irregularity of sliding windows into a spatially aligned matrix format, deliberately leveraging memory redundancy to guarantee the contiguous access patterns essential for maximizing VLIW throughput. By transforming temporal dependencies into a fixed spatial layout, this approach eliminates unaligned access penalties and enables a deterministic, fully pipelined instruction schedule that maximizes the theoretical throughput of the AIE-ML vector units. Moreover, its matrix-oriented formulation inherently maps channel dimensions to the processor's vector lanes, ensuring maximal SIMD utilization regardless of the temporal stride, making it the preferred implementation strategy for STANN-AIEML.

The implementation uses a memory-centric explicit im2row, a variant of the standard im2row algorithm optimized for accelerating 1D convolution on VLIW architectures [4]. Instead of the conventional sliding window, computation is reorganized, as discussed below, to fully exploit the AIE-ML architecture and minimize irregular memory accesses. The vector processing unit (VPU) has a 512-bit data path, configurable for 32 lanes with bfloat16 or 16 lanes with float, providing flexibility to match different data types.

Suppose we have the following example for a 1D convolution with an input length N, kernel size 3, and stride 1. To improve efficiency, we transform the temporal structure of the sliding window into a fixed spatial layout within local memory. The input sequence is distributed across multiple parallel buffers, where the k-th buffer holds the input shifted by k positions. Meanwhile, the kernel weights are broadcast from scalar to vector form to match the entire SIMD lane width, preparing them for vectorized computation.

The core computation uses the `aie::mac` (multiply-and-accumulate) intrinsic primitive of the Versal AIE-ML, referred to as a processing element (PE) in the context of STANN. Each PE multiplies the broadcasted weight vectors by the pre-aligned input vectors in the shift buffers, effectively performing the sliding-window calculation across multiple data points simultaneously. This vectorization strategy reduces memory access overhead and maximizes arithmetic intensity. The STANN-AIEML framework is fully parameterizable, supporting different input lengths, kernel sizes, and stride values. Additionally, it is highly scalable: adjusting the number of PEs allows the workload to be spatially distributed, which enables the computational throughput and latency to be tuned to meet specific performance requirements. Scaling the PE count inherently partitions the workload by mapping concurrent `aie::mac` intrinsic calls to available SIMD lanes for spatial scaling and interleaving their execution through optimized instruction-level pipelining for temporal scheduling within a single AIE tile. Rather than increasing the tile count, scaling the PE count enhances intra-tile parallelism by leveraging the AIE-ML SIMD architecture for spatial scaling and by using extensive loop unrolling to optimize temporal instruction scheduling.

3.6 Implementation of Max Pooling Layers

The 1D max pooling layers are implemented on the AIE-ML architecture using a configurable C++ kernel that supports various input sequence lengths, kernel sizes, and stride values. To achieve high efficiency without the overhead of conditional branching, the implementation leverages the `aie::max` intrinsic, a hardware-native instruction that performs single-cycle, element-wise comparisons across all vector lanes. This approach ensures deterministic latency and full utilization of vector resources, replacing complex control flow with a simple, parallel operation.

Suppose we have the following example. For an input sequence of length N with kernel size 2 and stride 2, local maxima are identified by comparing adjacent input pairs, e.g., (x_0, x_1). The instruction schedule is fully pipelined, allowing a new operation to start every clock cycle. Data loading, computation, and write-back stages are overlapped so that sequential operations become a steady-state parallel process. For example, while the Compute Unit applies

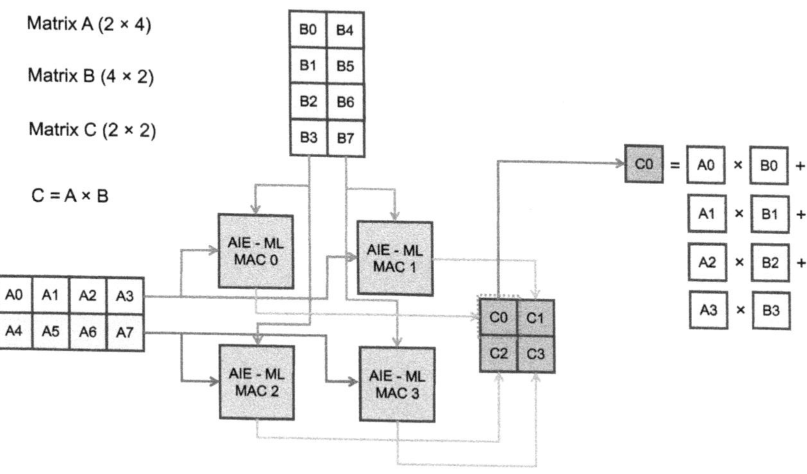

Fig. 5. Implementation of Block Matrix Multiplications.

`aie::max` to (x_2, x_3), the Load Unit fetches (x_4, x_5) and the Store Unit writes back (x_0, x_1). This concurrent execution hides memory latency, maintains continuous throughput, and produces a new max-pooled output vector every cycle.

3.7   Implementation of Dense Layers

The dense layer is implemented as a General Matrix Multiplication (GEMM), optimized through a configurable block matrix multiplication strategy. Instead of processing the entire weight and input matrices at once, the operation partitions them into smaller sub-blocks with tunable dimensions. Each sub-block is multiplied in parallel to produce partial result vectors, which are then accumulated into the final outputs. This parametric tiling scheme is essential for performance, enabling sub-block dimensions to be adaptively configured in accordance with the limitations of local memory and the vectorization width of the hardware.

Figure 5 illustrates the architectural design of a block matrix multiplication. The kernel executes a matrix multiplication $C = A \times B$, where the input sub-matrix A is 2×4 and the weight sub-matrix B is 4×2, producing a 2×2 output matrix. To maximize hardware utilization, the computation is distributed across four parallel AIE-ML MAC units, MAC_0 to MAC_3. Data efficiency is improved through broadcasting: each input row is shared horizontally across MAC units, while each weight column is shared vertically. Specifically, the first row of A, $[A_0, \ldots, A_3]$, is provided to both MAC_0 and MAC_1 to compute the top row of C, and the second row, $[A_4, \ldots, A_7]$, is delivered to MAC_2 and MAC_3. Similarly, the first column of B, $[B_0, \ldots, B_3]^\top$, is sent to MAC_0 and MAC_2, and the second column, $[B_4, \ldots, B_7]^\top$, to MAC_1 and MAC_3. Each MAC unit performs a vectorized multiply-accumulate operation, summing products of the input row and weight column. By resolving all four output elements simultaneously, this

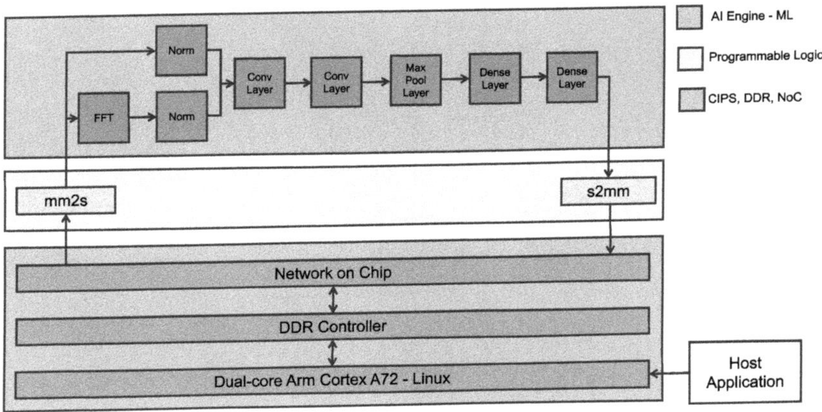

Fig. 6. The algorithm is implemented on the VE2302 Versal device.

parallelized design greatly reduces the latency of block multiplications and dense layer computations. Moreover, this approach improves memory reuse by keeping input and weight submatrices local to each MAC unit, minimizing global memory accesses. The fully pipelined execution ensures continuous throughput, allowing new blocks to be processed every cycle.

The dense layer on AIE-ML tiles is implemented using block matrix multiplication to accelerate fully connected operations. Consider an input sequence of length 8 with a batch size of 2, forming an input matrix A of dimensions 2×8, and an output length of 4, corresponding to a weight matrix B of dimensions 4×8. The kernel performs the matrix multiplication $C = B \times A^\top$. Both matrix B and matrix $A^\top$ are decomposed into sub-blocks along the dimensions, allowing multiple PEs to calculate partial results concurrently. These partial outputs are then accumulated element-wise to produce the final matrix. This block-wise execution maximizes SIMD resource utilization and ensures scalable performance with high throughput and minimal latency.

3.8   Hardware Acceleration Based on STANN-AIEML

The STANN-AIEML-based implementations are evaluated on the Trenz TE0950 AMD Versal AI Edge evaluation board. The integrated Versal VE2302 device combines 34 AIE-ML tiles, an FPGA fabric, and a dual-core Arm Cortex-A72 processing system within a single system-on-chip device. Figure 6 presents the heterogeneous hardware architecture deployed on the Versal AI Edge platform. The system is coordinated by the Control, Interfaces, and Processing System (CIPS), which serves as the supervisory controller. The dual-core Arm Cortex-A72 executes the Linux operating system and manages high-level host applications. High-bandwidth on-chip communication is enabled by the NoC, which interconnects the processing subsystems with the external DDR memory controller. The PL region operates as a data movement and acceleration bridge, incorporating dedicated memory-mapped-to-stream (mm2s) and stream-

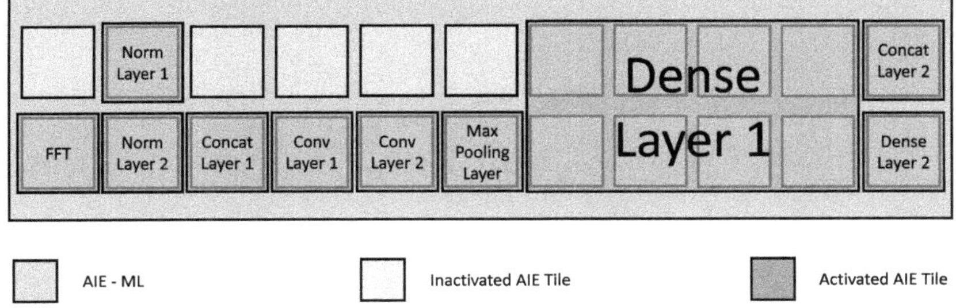

Fig. 7. The AIE tiles usage for the algorithm on the VE2302 Versal device.

to-memory-mapped (s2mm) kernels for high-throughput data transfer and protocol conversion, thereby offloading direct memory access tasks from the CPU. The AIE-ML array forms the computational core, executing the detection algorithm in a pipeline. During operation, CIPS schedules the tasks, the PL facilitates data streaming from memory, and the AIE-ML array performs inference computation before the results are written back to DDR. Task execution is synchronized to maintain continuous dataflow between the PL and AIE-ML tiles, minimizing idle cycles. Shared buffers within the AIE-ML array enable neighboring tiles to exchange intermediate results efficiently, supporting a pipelined processing graph, enabling high throughput and low latency.

Figure 7 illustrates the mapping of the algorithm onto the AIE-ML. It shows a part of the VE2302 Versal device in light green. There are two rows of AIE tiles on the device. The unused AIE tiles are gray while the activated AIE tiles are marked in green. The kernels communicate intermediate results via shared buffers. To deploy the detection algorithm on AIE-ML tiles, each computation kernel is mapped onto a dedicated AIE-ML tile, with the corresponding weights and biases stored in local data memory, allowing for concurrent execution and efficient utilization of the AI Engine's parallel resources. Due to the limited memory capacity of each AIE-ML tile, the first dense layer (Dense Layer 1) is decomposed into eight smaller dense layers (dimensions: from 256×128 to $8 \times 256 \times 16$), with each small dense layer deployed on a dedicated AIE-ML tile. A concatenation kernel (Concat Layer 1) is applied to merge the outputs of the two normalization kernels, each containing 256 elements, into a single 512-element 1D vector, which serves as the input to the first convolutional kernel. Another concatenation kernel (Concat Layer 2) is employed to merge the resulting 8 output vectors from kernel Dense Layer 1 into a one-dimensional array with 128 elements, which serves as the input to the second dense layer. In total, 17 AIE-ML tiles are utilized.

4   Evaluation and Comparison

This section presents the evaluation of the proposed architecture. The analysis focuses on inference latency, energy efficiency, and model accuracy under

Table 1. Resource usage, execution time, and power of implementations using float data type

Data Type	PE	LUT	FF	BRAM	Tile	Execution Time	On-Chip Power	Energy per Infer
Float	1	17951 (12%)	25426 (8%)	4.5 (3%)	17 (50%)	255 µs	6.58 W	1678 µJ
Float	2	17952 (12%)	25427 (8%)	4.5 (3%)	17 (50%)	143 µs	6.62 W	947 µJ
Float	4	17952 (12%)	25426 (8%)	4.5 (3%)	17 (50%)	71 µs	6.77 W	481 µJ
Float	8	17955 (12%)	25432 (8%)	4.5 (3%)	17 (50%)	41 µs	6.85 W	281 µJ

different model precisions with different hardware configurations. All the implementations are executed on the Trenz TE0950 AMD Versal AI Edge evaluation board, operating at 1 GHz for the AIE-ML tiles and 300 MHz for the FPGA fabric. Vivado 2024.1 is used for implementation and on-chip power estimation. Execution time refers to the end-to-end latency on the AI Engine, which includes FFT, normalization, and neural network inference stages. In addition, comparisons across different hardware platforms and with existing studies are provided.

Table 1 summarizes the resource utilization, inference latency, and energy consumption per inference of the accelerator using the floating-point data type across different numbers of PEs per layer. The utilization of PL resources (LUTs, FFs, BRAMs, and IOs) remains nearly constant across all configurations, as the PL is exclusively used to implement the mm2s and s2mm kernels for data movement. Increasing the number of PEs per layer significantly reduces inference latency while resulting in only minimal additional power consumption. As a result, the energy consumption per inference decreases dramatically with higher PE allocation per layer. Specifically, the configuration with 8 PEs per layer

Table 2. Resource usage, execution time, and power of implementations using bdloat16 data type

Data Type	PE	LUT	FF	BRAM	Tile	Execution Time	On-Chip Power	Energy per Infer
Bfloat16	1	17943 (12%)	25432 (8%)	4.5 (3%)	17 (50%)	136 µs	6.46 W	879 µJ
Bfloat16	2	17941 (12%)	25430 (8%)	4.5 (3%)	17 (50%)	73 µs	6.51 W	475 µJ
Bfloat16	4	17945 (12%)	25431 (8%)	4.5 (3%)	17 (50%)	39 µs	6.63 W	259 µJ
Bfloat16	8	17940 (12%)	25428 (8%)	4.5 (3%)	17 (50%)	23 µs	6.68 W	153 µJ

Table 3. Accuracy of implementations using different data types across various hardware platforms

Hardware Platforms	AIE-ML	FPGA [16]	GPU [16]	CPU
Float	99.87 %	99.87 %	99.48 %	99.87 %
Half	–	99.78 %	–	–
Bfloat16	94.32 %	–	–	–

achieves a 5.7× speedup compared to the single-PE design and reduces the energy consumption per inference by 1397 µJ (5.9 times).

Table 2 shows the resource utilization, execution time, and energy consumption per inference of the accelerators using bfloat16 precision with varying numbers of PEs per layer. Similar to Table 1, the PL and AIE tile usage remains nearly constant across different configurations. Increasing the number of PEs per layer leads to shorter execution times and reduced energy consumption per inference. Specifically, the implementation with 8 PEs per layer achieves a 6.2× speedup compared to a single-PE configuration and reduces the energy per inference by 726 µJ (5.7 times). Moreover, the 8-PE implementation in bfloat16 executes nearly twice as fast as the corresponding float implementation. This performance benefit arises from the VPU on AIE-ML, which features a 512-bit data path. The VPU's vectorization factor is configurable, supporting 32 lanes for the bfloat16 data type and 16 lanes for the float data type. Consequently, with the same number of VPUs, twice as many bfloat16 elements can be processed per cycle compared to float.

Table 3 depicts the accuracy of the implementations using different data types across different hardware platforms based on the identical model [16]. Accuracy is evaluated across four hardware platforms: a Trenz TE0950 AMD Versal AI Edge evaluation board, an Avnet Ultra96-V2 FPGA board, an Nvidia Jetson Xavier NX GPU, and an AMD Ryzen 9 3900X CPU (via PyTorch). The floating-point implementation matches the FPGA and CPU baselines at 99.87%, while slightly exceeding the accuracy of the GPU implementation (99.48%). The accuracy divergence on the GPU is attributed to numerical precision trade-offs and operator fusion optimizations inherent in the Nvidia TensorRT C++ inference engine [15]. Half computations on FPGA yield an accuracy of 99.78%, whereas bfloat16 on AIE-ML achieves 94.32%. Compared to the half format, bfloat16 offers a wider dynamic range to prevent underflows. Nevertheless, for the arc detection dataset, its reduced fractional precision leads to significantly lower accuracy. Therefore, although bfloat16 offers shorter execution times and lower energy per inference, it is not the ideal choice for this scenario where high accuracy is most critical.

Table 4 presents a comparison with existing studies using different algorithms and architectures [16], [21] and [27]. The float implementation with the lowest execution time is selected for comparison. The results demonstrate that

Table 4. Comparison of implementations across hardware platforms and with existing studies [16, 21, 27]

Source	AIE-ML	FPGA [16]	GPU [16]	FPGA [21]	GPU [27]
Model	1D-CNN	1D-CNN	1D-CNN	FCNN	TCN
Data Points	256	256	256	160	512
Sampling Rate	16 kS/s	16 kS/s	16 kS/s	16 kS/s	250 kS/s
Accuracy	99.87%	99.87%	99.48%	99.07%	99.88%
Runtime	41 μs	87 μs	162 μs	60 μs	150 ms
Energy per Infer	281 μJ	292 μJ	361 μJ	182 μJ	–

the proposed implementation achieves comparable or even better accuracy than the state-of-the-art. The accuracy of the proposed implementation on AIE-ML exceeds the accuracy of 99.07% for the FCNN model used in [21], matching the baseline accuracy of 99.87% for the identical 1D-CNN model introduced in [16], while being comparable to the accuracy of 99.88% achieved with the TCN model in [27]. In terms of runtime, a single inference on AIE-ML takes 41 μs, which is approximately 2.1× faster than the latency of 87 μs for the identical 1D-CNN model on an Avnet Ultra96-V2 FPGA and 3.9× faster than the latency of 162 μs for the same model on an Nvidia Jetson Xavier NX GPU [16]. Compared to the FCNN model on an Avnet Ultra96-V2 FPGA [21], a speedup of 1.5 is achieved and with 150 ms, the TCN model [27] on an Nvidia Jetson Nano GPU requires significantly more time than the other implementations. Regarding energy efficiency, the energy consumption per inference on AIE-ML is 281 μJ, slightly lower than that of 292 μJ for the same 1D-CNN model on an Avnet Ultra96-V2 FPGA [16], and also lower than that of 361 μJ for the same 1D-CNN model on an Nvidia Jetson Xavier NX GPU [16]. These results highlight the effectiveness of the AIE-ML architecture for real-time DC series arc fault detection, offering high precision, low-latency execution, and energy efficiency.

5   Conclusion

This work presents the design and evaluation of a high-performance DC series arc fault detection system accelerated on the AMD Versal AI Edge platform using the STANN-AIEML framework. By offering support for various neural network architectures and configurable parameters, the framework significantly streamlines the rapid deployment and acceleration of arc detection models. The AIE-ML implementation exhibits superior performance, achieving a competitive accuracy of 99.87% while significantly reducing inference latency to 41 μs. This represents a 1.5×–2.1× speedup over existing FPGA implementations and at least a 3.9× improvement over GPU-based benchmarks. These results validate that the proposed mapping strategy effectively exploits the spatial parallelism of the Versal architecture, establishing a new benchmark for high-throughput, low-latency DC series arc fault detection.

Future work will expand the STANN-AIEML library to include high-demand neural network layers. Additionally, we plan to evaluate the implementations directly in the testbench, integrating an ADC and all required peripherals.

Acknowledgments. This work is supported by the "HybrInt – Hybrid Intelligence through Interpretable Artificial Intelligence in Machine Perception and Interaction" project (Zukunft Nds, Niedersächsisches Ministerium für Wissenschaft, Grant ID: ZN4219).

References

1. Agiakatsikas, D., et al.: Evaluation of Xilinx Deep Learning Processing Unit under Neutron Irradiation (2022). https://arxiv.org/abs/2206.01981
2. Alam, S.A., et al.: Winograd Convolution for Deep Neural Networks: Efficient Point Selection (2022). https://arxiv.org/abs/2201.10369
3. AMD: AIE-ML Architecture – AM020 Versal Adaptive SoC AIE-ML Architecture Manual. AMD (2025). https://docs.amd.com/r/en-US/am020-versal-aie-ml/AIE-ML-Architecture. Accessed 05 Feb 2026
4. Anderson, A., et al.: Low-memory GEMM-based Convolution Algorithms for Deep Neural Networks (2017). https://arxiv.org/abs/1709.03395
5. Blott, M., et al.: FINN-R: an end-to-end deep-learning framework for fast exploration of quantized neural networks. ACM Trans. Reconfigurable Technol. Syst. **11**(3) (2018). https://doi.org/10.1145/3242897
6. Burgess, N., Milanovic, J., Stephens, N., Monachopoulos, K., Mansell, D.: Bfloat16 processing for neural networks. In: 2019 IEEE 26th Symposium on Computer Arithmetic (ARITH), pp. 88–91 (2019). https://doi.org/10.1109/ARITH.2019.00022
7. Dang, H.L., Kim, J., Kwak, S., Choi, S.: Series DC arc fault detection using machine learning algorithms. IEEE Access **9**, 133346–133364 (2021). https://ieeexplore.ieee.org/document/9548085/
8. Danopoulos, D., et al.: AIE4ML: An End-to-End Framework for Compiling Neural Networks for the Next Generation of AMD AI Engines (2026). https://arxiv.org/abs/2512.15946
9. Deng, X., Wang, S., Gao, T., Liu, J., Liu, L., Zheng, N.: AMA: an analytical approach to maximizing the efficiency of deep learning on versal AI engine. In: 2024 34th International Conference on Field-Programmable Logic and Applications (FPL), pp. 227–235 (2024). https://doi.org/10.1109/FPL64840.2024.00039
10. Duarte, J., et al.: Fast inference of deep neural networks in FPGAs for particle physics. JINST **13**(07), P07027 (2018). https://doi.org/10.1088/1748-0221/13/07/P07027
11. Gaide, B., Gaitonde, D., Ravishankar, C., Bauer, T.: Xilinx adaptive compute acceleration platform: versaltm architecture. In: Proceedings of the 2019 ACM/SIGDA International Symposium on Field-Programmable Gate Arrays, pp. 84–93 (2019)

12. Hu, Y., Liu, Y., Liu, Z.: A survey on convolutional neural network accelerators: GPU, FPGA and ASIC. In: 2022 14th International Conference on Computer Research and Development (ICCRD), pp. 100–107 (2022). https://doi.org/10.1109/ICCRD54409.2022.9730377
13. Jia, X., et al.: XVDPU: a high-performance CNN accelerator on the versal platform powered by the AI engine. ACM Trans. Reconfig. Technol. Syst. **17**(2), 1–24 (2024)
14. Kalamkar, D.D., et al.: A study of BFLOAT16 for deep learning training. CoRR arxiv:1905.12322 (2019)
15. Li, Y., Mao, Y., Rothmann, M., Weiss, R., Porrmann, M.: FPGA-enabled deep learning for real-time DC series arc fault detection. IEEE Open J. Ind. Appl. 1–24 (2026). https://doi.org/10.1109/OJIA.2026.3671845
16. Li, Y., Mao, Y., Weiss, R., Porrmann, M.: High-performance FPGA-based CNN acceleration for real-time DC arc fault detection. In: Rojas, I., Joya, G., Catala, A. (eds.) Advances in Computational Intelligence, pp. 192–204. Springer, Cham (2026)
17. Li, Y., Rothmann, M., Porrmann, M.: Resource-efficient implementation of convolutional neural networks on FPGAs with STANN. In: Rojas, I., Joya, G., Catala, A. (eds.) Advances in Computational Intelligence, pp. 179–191. Springer, Cham (2026)
18. Lu, S.: Intelligent DC Series Arc Fault Detection Using Deep Learning in Photovoltaic Systems. Ph.D. thesis, UNSW Sydney (2021). https://doi.org/10.26190/UNSWORKS/2236. http://hdl.handle.net/1959.4/70737
19. Lu, S., Phung, B., Zhang, D.: A comprehensive review on DC arc faults and their diagnosis methods in photovoltaic systems. Renew. Sustain. Energy Rev. **89**, 88–98 (2018). https://doi.org/10.1016/j.rser.2018.03.010. https://linkinghub.elsevier.com/retrieve/pii/S1364032118300996
20. Mao, Y., Safa, S., Smith, G., Wurth, L., Weiss, R., Hagemeyer, J.: Why AI: a comparative study for detection methods in DC series arc fault. IEEE Access **13**, 42703–42722 (2025). https://doi.org/10.1109/ACCESS.2025.3548309
21. Mao, Y., Weiss, R., Zhang, Y., Li, Y., Rothmann, M., Porrmann, M.: FPGA acceleration of DL-based real-time dc series arc fault detection. In: 2024 IEEE International Parallel and Distributed Processing Symposium Workshops (IPDPSW), pp. 92–98 (2024). https://doi.org/10.1109/IPDPSW63119.2024.00031
22. Rothmann, M., Porrmann, M.: STANN - synthesis templates for artificial neural network inference and training. In: 17th International Work-Conference on Artificial Neural Networks (IWANN2023). Springer, Heidelberg (2023)
23. Tian, H., Yang, S., Cha, Y., Huang, S.: Late breaking results: Pyaie: a python-based programming framework for versal ACAP platforms. In: 2023 60th ACM/IEEE Design Automation Conference (DAC), pp. 1–2. IEEE (2023)
24. Umuroglu, Y., et al.: FINN: a framework for fast, scalable binarized neural network inference. In: Proceedings of the 2017 ACM/SIGDA International Symposium on Field-Programmable Gate Arrays, FPGA '17, pp. 65–74. ACM (2017)
25. Underwriters Laboratories: UL1699B, UL Standard for safety Photovoltaic DC Arc-Fault Circuit Protection (2018)
26. Vissers, K.: Versal: the xilinx adaptive compute acceleration platform (ACAP). In: Proceedings of the 2019 ACM/SIGDA International Symposium on Field-Programmable Gate Arrays, pp. 83–83 (2019)
27. Yan, J., Li, Q., Duan, S.: A simplified current feature extraction and deployment method for DC series arc fault detection. IEEE Trans. Ind. Electron. **71**(1), 625–634 (2024). https://doi.org/10.1109/TIE.2023.3247721. https://ieeexplore.ieee.org/document/10054597/

28. Yvinec, E., Dapogny, A., Bailly, K.: To fold or not to fold: a necessary and sufficient condition on batch-normalization layers folding. In: Thirty-First International Joint Conference on Artificial Intelligence (IJCAI 22), pp. 1601–1607. International Joint Conferences on Artificial Intelligence Organization, Vienna (2022). https://doi.org/10.24963/ijcai.2022/223. https://hal.science/hal-03953581

LiveFIFO: FPGA-in-the-Loop Buffer Sizing for Dataflow Accelerators

Felix Jentzsch[1]([✉]), Thomas B. Preußer[2], Lukas Stasytis[3], Yaman Umuroğlu[4], Jakoba Petri-Koenig[2], Christoph Berganski[1], and Marco Platzner[1]

[1] Computer Engineering Group, Paderborn University, Paderborn, Germany
{felix.jentzsch,christoph.berganski,platzner}@upb.de
[2] Advanced Micro Devices (AMD) Research, Dublin, Ireland
{thomas.b.preusser,jakoba.petri-Koenig}@amd.com
[3] Systems Group, Technical University of Darmstadt, Darmstadt, Germany
lukas.stasytis@tu-darmstadt.de
[4] Norwegian University of Science and Technology, Trondheim, Norway
yaman.umuroglu@ntnu.no

Abstract. Sizing intermediate data buffers has been a long-standing challenge in building FPGA dataflow accelerators. Current techniques rely on imperfect analytical models or time-intensive simulation, often choosing suboptimal buffer sizes, which either waste valuable resources or risk performance degradation. We introduce an FPGA-accelerated buffer-sizing approach that finds locally optimal first-in-first-out (FIFO) buffer sizes by synthesizing and profiling a lean but faithful surrogate of the target dataflow design. Contrary to existing simulation-based or model-based techniques, our approach guarantees optimal throughput and latency results using a search-based fine-tuning step, which is enabled by our ability to evaluate any FIFO depth configuration five orders of magnitude faster than in simulation. We fully integrate our approach into the open-source deep neural network (DNN) accelerator compiler FINN and evaluate it on a suite of 12 example DNNs, achieving a total FIFO size reduction of up to 86% compared to the best prior technique.

1 Introduction

FPGA-based dataflow architectures have become a promising alternative to traditional instruction-driven architectures (e.g., CPU, GPU, NPU) for certain signal processing and deep neural network (DNN) inference applications. They unlock a unique low-latency and high-efficiency potential by instantiating compute operators in parallel and streaming intermediate results between them, thereby minimizing costly off-chip memory access and enabling per-operator architecture specialization. However, dataflow accelerators still need to buffer intermediate data between operators for two primary reasons: 1) as a structural

Y. Umuroğlu—Part of the work was carried out while the author worked at AMD.

necessity to avoid deadlocks between fork-join paths with unbalanced latency and 2) as a performance optimization to allow each operator to run at its peak rate by absorbing bursty I/O behavior. Optimally sizing these first-in-first-out (FIFO) buffers poses a challenge, especially on FPGAs, where each buffer must be allocated to fixed resources of the logic fabric. In the context of FPGA dataflow neural network accelerator (FDNA) compilers (such as FINN [7] or hls4ml [9]) FIFO sizing poses an increasingly pressing problem as typical DNN topologies become larger and more complex (e.g., featuring re-convergent paths [12] or transpose operations [5]). Current FIFO sizing techniques in FINN, which are based on simulation, heuristics, and manual modeling of I/O behavior, are inadequate for these models. We demonstrate this on a wide range of example DNNs, where we routinely observe hours-long FIFO sizing durations and designs with wasted FPGA resources or degraded performance.

In this work, we present "LiveFIFO" as a method for FIFO sizing in dataflow designs, where control flow is governed solely by token availability and follows a data-oblivious schedule with no inter-frame state. This generally applies to FDNAs due to their statically-defined computation graph. By utilizing an FPGA in-the-loop for iterative performance profiling, we can emulate and evaluate different FIFO configurations to search for locally optimal FIFO depths within seconds where a simulation would take hours. In doing so, we give guarantees for both key performance metrics of the accelerator: the frame initiation interval, which is the inverse of throughput and determined by the pipeline bottleneck (i.e., the operator with maximum interval), and the frame processing latency. The LiveFIFO approach comes at the cost of an additional synthesis of a "profiling surrogate" design, which we deem acceptable if used sparingly during design space exploration or as a gold standard for calibrating faster, approximate FIFO sizing methods. More specifically, our contributions include:

1. We design hardware components (virtual FIFO, controller, and profiler) to facilitate profiling of stream-based accelerators via a surrogate design.
2. We propose a configurable three-phase FIFO sizing algorithm that operates on an FPGA programmed with the synthesized profiling surrogate.
3. We integrate LiveFIFO into the open-source FINN+ framework [14] and evaluate it on a suite of 12 example DNN models against existing techniques.

In the following, we provide an overview of related work (Sect. 2) and FIFO sizing in FINN (Sect. 3). Then, we present our design and algorithm (Sect. 4) and evaluate it (Sect. 5). Finally, Sect. 6 concludes the paper.

2 Related Work

Buffer sizing in dataflow applications is an NP-hard problem [4] that is generally approached using formal or search-based techniques. Formal methods define models of the dataflow application which capture the underlying operator production and consumption characteristics. These are then used to formulate a buffer minimization problem as input to a solver. Examples of such models include the synchronous dataflow graph (SDF) [16], cyclo-static dataflow graph (CSDF) [6,18], and SDF with access patterns (SDF-AP) [11]. These methods differ in the expressiveness of the underlying operator characterization. Restricted models like SDF abstract operator behavior into fixed, aggregate token rates per firing, which cannot capture the fine-grained, cycle-accurate access patterns of hardware operators. Modeling at this level of abstraction can cause significant buffer size overestimation, which is particularly undesirable in memory-constrained devices such as FPGAs. CSDF increases expressiveness by allowing rates to vary periodically across firings, but still treats each firing as atomic and therefore cannot represent intra-firing access patterns at clock-cycle granularity. SDF-AP can express the fine-grained I/O behavior of the operators under consideration, but results in prohibitive solver runtimes when modeled at clock-cycle granularity [11,24]. We refer to Roumage et al. [20] for a survey of alternative models.

Search-based approaches rely on compiling the application and simulating it with varied buffer sizes to assess the resulting performance. Recently, multiple HLS-based buffer exploration frameworks have been proposed, which are unfortunately not directly applicable to the FINN compiler, as it is based on a mixed back-end of HLS and RTL operators. One example is the hybrid approach by Honorat et al. [13], which starts with an ILP solver over a coarse-grained application model to obtain an upper bound on buffer sizes, followed by an iterative co-simulation to reduce the buffer sizes. Even with multiple optimizations, this search takes hours to complete, despite their benchmark workloads being relatively light compared to typical DNN accelerators. In contrast to this, the tool FIFOAdvisor [1] aims to avoid costly co-simulation altogether by building the exploration process on top of a near cycle-accurate HLS simulation tool [21].

In the context of on-FPGA profiling, our approach bears conceptual resemblance to a buffer sizing study [3] from the networking domain, where FPGA-based routers are not just monitored to assess buffer occupancy (also referred to as "fullness"), but buffer size is actively adjusted to evaluate its effect on system performance. More closely related to our domain is the SPRING profiling framework [22] integrated into the hls4ml FDNA compiler [9]. On an HLS level, the authors introduce a dedicated profiling stream alongside the data stream to monitor internal signals of compute operators. More specifically, they observe the FIFO occupancy during runtime—which we also do as an intermediate step in our algorithm—and characterize the maximum occupancy distribution for a set of randomly interconnected DNNs to understand their post-implementation behavior. While they offer design guidance based on this characterization, their method does not emulate or search for optimized FIFO sizes. Also, SPRING introduces a resource overhead for the profiling logic that may prevent the design from fitting on the target device. Our solution does not face this limitation, as the profiling surrogate design is always smaller than the profiled accelerator due to data-path pruning.

3   Review of FIFO Sizing in FINN

Figure 1 shows a taxonomy of FIFO sizing tools in FINN. In the following, we identify shortcomings of both existing approaches that we aim to address.

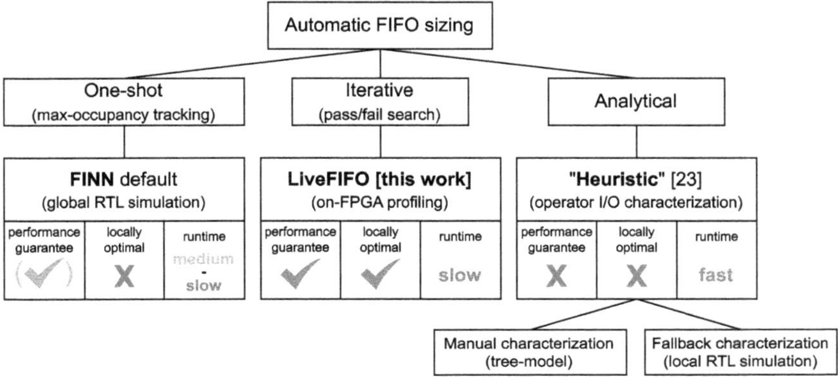

Fig. 1. Taxonomy of FIFO sizing in FINN, categorized into one-shot approaches based on a single profiling run, iterative approaches performing multiple measurements, and analytical approaches relying on a-priori knowledge of operator behavior.

3.1   FINN Default

The default method for computing FIFO sizes in FINN, referred to simply as "FINN" baseline for the remainder of this paper, is a one-shot approach based on monitoring maximum occupancy of each FIFO in a model via simulation. This method has also been used in hls4ml [8]. It relies on simulating the entire model by processing a series of frames and monitoring the FIFO occupancy between each operator pair. The maximum count of buffered values in each FIFO over the course of this simulation is used as the size for its final implementation. This approach, however, is extremely time-consuming as large FDNAs with hundreds of layers can require hundreds of thousands to millions of cycles to process a frame. The method usually leads to a severe over-estimation of buffer sizes. In many cases, shrinking FIFO space between operators may not lead to any decrease in throughput of the model if the operators were not a pipeline bottleneck to begin with [23]. On the other hand, two further imperfections of the implementation can still lead to insufficiently sized FIFOs, degrading throughput or even causing a deadlock:

1. During the simulation, the primary input frame rate must be throttled to the nominal throughput of the pipeline. Otherwise, FIFO occupancy will grow without bound in front of bottleneck layers with increased simulation duration. However, this throttling interval is determined by analytical estimates

of the individual compute operators, which is not always cycle-accurate. In our approach (4.4), we also rely on maximum occupancy measurement, but use the measured bottleneck interval for cycle-accurate throttling.

2. There exists no stable-state detection or proper heuristic for determining the simulation duration. Instead, it defaults to the processing of N=2 input frames, a value that is often too small and must be overwritten by the user.

3.2 Heuristic FIFO Sizing

A recent addition to FINN's FIFO sizing toolkit was presented by Stasytis et al. [23]. It focuses on a heuristic approach which avoids simulations and solvers entirely. We will refer to this method as "Heuristic" baseline throughout the paper. The approach is based on token access vectors (TAVs) [11], which are execution traces of the model operators limited to stream read and write operations. These TAVs are usually generated by traversing hand-crafted tree-based models of the operators but may also be generated using local (i.e., per-operator) RTL simulation as a fallback. The TAVs are then manipulated and compared by a heuristics-driven algorithm to compute approximate buffer sizes, without giving guarantees about the tightness of the buffer sizes or the resulting accelerator performance. In contrast, our approach determines tight buffer sizes with performance guarantees and requires no prior knowledge of either model-level performance characteristics or operator-level access patterns, making it more general.

4 LiveFIFO Methodology

Our methodology hinges on a special variant of a FIFO buffer operator that we call "virtual FIFO." This component does not actually buffer any data—the stream data signals remain unconnected and are pruned during synthesis as part of default logic optimization. Instead, it allows us to operate the control flow of the pipeline, which is based on the stream ready and valid signals, in various operating modes while profiling its interval and latency.

Figure 2 gives an overview of our modified FINN tool flow. The FINN front-end remains unmodified. A quantized DNN in QONNX format is ingested, streamlined, mapped to hardware operators and folded, which is a step that automatically configures the parallelism of each operator to achieve a balanced pipeline at the target throughput. To synthesize the profiling surrogate design, we then run the usual sequence of back-end transformation steps with a configuration flag set that enables our extensions. Most importantly, we 1) insert the virtual FIFO operators in place of regular FIFOs and 2) instantiate the FIFO Controller and Profiler IP Cores and connect all signals on the block-design level. The generated bitstream and driver are passed to an FPGA in-the-loop to run the accelerated buffer sizing algorithm. The output is a set of locally optimal FIFO sizes used to configure the regular FIFO sizes to build the real accelerator bitstream.

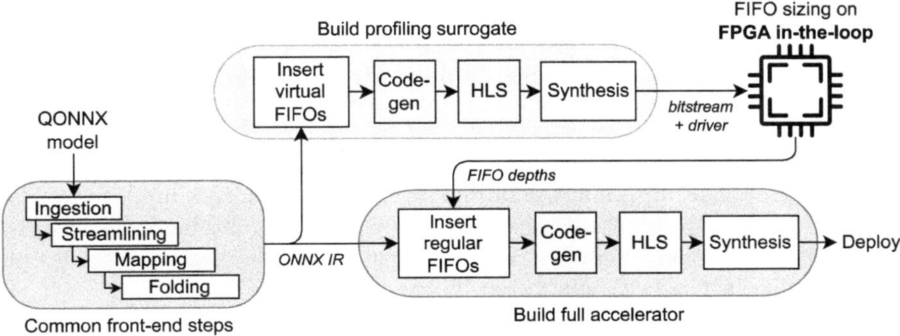

Fig. 2. Simplified FINN tool flow incorporating FPGA-accelerated FIFO sizing. Steps colored in blue can be re-used between both builds. (Color figure online)

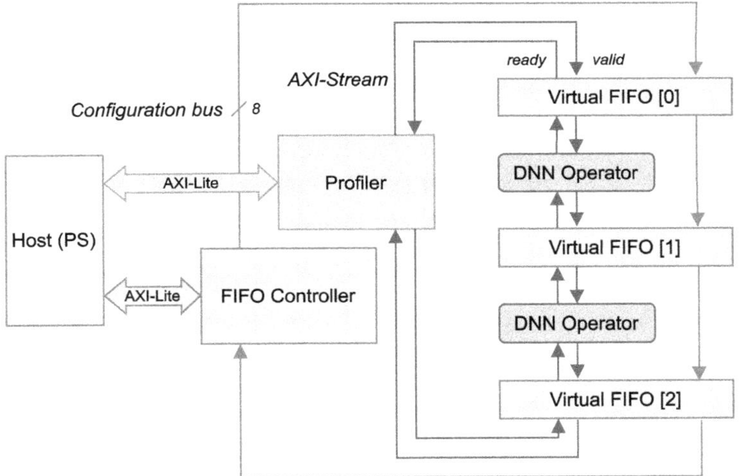

Fig. 3. Simplified block diagram of the profiling surrogate design. The AXI-Stream data path is unconnected, leaving only the control flow to be implemented.

In the following, we explain our solution in detail, covering the virtual FIFO (Sect. 4.1) and its controller (Sect. 4.2), the profiler (Sect. 4.3), and the FIFO sizing algorithm itself (Sect. 4.4). Figure 3 shows a schematic overview of how these components interface with the layer-parallel DNN operators within a FINN accelerator, where communication is implemented via the AXI-Stream protocol. Note that the proposed components are not FINN-specific but generic in nature and could be applied to other streaming-based designs.

4.1   Virtual FIFO

As already mentioned, the virtual FIFO operates the stream control flow in different ways while leaving the data path (i.e., AXI-Stream tDATA signals) unconnected. This component is controlled by a single-byte-wide, synchronous ring bus without flow control. Each packet transmitted over this bus consists of a 1-byte opcode, optionally followed by a 2-byte address and/or payload. Bus participants must pass-through packets without modifying their size, but they may modify their contents. Table 1 shows the three operating modes and corresponding instructions supported by the virtual FIFO.

Table 1. Operating modes and instructions of the virtual FIFO.

Mode	Instructions	Opcode	Payload (Bytes)
Idle	NOP	0x00	-
1) Run detached	RUN_DETACHED	0x07	–
	BARRIER_CLEAN	0x08	–
	BARRIER_DIRTY	0x09	–
	COMP_PERIOD	0x0A	Period (4)
2) Run paced	RUN_PACED	0x05	–
	READ_FILL	0x0C	ID (2), max. fill (4)
3) Run bounded	RUN_BOUNDED	0x04	–
	WRITE_FILL	0x0E	ID (2), capacity (4)
	READ_STALL	0x0D	ID (2), stall status (1)

RUN_DETACHED. This mode turns the FIFO into a free-running source and sink for its adjacent operators, measuring the frame initiation interval while feeding four frames worth of transactions, which is sufficient to profile all FINN operators, the deepest of which are normalization operators with an internal pipeline depth of two frames. The completion of this measurement can be polled via the BARRIER_CLEAN instruction, which is overwritten with BARRIER_DIRTY by any FIFO that is still processing transactions. Once a BARRIER_CLEAN reaches the controller at the end of the ring, the COMP_PERIOD instruction can be issued to perform a distributed computation of the global maximum of the feature map initiation period. This global bottleneck period determines the theoretical peak throughput of the entire dataflow pipeline.

RUN_PACED. In this mode, the FIFO behaves like a buffer with infinite size. It keeps track of its maximum fill level, which can be read out via the READ_FILL command.

RUN_BOUNDED. In this mode, the FIFO emulates the behavior of a normal FIFO with a maximum capacity configured via the WRITE_FILL instruction. The READ_STALL can be used to ascertain the stall signature, which uses four sticky bits to indicate on which ready or valid channel the FIFO stalled or received/exerted back-pressure during its operation. This can be helpful for in-depth profiling of a pipeline but is not used in our FIFO sizing approach.

4.2 FIFO Controller

This component serves as an adapter from AXI-Lite to the FIFO configuration ring bus. To simplify its design, it is synchronous and only allows a single instruction to be in flight at a time. It converts an AXI read or write command to the corresponding configuration bus instruction and only answers the AXI request once the packet arrives back at the controller. This means that the response time for each command scales linearly with the number of FIFOs on the ring, but since this number is usually well below 1000 cycles, the controller is still faster than necessary for this application.

The AXI-Lite peripheral exposes a 24-bit address aperture, which encodes both the opcode and FIFO ID for READ/WRITE instructions. It is controlled by a host CPU running the FIFO sizing algorithm. In our case, we use a ZYNQ platform-FPGA running a PYNQ-based driver on the processing system (PS).

4.3 Profiler

The profiler is also controlled via AXI-Lite and is attached to the primary input and output streams of the accelerator under test. It feeds data frames of fixed size and measures their initiation interval and processing latency by counting clock cycles and keeping track of frame initiation timestamps in a fixed-size buffer. The data rate applied to the accelerator input can be throttled based on a minimum interval between frames (i.e., the profiler will feed each frame as fast as possible and then wait until the minimum interval has been reached before continuing with the next frame). For real accelerators with data-path, the profiler also generates pseudo-random input data using a linear-feedback-shift-register (LFSR) and computes a checksum on the output data.

4.4 FIFO Sizing Algorithm

To perform FIFO sizing on the profiling surrogate, we apply a three-phase approach: First, we measure the pipeline bottleneck interval by running in detached mode as described in Sect. 4.1. Next, we measure the maximum occupancy as an upper bound of the depth for each FIFO by running the pipeline in paced mode while throttling the primary input to the bottleneck interval. Throttling ensures that, with increasing runtime, observed FIFO occupancy is bounded and does not approach infinity, as it otherwise would for FIFOs placed in front of a bottleneck. As a result, we can run the pipeline for a fixed time much greater than its latency, usually 1 s, to measure the asymptotic maximum occupancies.

Finally, starting from the upper bound on FIFO depths, we iteratively decrease and test the depth of individual FIFOs via binary search until a stop condition is reached, which can be set to either a) any (≥ 1 clock cycle) interval degradation, or b) any interval or latency degradation. For the latter, we always allow a slight latency degradation of 0.05%, because we observed a latency fluctuation of this magnitude for some of our experiments that could otherwise lead to early stopping. Optionally, the stop condition can be relaxed by a given percentage, which allows us to potentially trade off insignificant performance degradation against significant FIFO size savings. To test the FIFO depth configuration in each search iteration, we run the accelerator in bounded mode for an iteration runtime determined by the following conservative heuristic based on the measured latency and minimum ~ 1 ms response time of the Python driver:

$$iteration\_runtime = \max\{1\ ms,\ latency * 4\} \tag{1}$$

The search is performed on a per-FIFO basis (i.e., one FIFO is minimized until any further decrease in depth would result in a violation of the stop condition). The depth of this FIFO is then fixed and the search moves on to the next FIFO. Because this approach produces FIFO depth configurations that cannot be further optimized by decreasing any single FIFO alone (i.e., without changing the capacity distribution between FIFOs), we consider it locally optimal. As such, the search order has an impact on how close the result will be to the unknown global optimum. We allow to choose from five intuitive orders: forward, reverse, or alternating (i.e., outside-in) topological order, largest FIFO first, or deepest FIFO first. We compare the performance of these search orders under the different stop conditions in the next section.

5   Evaluation

We evaluate our FIFO sizing approach on a suite of 12 example DNN accelerators, consisting of nine models based on the finn-examples repository [2] and three transformer models based on FINN-T [5]. All syntheses target the AMD Zynq UltraScale+ RFSoC2x2 development board at a clock frequency of 100 MHz, using Vivado 2024.2 on an AMD EPYC 9655 CPU with 32 FINN worker threads. We use the latest version of FINN+ [14], our fork of FINN, to produce all results. FIFO sizes are validated by applying them to the full accelerator builds and measuring the resulting performance on hardware.

In the following, we evaluate the resource utilization of our solution (Sect. 5.1), analyze the impact of search orders and stop conditions (Sect. 5.2), and compare against existing methods (Sect. 5.3).

5.1   Resource Utilization

To show the breadth of our example model suite, Table 2 lists the number of FIFOs (which equals the number of FINN hardware operators in the accelerator),

Table 2. Overview of example models and comparison of runtime and resource cost of their real build (full accelerator synthesis) and surrogate build (FIFO sizing). For the real build, resource percentage used for FIFOs is given to gauge their impact.

Model (Topology)	# FIFOs	FPS	Real				Real (FIFOs)		Surrogate	
			Time [min]	LUT [k]	BRAM18	DSP	LUT [%]	BRAM [%]	Time [min]	LUT [k]
KWS (MLP)	11	204k	12	45	77	0	1.4%	0.0%	11	11
CyberSec (MLP)	7	1.4M	10	17	40	0	1.4%	0.0%	9	3
TFC-1bit (MLP)	11	1.4M	10	17	29	0	4.0%	0.0%	11	5
TFC-2bit (MLP)	11	1.4M	12	28	51	0	2.9%	0.0%	11	5
CNV-1bit (CNN)	33	3.1k	12	29	162	0	3.1%	0.6%	16	12
CNV-2bit (CNN)	34	868	13	36	214	0	5.7%	1.4%	16	13
VGG10 (1D-CNN)	65	97k	27	96	36	1098	9.5%	0.0%	26	22
MobileNetV1 (DSCNN)	142	254	39	139	1039	696	9.5%	0.7%	43	35
ResNet-50*	269	110	222	356	4557	11	16.4%	1.0%	95	72
RadioML Transformer	87	19k	43	256	595	240	4.9%	0.2%	34	45
Vision Transformer	147	1.2k	33	153	206	120	16.7%	9.7%	48	50
Language Transformer	140	1.2k	45	269	375	120	9.7%	4.8%	49	53

ResNet-50 is synthesized for Alveo U250 as it does not fit our target device.

the throughput in frames per second (FPS), and the build time and resource utilization of the full accelerator build for each model. This build is based on the minimal FIFO sizes without performance degradation found by our approach. As can be seen in the resource breakdown, FIFOs account for 1.4% to 16.7% of the total accelerator LUT utilization and 0% to 9.7% of the BRAM utilization.

Also shown in Table 2 is the build time and LUT utilization of the corresponding surrogate designs. Since the data-path is pruned, the surrogate does not require DSP or BRAM resources (except two BRAM18 for the timestamp buffer of the profiler). Its LUT cost is composed of approximately 2k LUTs for the Profiler, which is implemented in C++ HLS, 175 LUTs for the FIFO controller, and 200 LUTs per virtual FIFO, both implemented in SystemVerilog. The remaining LUT resources are spent on the pipeline control path, which amounts to 140 LUT per operator on average over all models. Extrapolating these numbers, our mid-size FPGA board could accommodate surrogate designs with up to 1200 operators, which, to the best of our knowledge, is larger than any model ever implemented with FINN [17]. This makes it feasible to permanently deploy such a board as an accelerator for FIFO sizing, regardless of the final target device. Our experimental setup is constructed this way, using GitLab continuous integration (CI) with an FPGA-board runner next to our build servers.

5.2 Search Parameter Analysis

The binary search phase of our algorithm is crucial for reducing FIFO depths from the upper bound given by the maximum occupancy to a minimum that

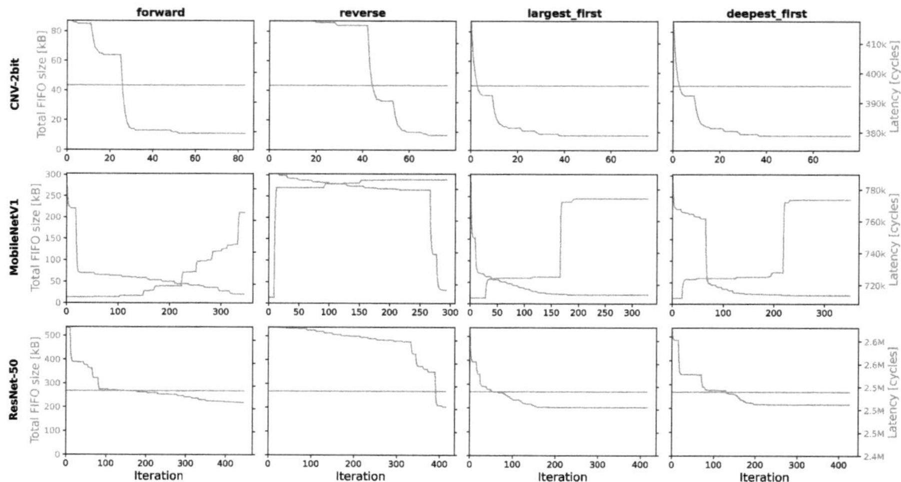

Fig. 4. Binary search phase for select models and search orders. The stop condition is set to interval degradation. Only passing iterations are shown.

still yields nominal interval and/or latency. To provide intuition about this process, Fig. 4 shows the search phase for some example models with only interval degradation set as the stop condition. We report total FIFO size as the key metric, as it accounts for both, the found depth and the fixed bitwidth of each FIFO. For most models, the search is able to reduce FIFO sizes substantially (42% on average). For example, looking only at the forward search order, the initial total size for MobileNetV1 is 303 kB, which is reduced by 93% to 21 kB in 429 search iterations without any interval degradation. However, latency starts to increase slightly after a total FIFO size of 64 kB is reached, resulting in 7% latency degradation at the end of the search. This effect of latency increasing before interval/throughput increases is not present for every model and can be explained as follows: Shrinking FIFOs can reduce pipeline parallelism between stages operating faster than the bottleneck, decreasing overlap and increasing latency as these stages must wait more often. Throughput only drops once a FIFO has been shrunk so much that it creates a new bottleneck by disrupting the natural rhythm of the pipeline.

Effects like this are highly dependent on the pipeline topology, folding, and I/O access patterns of each individual operator. The search order also effects the final FIFO size, latency degradation (if allowed), and number of search iterations needed, because it can change how buffer volume is distributed across FIFOs. Figure 5 shows how five different search orders compare in terms of result quality for both stop conditions. Five models have been omitted, as they feature very small FIFO sizes and are not sensitive to these search parameters at all. The results show that, at least for the "both" stop condition, all tested search orders perform similarly, suggesting close proximity to the global optimum. Still, since

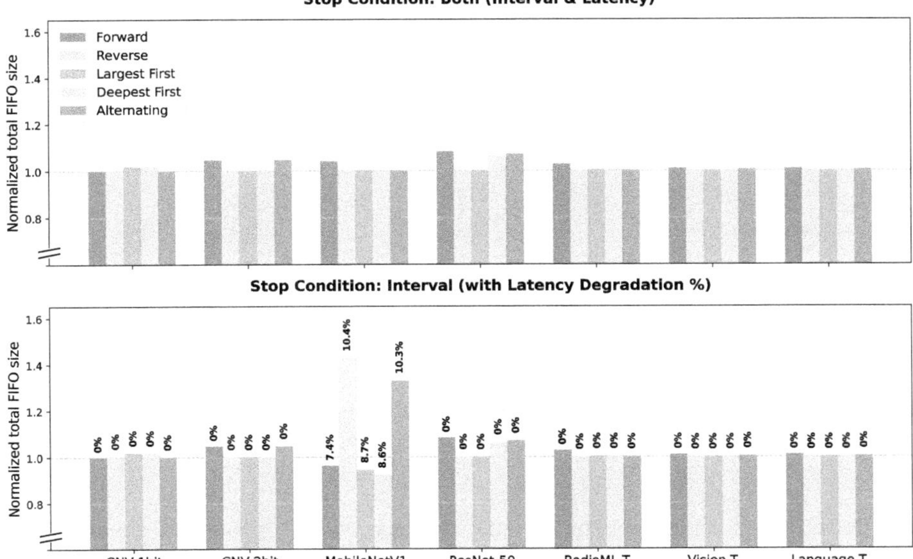

Fig. 5. Comparison of search orders for different stop conditions. Total FIFO size is normalized to the minimum total FIFO size achieved for the "both" stop condition for each model respectively. Relative latency degradation is annotated where applicable.

the FIFO sizing algorithm runs quickly (maximum 107 s for ResNet-50 and 12 s on average), we recommend to run the algorithm with multiple search orders and pick the best result.

Looking at the results for the "interval" stop condition, we don't recommend to allow latency degradation during the search, as it doesn't make a difference for any model except MobileNetV1, where the FIFO size savings are small ($<10\%$) but latency degradation is significant ($\geq 7.4\%$). Instead, allowing a preset interval and latency degradation via the stop condition relaxation is a better option. We demonstrate this in Fig. 6, where we plot how the required total FIFO size behaves as we sweep the relaxation for the "both" stop condition and largest-first search order. Note that a 100% interval degradation means a 50% throughput degradation. The results show that a slight performance degradation can be traded against significant FIFO size savings for certain models, in this case MobileNetV1, where a 3% relaxation reduces FIFO size by over 80%. Depending on the situation, trade-offs like this might be attractive, for example if the accelerator performance overshoots the application requirements due to limited flexibility of the pipeline parallelism configuration (i.e., folding).

5.3 Baseline Comparison

Table 3 compares the result quality of our approach with the "FINN" and "Heuristic" [23] baselines described in Sect. 3. Note that the numbers shown here might

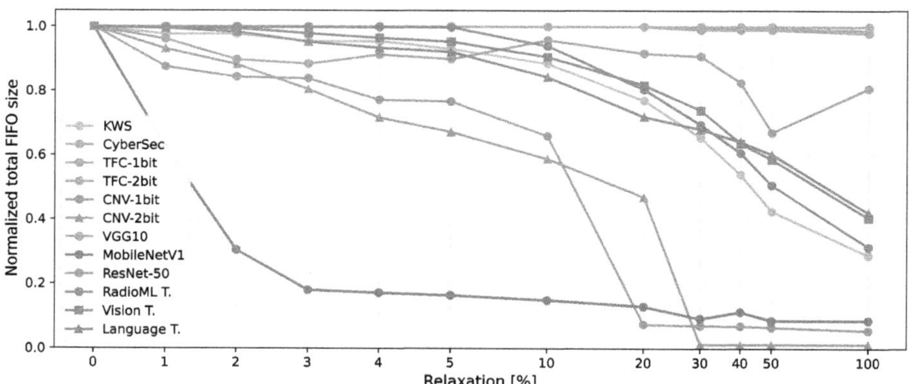

Fig. 6. Sweep over relaxation for largest-first search order and "both" (interval degradation or latency degradation) stop condition. Logarithmic x-axis from 5% onwards.

not match the results reported in [23] because we (re-)produced them on the most recent implementation version. As one can see, some models barely require any buffering, such as CyberSec, TFC, and VGG-10, where all FIFOs could be set to the minimum possible depth of two. For these models, all methods arrive practically at the same result. For the other models though, the FINN baseline at default settings ($N = 2$ frames simulation duration, input throttling enabled) is essentially unusable, as we observe interval degradation between 10% and 91% for eight models and up to 13x larger total FIFO size than our best solution. The largest Transformer model failed synthesis due to an excessively deep FIFO. As a consequence, we experimented with different settings: The results for N=4 and disabled throttling largely avoid interval degradation, but introduce even larger FIFOs, with a 33.6x size overhead for MobileNetV1.

For the Heuristic method, we show two configurations: 1) the "rtlsim" operating mode with no relaxation selected and 2) the "tree-model" mode with "aggressive" relaxation. Among all possible configurations, these performed generally the best in terms of interval degradation and FIFO size over-estimation, respectively. Still, the Heuristic method either over-estimates FIFO sizes by up to 18.9x (for ResNet-50) and/or incurs an interval degradation by up to 21% (for CNV-2bit). Crucially, the large and complex models, where FIFOs are most impactful, suffer from at least a 4.9x FIFO size overhead (MobileNetV1) or are not supported by this FIFO sizing method at all. This is the case for the Transformer models, whose topology includes nested branches that are not currently supported by the FIFO sizing algorithm.

To compare the FIFO sizing runtime, we report two distinct metrics in Table 4: 1) The effective FIFO sizing time, which does not include time spent on build steps that need to be performed anyway for the final build or, in our case, can be shared between surrogate and final build. 2) The end-to-end build time, which is the time to generate the final accelerator from scratch, including

Table 3. Comparison against FINN and Heuristic [23] baselines, showing total FIFO size and interval degradation relative to our solution.

Method	LiveFIFO		FINN		FINN		Heuristic		Heuristic	
Mode	best order		$N = 2$		$N = 4^\dagger$		rtlsim		tree-model	
Relaxation	no degradation		–		–		none		aggressive	
Model	Size [kB]	Intvl [cycles]	Size [rel.]	Intvl [degr.]	Size [rel.]	Intvl [degr.]	Size [rel.]	Intvl [degr.]	Size [rel.]	Intvl [degr.]
KWS	0.4	490	1.0x	62%	1.4x	1%	1.6x	0%	1.0x	0%
CyberSec	0.1	70	1.0x	0%	1.0x	0%	1.0x	0%	1.0x	0%
TFC-1bit	0.2	70	1.0x	10%	1.0x	0%	1.0x	0%	1.0x	0%
TFC-2bit	0.2	70	1.0x	10%	3.4x	0%	1.0x	0%	1.0x	0%
CNV-1bit	2.7	32774	1.8x	91%	1.8x	4%	1.2x	0.2%	0.7x	8%
CNV-2bit	10.1	115206	1.2x	14%	1.1x	13%	0.6x	0%	0.3x	21%
VGG10	2.2	1027	1.0x	0%	1.1x	0%	1.2x	0%	1.0x	0%
MobileNetV1	22.1	394272	13.0x	17%	33.6x	16%	8.6x	0.3%	4.9x	1%
ResNet-50	202.7	903174	2.7x	0%	4.8x	0%	18.9x	0%	6.9x	0%
RadioML T.	17.7	5120	1.3x	15%	1.7x	0%	–	–	–	–
Vision T.	85.0	81920	0.9x	60%	1.4x	0%	–	–	–	–
Language T.	84.5	81920	2.5x	–	4.6x	–	–	–	–	–

† *Input throttling disabled.*

Table 4. FIFO sizing runtime of our approach (including surrogate synthesis, search time on FPGA shown in brackets) compared to existing methods. End-to-end build time is spent on generating a fully functional and FIFO-sized accelerator from scratch.

	Effective FIFO sizing time [s]				End-to-end build [min]	
Method	**LiveFIFO**	FINN	Heuristic	Heuristic	**LiveFIFO**	Heuristic
Mode	best order	$N = 4$	rtlsim	tree-model	best order	tree-model
KWS	584 (1)	153	<1	<1	22	18
CyberSec	489 (1)	77	2	<1	18	13
TFC-1bit	576 (1)	113	<1	<1	20	16
TFC-2bit	573 (1)	88	<1	1	21	15
CNV-1bit	845 (1)	218	8	2	26	18
CNV-2bit	850 (2)	301	27	4	27	15
VGG10	1487 (1)	343	6	<1	52	29
MobileNetV1	2492 (16)	5008	470	110	80	47
ResNet-50	5140 (107)	19439	8104	324	307	227
RadioML T.	1964 (2)	279	–	–	75	–
Vision T.	2754 (10)	1314	–	–	79	–
Language T.	2768 (9)	1419	–	–	91	–

the entire FIFO sizing procedure. Considering the synthesis time of the profiling surrogate, our solution is always the slowest, except for the MobileNetV1 and ResNet-50 models, which require extreme simulation durations due to their large size and long interval. The Heuristic method is much faster, at least when using the tree-model based operator characterization as originally intended. However, when considering the big picture, our method extends the ResNet-50 end-to-end build time by only about 35% over this baseline, which is largely due to the fast synthesis of the lean profiling surrogate.

Overall, our approach delivers locally optimal FIFO sizes with guaranteed performance while keeping end-to-end runtimes manageable and generally within the same order as the original synthesis time, albeit at the cost of some additional runtime and requiring an FPGA in the loop. Since most design decisions, such as folding or resource selection, do not directly depend on the FIFO configuration, we recommend to skip FIFO sizing during early design iterations, or to consider fast FIFO sizing methods as a rough approximation, before employing our method for fine-tuning of the final accelerator candidates.

6   Conclusion

In this work, we recognize FIFO sizing as a critical aspect of dataflow accelerator compilation. As shown by our experimental evaluation, existing methods are time-consuming and/or inaccurate, leading to over-sized FIFOs or performance degradation. Our unique approach places an FPGA in the design loop, accelerating the evaluation of individual FIFO configurations by five orders of magnitude compared to simulation. This enables a search-based algorithm that finds locally optimal FIFO depth configurations within seconds. We integrate our technique into the open-source FINN+ framework [14] as a principled solution to FIFO sizing with tight buffer bounds and guaranteed performance—addressing a longstanding limitation of existing methods.

The primary limitation is the need for synthesis and deployment of an additional profiling surrogate design before the final FDNA can be generated. While still faster than existing simulation-based FIFO sizing methods in some cases, future work could explore if massively parallel simulation [10,25] paired with optimized search algorithms could reach similar results in a reasonable time frame without requiring an FPGA. Other avenues for future research could be to use our approach as a gold standard to calibrate other FIFO sizing methods [23] or quality-of-result estimation tools [15,19], or to guide further optimization of FDNA compilers by providing insights into optimal FIFO distribution within a pipeline.

Acknowledgments. This work has been funded by the German Federal Ministry for the Environment, Nature Conservation, Nuclear Safety and Consumer Protection under the EKI project [67KI32004A], the LOEWE initiative (Hesse, Germany) within the emergenCITY center [LOEWE/1/12/519/03/05.001(0016)/72], and the Ministry of Culture and Science of the State of North Rhine-Westphalia under the SAIL project [NW21-059D]. We gratefully acknowledge the computing time provided to us on the high-performance computers Noctua 2 and Otus at the NHR Center PC2, which is funded by the Federal Ministry of Education and Research and the state governments.

Disclosure of Interests. The authors have no competing interests to declare that are relevant to the content of this article.

References

1. Abi-Karam, S., Sarkar, R., Basalama, S., Cong, J., Hao, C.: FIFOAdvisor: a DSE framework for automated FIFO sizing of high-level synthesis designs. In: Proceedings of the 31th Asia and South Pacific Design Automation Conference, ASPDAC 2026 (2026). https://arxiv.org/abs/2510.20981, to appear
2. AMD: finn-examples repository. https://github.com/Xilinx/finn-examples
3. Beheshti, N., Ganjali, Y., Ghobadi, M., McKeown, N., Salmon, G.: Experimental study of router buffer sizing. In: Proceedings of the 8th ACM SIGCOMM Conference on Internet Measurement, IMC 2008, pp. 197–210. Association for Computing Machinery, New York (2008). https://doi.org/10.1145/1452520.1452545
4. Benazouz, M., Marchetti, O., Munier-Kordon, A., Michel, T.: A new method for minimizing buffer sizes for cyclo-static dataflow graphs. In: 2010 8th IEEE Workshop on Embedded Systems for Real-Time Multimedia, pp. 11–20 (2010). https://doi.org/10.1109/ESTMED.2010.5666980
5. Berganski, C., Jentzsch, F., Platzner, M., Kuhmichel, M., Giefers, H.: FINN-T: compiling custom dataflow accelerators for quantized transformers. In: 2024 International Conference on Field Programmable Technology (ICFPT), pp. 01–10 (2024). https://doi.org/10.1109/ICFPT64416.2024.11113391
6. Bilsen, G., Engels, M., Lauwereins, R., Peperstraete, J.: Cyclo-static data flow. In: 1995 International Conference on Acoustics, Speech, and Signal Processing, vol. 5, pp. 3255–3258 (1995). https://doi.org/10.1109/ICASSP.1995.479579
7. Blott, M., et al.: FINN-R: an end-to-end deep-learning framework for fast exploration of quantized neural networks. ACM Trans. Reconfigurable Technol. Syst. **11**(3) (2018). https://doi.org/10.1145/3242897
8. Borras, H., et al.: Open-source FPGA-ML codesign for the MLPerf tiny benchmark (2022). https://arxiv.org/abs/2206.11791
9. Duarte, J., et al.: Fast inference of deep neural networks in FPGAs for particle physics. JINST **13**(07), P07027 (2018). https://doi.org/10.1088/1748-0221/13/07/P07027
10. Emami, M., Bourgeat, T., Larus, J.R.: Parendi: thousand-way parallel RTL simulation. In: Proceedings of the 30th ACM International Conference on Architectural Support for Programming Languages and Operating Systems, vol. 2, pp. 783–797. Association for Computing Machinery, New York (2025). https://doi.org/10.1145/3676641.3716010
11. Ghosal, A., et al.: Static dataflow with access patterns: semantics and analysis. In: Proceedings of the 49th Annual Design Automation Conference, DAC 2012, pp. 656–663. Association for Computing Machinery, New York (2012). https://doi.org/10.1145/2228360.2228479
12. He, K., Zhang, X., Ren, S., Sun, J.: Deep residual learning for image recognition. In: 2016 IEEE Conference on Computer Vision and Pattern Recognition (CVPR), pp. 770–778 (2016). https://doi.org/10.1109/CVPR.2016.90
13. Honorat, A., Dardaillon, M., Miomandre, H., Nezan, J.F.: Automated buffer sizing of dataflow applications in a high-level synthesis workflow. ACM Trans. Reconfigurable Technol. Syst. **17**(1) (2024). https://doi.org/10.1145/3626103
14. Jentzsch, F., Berganski, C., Jungemann, L., Wintermann, B.: FINN+ (2026). https://doi.org/10.5281/zenodo.19100351, https://github.com/eki-project/finn-plus
15. Jentzsch, F., Platzner, M.: Empirical QoR estimation flow for fast design space exploration of DNN dataflow accelerators. In: 2025 International Conference on

Field Programmable Technology (ICFPT), pp. 231–232 (2025). https://doi.org/10.1109/ICFPT67023.2025.00044

16. Lee, E.A., Messerschmitt, D.G.: Synchronous data flow. Proc. IEEE **75**(9), 1235–1245 (1987)

17. Mrahorović, M.: Integration of a convolutional neural network for speech-to-text recognition in an FPGA compiler flow. Master's thesis, TU Delft (2021). https://resolver.tudelft.nl/uuid:b6c889b1-e06f-447c-af69-55708555bf90

18. Parks, T., Pino, J., Lee, E.: A comparison of synchronous and cycle-static dataflow. In: Conference Record of the Twenty-Ninth Asilomar Conference on Signals, Systems and Computers, vol. 1, pp. 204–210 (1995). https://doi.org/10.1109/ACSSC.1995.540541

19. Rahimifar, M.M., Rahali, H.E., Therrien, A.C.: Rule4ML: an open-source tool for resource utilization and latency estimation for ML models on FPGA. Mach. Learn.: Sci. Technol. **6**(1), 015009 (2025). https://doi.org/10.1088/2632-2153/ada71c

20. Roumage, G., Azaiez, S., Faure, C., Louise, S.: An extended survey and a comparison framework for dataflow models of computation and communication (2025). https://arxiv.org/abs/2501.07273

21. Sarkar, R., Hao, C.: LightningSim: fast and accurate trace-based simulation for high-level synthesis. In: 2023 IEEE 31st Annual International Symposium on Field-Programmable Custom Computing Machines (FCCM), pp. 1–11. IEEE Computer Society, Los Alamitos (2023). https://doi.org/10.1109/FCCM57271.2023.00010

22. Shi, R., Ogrenci, S.: SPRING: systematic profiling of randomly interconnected neural networks generated by HLS. In: 2025 IEEE 43rd VLSI Test Symposium (VTS), pp. 1–5. IEEE Computer Society, Los Alamitos (2025). https://doi.org/10.1109/VTS65138.2025.11022878

23. Stasytis, L., Jentzsch, F., Preusser, T., Umuroglu, Y., Petri-Koenig, J., István, Z.: Heuristic & expert-guided buffer sizing for neural network inference applications on FPGAs. In: 2025 International Conference on Field Programmable Technology (ICFPT), pp. 189–197 (2025). https://doi.org/10.1109/ICFPT67023.2025.00032

24. Wang, G., Allen, R., Andrade, H., Sangiovanni-Vincentelli, A.: Communication storage optimization for static dataflow with access patterns under periodic scheduling and throughput constraint. Comput. Electr. Eng. **40**(6), 1858–1873 (2014). https://doi.org/10.1016/j.compeleceng.2014.05.002

25. Wang, H., Beamer, S.: RepCut: Superlinear parallel RTL simulation with replication-aided partitioning. In: Proceedings of the 28th ACM International Conference on Architectural Support for Programming Languages and Operating Systems, ASPLOS 2023, vol. 3, pp. 572–585. Association for Computing Machinery, New York (2023). https://doi.org/10.1145/3582016.3582034

StreamLearn-FPGA: An Elastic Weight Consolidation Accelerator for Online Continual Learning on Reconfigurable SoCs

Saher Elsayed[(✉)]

University of Pennsylvania, Philadelphia, PA, USA
`selsayed@seas.upenn.edu`

Abstract. Online continual learning (CL), where a model must learn new tasks sequentially without forgetting prior ones, is a fundamental capability for adaptive edge AI systems. Elastic Weight Consolidation (EWC) is among the most principled algorithmic approaches, using the Fisher information matrix to identify and protect task-critical parameters, but its per-task Fisher computation incurs a $4.7\times$ runtime overhead over standard fine-tuning that makes it impractical on embedded CPU platforms. We present **StreamLearn-FPGA**, a dedicated hardware architecture for EWC-based continual learning targeting the Xilinx Zynq UltraScale+ ZU3EG SoC. StreamLearn-FPGA introduces three architectural innovations: (1) a pipelined *Importance Scoring Unit* (ISU) that computes per-parameter Fisher diagonal estimates at 41.7 M parameters/second, (2) a *Gated Update Engine* (GUE) that enforces EWC parameter protection in hardware at 12.4 ns per parameter, and (3) an *Elastic Threshold Controller* (ETC) that automatically adjusts the regularisation penalty λ based on running task-loss trajectories. Evaluated on a 10-task sequential classification scenario with a 0.5M-parameter CNN on the ZCU104 board, StreamLearn-FPGA achieves **8.2×** faster per-task training and **7.2×** lower energy versus EWC-CPU, while delivering 84.58% average accuracy—exceeding EWC-CPU (79.93%) and approaching PackNet (85.55%) at **12.9×** PackNet's speed. The design occupies 38.4% LUTs, 52.1% DSPs, and 61.3% BRAMs of the ZU3EG at 250 MHz and 5.9 W.

Keywords: continual learning · FPGA · elastic weight consolidation · reconfigurable SoC · hardware accelerator · catastrophic forgetting · edge AI · Fisher information

1 Introduction

Deployed edge AI systems increasingly operate in non-stationary environments where input distributions shift over time. An industrial inspection system must adapt to new defect categories; a medical device must incorporate new diagnostic

© The Author(s), under exclusive license to Springer Nature Switzerland AG 2027
G. Leone et al. (Eds.): ARC 2026, LNCS 16514, pp. 51–62, 2027.
https://doi.org/10.1007/978-3-032-29365-7_4

criteria; a robotics platform must learn new manipulation tasks without human redeployment. The naive response, fine-tuning the deployed model on new data, leads to *catastrophic forgetting* [6,13], where gradient updates for new tasks overwrite weights critical to previously mastered objectives.

Continual learning (CL) algorithms address this via three broad families: (i) regularisation-based methods [1,8,9,21] that penalise changes to task-critical parameters, (ii) memory-replay methods [4,11] that interleave stored exemplars, and (iii) expansion-based methods [12,15] that grow or partition the network per task. Among regularisation approaches, Elastic Weight Consolidation (EWC) [8] is particularly suited to embedded deployment: it requires no replay buffer, does not expand the model, and is grounded in a principled Bayesian posterior approximation.

EWC augments the training loss with a quadratic penalty:

$$\mathcal{L}(\theta) = \mathcal{L}_{\text{new}}(\theta) + \frac{\lambda}{2} \sum_i F_i \big(\theta_i - \theta^*_{A,i}\big)^2 \tag{1}$$

where θ is the full parameter vector, $\lambda > 0$ is the global regularisation strength, $\theta^*_{A,i}$ is the i-th parameter after training on the prior task A, and $F_i = \mathbb{E}\big[(\nabla_{\theta_i} \log p(\mathcal{D}_A \mid \theta))^2\big]$ is the diagonal Fisher information for parameter i estimated over prior task dataset $\mathcal{D}_A$. The critical bottleneck is computing F_i: for a 0.5M-parameter model, a full Fisher pass adds 198.4 s per task on an ARM Cortex-A53 versus 42.1 s for simple fine-tuning—a 4.7× overhead prohibitive for real-time edge deployment.

Existing FPGA accelerators target standard supervised training [10,22,23] or inference [18,19]. None addresses CL-specific compute: Fisher diagonal estimation, importance-gated parameter updates, or adaptive regularisation control. StreamLearn-FPGA fills this gap.

Contributions:

1. The first FPGA accelerator designed for EWC-based CL, co-integrating ISU, GUE, and ETC on a single Zynq UltraScale+ ZU3EG SoC.
2. A 32-lane pipelined ISU computing diagonal Fisher estimates at 41.7 M parameters/s, achieving 8.2× speedup over ARM EWC.
3. A hardware-enforced GUE applying per-parameter EWC gating at 12.4 ns latency with zero overhead over standard gradient updates.
4. An adaptive ETC modulating the EWC penalty from per-epoch loss trajectories, improving accuracy by 2.24 pp over a fixed penalty.
5. A 10-task evaluation: 8.2× time reduction, 7.2× energy reduction, 84.58% average accuracy.

2 Background and Related Work

2.1 Catastrophic Forgetting and Continual Learning

Catastrophic forgetting [6,13] arises because gradient descent steps for new task data perturb parameters shared with prior task representations. Regularisation methods such as EWC [8], SI [21], MAS [1], and LwF [9] impose soft constraints on parameter updates. Replay methods including GEM [11] and ER [4] replay past exemplars during new-task training. Expansion methods such as PNN [15] and PackNet [12] partition or grow the model per task.

2.2 Elastic Weight Consolidation

EWC [8] approximates the diagonal Fisher as:

$$\hat{F}_i = \frac{1}{|\mathcal{D}_A|} \sum_{(x,y)\in\mathcal{D}_A} \left(\frac{\partial \log p(y \mid x, \theta_A^*)}{\partial \theta_i} \right)^2 \tag{2}$$

where $|\mathcal{D}_A|$ is the dataset cardinality. This requires one forward-backward pass over $\mathcal{D}_A$ per task boundary. For a 0.5M-parameter model at FP32 precision the Fisher vector is 2 MB—within the BRAM budget of mid-range UltraScale+ devices. Online EWC [16] and the quadratic-penalty correction of Huszár [7] propose recursive Fisher approximations that share the same per-step computational structure as Eq. (2) and would benefit equally from ISU-style acceleration.

2.3 FPGA Accelerators for Neural Network Training

Early work demonstrated FPGA training viability for small networks [23]. Subsequent systems targeted few-shot learning [5], online adaptation [10], and transfer learning [17]. Inference accelerators such as FINN [18], DeepBurning [20], and Caffeine [22] show FPGAs can match GPU throughput-per-watt for structured workloads. Dynamic Partial Reconfiguration [2,19] supports model switching at runtime, but none of these works addresses CL-specific overheads. StreamLearn-FPGA co-designs Fisher estimation, importance-gated updates, and adaptive regularisation directly with the training datapath.

2.4 Importance-Based Parameter Protection

SI [21] accumulates online importance as the parameter-specific contribution to loss reduction. MAS [1] computes importance from output-function sensitivity, enabling unsupervised estimation. Both share the squared-gradient accumulation structure of EWC and are architecturally compatible with the ISU.

3 StreamLearn-FPGA Architecture

3.1 System Overview and Hardware–Software Partition

StreamLearn-FPGA targets the Xilinx Zynq UltraScale+ ZU3EG (71K LUTs, 360 DSPs, 216 BRAMs, dual ARM Cortex-A53 at 1.5 GHz). The design partitions computation along a clear principle: *data-parallel, numerically intensive operations execute in PL; lightweight scalar control operations execute in PS.*

Three PL units reside on the fabric: the Gradient Datapath (forward/backward pass), the ISU (Fisher accumulation), and the GUE (EWC gradient modification). The PS runs the ETC, updating the scalar penalty λ once per epoch. This partition is deliberate: (i) Fisher normalisation by the scalar $|\mathcal{D}_{t-1}|$ takes < 0.1 ms on the ARM PS and benefits from no PL routing; (ii) the ETC reads one scalar loss value, evaluates Eq. (5), and writes two scalars back, completing during inter-epoch DMA setup without any PL fabric stall. The PS–PL interface uses AXI4-Stream for gradient data and AXI4-Lite for control registers. Task checkpoints θ^* and Fisher vectors $\hat{F}$ reside in BRAM banks shared between the ISU and GUE via a banked 32×32-bit port.

Figure 1 shows the complete system block diagram with all inter-module connections, bus types, and data-flow directions.

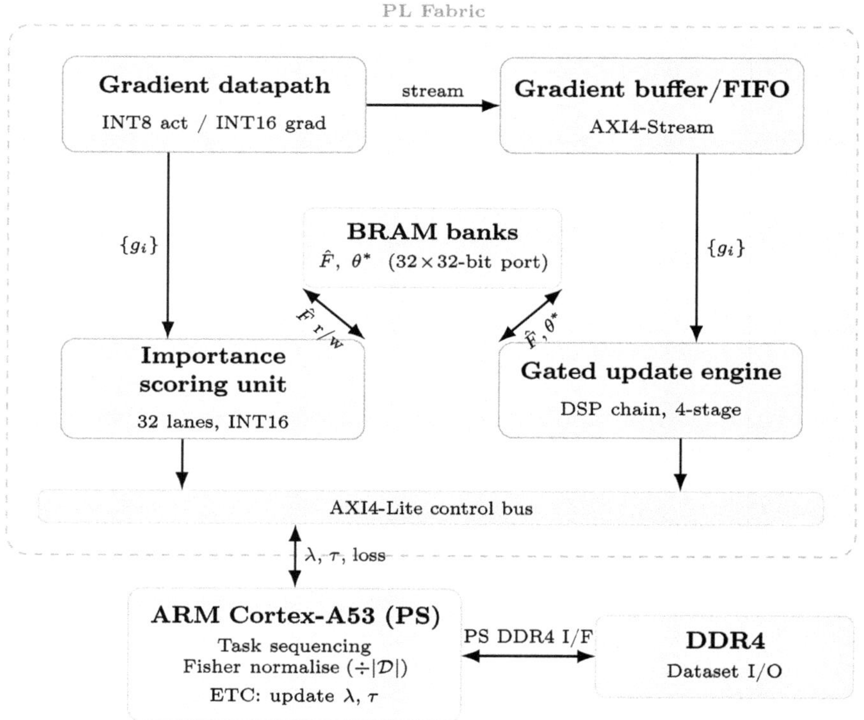

Fig. 1. StreamLearn-FPGA system block diagram on the Zynq UltraScale+ ZU3EG. The PL fabric (blue dashed region) hosts the Gradient Datapath (INT8 activations / INT16 gradients), Importance Scoring Unit (ISU, 32 lanes), Gated Update Engine (GUE, DSP chain), and shared BRAM banks storing $\hat{F}$ and θ^* via a 32×32-bit port, interconnected via AXI4-Stream for gradient flow. The ARM PS handles task sequencing, Fisher normalisation by the scalar dataset size $|\mathcal{D}|$ (< 0.1 ms), and ETC updates—writing λ and τ to GUE control registers via AXI4-Lite. DDR4 provides dataset I/O through the PS memory interface. (Color figure online)

StreamLearn-FPGA system block diagram on the Zynq UltraScale+ ZU3EG. The PL fabric (blue dashed region) hosts the Gradient Datapath (INT8 activations / INT16 gradients), Importance Scoring Unit (ISU, 32 lanes), Gated Update Engine (GUE, DSP chain), and shared BRAM banks storing $\hat{F}$ and θ^* via a 32×32-bit port, interconnected via AXI4-Stream for gradient flow. The ARM PS handles task sequencing, Fisher normalisation by the scalar dataset size $|\mathcal{D}|$ (< 0.1 ms), and ETC updates — writing λ and τ to GUE control registers via AXI4-Lite. DDR4 provides dataset I/O through the PS memory interface.

3.2 Importance Scoring Unit (ISU)

The ISU accelerates the most expensive EWC operation: accumulating squared per-parameter gradients across the prior-task dataset:

$$\hat{F}_i^{(t+1)} = \hat{F}_i^{(t)} + \left(g_i^{(t)}\right)^2, \quad i = 1, \ldots, |\theta| \tag{3}$$

where $g_i^{(t)}$ is the gradient of parameter i on sample t. The ISU implements a 32-lane vectorised pipeline. INT8 activations reduce forward-pass bandwidth and MAC cost; INT16 gradients provide sufficient dynamic range for Fisher accumulation without FP32 cost; INT32 accumulation prevents overflow. Each lane processes one parameter per clock cycle. At $250\,\mathrm{MHz}$ the ISU sustains $32 \times 250 = 8$ Gops/s, completing the full 0.5M-parameter Fisher in ~ 12 ms per dataset pass, a $71\times$ improvement over ARM Cortex-A53 scalar execution. The 0.5M-parameter Fisher vector (2 MB) is stored in 32 BRAMs configured as a 32×32-bit-wide port matching the ISU lane count for stall-free access. The ISU pipeline is 5 stages: gradient load, square (INT16→INT32), accumulate (INT32), normalise (ARM PS, < 0.1 ms), BRAM write-back.

3.3 Gated Update Engine (GUE)

The GUE enforces the EWC update rule in hardware:

$$\tilde{g}_i = g_i - \lambda \cdot \hat{F}_i \cdot (\theta_i - \theta_{A,i}^*) \tag{4}$$

where $\tilde{g}_i$ is the EWC-modified gradient, θ_i is the current parameter value, and $\theta_{A,i}^*$ is the prior-task checkpoint. The GUE fetches $\hat{F}_i$ and $\theta_{A,i}^*$ from BRAM, computes the penalty via a 3-DSP chain (multiply, scale by λ, subtract from g_i), and delivers $\tilde{g}_i$ within the same pipeline cycle as a standard update, achieving zero overhead once the pipeline is full. The 4-stage, 32-lane, $250\,\mathrm{MHz}$ configuration gives 12.4 ns per-parameter latency. The primary advantage over ARM PS gradient modification is latency hiding: the EWC subtraction executes inside the gradient datapath pipeline, eliminating the AXI read-modify-write round-trip that would stall the weight update step.

3.4   Elastic Threshold Controller (ETC)

Static EWC fixes λ across all tasks and epochs, under-protecting during early training and over-protecting near convergence. The ETC dynamically adjusts λ once per epoch:

$$\lambda^{(t+1)} = \lambda^{(t)} \cdot \exp\!\Big(\beta \cdot \mathrm{sign}\big(\Delta\mathcal{L}^{(t)} - \gamma\big)\Big) \tag{5}$$

Table 1. Resource utilisation on Zynq UltraScale+ ZU3EG (71K LUTs, 360 DSPs, 216 BRAMs).

Unit	LUT (%)	DSP (%)	BRAM (%)	FF (%)
Importance Scoring Unit	18.1	21.4	38.2	14.8
Gated Update Engine	12.4	22.7	9.7	9.6
Gradient Buffer / FIFO	4.2	4.8	10.6	4.8
Controller & AXI Comms	3.7	3.2	2.8	2.5
Total	**38.4**	**52.1**	**61.3**	**31.7**

where $\Delta\mathcal{L}^{(t)} = \mathcal{L}^{(t)} - \mathcal{L}^{(t-1)}$ is the per-epoch loss improvement, $\beta = 0.05$ is the multiplicative step size, and $\gamma = 0.005$ is the minimum-improvement threshold. When $\Delta\mathcal{L}^{(t)} < \gamma$ (convergence), λ increases to tighten protection; when $\Delta\mathcal{L}^{(t)} > \gamma$ (active learning), λ decreases to allow plasticity. The ETC runs on the ARM PS, reading the task loss from a GUE AXI-Lite status register, evaluating Eq. (5), and writing $\lambda^{(t+1)}$ back to the GUE control register in < 0.1 ms during inter-epoch DMA setup. An importance threshold τ, updated proportionally to λ, gates which parameters receive the full EWC penalty.

3.5   Resource Utilisation

Table 1 reports utilisation on the ZU3EG. The ISU dominates BRAM usage (38.2%) for Fisher vector storage; the GUE dominates DSP usage (22.7%) for the penalty chain. A total of 61.6% LUTs and 47.9% DSPs remain available for the gradient datapath and future extensions.

Power Measurement. CPU baseline power (5.2 W) is measured with PL fabric configured but idle, so that PL static power is included in both conditions, ensuring a fair comparison. Energy figures use separate on-board INA226 monitors on the PS and PL rails at 1 kHz.

4   Per-Task Continual Learning Algorithm

Algorithm 1 gives the per-task CL loop. Each task boundary triggers Phase 1 (Fisher computation via ISU) followed by Phase 2 (EWC-regularised training with GUE active and ETC updating λ per epoch).

4.1 Phase 1: Fisher Computation

Phase 1 triggers once at each task boundary. The ISU performs one forward-backward pass over $\mathcal{D}_{t-1}$, holding $|\mathcal{D}_{t-1}| = 1{,}000$ training samples per task, representative of resource-constrained edge scenarios where data arrives in bounded streaming batches. The gradient datapath operates at INT8 activations and INT16 gradients. After ISU accumulation, the ARM PS reads the Fisher total via AXI-Lite and divides by 1,000 to normalise per Eq. (2) in < 0.1 ms. Phase 1 completes in ≈ 2.2 s, contributing 9.1% of total per-task time versus 78.8% Fisher overhead on ARM CPU EWC, reversing the bottleneck from Fisher-dominated to training-loop-dominated.

Algorithm 1. StreamLearn-FPGA Per-Task CL Loop

1: **Input:** $\mathcal{D}_t$ (1,000 samples), θ^*_{t-1}, $\hat{F}_{t-1}$
2: // **Phase 1: Fisher computation (ISU)**
3: **for** each mini-batch $(x, y) \in \mathcal{D}_{t-1}$ **do**
4:     Forward + backward $\rightarrow \{g_i\}$
5:     ISU: $\hat{F}_i \mathrel{+}= g_i^2 \; \forall i$ // *32-lane, INT16 sq., INT32 acc.*
6: **end for**
7: ARM PS: $\hat{F} \leftarrow \hat{F}/|\mathcal{D}_{t-1}|$ // *scalar normalise, < 0.1 ms*
8: // **Phase 2: EWC training (GUE + ETC active)**
9: **for** each epoch $e = 1, \ldots, 5$ **do**
10:     **for** each mini-batch $(x, y) \in \mathcal{D}_t$ **do**
11:         Forward $\rightarrow \mathcal{L}_{\text{new}}$; backward $\rightarrow \{g_i\}$
12:         GUE: $\tilde{g}_i \leftarrow g_i - \lambda \hat{F}_i(\theta_i - \theta^*_{t-1,i})$ // *12.4 ns/param*
13:         $\theta \leftarrow \theta - \eta\tilde{g}$
14:     **end for**
15:     ETC (ARM PS): read loss; update λ per Eq. (5); write λ, τ to GUE registers
16: **end for**
17: $\theta^*_t \leftarrow \theta$; $\hat{F}_{\text{acc}} \leftarrow \hat{F}_{t-1} + \hat{F}_t$ // *online EWC [16]*

4.2 Phase 2: EWC-Regularised Training

Phase 2 trains on $\mathcal{D}_t$ for $E = 5$ epochs. At each mini-batch, raw gradients are piped directly to the GUE, which applies Eq. (4) in-pipeline and delivers modified gradients to the weight update unit. At each epoch boundary, the ETC (ARM PS) reads the task loss scalar, evaluates Eq. (5), and writes updated λ and τ to GUE registers via AXI-Lite during inter-epoch DMA setup, adding no pipeline stall.

4.3 Task Checkpoint Management

At Phase 2 completion the ARM PS saves θ^*_t. A parallel ISU accumulation channel running during Phase 2 simultaneously computes $\hat{F}_t$, requiring no additional dataset pass. Fisher vectors are combined via the online approximation [16]: $\hat{F}_{\text{acc}} = \hat{F}_{t-1} + \hat{F}_t$, storing only two Fisher vectors regardless of task count.

5 Experimental Evaluation

5.1 Experimental Setup

Hardware. Xilinx Zynq UltraScale+ ZU3EG on a ZCU104 evaluation board, synthesised with Vivado 2023.2. PL clock: 250 MHz; PS clock: 1.5 GHz.

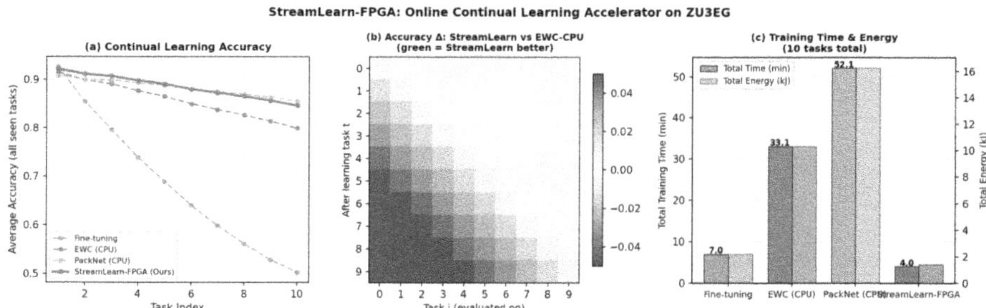

Fig. 2. StreamLearn-FPGA vs. baselines over 10 sequential tasks. (a) Average accuracy retention: StreamLearn-FPGA accumulates a growing advantage over EWC-CPU, reflecting the ETC's compounding adaptive protection. (b) Per-task accuracy difference matrix (StreamLearn-FPGA minus EWC-CPU); green cells indicate tasks where StreamLearn-FPGA achieves higher accuracy. (c) Total training time and energy: 8.2× time reduction and 7.2× energy reduction versus EWC-CPU. (Color figure online)

Model. A 0.5M-parameter CNN: three convolutional layers (32/64/128 filters), ReLU activations, batch normalisation after each convolutional layer, two fully connected output layers.

CL Benchmark. 10-task sequential classification: each task presents a new disjoint class subset from a shuffled image classification corpus, with 1,000 training and 200 test samples per task. The 10-task protocol is standard in the CL literature [8, 16] and provides sufficient depth to reveal multi-task forgetting dynamics.

Baselines. (1) *Fine-tuning* (CPU, no CL defence); (2) *EWC-CPU* (software EWC, ARM Cortex-A53 at 1.5 GHz); (3) *PackNet-CPU* [12] (structured pruning-based CL). All use the same model, $\eta = 0.01$, and 5 epochs per task.

Metrics. Average accuracy (mean test accuracy across all tasks after the final task); backward transfer $\mathrm{BWT} = \frac{1}{T-1} \sum_{j<T} [\mathrm{acc}(j|\text{after } T) - \mathrm{acc}(j|j)]$ (lower magnitude = less forgetting); total training time (s); total energy (J) via INA226 at 1 kHz on separate PS/PL rails.

5.2 Main Results

Table 2 summarises results. StreamLearn-FPGA achieves **84.58%** average accuracy: 4.65 pp above EWC-CPU (79.93%) and only 0.97 pp below PackNet

(85.55%), at 8.2× lower training time (243 s vs. 1,984 s) and 7.2× lower energy (1,430 J vs. 10,310 J). Compared to PackNet, StreamLearn-FPGA is 12.9× faster and 11.4× more energy-efficient sacrificing < 1% accuracy. The accuracy advantage over EWC-CPU grows across tasks (Fig. 2a), confirming the ETC's compounding benefit.

Table 2. Continual learning results: 10-task sequential benchmark. BWT: backward transfer (lower magnitude = less forgetting).

Method	Avg Acc (%)	BWT	Time (s)	Energy (J)	Power (W)
Fine-tuning (CPU)	50.32	−0.462	421	2,180	5.2
EWC-CPU [8]	79.93	−0.121	1,984	10,310	5.2
PackNet-CPU [12]	85.55	−0.051	3,127	16,230	5.2
StreamLearn-FPGA	**84.58**	**−0.077**	**243**	**1,430**	**5.9**
vs. EWC-CPU	+4.65 pp	+0.044	8.2× faster	7.2× less	—
vs. PackNet	−0.97 pp	−0.026	12.9× faster	11.4× less	—

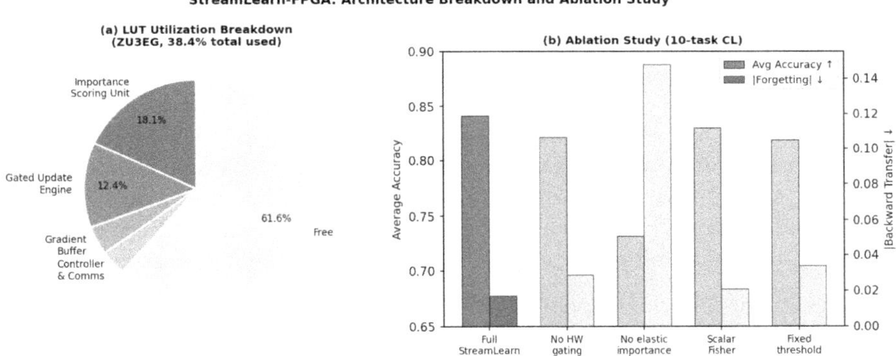

Fig. 3. (a) LUT utilisation by hardware unit: ISU and GUE together consume 79.4% of used fabric. (b) Ablation study: removing elastic importance scoring degrades accuracy to 73.18% (near fine-tuning baseline), confirming ISU+GUE as the critical components; removing the ETC costs 2.24 pp at no additional resource overhead.

5.3   Ablation Study

Table 3 quantifies each component's contribution. Removing elastic importance scoring ("No elastic importance") drops accuracy to 73.18% and BWT to −0.148, confirming ISU+GUE as indispensable. Removing hardware gating costs 2.44 pp: software-side gradient modification on the ARM PS introduces AXI round-trip latency that disrupts batch-level gradient coherence. Removing the ETC costs 2.24 pp at no additional resource or time overhead (Fig. 3).

5.4   Fisher Throughput and Energy Analysis

The ISU achieves 41.7 M parameters/s, completing Phase 1 in 2.2 s (9.1% of per-task time) versus 156.3 s (78.8%) on ARM CPU EWC. Peak power is 5.9 W: 3.1 W PL fabric, 1.4 W PS, 0.8 W DRAM, 0.6 W I/O. Despite higher peak power than the 5.2 W CPU baseline, the 8.2× time reduction yields 7.2× lower total energy.

Table 3. Ablation study (10-task sequential CL).

Configuration	Avg Acc (%)	BWT	Time (s)
Full StreamLearn-FPGA	**84.58**	**−0.077**	**243**
No hardware gating (SW GUE)	82.14	−0.029	243
Scalar Fisher (no ISU vectorisation)	83.01	−0.021	312
Fixed threshold (no ETC)	81.88	−0.034	243
No elastic importance (fine-tune only)	73.18	−0.148	181

6   Discussion

Scalability. For models beyond 0.5M parameters, on-chip BRAM storage for $\hat{F}$ is exhausted. Scaling to 5M parameters requires DRAM-backed Fisher storage; at 15 GB/s LPDDR4 bandwidth a 5M-parameter Fisher pass takes ≈ 53 ms, still 3× faster than CPU equivalents. Block-sparse or quantised Fisher approximations [14] offer an alternative path to maintaining on-chip storage.

Quantisation. The ISU operates at INT16/INT32. We observe no accuracy degradation at this precision, consistent with prior work [3]. A systematic INT16-vs-FP32 study across Split-CIFAR and Permuted-MNIST is valuable future work.

Generalisability. SI [21] and MAS [1] are natural ISU extensions. Online EWC [16] recursive Fisher updates are structurally identical to Eq. (3). Moving the ETC to PL fabric would enable per-mini-batch λ updates and is a target for a follow-on design.

7   Conclusion

We presented StreamLearn-FPGA, the first FPGA accelerator for EWC-based online continual learning. Co-integrating ISU, GUE, and ETC on a Zynq Ultra-Scale+ ZU3EG reduces per-task training time by 8.2× and energy by 7.2× versus ARM CPU EWC, while delivering 84.58% average accuracy over 10 sequential tasks—within 1% of PackNet at 12.9× PackNet's speed. EWC's Fisher computation is an embarrassingly parallel accumulation of squared gradients, naturally matched to FPGA vectorised datapaths; per-parameter EWC gating maps directly to DSP-chain operations. StreamLearn-FPGA establishes reconfigurable SoCs as practical targets for continual learning at the edge.

Acknowledgments. The authors declare no external funding.

Disclosure of Interests. The authors have no competing interests.

References

1. Aljundi, R., Babiloni, F., Elhoseiny, M., Rohrbach, M., Tuytelaars, T.: Memory aware synapses: learning what (not) to forget. In: Ferrari, V., Hebert, M., Sminchisescu, C., Weiss, Y. (eds.) ECCV 2018. LNCS, vol. 11207, pp. 144–161. Springer, Cham (2018). https://doi.org/10.1007/978-3-030-01219-9_9
2. AMD/Xilinx: Dynamic Function eXchange User Guide (UG909), v2023.2 (2023). https://docs.xilinx.com/r/en-US/ug909-vivado-partial-reconfiguration. Accessed: March 2026
3. Banner, R., Nahshan, Y., Soudry, D.: Post training 4-bit quantization of convolutional networks for rapid-deployment. In: Advances in Neural Information Processing Systems (NeurIPS). vol. 32, pp. 7948–7956 (2019)
4. Chaudhry, A., et al.: On tiny episodic memories in continual learning. arXiv preprint arXiv:1902.10486 (2019)
5. Fang, Z., Zhao, J., Liu, S., Liu, C., Geng, T.: FPGA-based few-shot learning accelerator for edge AI. In: Proceedings of the 32nd International Conference on Field-Programmable Logic and Applications (FPL). pp. 1–7 (2022). https://doi.org/10.1109/FPL57034.2022.00019
6. French, R.M.: Catastrophic forgetting in connectionist networks. Trends Cogn. Sci. **3**(4), 128–135 (1999). https://doi.org/10.1016/S1364-6613(99)01294-2
7. Huszár, F.: Note on the quadratic penalties in elastic weight consolidation. Proc. Natl. Acad. Sci. **115**(11), E2496–E2497 (2018). https://doi.org/10.1073/pnas.1717042115
8. Kirkpatrick, J., et al.: Overcoming catastrophic forgetting in neural networks. Proc. Natl. Acad. Sci. **114**(13), 3521–3526 (2017). https://doi.org/10.1073/pnas.1611835114
9. Li, Z., Hoiem, D.: Learning without forgetting. IEEE Trans. Pattern Anal. Mach. Intell. **40**(12), 2935–2947 (2018). https://doi.org/10.1109/TPAMI.2017.2733150
10. Liu, Z., Cheng, J., Huang, Y., Shen, L., Li, G.: Online training accelerator for adaptive edge inference. In: Proceedings of the 58th ACM/IEEE Design Automation Conference (DAC), pp. 1–6 (2021). https://doi.org/10.1109/DAC18074.2021.9586289
11. Lopez-Paz, D., Ranzato, M.: Gradient episodic memory for continual learning. In: Advances in Neural Information Processing Systems (NeurIPS). vol. 30, pp. 6467–6476 (2017)
12. Mallya, A., Lazebnik, S.: PackNet: Adding multiple tasks to a single network by iterative pruning. In: Proceedings of the IEEE/CVF Conference on Computer Vision and Pattern Recognition (CVPR), pp. 7765–7773 (2018). https://doi.org/10.1109/CVPR.2018.00810

13. McCloskey, M., Cohen, N.J.: Catastrophic interference in connectionist networks: the sequential learning problem. Psychol. Learn. Motiv. **24**, 109–165 (1989). https://doi.org/10.1016/S0079-7421(08)60536-8
14. Rhu, M., Gimelshein, N., Clemons, J., Zulfiqar, A., Keckler, S.W.: vDNN: virtualized deep neural networks for scalable, memory-efficient neural network design. In: Proceedings of the 49th Annual IEEE/ACM International Symposium on Microarchitecture (MICRO), pp. 1–13 (2016). https://doi.org/10.1109/MICRO.2016.7783721
15. Rusu, A.A., et al.: Progressive neural networks. arXiv preprint arXiv:1606.04671 (2016)
16. Schwarz, J., et al.: Progress and compress: A scalable framework for continual learning. In: Proceedings of the 35th International Conference on Machine Learning (ICML), pp. 4528–4537. PMLR (2018)
17. Sharma, H., et al.: FPGA-based transfer learning acceleration for edge inference. In: Proceedings of the Design, Automation and Test in Europe Conference (DATE), pp. 1–6 (2022). https://doi.org/10.23919/DATE54114.2022.9774692
18. Umuroglu, Y., et al.: FINN: a framework for fast, scalable binarized neural network inference. In: Proceedings of the ACM/SIGDA International Symposium on Field-Programmable Gate Arrays (FPGA), pp. 65–74 (2017). https://doi.org/10.1145/3020078.3021744
19. Venieris, S.I., Bouganis, C.S.: fpgaConvNet: mapping regular and irregular convolutional neural networks on FPGAs. IEEE Trans. Neural Networks Learn. Syst. **30**(2), 326–342 (2019). https://doi.org/10.1109/TNNLS.2018.2844093
20. Wang, N., et al.: DeepBurning: automatic generation of FPGA-based learning accelerators for the neural network family. In: Proceedings of the 53rd ACM/IEEE Design Automation Conference (DAC), pp. 1–6 (2016). https://doi.org/10.1145/2897937.2898002
21. Zenke, F., Poole, B., Ganguli, S.: Continual learning through synaptic intelligence. In: Proceedings of the 34th International Conference on Machine Learning (ICML), pp. 3987–3995. PMLR (2017)
22. Zhang, C., Fang, Z., Zhou, P., Pan, P., Cong, J.: Caffeine: towards uniformly accelerating all CNN layers on FPGA. In: Proceedings of the IEEE/ACM International Conference on Computer-Aided Design (ICCAD), pp. 1–8 (2016). https://doi.org/10.1145/2966986.2967011
23. Zhang, C., Li, P., Sun, G., Guan, Y., Xiao, B., Cong, J.: Optimizing FPGAbased accelerator design for deep convolutional neural networks. In: Proceedings of the ACM/SIGDA International Symposium on Field-Programmable Gate Arrays (FPGA), pp. 161–170 (2015). https://doi.org/10.1145/2684746.2689060

Softcores and Optimization

FACETs: Fast and Efficient Compilation for Control–Dataflow Mapping on CGRAs

Yuxuan Wang[1]([✉]), Rubén Rodríguez Álvarez[1], Cristian Tirelli[2],
Rodrigo Otoni[3], Giovanni Ansaloni[1], Laura Pozzi[2], and David Atienza[1]

[1] EPFL, Lausanne, Switzerland
yuxuan.wang@epfl.ch
[2] Università della Svizzera italiana, Lugano, Switzerland
[3] University of Groningen, Groningen, The Netherlands

Abstract. Reconfigurable computing bridges the gap between the flexibility of general-purpose processors and the efficiency of application-specific hardware. Among reconfigurable architectures, Coarse-Grained Reconfigurable Arrays (CGRAs) are particularly promising because they offer high efficiency and low configuration overhead, while maintaining programmability at the operation level. However, mapping high-level applications onto CGRAs remains challenging, as most state-of-the-art approaches either have a limited compilation scope or incur a very high compilation time. To address this challenge, we propose a compilation framework that supports generic control–dataflow graphs by scheduling dataflow graphs under explicit control-flow constraints. The framework adopts a flexible approach that comprises a fast heuristic mapping strategy for non-critical code regions, while enabling aggressive optimizations for performance-critical regions. Experimental results show up to $10\times$ faster compilation for applications with complex control–dataflow graph structures, while achieving comparable or better runtime performance relative to existing approaches.

1 Introduction

Modern computing workloads require hardware platforms that deliver high performance, energy efficiency, and flexibility. Coarse-Grained Reconfigurable Arrays (CGRAs) address these requirements by combining efficient parallel execution with architectural reconfigurability [1]. Composed of a grid of reconfigurable processing elements (PEs), CGRAs execute time-multiplexed operations to achieve high performance and energy-efficient data propagation [2].

CGRAs compilers are tasked with mapping applications in PEs at given time slots, taking into account both spatial (e.g. connectivity) and temporal (e.g. def-use relationships) constraints. To this end, applications are usually translated from high level languages such as C to Intermediate Representations (IRs) using standard compilation chains. IR statements are then mapped on hardware resources [3]. Goal of the CGRA compilation process is to efficiently deploy

G. Leone et al. (Eds.): ARC 2026, LNCS 16514, pp. 65–81, 2026.
https://doi.org/10.1007/978-3-032-29365-7_5

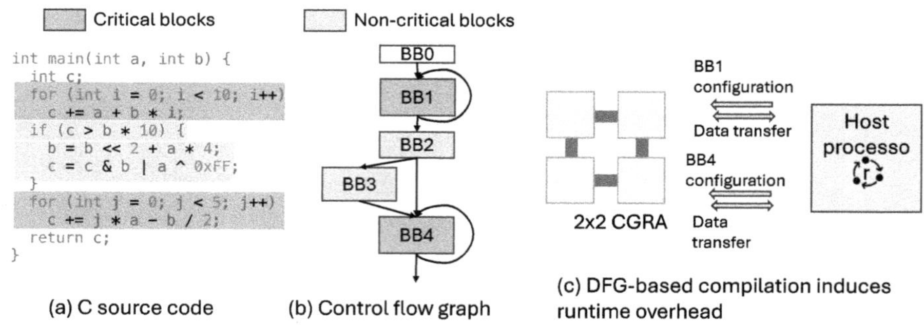

Fig. 1. Deployment of applications onto CGRA: limited mapping ranges introduce high reconfiguration and data transfer overhead at runtime.

operations on the available PEs, effectively exploitation parallelism. A prevalent compilation strategy is modulo scheduling (MS), which targets control-free loops represented as dataflow graphs (DFGs) [4]. This restriction limits the range of applications that can be mapped onto CGRA hardware. Consequently, application developers must either manually or automatically isolate compilable regions [5], and additional runtime overhead is introduced due to frequent reconfiguration. Figure 1 illustrates this limitation with an application composed of five basic blocks (BBs). As shown in Fig. 1(b), only BB1 and BB4 are mapped onto the CGRA, while the remaining blocks execute on the host processor. Hence, DFG-based approaches require the blocks to be compiled and executed independently. As depicted in Fig. 1(c), instructions configuration and data transfer are required before/after the CGRA execution of each BB. Even when BB4 consumes the data produced by BB1, the data must be transferred back to the host and reloaded, leading to redundant reconfiguration and unnecessary runtime overhead.

Control dataflow graph (CDFG) compilation expands the mapping scope to support general applications by enabling multiple basic blocks (e.g., BB0–BB4 in Fig. 1) to be mapped onto the CGRA. Marionette [6] adopts this approach by introducing dedicated reconfiguration hardware to support basic block switching, which reduces—but does not eliminate—reconfiguration overhead. In contrast, CDFG-aware compilation eliminates runtime reconfiguration by switching basic blocks via the program counter [7]. However, this approach results in a very high compilation time as a result of the high mapping complexity. Moreover, a single high-complexity basic block can prevent the entire CDFG from being successfully compiled. For example, if BB3 in Fig. 1 is too complex for the compiler to map, the entire application cannot be mapped to the CGRA.

Our approach is driven by the insight that critical blocks in a CDFG constitute only a subset of all basic blocks, and that this subset has a large impact on overall performance. As shown in Fig. 1, the blocks highlighted in orange correspond to critical blocks that dominate runtime due to frequent execution and therefore determine the achievable performance of the application [8]. For these blocks, longer compilation time is justified to enable performance optimization using techniques such as modulo scheduling. In contrast, low-impact blocks (e.g., BB2 and BB3) are executed infrequently–often only once or not at all—and have negligible influence on overall performance. For such blocks, it is acceptable to tolerate suboptimal mappings that incur a few additional clock cycles, as their impact on end-to-end performance is negligible.

Building on these observations, we propose FACETs - a CDFG mapping approach that maps each basic block while preserving correct data propagation across blocks. Inter-block dependencies are captured at basic block boundaries, enabling efficient CGRA execution as a single accelerated CDFG. FACETs is based on a heuristic approach that reduces compilation complexity and expands the compilation scope to CDFG, while enabling the integration of high-performance, but time-consuming, compilers for critical BBs only. Moreover, it effectively reduces the runtime required for data transfers between the host processor and the CGRA and for reconfiguration.

2   Related Works

2.1   DFG Mappers

Existing DFG mapping techniques for CGRAs primarily differ in how they formulate and solve the spatial–temporal assignment of operations to PEs under data-dependency and routing constraints. Exact-based approaches can be broadly classified into Integer Linear Programming (ILP) formulations [9, 10] and Satisfiability Modulo Theories (SMT)–based methods [11–13]. These methods determine spatial and temporal mappings by solving explicitly constructed optimization models. However, their computational complexity grows exponentially with increasing problem size [14]. To alleviate this limitation, another class of mappers adopts heuristic placement policies guided by cost functions to determine the placement of DFG nodes on CGRA processing elements [15]. In this category, E2EMap [16] leverages reinforcement learning to learn placement policies for DFG mapping, where neural networks are trained through reward-driven optimization to guide placement decisions. Although the generated solutions are effective, training such models is challenging, and the mapping time typically ranges from 10^3 to 10^4 seconds [17, 18]. Moreover, DFG-only mapping approaches face inherent limitations in supporting broader program scopes. These issues stem from the restricted mapping scope of DFG mappers, which typically operate on a single loop body: data initialization and write-back operations often lie outside the loop DFG and therefore cannot be mapped automatically.

2.2   Control Dataflow Compilation

To address these limitations, compilation must be extended beyond isolated DFGs to the CDFG level. HDCC [19] addresses this by identifying DFGs suitable for CGRA deployment and analyzing their live-in and live-out values to insert the required load and store operations. This automates memory accesses and

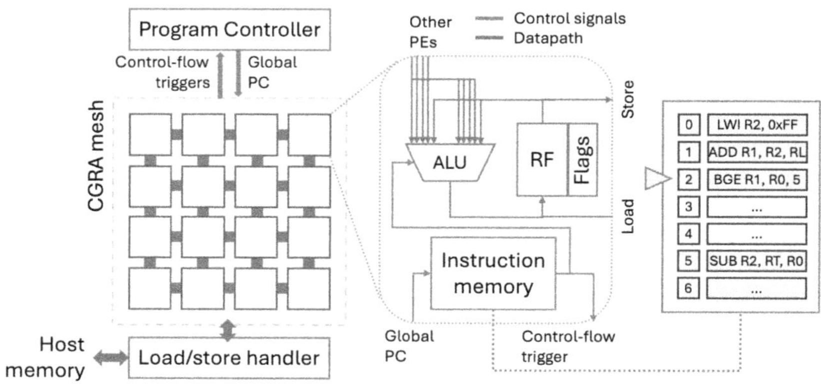

Fig. 2. Architectural overview of the targeted instruction-based CGRA. The datapath is represented in blue, while control-flow signals are depicted in green. (Color figure online)

accelerates only the selected kernels, while leaving a substantial portion of the application to execute on the host processor.

To overcome this limitation, several works propose specialized architectures and compilation techniques targeting common control patterns, such as divergent branches and nested loops. Cao et al. [20] propose a Speculative Iteration Execution (SIE) CGRA architecture that decouples path selection from condition evaluation. In this design, the SIE controller speculatively issues and executes loop iterations, enabling support for divergent branches within loops. However, this approach requires rollback mechanisms when predication errors occur, constraining its applicability and efficiency. The Adora compiler [21] employs loop transformations to enable efficient dataflow-level execution and optimizes data communication at the task level, with a particular focus on improving the execution of nested loop structures.

These approaches typically treat common control-flow patterns, such as if-then-else constructs and nested loops, as independent problems, leaving more general cases—such as dynamic-boundary loops or multiple branches— unaddressed. Conversely, Marionette [6] relies on reconfiguration-based techniques that can adapt the CGRA configuration at runtime according to conditions, but they incur considerable hardware and configuration overhead. Finally, static approaches that compile the entire CDFG with general control flows are often based on ILP models, which result in long compilation time [22].

3   Target CGRA Architecture

We assume as compilation target a prototypical CGRA consisting of a 2D mesh of interconnected PEs. Each PE contains a register file (RF) with data and zero/negative/overflow fields, an ALU, and a private instruction memory. To support CDFG execution, a program counter (PC) directs the control flow, as illustrated in Fig. 2. Supported operations include arithmetic and logic operations, flag-based select operations, conditional branches, jumps and load/store accesses to host memory.

At each instruction step, each PE issues one operation from its private instruction memory as dictated by a global program counter. All PEs simultaneously process their current instruction. ALU operations may consume operands either from the local RF or from other PEs, and the result is written back to the RF. A memory controller interfaces PEs to memory for load and store operations. Once all PEs complete their current operation, the program controller updates the global PC to the next instruction. Each PE can overwrite the PC by issuing a control operation (i.e., branch, jump, and exit). For example, in PC=2 in Fig. 2, if the value in R1 $\geq$ R0, the next value for the PC is set to PC=5. Such mechanism enables the deployment of applications with generic control flows, including if-clauses and loop nests.

4   Methodology

FACETs manages data placement and propagation at the CDFG level, enabling seamless BB transitions via the PC and eliminating reconfiguration overhead during BB switches. Specifically, Sect. 4.1 presents our approach to manage inter–basic-block data propagation in the CDFG. Section 4.2 details the scheduling strategy used to efficiently map each basic block, and Sect. 4.3 describes the data propagation mechanism that updates shared constraints after the DFG of a basic block has been scheduled.

4.1   Overview: Control Flow Management

The CDFG captures inter-block data propagation subject to the underlying CDFG structure, which consists of multiple basic blocks connected by control operations that define block transitions. Each block contains a DFG that is executed when control reaches the block—for example, when a predecessor executes a branch operation targeting it. Figure 3 illustrates an example of mapping a CDFG onto CGRA hardware, with the CDFG shown in Fig. 3a. The bold grey lines indicate the CDFG transitions of an outer loop with a divergent branch (BB0 $\rightarrow$ BB1 $\rightarrow$ BB3 or BB0 $\rightarrow$ BB2 $\rightarrow$ BB3). In this structure, one path forms a self-loop within BB2, while the thin black lines represent the corresponding data dependencies. Within this execution flow, BB0 and BB2 evaluate the control conditions that determine which successor block is triggered.

To manage control flow while coordinating the DFG execution within each basic block, we define two graph states for every basic block to represent the spatial mapping of operations onto the CGRA hardware:

- **Entry graph** ($\mathcal{G}^E$): the spatial mapping graph when PC enters a block.
- **Exit graph** ($\mathcal{G}^X$): the spatial mapping graph after the DFG of the basic block has completed execution.

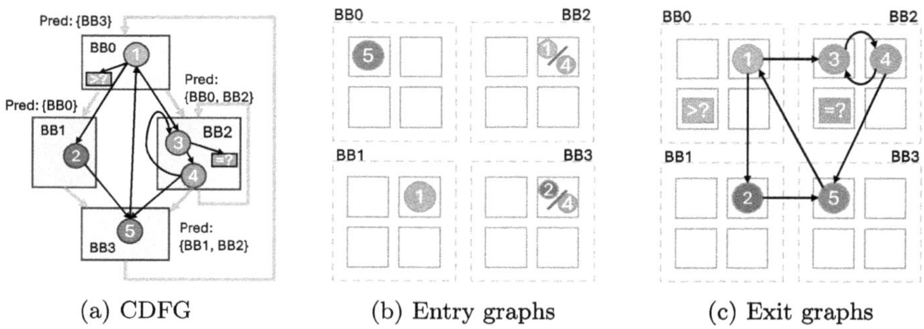

(a) CDFG   (b) Entry graphs   (c) Exit graphs

Fig. 3. Mapping solutions for a nested loop with divergent branches with livein/liveout mapped in the BB boundaries: the control operation determines the next BB to be executed. (Op①/Op① denotes either ① or ① is used, depending on the control flow.)

Figure 3b and Fig. 3c present the entry and exit graphs of each basic block, integrating both control and data-flow operations to support CDFG mapping. The objective of this spatial mapping is to ensure that values produced or propagated in a basic block are available at the end of its execution such that they can be correctly consumed by operations in successor DFGs. For example, the consumer operations in BB1 and BB2 can access the producer value (operation ①) defined in BB0, regardless of whether control transfers, as shown in their entry graphs. Operation ⑤ receives its input from operation ② when BB1 is taken, or from operation ④ when BB2 is taken; in both cases, the value is routed from the right neighboring processing element, as shown in the exit graphs.

To guarantee the correct execution of a DFG, its entry graph must provide all live-in values required for computation. Accordingly, control-flow management across basic blocks is defined by the following constraint:

$$\mathcal{G}^{E}_{B_n} \subseteq \mathcal{G}^{X}_{B_m}, \quad B_m \in Pred(B_n) \tag{1}$$

The entry graph of a block is a subgraph of its predecessors' exit graphs, ensuring that live-in values are available to perform the block's computation. For example, BB3 has two predecessors BB1 and BB2. Therefore, the entry graphs of BB3 should be the subset of both the exit graphs of BB1 and BB2.

4.2 Data Flow Mapping

Data flow graph mapping incorporates entry and exit graph prerequisites that encode CDFG-level constraints from other basic blocks, producing temporal–spatial solutions that conform to these requirements. Figure 4 shows the heuristic process of mapping one DFG to the hardware, considering the CDFG constraints.

Temporal Scheduling Candidates. An operation is eligible for scheduling if and only if all of its producer values are available in the CGRA registers.

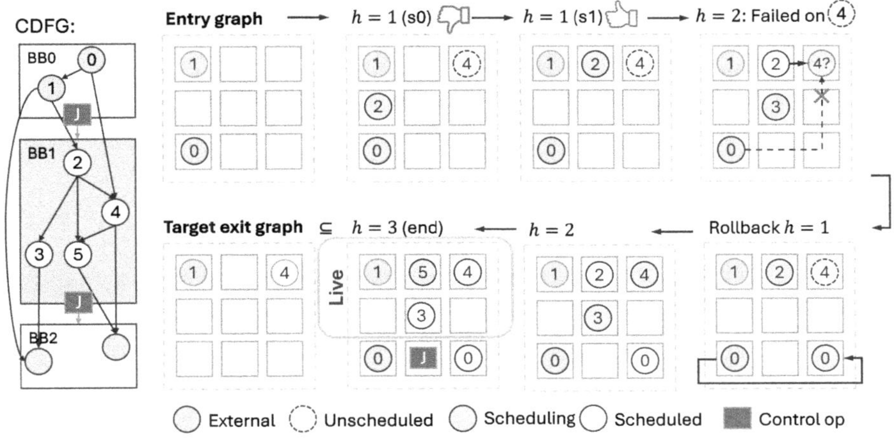

Fig. 4. Heuristic mapping process of BB1, following the prerequisites of its entry graph and exit graph.

Under the as-soon-as-possible (ASAP) policy, all schedulable operations are first retrieved, thereby allowing greater flexibility in the subsequent mapping decisions. The yellow operations in Fig. 4 show the set of temporal scheduling candidates in each height, which are denoted as $\mathcal{I}_C$ and defined as follows:

$$\mathcal{I}_C = \{I_k \,|\, \mathrm{Prod}(I_k) \subseteq V_I \cup \mathcal{I}_D, \}, \tag{2}$$

where $Prod(I_k)$ denotes the producer operations of the candidate operation I_k, $\mathcal{I}_D$ is the set of operations already scheduled within the current DFG, and V_I represents the set of live-in values that are not produced internally within the basic block. More generally, an operation becomes schedulable once all of its producers are either live-in values or operations that have already been scheduled in the same DFG. The availability of live-in values is ensured by Eq. 1, which guarantees that they are prepared in the entry graph.

Control operations (e.g., branch or jump instructions) are required to be scheduled at the end of each basic block, following the conventional compiler design principle. This constraint arises because control operations determine the next PC value and thus define the boundary of a basic block. Scheduling control operations earlier would prematurely redirect control flow, potentially preventing the execution of remaining data operations in the block and violating the single-entry–single-exit semantics of a basic block. Moreover, in CGRA architectures, the effects of control operations must be resolved only after all data computations in the block have completed, ensuring that live-out values are fully produced before control is transferred to successor blocks.

Spatial Placement Space. The spatial placement space of an operation is determined by both data dependencies and the architectural constraints of the

CGRA. An operation must be placed on a PE that can receive its input operands from the PEs hosting its producer operations and forward its output values to the PEs hosting its consumer operations, subject to the availability of routing resources. In addition, the selected PE must provide sufficient register capacity to store newly generated live values without overwriting existing ones. Formally, for an operation I, its spatial placement space $\mathcal{S}(I)$ is defined as

$$\mathcal{S}(I) = \mathcal{A}_{\mathrm{Prod}}(I) \cap \mathcal{A}_{\mathrm{Cons}}(I) \cap \mathcal{A}_{\mathrm{Reg}}, \tag{3}$$

where $\mathcal{A}_{\mathrm{Prod}}(I)$ and $\mathcal{A}_{\mathrm{Cons}}(I)$ denote the sets of PEs that can communicate with the scheduled producer and consumer operations of I, respectively, and $\mathcal{A}_{\mathrm{Reg}}$ denotes the set of PEs with sufficient register resources to accommodate additional live values.

Both producer- and consumer-side constraints are considered because the BB scheduling does not strictly follow dominance order, which traditionally requires that a block in the control-flow graph be scheduled only after all of its dominating predecessors have been placed. Therefore, a producer operation from other BB may not yet be assigned to a physical PE and does not impose immediate spatial restrictions on its consumers. Conversely, once a consumer operation has been spatially scheduled, its placement introduces concrete communication constraints that must be satisfied by its producers. For example, as shown in Fig. 3, when the DFG of BB2 is scheduled first and the placement of operation ① in BB0 remains undecided, the mapping of operation ③ retains greater spatial flexibility. However, when operation ① is scheduled at a later stage, it must be placed in a manner that satisfies the constraints established by operation ③.

This scheduling strategy enables BB scheduling without strictly adhering to dominance order. By deferring the spatial binding of values originating from unscheduled basic blocks, the approach preserves greater placement flexibility for performance-critical regions such as loops. The algorithm for maintaining Eq. 1 after each basic block is scheduled is described in Sect. 4.3.

Height-Based Scheduling. To enable CDFG mapping, DFG scheduling must explicitly account for inter-BB data dependencies. This is achieved by enforcing compatibility between the entry and exit graphs of the basic block being scheduled, as shown in Fig. 4. Scheduling starts from the entry graph, which specifies live-in value placements, and aims to produce an exit graph satisfying successor-block requirements, with the target exit graph constrained to be a subgraph of the final exit graph after scheduling ($\mathcal{G}_{\mathrm{target}}^{X} \subseteq \mathcal{G}^{X}$).

Algorithm 1 describes the DFG scheduling procedure under the constraints imposed by the entry and exit graphs. The algorithm initializes scheduling from the entry graph and proceeds in a layer-by-layer manner following data dependencies. At each scheduling height, it identifies the schedulable operation set $\mathcal{I}_C$ and randomly selects a spatial mapping from the placement scheduling space S. To identify an optimal placement, the algorithm performs N_{SA} iterations, perturbing the placement within the search space to minimize the cost. In each iteration, the resulting layout is evaluated using the following cost function:

Algorithm 1: Priority-Guided Spatial-Temporal Scheduling

Input: Entry graph $\mathcal{G}^E$, Exit graph $\mathcal{G}^X$, Full operation sets I_{full},
Exploration steps N_{SA}

1 scheduled operation sets $I_S \leftarrow \emptyset$;
2 Unscheduled operation sets $I_U \leftarrow I_{full}$;
3 $h \leftarrow 1$; $\mathcal{G}^{\mathrm{before}} \leftarrow \mathcal{G}^E$;
4 **while** I_U *not empty* **do**
5   Get schedulable operations at time h: $\mathcal{I}_C$;
6   Randomly place operations under spatial constraints $\mathcal{S}(I)$ to generate
      current placement graph $\mathcal{G}_{\mathrm{after}}$ and record initial cost C_{best};
7   **for** $iter = 1$ *to* N_{SA} **do**
8   Compute $\mathcal{S}(I)$ based on $\mathcal{G}^{\mathrm{before}}$ and $\mathcal{G}^X$;
9   Randomly perturb placement within search space to get $\mathcal{G}^{\mathrm{cur}}$;
10   Evaluate new cost C_{cur};
11   **if** $\mathrm{ACCEPT}(C_{best}, C_{cur})$ **then**
12           $C_{\mathrm{best}} \leftarrow C_{\mathrm{cur}}$; $\mathcal{G}^{\mathrm{after}} \leftarrow \mathcal{G}^{\mathrm{cur}}$;
13   **if** *convergence detected* **then**
14   **break**;
15     $\mathcal{T} \leftarrow \{I \in \mathcal{I}_C \mid I \notin \mathrm{scheduledOps} \wedge \mathrm{latest\ schedule}(I) \leq h\}$;
16   **if** $\mathcal{T} \neq \emptyset$ **then**
17   Apply graph transformations;
18   Roll back schedule and graph to height h_{rb};
19   **continue**;
20   Commit scheduling results at time h;
21     $I_D \leftarrow \mathcal{I}_C - \mathcal{T}$; $I_U \leftarrow I_U - I_D$
22     $G_{\mathrm{before}} \leftarrow G_{\mathrm{after}}$; $h \leftarrow h + 1$;
23 **return** $\mathcal{S}$ *and* $\{\mathcal{G}^{after}\}$

$$\sum_{I_U} 2^{-priority} \log_2(1 + d) \tag{4}$$

$$priority = \frac{max(h_0, h) + h_1}{2} \tag{5}$$

The scheduling priority reflects the urgency of scheduling an operation at height h, where h_0 and h_1 represent its earliest and latest possible schedule time, respectively. I_U denotes the set of unscheduled operations, and d is the distance between an unscheduled operation and its producers. This cost function evaluates the impact of the current layout on the remaining operations, accounting for both the availability of suitable PEs for direct mapping and the additional routing required when placement is constrained. Figure 4 illustrates this concept: at $h = 1$, operation ② is successfully mapped in both scenarios s1 and s2. However, in situation s1, operation ④ is positioned closer to its producer than in s0, yielding a lower cost and a more favorable layout, which is thus accepted.

If the scheduling space for an operation is empty, i.e., $S(I) = \emptyset$, the operation cannot be scheduled at the current height h. If $h < h_1$, scheduling can be deferred and potentially resolved in later layers. For example, if two operations must be executed on the same PE, the conflict can be resolved by executing one operation in the current layer and the other in a subsequent layer. However, if the operation has reached its latest allowable schedule time (i.e., it lies on the critical path), deferring is no longer feasible. As illustrated in Fig. 4, failing to map operation ④ would block the scheduling of all subsequent operations, since it lies on the critical path. To resolve this, additional routing is performed. When scheduling the routing operation, the height is rolled back to $\max(h_p + 1, h - l_R)$, where h_p is the scheduling height of the producer and l_R is the routing length. This approach minimizes the rollback required for rescheduling while allowing routing operations to execute in parallel with other operations. As a result, the final temporal schedule is not affected, provided that the routing operations do not extend the critical path.

The placement is performed in a layer-by-layer manner until all operations are scheduled. The exit graph captures all live-out values required for the placement of successor blocks, including both the prerequisites specified by the target exit graph and the new values produced during scheduling. These values are then used to update the entry and exit graphs of all basic blocks to maintain CDFG consistency, as discussed in Sect. 4.3.

4.3   Update the Entry and Exit Graphs

The scheduling of basic blocks derives their constraints from the corresponding entry and exit graphs, preserve consistency across the CDFG, i.e. if a basic block (B) produces an exit graph $(\mathcal{G}_B^X)$, for each successor block $(S(B))$ the live-in values in its entry graph must conform to the operations mapped in $\mathcal{G}_B^X$. If a value is propagated through the successor block—i.e., it remains live in the successor's exit graph—it must also live in its exit graph.

$$\mathcal{G}_{S(B)}^E \leftarrow Live(\mathcal{G}_B^X), \ \mathcal{G}_{S(B)}^X \leftarrow Live(\mathcal{G}_B^X) \tag{6}$$

Here, $Live$ notates the live value sets that should be kept if it is used by its successors. This propagation process is applied recursively to successor blocks until no successors remain or a block has already been visited.

Similarly, if an operation assumes that a live-in value is sourced from a specific spatial PE, this requirement is propagated backward to its predecessor blocks to ensure that they produce consistent results. The exit graph of each predecessor is updated accordingly. If the required value is not produced within a given predecessor block, the update is further propagated through its predecessors. The backward propagation proceeds recursively until the block that produces the value is reached:

$$\mathcal{G}_{P(B)}^X \leftarrow Live(\mathcal{G}_B^E), \ \mathcal{G}_{P(B)}^E \leftarrow Live(\mathcal{G}_B^E) \tag{7}$$

CDFG consistency is maintained through updates to the entry and exit graphs, where unscheduled blocks only need to satisfy the prerequisites imposed by scheduled blocks. In Fig. 4, the yellow block highlights the live sets at the end of scheduling ($h = 3$), which are used to update the entry graph of its successor, BB2. Values that are no longer live and unused, such as Operation ⓪, do not affect subsequent scheduling.

This separation enables independent scheduling of different blocks: critical blocks can devote greater compilation effort to exploit optimizations. For example, modulo scheduling can be used to improve runtime performance without initially considering inter–basic-block constraints. Once these blocks produce their scheduling solutions, non-critical blocks can then be mapped using height-based scheduling while adhering to the generated constraints, thereby quickly obtaining feasible solutions. As a result, the overall compilation time is reduced, allowing the approach to scale to large CDFGs. Moreover, it helps avoid unnecessary communication overhead between the CGRA and the host processor.

5   Experiments

5.1   Experimental Setup

Benchmarks: We evaluate our framework using a set of applications that exhibit a variety of control-flow patterns, selected from the MiBench suite [23] and Rodinia [24]. We select the benchmarks with divergent control flow patterns including multi-level nested and sequential loops, dynamic loop boundaries, runtime selection, and their combinations. The characteristics of the selected applications are summarized in Table 1, including the number of basic blocks, and the number of operations.

Table 1. Benchmarks.

Benchmarks	# BBs	# Ops	CFG attributes
bicg	7	61	2-level nested loops
2mm	17	107	Sequential nested loops
sha	5	41	Sequential loops
gsm	3	32	Loop with selection
hotspot3D	9	84	3-level nested loops with selection
isqrt	3	27	DFG loop with data initialization
lud	14	77	Sequential 3-level nested loops with dynamic boundaries

Baseline: We compare our methodology against Compigra [22]. Compigra is built on an ILP-based scheduling framework that consider for inter BB data propagation at compile time. For MS of loop DFGs, Compigra integrates SATMapIt [12], whereas our approach adopts MonoMap [25], which to the best of our knowledge is the fastest open-source MS tool. For assessing the runtime of

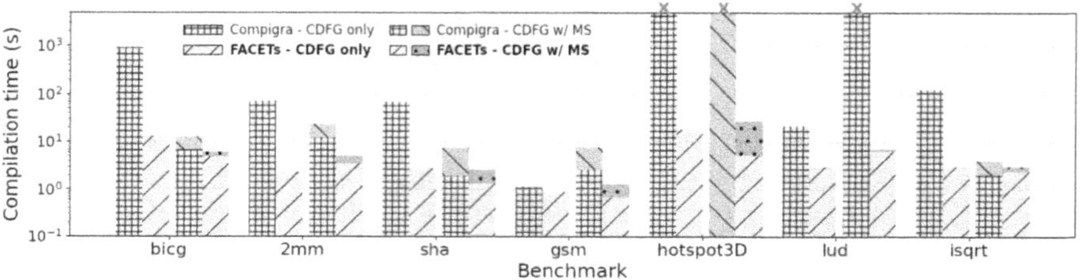

Fig. 5. Compilation time across benchmarks. For each benchmark, the four bars represent Compigra CDFG mapping, our CDFG mapping, Compigra CDFG mapping with MS, and our CDFG mapping with MS.

scheduled application, we further compare with Marionette [6], which, as opposed to the simple PC-based strategy of FACETs (Sect. 3) relies on specialized hardware support for control-flow management.

Testbed: Our experimental evaluation is conducted on a 4×4 CGRA implementation derived from OpenEdgeCGRA [26], an open-source, silicon-validated CGRA design. The PEs are arranged in a 2D mesh and connected using nearest-neighbor links with wrap-around connectivity. In the considered implementation, each PE has read-only access to the full RF of its neighboring PEs. Furthermore, PEs operate in lockstep under a shared global program counter, and all instruction complete in a single clock cycle. We use 6-entry register files for each PE and an instruction memory capacity of 128 instructions, which suffuce for all considered benchmarks.

5.2   Compilation Time

Figure 5 compares the compilation latency of our approach against Compigra under two settings: (1) standalone CDFG compilation with height-based scheduling introduced in Sect. 4.2, and (2) integrated compilation with MS for critical blocks. In both settings, our method consistently outperforms Compigra's ILP-based mapping, typically completing in under 10 s, while DFG solvers such as Morpher [15] and E2EMap [16] require over 100 s for the DFG loop alone for `bicg`. While incorporating DFG optimization introduces a slight overhead, the impact is modest. With MS enabled, the compilation time for the remaining blocks is reduced, as the computation-intensive blocks are already mapped, leaving fewer blocks to schedule. For CDFG-only compilation with height-based scheduling, our approach is faster by several orders of magnitude (as shown by the logarithmic scale in Fig. 5). This efficiency enables our method to successfully process all benchmarks, whereas Compigra suffers from timeouts on larger kernels such as `hotspot3D` and `lud`.

To further analyze these timing components, Fig. 6 illustrates compilation time as a function of the number of operations per basic block. The ILP model

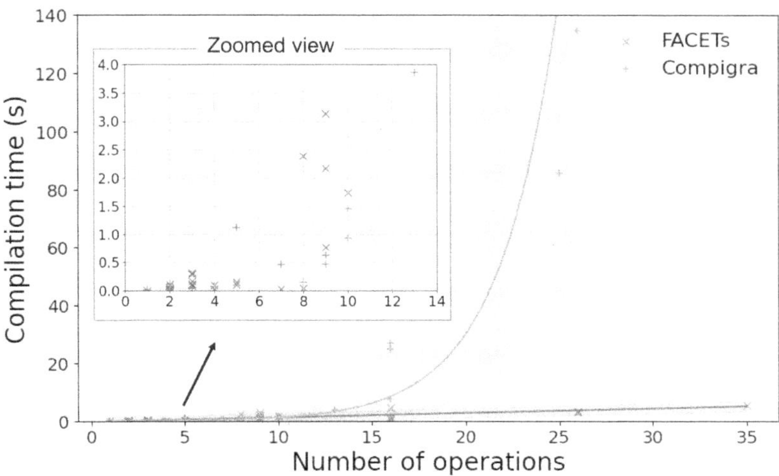

Fig. 6. Compilation time VS number of operations per DFG.

in Compigra exhibits exponential growth ($R^2 = 0.9210$), driven by the rapid increase in constraints as the number of operations increases. Conversely, our heuristic approach scales gracefully, with small increases in compile time due to more complex data dependencies for larger benchmarks. While Compigra is marginally faster (by only a few seconds) for small-scale problems, for higher number of operations the ILP model's compilation time is orders of magnitude higher than ours—a critical bottleneck that makes it less practical for complex CDFG applications.

5.3   Runtime Analysis

To assess the quality of FACETs schedules, we compared the achieved result with the lower bound derived from data dependencies and hardware constraints. The lower bound is defined by:

$$L_{\text{non-loop}} = \max(l_d, l_h); \quad II_{\text{loop}} = \max(ResII, RecII)$$

For a non-loop basic block, the latency lower bound L is determined by the maximum of the data-dependency bound l_d and the hardware bound l_h. The data-dependency bound l_d corresponds to the length of the critical path (i.e., the longest data-dependency path) in the corresponding DFG, while the hardware-constraint bound l_h is computed as $N_{\text{op}}/N_{\text{PE}}$. For a loop basic block, the runtime lower bound is instead determined by the initiation interval II, which represents the minimum gap between the start of successive iterations. The II is constrained by both loop-carried data dependencies (captured by $RecII$) and the availability of hardware resources (captured by $ResII$) [4].

Figure 7 shows the lower bound and implemented scheduling metrics of 2mm, which shows the largest BB and operation counts. The achieved schedules are

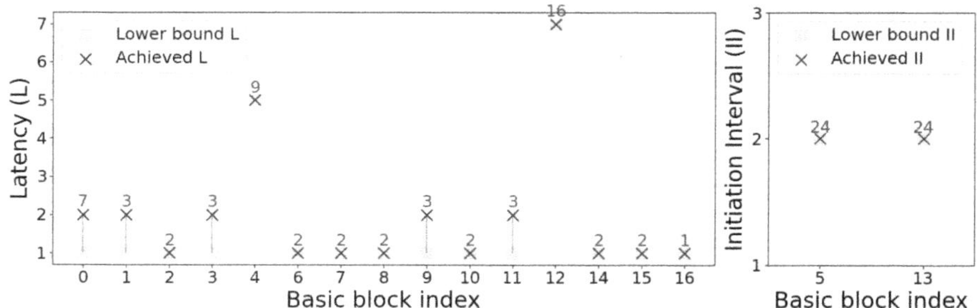

Fig. 7. Runtime analysis of 2mm for nonloop blocks (left) and loop blocks (right), showing the blocks latency and initiation interval, respectively for the two cases. The $\times$ indicates achieved scheduling, $\square$ indicates the scheduling lower bounds. The number of operations per BB is noted above each data point.

close to the runtime lower bounds in most cases, resulting in small gaps despite the large variation in operation counts. This indicates that the proposed scheduling approach efficiently exploits available parallelism and approaches the optimal scheduling limit under realistic resource constraints for 2mm, which has a complex CFG structure. For performance-critical basic blocks, such as BB5 and BB13, which correspond to the innermost loops, DFG optimizations are applied first to simplify CFG constraints. The remaining basic blocks are then mapped while enforcing the required data-propagation patterns across the CFG. Basic blocks that exhibit gaps to the theoretical bounds are executed only once for data initialization or for data propagation between sequential loops, or they belong to outer loops with significantly fewer executions. Consequently, their scheduling overhead has a limited impact on overall runtime performance.

5.4   Runtime Comparison with SoA Methods

Figure 8 presents the runtime performance normalized to the baseline configuration, in which no MS is applied. Across most benchmarks, enabling DFG optimization achieves more than a $2\times$ speedup. This improvement is attributed to MS attaining an initiation interval [4] ($II < \frac{1}{2}L$), where L denotes the length of the longest loop-carried data dependency, thereby enabling effective loop folding. Consequently, each loop iteration completes in fewer cycles than in the baseline execution, which requires at least L cycles per iteration, resulting in substantially improved basic-block execution efficiency. The flexibility of integrating fast compilers for non-critical blocks and highly optimizing (slower) ones for critical ones is therefore key for achieving high runtime performance while targeting complex CFGs.

FACETs with MS consistently outperforms Marionette on benchmarks with deep loop nesting, such as 2mm and hotspot3D. Marionette incurs runtime overhead due to data reconfiguration during basic-block switching, which becomes a performance bottleneck in nested-loop scenarios. In particular, for a three-level

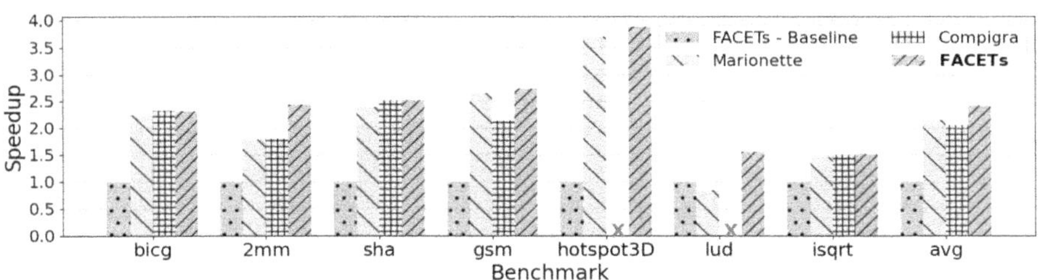

Fig. 8. Runtime comparison with state-of-the-art.

nested loop, the innermost loop requires reconfiguration $N_0 \times N_1$ times, where N_i denotes the iteration count at loop level i. This frequent reconfiguration significantly degrades runtime performance. For `lud`, Marionette fails to achieve speedup over the baseline because the innermost loop has a dynamic bound and the second-level loop has a dynamic start value, which prevents the scheduler from constructing a schedule with $II < L$.

Compared to Compigra, our approach slightly underperforms only on `bicg`, where Compigra's ILP formulation is able to find an optimal placement within a reasonable solving time. However, when the optimal solution exceeds the ILP time limit, Compigra resorts to splitting the DFG via load/store operations, introducing additional overhead. In the worst cases, such as `hotspot3D` and `lud`, Compigra fails to produce a result within a reasonable time, as reflected by the missing data points in the figure.

6   Conclusion

We presented FACETs, a fast control–dataflow mapping framework for CGRAs that broadens the scope of compilation for applications with complex control flow. By combining heuristic mapping for non-critical regions with targeted optimization of performance-critical code under explicit control-flow constraints, the proposed approach significantly reduces compilation time while preserving execution efficiency. FACETs ultimately enables the acceleration of complex CDFGs as single CGRA functions, minimizing costly host/CGRA data and configuration transfers overhead. Experimental results demonstrate up to 10× faster compilation with comparable or improved runtime performance over existing methods.

Acknowledgment. This work was supported in part by the Swiss NSF Edge-Companions project (GA No. 10002812) and the Swiss NSF grant no. 200021E_220194: "Sustainable and Energy Aware Methods for SKA (SEAMS)"; in part by the EC Horizon project CERBERUS under Grant 101223271; in part by the ACCESS—AI Chip Center for Emerging Smart Systems, sponsored by InnoHK funding, Hong Kong, SAR; in part by the Swiss National Science Foundation via project ADApprox (grant 200020_188613); and in part by the Swiss State Secretariat for Education, Research, and Innovation (SERI) through the SwissChips Research Project.

References

1. Bouwens, F., Berekovic, M., Kanstein, A., Gaydadjiev, G.: Architectural exploration of the ADRES coarse-grained reconfigurable array. In: Diniz, P.C., Marques, E., Bertels, K., Fernandes, M.M., Cardoso, J.M.P. (eds.) ARC 2007. LNCS, vol. 4419, pp. 1–13. Springer, Heidelberg (2007). https://doi.org/10.1007/978-3-540-71431-6_1
2. Vipperla, A., Murugan, N., Akoglu, A., Chakrabarti, C.: Compilation framework for dynamically reconfigurable array architectures. IEEE Access **13**, 196415–196432 (2025)
3. Wang, Y., et al.: An MLIR-based compilation framework for CGRA application deployment. In: International Symposium on Applied Reconfigurable Computing, pp. 33–50. Springer, Cham (2025)
4. Ramakrishna Rau, B.: Iterative Modulo Scheduling. **24**(1), 3–64 (1996)
5. Zacharopoulos, G., Ferretti, L., Giaquinta, E., Ansaloni, G., Pozzi, L.: Region-seeker: automatically identifying and selecting accelerators from application source code. IEEE Trans. Comput. Aided Des. Integr. Circ. Syst. **38**(4), 741–754 (2019)
6. Deng, J., et al.: Towards efficient control flow handling in spatial architecture via architecting the control flow plane. In: Proceedings of the 56th Annual IEEE/ACM International Symposium on Microarchitecture, MICRO 2023, pp. 1395–1408. Association for Computing Machinery, New York (2023)
7. Das, S., Martin, K.J.M., Rossi, D., Coussy, P., Benini, L.: An energy-efficient integrated programmable array accelerator and compilation flow for near-sensor ultralow power processing. IEEE Trans. Comput. Aided Des. Integr. Circ. Syst. **38**(6), 1095–1108 (2019)
8. Zacharopoulos, G., Pozzi, L.: Clrfreqcfgprinter: a tool for frequency annotated control flow graph generation. In: European LLVM Developers Meeting (2017)
9. Guo, Y., Wang, J., Zhang, J., Luo, G.: Formulating data-arrival synchronizers in integer linear programming for CGRA mapping. In: 2021 58th ACM/IEEE Design Automation Conference (DAC), pp. 943–948 (2021)
10. Chin, A., Anderson, J.: An architecture-agnostic integer linear programming approach to CGRA mapping. In: 2018 55th ACM/IEEE Design Automation Conference (DAC), pp. 1–6 (2018)
11. Donovick, C., Mann, M., Barrett, C., Hanrahan, P.: Agile SMT-based mapping for CGRAS with restricted routing networks. In: 2019 International Conference on ReConFigurable Computing and FPGAs (ReConFig), pp. 1–8. IEEE (2019)
12. Tirelli, C., et al.: Sat-based exact modulo scheduling mapping for resource-constrained CGRAS. J. Emerg. Technol. Comput. Syst. **20**(3) (2024)
13. Tirelli, C., Ferretti, L., Pozzi, L.: SAT-MapIt: a SAT-based modulo scheduling mapper for coarse grain reconfigurable architectures. In: 2023 Design, Automation & Test in Europe Conference & Exhibition (DATE), pp. 1–6. IEEE (2023)
14. Tirelli, C., Ferretti, L., Pozzi, L.: SAT-MapIt: an open source modulo scheduling mapper for coarse grain reconfigurable architectures. In: Proceedings of the 20th ACM International Conference on Computing Frontiers, pp. 383–384 (2023)
15. Wijerathne, D., Li, Z., Karunaratne, M., Peh, L-S., Mitra, T.: Morpher: An open-source integrated compilation and simulation framework for CGRA. In: Fifth Workshop on Open-Source EDA Technology (WOSET) (2022)
16. Liu, D., Xia, Y., Shang, J., Zhong, J., Ouyang, P., Yin, S.: E2EMap: end-to-end reinforcement learning for CGRA compilation via reverse mapping. In: 2024 IEEE International Symposium on High-Performance Computer Architecture (HPCA), pp. 46–60 (2024)

17. Ramos, F.T., et al.: Smartmap: architecture-agnostic CGRA mapping using graph traversal and reinforcement learning. In: 2025 Design, Automation & Test in Europe Conference (DATE), pp. 1–7 (2025)
18. Mu, Y., Li, S., Fan, Z., Li, W., An, X., Ye, X.: Nfmap: node fusion optimization for efficient CGRA mapping with reinforcement learning. In: Li, C., Qian, X., Gizopoulos, D., Grot, B., (eds.) Advanced Parallel Processing Technologies, pp. 61–73. Springer, Cham (2026)
19. Li, S., Xing, M., Wu, Y.: HDCC: a hierarchical dataflow-oriented CGRA compiler for complex applications. In: Proceedings of the 30th Asia and South Pacific Design Automation Conference, ASPDAC 2025, pp. 265–271. Association for Computing Machinery, New York (2025)
20. Cao, H., Wu, Z., Li, D., Jing, P., Pun, S.H., Liu, Y.: Accelerating control flow on CGRAS via speculative iteration execution. IEEE Comput. Archit. Lett. **24**(1), 109–112 (2025)
21. Lou, J., Zhu, Q., Dai, Y., Zhong, Z., Yin, W., Wang, L.: Adora compiler: end-to-end optimization for high-efficiency dataflow acceleration and task pipelining on CGRAS. In: 2025 62nd ACM/IEEE Design Automation Conference (DAC), pp. 1–7 (2025)
22. Wang, Y., Tirelli, C., Ansaloni, G., Pozzi, L., Atienza, D.: An MLIR-based compilation framework for control flow management on coarse grained reconfigurable arrays. arXiv preprint arXiv:2508.02167 (2025)
23. Guthaus, M.R., Ringenberg, J.S., Ernst, D., Austin, T.M., Mudge, T., Brown, R.B.: Mibench: a free, commercially representative embedded benchmark suite. In: Proceedings of the Fourth Annual IEEE International Workshop on Workload Characterization. WWC-4 (Cat. No.01EX538), pp. 3–14 (2001)
24. Che, S., et al.: Rodinia: a benchmark suite for heterogeneous computing. In: 2009 IEEE International Symposium on Workload Characterization (IISWC), pp. 44–54 (2009)
25. Tirelli, C., Otoni, R., Pozzi, L.: Monomorphism-based CGRA mapping via space and time decoupling. In: 2025 Design, Automation & Test in Europe Conference (DATE), pp. 1–7. IEEE (2025)
26. Álvarez, R., Denkinger, B., Sapriza, J., Calero, J.M., Ansaloni, G., Alonso, D.A.: An open-hardware coarse-grained reconfigurable array for edge computing. In: Proceedings of the 20th ACM International Conference on Computing Frontiers, pp. 391–392 (2023)

Characterising Physical Memory Access Pattern Impact on RISC-V Softcore Performance: A Microbenchmark Study

Hsin-Kun Lin[(✉)] , Wadid Foudhaili , Rainer Buchty , Mladen Berekovic ,
and Saleh Mulhem

Institute of Computer Engineering, Universität zu Lübeck, Lübeck, Germany
`h.lin@uni-luebeck.de`

Abstract. Modern processor performance is strongly constrained by the memory hierarchy and memory access patterns, and this sensitivity is particularly pronounced for FPGA-based soft-core CPUs with configurable memory subsystems. This paper presents a systematic experimental study of how physical memory access patterns interact with DRAM controllers and cache hierarchies to shape the performance of RISC-V soft cores on FPGA platforms with DDR4 memory. We evaluate representative access patterns including row-major sequential, column-major, small and large strides, and blocked traversal across STREAM kernels, dense matrix multiplication and transpose, and vector reduction workloads. The analysis compares an in order Rocket core and an out-of-order BOOM core instantiated on a Xilinx VCU118 board, using only standard RISC-V hardware performance counters to ensure portability. Row-major scans attain up to 163.91 MB/s on BOOM, while column-major traversal and large strides can increase per-element execution cost by up to 68% and reduce effective bandwidth by more than an order of magnitude. Blocked algorithms deliver up to 2.67× speedup for matrix multiplication by keeping working sets within the 32 KB L1 cache, largely independent of core microarchitecture. Contrary to the common assumption that out-of-order cores are always more sensitive to memory pressure, we find that BOOM's overhead can be higher or lower than Rocket's depending on the workload, despite identical L1 caches and DRAM interfaces. The proposed microbenchmark suite and methodology form a reproducible framework for characterising memory-subsystem behavior of FPGA-based RISC-V systems and provide practical guidelines for designing locality-aware kernels on reconfigurable platforms.

Keywords: RISC-V · FPGA · Memory Access Patterns · Performance Benchmarking · DDR Memory · Cache Locality · Row Buffer Locality

H-K. Lin and W. Foudhaili—These authors contributed equally to this work.
This work was partially supported by the ISOLDE project (Grant No. 101112274), funded by the Chips Joint Undertaking and participating states, and by the RILKOSAN project (Grant No. 16KISR010K), funded by the Federal Ministry of Research, Technology and Space (BMFTR).

G. Leone et al. (Eds.): ARC 2026, LNCS 16514, pp. 82–99, 2026.
https://doi.org/10.1007/978-3-032-29365-7_6

1   Introduction

Soft CPU cores (SC) implemented on field-programmable gate arrays (FPGAs) are widely used in embedded and high-performance systems. Unlike fixed-function ASIC processors [6], SC must be tailored to FPGA resource constraints, memory interfaces, and board-specific DRAM controllers, which complicates fair performance comparison across platforms. Existing evaluation approaches typically either correlate resource utilization with throughput [4] or isolate cache and on-chip memory effects using standardized or parameterized memory models [10]. However, both directions overlook the combined influence of software memory-access patterns and FPGA DRAM controllers on end-to-end processor behavior under realistic workloads. In particular, benchmark memory-access patterns and their performance impact under realistic workloads on FPGA remain insufficiently studied. While data locality and sequential access has been extensively studied for general-purpose CPUs, existing work rarely considers open-source RISC-V SC with configurable DDR controllers. Prior RISC-V evaluations focus on CoreMark/Embench-style benchmarks [3,5,7,24] and do not systematically vary physical access patterns or isolate memory-subsystem behavior.

This work addresses this gap by asking: *"How do physical memory access patterns interact with DRAM controllers and cache hierarchies to shape quantitative evidence of the observable performance of FPGA-based RISC-V SC across representative workloads?"*
We advance the state of the art with the following contributions:

1. We analyze memory-access patterns of RISC-V soft cores on FPGA and measure how the DDR4 memory controller affects deployed core performance. We show that controller behavior is a major factor influencing the consistency of FPGA-based performance measurements.
2. To enable objective evaluation, we develop and tune a portable microbenchmark suite spanning sequential, column-major, small/large-stride, and blocked patterns across STREAM[1] kernels [13], dense matrix operations, and reductions.
3. We conduct an empirical evaluation on in-order and out-of-order (OoO) RISC-V cores using the proposed microbenchmarks suite. The results show that under identical row-major sequential access, effective STREAM bandwidth varies by 20% between kernels for both cores, and that blocked matrix multiplication achieves $2.31\times$ and $2.67\times$ speedup on in-order core and OoO core, respectively.
4. We show that OoO execution does not uniformly exacerbate memory sensitivity: for some benchmarks, OoO exhibits higher overhead under adverse patterns, whereas for other in-order core is more affected despite identical L1 caches and DRAM interfaces.

---

[1] based on a variant of the STREAM benchmark code.

2 Background and Motivation

2.1 DRAM Architecture and Row Buffer Locality

Modern DRAM is hierarchically organized into channels, ranks, banks, rows, and columns, with each bank containing a row buffer that caches the most recently accessed row [16,18,23]. Accesses to the open row (row hits) avoid precharge and activation, while accesses to a different row in the same bank (row conflicts) incur roughly twice the latency. Prior work reports row-buffer hit rates between 10–80% depending on access pattern, and shows that scheduling policies that favor hits can improve bandwidth-bound workloads by 30–50% [18]. Address mapping therefore critically influences performance: most controllers distribute consecutive addresses across banks and channels to exploit parallelism, but irregular patterns can induce bank conflicts and degrade throughput.

2.2 Memory Access Pattern Optimization

The "memory wall" study [15] quantified the widening processor-memory speed gap, identifying data movement as a dominant performance bottleneck. STREAM analysis [14] demonstrated that even simple vector kernels achieve widely varying bandwidth depending on layout and traversal order. Cache efficiency depends on spatial and temporal locality, motivating loop transformations such as interchange, tiling, and fusion [21], which can reduce miss rates from 30–40% to below 5% in favorable cases. Compiler-driven blocking can approach the performance of manual optimization for linear algebra kernels. Hardware prefetchers mitigate latency only for predictable patterns (e.g., unit stride), but perform poorly for irregular or large-stride accesses, leading to stalls. Fine-grained profiling methods [19] further show that reorganizing data structures can reduce cache misses by 20–40%.

2.3 RISC-V on FPGA and Memory Subsystems

RISC-V has emerged as a widely adopted open ISA for both research and industrial use. The Rocket generator produces configurable in-order cores with modest L1 caches and competitive CoreMark/MHz [1], while BOOM extends Rocket with OoO execution, superscalar issue, and a reorder buffer, achieving 2–3× higher IPC on compute-intensive workloads at similar FPGA frequencies [4]. FPGAs interface with DRAM through configurable memory controllers; Xilinx UltraScale devices, for example, support DDR4 up to 2400 MT/s with tunable address mapping and refresh timing [22]. Empirical studies show that random 64-byte accesses may achieve only 15–20% of sequential bandwidth due to row-buffer conflicts, and non-sequential patterns can incur up to 4× higher latency [11,20]. Existing FPGA studies, however, largely focus on controller and PHY behavior rather than end-to-end processor performance under software-executed workloads. Most prior RISC-V evaluations on FPGA benchmark cores [4,8,12] with standard suites such as CoreMark [5] and Embench [3]. These works generally do not systematically vary memory-access patterns or explicitly isolate memory-subsystem effects. The combined impact of software access patterns and FPGA memory subsystems on RISC-V processor performance therefore remains insufficiently characterized. This work addresses that gap by conducting a dedicated and tailored microbenchmarks that analyzes how diverse access patterns influence RISC-V performance on FPGA platforms with DDR4 memory across multiple computational kernels.

3   The Proposed Approach

In this section, we present our approach to evaluating memory-controller impact on FPGA-based RISC-V SC. A central design goal of this study is to make the evaluation methodology portable across RISC-V implementations and reproducible on different FPGA platforms. The proposed approach is illustrated in Fig. 1. To ensure reliable evaluation across different RISC-V implementations, we deliberately base our approach solely on standard hardware performance counters (HPC). Then, we drive metrics to determine the memory-controller impact on FPGA-based RISC-V SC. To enable such an impact evaluation, we propose a portable microbenchmark suite.

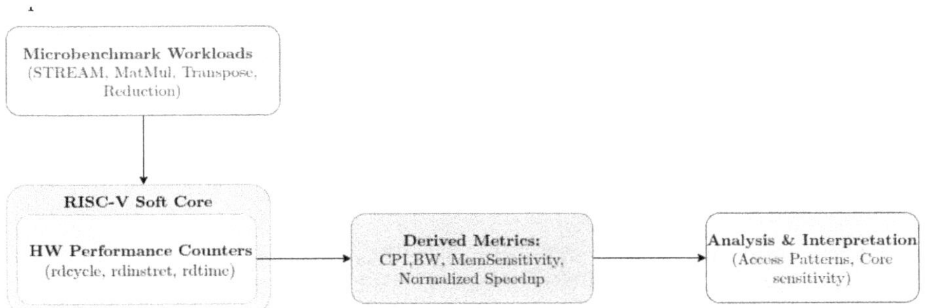

Fig. 1. Proposed Approach for Memory-Controller Impact Evaluation.

3.1   HPC as Memory Impact Measurement Enablers

Concretely, we deploy three architectural counters exposed via pseudo-instructions, as follows:

- `rdcycle` is indispensable for lightweight performance monitoring and cycle-accurate timing. It exposes a 64-bit cycle counter incremented every processor clock. By invoking `rdcycle` only at kernel boundaries to minimize measurement overhead, we can capture the current CPU cycle count, allowing to precisely gauge the latency of particular code blocks or kernels.

- **rdinstret** reads a hardware counter that tracks the number of retired instructions (successfully executed). It allows to calculate exactly how many instructions were executed.
- **rdtime** (Read Time) provides a reference timer for latency measurement. It provides a timer driven by a fixed-frequency reference.

The deployed HPC pseudo-instructions provide real-time, low-overhead monitoring of microarchitectural events.

3.2 Memory Sensitivity Metrics

We can derive the following metrics based on the values of HPCs and define them as follows:

- **Cycles Per Instruction (CPI):** CPI = cycles/instructions_retired. CPI captures the aggregate impact of memory stalls on pipeline throughput.
- **Effective Memory Bandwidth:** BW = data_bytes_accessed/execution_time, where execution time is derived from cycle counts and the known clock frequency. Data bytes are computed analytically for each kernel (e.g., $2 \times$ array_size for Copy, $3 \times$ array_size for Triad).
- **Memory Sensitivity (MemSensitivity):** the relative cycle-count degradation when transitioning from the baseline pattern (Row-Major Sequential, RM-SEQ) to an alternative pattern:

$$\text{MemSensitivity} = \frac{\text{Cycles}_{\text{pattern}} - \text{Cycles}_{\text{baseline}}}{\text{Cycles}_{\text{baseline}}} \qquad (1)$$

Positive values indicate degradation; negative values indicate that the alternative pattern is more efficient (as can occur for transpose under column-major traversal).
- **Normalized Speedup:** Speedup = $\text{Cycles}_{\text{baseline}}/\text{Cycles}_{\text{pattern}}$. Values > 1 indicate the pattern executes faster than the baseline; values < 1 indicate slowdown.

These metrics are intentionally derived from cycle and instruction counters alone, avoiding reliance on cache-miss counters or other implementation-specific events that may not be available across all RISC-V cores. This choice maximizes portability and reproducibility of the framework.

3.3 Benchmark Requirements and Design

We target the following properties:

- **Sustained memory throughput** under varying access regularity, to quantify effective bandwidth as a function of access pattern.
- **Cache and row-buffer locality sensitivity**, to distinguish patterns that exploit spatial and temporal reuse from those that defeat caching and trigger row-buffer conflicts.

– **Prefetcher interaction**, to identify the stride regimes where hardware prefetching remains effective versus where it fails.
– **Pipeline utilization**, to assess how in-order and OoO execution respond differently to memory pressure.

The design follows four principles: (1) *Portability:* kernels use standard C with minimal platform-specific code to facilitate deployment on any RISC-V target (2) *Simplicity:* each kernel isolates a single computational pattern to avoid confounding effects (3) *Parameterizability:* array sizes, strides, and tile dimensions are compile-time constants to ease systematic sweeps (4) *Analyzability:* each kernel's memory traffic is analytically predictable to enable direct comparison between expected and measured behavior.

We employ three categories of computational kernels spanning distinct memory-access characteristics.

1. **STREAM Bandwidth Kernels**: We tune the STREAM benchmark [14] to measure sustainable memory bandwidth through four kernels of increasing arithmetic intensity: `Copy` ($b[i] = a[i]$), `Scale` ($b[i] = s \cdot a[i]$), `Add` ($c[i] = a[i] + b[i]$), and `Triad` ($a[i] = b[i] + s \cdot c[i]$). Under row-major sequential (RM-SEQ) access, these kernels generate highly predictable, unit-stride memory traffic ideal for prefetcher exploitation. Irregular patterns introduce cache misses and reduce throughput.
2. **Dense Matrix Operations**: We propose two workloads: (1) *Matrix Multiplication* (MM) of 512×512 matrices ($C = A \times B$, requiring $512^3 \approx 134\,\mathrm{M}$ multiply-add operations), tested with row-major (`ijk`), column-major (`jik`), and blocked (tiled, 32×32) loop orderings, and (2) *Matrix Transpose* (MT) of 512×512 matrices, generating either sequential or strided access depending on traversal order.
3. **Reduction Operations**: We propose a vector reduction (sum $= \sum_i v_i$) over 262,144 elements that tests sensitivity to memory-latency hiding: OoO cores can potentially overlap independent loads, whereas in-order cores stall on each miss.

Each workload stresses different parts of the memory hierarchy. STREAM kernels are bandwidth-limited with minimal compute, making them sensitive to row-buffer locality and prefetcher effectiveness. Matrix multiplication combines high computational intensity with large working sets, exposing the interaction between cache capacity and access ordering. Transpose produces inherently mismatched read and write strides, revealing asymmetries in cache write-back behavior. Reduction isolates the impact of instruction-level parallelism on memory-latency tolerance. We evaluate five distinct access patterns across these workloads: **(1) Row-Major Sequential (RM-SEQ):** stride-1 element traversal, maximizing row-buffer locality and prefetcher accuracy. **(2) Column-Major Sequential (CM-SEQ):** stride equal to matrix dimension ($512 \times 4 = 2{,}048$ bytes), crossing row boundaries on nearly every access. **(3) Small Stride (STRIDE-4):** stride of 4 elements (16 bytes), partially defeating prefetchers while remaining within cache-line boundaries. **(4) Large Stride**

(STRIDE-64): stride of 64 elements (256 bytes), accessing exactly one element per cache line before advancing, defeating both prefetching and spatial locality. **(5) Blocked (BLOCKED):** for matrix operations, computation proceeds on 32×32 sub-matrices fitting entirely in L1 data cache (32 KB), with row-major intra-block access. Figure 2 visualizes these five access patterns on a row-major 2D matrix, highlighting how RM-SEQ and BLOCKED preserve row locality while CM-SEQ and large-stride patterns repeatedly cross row boundaries.

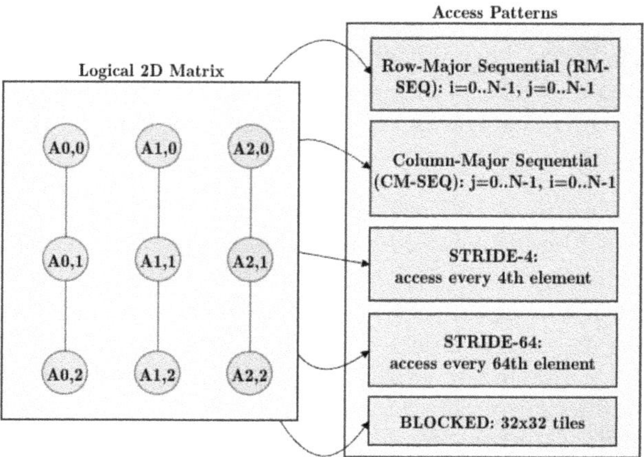

Fig. 2. Illustration of the evaluated memory access patterns on a row-major 2D matrix.

4   Implementation Protocol and Experimental Setup

4.1   Hardware Platform Configuration

Experiments run on a Xilinx VCU118 FPGA board with 4 GB DDR4 SDRAM at 2400 MT/s. The DDR4 subsystem exposes four 64-bit channels, each with 8 banks and 64 KB row buffers, with typical access latencies of $\approx$40–50 ns (row hit) and $\approx$80–100 ns (row conflict). The FPGA bitstream instantiates either a Rocket or BOOM RISC-V core configured as in Table 1; both use 32 KB instruction and data caches with 64-byte lines and connect directly from L1 to DDR4 (no L2), enabling direct observation of memory access behavior. The DDR controller employs a default address mapping that interprets physical addresses from least significant bit (LSB) to most significant bit (MSB) as column, bank, row, channel, and rank. This mapping distributes consecutive cache-line addresses across banks and channels to exploit parallelism while preserving row-buffer locality for sequential accesses:

$$\underbrace{\text{Column}}_{11} \mid \underbrace{\text{Bank}}_{3} \mid \underbrace{\text{Row}}_{16} \mid \underbrace{\text{Channel}}_{2} \mid \underbrace{\text{Rank}}_{1} \quad \text{(from LSB to MSB)}.$$

Table 1. Configuration comparison between Rocket and BOOM cores.

Feature	Rocket Core	BOOM Core
Pipeline	5-stage in-order scalar	2-way superscalar out-of-order
Instruction Fetch Width	$1 \times$ 32-bit instr./cycle	$2 \times$ 32-bit instr./cycle
Reorder Buffer	N/A	32 entries
L1 I\$/D\$ Cache	32 KB, 4-way, 64B lines	32 KB, 4-way, 64B lines
L2 Cache	None (L1 $\rightarrow$ DDR)[a]	None (L1 $\rightarrow$ DDR)[1]
Data Memory Width	64-bit per load/store	64-bit per load/store
Runtime Environment	Minimal Linux, compiled with -O2	

[a] Same DDR interface (64-bit).

4.2 Workloads and Access Patterns

All workloads use a working set of 262,144 elements (1 MB for 4-byte floats), exceeding the 32 KB L1 cache to enforce main-memory traffic. The benchmark kernels and access patterns are defined in Sect. 3.3.

Across these workloads we evaluate five memory access patterns: row-major sequential (RM-SEQ), column-major sequential (CM-SEQ), small stride (STRIDE-4), large stride (STRIDE-64), and blocked (BLOCKED) access for matrix operations, as illustrated in Fig. 2.

4.3 Performance Measurement and Data Collection

We use RISC-V performance counters to avoid external instrumentation overhead: `rdcycle` (64-bit cycle counter), `rdinstret` (retired instructions), and `rdtime` (timer). From these we derive execution cycles, instructions retired, CPI (cycles/instruction), execution time (cycles/fixed clock frequency), and effective memory bandwidth (bytes/time).

To ensure statistical validity, each configuration is executed 10 times after a three-iteration warmup. Before each measurement, we flush L1 caches using a buffer larger than 32 KB and insert memory fences around the timed region. Benchmarks run in a single thread in a minimal Linux system with CPU affinity and interrupts disabled. Both Rocket and BOOM cores are clocked at 50 MHz. We report mean cycles, CPI, and bandwidth; coefficients of variation are typically below 2%. Memory bandwidth calculations assume a specific data volume per kernel (e.g., $2 \times$ array_size for Copy, $3 \times$ array_size for Triad).

4.4 Experimental Procedure

We evaluate seven benchmarks (the four STREAM kernels, matrix multiplication, matrix transpose, and reduction) across five access patterns (RM-SEQ, CM-SEQ, STRIDE-4, STRIDE-64, BLOCKED) on both Rocket and BOOM, for 70 configurations in total. Each configuration is run 10 times, yielding 700 measurements. All code is compiled for RV64GC with -O2, deployed from SD card, and executed on the VCU118 board; standard output is logged for offline analysis. Complete source code, build scripts, and experimental procedures will be made publicly available to facilitate reproducibility.

5   Experimental Results

5.1   STREAM Benchmark: Row-Major Baseline

Table 2 presents the STREAM benchmark results under the baseline access pattern, row-major sequential (RM-SEQ). Using this baseline, we **analyze** how kernel characteristics affect measured bandwidth before comparing other access patterns in Sect. 5.2. On BOOM, Copy achieves the highest bandwidth (BW) at 163.91 MB/s with a CPI of 0.90, confirming that the OoO pipeline sustains more than one useful operation per cycle on this memory-streaming workload. Scale follows closely at 160.61 MB/s (CPI = 0.77), while Add and Triad, which require three memory operands each, drop to 132.65 and 130.54 MB/s, respectively, due to increased memory pressure. On Rocket, the same four kernels achieve 44.45, 35.41, 42.29, and 42.10 MB/s, respectively. The in-order pipeline's CPI remains between 3.03 and 3.20, reflecting its limited ability to overlap memory latency with computation.

A key observation is the *bandwidth spread* across the four RM-SEQ kernels. Despite using the same sequential access pattern, effective bandwidth varies by 20.3% on Rocket (35.41 to 44.45 MB/s) and 20.4% on BOOM (130.54 to 163.91 MB/s). This variation arises from differences in arithmetic intensity and the number of memory streams per kernel, showing that benchmark selection can significantly affect measured bandwidth even under ideal access conditions. Table 2 provides the reference point for the pattern-impact comparisons in Sect. 5.2.

Table 2. STREAM Benchmark Performance—Row-Major Sequential (RM-SEQ) Pattern.

Kernel	Rocket			BOOM		
	Cycles (avg)	CPI	BW	Cycles (avg)	CPI	BW
Copy	4,498,986	3.06	44.45	1,220,202	0.90	163.91
Scale	5,647,973	3.20	35.41	1,245,269	0.77	160.61
Add	7,094,599	3.03	42.29	2,261,560	1.04	132.65
Triad	7,125,505	3.04	42.10	2,298,232	1.05	130.54

The bandwidth achieved by STREAM Copy on BOOM (163.91 MB/s) represents approximately 0.85% of the theoretical peak DDR4 single-channel bandwidth (19.2 GB/s at 2400 MT/s). This low utilization is expected: the SC pipeline issues at most one 8-byte load or store per cycle at 50 MHz, yielding a theoretical processor-side ceiling of 400 MB/s BOOM achieves 41% of this processor-side ceiling, while Rocket achieves 11%, consistent with their respective CPI values.

5.2 Impact of Access Patterns on STREAM Performance

Table 3 presents normalized performance (RM-SEQ = 1.0) for all patterns.

STRIDE-4 Degradation: Small-stride access (16 bytes) degrades STREAM performance by up to 35% depending on kernel and core. On Rocket, Copy suffers the most (normalized speedup 0.74, i.e., 35% more cycles), while Triad is nearly unaffected (0.98). BOOM exhibits similar trends (Copy: 0.73, Triad: 0.94).

STRIDE-64 Behavior: Large-stride access (256 bytes) processes only 1/64 of the array elements, touching one element per cache line. Although the raw cycle counts are much lower (fewer elements are accessed), the *per-element cost* reveals severe penalties. The normalized speedup values in Table 3 (7.56–9.75× for Rocket, 10.05–16.42× for BOOM) reflect that fewer cycles are spent in total because fewer elements are touched. Per-element execution cost increases by up to 68% compared to row-major sequential access, even though fewer elements are accessed overall. These comparisons show how changes in access pattern affect the measured behavior of the DDR4 controller path, which can change the consistency of FPGA-based performance measurements.

Table 3. Normalized Performance Comparison: Rocket (R) vs. BOOM (B) by Access Pattern. (RM-SEQ = 1.0). Values >1 indicate fewer total cycles than RM-SEQ.

Pattern	Copy		Scale		Add		Triad		MatMul	
	R	B	R	B	R	B	R	B	R	B
RM-SEQ	1.00	1.00	1.00	1.00	1.00	1.00	1.00	1.00	1.00	1.00
CM-SEQ	—	—	—	—	—	—	—	—	0.94	1.00
STRIDE-4	0.74	0.73	0.75	0.79	0.82	0.77	0.98	0.94	—	—
STRIDE-64	7.56	10.11	8.80	10.70	8.28	14.27	9.75	16.42	—	—
BLOCKED	—	—	—	—	—	—	—	—	2.31	2.67

5.3   Matrix Operation Results

Matrix Multiplication: Row-major (`ijk`) matrix multiplication requires approximately 8.94 billion cycles on Rocket (CPI = 7.79) and 4.50 billion cycles on BOOM (CPI = 4.59), yielding a BOOM-over-Rocket speedup of ~2×. Column-major (`jik`) ordering adds 5.8% overhead on Rocket but has negligible effect on BOOM (<0.1%). Blocked (tiled) multiplication provides substantial speedups: 2.31× on Rocket (CPI drops from 7.79 to 3.37) and 2.67× on BOOM (CPI drops from 4.59 to 1.72).

Matrix Transpose: Column-major traversal is faster than row-major on both cores, by 16.1% on Rocket (17.96 M vs. 21.40 M cycles) and 7.8% on BOOM (8.86 M vs. 9.61 M cycles). Blocked transpose achieves further improvement: 1.56× speedup on Rocket and 1.73× on BOOM relative to RM-SEQ, with CPI dropping from 10.24 to 6.56 (Rocket) and from 5.79 to 3.35 (BOOM).

Reduction: Vector reduction achieves 19.96 MB/s on Rocket (CPI = 2.52) and 25.30 MB/s on BOOM (CPI = 1.76), a 1.47× BOOM advantage.

5.4   Cross-Core Comparison

Table 4 compares CPI and core speedup across all benchmarks under RM-SEQ access. BOOM achieves its largest advantage on STREAM Copy and Scale (3.7–4.5×), where the workload is a simple memory transfer with minimal computation. For STREAM Add and Triad, the advantage narrows to ~3.1× as the three-operand kernels increase memory pressure. Matrix multiplication shows a consistent ~1.9× speedup. This reflects BOOM's ability to overlap independent multiply-add operations. Reduction yields only 1.47×, confirming that the sequential accumulation chain limits OoO benefit.

Table 4. CPI comparison and BOOM-over-Rocket speedup under RM-SEQ access.

Benchmark	Rocket CPI	BOOM CPI	Speedup
STREAM Copy	3.06	0.90	3.69×
STREAM Scale	3.20	0.77	4.54×
STREAM Add	3.03	1.04	3.14×
STREAM Triad	3.04	1.05	3.10×
Matrix Mult (RM)	7.79	4.59	1.93×
Matrix Trans (RM)	10.24	5.79	2.16×
Reduction	2.52	1.76	1.47×

5.5   Memory Sensitivity Analysis

We compute per-benchmark memory sensitivity as the cycle-count overhead introduced by the worst-performing directly comparable pattern relative to RM-SEQ (Eq. 1). For STREAM kernels, STRIDE-4 represents the worst directly comparable pattern (STRIDE-64 processes a different element count). For matrix operations, CM-SEQ serves as the comparison pattern.

Table 5. Memory sensitivity: cycle-count overhead of worst-case pattern relative to RM-SEQ.

Benchmark	Rocket	BOOM
STREAM Copy (STRIDE-4)	+35.1%	+37.3%
STREAM Scale (STRIDE-4)	+33.0%	+26.9%
STREAM Add (STRIDE-4)	+21.6%	+29.7%
STREAM Triad (STRIDE-4)	+2.0%	+6.2%
Matrix Mult (CM-SEQ)	+5.8%	<0.1%
Matrix Transpose (CM-SEQ)	−16.1%	−7.8%

STREAM Copy and Scale exhibit the highest sensitivity (26–37% overhead under STRIDE-4), while Triad is nearly insensitive (2–6%). For matrix multiplication, column-major ordering adds 5.8% overhead on Rocket but is effectively neutral on BOOM thanks to its OoO scheduling which masks the penalty. Transpose sensitivity is negative under CM-SEQ (i.e., column-major is beneficial), as discussed above. An important finding is that BOOM does *not* consistently exhibit higher memory sensitivity than Rocket across all benchmarks. While BOOM shows greater sensitivity for STREAM Add (+29.7% vs. +21.6%) and Triad (+6.2% vs. +2.0%), Rocket is more sensitive for STREAM Scale (+33.0% vs. +26.9%) and for matrix multiplication (+5.8% vs. ∼0%). This contradicts the common expectation that OoO cores uniformly suffer more under memory pressure; instead, the shared DDR interface and identical cache configuration mean that the memory-system bottleneck affects both cores comparably, with workload-specific differences determining which core is more exposed.

5.6   Robustness and Measurement Variability

Measurement variability is low across all configurations. STREAM benchmarks on BOOM show cycle-count ranges of less than 5% between minimum and maximum across 10 iterations (e.g., Copy: 1,207,915–1,257,064 cycles, a 4.1% range). Matrix multiplication variability is even smaller (<0.01% for both cores), reflecting the deterministic nature of large, compute-bound workloads. The use of 10 iterations and mean-based reporting effectively mitigates rare outlier events such as Linux interrupts. Coefficients of variation are typically below 2%, confirming the statistical robustness of our measurement framework.

6   Discussion: µ-architectural Implications and Use Cases

Prior work on DRAM architectures and memory scheduling studies synthetic traffic patterns, controller policies, or standalone memory subsystems. Our results complement these efforts by providing a counter-based framework that links physical access patterns, DRAM row-buffer locality, and the observable performance of FPGA-hosted RISC-V soft cores.

6.1   Row-Buffer Locality as Primary Performance Factor

Our measurements confirm that row-buffer locality is the dominant factor governing memory-access performance across all evaluated benchmarks and core architectures, consistent with prior work on DRAM access behavior [16,18,23]. Sequential row-major traversal (RM-SEQ) yields peak bandwidths of 44.45 MB/s on Rocket and 163.91 MB/s on BOOM for the Copy kernel, because incrementing column addresses keeps all accesses within a single DRAM row and avoids repeated precharge-activate cycles. In contrast, column-major traversal (CM-SEQ) produces a measurable penalty for matrix multiplication (5.8% overhead on Rocket and near-zero on BOOM). With a stride equal to the matrix dimension 2,048 B for our 512×512 matrices) nearly every access crosses a row boundary, producing frequent row-buffer conflicts. Intermediate stride patterns STRIDE-4 (16 B stride) remains within a 64 B cache line across multiple accesses and incurs modest penalty, while STRIDE-64 (256 B stride) touches one element per cache line, defeating both spatial locality and prefetching. Using a simple analytical model,

$$\mathrm{ExpectedHitRate} = \frac{\mathrm{RowBufferSize/Stride}}{\mathrm{WorkingSetSize}}$$

we estimate a hit rate of approximately 99% for RM-SEQ ($65{,}536/64/262{,}144 \approx 0.99$) and approximately 12% for CM-SEQ with a 2,048 B stride ($65{,}536/2{,}048/262{,}144 \approx 0.12$). These estimates closely match the observed performance ratios, reinforcing that DRAM row locality is the primary determinant of sustained memory performance.

6.2   Prefetching Effectiveness and Stride Patterns

Hardware prefetchers exhibit clear operational limits in our stride-pattern experiments [9]. Under unit-stride access (RM-SEQ), both Rocket and BOOM benefit substantially: prefetchers accurately track the sequential pattern and fetch the next cache line before the current access completes, yielding CPIs of 3.03–3.20 on Rocket and 0.77–1.05 on BOOM. With a stride of four elements (16 B), prefetchers remain only partially effective, causing a $\approx 1.3\times$ slowdown for Copy relative to RM-SEQ, consistent with reported 40–70% prefetch accuracy on small but non-contiguous strides. At a stride of 64 elements (256 B), each access touches a new cache line and predictive mechanisms are effectively defeated, increasing per-element cost by 6–8× as the cores repeatedly stall on memory responses.

Thus, compilers and algorithm designers should not rely on hardware prefetchers to rescue irregular patterns; locality-enhancing transformations such as tiling, fusion, blocking, and data-layout restructuring offer more robust gains [2,21].

6.3   Blocked Algorithms and Cache-Aware Optimizations

Blocked (tiled) matrix multiplication demonstrates the efficacy of cache-conscious algorithm design [21]. By restructuring computation to operate on 32×32 sub-matrices that fit within L1 data cache (32 KB), the kernel dramatically reduces main memory traffic despite identical algorithmic complexity.

Performance Improvement: Blocked matrix multiplication achieves $2.31\times$ speedup (**S**) on Rocket and $2.67\times$ on BOOM over naive `ijk` loop ordering:

$$S_{\text{Rocket}} = \frac{8{,}935{,}128{,}361}{3{,}866{,}980{,}940} = 2.31, \qquad S_{\text{BOOM}} = \frac{4{,}499{,}067{,}086}{1{,}685{,}162{,}292} = 2.67.$$

Mechanism: Simple `ijk` ordering accesses matrix B with column-major traversal despite row-major storage. Blocked ordering partitions matrices into tiles which allows all three matrices to reside in L1 cache when :

$$\text{tile\_size}^2 \leq \frac{\text{cache\_size}}{3} \tag{2}$$

This yields a maximum tile dimension of $\sqrt{32{,}768/3} \approx 104$ elements for our 32 KB L1 cache, well above 32. we therefore choose 32×32 tiles. This increases arithmetic intensity from roughly 0.015 FLOP/byte (naive, cache-miss-dominated) to about 0.5 FLOP/byte (blocked, cache-resident).

Core Parity: Both cores exhibit similar relative speedup from blocking ($2.31\times$ and $2.67\times$), indicating that cache-locality benefits are largely independent of microarchitectural sophistication. Blocked transpose shows a similar pattern ($1.56\times$ on Rocket and $1.73\times$ on BOOM), with BOOM's larger improvement attributable to its ability to overlap the remaining cache misses with computation.

6.4   In-Order vs. OoO: Microarchitectural Implications

IPC Across Workloads: BOOM achieves its highest speedup on STREAM Copy and Scale (3.7–$4.5\times$ over Rocket), where simple streaming allows extensive latency hiding via OoO execution and multiple outstanding memory requests. For STREAM Add and Triad the advantage narrows to $\approx3.1\times$, as additional memory streams bring both cores closer to the DDR bandwidth ceiling. Matrix multiplication and transpose show more modest speedups of 1.9–$2.2\times$, and reduction only $1.47\times$, because high arithmetic intensity or strict data dependencies limit exploitable instruction-level parallelism. BOOM does not uniformly exhibit higher memory sensitivity than Rocket (Table 5). BOOM is more sensitive for STREAM Add (29.7% vs. 21.6%) and Triad (6.2% vs. 2.0%), while Rocket is more sensitive for STREAM Scale (33.0% vs. 26.9%) and matrix multiplication (5.8% vs. ~0%). This contradicts the common assumption that OoO cores always suffer more under memory pressure; instead, the shared DDR interface and identical L1 configuration mean that the memory-system bottleneck affects both architectures comparably, with workload-specific characteristics determining which core is more exposed.

Reorder Buffer Pressure: BOOM's 32-entry reorder buffer can fill during prolonged memory stalls. Under severe memory pressure (e.g., STRIDE-64 with frequent row-buffer misses), reorder-buffer saturation causes fetch stalls and prevents instruction prefetching, eroding the advantage of the OoO pipeline. Conversely, on compute-rich operations with good locality (e.g., blocked matrix multiplication), BOOM maintains its higher 2.3–2.7× speedup. Overall, these findings indicate that microarchitectural sophistication alone cannot compensate for adverse memory access patterns, and that the benefits of OoO execution on FPGA-based RISC-V cores are strongly workload dependent rather than universally positive.

6.5   Generalizability

Our experiments were conducted on a Xilinx Virtex UltraScale+ VCU118 FPGA board with Rocket and BOOM cores and DDR4 memory at 2400 MT/s. Absolute bandwidth scales with memory technology and cache sizes, but prior work suggests that relative differences across access patterns are stable across DRAM generations [17, 18]. We therefore expect the qualitative trends observed here (strong dependence on row-buffer locality, limited prefetching effectiveness, and substantial benefits from blocking) to generalize to other FPGA-based systems with DDR3, DDR4, or DDR5 memory and comparable cache hierarchies.

Workload Coverage: Our benchmark focuses on memory-bandwidth-limited kernels (STREAM) and cache-sensitive operations (matrix multiplication, transpose, reduction). Measurement uncertainty from clock variation, context switches, and cache flush overhead is around 2%, and coefficients of variation are typically below 2%, which confirms the reproducibility of our measurements. Based on our results, we offer the following practical guidelines for software and system designers targeting RISC-V FPGA systems:

1. **Prioritize sequential access:** traverse data structures with unit stride and avoid column-major access to row-major matrices unless cache is sufficiently large, yielding up to 35% improvement vs. STRIDE-4 and 6–8× per-element improvement vs. STRIDE-64.
2. **Apply loop blocking for cache-limited kernels:** tile matrix operations so working sets fit in L1 (32 KB), typically with 32–64 elements per dimension, achieving 2.3–2.7× speedup.

3. **Use OoO cores selectively:** BOOM provides 3.7–4.5× speedup on simple streaming but only 1.5–2.2× on compute-intensive workloads; in-order cores can suffice for memory-bound applications.
4. **Avoid large strides:** strides $\geq 256\,$B defeat prefetching and increase per-element cost by 6–8×; when unavoidable, consider software prefetching or data-layout changes.
5. **Profile with hardware counters:** use `rdcycle` and `rdinstret` to compute CPI and distinguish memory-bound (CPI $\gg$ 1) from compute-bound (CPI $\approx$ 1) kernels, then apply pattern or parallelism optimizations accordingly.

Many of our qualitative conclusions are consistent with classical memory-optimization literature for x86/ARM processors. The novelty of our work lies in showing that these principles manifest in distinct, quantifiable ways on RISC-V SC with minimal caching, and in demonstrating that widely used open-source cores exhibit non-trivial, workload-dependent memory sensitivity despite having identical L1 caches and DDR interfaces.

7   Conclusion

This paper presented how physical memory access patterns affect RISC-V soft-core performance on FPGA platforms with DDR4 memory. By benchmarking sequential, strided, and blocked patterns across STREAM kernels, matrix operations, and reductions on in-order (Rocket) and out-of-order (BOOM) cores, we showed (i) Row-buffer locality is the dominant performance driver: sequential access reaches 163.91 MB/s on BOOM, while non-unit strides increase per-element cost by 6–8× due to row conflicts and prefetcher failure. (ii)Hardware prefetchers are effective only for unit-stride access and fail once strides exceed the 64-byte cache-line size, motivating algorithms that emphasize spatial locality. (iii) Blocked (tiled) algorithms provide 2.3–2.7× speedup by keeping working sets in L1 cache; this benefit appears on both in-order and out-of-order cores. (iv) Out-of-order execution offers 3.7–4.5× speedup on simple streaming workloads but only 1.5–2.2× on compute-intensive matrix operations and reduction, indicating that in-order cores are competitive for memory-bound workloads. (v) On these RISC-V SC, microarchitectural sophistication cannot compensate for poorly structured access patterns;careful memory organization remains the primary optimization frontier, and our measurements quantify its impact under realistic DDR4 operation. And, (vi) The proposed methodology, based on RISC-V hardware counters (`rdcycle`, `rdinstret`) and 700 measurements, forms a reproducible basis for future studies of memory-subsystem behavior on FPGA-based RISC-V platforms.

Our benchmark design and methodology constitute a reusable framework for characterizing memory-subsystem behavior of future RISC-V FPGA platforms and for comparing new core or memory-controller designs.

References

1. Asanović, K., et al.: The rocket chip generator. Technical report. UCB/EECS-2016-17, EECS Department, University of California, Berkeley (2016)
2. Bacon, D.F., Graham, S.L., Sharp, O.J.: Compiler transformations for high-performance computing. ACM Comput. Surv. (CSUR) **26**(4), 345–420 (2000)
3. Bennett, J., Patterson, D., et al.: Embench: a free, open benchmark suite for embedded systems. In: 2020 IEEE International Symposium on Workload Characterization (IISWC). IEEE (2020). https://doi.org/10.1109/IISWC50251.2020.00016
4. Dörflinger, A., et al.: A comparative survey of open-source application-class risc-v processor implementations. In: Proceedings of the 18th ACM International Conference on Computing Frontiers, pp. 12–20 (2021)
5. Embedded Microprocessor Benchmark Consortium (EEMBC): CoreMark: A Benchmark that Tests the Efficiency of Microcontrollers. Technical report, EEMBC (2010). https://www.eembc.org/coremark/
6. Ewert, C., et al.: Sailor: a scalable and energy-efficient ultra-lightweight risc-v for IoT security (2026). https://arxiv.org/abs/2602.24166
7. Foudhaili, W., et al.: Reconfigurable edge hardware for intelligent ids: systematic approach. In: Skliarova, I., Brox Jiménez, P., Véstias, M., Diniz, P.C. (eds.) Applied Reconfigurable Computing. Architectures, Tools, and Applications, pp. 48–62. Springer, Cham (2024)
8. Gachomba, M.L., et al.: Comparative performance analysis of risc-v architectures. In: Proceedings of the International Conference on Computer Architecture. IEEE (2022)
9. Hashemi, M., et al.: Learning memory access patterns. In: International Conference on Machine Learning (ICML), pp. 1924–1933. PMLR (2018)
10. Heinz, C., Lavan, Y., Hofmann, J., Koch, A.: A catalog and in-hardware evaluation of open-source drop-in compatible risc-v softcore processors. In: 2019 International Conference on ReConFigurable Computing and FPGAs (ReConFig), pp. 1–8 (2019). https://doi.org/10.1109/ReConFig48160.2019.8994796
11. Koch, D., Torresen, J., Pham, K.: Understanding and mitigating memory interference in FPGA-based heterogeneous socs. In: IEEE International Symposium on Field-Programmable Custom Computing Machines (FCCM), pp. 145–156. IEEE (2020)
12. Lehnert, S., et al.: Evaluating the feasibility of a risc-v core for real-time applications. In: Fraunhofer Research Publication (2021)
13. McCalpin, J.D.: Stream: sustainable memory bandwidth in high performance computers. Technical report, University of Virginia, Charlottesville, Virginia (1991–2007). http://www.cs.virginia.edu/stream/. a continually updated technical report
14. McCalpin, J.D.: Memory bandwidth and machine balance in current high performance computers. In: IEEE Computer Society Technical Committee on Computer Architecture (TCCA) Newsletter, vol. 2, no. 19–25 (1995)
15. McKee, S.A.: Reflections on the memory wall, p. 162 (2004). https://doi.org/10.1145/977091.977115
16. Mutlu, O., Moscibroda, T.: Stall-time fair memory access scheduling for chip multiprocessors. In: 40th Annual IEEE/ACM International Symposium on Microarchitecture (MICRO), pp. 146–160. IEEE (2007)
17. Mutlu, O., Moscibroda, T.: Parallelism-aware batch scheduling: enhancing both performance and fairness of shared dram systems. ACM SIGARCH Comput. Archit. News **36**(3), 63–74 (2008)

18. Rixner, S., Dally, W.J., Kapasi, U.J., Mattson, P., Owens, J.D.: Memory access scheduling. In: Proceedings of the 27th Annual International Symposium on Computer Architecture (ISCA), pp. 128–138. ACM (2000)
19. Sanchez, D., Aragón, J.L., Kozyrakis, C.: Understanding object-level memory access patterns across diverse workloads. In: IEEE International Symposium on Performance Analysis of Systems and Software (ISPASS), pp. 234–246. IEEE (2017)
20. Weisgut, A., Rabl, T.: Cxl-bench: benchmarking shared cxl memory access. In: Proceedings of the HPI Systems Seminar, pp. 1–15 (2025)
21. Wolf, M.E., Lam, M.S.: A data locality optimizing algorithm. In: Proceedings of the ACM SIGPLAN Conference on Programming Language Design and Implementation (PLDI), pp. 30–44. ACM (1991)
22. Xilinx Inc.: Zynq ultrascale+ mpsoc - processing system (PS) DDR controller (2023). https://adaptivesupport.amd.com/s/article/66194?language=en_US
23. Zuravleff, W.K., Robinson, T.: Controller for a synchronous dram that maximizes throughput by allowing memory requests and commands to be issued out of order. US Patent 5,630,075 (1997)
24. Čejić, I., Nešković, A., Berekovic, M., Mulhem, S., Vranjković, V.: Area-optimized risc-v matrix extension implementation for edge devices. In: 2025 33rd Telecommunications Forum (TELFOR), pp. 1–4 (2025). https://doi.org/10.1109/TELFOR67910.2025.11314483

JACABench - The JACA Benchmark Suite for Embedded Computing

José A. M. de Holanda[1]([✉]), Vanderlei Bonato[2], João M. P. Cardoso[3], and José Mendes[3]

[1] Federal Institute of Education, Science and Technology of São Paulo,
São Paulo, Brazil
`arnaldomh@ifsp.edu.br`
[2] Institute of Mathematics and Computer Science, University of São Paulo,
São Paulo, Brazil
`vbonato@usp.br`
[3] Faculty of Engineering, University of Porto, Porto, Portugal
`jmpc@fe.up.pt, up201603781@up.pt`

Abstract. This paper introduces JACABench, the JACA Benchmark Suite for embedded computing systems. JACABench is a C-based benchmark suite designed to complement existing evaluation frameworks. JACABench incorporates a set of features that support the systematic assessment of compilers, code transformations and optimizations, high-level synthesis (HLS) tools, hardware accelerators, and embedded computer architectures, as well as the impact of code variants on performance and energy consumption. For each benchmark, the suite provides multiple code variants that capture relevant dimensions, including alternative code transformations, data types, scenario-specific specializations, and configurable parameters. JACABench is conceived as a continuously evolving benchmark suite, with a particular emphasis on FPGA-based embedded computing. We present the initial set of benchmarks currently included in the suite and show the impact of selected code variants on FPGA implementations.

Keywords: benchmarks · performance · evaluation · FPGA · compilers · high-level synthesis · embedded computing

1 Introduction

Benchmark suites are essential for evaluating computer architectures, compiler optimizations, and high-level synthesis (HLS) methodologies. Existing suites, including SPEC [1], PolyBench [2], MiBench [3], MediaBench [4], PARSEC [5], RODINIA [6], CortexSuite [7], MachSuite [8], CHStone [9], Rosetta [10], and HeteroBench [11], span a broad range of application domains and computational patterns. Their design purposes vary from full applications to kernel-focused workloads, often shaped by the capabilities and limitations of HLS tools and target hardware platforms.

G. Leone et al. (Eds.): ARC 2026, LNCS 16514, pp. 100–115, 2026.
https://doi.org/10.1007/978-3-032-29365-7_7

With recent advances in FPGAs and HLS tools, the research community increasingly requires benchmark suites that capture both realistic application behavior and the fine-grained variants needed for compiler, toolchain, and hardware/software (hw/sw) co-design evaluations. Such suites should balance kernel-level simplicity with application-level structure, incorporate multi-stage computations and real datasets, expose meaningful optimization opportunities, and remain extensible and up-to-date.

JACABench addresses this need by providing a C-based benchmark suite focused on embedded computing systems, particularly those involving sensing data and FPGA-accelerated execution. The suite includes multiple code variants that target different optimization strategies, data representations, and deployment scenarios, supporting both CPU and HLS execution environments. Multi-threaded CPU versions offer baselines for comparison against hardware acceleration, while bare-metal variants emulate realistic embedded execution conditions.

This paper introduces the first release of JACABench, detailing its benchmarks, design principles, and variant space. We also demonstrate its versatility through FPGA-based experimental results obtained from representative variants synthesized with Vitis HLS. Specifically, the JACABench suite presented in this paper provides:

- Code variants considering typical code transformations, code specialization regarding deployment scenarios.
- Both kernels and parts of applications consisting of multiple computing stages and data streaming options.
- Different options for loading/storing input/output data (e.g., static initialization of arrays vs. reading from files), which may better emulate the real system, and alternatives for dataset sizes.
- Clear interfaces that provide the selection of the options for each benchmark and the automatic preparation of the code for a given option.
- Variants addressing bare metal implementations.

This paper is organized as follows. Section 2 gives an overview of the current benchmarks provided by JACABench. Section 3 details each benchmark, provides a roadmap, and identifies potential optimization opportunities. Section 4 presents FPGA results from HLS for some of the JACABench benchmark variants. Section 5 summarizes the most relevant benchmark suites and compares them to JACABench. Finally, Sect. 6 concludes the paper.

2   About the JACA Benchmark Suite

The idea of JACABench is to complement other existing benchmark suites with benchmarks including:

- Both kernels and representative sections of applications with multiple computing stages/tasks for exploring efficient optimizations addressing stages and task-level pipelining;

- CPU and HLS versions for analyzing software and hardware compilers;
- Input/output code variants and different options for loading/storing input/output data, which may better emulate the real system.
- Code variants based on distinct code transformations and optimizations and making it possible to analyze the impact of compiler optimizations in terms of software and hardware;
- Bare metal versions for analyzing the impact on CPUs with minimum system and operating system support features;
- Clear interfaces (e.g., Jupyter notebooks) that provide the selection of the options for each benchmark and the automatic preparation of the code for a given option.
- A low to middle code complexity and size in order to be manageable by HLS tools and by researchers intending to evaluate specific code transformations and/or compiler optimizations.

Table 1 briefly describes the current JACABench benchmarks. We note that JACABench also focuses on an open and active benchmark repository, with the intention of evolving and accepting contributions rather than becoming a static benchmark suite without regular updates and additions. Thus, our goal is to continually add new benchmarks and variants of existing benchmarks and to involve other contributors.

The complexity of the benchmarks varies from 319 SLOC (source lines of code) and 21 loops (smooth) to 1,006 SLOC and 44 loops (har-knn). The har-knn benchmark is the most complex and consists of 4 top-level computing stages, with the feature extraction stage including 15 and 89 sub-stages for the WISDM [12] and PAMAP2 [13] dataset scenarios, respectively. It consists of 55 functions and 176 function calls, and a cyclomatic complexity of 106.

Table 1. Current JACABench benchmarks

Bench.	Brief description	Type	#stages
Smooth	smooth image kernel (also commonly known as 2D FIR) using a 3×3 coefficient window	kernel	1
knn	A *kNN* classifier using as input vectors from datasets from HAR	application	2 (3)
har-knn	An HAR *kNN*-based classifier including feature extraction and normalization stages	application	4 top-level (one w/ 15 or 89)
har-cnn	An HAR CNN-based classifier including feature extraction by convolution operations and classification by fully connected neurons	application	$x \in [5, 8]$
hog	A sliding-window object detector using HOG-based feature extraction from local gradient distributions and classification via a linear SVM.	application	9

3 Overview of Current JACABench Benchmarks

This section summarizes the current benchmarks included in the first version of JACABench.

3.1 Smooth Benchmark

The smooth benchmark represents an image processing kernel (also commonly known as 2D FIR). The implementation uses a 3×3 Gaussian blur kernel (convolution matrix). This simple benchmark consists of only a processing stage, but it represents some of JACABench's goals. For each image representation (pointer-based or 2-D arrays), the benchmark provides the original (v1) and 4 code variants representing increasing levels of optimization (including data reuse). Specifically, versions v2–v5 differ in the number and structure of nested loops and in how the 3×3 sliding window reuses buffered pixels: one (v2) reusing the 6 overlapping pixels for each sliding step of the window; the other three (v3-5) consider 3 line buffers with differences in the amount of data-reuse of pixels among them. Specifically, v3 reuses data in the buffers; v4 reuses data in the buffers and 6 pixels for each sliding window step; and v5 reuses data in the buffers, 6 pixels for each sliding window step, and 6 pixels when starting a new row of pixels.

The kernel code provided includes from v1 to v5: 4 nested FOR loops, 2 nested FOR loops, 7, 8, and 9 FOR loops, respectively.

Although the benchmark can be used with any gray image size, the input images provided are 5: Small (320×480 - VGA), Large (1024×768 - XGA/EVGA), Extra large (1920×1080: Full HD), and Extra extra large (3840×2160 - 4K Digital Cinema).

3.2 kNN and HAR-kNN Benchmarks

The k-Nearest Neighbors (kNN) algorithm [14] is a widely used machine learning technique for classification and regression. For classification, a basic version of kNN involves storing the n training instances, each represented as a vector of d features (dimensions), labeled by their respective class. For each instance to classify, kNN determines the k nearest instances, i.e., the k training instances nearest the instance, and then classifies based on the classes of those k instances. A common strategy is to assign the class that is most frequent among the k nearest training instances.

The benchmark implements kNN in C, targeting the classification of m instances. All instances consist of vectors of d features represented in single- or double-precision floating point numbers (float or double types in C). Training considers c classes, and Euclidean or Manhattan distances are used for the distance between the instance to classify and each of the training instances. For feature normalization, the benchmark uses min-max scaling.

The knowledge base consists of all or a subset of vectors of features from the training set, and no model is built from the training set. However, the typical implementation is computationally intensive because it calculates the distance between each new instance and every instance in the knowledge base. The kNN's wide use, simplicity, and potential for optimizations and variants make it an interesting and relevant benchmark. The actual benchmark is a starting point for other *kNN* implementations, such as the ones representing the knowledge base in other data structures (e.g., KD-tree) that make the classification/regression more efficient, and approximate *kNN* implementations (i.e., implementations that may not give exact results).

JACABench provides different variants of *kNN* addressing classification, tailored to specialization and optimization scenarios. Although it can be used with other datasets, the ones provided address Human Activity Recognition (HAR) systems [15]. Specifically, two datasets are used, WISDM [12] and PAMAP2 [13]. They represent raw data collected from different sensors and inertial measurement units (IMUs). For each input instance, the algorithm infers/outputs its class. Although the benchmark can be used in a non-streaming context, its primary scenario involves streaming instances for classification and streaming classification outputs.

WISDM uses data collected from a 3-axis accelerometer, a window size of 200, an overlap of 50%, considers 6 activities, and 43 features. PAMAP2 uses data from 3 3-axis sensors (accelerometer, magnetometer, gyroscope) in each of the 3 IMUs, considers 22 activities, and 90 features. The benchmark uses data from 8 users for training, data from user #5 for testing, a window size of 300, and an overlap of 10%. The datasets used consist of $738,400$ and $1,670,250$ raw training data instances, and $316,400$ and $272,190$ raw test data instances for WISDM and PAMAP2, respectively. The instances for kNN consist of $3,163$ and $1,008$ feature vectors for WISDM and PAMAP2, respectively.

Two main *kNN* variants are included (see block diagrams in Fig. 1(a) and (b)):

- knn: the input data represents the data after the calculation of the features.
- har-knn: the input is raw data from sensors, and the code includes the calculation of the features.

Each one of these benchmark variants has various versions (see Table 2): a core version where all distances are stored, and only after that, the k nearest ones are determined; OpenMP version, which parallelizes the loop calculating all the distances; version that for each distance calculated, the algorithm verifies if it is one of k nearest and updates the k nearest neighborhoods (NNs) accordingly, and thus does not store all distances calculated; OpenMP version, which parallelizes in a statically defined m threads, the distance calculation and the update of m k-NNs, and then merges the m k-NNs into one k-NN.

3.3 HAR-CNN Benchmark

The har-cnn benchmark implements a basic Convolutional Neural Network (CNN) trained for the HAR application on the WISDM dataset. Figure 2 shows

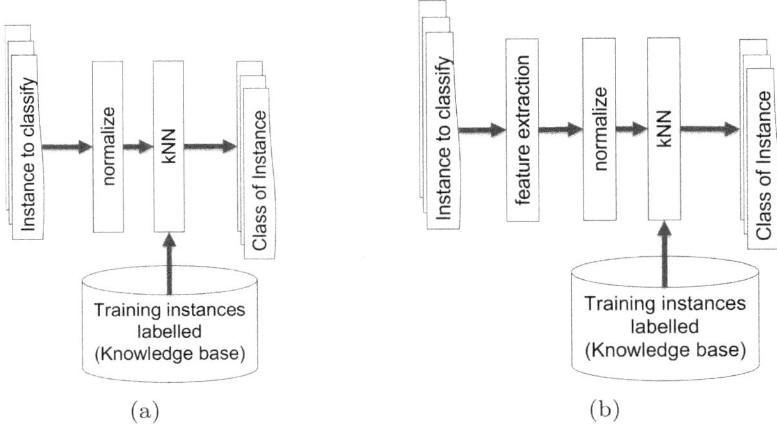

Fig. 1. har-knn benchmark: (a) *kNN* considering vectors of features as input for inference; (b) har-knn considering raw data sensors as input for inference.

Table 2. Code variants of the *kNN* benchmark

Variant	Description
knn-a	Distances are fully computed and stored before selecting the k nearest points. Supports insertion, bubble, and selection sort for top-k selection. Variants include double vs. float data types, streaming vs. batch normalization, Euclidean (with/without $\sqrt{\cdot}$) and Manhattan distances, and specialized implementations for $k = 3$.
knn-b	Distances are processed one at a time, updating the k nearest points on the fly without storing all distances. Top-k maintenance is performed using insertion sort or by replacing the farthest neighbor when required.
knn-a-omp	OpenMP-parallelized version of knn-a.
knn-b-omp1	OpenMP-parallelized version of knn-b using a shared top-k structure protected by a critical section.
knn-b-omp2	OpenMP-parallelized version of knn-b with thread-local top-k computation followed by a merge into a global top-k set.
knn-{a,b}-deploy{1,2,3}	Deployment-oriented variants: deploy1 defines most parameters as compile-time constants; deploy2 additionally initializes max–min vectors inside the main kNN function; deploy3 further initializes the training set inside the main function to enable on-chip storage.

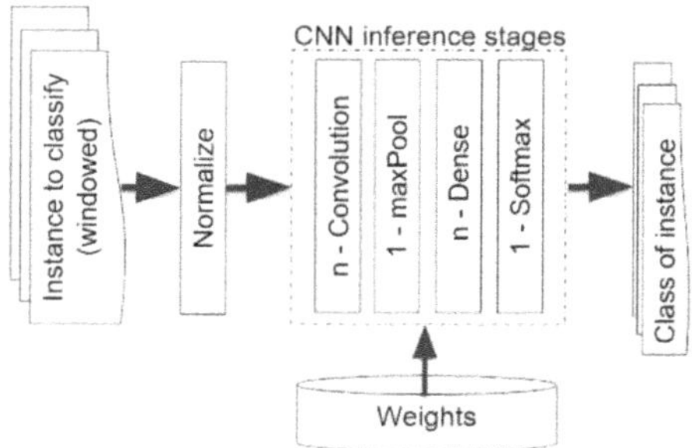

Fig. 2. har-cnn inference dataflow considering time-windowed raw sensor data as input.

the har-cnn inference stages, along with network weights (which include bias) and normalized input data to perform classification.

The benchmark provides three primary architectural variants, each with varying numbers of NN layers and their respective parameters, aiming to achieve different trade-offs between computational cost and classification quality. These variants are presented in Table 3, where 1CONV_2FC has the lowest computational cost, while 5CONV_1FC has the highest one.

The code provided targets CPU and HLS platforms. The CPU version supports only the floating-point format, while the HLS version supports both fixed- and floating-point formats. The default fixed-point format is $ap\_fixed < 32, 16 >$, and for the floating-point is $float32$.

Weights are decoupled from the logic, and two versions are provided, named internalWeights and externalWeights. The former has the weights hardcoded, while the latter reads them from files via testbench. Thus, for each har-cnn variant presented in Table 3, there are four HLS and two CPU versions available to perform inference/classification. All versions are configured to process 3 sensor channels/axes with a window size of 10 samples, and the output has 6 classes, each corresponding to a human activity.

Each CNN layer is implemented as an independent C function, where parameters are passed by reference: the input data from the previous layer, the weights, and the bias. The training dataset is provided, along with the necessary code to retrain the model using a backpropagation algorithm implemented in C using the Adam optimizer. For the fixed-point versions, training is conducted in floating-point, and the final weights are converted to fixed-point at compilation time using a standard VitisHLS data conversion.

Although the backpropagation code is not currently intended for HLS synthesis, users can retrain the model whenever required, for example, when changing the fixed-point format or modifying the model architecture, both of which may need a new training process.

3.4 HOG Benchmark

The Histogram of Oriented Gradients (HOG) [16] is a traditional method and a popular feature descriptor in computer vision for object detection applications.

The original algorithm calculates the normalized histograms of oriented gradients for dense and overlapping image regions. The object detection process typically involves extracting HOG features and the use of an SVM classifier.

The benchmark implements the HOG in C targeting pedestrian detection on RGB images. The detector is a multi-stage pipeline consisting of three major computational levels: image pyramid generation, sliding-window scanning, and feature descriptor computation.

First, an image pyramid is constructed to enable detection at multiple scales. The entire detection process is performed at each scale level, forming the outermost loop of the algorithm. For each scale, a fixed-size detection window slides over the image with a specified spatial stride. This nested loop over the horizontal and vertical coordinates generates a very dense set of candidate regions. Because feature description and classification are performed at each window position, the sliding window stage is responsible for a significant fraction of the total computational workload.

Table 3. Architecture details for the CNN models of the har-cnn benchmark

Layer	In shape	Out shape	Details
1CONV_2FC			
Conv1	3×10	16×10	ReLU
MaxPool	16×10	16×5	$K = 2, S = 2$
Flatten	16×5	80	–
Dense1	80	64	ReLU
Dense2	64	6	Softmax
3CONV_2FC			
Conv1	3×10	6×10	ReLU
Conv2	6×10	12×10	ReLU
Conv3	12×10	16×10	ReLU
MaxPool	16×10	16×5	$K = 2, S = 2$
Flatten	16×5	80	–
Dense1	80	64	ReLU
Dense2	64	6	Softmax
5CONV_1FC			
Conv1	3×10	6×10	ReLU
Conv2	6×10	12×10	ReLU
Conv3	12×10	16×10	ReLU
Conv4	16×10	24×10	ReLU
Conv5	24×10	32×10	ReLU
MaxPool	32×10	32×5	$K = 2, S = 2$
Flatten	32×5	160	–
Dense1	160	6	Softmax

Within each window, the algorithm calculates the HOG feature descriptor by a series of fine-grained loops. It accumulates the gradient magnitudes and orientations into cell histograms using trilinear interpolation. The approach then combines neighboring cells into overlapping blocks and performs L2-Hys normalization to enhance the robustness against illumination changes. Finally, it concatenates the normalized block histograms into a feature vector and evaluates it using a linear SVM classifier.

The linear SVM classifier was trained on the INRIA Person Dataset [17], which offers annotated positive and negative samples particularly suited for testing human detection algorithms in natural environments. The training dataset includes $2,474$ positive samples (including horizontally flipped samples), all normalized to 64×128 pixels, and $9,120$ negative samples selected from background images. We trained the SVM using the SVMlight tool [18], which produced the final weight vector and bias term that define the linear decision function.

The code is available in two implementations: a dynamic one using runtime memory allocation and a static one that uses only fixed-size memory structures, including an HLS-targeted implementation. These versions are used as baseline references for benchmarking compilers and HLS tools. We also include, as a benchmark, the part of the HOG pipeline responsible for processing an image of size 64×128. It is a simplified version that does not build an image pyramid because the image size equals the size of the HOG detection window given to the SVM classifier.

The static hog implementation exhibits higher structural complexity than the dynamic hog implementation, as indicated by the number of lines of code (476 vs. 408), decision points (69 vs. 55), and loops (36 vs. 28). This is because more control logic is needed in the static HOG implementation to avoid dynamic memory allocation and ensure deterministic memory access patterns that are required in HLS.

Both implementations include a specific testbench that provides input images to the detection pipeline and extracts the output bounding box coordinates and corresponding confidence scores. This allows functional verification and performance analysis of the detection system. The implementation allows configuration of several algorithmic parameters, such as the initial scale and scale factor of the image pyramid, as well as the width and height of the input image. Other structural parameters, such as the detection window size, block size, and cell size, can also be set. However, changing these parameters requires retraining the SVM classifier to maintain consistency between the feature extraction algorithm and the trained classifier (Fig. 3).

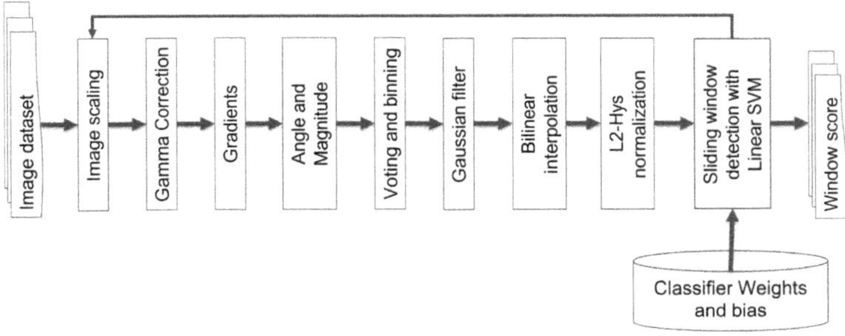

Fig. 3. HOG benchmark.

3.5 JACABench Roadmap

Table 4 presents optimization opportunities for the current JACABench benchmarks, as well as planned optimizations and code variants. The current benchmarks have extensive optimization opportunities, spanning, e.g., data reuse, data distribution, and loop optimizations. As an example of the number of possible implementations resulting from the different algorithms and specialization opportunities, the knn benchmark can provide more than 30 variants. Although this provides useful options for evaluation, knn, har-knn, har-cnn and hog have significant potential for further optimization and code variants, which could extend their usefulness for evaluation purposes.

Table 4. Current and planned optimizations.

Benchmark	Current optimization opportunities	Planned optimizations
smooth	Data reuse.	Rotating buffers sized to image dimensions; rotating registers; loop unrolling and vectorization.
knn	Function inlining; loop unrolling and vectorization; data and functional parallelism; floating- and fixed-point quantization; specialization; reduced communication for hw/sw partitioning and offloading.	Fixed-point and reduced-precision floating-point quantization; AoS to SoA conversion; on-chip knowledge-base buffering with double buffering; contiguous external memory accesses.
har-knn	All *knn* optimizations; removal of redundant function calls; function and loop merging; excessive feature extraction calls; inefficient buffering of raw data; task-level pipelining.	All kNN optimizations; FIFO-based or per-source buffering of raw data windows.
har-cnn	Loop unrolling and pipelining; loop merging; task-level pipelining; CNN parameter hardcoding or external loading; fixed-point quantization tuning ($(\langle 32, 16 \rangle)$).	Scratchpad memories inside nested loops; reuse of windowed input data; adoption of 2D CNN kernels; integration of off-chip memory banks.
hog	Loop unrolling and pipelining; loop and function merging; function inlining.	AoS to SoA conversion; fixed-point quantization; memory partitioning; dataflow optimization; data and task-level parallelism.

4 Experimental Results

Table 5 presents post-HLS estimated FPGA-based results for a subset of JACABench benchmarks synthesized using Vitis HLS 2025.1 targeting an AMD xczu9eg-ffvb1156-1-e device. The target clock period was defined as 5 ns, and all the designs presented have post-HLS estimated periods below 5 ns. The HLS directives applied to the benchmarks were automatically selected by VitisHLS using the default parameters. The selected implementations highlight the diversity of code structures, optimization strategies, and dataflow characteristics represented within the suite.

The smooth benchmark shows that increasing data reuse through line buffers and sliding-window optimizations yields significant latency reductions while incurring predictable increases in BRAM utilization. These variants illustrate HLS optimization trade-offs, where loop restructuring and buffering patterns directly influence pipeline efficiency and memory footprint.

For knn and har-knn, distinct strategies for distance computation, top-k maintenance, data streaming, and memory organization lead to wide variation in the quality of results (QoR). Variants that process distances sequentially while updating the nearest-neighbor set on-the-fly tend to reduce memory requirements, whereas storing all distances enables simpler logic at the expense of higher bandwidth needs. The reported results confirm that the suite captures diverse computation/memory trade-offs relevant to both compiler and accelerator studies. The knn and har-knn variants demonstrate meaningful differences and non-trivial achievements. They highlight the potential for further improvements, only partially illustrated here, and reinforce the need for more advanced tools.

The har-cnn experiments further highlight architectural flexibility: moving from shallow to deeper convolutional pipelines significantly alters DSP usage, BRAM footprint, and latency. The availability of floating- and fixed-point variants enables analysis of precision-related design choices common in embedded inference.

Although these experiments do not aim to exhaustively explore the design space, they clearly illustrate the richness of the benchmark variants and their relevance for evaluating compilers, HLS optimizations, and heterogeneous architectures.

Table 5. Performance and resource utilization of some benchmarks. TK = 1 (top-k sorting w/ selection sort), ai = knn-a-deployi, bi = knn-b-deployi, W = WISDM, U = 1 (top-k points by incrementally substituting the farthest one), S = specialized, F = float, Fp = fixed-point.

Bench.	Ver.	Lat. #ccs (min/max)		Speedup	#BRAM	#DSP	#FF	#LUT
smooth-img-array (320×240)								
	v1	681,300	681,300	1.00	2	0	1,701	2,340
	v2	295,835	295,835	2.30	2	0	2,784	4,497
	v3	95,356	172,230	3.96	29	2	8,347	8,748
	v4	95,594	172,468	3.95	32	0	8,097	7,095
	v5	95,832	172,706	3.94	32	0	8,167	7,147
knn (k = 3)								
a2,TK=1,W,F	v1	392,174	392,195	1.00	24	7	16,463	13,370
a3,TK=1,W,F	v2	384,677	384,698	1.02	712	7	9,015	5,716
a2,W,S,F	v3	347,867	347,867	1.13	24	7	16,745	13,558
a3,W,S,F	v4	340,370	340,370	1.15	712	7	9,334	5,971
b2,U=1,W,S,F	v5	325,707	325,707	1.20	4	7	16,520	13,142
b3,U=1,W,S,F	v6	318,210	318,210	1.23	694	7	9,178	5,720
har-knn (k = 3)								
a1,TK=1,W,F	v1	4,153,288	4,225,053	1.00	29	69	32,771	53,406
a1,W,S,F	v2	4,175,428	4,180,708	1.01	29	69	32,750	53,468
a3,TK=1,W,F	v3	126,220	126,928	33.29	725	361	73,995	82,205
hog stage (128×64)								
F	v1	984,493	984,562	–	195	90	27,051	40,666
har-cnn: 5CONV_1FC (1D)								
W, F	v1	61,305	67,065	1.00	33	383	142,681	221,204
W, F	v2	16,230	21,990	3.05	33	313	102,284	197,507
W, F	v3	10,644	10,644	6.30	90	383	124,526	100,536
W, Fp	v4	5,042	5,042	13.30	45	171	77,638	76,805

5   Benchmark Suites

A wide range of benchmark suites has been developed to support research in computer architecture, heterogeneous execution, and HLS. Their design goals differ substantially across domains, levels of abstraction, and optimization capabilities.

PolyBench [2] focuses on parametric kernels suited for compiler transformations; PARSEC [5] and Rodinia [6] provide multicore and heterogeneous workloads, respectively; MachSuite [8] emphasizes accelerator-centric kernels; Rosetta [10] and HLSyn [19] specifically target HLS design-space exploration with pragma-controlled variants; and HeteroBench [11] provides cross-platform CPU/GPU/FPGA equivalents. Additional collections—including CHStone [9], S2CBench [20], and specialized libraries such as HiFlipVX [21] serve as baselines for evaluating synthesis tools and low-level optimizations.

Table 6. Comparison of a selection of benchmark suites (part I)

Bench.	Lang.	Target	Target dom.	Applic. dom.	Focus
PolyBench/ PolyBench- ACC	C; CUDA; OpenCL; OpenACC; OpenMP	CPU; GPU	HPC; compilers	Lin. alg., stencils, DSP, stats	Loop transf.; polyhedral kernels
PARSEC	C/C++	CPU	Shared- mem. multicore	RMS; system apps	Parallel workloads
Rodinia	C/C++ (OpenMP); CUDA; OpenCL	CPU; GPU	CPU+GPU heterog.	Med. img., data mining, bioinf.	Heterog. prog. models
MachSuite	C	CPU; FPGA (HLS)	Accelerator- centric	AES, FFT, GEMM, SPMV, BFS	Std. kernels
Rosetta	C++; OpenCL (HLS pragmas)	Xilinx SDx	Embedded; cloud FPGA	ML; vision	Realistic HLS apps
HLSyn	C/C++ kernels + pragmas	FPGA HLS tools	HLS QoR pred.	General kernels	DSE
HeteroBench	Python; C++; OpenMP; OpenACC; CUDA; VitisHLS	CPU; GPU; FPGA	Heterog.; HPC	Img. proc., ML, numerics	Cross-accel. comp.
JACABench (this paper)	C	CPU; FPGA	Embedded comp.	Sensing	Comp. stages; variants

While these suites offer valuable capabilities, they generally lack multi-stage application pipelines, embedded sensing workloads, and matched CPU/HLS code variants designed for modern FPGA-accelerated systems. JACABench complements these existing efforts by providing algorithmic and code-level variants, bare-metal and multithreaded CPU versions, and flexible I/O configurations suited for evaluating compiler optimizations, HLS flows, and hardware/software co-design methodologies.

Tables 6 and 7 summarize the distinguishing characteristics of the surveyed benchmark suites and highlight how JACABench fills an important gap within the current benchmark suite ecosystem. JACABench distinguishes itself from

Table 7. Comparison of a selection of benchmark suites (part II)

Bench.	Comp. stages	Variants/ algorithms	OpenMP	Bare-metal	I/O sizes and interfaces	HLS prep.
PolyBench/ PolyBench-ACC	Mostly single-kernel	Algorithmic variants; parametric sizes	Yes	No	Parametric sizes; optional file I/O	Partial
PARSEC	Application-level pipelines (subset)	Multiple build configurations	Yes (subset)	No	Varied inputs	No
Rodinia	Multi-kernel pipelines	Multiple models and algorithms	Yes	No	Provided generators	No
MachSuite	Kernel-level only	Algorithmic variants (e.g., GEMM, BFS, SPMV)	No	Possible	Small reference inputs	Yes
Rosetta	Multi-kernel application pipelines	Optimized vs. unoptimized versions	No	No	Platform-specific harness	Yes
HLSyn	Kernel-level	Extensive pragma-driven variants	No	N/A	Not primary	Yes
HeteroBench	Multi-kernel applications	Backend-consistent variants	Yes	No	Configurable files	Yes
JACABench (this paper)	Multi-kernel application pipelines	Algorithmic and code variants	Yes	Yes	Configurable files	Yes

other benchmark suites by providing a comprehensive end-to-end evaluation pipeline rather than isolated tasks. Unlike typical benchmarks that focus on a single stage of processing, JACABench encompasses multiple stages of algorithm development, from initial data collection and feature extraction to the final classification. This means each benchmark in the suite represents a complete solution, mirroring real-world applications where data flows through every step of the process. Another key differentiator is JACABench's built-in support for both fixed- and floating-point arithmetic. This dual-arithmetic capability is particularly beneficial for embedded systems, where fixed-point calculations are often required to meet strict resource and performance constraints. Furthermore, the JACABench codebase is organized into clear, modular stages, enabling researchers and developers to easily explore and experiment with different methods at each pipeline stage. This structured, multi-stage approach not only promotes detailed performance analysis at each step, but also facilitates the iterative optimization of algorithms in both simulation and real embedded environments, setting JACABench apart from more narrowly focused benchmarks.

6 Conclusion

The evolution of heterogeneous computing spanning multicore CPUs, GPUs, and FPGA-based accelerators demands benchmark suites that expose diverse code variants, optimization opportunities, and execution models. JACABench addresses this need by providing a C-based suite developed for embedded computing and FPGA-oriented evaluation, featuring kernels and multi-stage applications, configurable datasets, and CPU/HLS code variants aligned with realistic deployment scenarios. Designed as an open and evolving repository, JACABench aims to encourage contributions and the continuous expansion of benchmarks, variants, and datasets. Its design supports studies of compiler transformations, hardware/software co-design techniques, and HLS workflows.

JACABench Suite: *GitHub link:* https://github.com/jacabench.

References

1. Kounev, S., Lange, K., von Kistowski., J.: The –SPEC CPU benchmark suite. In: Systems Benchmarking, pp. 231–250. Springer (2020). https://doi.org/10.1007/978-3-030-41705-5_10
2. Pouchet, L., Yuki, T.: "PolyBench/C" dataset. TIB Leibniz Information Centre for Science and Technology (2025). https://doi.org/10.57702/ie5povaq
3. Guthaus, M.R., et al.: MiBench: a free, commercially representative embedded benchmark suite. In: Proceedings of 4th Annual IEEE Int'l Workshop on Workload Characterization. WWC-4 (Cat. No. 01EX538), pp. 3–14 (2001). https://doi.org/10.1109/WWC.2001.990739
4. Lee, C., Potkonjak, M., Mangione-Smith, W.H.: MediaBench: a tool for evaluating and synthesizing multimedia and communications systems. In: Proceedings of 30th Annual International Symposium on Microarchitecture, pp. 330–335 (1997). https://doi.org/10.1109/MICRO.1997.645830
5. Bienia, C., et al.: "The –PARSEC benchmark suite: characterization and architectural implications. In: Proceedings of the 17th International Conference on Parallel Architectures and Compilation Techniques (PACT), pp. 72–81. ACM (2008). https://doi.org/10.1145/1454115.1454128
6. Che, S., et al.: Rodinia: a benchmark suite for heterogeneous computing. In: Proceedings of IEEE International Symposium on Workload Characterization (IISWC), pp. 44–54. IEEE (2009). https://doi.org/10.1109/IISWC.2009.5306797
7. Thomas, S., et al.: CortexSuite: a synthetic brain benchmark suite. In: International Symposium on Workload Characterization (IISWC), pp. 76–79. IEEE (2014). https://doi.org/10.1109/IISWC.2014.6983043
8. Reagen, B., et al.: MachSuite: benchmarks for accelerator design and customized architectures. In: Proceedings of IEEE International Symposium on Workload Characterization (IISWC), pp. 110–119 (2014). https://doi.org/10.1109/IISWC.2014.6983050
9. Hara, Y., et al.: CHStone: a benchmark program suite for practical C-based high-level synthesis. In: IEEE International Symposium on Circuits and Systems (ISCAS), pp. 1192–1195 (2008). https://doi.org/10.1109/ISCAS.2008.4541637

10. Zhou, Y., et al.: Rosetta: a realistic high-level synthesis benchmark suite for software programmable FPGAs . In: Proceedings of the 2018 ACM/SIGDA International Symposium on Field-Programmable Gate Arrays (FPGA), pp. 269–278. ACM (2018). https://doi.org/10.1145/3174243.3174255

11. Tian, H., et al.: HeteroBench: multi-kernel benchmarks for heterogeneous systems. In: Proceedings of the 16th ACM/SPEC International Conference on Performance Engineering. ICPE '25, Toronto ON, Canada, pp. 320–333. ACM (2025). https://doi.org/10.1145/3676151.3719366

12. Kwapisz, J.R., Weiss, G.M., Moore, S.A.: Activity recognition using cell phone accelerometers. SIGKDD Explor. Newsl. **12**(2), 74–82 (2011). https://doi.org/10.1145/1964897.1964918

13. Reiss, A., Stricker, D.: Introducing a new benchmarked dataset for activity monitoring. In: 2012 16th International Symposium on Wearable Computers, pp. 108–109 (2012). https://doi.org/10.1109/ISWC.2012.13

14. Cover, T., Hart, P.E.: Nearest neighbor pattern classification. IEEE Trans. Inf. Theory **13**(1), 21–27 (1967). https://doi.org/10.1109/TIT.1967.1053964

15. Lara, O.D., Labrador, M.A.: A survey on human activity recognition using wearable sensors. IEEE Commun. Surv. Tutor. **15**(3), 1192–1209 (2013). https://doi.org/10.1109/SURV.2012.110112.00192

16. Dalal, N., Triggs, B.: Histograms of oriented gradients for human detection. In: Proceedings of IEEE Computer Society Conference on Computer Vision and Pattern Recognition (CVPR'05), Computer Society, USA. vol. 1, pp. 886–893. IEEE (2005). https://doi.org/10.1109/CVPR.2005.177

17. INRIA Person Dataset. http://pascal.inrialpes.fr/data/human/. Accessed 13 Feb 2026

18. Joachims, T.: Making large-scale support vector machine learning practical. In: Advances in Kernel Methods: Support Vector Learning. The MIT Press (1998). https://doi.org/10.7551/mitpress/1130.003.0015

19. Bai, Y., et al.: Towards a comprehensive benchmark for high-level synthesis targeted to FPGAs. In: Proceedings of 37th Int'l Conf. on Neural Information Processing Systems. NIPS '23. New Orleans, LA, USA. Curran Associates Inc., (2023)

20. Carrion Schafer, B., Mahapatra, A.: S2CBench: synthesizable systemc benchmark suite for high-level synthesis. IEEE Embedded Syst. Lett. **6**(3), 53–56 (2014). https://doi.org/10.1109/LES.2014.2320556

21. Kalms, L., Podlubne, A., Gohringer, D.: HiFlipVX: an open source high-level synthesis FPGA library for image processing. In: Applied Reconfigurable Computing. ARC 2019, LNCS. vol. 11444, pp. 149–164. Springer, Heidelberg (2019). https://doi.org/10.1007/978-3-030-17227-5_12

Neural Networks and Artificial Intelligence

End-to-End Keyword Spotting on FPGA Using Graph Neural Networks with a Neuromorphic Auditory Sensor

Wiktor Matykiewicz[1], Piotr Wzorek[1,2], Kamil Jeziorek[1,2(✉)],
Tomás Muñoz[3], Antonio Rios-Navarro[3], Angel Jiménez-Fernández[3],
and Tomasz Kryjak[1,2]

[1] AGH University of Kraków, Kraków, Poland
`kjeziorek@agh.edu.pl`
[2] Embedded Vision Systems Group, Computer Vision Laboratory, Kraków, Poland
[3] Robotics and Technology of Computers Lab., ETSII, EPS, SCORE, I3US,
Universidad de Sevilla, Sevilla, Spain

Abstract. With the rapid growth of mobile robotics and embedded intelligence, there is an increasing demand for efficient on-device data processing on edge platforms. A promising research direction is the use of neuromorphic sensors inspired by human sensory systems, which generate sparse, event-based data encoding changes in the environment. In this work, we present the first end-to-end FPGA implementation of a keyword spotting system that integrates a Neuromorphic Auditory Sensor (NAS) and a graph neural network (GNN) on a single FPGA device, enabling real-time processing of raw audio data. The proposed architecture eliminates conventional signal preprocessing and operates directly on event-based audio streams. Leveraging a compute-near-memory network architecture, the system achieves efficient inference with low latency and low power consumption. Experimental results demonstrate an accuracy of 87.43% after quantization on the Google Speech Commands v2 dataset processed through the neuromorphic sensor, with end-to-end latency below 35 μs and average power consumption of 1.12 W. The processed datasets, software models, and hardware modules are available at https://github.com/vision-agh/NAS-GNN-KWS.

Keywords: neuromorphic auditory sensor · FPGA · keyword spotting · graph neural network · hardware-aware design · event-based processing

1 Introduction

Edge perception has become a key requirement in modern embedded systems, including mobile robotics and IoT applications. In such scenarios, audio processing plays an important role and must ensure high prediction accuracy while

G. Leone et al. (Eds.): ARC 2026, LNCS 16514, pp. 119–136, 2026.
https://doi.org/10.1007/978-3-032-29365-7_8

maintaining low energy consumption and minimal latency. In this context, neuromorphic sensors are gaining increasing attention, as they generate events representing changes in the environment. The resulting data are inherently sparse in both space and time, and preserving this sparsity during processing enables a substantial reduction in computational complexity.

An example of such a device for audio processing is the Neuromorphic Auditory Sensor (NAS) [16], whose FPGA-based implementation enables direct conversion of a raw digital audio stream into event-based representations. Among the methods capable of efficiently processing sparse event data, spiking neural networks and graph neural networks (GNN) have been widely investigated. In [14], an FPGA-based architecture for keyword spotting (KWS) utilizing GNN and operating on simulated event-based data was proposed, demonstrating low latency and reduced energy consumption.

In this work, our main objective is to demonstrate the feasibility of integrating the NAS and a GNN within a single FPGA device, forming a unified end-to-end system suitable for mobile robotics applications. The main contributions of this paper are as follows:

- We present and publicly release a set of event-based audio datasets recorded using multiple NAS configurations. The datasets correspond to the popular Google Speech Commands v2 benchmark [33] for keyword spotting.
- We provide detailed statistical analysis of the recorded data and propose an event filtering method that reduces the number of processed events by approximately 47%, while simultaneously improving prediction accuracy. The method is designed for efficient hardware implementation.
- We introduce a set of architectural modifications to the GNN, derived from extensive ablation studies, enabling integration of the sensor and network on a single device while ensuring sufficient throughput. The proposed changes improve latency while reducing energy consumption.
- We present the first end-to-end KWS system operating on real event-based data from a neuromorphic auditory sensor, integrating both the sensor and a graph neural network on the same FPGA device. The system is evaluated in simulation and on the target hardware platform, achieving high accuracy, low latency, and low energy consumption.

The remainder of this paper is organized as follows. Section 2 reviews related work. Section 3 describes the proposed method. Section 4 presents the experimental evaluation. Finally, Sect. 5 concludes the paper.

2   Related Work

2.1   Neuromorphic Auditory Sensors

Biological auditory systems operate asynchronously, generating sparse spikes only when spectral energy changes occur—unlike conventional pipelines that rely on fixed-rate sampling and computationally intensive DSP. This event-driven principle significantly reduces redundant data transmission and enables efficient processing of dynamic acoustic environments. Such bio-inspired systems offer the high dynamic range and low power consumption required for edge applications.

Early hardware realizations employed analog VLSI circuits to mimic cochlear functionality [6,18,20,32], but such systems suffer from transistor mismatch and noise, and key platforms are no longer commercially available. Digital alternatives on FPGAs offer greater scalability, though conventional filter-bank implementations retain significant arithmetic overhead [10,31]. In this work, we adopt the spike signal processing (SSP) paradigm [15] using the Neuromorphic Auditory Sensor (NAS) [16]. This architecture processes information directly in the spike domain, avoiding conventional numerical signal representations. By replacing complex arithmetic operations with simple logic gates and counters, SSP enables efficient event-based computation, allowing for fully parallel auditory processing with minimal power consumption.

2.2 Processing Event-Based Audio Data

Event-based audio from NAS is sparse, asynchronous, and temporally irregular, posing challenges for standard DSP pipelines. Learning-based methods therefore either operate directly on the event stream or convert events into temporally accumulated representations suitable for tensor-based processing.

Spiking neural networks (SNNs) remain a central modelling paradigm for event-based audio due to their native compatibility with spike-domain inputs. Existing work includes convolutional [11,27,28] and recurrent [4,8,9,24,35] architectures. More recently, state-space models (SSMs) have been investigated as an alternative framework for event-driven sequences [13,29]. SSMs provide a structured mechanism for representing evolving latent states over time and can capture long-range temporal dependencies without relying on explicit recurrence.

Another emerging direction is the use of graph neural networks (GNNs), where event streams are interpreted as collections of interacting elements rather than uniformly sampled time series [23,26]. By representing events as nodes and encoding relationships through edges, these methods can express locality and interaction patterns that are difficult to encode with fixed-grid representations. Work [14] extends this approach by integrating GNNs with recurrence to increase temporal dependency over longer contexts, which is the baseline for our study.

Alongside these algorithmic developments, a number of recent studies have focused on efficient hardware realization of event-driven processing pipelines, particularly on FPGA platforms [5,14,22,23]. Event-driven computation aligns well with FPGA architectures because sparse activity can reduce unnecessary switching and memory operations, improving energy efficiency and latency.

A recurring limitation of prior work is the reliance on synthetically generated event streams. Benchmarks such as SHD and SSC [7] are frequently used for SNN evaluation but they may not fully capture the variability, noise characteristics, and timing irregularities present in real NAS outputs. In contrast, our system processes event-based audio from a physical neuromorphic sensor integrated with a GNN on a single FPGA, alongside an efficient hardware realisation of the full processing pipeline.

3   The Proposed Method

The main goal of this work is to build an end-to-end keyword spotting system on a single FPGA device that processes raw audio data from a neuromorphic auditory sensor. Our system consists of three main components: the neuromorphic sensor that generates event-based audio data from raw audio input (Sect. 3.1), the filtration stage that reduces the number of events (Sect. 3.2), and the graph generation and GNN architecture that processes the event-based data (Sect. 3.3). In this section, we describe the implementation of each component and the overall architecture of the system.

3.1   Sensor

The input stage of our system utilizes a fully digital FPGA-based NAS architecture following the spike signal processing principles described in [15] and [16]. This module is responsible for converting continuous audio signals into a sparse, asynchronous stream of Address-Event Representation (AER) packets.

The signal acquisition pipeline begins with an analog audio input provided via a standard jack interface. An external audio codec digitizes the analog signal and transmits it to the FPGA via an I2S digital audio interface. Inside the FPGA, the pulse coded modulation (PCM) samples are immediately converted into a high-frequency spike train using pulse frequency modulation (PFM). This spike train serves as the input to a bank of digital spike-based filters that decompose the signal into distinct frequency bands (channels).

To investigate the trade-offs between biological plausibility, latency, and event throughput, we implemented and evaluated the NAS in two distinct topological configurations:

- **Cascade Architecture:** Inspired by the biological cochlea and [16], this configuration chains spike low-pass filters (SLPFs), each feeding into the next to progressively remove higher frequencies. However, cumulative latency scales with the number of channels, and non-ideal filter charachteristics cause compounding signal attenuation, reducing the event rate.
- **Parallel Architecture:** Here, the input spike train feeds simultaneously into a bank of independent spike band-pass filters (SBPFs). This eliminates cumulative delay and avoids compounding signal degradation, yielding similar latency across frequency channels and higher event density (Table 1).

The output of the filter banks is transmitted via an asynchronous AER interface. Natively, the sensor encodes each event as a tuple (c, p), representing the frequency channel index and signal polarity, respectively. To incorporate temporal information, we designed and implemented a custom timestamping module

Table 1. Statistics of the generated neuromorphic version of the Google Speech Commands v2 dataset [34]. Reported values are the mean ± standard deviation and the maximum number of events, expressed in kilo-events (kEv.).

Version	Max. kEv./sample	Avg. kEv./sample	Max. kEv./s	Avg. kEv./s
32-cascade	204.84	17.22 ± 9.58	151.21	15.03 ± 8.21
32-parallel	227.22	39.19 ± 12.65	174.82	28.08 ± 9.12
64-cascade	227.99	31.67 ± 13.96	194.64	24.63 ± 11.15
64-parallel	245.35	75.40 ± 21.41	277.07	54.01 ± 16.14
128-cascade	254.67	61.27 ± 20.94	240.57	45.49 ± 16.01
128-parallel	265.96	126.69 ± 24.11	518.69	92.18 ± 21.03

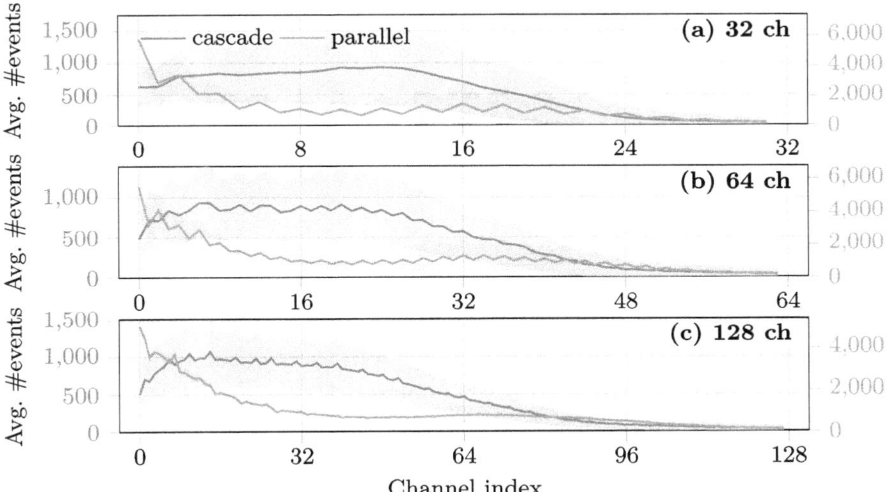

Fig. 1. Average events per channel with standard deviation for different configurations of the neuromorphic auditory sensor. For all configurations the number of events is higher for low channel (higher frequency) indices.

on the FPGA. This module assigns a timestamp t with a resolution of $1\,\mu s$ to each event immediately upon generation, yielding the final event representation (t, c, p) used for subsequent processing.

We synthesized and tested the system in six different variations to analyze the impact of spectral resolution on KWS performance. Specifically, we implemented both cascade and parallel architectures for 32, 64, and 128 frequency channels. Increasing the number of channels improves frequency resolution but results in higher FPGA resource utilization (Slices and LUTs) and increased power consumption. The resulting event streams undergo a filtration stage before serving as the input to our graph neural network pipeline.

Algorithm 1: Per-channel filtration with decayed potential

Input: Event stream $\{(t_i, c_i, p_i)\}_{i=1}^{N}$ with time $t_i \in \mathbb{N}$, channel $c_i \in \{0, \ldots, C-1\}$ and polarity $p_i \in \{-1, 1\}$
Input: Parameters: `div_factor` $\in \mathbb{N}$, weight $w \geq 0$, thresholds $\{\theta_c\}_{c=0}^{C-1}$
Output: Accepted events $\mathcal{P}$ (each as (t, c, p))

State: per-channel last timestamp $t_{\text{last}}[c]$ and potential $v[c]$

Initialization:
for $c \leftarrow 0$ **to** $C - 1$ **do**
$\quad t_{\text{last}}[c] \leftarrow 0$
$\quad v[c] \leftarrow 0$

$\mathcal{P} \leftarrow \emptyset$
$q \leftarrow 2^{\texttt{div\_factor}}$ `// time quantization for decay`

for $i \leftarrow 1$ **to** N **do**
$\quad t \leftarrow t_i; \quad c \leftarrow c_i; \quad p \leftarrow p_i$
$\quad \Delta t \leftarrow t - t_{\text{last}}[c]$

$\quad v[c] \leftarrow \max\left(0, \; v[c] - \left\lfloor \dfrac{\Delta t}{q} \right\rfloor\right) + w$ `// decay + integrate`

$\quad t_{\text{last}}[c] \leftarrow t$
$\quad$ **if** $v[c] < \theta_c$ **then**
$\quad\quad$ **continue**
$\quad \mathcal{P} \leftarrow \mathcal{P} \cup \{(t, c, p)\}$ `// accept event and reset potential`
$\quad v[c] \leftarrow 0$

return $\mathcal{P}$

3.2 Filtration

As shown in Sect. 3.1, the sensor produces a large number of events (Table 1), and their distribution is highly uneven across channels (Fig. 1). This variability increases the computational cost of subsequent processing and can bias the graph construction toward channels with the highest activity. Therefore, before graph generation, we apply a dedicated filtration stage that reduces the event rate.

The proposed filtration is designed to mimic the behavior of a leaky integrate-and-fire (LIF) neuron model [1]. Each channel maintains an internal state that integrates incoming events as a discrete potential and decays over time; once the potential exceeds a channel-specific threshold, the event is accepted and the potential is reset.

In our implementation, the filtration is controlled by three parameters: `div_factor`, which defines the time quantization used for the decay; the weight w added to potential; and the per-channel thresholds θ_c. The overall procedure is summarized in Algorithm 1, which performs a per-channel update for every event and outputs a filtered event set $\mathcal{P}$.

A key element of the filtration is the selection of per-channel thresholds θ_c. To generate these thresholds, we consider three simple strategies: constant, linear, and exponential, whose effect on the event reduction and downstream performance is evaluated in the Sect. 4.3.

3.3 Graph Generation and GNN Architecture

In our work, we adopted the FPGA-based hardware implementation proposed in [14] (for detailed description refer to full paper), designed for the keyword spotting task using event-driven audio data. The architecture follows a dataflow paradigm, where consecutive modules process the recorded event streams.

In the considered system, each input event is first forwarded to the graph generation module, where it is represented as a vertex. For every newly registered event, directed edges are created toward previously recorded events (time-directed graph) that lie within a half-sphere defined by the search radius along the channel dimension (R_c) and the temporal dimension (R_t - we support both the lower time radius R_t^{low} and the upper time radius R_t^{high}). For this work, the values of these parameters were determined through ablation studies (see Sect. 4.3). This design enables sparse, event-driven processing immediately after acquisition and dynamic graph updates.

The resulting vertex, together with its edge list, is subsequently processed by the feature extraction stage composed of four consecutive `PointNetConv` modules [25]. The operation of `PointNetConv` can be expressed as:

$$\mathbf{x}_i' = \left(\max_{j \in \mathcal{N}(i) \cup \{i\}} \phi_\Theta \left(\mathbf{x}_j, \mathbf{p}_j - \mathbf{p}_i \right) \right), \tag{1}$$

where $\mathbf{x}_i$ denotes the input feature vector of node i, $\mathbf{p}_i$ its position, $\mathcal{N}(i)$ the neighborhood of node i, and ϕ_Θ is a learnable function.

For the first `PointNetConv` layer, two input features are used, corresponding to the mean neighbor position (channel and timestamp). The ablation studies were conducted to select the number of output features in each `PointNetConv` module in a way that guaranties efficient BRAM utilization, enabling full use of the memory word width.

The subsequent module is a MaxPool layer that aggregates events within 10 ms temporal windows. After this interval, the aggregated feature vector is forwarded to the network head, which consists of four linear layers and GRU-based memory unit. Every 10 ms the GNN generates prediction consisting of:

- **class**: For the keyword spotting task, we selected a set of target keywords and an additional *unknown* class that includes all remaining words, silence, and noise. The number of outputs depends on the number of selected keywords.
- **conf**: An additional single-valued output representing the confidence that a keyword has been detected within a given time window. This end-of-word temporal localization significantly improves the practical performance.

In [14], the system was evaluated on the Spiking Heidelberg Digits and Spiking Speech Commands datasets [7], which are synthetic spiking datasets obtained through simulation (with 700 audio channels each). In this work, we introduced a series of modifications to enable deployment on data recorded directly by the NAS on the same target device. To this end, we defined system-level requirements and proposed necessary optimizations.

Due to the targeted application in mobile robotics and edge processing, we identified energy consumption and system latency as the key design constraints. The proposed system must therefore exhibit low resource utilization. To further minimize energy consumption, we implemented the entire processing pipeline

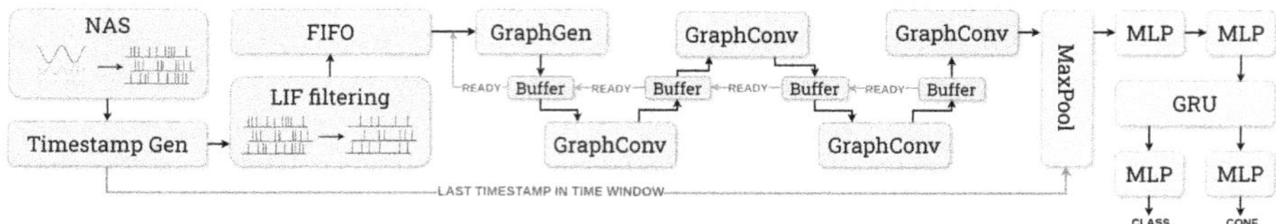

Fig. 2. The proposed architecture is illustrated with the sensor and filtering modules highlighted in green, the feature extraction stage in blue, and the MaxPool and network head modules in yellow. The scheduling mechanism is marked in purple, while the timestamp propagation mechanism is indicated in red. (Color figure online)

exclusively in reconfigurable logic, avoiding the programmable processing system of the heterogeneous platform. The raw audio signal can be acquired directly on the FPGA and processed up to prediction without CPU involvement.

At the same time, the graph neural network must ensure sufficient system throughput. To determine precise performance requirements, we analyzed the event rate after filtering (see. Sect. 3.3). The system must sustain real-time processing even during periods of increased activity, which are often critical for accurate keyword spotting.

Performed Modifications. The hardware architecture was designed to support all considered configurations. The NAS provides an extra attribute for each event: polarity, which we incorporated as an additional input feature to the first convolutional layer. To enable deployment on the target platform while minimizing energy consumption—without violating latency and throughput constraints—we optimized the feature extraction module of the GNN.

LUT utilization in considered architecture is dominated by vector multipliers, which are the core computational elements of the `PointNetConv` layers. While [14] employed an architecture supporting four parallel feature-vector multiplications per graph convolution (74 8-bit elements each), we reduced the number of parallel multipliers to decrease resource usage. Since graph convolution forms the system bottleneck, increasing sequential processing impacts both latency and throughput. The final number of multipliers was selected based on the measured average and maximum post-filter event rates for each NAS configuration, defining explicit requirements (see Table 3).

Moreover, the computational load of a single `PointNetConv` operation depends on the number of edges, as linear transformations must be applied to the processed vertex and each of its neighbors. In the [14] design, input events were accepted at a fixed interval (in clock cycles) determined by the worst-case neighborhood size, ensuring no internal congestion. This conservative approach resulted in constant (yet limited) throughput and unnecessary latency.

We therefore introduced a back-pressure scheduling mechanism with inter-module buffering (see Fig. 2). Each processing stage is equipped with a local buffer and signals readiness upon completing the current convolution. As the latency of each operation depends on the actual number of neighbors, events are admitted dynamically once downstream resources become available. Consequently, latency becomes event-dependent, and the input rate adapts to instantaneous workload conditions. Despite reducing the number of parallel multipliers, the effective throughput satisfies system requirements.

It is important to note that introducing the scheduling mechanism disrupts a fixed throughput. In the original design, the MaxPool module relied on a constant convolution latency, triggering feature extraction every 10 ms based on a real-time counter. After our modifications, it became necessary to implement a *timestamp propagation mechanism*, in which the NAS output timestamps are monitored and the last timestamp within each time window is propagated to the MaxPool module. The MaxPool then forwards features to the network head only when the final event of the corresponding 10 ms window has been processed.

4   Evaluation

This section evaluates the proposed keyword spotting system in terms of both classification performance and end-of-word temporal localization. We first describe the training and evaluation setup and define the metrics used throughout the experiments. We then conduct software-based ablation studies to quantify the impact of key design choices, including model capacity, graph construction, and filtration parameters, and to identify a configuration suitable for the subsequent hardware implementation.

4.1   Dataset Generation

To train the proposed GNN, we utilized the Google Speech Commands v2 (GSCv2) dataset [34], comprising over 100,000 one-second utterances. To capture the precise noise characteristics and temporal dynamics of the sensor, we generated a neuromorphic version of the dataset by processing the full audio corpus through the physical NAS hardware rather than relying on software simulations.

The acquisition pipeline involved streaming GSCv2 audio samples via an I2S codec to the NAS, which decomposed the signal into asynchronous AER events. These events were captured by an Opal Kelly XEM6310 FPGA module. Utilizing the FrontPanel SDK, we established a high-bandwidth USB 3.0 communication link between the FPGA and a host PC. The FPGA logic was programmed to append microsecond-resolution timestamps to the incoming AER packets, producing (t, c, p) tuples. A dedicated Python script automated the process, synchronizing audio playback with event acquisition and converting the stream into .aedat format.

The generated datasets were approximately 15–30% longer than the original audio corpus. This extension resulted from intentional padding introduced during the hardware recording process, comprising pre-sample delays for error-free sequential acquisition, and post-sample delays to avoid positioning keywords at the end of the recording window, which degraded learning process.

4.2 Implementation Details

Training Setting. The keyword spotting system was trained for 50 epochs in floating point (FP32) using the Adam optimizer [17] with a learning rate of 1*e*-3 and weight decay of 1*e*-4, together with a cosine-annealing learning-rate schedule [19]. The network was then fine-tuned for 5 additional epochs using 8-bit quantization-aware training (QAT) with a constant learning rate of 1*e*-4. All experiments used a batch size of 16 and were run on an NVIDIA GH200 GPU. The model was implemented using PyTorch [2]. Checkpoints were selected based on the minimum validation loss and evaluated on the test set.

4.3 Ablation Studies

We perform ablation studies to quantify the impact of key design choices on keyword spotting performance and to select a configuration suitable for hardware implementation. We consider three factors: model size, graph-generation settings, and filtration parameters. Unless stated otherwise, results are obtained on the test set (64-cascade configuration) using the baseline configuration: 72 channels per layer; channel radius (R_c) 20 with skip step 2; low/high time radius ($R_t^{low/high}$) of 2000/10000; and filtration parameters with division factor 8, weight 32 and thresholds exponentially spaced from 64 to 32.

We evaluate both keyword classification and end-of-word temporal localization. We report classification accuracy (Acc.) and macro F1, as well as timestamp-conditioned accuracy (Ts-acc$_k$), which counts a prediction as correct only if the class matches and the predicted end-of-word time falls within $\pm k$ bins (10 ms each). For the filtration ablation, we additionally report event-rate statistics. All results are in FP32 (quantized models are evaluated in Sect. 4.4). Formal definition of all metrics, complete sweep results and model weights are released as open-source materials[1].

Model Size. We vary only the number of channels per layer in the set {18, 36, 54, 72, 90, 108, 126}. Performance improves with increasing width, reaching the best results at 126 channels per layer (79.45% accuracy, 65.51% F1). However, gains beyond 72 channels are modest: the 72-channel model achieves 78.70% accuracy and 62.29% F1, while being substantially smaller (59.84 k parameters vs. 179.56 k for 126 channels). We therefore select 72 channels for hardware implementation.

Graph Generation. We next examine the effect of graph-generation parameters.

- *Time radius.* Figure 3 shows the effect of varying the lower time radius R_t^{low} (0–5000) and upper time radius R_t^{high} (1000–10000). Increasing R_t^{low} consistently degrades all metrics: relative to $R_t^{low} = 0$, setting it to 500 or 1000 decreases

---

[1] https://github.com/vision-agh/NAS-GNN-KWS.

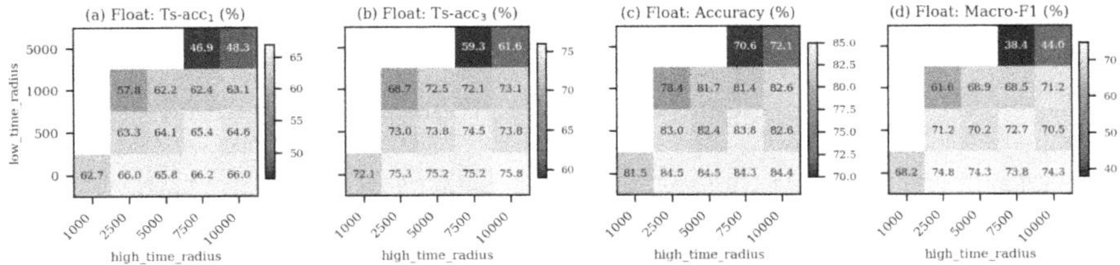

Fig. 3. Influence of the low and high time radius on the keyword-spotting metrics.

Table 2. Ablation results for (a) channel radius / skip step and (b) filtration division factor. Bold marks the selected configuration; "–" denotes no filtration.

(a) $R_t^{low/high}=0/5000$

R_c / skip	Ts-acc$_1$	Ts-acc$_3$	Acc. (%)	F1 (%)
10 / 1	**67.4**	**77.0**	**85.9**	**77.0**
20 / 1	66.6	76.0	85.0	74.9
20 / 2	58.3	68.6	78.7	62.3
30 / 3	63.4	72.9	82.0	69.5
40 / 4	63.5	72.7	82.1	70.2
50 / 5	63.8	72.9	81.7	69.0

(b) $R_c=10$, skip 1, $R_t^{low/high}=0/5000$

Div. fact.	Ts-acc$_1$	Ts-acc$_3$	Acc. (%)	F1 (%)	Avg. kEv/s
–	51.2	62.8	74.4	49.1	24.6
6	66.5	76.0	83.6	72.6	7.9
7	65.5	75.2	83.4	72.3	9.9
8	**65.8**	**75.2**	**84.5**	**74.3**	**11.2**
9	66.2	75.9	84.7	74.6	11.8
10	66.1	76.0	84.9	75.2	12.1

the average F1 by 1.93% and 5.53%, respectively. The best results are achieved with $R_t^{low} = 0$ and $R_t^{high} \in \{2500, 5000\}$ (84.5% accuracy). We set $R_t^{low/high} = 0/5000$ for subsequent experiments.

- *Channel radius and skip step.* Table 2a reports performance for different channel-radius/skip-step pairs, with $R_t^{low/high}$ fixed to 0/5000. We consider paired settings (10/1, 20/2, 30/3, 40/4, 50/5) that keep the maximum number of neighbours constant (20 plus a self-loop), alongside a baseline with $R_c = 20$ and skip step 1 (dense neighbourhood). Overall, increasing either the radius or the skip step reduces performance. The best configuration is $R_c = 10$ with skip step 1 (85.89% accuracy, 76.99% F1). Together with the time-radius results, this suggests that the model benefits from a restricted spatiotemporal context, as broader neighbourhoods incorporate more irrelevant events.

Filtration. We evaluate the division factor and the threshold configuration, while keeping the weight parameter constant and setting the $R_t^{low/high}$ to 0/5000.

- *Division factor.* Table 2b shows the effect of the division factor. Disabling filtration (–) substantially degrades performance (74.36% accuracy) and produces the highest event rate (24.63 avg. kEv/s). Introducing filtration improves all metrics while reducing the event count. As the division factor increases from 6 to 10,

Table 3. Best ablation-selected configurations for cascade and parallel variants across datasets, reporting configuration, performance and throughput.

Dataset	Configuration						Performance (%)				Throughput		
	R_c	Skip step	R_t^{low}	R_t^{high}	div. factor	Thresholds	Ts-acc$_1$	Ts-acc$_3$	Acc.	F1	Max. kEv./s	Avg. kEv./s	Avg. edges/Ev
32-cascade	5	1	0	5000	8	exp.: 64 → 32	67.02	76.68	84.28	75.55	76.28	7.88	10.53
32-parallel	5	1	0	5000	8	exp.: 64 → 32	68.57	75.58	88.03	79.36	92.87	18.68	9.05
64-cascade	10	1	0	5000	8	exp.: 64 → 32	67.41	77.01	85.89	76.99	99.45	14.33	18.77
64-parallel	10	1	0	5000	8	exp.: 64 → 32	75.12	81.85	87.87	80.29	147.69	36.33	17.61
128-cascade	20	2	0	5000	8	exp.: 64 → 32	66.34	75.52	85.13	75.63	119.64	27.55	19.62
128-parallel	20	2	0	5000	8	exp.: 64 → 32	67.94	76.29	83.15	78.54	258.76	43.74	18.05

accuracy improves (83.59%→84.93%) while Ts-acc changes only marginally, indicating a trade-off between noise suppression and removal of informative events. We select division factor 8, which achieves 84.46% accuracy with an approximately twofold reduction in event rate.

- *Threshold configuration.* We compare exponential, linear, and constant threshold schedules (weight 32, division factor 8). Note that thresholds $\leq w$ effectively disable filtration (e.g. the constant-32 setting). Among all tested schedules (detailed results in the additional material), linear thresholds of 48→16 achieve the best performance (85.22% accuracy, 75.61% F1), slightly outperforming constant 48 (84.29% accuracy). This indicates that stronger filtration is beneficial for lower channels (higher frequency), whereas higher channels (lower frequency) require less suppression.

Best Configurations. Based on the ablation studies, we select one configuration for each dataset variant and report the corresponding metrics in Table 3. Across all selected configurations, the time radius, division factor, and threshold settings remain identical; only the channel radius and skip step differ. The best results are achieved by the parallel configurations, which generate more than twice as many events on average as the cascade configurations. Moreover, the frequency-dependent latency introduced by the cascade configuration (see Sect. 3.1) hinders precise end-of-word detection, negatively affecting metrics that explicitly account for this parameter (Ts-acc$_1$, Ts-acc$_3$).

Comparison with State-of-the-Art. To contextualize our results, we compare the best-performing configuration identified in the ablation studies with previously reported state-of-the-art results. For consistency, we use *accuracy* as the primary metric and restrict the comparison to works reporting accuracy on the SSC dataset, which is the closest match to our dataset. In addition, we report the number of parameters as an indicator of model size (see Table 4).

Following the categorization used above, [3, 4, 9, 11, 21, 28, 30] report SNN-based models, [13, 29] report state-space models; and [14] report a graph-based approach. For our method, we report results for the best-performing configura-

Table 4. Accuracy and parameter-count comparison. Results for prior work are reported on the SSC dataset, while our models are evaluated on our dataset. Ranges indicate results reported for multiple model settings in the cited work.

Category	Reference	Model	#Params	Acc. (%)
SNN	Dampfhoffer et al. [9]	SpikGRU	280k	77.0
	Bittar et al. [4]	Recurrent SNN	3.9M	77.4
	Sadovsky et al. [28]	SNN-CNN	–	72.0
	Hammouamri et al. [11]	DCLS-Delays	0.7–2.5M	79.8–80.7
	Malettira et al. [21]	Temporal skips with delay learning	1.4M	80.2
	Baronig et al. [3]	SE-adLIF	1.6M	80.4
	Sun et al. [30]	PfA SNN	0.1/0.7M	77.4/80.2
SSM	Schone et al. [29]	Event-State-Space Model	0.1/0.6M	85.3/88.4
	Huber et al. [13]	S5-RF	1.8M	78.8
GNN	Jeziorek et al. [14]	Spectro-temporal graph on SoC FPGA	8.6k–272k	78.4–84.3
Our	32-cascade	End-to-end GNN with NAS on FPGA	59.84k	84.61
	32-parallel		59.84k	88.03
	64-cascade		59.84k	85.89
	64-parallel		59.84k	87.87
	128-cascade		59.84k	85.03
	128-parallel		59.84k	83.15

tion within each NAS setting (32, 64, and 128 channels) and for both cascade and parallel variants, where available.

Overall, our approach achieves higher accuracy than almost all previously reported methods, including all SNN-based models and the prior graph-based implementation on SoC FPGA, while using substantially fewer parameters (59.84 k). The only exception is Event-SSM [29], which reports a slightly higher peak accuracy (88.4%) than our best configuration (32-parallel, 88.03%). Importantly, our model is considerably smaller and is designed for end-to-end deployment on SoC FPGA, making it well suited for full hardware implementation under tight resource constraints.

4.4 Hardware Implementation

Based on the ablation studies (Sect. 4.3) and the system requirements (Sect. 3.3), we developed a hardware implementation integrating both the NAS and the GNN on the same device, building upon the modules provided in [14].

The graph neural network module supports all considered NAS configurations (32, 64, or 128 channels, in both parallel and serial variants). Due to efficient memory organization for storing features of previously processed events—required for the `PointNetConv` operation—BRAM usage remains independent of the channel count. Each memory entry stores nine 8-bit features (72 bits in total), resulting in a required depth of 1024 for the 128-channel configuration.

Table 5. Evaluation of proposed design compared with GNN from [14].

Metric	GNN [14]	64-parallel This work	32-parallel This work
LUT	125,130	88,370	82,739
FF	82,372	84,031	77,457
BRAM	75.5	55.5	55.5
DSP	140	83	83
Latency [μs]	10.53	25 (42)	25 (35)
Throughput [keps]	555	245	440
Power [W]	1.18	1.16	1.12
Accuracy	73.5%	86.9%	87.43%

Based on measured event statistics, we selected the number of parallel multipliers per graph convolution to process two 72-element feature vectors concurrently. With this configuration, a new event can be accepted every $0.47\,\mu s$ to $4.07\,\mu s$ (depending on the number of edges) at 200 MHz. The resulting throughput is estimated between 2.1 MEv./s and 245 kEv./s, significantly exceeding the measured event rates for all considered datasets (see Table 3). To handle short bursts of higher activity, we introduced a FIFO buffer between the filtering and graph generation modules.

The complete system was implemented on AMD US+ ZCU104 and validated against the software reference model. For evaluation purposes, we selected the 32-channel and 64-channel parallel NAS configurations due to their high accuracy of 87.43% and 86.9% respectively (after 8-bit quantization). An additional advantage of the parallel variants is the elimination of additional low-frequency latency effects that are characteristic of the cascaded configuration. Both implementations were evaluated with respect to the following metrics (Table 5):

- **Resource utilization** The proposed optimizations enabled a significant reduction in resource utilization compared to the GNN proposed in [14]. This resource efficiency allowed the full system to be deployed on the target platform without timing violations at a 200 MHz clock frequency.
- **Latency**. Due to the MaxPool architecture, the system generates predictions every 10 ms, invoking the network head once per window. With the timestamp propagation mechanism (see Sect. 3.3), the effective GNN latency—defined as the time between the end of a 10 ms window and the prediction—is typically equal to the head latency, i.e., $2.11\,\mu s$. In the worst case (when the last event occurs near the very end of the time window), it increases to a maximum of $18.62\,\mu s$. The NAS exhibits an input-to-event latency of $23\,\mu s$ resulting in overall end-to-end latency between 25 and $42\,\mu s$ (for 32-channels between 25 and $35\,\mu s$).
- **Power consumption**. Average power of the KWS modules was estimated in Vivado using post-implementation simulation toggle-rates under 40 kEv/s

load. For 64-channel coniguration (simulated with an average of 18 edges/Ev.) yielding 0.539 W dynamic and 0.595 W static, and for 32-channels (avg. 9.8 edges/Ev.) – 0.494 W dynamic and 0.595 W static. With NAS power reported as 29.7 mW in [16], the total average power is estimated at 1.16 W and 1.12 W, for 64-channel and 32-channel configurations respectively.

To the best of our knowledge, this is the first system enabling fully integrated, end-to-end keyword spotting on event-based audio with both the sensor and neural network implemented on a single FPGA device. There are, however, recent works on efficient KWS implementations for FPGA platforms evaluated on the original Google Speech Commands Dataset (not the spiking one) that report higher accuracies, e.g., a binary neural network accelerator on a Xilinx VC707 achieving 97.29% in 536 clock cycles [36], and a configurable temporal-efficient neural network reaching 95.36% [12]. However, both approaches rely on precomputed features rather than processing raw audio directly, which introduces additional preprocessing overhead, power consumption, and latency. Furthermore, their predictions are generated once per 1 s input sample.

In contrast, our approach eliminates the need for explicit aggregation or conventional preprocessing stages, thereby avoiding the associated latency and computational overhead. Furthermore, we generate predictions every 10 ms, significantly increasing the temporal resolution of keyword detection. This combination of raw audio handling, frequent prediction updates, and adaptive scheduling distinguishes our architecture from existing FPGA-based KWS systems.

5   Summary

This paper presents an end-to-end, real-time keyword spotting system implemented entirely on a single FPGA through tight integration of a Neuromorphic Auditory Sensor (NAS) with a graph neural network (GNN). We publicly release both software and hardware implementations, together with recorded event-based versions of the GSCD for multiple NAS configurations.

We propose a hardware-friendly event filtering method that reduces the number of processed events by approximately 47% while improving classification accuracy. Furthermore, we introduce GNN architectural modifications derived from extensive ablation studies to reduce resource utilization, latency, and power consumption while maintaining high throughput. On hardware, the selected 64-channel parallel NAS configuration achieves 87.43% accuracy after 8-bit quantization. The system produces predictions every 10 ms, with an effective postwindow inference latency of 35 µs and low average power consumption at 1.12 W.

The proposed design enables accurate and high-speed inference directly from raw audio on a single device, making it well suited for edge computing applications in mobile robotics and IoT. In future work, we plan to validate the proposed approach in real-world robotic human–machine interaction scenarios. Additionally, we intend to investigate the feasibility of an ASIC implementation to achieve an even more efficient and optimized solution.

Acknowledgments. This work was supported by: the Polish National Science Centre projects no. 2024/53/N/ST6/04254 and no. 2024/53/N/ST6/04331, the "Excellence initiative – research university" programme, 16.16.120.773 for the AGH University of Krakow. This work is a part of the projects PID2023-149071NB-C54 (NEKOR) funded by "Ministerio de Ciencia, Innovación y Universidades"/AEI/10.13039/501100011033, by "ERDF A way of making Europe" and by the European Union NextGenerationEU/PRTR, by grant USECHIP (TSI-069100–2023-001), project funded by the Secretary of State for Telecommunications and Digital Infrastructure, Ministry for Digital Transformation and Civil Service and by the European Union–NextGenerationEU/PRTR. We gratefully acknowledge Polish high-performance computing infrastructure PLGrid (HPC Center: ACK Cyfronet AGH) for providing computer facilities and support within computational grant no. PLG/2026/019156.

References

1. Abbott, L.F.: Lapicque's introduction of the integrate-and-fire model neuron (1907). Brain Res. Bull. **50**(5–6), 303–304 (1999)
2. Ansel, J., et al.: PyTorch 2: faster machine learning through dynamic python bytecode transformation and graph compilation. In: 29th ACM International Conference on Architectural Support for Programming Languages and Operating Systems, vol. 2 (ASPLOS '24). ACM (2024). https://doi.org/10.1145/3620665.3640366, https://docs.pytorch.org/assets/pytorch2-2.pdf
3. Baronig, M., Ferrand, R., Sabathiel, S., Legenstein, R.: Advancing spatio-temporal processing through adaptation in spiking neural networks. Nat. Commun. **16**(1), 5776 (2025). https://doi.org/10.1038/s41467-025-60878-z
4. Bittar, A., Garner, P.N.: A surrogate gradient spiking baseline for speech command recognition. Front. Neurosci. **16** (2022). https://doi.org/10.3389/fnins.2022.865897
5. Carpegna, A., Savino, A., Carlo, S.D.: Spiker+: a framework for the generation of efficient spiking neural networks FPGA accelerators for inference at the edge. IEEE Trans. Emerg. Top. Comput. **01**, 1–15 (2024). https://doi.org/10.1109/TETC.2024.3511676
6. Chan, V., Liu, S.C., van Schaik, A.: Aer ear: a matched silicon cochlea pair with address event representation interface. IEEE Trans. Circuits Syst. I Regul. Pap. **54**(1), 48–59 (2007). https://doi.org/10.1109/TCSI.2006.887979
7. Cramer, B., Stradmann, Y., Schemmel, J., Zenke, F.: The heidelberg spiking data sets for the systematic evaluation of spiking neural networks. IEEE Trans. Neural Netw. Learn. Syst. 1–14 (2020). https://doi.org/10.1109/TNNLS.2020.3044364
8. Cramer, B., Stradmann, Y., Schemmel, J., Zenke, F.: The heidelberg spiking data sets for the systematic evaluation of spiking neural networks. IEEE Trans. Neural Netw. Learn. Syst. **33**(7), 2744–2757 (2022). https://doi.org/10.1109/TNNLS.2020.3044364, https://zenkelab.org/resources/spiking-heidelberg-datasets-shd/
9. Dampfhoffer, M., et al.: Investigating current-based and gating approaches for accurate and energy-efficient spiking recurrent neural networks. In: Aydin, M. (ed.) Artificial Neural Networks and Machine Learning - ICANN 2022, pp. 359–370. Springer Nature Switzerland, Cham (2022). https://doi.org/10.1007/978-3-031-15934-3_30
10. Gambin, I., Grech, I., Casha, O., Gatt, E., Micallef, J.: Digital cochlea model implementation using xilinx xc3s500e spartan-3e FPGA. In: 2010 17th IEEE International Conference on Electronics, Circuits and Systems, pp. 946–949 (2010). https://doi.org/10.1109/ICECS.2010.5724669

11. Hammouamri, I., Khalfaoui-Hassani, I., Masquelier, T.: Learning delays in spiking neural networks using dilated convolutions with learnable spacings (2023). https://arxiv.org/abs/2306.17670
12. He, K., Chen, D., Su, T.: A configurable accelerator for keyword spotting based on small-footprint temporal efficient neural network. Electronics **11**(16), 2571 (2022)
13. Huber, T.E., Lecomte, J., Polovnikov, B., von Arnim, A.: Scaling up resonate-and-fire networks for fast deep learning. In: Del Bue, A., Canton, C., Pont-Tuset, J., Tommasi, T. (eds.) Computer Vision - ECCV 2024 Workshops, pp. 241–258. Springer Nature Switzerland, Cham (2025). https://doi.org/10.1007/978-3-031-92460-6_15
14. Jeziorek, K., et al.: Hardware-accelerated graph neural networks: an alternative approach for neuromorphic event-based audio classification and keyword spotting on soc FPGA (2026). https://arxiv.org/abs/2602.16442
15. Jimenez-Fernandez, A., Linares-Barranco, A., Paz-Vicente, R., Jiménez, G., Civit, A.: Building blocks for spikes signals processing. In: The 2010 International Joint Conference on Neural Networks (IJCNN), pp. 1–8 (2010). https://doi.org/10.1109/IJCNN.2010.5596845
16. Jiménez-Fernández, A., et al.: A binaural neuromorphic auditory sensor for FPGA: a spike signal processing approach. IEEE Trans. Neural Netw. Learn. Syst. **28**(4), 804–818 (2017)
17. Kingma, D.P., Ba, J.: Adam: a method for stochastic optimization arXiv preprint arXiv:1412.6980 (2014)
18. Liu, S.C., van Schaik, A., Minch, B.A., Delbruck, T.: Asynchronous binaural spatial audition sensor with $2 \times 64 \times 4$ channel output. IEEE Trans. Biomed. Circuits Syst. **8**(4), 453–464 (2014). https://doi.org/10.1109/TBCAS.2013.2281834
19. Loshchilov, I., Hutter, F.: SGDR: stochastic gradient descent with warm restarts. arXiv preprint arXiv:1608.03983 (2016)
20. Lyon, R., Mead, C.: An analog electronic cochlea. IEEE Trans. Acoust. Speech Sign. Process. **36**(7), 1119–1134 (1988). https://doi.org/10.1109/29.1639
21. Malettira, P.G., Negi, S., Ponghiran, W., Roy, K.: TSkips: efficiency through explicit temporal delay connections in spiking neural networks (2024). https://arxiv.org/abs/2411.16711
22. Matinizadeh, S., et al.: A fully-configurable open-source software-defined digital quantized spiking neural core architecture (2024). https://arxiv.org/abs/2404.02248
23. Nakano, H., et al.: Hardware-accelerated event-graph neural networks for low-latency time-series classification on soc FPGA. In: International Symposium on Applied Reconfigurable Computing, pp. 51–68. Springer (2025)
24. Perez-Nieves, N., Leung, V.C.H., Dragotti, P.L., Goodman, D.F.M.: Neural heterogeneity promotes robust learning. Nat. Commun. **12**(1), 5791 (2021). https://doi.org/10.1038/s41467-021-26022-3
25. Qi, C.R., Yi, L., Su, H., Guibas, L.J.: Pointnet++: deep hierarchical feature learning on point sets in a metric space (2017). https://arxiv.org/abs/1706.02413
26. Rafeldt, L., et al.: Event-based audio prediction with spectro-temporal event-graphs. In: 2025 IEEE International Symposium on Circuits and Systems (ISCAS), pp. 1–5 (2025). https://doi.org/10.1109/ISCAS56072.2025.11043865
27. Rossbroich, J., Gygax, J., Zenke, F.: Fluctuation-driven initialization for spiking neural network training. Neuromorphic Comput. Eng. **2**(4), 044016 (2022). https://doi.org/10.1088/2634-4386/ac97bb

28. Sadovsky, E., Jakubec, M., Jarina, R.: Speech command recognition based on convolutional spiking neural networks. In: 2023 33rd International Conference Radioelektronika (RADIOELEKTRONIKA), pp. 1–5 (2023). https://doi.org/10.1109/RADIOELEKTRONIKA57919.2023.10109082
29. Schöne, M., Sushma, N.M., Zhuge, J., Mayr, C., Subramoney, A., Kappel, D.: Scalable event-by-event processing of neuromorphic sensory signals with deep state-space models. In: 2024 International Conference on Neuromorphic Systems (ICONS), pp. 124–131 (2024). https://doi.org/10.1109/ICONS62911.2024.00026
30. Sun, P., Wu, J., Devos, P., Botteldooren, D.: Towards parameter-free attentional spiking neural networks. Neural Netw. **185**, 107154 (2025). https://doi.org/10.1016/j.neunet.2025.107154, https://www.sciencedirect.com/science/article/pii/S0893608025000334
31. Thakur, C.S., Hamilton, T.J., Tapson, J., van Schaik, A., Lyon, R.F.: FPGA implementation of the car model of the cochlea. In: 2014 IEEE International Symposium on Circuits and Systems (ISCAS), pp. 1853–1856 (2014). https://doi.org/10.1109/ISCAS.2014.6865519
32. Wang, S., Koickal, T.J., Enemali, G., Gouveia, L., Wang, L., Hamilton, A.: Design of a silicon cochlea system with biologically faithful response. In: 2015 International Joint Conference on Neural Networks (IJCNN), pp. 1–7 (2015). https://doi.org/10.1109/IJCNN.2015.7280828
33. Warden, P.: Speech commands: a dataset for limited-vocabulary speech recognition. arXiv preprint arXiv:1804.03209 (2018)
34. Warden, P.: Speech commands: a dataset for limited-vocabulary speech recognition (2018). https://arxiv.org/abs/1804.03209
35. Yin, B., Corradi, F., Bohté, S.M.: Accurate and efficient time-domain classification with adaptive spiking recurrent neural networks. Nat. Mach. Intell. **3**(10), 905–913 (2021). https://doi.org/10.1038/s42256-021-00397-w
36. Zhang, A., Shi, J., Qian, H., Wang, J.: High precision speech keyword spotting based on binary deep neural network in FPGA. Entropy **27**(11), 1143 (2025)

A Compact Spiking Neural Network for Real-Time Swimming Style Recognition on Low-Power FPGA

Matteo Antonio Scrugli$^{(\boxtimes)}$ and Paolo Meloni

Università degli studi di Cagliari, 09124 Cagliari, CA, Italy
`{matteoa.scrugli,paolo.meloni}@unica.it`

Abstract. Accurate and energy-efficient recognition of swimming styles is essential for real-time training analysis in wearable systems. This work introduces an end-to-end, spike-driven approach for swimming style classification, in which a Spiking Neural Network (SNN) operates on event-based inertial inputs. To the best of our knowledge, this is the first application of neuromorphic computing to swimming style recognition.

The signal encoding employs delta modulation on accelerometer, gyroscope, and magnetometer axes, converting continuous sensor streams into sparse binary spike trains that capture temporal dynamics of swimming movements without requiring explicit filtering or feature extraction. A compact fully connected SNN with leaky integrate-and-fire neurons classifies four swimming styles (freestyle, breaststroke, backstroke, and butterfly) using only 18,176 trainable parameters.

The approach is validated on a publicly available benchmark of 40 swimmers recorded in realistic training conditions, achieving an F1 of 0.945 under Leave-One-Subject-Out cross-validation.

To support deployment on resource-constrained wearable devices, we implement an optimized hardware architecture on a low-power Lattice iCE40-UltraPlus FPGA. The event-driven nature of the SNN enables efficient inference by processing only active spikes, reducing power consumption while maintaining low latency. Performance evaluations indicate an execution time of 7.8 ms per classification, with energy usage of 93.6 µJ, demonstrating the feasibility of on-device real-time swimming analysis.

Keywords: Spiking neural networks · Real-time monitoring · Edge computing · Sport analytics

1 Introduction

Wearable devices equipped with inertial measurement units (IMUs) have become a standard tool for monitoring athletic performance [3]. Modern smartwatches integrate accelerometers, gyroscopes, and magnetometers [1] capable of capturing multi-axis motion at sampling rates suitable for human activity recognition [2]. Among individual sports, swimming presents a particularly compelling

G. Leone et al. (Eds.): ARC 2026, LNCS 16514, pp. 137–153, 2026.
https://doi.org/10.1007/978-3-032-29365-7_9

use case: each stroke style exhibits distinctive cyclic kinematic patterns that are well-suited for automatic classification from wrist-worn inertial sensors [1]. Accurate real-time recognition of swimming styles enables objective training analysis, automatic lap counting, and personalized feedback, replacing manual observation by coaches. However, deploying such classification systems on battery-powered wearables imposes strict constraints on computational cost and power consumption, as continuous processing of multi-axis sensor streams must be sustained over extended training sessions. In swimming, this challenge is compounded by the strong attenuation of radio-frequency signals in water, which limits wireless data transfer from submerged sensors [8] and demands fully on-device inference.

Several deep learning approaches have been proposed for swimming style recognition from smartwatch sensor data. Brunner et al. [1] established the primary public benchmark of 40 swimmers, on which subsequent CNN and LSTM architectures [14,17] have achieved high classification accuracy. However, these models rely on dense floating-point computation with large parameter counts, and none addresses deployment on ultra-low-power wearable hardware suitable for continuous on-device inference.

Spiking Neural Networks (SNNs) offer a fundamentally different computing paradigm in which neurons communicate through sparse, asynchronous binary events (spikes) rather than continuous-valued activations [13]. Computation is triggered only when input changes exceed a significance threshold, making SNNs inherently suited for event-driven processing of temporal signals. In this work, we apply delta modulation to accelerometer, gyroscope, and magnetometer axes, converting continuous inertial streams into sparse binary spike trains that capture the temporal dynamics of swimming movements without requiring explicit filtering or handcrafted feature extraction. The resulting event-based representation naturally matches the SNN computation model: the network processes only active spikes, achieving high sparsity throughout the inference pipeline. To the best of our knowledge, this is the first application of neuromorphic computing to swimming style recognition.

Figure 1 illustrates the architecture of the proposed system. Raw inertial signals from a wrist-worn smartwatch are encoded into binary spike trains via delta modulation applied to accelerometer, gyroscope, and magnetometer data. A compact four-layer fully connected SNN with Leaky Integrate-and-Fire (LIF) neurons classifies four swimming styles (freestyle, backstroke, breaststroke, and butterfly) from the encoded spikes. The entire pipeline, from encoding to classification, is deployed on the open-source SYNtzulu platform [11], targeting a Lattice iCE40-UltraPlus Field Programmable Gate Array (FPGA).

To summarize, this work presents the following main contributions:

- We introduce the first neuromorphic approach for swimming style classification, employing a compact LIF-based SNN to classify four swimming styles from wrist-worn smartwatch IMU data.
- We apply delta modulation encoding to multi-sensor inertial data (accelerometer, gyroscope, and magnetometer), producing 24 sparse binary spike channels that preserve temporal dynamics without explicit feature engineering.

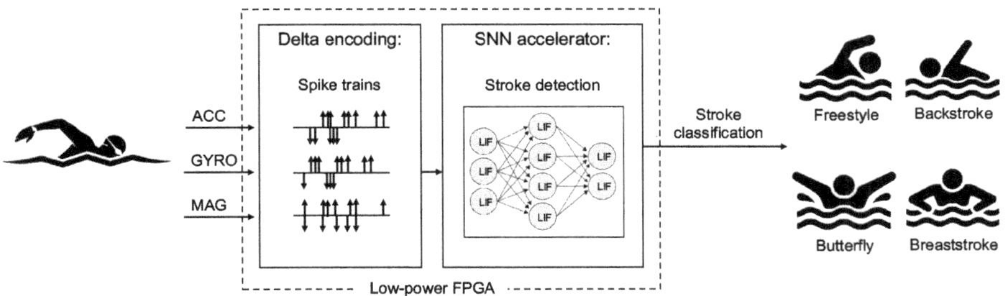

Fig. 1. "Overview of the proposed swimming style classification system. Raw inertial signals (accelerometer, gyroscope, magnetometer) from a wrist-worn smartwatch are encoded into sparse binary spike trains via per-axis delta modulation (24 channels). A four-layer fully connected SNN with LIF neurons classifies four swimming styles. The entire pipeline is deployed on a Lattice iCE40-UltraPlus FPGA via the SYNtzulu platform.

- We validate the approach on a publicly available benchmark of 40 swimmers under LOSO cross-validation, achieving an F1 of 0.945 with temporal voting, within 3% points of the state-of-the-art CNN [1].
- We demonstrate deployment on a Lattice iCE40-UltraPlus FPGA via the SYNtzulu platform, achieving real-time inference in 7.8 ms with 93.6 μJ energy consumption per classification, enabling always-on monitoring on ultra-low-power wearable devices.

2   Related Work

Wearable inertial sensors have become increasingly prevalent in sport analytics, enabling continuous monitoring of athletic performance outside laboratory settings [3]. The standard approach to sensor-based activity recognition segments continuous data streams into fixed-length sliding windows, from which a classifier predicts the activity label [2]. Deep learning methods, particularly convolutional and recurrent neural networks, have largely superseded handcrafted feature pipelines in this domain, achieving high accuracy across a variety of sports and daily activities, including swimming style recognition [1,5,17,19]. Swimming is a particularly well-suited target for IMU-based recognition, as the four competitive strokes produce distinct cyclic kinematic patterns at the wrist that differ in arm trajectory, body rotation, and stroke frequency.

Brunner et al. [1] established the primary benchmark for swimming style recognition by collecting 17 h of smartwatch sensor data from 40 swimmers. Their four-layer CNN with approximately 128,000 parameters achieves an F1 of 0.974 under 40-fold LOSO cross-validation on five classes (four strokes plus transitions), employing four data augmentation techniques and an 83% window overlap. Tarasevicius and Serackis [17] applied a three-layer bidirectional LSTM to the same dataset under the same LOSO protocol, reaching an F1 of 0.914

without data augmentation. Meng [14] improved per-class accuracies to 97.4–98.8% with an enhanced CNN under the same protocol.

Beyond the Brunner dataset, several works have addressed swimming recognition with different sensor placements. Delhaye et al. [5] placed a single IMU at the sacrum and trained a Bi-LSTM to classify eight swimming activities, reporting an F1 of 0.96 after post-processing on a single hold-out subject. Zhang et al. [19] combined a 1D-CNN with a Bi-LSTM and attention on hip-mounted data from four coaches, reaching 93.53% accuracy. Hamidi Rad et al. [9] applied rule-based thresholds on multiple body-worn sensors, highlighting the difficulty of wrist-based classification without learned features. Zhuang and Xue [20] improved accuracy by 3.9% points through periodic matching that segments signals by stroke cycle. Across all these works, the models rely on dense floating-point computation, and none explores event-driven or neuromorphic processing.

Deploying these models on ultra-low-power wearable hardware remains an open challenge, as continuous on-device inference demands power budgets in the order of tens of milliwatts. Yeon et al. [18] demonstrated general activity recognition on an Apple Watch GPU with approximately 7 million parameters and 21.1 ms total inference; however, smartwatch-class processors typically consume hundreds of milliwatts, limiting battery life for continuous monitoring. These constraints motivate the exploration of alternative computing paradigms that can reduce both model size and inference energy.

SNNs offer one such paradigm, in which neurons communicate through sparse binary events rather than dense real-valued activations [13,15]. This event-driven computation model inherently exploits the temporal sparsity of sensor signals: inference cost scales with the number of active spikes rather than the total number of synapses, enabling substantial energy savings when input activity is sparse. Delta modulation provides a natural interface between continuous sensor streams and SNN inputs by encoding signal changes that exceed a fixed threshold as binary spike events, preserving temporal dynamics while suppressing redundant information. Recent work has shown that SNNs can match or approach ANN accuracy on activity recognition tasks at a fraction of the computational cost, with applications to wearable human activity recognition [12], energy-efficient early-exit inference [7], and event-driven action recognition [4]. However, to the best of our knowledge, no prior work has applied SNNs to swimming style recognition or, more broadly, to sport-specific activity classification from wearable inertial sensors.

FPGA platforms offer a practical middle ground between the flexibility of general-purpose processors and the efficiency of custom ASICs, with reconfigurable logic that can be adapted as SNN architectures evolve [11]. In our previous work [16], we demonstrated the viability of this approach for wearable biosignal processing, deploying an SNN for real-time sEMG gesture recognition on a Lattice iCE40-UltraPlus FPGA at 11.3 mW inference power and 44.6 μJ per classification. This device provides 5,280 look-up tables and 128 KB of single-port RAM at an operating power in the order of 10 mW, making it a suitable target for always-on wearable inference.

Table 1. Class distribution of the Brunner et al. dataset [1]. The four swimming styles exhibit a pronounced imbalance in the number of swimmers who performed each style. Only 18 out of 40 swimmers performed all four styles.

Style	Swimmers
Freestyle	39
Breaststroke	24
Backstroke	37
Butterfly	23
All 4 styles	18

3 Method

In this section, we describe the proposed swimming style classification system. We introduce the reference dataset, detail the spike-based encoding scheme, present the SNN architecture and training procedure, and define the evaluation protocol.

3.1 Dataset

This study employs the publicly available swimming dataset introduced by Brunner et al. [1], which comprises 17 h of smartwatch sensor data collected from 40 swimmers in an indoor swimming pool. Recordings were acquired using a commercial wrist-worn smartwatch, capturing five sensor modalities: three-axis accelerometer (ACC), gyroscope (GYRO), magnetometer (MAG), barometric pressure, and ambient light, resampled to a uniform 30 Hz.

The dataset annotates four competitive swimming styles (freestyle, breaststroke, backstroke, and butterfly) alongside transition periods encompassing rest phases and wall turns. We retain only the four stroke labels and discard transition segments, reducing the classification task to four classes, whereas prior works on this benchmark evaluate five [14,17]. The class distribution is notably imbalanced: freestyle is the most represented style, performed by 39 out of 40 swimmers, whereas butterfly is absent in 17 swimmers and breaststroke in 16. Only 18 out of 40 swimmers recorded all four styles during their sessions. Table 1 summarizes the per-class swimmer coverage.

From the five available sensor modalities, we select accelerometer, gyroscope, and magnetometer (3 sensors), discarding pressure and ambient light. The three retained sensors capture complementary aspects of wrist kinematics (linear acceleration, angular velocity, and orientation), and Brunner et al. [1] reported that excluding pressure and light does not degrade classification accuracy. For each sensor, we extract three spatial axes and compute the Euclidean magnitude, yielding 4 signals per sensor and 12 signals in total before encoding.

Algorithm 1: Delta Encoding with Reset

Input: Normalized signal $x = [x_0, x_1, \ldots, x_{T-1}]$, threshold δ
Output: Binary spike trains s^+ and s^- of length T
$\ell \leftarrow x_0$;   // Initialize reference level
for $t \leftarrow 1$ **to** $T - 1$ **do**
   if $x_t - \ell \geq \delta$ **then**
      $s_t^+ \leftarrow 1$;
      $\ell \leftarrow x_t$;   // Positive spike, reset reference
   else if $x_t - \ell \leq -\delta$ **then**
      $s_t^- \leftarrow 1$;
      $\ell \leftarrow x_t$;   // Negative spike, reset reference

end

3.2 Signal Preprocessing and Encoding

Prior to spike generation, each sensor's raw signals are normalized by dividing by a physical-unit constant that brings the three modalities into comparable ranges: accelerometer values are divided by 9.81 (gravitational acceleration in m/s^2), gyroscope values by π (maximum expected angular velocity in rad/s), and magnetometer values by 18 (empirically determined scale in μT). This per-sensor normalization preserves the relative dynamics within each modality while avoiding global z-score standardization.

The normalized signals are converted into binary spike trains using delta modulation, a well-established technique that encodes signal changes exceeding a fixed threshold as discrete binary events. As detailed in Algorithm 1, the encoder maintains a reference level ℓ initialized to the first sample. At each subsequent time step t, if the signal exceeds the reference by at least δ, a positive spike is emitted and the reference is reset to the current signal value; symmetrically, if the signal falls below the reference by at least δ, a negative spike is produced and the reference is updated. Time steps where neither condition is met generate no spike.

Delta encoding is applied independently to each of the 12 signals (three axes plus magnitude for each of the 3 sensors), with a fixed threshold $\delta = 0.05$ in normalized units. Each signal produces two spike trains (one for positive and one for negative threshold crossings), yielding $12 \times 2 = 24$ binary input channels. With $\delta = 0.05$, the average spike rate at the input layer is approximately 40% per channel, indicating a relatively dense input regime; the computational savings from spike sparsity arise primarily in the hidden layers, as discussed in Sect. 5.3.

Figure 2 illustrates the encoding process on a representative freestyle segment. The encoded spike trains are segmented into fixed-length windows of 6 seconds (180 time steps at 30 Hz) with 50% overlap between consecutive windows. Each window is assigned the label of the majority class among its constituent samples, provided that this class accounts for at least 80% of the samples within the window. Windows that do not meet this purity criterion are discarded.

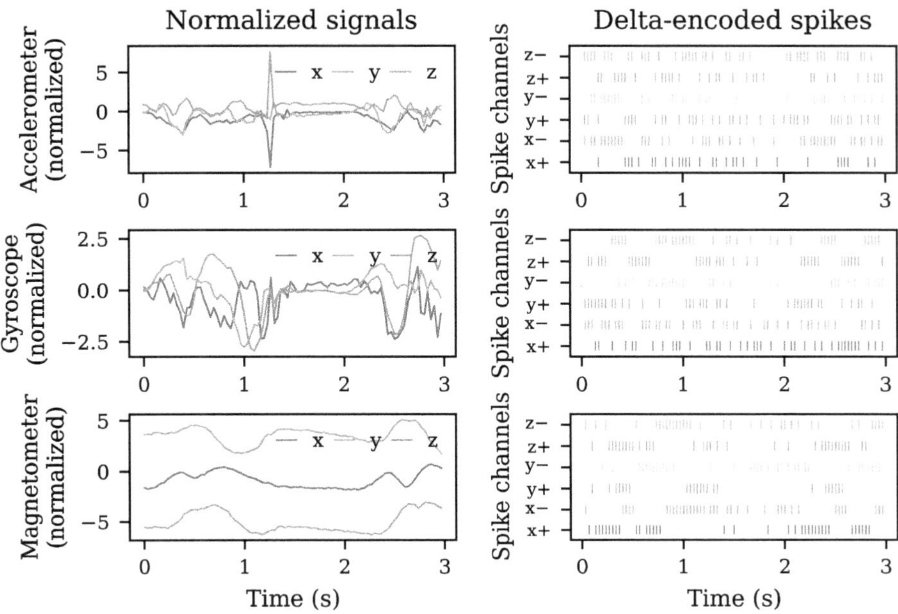

Fig. 2. Delta encoding of a representative freestyle segment. Left: normalized accelerometer, gyroscope, and magnetometer signals (three spatial axes per sensor). Right: corresponding binary spike trains produced by delta modulation with $\delta = 0.05$, with one positive and one negative channel per axis. The spike trains capture the temporal dynamics of the cyclic stroke pattern while suppressing constant-level intervals.

3.3   SNN Topology and Training

The proposed classifier is a 4-layer fully connected spiking neural network with LIF neurons, implemented using the SpikingJelly framework [6]. The network receives 24 input channels and produces 4 output neurons corresponding to the swimming styles. The three hidden layers (of 64, 128, and 64 neurons) are interposed between the input and output layers, each consisting of a fully connected (dense) synapse followed by a LIF neuron. Table 2 details the layer dimensions and the resulting parameter count.

Each LIF neuron integrates incoming weighted spikes into a membrane potential v that decays exponentially between time steps. The membrane dynamics, governed by a decay factor $\alpha = 1 - 1/\tau$ (where τ is the membrane time constant), follow the update rule of Eq. 1,

$$v'(t) = \alpha \cdot v(t) + \sum_{i} w_i \cdot s_i^{\text{in}}(t) \tag{1}$$

where w_i denotes the synaptic weight from presynaptic neuron i and $s_i^{\text{in}}(t) \in \{0, 1\}$ is its input spike at time t. When the updated potential exceeds the firing threshold θ, the neuron emits an output spike and the potential is reduced by θ through a soft reset (Eqs. 2–3).

$$v(t+1) = \begin{cases} v'(t), & \text{if } v'(t) < \theta \\ v'(t) - \theta, & \text{otherwise} \end{cases} \tag{2}$$

$$s^{\text{out}}(t+1) = \begin{cases} 1, & \text{if } v'(t) \geq \theta \\ 0, & \text{otherwise} \end{cases} \tag{3}$$

In our configuration, the time constant is set to $\tau = 2.0$ and the firing threshold to $\theta = 1.0$. Gradient computation through the non-differentiable spike function employs a sigmoid-based surrogate.

Table 2. Topology of the proposed 4-layer SNN. Each layer consists of a fully connected (dense) synapse without bias followed by a LIF neuron. The total number of trainable parameters (synaptic weights only) is 18,176.

Layer	Input	Output	Parameters
Dense + LIF 1	24	64	$24 \times 64 = 1{,}536$
Dense + LIF 2	64	128	$64 \times 128 = 8{,}192$
Dense + LIF 3	128	64	$128 \times 64 = 8{,}192$
Dense + LIF 4	64	4	$64 \times 4 = 256$
Total			**18,176**

Training is conducted using the Adam optimizer with an initial learning rate of 10^{-3} and a mini-batch size of 16. A plateau-based learning rate schedule monitors validation accuracy with a patience of 5 epochs: when no improvement is observed, the learning rate is multiplied by 0.5, for a maximum of 5 reductions. Training terminates via early stopping when the patience of 10 epochs is exhausted after the final learning rate reduction.

The loss function operates on the average output spike rate over the temporal window. A target spike-rate vector drives the true-class neuron toward 0.2 spikes per time step and all others toward 0.03; the mean squared error between observed and target rates defines the per-sample loss. At inference time, the class with the highest average firing rate is selected as the prediction.

Two data augmentation strategies are applied to improve generalization. First, the training set in each LOSO fold exhibits significant class imbalance, with freestyle windows outnumbering butterfly by up to 6×; minority classes are therefore oversampled by randomly duplicating windows with replacement until all classes match the majority count, yielding a balanced training set per fold. Second, LOSO analysis reveals that one swimmer (S33) exhibits an anomalous sensor orientation (inverted gyroscope axis), causing systematic misclassification; to address this, we apply random axis flipping during training of the S33 fold, where each of the 9 sensor axes is independently sign-inverted with 50% probability, producing 4 augmented copies per window. The remaining 39 folds use oversampling only.

To prepare the network for deployment on the SYNtzulu accelerator, all synaptic weights are quantized to signed 8-bit integers using per-layer symmetric scaling. Each weight matrix is multiplied by $s = 127/\max|w|$, rounded to the nearest integer, and divided back by s. This representation is natively supported by the 8-bit accumulation pipeline (Sect. 4), as evaluated in Sect. 5.3.

3.4   Evaluation Protocol

Model performance is assessed using LOSO cross-validation, the standard evaluation protocol for this dataset [1,14,17], which quantifies inter-subject generalization across the full swimmer population.

In the LOSO configuration, 40 folds are constructed, each leaving one swimmer out as the test set. Within each fold, 5 swimmers are drawn from the training pool as a validation set, selecting subjects that collectively cover all available classes, and the remaining swimmers constitute the training set. A separate model is trained from scratch for each fold.

Classification performance is reported using two metrics: overall accuracy (proportion of correctly classified windows) and macro-averaged F1 score (hereafter F1). To ensure comparability with Brunner et al. [1], we adopt their evaluation methodology: per-class F1 scores are first averaged within each swimmer, and the resulting per-swimmer F1 values are then averaged across all swimmers.

In addition to per-window classification, we evaluate temporal majority voting as a post-processing step, where the most frequent label over a sliding window of consecutive predictions is selected as the final output. The effect of different voting window sizes is analyzed in Sect. 5.

4   FPGA Deployment

To deploy the proposed classification pipeline on an ultra-low-power wearable device while leveraging the advantages of event-driven processing, we target the SYNtzulu platform, an open-source SNN processor designed for low-end FPGA implementation [11]. This device provides 5,280 Logic Cells (LCs), 128 KB of Single-Port RAM (SPRAM), 30 Embedded Block RAM (EBR) modules of 4 Kbit each, and 8 DSP blocks, at a typical operating power in the order of 10 mW.

The processor follows a System-on-Chip (SoC) architecture that integrates three main components. A RISC-V core based on the SERV microarchitecture [10] handles supervisory tasks, input/output peripheral management (sensor communication via SPI, classification output via UART), and system initialization, chosen for its minimal resource footprint. Two design-time configurable processing slots, termed *encoding* and *decoding* slots, implement the conversion of input sensor samples into binary spikes and the interpretation of output spikes into a classification result, respectively. An SNN accelerator module executes network inference in a clock-driven scheme while exploiting the event-based nature of spike inputs. The accelerator incorporates two pipelined neuron modules that share the workload by each processing half of the neurons in every layer. Each module accumulates four 8-bit synaptic weights per clock cycle, computes synaptic currents, updates membrane potentials according to LIF dynamics (Eqs. 1–3), and generates output spikes. An address generator module enables event-driven computation by dynamically fetching only the weights associated with active input synapses, skipping inactive channels and reducing the effective execution time in proportion to input sparsity.

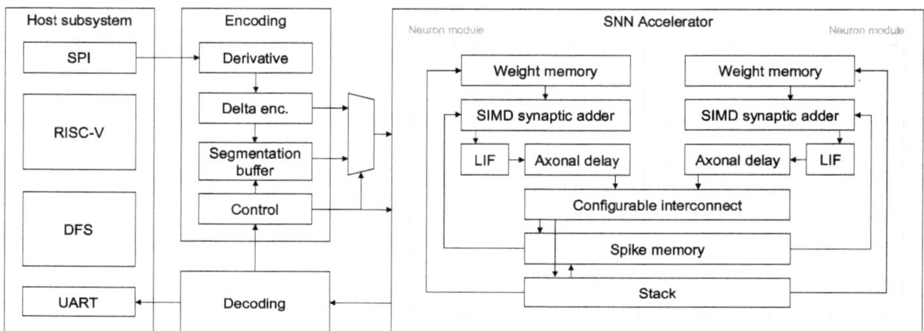

Fig. 3. Architecture of the SYNtzulu SNN processor configured for swimming style classification. The system integrates a RISC-V core (SERV) for supervisory tasks, an encoding slot that performs delta modulation on 12 IMU signals to produce 24 binary spike channels, an SNN accelerator with two pipelined neuron modules executing the 4-layer LIF network, and a decoding slot that accumulates per-class spike rates to output the predicted swimming style. All synaptic weights are quantized to 8-bit and stored in on-chip SPRAM.

Figure 3 illustrates the SYNtzulu architecture as configured for the swimming classification task. The encoding slot implements the delta modulation algorithm described in Sect. 3.2 independently on each of the 12 normalized IMU signals, producing 24 spike channels. A circular buffer continuously stores the most recent 180 spike vectors, occupying 4,320 bits (540 bytes), which fits within two EBR blocks. The decoding slot implements per-class spike-rate accumulation over the classification window, selecting the class with the highest average firing rate as the predicted swimming style.

The synaptic weights are represented in 8-bit fixed-point format and stored in on-chip SPRAM, occupying 18.4 KB of the available 128 KB capacity. Table 3 reports the resource utilization of the swimming classification system on the iCE40-UltraPlus.

The computational load per classification window amounts to 3,271,680 synaptic operations, obtained by summing the per-layer connection

Table 3. Resource utilization of the swimming classification system on the Lattice iCE40-UltraPlus FPGA.

Resource	Used	Available	Utilization
Logic Cells (LC)	3,718	5,280	70.4%
DSP Blocks	2	8	25%
EBR (4 Kbit)	20	30	66.7%
SPRAM (32 KB)	4	4	100%

counts (Table 2) over 180 time steps. Exploiting input sparsity, the accelerator skips groups of four inactive synapses, reducing the effective execution cycles according to Eq. 4,

$$cycles = \frac{ops \times (1 - sparsity\text{-}hw)}{modules \times parallel\_spikes} \tag{4}$$

where $modules = 2$ denotes the number of neuron modules, $parallel\_spikes = 4$ is the number of weights accumulated per cycle per module, and $sparsity\text{-}hw$ quantifies the fraction of four-synapse groups entirely skipped due to input inactivity (Sect. 5.3). In the worst case (zero sparsity), the 3,271,680 operations require approximately 409,000 execution cycles, corresponding to 17 ms at the 24 MHz system clock, already orders of magnitude below the inter-window interval imposed by the 6-second window duration and 50% overlap. The actual inference time and energy consumption, which depend on the measured spike sparsity, are reported in Sect. 5.3.

Between classification windows, the system enters a low-power standby state in which only the encoding slot and the sensor interface remain active, further reducing the average power consumption over extended swimming sessions.

The complete classification pipeline, from delta encoding of raw IMU samples to swimming style prediction, executes entirely within the FPGA fabric through the dedicated encoding, accelerator, and decoding modules. The RISC-V core is limited to supervisory duties (sensor communication, output transmission, and system initialization), ensuring deterministic inference latency and enabling duty-cycling during standby periods.

5   Experimental Results

This section presents the experimental evaluation of the proposed swimming style classification system. We first report LOSO cross-validation results with an analysis of per-swimmer variability and temporal voting, then compare with state-of-the-art approaches, and conclude with an analysis of spike sparsity and hardware performance.

5.1 LOSO Cross-Validation

Under the 40-fold LOSO protocol described in Sect. 3.4, the proposed system achieves 94.98% mean accuracy (standard deviation 4.79% across swimmers) and an F1 of 0.936 on per-window classification, where each 6-second window is classified independently.

Table 4. LOSO cross-validation results (40 folds). Per-window: each 6-s window is classified independently. Temporal voting selects the majority class over a sliding window spanning approximately 6 s. Accuracy and F1 follow the per-swimmer averaging methodology of Brunner et al. [1].

Configuration	Accuracy (%)	F1
Without augmentation (baseline)	89.70	0.880
Per-window (with augmentation)	94.98	0.936
+ Temporal voting (6 s)	96.27	0.945

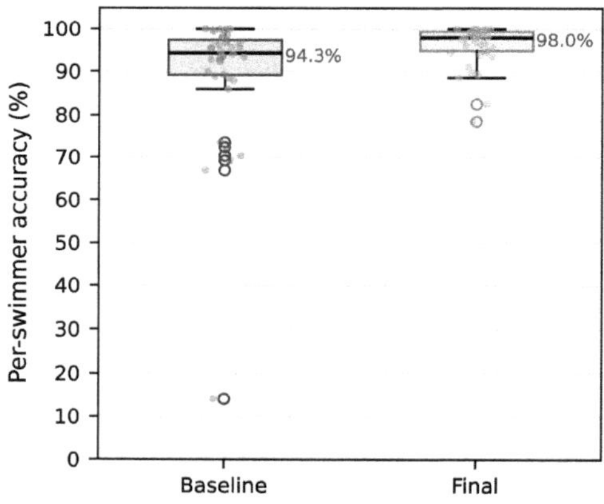

Fig. 4. Per-swimmer accuracy distribution under 40-fold LOSO cross-validation. Both configurations use 8-bit quantized weights. *Baseline*: per-window classification without augmentation. *Final*: with oversampling, data augmentation, and temporal voting. Each data point represents a single held-out swimmer.

The per-swimmer accuracy distribution (Fig. 4) shows that data augmentation substantially reduces the number of outliers compared to the unaugmented baseline. Without augmentation, six swimmers fell below 80% accuracy; with augmentation and temporal voting, only one swimmer (S11: 79%) remains below this threshold. The previously worst-performing swimmer (S33, 14% without augmentation) reaches 93% accuracy thanks to the combination of oversampling and random axis flipping. Former outliers S13, S9, S6, and S36 improve by 17–32% points each, confirming that class imbalance was a primary driver of their poor performance.

Applying temporal majority voting over a sliding window of approximately 6 seconds improves mean accuracy to 96.27% and F1 to 0.945 (Table 4).

Fig. 5. Normalized confusion matrix pooled across all 40 LOSO folds (per-window predictions, without temporal voting). Rows represent true labels and columns represent predicted labels. Values indicate the fraction of windows of each true class assigned to each predicted class.

Table 5. Comparison with state-of-the-art methods on the Brunner et al. dataset [1] under LOSO cross-validation. [†]Evaluated on 5 classes (including transitions); our model classifies 4 swimming styles. [*]Per-class accuracy of 97.4–98.8% reported; F1 not available. [**]Not reported by the authors; estimated from the described architecture (see text).

Method	Type	Parameters	LOSO F1
Brunner [1]	CNN	~128K	0.974[†]
Tarasevicius [17]	Bi-LSTM	0.5–2M[**]	0.914[†]
Meng [14]	CNN	≥200K[**]	–[*†]
Ours	**SNN (LIF)**	**18K**	**0.945**

Figure 5 presents the confusion matrix pooled across all 40 folds. Freestyle, the most represented style in the dataset (39/40 swimmers), achieves the highest per-class accuracy. Butterfly, which is absent in 17 out of 40 swimmers, exhibits the lowest recall due to limited training diversity. The dominant confusion pattern involves freestyle being misclassified as other styles (or vice versa) in swimmers whose stroke mechanics deviate from the population norm.

5.2   Comparison with State of the Art

Table 5 compares the proposed SNN with the three methods evaluated on the same dataset under LOSO cross-validation. The CNN of Brunner et al. [1] achieves the highest F1 of 0.974, followed by the Bi-LSTM of Tarasevicius and Serackis [17] at 0.914 and the enhanced CNN of Meng [14] (per-class accuracy 97.4–98.8%, F1 not reported). Our SNN achieves an F1 of 0.945 with temporal voting, narrowing the gap with the Brunner baseline to approximately 3% points.

The residual gap can be attributed to several factors. Brunner et al. classify five classes (including transitions) versus our four swimming styles, and their CNN uses z-score normalization computed across the full dataset, which may capture a broader input distribution than our per-sensor physical-unit normalization (designed to prevent information leakage across folds). Additionally, our model is the only approach in the comparison that applies 8-bit weight quantization at inference time.

Despite the accuracy gap, the proposed SNN offers substantial advantages in efficiency. With 18,176 parameters, our model is approximately 7× smaller than the Brunner CNN (~128K parameters), which is the most directly comparable baseline as it achieves the highest F1 in the comparison with a fully specified architecture. The remaining methods do not report their parameter counts explicitly; from the described architectures, we estimate 0.5–2M parameters for the Tarasevicius Bi-LSTM [17] (depending on weight sharing across the nine sensor streams) and at least 200K for the six-layer CNN of Meng [14]. In all cases, the proposed SNN is at least one order of magnitude smaller, and its compact footprint enables deployment on ultra-low-power FPGA hardware as detailed in Sect. 4.

5.3   Sparsity and Hardware Performance

A key advantage of SNN-based inference is the inherent sparsity of spiking activity, which reduces the number of synaptic operations that must be physically executed on the hardware accelerator. The overall sparsity across network layers and time steps is quantified according to Eq. 5,

$$Sparsity = \left(1 - \frac{\sum_{i=1}^{L} \sum_{t=1}^{T} \sum_{j=1}^{N_i} s_{itj}}{\sum_{i=1}^{L} N_i \cdot T}\right) \times 100 \tag{5}$$

where L is the number of layers, T is the number of time steps per window, N_i is the number of output neurons in layer i, and $s_{itj} \in \{0, 1\}$ is the spike output of neuron j in layer i at time step t. The measured sparsity of the swimming classification model, averaged over all LOSO test sets, is 73.6%.

As described in Sect. 4, the SYNtzulu accelerator processes spikes in groups of four, meaning that only groups of four consecutive inactive neurons at a given time step translate into actual computation savings. To capture this constraint, we define the hardware-aware sparsity in Eq. 6,

$$Sparsity\text{-}hw = \left(1 - \frac{\sum_{i=1}^{L}\sum_{t=1}^{T}\sum_{k=1}^{G_i} a_{itk}}{\sum_{i=1}^{L} G_i \cdot T}\right) \times 100 \qquad (6)$$

where $G_i = \lceil N_i/4 \rceil$ is the number of four-neuron groups in layer i and $a_{itk} = 1$ if at least one neuron in group k of layer i is active at time step t, and 0 otherwise. To maximize this metric, neurons within each layer are reordered by their average firing rate measured on the training set, clustering inactive neurons into the same groups; this permutation is mathematically equivalent (identical predictions) and only affects the physical layout seen by the accelerator. The measured hardware-aware sparsity after reordering is 54.2%, representing the fraction of computation that can be effectively skipped during inference.

Applying the measured sparsity-hw to the execution time model of Eq. 4, the 3,271,680 synaptic operations per classification window result in an effective execution time of 7.8 ms at the 24 MHz system clock. Combined with the measured average power consumption of 12.0 mW during active inference (Table 6), the energy per classification amounts to 93.6 μJ.

Table 6. Execution and power characteristics of the swimming classification system deployed on the iCE40-UltraPlus at 24 MHz. The energy per classification refers to a single 6-second window of 180 time steps.

Metric	Value
Synaptic operations/window	3,271,680
Hardware-aware sparsity	54.2%
Inference time	7.8 ms
Average power (during inference)	12.0 mW
Energy per classification	93.6 μJ

All accuracy figures reported in this work refer to 8-bit quantized inference; the weight quantization (Sect. 3.3) reduces on-chip storage to 18.4 KB.

These figures compare favorably with conventional inference solutions. Yeon et al. [18] demonstrated 21.1 ms total inference for general activity recognition on an Apple Watch GPU with approximately 7 million parameters, implying an energy cost per inference over one order of magnitude higher than our FPGA implementation.

6   Conclusion

This work presented the first neuromorphic approach to swimming style classification, combining delta modulation encoding of multi-sensor IMU data with a compact fully connected SNN deployed on a low-power FPGA. The system classifies four swimming styles from wrist-worn smartwatch data with approximately seven times fewer parameters than the leading CNN baseline.

Evaluated on a publicly available benchmark of 40 swimmers under LOSO cross-validation, the system achieves an F1 of 0.945 with temporal voting, approximately 3% points below the CNN baseline of Brunner et al. [1]. The proposed SNN operates at a fundamentally different efficiency regime: the entire model fits within on-chip SPRAM on the Lattice iCE40-UltraPlus FPGA, achieving real-time inference in 7.8 ms with 93.6 μJ per classification, over one order of magnitude below the energy cost of conventional alternatives.

Acknowledgments. This work has received funding from multiple European research initiatives. The project EdgeAI "Edge AI Technologies for Optimised Performance Embedded Processing" is supported by the Chips Joint Undertaking and its members including top-up funding by Austria, Belgium, France, Greece, Italy, Latvia, Netherlands, and Norway under grant agreement No 101097300.

This work was also supported in part by the European Union's Horizon 2020 Research and Innovation Program under Grant Agreement GA 101140052 (H2TRAIN), and in part by NextGenerationEU Mission 4, Component 2, Investment 1.5, CUP B83C22002820006.

Funded by the European Union. Views and opinions expressed are however those of the author(s) only and do not necessarily reflect those of the European Union or the Chips Joint Undertaking. Neither the European Union nor the granting authority can be held responsible for them.

Disclosure of Interests. The authors have no competing interests to declare that are relevant to the content of this article.

References

1. Brunner, G., Melnyk, D., Sigfússon, B., Wattenhofer, R.: Swimming style recognition and lap counting using a smartwatch and deep learning. In: Proceedings of the 2019 ACM International Symposium on Wearable Computers, pp. 23–31. ISWC '19, Association for Computing Machinery, New York, NY, USA (2019). https://doi.org/10.1145/3341163.3347719
2. Bulling, A., Blanke, U., Schiele, B.: A tutorial on human activity recognition using body-worn inertial sensors. ACM Comput. Surv. **46**(3) (2014). https://doi.org/10.1145/2499621
3. Camomilla, V., Bergamini, E., Fantozzi, S., Vannozzi, G.: Trends supporting the in-field use of wearable inertial sensors for sport performance evaluation: a systematic review. Sensors **18**(3), 873 (2018). https://doi.org/10.3390/s18030873
4. Chen, J., Yang, Y., Deng, S., Teng, D., Pan, L.: SpikMamba: when SNN meets mamba in event-based human action recognition. In: Proceedings of the 6th ACM International Conference on Multimedia in Asia (2024). https://doi.org/10.1145/3696409.3700204
5. Delhaye, E., Bouvet, A., Nicolas, G., Vilas-Boas, J.a.P., Bideau, B., Bideau, N.: Automatic swimming activity recognition and lap time assessment based on a single IMU: a deep learning approach. Sensors **22**(15), 5786 (2022). https://doi.org/10.3390/s22155786

6. Fang, W., et al.: SpikingJelly: an open-source machine learning infrastructure platform for spike-based intelligence. Sci. Adv. **9**(40), eadi1480 (2023). https://doi.org/10.1126/sciadv.adi1480

7. Fang, Z., Li, J., Wang, W.: CASNN: continuous adaptive SNN for human activity recognition. In: 2024 IEEE 19th Conference on Industrial Electronics and Applications (ICIEA), pp. 1–6 (2024). https://doi.org/10.1109/ICIEA61579.2024.10665045

8. Hagem, R.M., O'Keefe, S.G., Fickenscher, T., Thiel, D.V.: Self contained adaptable optical wireless communications system for stroke rate during swimming. IEEE Sens. J. **13**(8), 3144–3151 (2013). https://doi.org/10.1109/JSEN.2013.2262933

9. Hamidi Rad, M.: SmartSwim: a novel approach to swimming analysis and coaching assistance based on wearable inertial sensors. Ph.D. thesis, EPFL, Lausanne (2022). https://doi.org/10.5075/epfl-thesis-9931

10. Kindgren, O.: SERV - the serial RISC-V CPU (2019). https://github.com/olofk/serv. Accessed 17 Feb 2026

11. Leone, G., Scrugli, M.A., Badas, L., Martis, L., Raffo, L., Meloni, P.: SYNtzulu: a tiny RISC-V-controlled SNN processor for real-time sensor data analysis on low-power FPGAs. IEEE Trans. Circuits Syst. I Regul. Pap. **72**(2), 790–801 (2025). https://doi.org/10.1109/TCSI.2024.3450966

12. Li, Y., Yin, R., Kim, Y., Panda, P.: Efficient human activity recognition with spatio-temporal spiking neural networks. Front. Neurosci. **17** (2023). https://doi.org/10.3389/fnins.2023.1233037

13. Maass, W.: Networks of spiking neurons: the third generation of neural network models. Neural Netw. **10**(9), 1659–1671 (1997). https://doi.org/10.1016/S0893-6080(97)00011-7

14. Meng, Y.: Swimming style recognition with convolutional neural network with single IMU. World Sci. Res. J. **10**(11), 39–43 (2024)

15. Nunes, J.a.D., Carvalho, M., Carneiro, D., Cardoso, J.S.: Spiking neural networks: a survey. IEEE Access **10**, 60738–60764 (2022). https://doi.org/10.1109/ACCESS.2022.3179968

16. Scrugli, M.A., Leone, G., Busia, P., Raffo, L., Meloni, P.: Real-time sEMG processing with spiking neural networks on a low-power 5K-LUT FPGA. IEEE Trans. Biomed. Circuits Syst. **19**(1), 68–81 (2025). https://doi.org/10.1109/TBCAS.2024.3456552

17. Tarasevičius, D., Serackis, A.: Deep learning model for sensor based swimming style recognition. In: 2020 IEEE Open Conference of Electrical, Electronic and Information Sciences (eStream), pp. 1–4 (2020). https://doi.org/10.1109/eStream50540.2020.9108849

18. Yeon, T., Xu, V., Hoffmann, H., Ahuja, K.: WatchHAR: real-time on-device human activity recognition system for smartwatches, pp. 387–394. Association for Computing Machinery, New York, NY, USA (2025). https://doi.org/10.1145/3716553.3750775

19. Zhang, G., Xi, B., Hu, M., Zhu, X.: Wearable inertial sensor-based recognition of swimming movements and postures. In: Proceedings of the 2025 2nd International Conference on Big Data Analytics and Artificial Intelligence Application, pp. 178–183. Association for Computing Machinery, New York, NY, USA (2025). https://doi.org/10.1145/3788108.3788525

20. Zhuang, Z., Xue, Y.: Sport-related human activity detection and recognition using a smartwatch. Sensors **19**(22), 5001 (2019). https://doi.org/10.3390/s19225001

Enabling Plasticity in FPGA-Based SNNs: an EEG Seizure Detection Study

Paola Busia$^{(\boxtimes)}$, Andrea Matticola , Luigi Raffo , Paolo Meloni ,
and Gianluca Leone

DIEE Università degli Studi di Cagliari, 09123 Cagliari, CA, Italy
`{paola.busia,paolo.meloni,gianluca.leone94}@unica.it`

Abstract. Real-time classification or anomaly detection tasks on sensor data often represent a significant challenge, due to signal variability and noise levels corrupting the data in unpredictable ways. This issue is especially relevant in biomedical applications, where data acquisition is noticeably unbalanced, inter-person and inter-day signal variability is non-negligible, and data annotation is an extremely complex task to be completed by expert physicians. In this context, Spiking Neural Networks (SNNs) provide the interesting opportunity of mimicking the learning capabilities of the brain through different plasticity mechanisms, which allow an online refinement of the model's parameters in an unsupervised fashion. This work aims at leveraging plasticity to adjust on the fly the classification performance of a lightweight SNN model, targeting biological signal monitoring in the wearable domain, by relying on a specialized low-power SNN accelerator enabling signal classification within a power envelope of 0.25 mW. The efficacy of the approach is evaluated on a seizure recognition problem based on the real-time processing of the electroencephalography (EEG) signal, where ensuring a good trade-off between anomaly detection and false-alarms minimization is paramount, and seizure occurrences vary significantly. The plasticity rule is executed on the host RISC-V processor integrated in the FPGA-based accelerator, enabling efficient and self-adaptive always-on monitoring with a negligible impact on the system's power consumption.

Keywords: Plasticity · Spiking Neural Networks · FPGA · Low-power

1 Introduction

Spiking Neural Networks (SNNs) have recently emerged as third-generation neural networks, due to the inherent efficiency ensured by event-driven computations and binary data representation. Combined with the possibility of replacing resource-hungry multiplications with additions during real-time inference execution, these advantages make them especially promising as processing models for the wearable domain. Furthermore, their time-dependent evolution enables accounting for the context of previously processed data, which is especially interesting for sensor data processing.

G. Leone et al. (Eds.): ARC 2026, LNCS 16514, pp. 154–171, 2026.
https://doi.org/10.1007/978-3-032-29365-7_10

To enable efficient exploitation of this sparse and event-driven computation, specialized neuromorphic architectures have been developed, also focusing on low-power solutions [18]. Some recent efforts have considered efficient FPGA-based implementations suitable for the ultra-low-power domain, leveraging the flexibility of reconfigurable logic to allocate different encoding schemes and focusing on low-end devices fostering wide accessibility [15,19].

Nonetheless, the real-time processing of sensor data poses very specific challenges, connected to a significant variability of the acquired signals due to changing noise levels, sensor drift, etc., as can be observed in biomedical applications in terms of inter-session/inter-day variability. A promising approach to address this issue is to rely on online refinement techniques, enabling adaptivity to these changing conditions. A recently emerging line of research focuses on mimicking biologically inspired learning mechanisms in SNNs, through the definition of synaptic connections supporting plasticity as a weight modulation rule accounting for changes in conductivity caused by pre- and post-synaptic activity [16]. However, the integration of these mechanisms in devices at the wearable scale requires careful resource reuse.

With this objective, in this work, we start from the SYNtzulu [11] template for SNN acceleration on low-end FPGAs, integrating with minimal resource overhead the necessary logic to implement spike monitoring and online weight update. To minimize the resource usage, we exploit software/hardware interaction to access the hardware monitoring registers and compute weight update based on Short-Term-Plasticity (STP) on the host RISC-V processor.

The main contributions are listed in the following:

- we present an efficient neuromorphic system based on SYNtzulu [11], integrating support for online refinement through STP-based weight updates with negligible additional resource requirements;
- we demonstrate the feasibility of real-time weight update through efficient implementation on the RISC-V host processor in SYNtzulu, where STP execution does not impact the latency of signal classification;
- we validate the proposed STP-based update rule on a meaningful use-case, namely unobtrusive electroencephalography (EEG) monitoring for seizure detection, demonstrating a 70% reduction of the false alarms raised on the examined EEG records compared to the state-of-the-art static SNN model considered as baseline.

The paper is organized as follows: Sect. 2 summarizes the state of the art, Sect. 3 describes the implemented methodology, Sect. 4 presents the experimental results, and Sect. 5 discusses the comparison with the literature.

2   Related Work

Spike-Time-Dependent Plasticity (STDP) has been exploited in the literature to perform unsupervised training of SNN models by strengthening connections based on the causality between post- and pre-synaptic firing. An example is represented by the ASIC proposed in [13] for the training of an MNIST classifier. Another typical learning mechanism observed in neuroscience is STP, which produces transient changes in the importance of synaptic connections as a consequence of the pre-synaptic activity [16]. Along with long-term potentiation/depression rules, these temporary changes in synaptic connectivity have been considered to enhance the adaptivity of SNN models to new data. A solution combining an STDP-based training stage with an online refinement based on STP has been considered in [17], demonstrating an improved robustness in noisy MNIST and EMNIST images classification thanks to online STP. As another example, fatiguing STDP has been introduced in [16] as a learning rule combining both STDP and STP effects to improve SNN learning on weather correlations.

In this work, we explore the impact of STP as an online refinement mechanism to increase the robustness of biological sensor data classification, starting from a model pre-trained in a supervised fashion. A significant reference was provided by [4], where STP was exploited to enable continuous noise filtering in action potential and bursts detection from micro-electrode array (MEA) acquisition. Compared to the STP implementation exploited in [4], we refined the weight update rule to enable a more gradual recovery of the weight module. Furthermore, focusing on the near-sensor domain as a deployment target, we optimized the STP rule implementation to be efficiently integrated in an ultra-low-power FPGA-based SNN accelerator and executed on the simple host RISC-V processor. This solution represents an innovation compared to the FPGA-based alternatives in the literature supporting plasticity mechanisms, mostly oriented to high performance over the strict energy efficiency constraints required for wearable deployment [1,23,24]. On the contrary, the interesting architectural solution proposed in [4] is customized on a fixed two-neuron network topology. A detailed quantitative comparison is discussed in Sect. 5.

Due to the challenges connected to seizure data acquisition and annotation, as well as to seizure occurrence variability, EEG seizure detection represents a relevant use case to assess the advantages of online model refinement through plasticity. For this reason, autoencoder solutions for unsupervised training [5,25, 26] and support for continual learning buffering new seizure events along with previous training samples [20] have been proposed.

In this context, a detector leveraging the plasticity of its synaptic connections to adapt to signal corruption, due to noise or artifacts, represents a promising opportunity for long-term monitoring, combined with the efficiency of sparse and binary SNN inference, which have been recently explored as detection models [3,6,12,27]. To the best of our knowledge, the use of plasticity as an online refinement mechanism in this context was only previously considered in [27], integrating an STDP-based online learning module. In this work, we explore a different plasticity mechanism, STP, and we discuss its impact on the real-time seizure detection performance, considering it as an always-on weight update rule. Finally, compared to the FPGA implementation proposed in [27], we demonstrate an improved energy efficiency in real-time execution.

3 Method

This section describes the details of the proposed SNN model, the implemented STP rule, the hardware target, and the EEG seizure detection use-case.

3.1 Lightweight SNN Classifier

The proposed system integrates a state-of-the-art lightweight SNN model [2], suitable to reach an acceptable EEG classification performance with a power envelope compatible with wearable deployment. The input encoding follows the approach exploited in [2], where the amplitude of the signal sampled at time t on each of the acquisition channels is encoded into 16 one-hot amplitude levels, selected based on the typical amplitude observed in the training records.

The topology of the model is depicted in Fig. 1. It exploits two layers of Leaky-Integrate-and-Fire (LIF) neurons: the first layer is composed of 8 neurons, each integrating through time the input signal information received from 64 input synapses and combined through a 64×8 Dense layer; the output layer is fully connected to the previous stage and includes a single neuron, whose output rate is compared to a pre-trained discrimination threshold th_{class} to obtain the final classification into two different classes, *non-seizure* or *seizure*.

The LIF mechanism considered for the implementation is recalled in the following. The neuron membrane voltage stores the history of the previously processed input spikes, evolving based on Eq. 1.

$$\tilde{v}(t+1) = \alpha \cdot v(t) + \sum w \cdot s_{in}(t+1) \tag{1}$$

where $s_{in}(t+1)$ is the input train of spikes, w are the synaptic weights assigned to the input connections, and α is a decay factor.

$$s_{out}(t+1) = \begin{cases} 1, & \text{if } \tilde{v}(t+1) \geq \theta \\ 0, & \text{otherwise} \end{cases} \tag{2}$$

$$v(t+1) = \begin{cases} \tilde{v}(t+1), & \text{if } \tilde{v}(t+1) < \theta \\ \tilde{v}(t+1) - \theta, & \text{otherwise} \end{cases} \tag{3}$$

When the membrane voltage reaches a threshold value θ, the neuron produces an output spike s_{out}, according to Eq. 2. As a consequence, the membrane voltage is reset by subtracting the threshold value, as reported in Eq. 3.

The model was implemented exploiting the SnnTorch library [7], enabling LIF evolution modeling and supervised training with backpropagation through time on the PyTorch framework. Training execution was performed on Google Colaboratory.

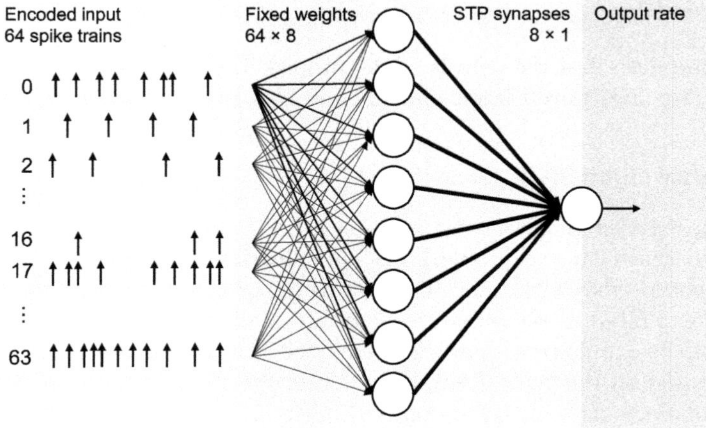

Fig. 1. Topology of the considered SNN model.

3.2   Short-Term Plasticity

STP models the effects of synaptic fatigue, due to a reduced concentration of the neurotransmitter in the pre-synaptic terminal, thus temporarily decreasing the weight of the connection with each spike transmitted [16].

Taking inspiration from [4], in this work, we focus on STP as a filtering mechanism for frequent synaptic activity, interpreted as noise and thus determining temporary synaptic depression. We focus on the synapses connecting to the output neuron, highlighted in Fig. 1, and particularly on those having learned a positive weight during the supervised training, whose activity contributes positively to the output rate of the classification neuron (i.e., seizure prediction). To define the frequency of the synaptic activity, we trace the number of spikes s_{io} transmitted along the plastic synapse within a rate observation window of T time steps. As reported in Eq. 4, this rate r_{io} is multiplied by the connection weight w_{io} to compute the input current transmitted to the output neuron along that connection during the last T steps.

$$c_i(n) = w_{io}(n) \cdot \sum_{t=0}^{T} s_{io}(t) = w_{io}(n) \cdot r_{io}(n) \qquad (4)$$

To evaluate the transient modification, the current c_i is compared to a typical current value C_i, expected on each connection based on the training data available for the normal class. The weight update rule is reported in Eq. 5, where D_i and P_i are synaptic-specific parameters, selected based on the training data to ensure that no relevant modification would be applied to the weights in a typical normal window.

$$w_{io}(n+1) = \begin{cases} w_{io}(n) - D_i \cdot r_{io}(n), & \text{if } c_i(n) > C_i \\ w_{io}(n) + P_i \cdot (1 - r_{io}(n)), & \text{otherwise} \end{cases} \tag{5}$$

The description of the selection process for the C_i. P_i, and D_i parameters in the seizure classification use-case is reported in Sect. 3.4.

As can be observed, after every evaluation window, the plastic weights are either increased or decreased, based on the observed input rate. This solution also enables a gradual potentiation of synaptic connections that exhibit reduced activity, compared to the synaptic behavior proposed in [4], where the effect of depression is reset immediately in the absence of spikes.

Finally, as the system aims at anomaly detection, we expect the neurons reacting to anomaly-specific patterns to increase their activity when the anomaly occurs. Since this increased activity should not be treated as noise, a stop criterion is needed for the STP weight updates. To this aim, we exploit the classification threshold applied to the output rate for anomaly recognition, th_{class}, assuming that the target is only reached in the presence of a seizure. To account for the impact of STP on the instantaneous output rate of the classification neuron, th_{class} is also updated with the same frequency as the connection weights, according to Eq. 6.

$$th_{class} = th_{class} \cdot (0.35 + 0.65 \cdot \frac{\sum_{i=0}^{C} w_{io}(n+1)}{\sum_{i=0}^{C} w_{io}(n)}) \tag{6}$$

The fundamental steps of the implemented STP update rule are summarized in Algorithm 1.

Algorithm 1: Implemented STP Update Rule

Input: *Synaptic Weights, Classification Threshold, Input Spike Rate, Output Spike Rate*

Result: *Updated Weights w, Updated Threshold th_{class}*

1 w = Pretrained Synaptic Weights;
2 th_{class} = Pretrained Classification Threshold;
3 Eval sum of Weights at previous step, S_{n-1};
4 **while** *Output Spike Rate* $< th_{class}$ **do**
5   **if** $w_i(n-1) > 0$ **then**
6   Evaluate Input Current c_i;
7   **if** $c_i > C_i$ **then**
8   Apply Weight Depression $w_i(n)$;
9   **else**
10   Apply Weight Potentiation $w_i(n)$;
11   Eval sum of Weights at current step, S_n;
12   Update Classification Threshold;

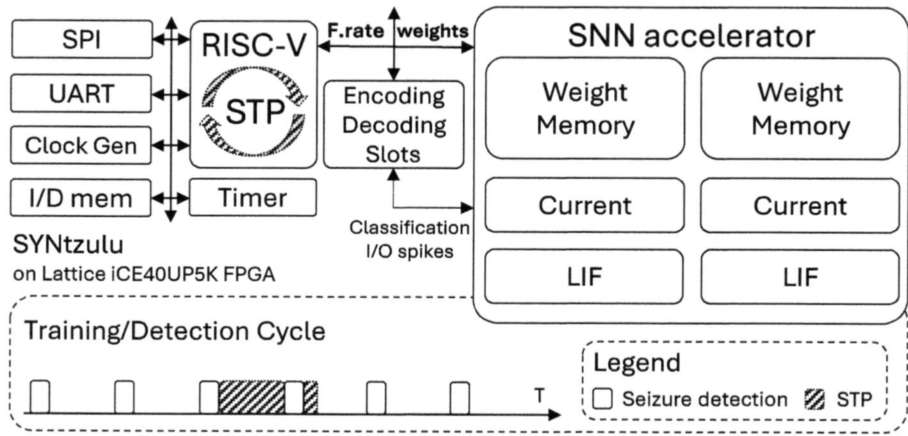

Fig. 2. Target hardware architecture and training/detection cycle overview.

3.3 Target Hardware

The algorithm has been deployed on SYNtzulu [11], an open-source[1] digital neuromorphic architecture optimized for low-cost and low-power FPGAs, such as the Lattice iCE40UP5K. SYNtzulu's architecture includes:

- A dual-core sparsity-aware accelerator of spiking dense layers, in charge of computing neuron input currents due to spike activity and of evaluating neuron dynamics in the SNN, updating the voltages, and applying thresholds. The accelerator goes idle as soon as all spikes are processed, thus maximizing energy efficiency;
- A compact bit-serial RISC-V core[2], responsible for managing input/output data flows, standby mode, and system initialization, such as model loading, at startup;
- Configurable encoding slot, to convert input samples into spikes;
- Configurable decoding slot, to interpret the classification results, e.g., to compute output spike rates.

In this work, we start from the implementation described in [2], already customized to implement the encoding and decoding algorithms of the considered use case. However, we regularly exploit the idle periods in the system, determined by the sparsity of spikes in the application at hand, to compute the STP learning mechanism in real time, leveraging the tiny RISC-V core already included in the architecture. The execution of the STP algorithm requires monitoring the neurons' firing rates and accessing the weight memory. Thus, we extended the hardware design, including eight 12-bit counters accessible by the microprocessor, one for each neuron of the first layer of the SNN model, and we granted the microprocessor write access to the weight memory.

---

[1] https://github.com/gianlucaleone/SYNtzulu.
[2] https://github.com/olofk/serv/.

The choice of deploying the plasticity task on the RISC-V processor is motivated by the need to keep the implementation as lightweight as possible, while ensuring significant flexibility thanks to software-based plasticity definition. As demonstrated by the results observed on the target use-case, weight updates can be evaluated on windows of signal, representing a low-frequency task compared to inference operations. Therefore, hardware acceleration is not strictly necessary, while requiring additional hardware resources, e.g., to support division, as well as additional design effort for any update on the considered plasticity rule. Furthermore, software-based support allows for fully leveraging the computing power of the RISC-V core, already available in the system, while retaining higher precision in intermediate weights representation (32-bit fixed point) than exploited in hardware (8-bit fixed point), thus allowing for accurate and gradual updates.

Figure 2 depicts the interaction between the RISC-V core and the hardware accelerator during STP execution, as well as an illustrative time diagram of the training/detection cycle.

3.4   EEG Seizure Detection Use-Case

For the considered seizure detection use case, we referenced the open-source CHB-MIT Scalp EEG dataset [9,21], curated by the Children's Hospital Boston and the Massachusetts Institute of Technology. The dataset includes a list of scalp EEG records from 23 epileptic patients, acquired with a 256 Hz sampling frequency and reporting a precise annotation of the onset of the occurred seizure events. Based on a typical unobtrusive behind-the-ear acquisition setup for continuous monitoring in everyday life with a wearable system [8,22], we limit the analysis to the signal acquired with the four temporal channels, namely F7-T7, T7-P7, F8-T8, T8-P8, according to the 10–20 international system. The encoding of these signals into 16 one-hot amplitude levels produces the 64 trains of spikes provided as input to the network in Fig. 1.

As seizure detection is commonly addressed as a patient-specific problem [10], we considered a subset of 6 patients and performed a different supervised training for each one. The training and validation set included all but the last seizure records available for the subject, whereas the last seizure record was left out to be included in the test set. To further assess the stability and robustness of the seizure detection, we also included in the test set consecutive non-seizure records, accounting for 5 h of test data per patient on average. This approach ensures a clear separation between the training and test sets, allowing us to evaluate the reliability of raised alarms, as well as the impact of event variability with time for the same subject, and the advantage of an online refinement approach.

The synaptic-specific parameters exploited in the STP update rule, i.e., C_i, D_i, and P_i, were selected with a patient-specific approach, based on the available training examples for the non-seizure data. In detail, the typical current C_i was defined according to Eq. 4, considering the average firing rate observed on the corresponding synapse when processing all the training non-seizure windows learned correctly, i.e., where the output firing rate of the trained model was under 0.05, compared to a training target of 0.03. Finally, the parameters P_i and D_i were selected to ensure that, when r_{io} equals the typical non-seizure rate, Eq. 5 does not produce any changes in the weight value. The values obtained for the considered subjects are reported in Table 1, referring to only the synaptic connections having learned a positive weight during supervised training. The code for model training and STP-based inference has been released as open source[3].

Table 1. STP parameters obtained from training data for the considered subjects. The value of D_i is obtained based on a P_i set to 3.13e-07.

Channel	chb01		chb02		chb03		chb05		chb07		chb08	
	D_i	C_i	D_i	C_i	D_i	C_i	D_i	C_i	D_i	C_i	D_i	C_i
	e-07	e-02	e-07	e-02	e-07	e-02	e-07	e-02	e-07	e-02	e-07	e-02
1	–	–	–	–	684.7	0.7	–	–	–	–	1724.4	0.3
2	9.01	9.1	1045	0.3	54.07	4	–	–	15.1	4.1	–	–
3	6.64	10.3	1024	0.2	–	–	–	–	129.4	1.1	1544	0.2
4	–	–	28.6	4.2	–	–	183.2	0.7	54.88	2	–	–
5	–	–	18.9	5.2	39.5	3.5	3.4	16.4	–	–	1465	0.3
6	7.19	5.7	–	–	10.19	8.3	–	–	–	–	1725	0.2
7	16.4	3.9	36.4	2.1	–	–	–	–	111.3	0.8	567.6	0.5
8	4.77	13.6	–	–	–	–	646.1	0.4	–	–	1288	0.2

4   Experimental Results

This section summarizes the assessment of STP impact on real-time classification and of the achievable on-hardware efficiency.

4.1   Impact on Real-Time Classification Performance

The classification performance is analyzed at the segment level and event level. We consider a segment a window of $T = 4096$ samples, corresponding to 16 s of data, which are processed to compute the output rate and evaluate the classification output. A new classification is produced for each new sample; therefore, the number of evaluated segments matches the number of acquired samples. Event-level metrics refer to the percentage of seizure occurrences detected and to the number of false-positives-per-hour (FP/h) raised, where we consider as a single FP event a sequence of FPs with less than 10 s distance, in alignment with [2]. The reported classification results consider a 20-s pre-ictal tolerance and a 15-min post-ictal tolerance.

As a baseline for the evaluation of the efficacy of STP, we first collected the classification performance of the static model obtained with supervised training, exploiting fixed-weighted synaptic connections to the output neuron [2]. The

---

[3] https://github.com/andem25/STPSNN.

Table 2. Test classification performance with static and STP inference.

| Subject | [2] Static (without STP) | | | | | | STP | | | | | |
| | Segment-level | | | | Event-level | | Segment-level | | | | Event-level | |
	Acc	Sens	Spec	AUC	Sens	FP/h	Acc	Sens	Spec	AUC	Sens	FP/h
chb01	99.9%	84.6%	99.99%	97.5%	100%	0.2	99.9%	82.3%	**100%**	96.5%	100%	**0**
chb02	99.7%	31.6%	99.7%	99.1%	100%	1.17	99.6%	**100%**	99.6%	**99.8%**	100%	**0.3**
chb03	99.9%	60.9%	100%	99.8%	100%	0	99.9%	**70.4%**	100%	99.8%	100%	0
chb05	99.8%	66.1%	100%	99.2%	100%	0	99.5%	20.1%	100%	98.4%	100%	0
chb07	99.8%	67.4%	100%	99.8%	100%	0	**99.9%**	**82%**	100%	98.6%	100%	0
chb08	99.1%	44.8%	99.9%	91.2%	100%	0.4	**99.2%**	**45.2%**	**100%**	**95.1%**	100%	**0**
Average	99.7%	59.9%	99.9%	97.8%	100%	0.2	99.7%	56.2%	99.9%	**98%**	100%	**0.06**

classification threshold for each subject was selected based on the output rate observed on training seizure segments, specifically as the minimum between mode and median, to enable event-level detection. The results are reported in the left half of Table 2. As can be observed, the model enables the detection of all the examined seizure events, reaching an accuracy of over 99% on the data from all considered subjects. Nonetheless, the tests on patients *chb01, chb02* and *chb08* show up to 1.17 FP/h are raised, which may represent an issue for the practical use of the monitoring device.

The same set of tests was repeated after enabling the online update of synaptic weights and classification threshold based on the STP rule described in Sect. 3.2. The results are reported in the right half of Table 2. The most noticeable advantage is the 70% reduction on average of the FP/h obtained on the whole test duration, compared to the static baseline model in [2], up to 0.06 FP/h. This result derives from an improved segment-level specificity in patients *chb01* and *chb08*, and a reduction of the FP events in patient *chb02*. This latter test is especially useful to highlight the advantages of the approach. Figure 3 shows the output rate obtained with static (Fig. 3a) and STP inference (Fig. 3b). At the beginning of the test, the spike patterns excited by the static model cause the output rate to grow and reach the seizure threshold, raising FPs around 2 h before the seizure onset. Synaptic weight plasticity enables us to distinguish these temporary patterns from actual seizure occurrence, thus removing these FPs, while gradual synaptic potentiation allows the seizure neurons to recover their importance and enables seizure detection with an improved segment-level sensitivity. Furthermore, the false alarms raised during STP inference are raised significantly closer to the seizure event, only 13 min before.

From a general perspective, the specificity improvement does not compromise sensitivity, which is increased in subjects *chb02, chb03, chb07,* and *chb08*. The only test where STP inference did not provide any advantages, while reducing both the accuracy and segment-level sensitivity of the classification, is the one on subject *chb05*. Nonetheless, despite a reduced efficacy on this subject's data, STP does not compromise the event-level seizure detection, preserving 100% of event-level seizure detection, and does not introduce any false alarms, demonstrating overall reliability.

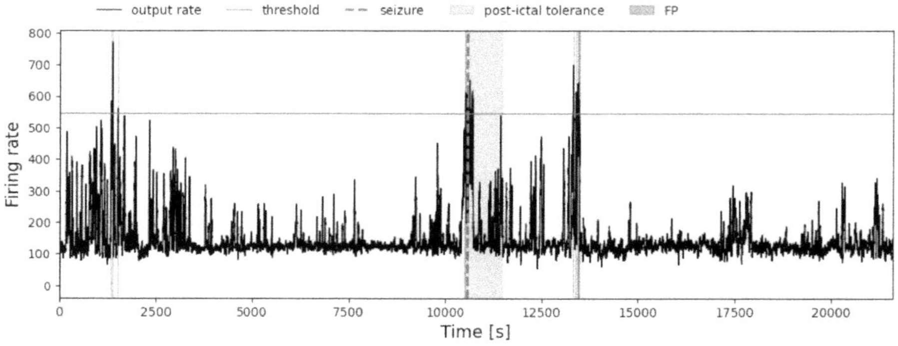

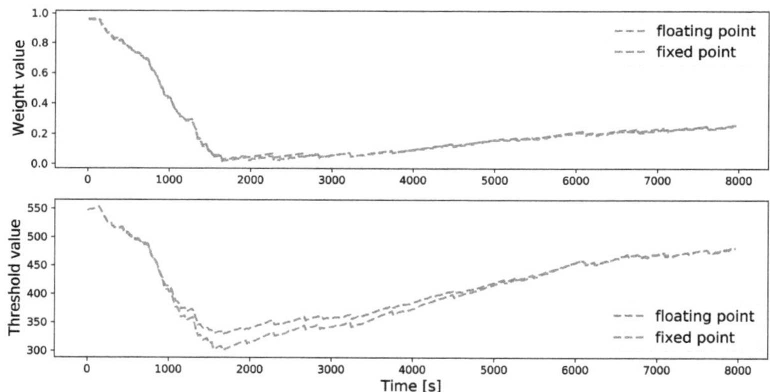

Fig. 3. Output firing rate and classification output with and without STP on test data from subject chb02.

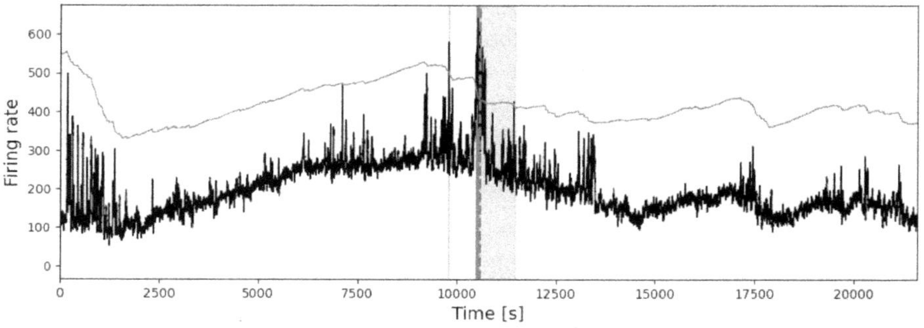

Fig. 4. Weight and classification threshold value over time during STP inference based on floating-point offline simulation and fixed-point execution on hardware.

4.2   Weight Quantization and Integer STP Rule Implementation

To enable efficient inference on the hardware accelerator integrated in SYNtzulu, all synaptic weights were quantized to 8-bit precision. Furthermore, as the targeted RISC-V core only supports integer operations, all STP update rules were implemented with fixed-point integer arithmetic.

To demonstrate the precision of the fixed-point approximation of the STP rule, an example of weight update behavior for one of the seizure weights is reported in the top plot of Fig. 4, which refers to the first 2 h of the test in Fig. 3. To retain sufficient precision, 32-bit fixed-point representation was exploited on the RISC-V processor: the updated weight value is stored until the next iteration for the evaluation of the next STP iteration, while a truncated 8-bit precision weight is offloaded to the local memory on the accelerator. As can be noticed, with this solution, the fixed-point implementation exploited on the RISC-V enables a precise approximation of the corresponding floating-point value, observed in the PyTorch-based simulated behavior, ensuring an accurate update of the weights based on the rule in Eq. 5.

Figure 4 also reports in the bottom plot the history of the classification threshold value obtained with the fixed-point implementation. In this case, the value is only stored in software with 32-bit precision, and the division in Eq. 6 is implemented with the restoring division algorithm. The plot shows a limited approximation error introduced by the fixed-point arithmetic in the system for the instantaneous classification threshold evaluation. Finally, the comparison with the full-precision classification results demonstrates a negligible impact on the system's accuracy.

4.3   Real-Time on-Hardware Efficiency

Real-time classification on SYNtzulu performs as in [2], since the SNN topology and the target hardware hyperparameters (such as the clock frequency and the number of parallel cores) have not been changed. A new inference is executed at every sample time by computing the evolution of the neuron state depending on the new spike activity. Inference computation requires 556 operations (OPS), however, due to an average sparsity of 82.8%, the typical workload running on the target hardware is 96 OPS. At 24 MHz working frequency, the average required inference time is 0.5 μs. Core power consumption during inference execution was directly measured with a Digital Analog Discovery 2 oscilloscope and a 3.3 ±0.033 Ω shunt resistor, resulting in 9.1 mW on average. The required energy per inference is therefore limited to 4.55 nJ. As soon as inference is completed, idle mode is activated; therefore, average power consumption over a sampling period is almost equal to idle power consumption, 0.25 mW, with a negligible impact resulting from STP execution, given the considered update frequency.

The execution of the STP algorithm on the RISC-V, performed once every 4096 samples (i.e., every 16 s), requires 4.23 ms, which exceeds the 3.9 ms sample period at 256 Hz. To address this, we split its computation across two sample times. Specifically, when a new sample arrives, the timer interrupt service routine is triggered, and the new weights computation is temporarily paused. The computation is then completed as soon as the core finishes its housekeeping tasks, effectively applying the weights update one sample period later, as shown in the training/detection cycle at the bottom of Fig. 2. As previously mentioned, the update happens during the idle cycles deriving from SNN sparsity, thus it has no impact on the real-time performance of the classification and a negligible impact on the energy dissipation.

The additional logic required to support STP execution is minimal, i.e., 258 Logic Cells (LCs), 7.9% more than the baseline design in [2], whereas the utilization of other FPGA resources remains unchanged. The overall hardware requirements of the design are shown in Table 3.

Table 3. Hardware Resources on Lattice ICE40UP5K

LC	DSP	BRAM [4 Kb]	SPRAM [256 Kb]	Frequency [MHz]
3529 (66%)	2 (25%)	14 (46%)	4 (100%)	24

5 Discussion

In this section, we evaluate the efficiency of the proposed neuromorphic system against relevant alternatives from the state of the art supporting plasticity mechanisms and implemented on an FPGA. Table 4 lists recent relevant works on this subject. As can be noticed, plasticity integration in neuromorphic FPGA processors has been considered with different objectives, ranging from brain activity simulation to unsupervised training for digit recognition. Based on the targeted use case, hardware design favors a different trade-off between performance maximization and power consumption minimization.

Starting from the work of [24], the proposed BiCoSS System-on-Chip (SOC) was developed as a large-scale cognitive supercomputing system for the real-time emulation of over 4 million neurons supporting STDP plasticity, thanks to the integration of up to 35 Intel EP4CE115 FPGAs, having an average power consumption of 10 W. On a smaller scale, in [1] the authors propose a system emulating context-dependent learning through STDP, exploiting over 34,000 LUTs. Support for plasticity has also been implemented as a solution for on-chip training targeting typical neuromorphic benchmarks, such as MNIST digit recognition [23], reporting 4 W power consumption. However, these solutions can not be easily adapted to the tight resource and power budgets typical of near-sensor processing at the wearable scale, as they generally dedicate different hardware structures for different sub-tasks in the system to increase parallelism.

On the contrary, this work aims at enabling the online model refinement capabilities offered by synaptic plasticity while fully exploiting the inherent efficiency of SNNs on low-end and low-power devices, such as the Lattice iCE40UP5K

Table 4. Comparison to state-of-the-art hardware implementation of online learning for SNNs.

Work	Use-case	Online Learning	Hardware	Frequency	Power	Energy
[24]	cerebellar motor learning	STDP	BiCoSS on Intel EP4CE115	N.R.	10 W	N.R.
[1]	context-dependent learning	STDP	Xilinx Kintex-7 XC7kt160t	143 MHz	1.91 W	N.R.
[23]	MNIST	STDP	Xlinx ZC706	125 MHz	4.4 W	N.R.
[4]	MEA spike detection	STP	Xilinx Kria KR260	585 MHz	0.36 W	N.R.
[14]	speech recognition	STDP	Xilinx ZC706	100 MHz	195 mW*	N.R.
[27]	EEG seizure	STDP	Xilinx ZCU102	100 MHz	–	3.73 µJ/class
this work	EEG seizure	STP	Lattice iCE40UP5K	24 MHz	9.1 mW	4.55 nJ/class

* Do not account for static power and ARM microprocessor power

Table 5. Comparison to state-of-the-art SNNs for seizure detection on the CHB-MIT dataset.

Model	Channels	Acc	Sens	Spec	OPS	Memory
[3]	22	97.1%	94.9%	99.3%	0.32 M	9.9 kB
[27]	23	98%	93.8%	98.64%	N.R.*	N.R.
[12]	2	93.3%	90.4%	96.7%	N.R.	2.4 kB
[6]	2	N.R.	78.7%	76.9%	57 k**	69 kB***
this work	4	99.7%	56.2%	99.9%	529	529 B

* Not Reported; ** Accounting for observed sparsity; *** Estimated from the paper.

FPGA. This is achieved through careful resource reuse on SYNtzulu's lightweight architecture, whose advantages are preserved by deploying the weight and classification threshold update task on the host RISC-V processor. Even compared to the works in the last half of the Table, reporting <1 W average power consumption for speech recognition [14] and real-time action potential and bursts detection [4] through STDP and STP, our work demonstrates the highest energy efficiency. Our approach shows a 20× reduction in power consumption, despite Lattice iCE40UP5K being implemented on 40 nm technology node, while [14] and [4] target 24 and 16 nm chips, respectively. Nonetheless, a considerable portion of power is not accounted for in [14], such as the static power of the FPGA and the overall power of the host ARM Cortex-A9 MPCore microprocessor used for input/output management. Moreover, the SNN accelerator in [4] is a custom implementation tailored to a two-neuron topology. In contrast, our solution accounts for both static and host processor power, while our processor–accelerator co-working strategy can be applied to a wide range of network topologies by simply reconfiguring the accelerator and reprogramming the firmware component. Finally, with respect to [27], which is the only other architecture evaluated on EEG seizure detection, our work shows lower classification energy by almost 3 orders of magnitude. [27] instantiates multiple engines for two-level detection and online learning, thus uses a higher number of resources and requires a bigger FPGA.

To provide a clear context for the evaluation of the performance achieved in the EEG seizure detection use-case, we summarize in Table 5 the state of the art for SNN-based solutions on the CHB-MIT dataset. Among the listed works, only [27] refers to online learning support. As anticipated, the network topology considered as baseline demonstrated competitive seizure detection performance [2], and the results in the previous section highlight the impact of online refinement through STP in false alarms reduction. Despite a reduced segment-level sensitivity, the proposed system ensures the detection of all the examined seizure events. Although referring to different test approaches and data subsets, the performance metrics reported in Table 5 show how the STP-version of the model, exploiting dynamically adapting synapses, reaches classification metrics comparable to the alternatives compatible with unobtrusive acquisition setups [6,12] and those exploiting full-montage setups [3,27]. The considered use case thus provides a meaningful benchmark for the efficiency of the proposed system.

6   Conclusions

In this work, we presented the efficient integration of plasticity support on SYNtzulu's architectural template, focusing on minimal resource overhead. Exploiting hardware/software interactions, we deploy the STP update rule on the host RISC-V processor, enabling online access to the local weight memory and to the newly introduced spike rate monitoring logic. The evaluation of the seizure detection use-case demonstrates an energy efficiency $20\times$ higher than the state-of-the-art alternative reporting the lowest power consumption among FPGA-based plasticity-supporting architectures. Furthermore, the classification performance assessment demonstrates the advantages of online STP in reducing the false-alarm rate of the static state-of-the-art SNN considered as baseline. These results provide a first validation of the efficacy of the proposed system. As future developments, we mean to further assess the impact of online plasticity by exploring additional use-cases, connected to real-time biological signal processing, and learning mechanisms, contributing to solving the issues connected to signal variability in sensor data processing. This further assessment aims at evaluating different accuracy and latency constraints, resulting in the definition of different network topologies, representing an additional benchmark for the proposed architecture.

Acknowledgments. This work was supported in part by the Key Digital Technologies Joint Undertaking (KDT JU) in EdgeAI "Edge AI Technologies for Optimized Performance Embedded Processing" Project under Grant 101097300; in part by European Union's Horizon 2020 Research and Innovation Program under Grant 101140052

(H2TRAIN). Funded by the European Union. Views and opinions expressed are however those of the author(s) only and do not necessarily reflect those of the European Union or the Chips Joint Undertaking. Neither the European Union nor the granting authority can be held responsible for them. We also acknowledge financial support under the National Recovery and Resilience Plan (NRRP), Mission 4 Component 2 Investment 1.5 - Call for tender No.3277 published on December 30, 2021 by the Italian Ministry of University and Research (MUR) funded by the European Union – NextGenerationEU. Project Code ECS0000038 – Project Title eINS Ecosystem of Innovation for Next Generation Sardinia – CUP F53C22000430001- Grant Assignment Decree No. 1056 adopted on June 23, 2022 by the Italian Ministry of University and Research (MUR).

References

1. Asgari, H., Maybodi, B.M.N., Payvand, M., Azghadi, M.R.: Low-energy and fast spiking neural network for context-dependent learning on FPGA. IEEE Trans. Circuits Syst. II Express Briefs **67**(11), 2697–2701 (2020). https://doi.org/10.1109/TCSII.2020.2968588

2. Busia, P., Leone, G., Matticola, A., Raffo, L., Meloni, P.: Wearable epilepsy seizure detection on FPGA with spiking neural networks. IEEE Trans. Biomed. Circuits Syst., 1–11 (2025). https://doi.org/10.1109/TBCAS.2025.3575327

3. Chen, Q., Sun, C., Gao, C., Liu, S.C.: Epilepsy seizure detection and prediction using an approximate spiking convolutional transformer. In: 2024 IEEE International Symposium on Circuits and Systems (ISCAS), pp. 1–5 (2024). https://doi.org/10.1109/ISCAS58744.2024.10558341

4. Cheslet, J., et al.: FPGA implementation of a spiking neural network for real-time action potential and burst detection. In: 2023 IEEE Biomedical Circuits and Systems Conference (BioCAS), pp. 1–5 (2023). https://doi.org/10.1109/BioCAS58349.2023.10388622

5. Emami, A., Kunii, N., Matsuo, T., Shinozaki, T., Kawai, K., Takahashi, H.: Autoencoding of long-term scalp electroencephalogram to detect epileptic seizure for diagnosis support system. Comput. Biol. Med. **110**, 227–233 (2019). https://doi.org/10.1016/j.compbiomed.2019.05.025, https://www.sciencedirect.com/science/article/pii/S0010482519301933

6. Erickson, X., Bastani, S., Aminifar, A.: Personalized seizure detection using spiking neural networks. In: 2023 IEEE International Conference on Omni-layer Intelligent Systems (COINS), pp. 1–6 (2023). https://doi.org/10.1109/COINS57856.2023.10189269

7. Eshraghian, J.K., et al.: Training spiking neural networks using lessons from deep learning. Proc. IEEE **111**(9), 1016–1054 (2023)

8. Frey, S., et al.: GAPSES: versatile smart glasses for comfortable and fully-dry acquisition and parallel ultra-low-power processing of EEG and EOG. IEEE Trans. Biomed. Circuits Syst. 1–11 (2024). https://doi.org/10.1109/TBCAS.2024.3478798

9. Goldberger, A.L., et al.: Physiobank, physiotoolkit, and physionet: components of a new research resource for complex physiologic signals. Circulation **101**, e215–e220 (2000)

10. Ingolfsson, T.M., et al.: Towards long-term non-invasive monitoring for epilepsy via wearable EEG devices. In: 2021 IEEE Biomedical Circuits and Systems Conference (BioCAS), pp. 01–04 (2021). https://doi.org/10.1109/BioCAS49922.2021.9644949

11. Leone, G., Antonio Scrugli, M., Badas, L., Martis, L., Raffo, L., Meloni, P.: Syntzulu: a tiny RISC-v-controlled SNN processor for real-time sensor data analysis on low-power FPGAs. IEEE Trans. Circuits Syst. I Regul. Pap. **72**(2), 790–801 (2025). https://doi.org/10.1109/TCSI.2024.3450966
12. Li, R., et al.: Real-time sub-milliwatt epilepsy detection implemented on a spiking neural network edge inference processor. Comput. Biol. Med. **183**, 109225 (2024)
13. Liu, S., et al.: An area- and energy-efficient spiking neural network with spike-time-dependent plasticity realized with SRAM processing-in-memory macro and on-chip unsupervised learning. IEEE Trans. Biomed. Circuits Syst. **17**(1), 92–104 (2023). https://doi.org/10.1109/TBCAS.2023.3242413
14. Liu, Y., Yenamachintala, S.S., Li, P.: Energy-efficient FPGA spiking neural accelerators with supervised and unsupervised spike-timing-dependent-plasticity. J. Emerg. Technol. Comput. Syst. **15**(3) (2019). https://doi.org/10.1145/3313866
15. Martis, L., Leone, G., Raffo, L., Meloni, P.: Low-power fpga-based spiking neural networks for real-time decoding of intracortical neural activity. IEEE Sens. J. **24**(24), 42448–42459 (2024). https://doi.org/10.1109/JSEN.2024.3487021
16. Moraitis, T., Sebastian, A., Eleftheriou, E.: The role of short-term plasticity in neuromorphic learning: Learning from the timing of rate-varying events with fatiguing spike-timing-dependent plasticity. IEEE Nanatechnol. Mag. **12**(3), 45–53 (2018). https://doi.org/10.1109/MNANO.2018.2845479
17. Naderi, R., Rezaei, A., Amiri, M., Peremans, H.: Unsupervised post-training learning in spiking neural networks. Sci. Rep. **15**, 17647 (2025). https://doi.org/10.1038/s41598-025-01749-x
18. Orchard, G., et al.: Efficient neuromorphic signal processing with loihi 2. In: 2021 IEEE Workshop on Signal Processing Systems (SiPS), pp. 254–259. IEEE (2021)
19. Scrugli, M.A., Leone, G., Busia, P., Raffo, L., Meloni, P.: All-spiking ECG analysis for arrhythmia classification on low-power FPGA. IEEE Sensors J. 1–1 (2026). https://doi.org/10.1109/JSEN.2026.3663715
20. Shahbazinia, A., Ponzina, F., Miranda, J.A., Dan, J., Ansaloni, G., Atienza, D.: Resource-efficient continual learning for personalized online seizure detection. In: 2024 46th Annual International Conference of the IEEE Engineering in Medicine and Biology Society (EMBC), pp. 1–7 (2024). https://doi.org/10.1109/EMBC53108.2024.10781699
21. Shoeb, A.H.: Application of machine learning to epileptic seizure onset detection and treatment. Ph.D. dissertation, MIT (2009)
22. Sopic, D., Aminifar, A., Atienza, D.: e-glass: a wearable system for real-time detection of epileptic seizures. In: 2018 IEEE International Symposium on Circuits and Systems (ISCAS), pp. 1–5 (2018). https://doi.org/10.1109/ISCAS.2018.8351728
23. Vallejo-Mancero, B., Madrenas, J., Zapata, M.: Real-time execution of SNN models with synaptic plasticity for handwritten digit recognition on simd hardware. Front. Neurosci. **18** (2024). https://doi.org/10.3389/fnins.2024.1425861, https://www.frontiersin.org/journals/neuroscience/articles/10.3389/fnins.2024.1425861
24. Yang, S., et al.: Bicoss: toward large-scale cognition brain with multigranular neuromorphic architecture. IEEE Trans. Neural Netw. Learn. Syst. **33**(7), 2801–2815 (2022). https://doi.org/10.1109/TNNLS.2020.3045492
25. You, S., Hwan Cho, B., Shon, Y.M., Seo, D.W., Kim, I.Y.: Semi-supervised automatic seizure detection using personalized anomaly detecting variational autoencoder with behind-the-ear EEG. Comput. Methods Programs Biomed. **213**, 106542 (2022). https://doi.org/10.1016/j.cmpb.2021.106542, https://www.sciencedirect.com/science/article/pii/S0169260721006167

26. İlkay Yıldız, Garner, R., Lai, M., Duncan, D.: Unsupervised seizure identification on EEG. Comput. Methods Programs Biomed. **215**, 106604 (2022). https://doi.org/10.1016/j.cmpb.2021.106604, https://www.sciencedirect.com/science/article/pii/S0169260721006787
27. Zhang, Q., Cui, M., Liu, Y., Chen, W., Yu, Z.: Low-power and low-cost ai processor with distributed-aggregated classification architecture for wearable epilepsy seizure detection. IEEE Trans. Biomed. Circuits Syst. **19**(1), 28–39 (2025). https://doi.org/10.1109/TBCAS.2024.3450896

Optimizing FPGA-Based Neural Network Ensemble

Bowen P. Y. Kwan[(✉)][iD], Ce Guo[iD], and Wayne Luk[iD]

Department of Computing, Imperial College London, SW7 2AZ London, UK
{pyk12,c.guo,w.luk}@imperial.ac.uk

Abstract. This paper introduces a novel divide-and-conquer approach to optimize a neural network ensemble. The approach would optimize the available resources to implement multiple neural networks in the ensemble. Three algorithms are proposed to explore the structure of neural networks and to estimate the optimal parallelism configuration for an ensemble; they provide a configuration design guide to facilitate the study of trade-offs between resource usage and run time. Our approach also supports variable widths of input data, further improving the diversity of the ensemble. The proposed approach shows promise in the evaluation against related work and baseline implementations, especially when used to process input data streams, with the ensemble utilizing the available resources to achieve 33 times speed up with 10% increase in accuracy over its members, and 5% improvement in speed and 2% in accuracy compared to the best performing single network. The FPGA implementation of a 3-bit ensemble is 23.49 times faster than the CPU implementation.

Keywords: Neural network ensemble · FPGA · Ensemble optimization

1 Introduction

Artificial Intelligence (AI) has become a popular and powerful tool, providing a convenient solution to many real-life scenarios, including GPT4 [1] for text generation, Generative Adversarial Networks (GAN) for video generation [2], and Vision Large Language Models (VLLMs) for image captioning [3]. The complexity of neural networks has increased drastically to achieve the desired functionality and accuracy; for example, GPT4 has 1.8 trillion parameters. Training and deployment of such a massive system is expensive and is not always affordable, especially for small businesses and individuals.

Recent research shows that an ensemble of weak learners [4] can significantly reduce the size of a network while improving accuracy compared to a deep and massive model. This type of improvement is also observed in ensembles for multimodal learning [5] and multi-class classification [6], with different networks in the ensemble focusing on different modes or classes.

© The Author(s), under exclusive license to Springer Nature Switzerland AG 2026
G. Leone et al. (Eds.): ARC 2026, LNCS 16514, pp. 172–188, 2026.
https://doi.org/10.1007/978-3-032-29365-7_11

Although extensive research has covered ensemble structure, network selection, and training strategies, network configuration is still a rarely explored topic, hindering the full potential of ensemble deployment.

The key challenge in determining the ensemble configuration of the neural networks is co-optimizing different neural networks, as design decision for one network could affect other networks. With such a rippling effect, it is not trivial to find out how each decision affects the overall performance of the ensemble. It cannot be seen as a simple divide-and-conquer problem in which each network is optimized independently and sequentially. All neural networks in the ensemble must be optimized at the same time, increasing the complexity of the problem.

To address the dependency among the ensemble members during optimization, all networks are iteratively optimized at the same time. For heterogeneous ensembles, in each optimization step, one component of the slowest network would be accelerated. This guaranties that the latency bottleneck of the ensemble is being treated in every optimization step to ensure resources are not wasted. The optimization procedure terminates when the target latency is met or when no more resources are available for further acceleration. Each network is optimized individually and independently to reduce the complexity, while the dependency between different networks is addressed by the choice of network to accelerate and the available resource in each optimization step.

For homogeneous ensembles, since they consist of identical members with the same structure (including the number and types of layers and precision used, but not the value of the weights and bias), the critical paths of the networks are the same. Optimizing an ensemble with k networks can be further simplified as optimizing one neural network with $1/k$ times resource available. The optimization of a homogeneous ensemble is transformed as a single-network optimization with a tighter bound on resources.

The key novelty of this paper is simplifying the ensemble optimization problem by transforming it into multiple single network optimizations with extra constraints, allowing the use of divide-and-conquer to reduce complexity. Three algorithms are introduced to explore the structure of neural network and estimate the optimal parallelism configuration for the ensemble, providing a configuration design guideline. The effects of having different network architectures and precisions on ensemble performance are illustrated using a real-life financial trading application implemented using FINN [7,8].

The major contributions are:

1. Three algorithms for different cases exploring the neural network structure and estimate the optimal parallelism configuration for the ensemble (Sect. 3)
2. Illustration of the effect of different design choices on ensemble performance for real-life financial trading applications (Sect. 4)
3. Evaluation of the ensemble configuration determination algorithm (Sect. 5)

2   Related Work

Different research has been done with ensemble learning to boost the accuracy of neural networks. A hierarchical approach to selecting and combining desirable member networks from a pool of candidates is discussed in [9]. However, little discussion is conducted on the trade off among resource usage, latency, tree retained, and accuracy. There is no clear guide on how to select the parameters.

Investigation has been done in searching for the optimal number of members in an ensemble to improve prediction accuracy [10]. Each member of the ensemble is trained with a specific state and is used only for the same state during inference. However, since this method separates the input space and handles each partition with a different member network, it cannot take advantage of the boosting effect of the ensemble to improve the reliability of the individual network.

The number of layers used for each member of the ensemble is being investigated to improve the reliability of neural networks with the trade off among accuracy, resource usage, and execution time [11]. All of the members have the same level of parallelism, making the overall execution time lower bounded by the slowest member. From the experimental result, the ensemble may even be slower than the slowest member when the number of members increases, as more processing is required to combine the increasing number of individual network result.

Partial reconfiguration technique is also used to improve the implementation of neural network ensemble [12]. Some members would first be implemented on the hardware. Once the computation of the particular member is done, it would be reconfigured to be the next member, this process repeats until every member is executed. With run-time partial reconfiguration in place, it relaxes the restriction of resource usage on the individual members. However, this approach traded off time for resources. It would not be suitable for any dataflow application, especially those requiring high frequency and low latency. [13] discusses the feasibility of a similar approach to explore partial reconfigurability to map a variety of neural networks on the same hardware. [14] explores adaptive switching between shallow and deep networks to reach the highest throughput on a resource-constrained system with CPU and FPGA.

3   Proposed Algorithms

To reduce the latency of the ensemble, parallelism is a common technique used in FPGA implementation. Effective exploration of the trade off between latency and resource is a key factor in deciding where and how much parallelism is applied in the system.

The novelty of this work is to determine the optimal configuration for each member network in the ensemble given their pre-defined structures. In the scope of this paper, only ensembles that can fit entirely on the target FPGA are being discussed.

3.1   Determining the Unfolding Factor of Network Component

Unfolding is a common technique for increasing parallelism, where exact copies of the same hardware are instantiated to allow parallel computation. Any functional block in the network, including convolution (conv), matrix multiplication (fully connected layer, FC), max pooling, etc., can be unfolded to allow parallel computation. Each block is considered a component. The goal of the algorithm is to determine the optimal configuration of the ensemble, i.e. the unfolding factor of every component in every network.

Apart from instantiating more copies, parallelism can be achieved by employing the Single Instruction Multiple Data (SIMD) approach. SIMD is a parallel processing approach that allows a single instruction to operate on multiple data elements simultaneously.

In this paper, we denote PE as the number of processing elements (PE) used, i.e. the number of copies instantiated, and $SIMD$ for the number of SIMD lanes within the PE. The overall unfolding factor of a particular component would be its $PE * SIMD$. In general, increasing PE and $SIMD$ has the same effect in reducing latency, as the latency with parallelism is defined as follows.

$$\text{new latency} = \frac{\text{latency}}{PE * SIMD} \tag{1}$$

In order to minimize the idle time of the hardware and additional control, it is assumed that the dimension of the input of the component is divisible by the unfolding factor. In this case, all unfolded components would be active all the time and finish processing the input at the same time, utilizing the resources with no extra control needed to take care of buffering.

The algorithm determining the next available unfolding is shown in Algorithm 1. In order not to store all the possible folding combinations of every component, the folding is dynamically explored on the fly. A 4-element tuple is used to notate the folding pair, [SIMD unfolding, PE unfolding, Speedup, Resource usage]. Speed up is the multiple of the PE and SIMD unfolding, and resource usage is calculated as the weighted sum of PE and SIMD usage.

For each component, an array is used to store a set of candidates. The array is initialized with elements having every feasible SIMD unfolding and no PE unfolding. The elements are arranged in ascending order of resource, minimizing the chance of going over the resource limit.

At each iteration, the first element of the array is chosen as the current candidate, and used to check against subsequent elements until the first element with larger speed up is found. All elements before that would be removed from the array, and updated with their respective next available PE unfolding before being added back to the array in ascending resource usage order. If there is a tie in resource usage, the tuple with higher speed up would be prioritized and placed closer to the head of the array to reduce redundant checking of the unfolding.

This method of exploring can ensure every possible unfolding would be checked, while not having to fully explore them at the start, which may lead to a huge memory footprint. This algorithm would also prioritize using components and unfolding with the least resource consumption.

Algorithm 1. Get Next Unfolding

Input:

$PE[\ ]$	Sorted array of feasible PE unfolding
$SIMD[\ ]$	Sorted array of feasible SIMD unfolding
Res_{PE}	Average resource usage per PE
Res_{SIMD}	Average resource usage per SIMD
$C[\ ]$	Array of unfolding candidates
$bits$	Data bit width

Output:

Next unfolding	Chosen unfolding candidate
Fully Unfolded	Indicate the component is fully unfolded

1: Unfolding $\leftarrow C[0][2]$
2: Next unfolding $\leftarrow C[0]$
3: **repeat**
4:    Remove $C[i]$ from $C[\ ]$
5:    $PE' \leftarrow PE[C[i][1]+1]$
6:    $C'[i] \leftarrow [C[i][0], PE', C[i][0] * PE', \text{Res}_{SIMD} * C[i][0] + \text{Res}_{PE} * PE']$
7:    Add updated $C'[i]$ to $C[\ ]$ in ascending resource usage, if tied on resource, add
         to descending speed up
8: **until** unfolding of $C[i] >$ Unfolding
9: **if** Unfolding$> min(PE[\text{last}]*SIMD[\text{last}],$max bit size of 1 component$/bits)$ **then**
10:    Fully Unfolded $\leftarrow 1$
11: **end if**
12: **return** Next unfolding, $C[\ ]$, Fully Unfolded

3.2   Estimating the Optimal Configuration for Ensembles

For a heterogeneous ensemble, every network in the ensemble is different. The overall execution time for the heterogeneous ensemble is determined by the slowest network in the ensemble. Equally distributing the resources to every network would not be the most sensible way to allocate resources, as the speed up gained from individual networks would be wasted as all of the networks need to wait for the slowest one to finish. Applying the same unfolding to every network would also not be ideal for the same reason.

Algorithm 2 shows the algorithm to explore the optimal configuration for a heterogeneous ensemble. Each network is initialized with no unfolding ($PE = SIMD = 1$) for all components, as it consumes the least resources and the longest latency. At each optimization step, only the slowest network would be accelerated using the next unfolding with the least resource usage, minimizing the chance of exceeding the resource limit and avoiding missing any potential optimal configuration. This also ensures that the bottleneck of the ensemble is being speeded up every step, making sure that any extra resources used would improve the overall latency of the ensemble. The optimization process is repeated until the target latency is met or there is no further acceleration available.

Homogeneous ensembles can be considered as a special case, as the critical path, latency, and resource usage would be the same for every member network.

Algorithm 2. Estimating the Optimal Configuration for Heterogeneous Neural Network Ensemble

1: **repeat**
2:     **for** the slowest network i **do**
3:         **for all** component **do**
4:             **if** not fully unfolded **then**
5:                 Get next unfolding
6:             **end if**
7:         **end for**
8:         **if** new resource used $\leq$ total resource **then**
9:             Apply the next unfolding with least resource usage
10:        **else**
11:            no further acceleration available
12:        **end if**
13:    **end for**
14: **until** desired target latency is met **or** no further acceleration available

---

Algorithm 3. Estimating the Optimal Configuration for Homogeneous Neural Network Ensemble with k members

1: **repeat**
2:     **for all** component **do**
3:         **if** not fully unfolded **then**
4:             Get next unfolding
5:         **end if**
6:     **end for**
7:     **if** new resource used $<$ total resource$/k$ **then**
8:         Apply the next unfolding with the least resource usage
9:     **end if**
10: **until** desired target latency is met **or** no further acceleration available

---

The algorithm can be simplified to optimize a single network with $1/k$ times the available resources, as seen in Algorithm 3.

3.3   Evaluation of Get Next Unfolding Algorithm

A simple example is shown here to demonstrate the effectiveness and benefit of using the Get Next Unfolding Algorithm.

A matrix vector multiplication with matrix size 64x600 in FINN is taken as an example, with PE array being factors of 64 (7 in total) and SIMD array being factors of 600 (24 in total). There are a total of 168 different possible PE-SIMD configurations available. The black crosses in Fig. 1a represent all possible configurations, with the red * on the top left being the base case with no unfolding, i.e. PE = SIMD = 1. Resource usage and latency are based on the linear estimation values of the mathematical model as stated in line 6 of Algorithm 1,

$$Resource = PE * Res_{PE} + SIMD * Res_{SIMD} \tag{2}$$

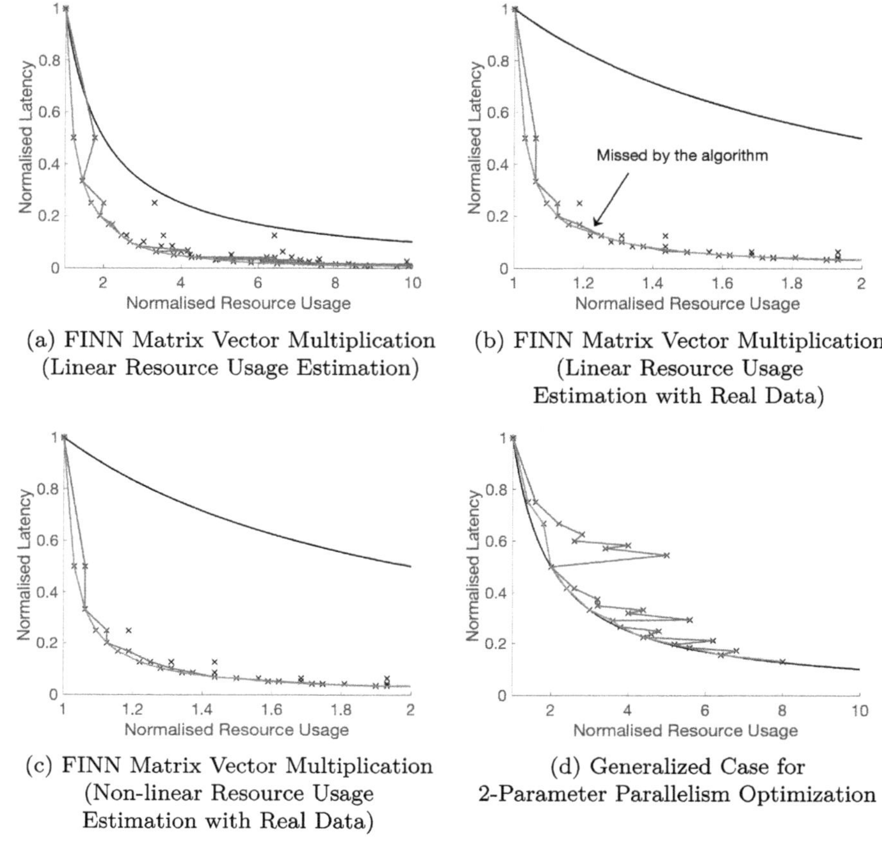

(a) FINN Matrix Vector Multiplication (Linear Resource Usage Estimation)

(b) FINN Matrix Vector Multiplication (Linear Resource Usage Estimation with Real Data)

(c) FINN Matrix Vector Multiplication (Non-linear Resource Usage Estimation with Real Data)

(d) Generalized Case for 2-Parameter Parallelism Optimization

Fig. 1. Search Frontier for Get Next Unfolding Algorithm. (Color figure online)

The black line shows latency * resource $=1$, which means n times increases in resource leading to n times speed up in latency. Usually designs would be above the line, as doubling the resource would seldom translate directly into reducing the latency by half, due to various reasons such as design overhead, extra control/ management unit, and additional communication among the modules. It is very rarely achieved that the designs are below the black line, showing more speed up than expected given the resource usage. However, in the case for FINN, as there is a relatively large overhead in setting up the Matrix Vector Multiplication, the increases in resources due to unfolding are comparatively small, and hence most of the candidate designs are below the line. In general, configurations towards the bottom left corner are more desirable, as it means they achieve more speed up with fewer resources.

The blue line in Fig. 1a shows that search path when resource usage is not taken into consideration. Although the designs are explored in order of ascending speed up, designs of the same overall speed up are accessed in the order of the node generation, i.e. the order of when the node is added to the candidate list. Since resource usage is not taken into account, nodes with same overall speed up would be discarded after the first one has been evaluated. This reduces the total configuration to check from 168 to 60, however, there is no guarantee that the node being examined would be the one with the best speed up to resource usage ratio.

On the contrary, when resource usage is taken into account, it can be seen from the red line in Fig. 1a, the search path is always on the left-most configuration, ensuring the next unfolding with the best possible ratio. The reason for line 7 in Algorithm 1 to add the node to the list with ascending resource usage is to ensure the left-most node is always explored first. Having the speed up to be added in descending order when tied on resource usage is to explore the node with better speed up to resource usage ratio first, so that the node with less speed up would be immediately discarded in the next iteration, reducing search time and space. With this algorithm, the number of configuration to check is further reduced to 44, which is a quarter of the original search space of configuration, while always ensuring to search the frontier with the best possible ratio. In actual implementation, every component in the system is expected to have more feasible PE and SIMD unfolding, which exponentially increases the search space. With the proposed algorithm, the search space can be greatly reduced to only frontier with the best ratio from every component, reducing the search complexity while improving the search space exploration efficiency.

Figure 1b shows our linear estimation search path with FINN resource estimation from compilation. Although the red line still closely approaches the search frontier of the FINN compilation data, there are some points that are missed by the proposed algorithm. This is due to the inaccuracy of the linear resource estimation.

To further improve the mathematical model, a non-linear estimation is used, as shown in Fig. 1c. Instead of simply having the linear estimation as stated in Eq. 2, the updated resource estimation is as follows,

$$\begin{aligned}
Resource = &Overhead + PE * SIMD * Res_{PE,SIMD} \\
&+ PE * Res_{PE} + SIMD * Res_{SIMD}
\end{aligned} \tag{3}$$

With the addition of the overhead term and non-linear PE*SIMD term, the estimation of the mathematical model is much closer to the FINN estimation from compilation. The red line in Fig. 1c would always ensuring the frontier with the best possible ratio is searched.

The proposed algorithm can be generalized for any 2-parameter parallelism optimization for speed up, assuming each accelerator is responsible for a certain part of the program. The two accelerators can replace SIMD and PE respectively in the algorithm, and the resource usage computation would remain the same.

Figure 1d shows all the possible parallelism combinations for A and B, with accelerator A and B each having their own cost for parallelism, and would accelerate different parts of the program. With a more realistic cost to unroll the two accelerators, all the candidates are now above the black line. The search frontier provided by the proposed algorithm is able to capture all the design closet to the line, yielding the best possible latency to resource usage ratio. Similar to the FINN case, only one-third of the nodes are being visited.

As seen from the 2 examples, the proposed algorithm can guide the exploration of search space towards the best possible latency to resource usage ratio, providing an efficient way to determine the desired unfolding configuration.

3.4   Evaluation of Ensemble Algorithms

Although homogeneous and heterogeneous algorithms share many similarities, the heterogeneous ensemble cannot simply be seen as a larger model for optimization. In the homogeneous case, the slowest component is always the bottleneck and in the critical path of the network, thus speeding up the slowest module would definitely improve the overall latency. However, the same cannot be said for the heterogeneous case. Consider an ensemble with two networks, A and B, each having 3 components, with latency A1=4, A2=5, A3=6, B1=7, B2=1, B3=1. The overall latency for A would be 4+5+6=15, while B=7+1+1=9. The latency of the ensemble would be 15 as it is limited by network A. To improve the overall latency, one of the components in A should be speeded up next. However, this cannot be guaranteed if the ensemble is simply treated as a larger network. The key of the heterogeneous algorithm is that it is always working on the critical path of the member network, and since the critical path of the ensemble is the critical path of the slowest network, each optimization step would be acting on the critical path of the ensemble, hence improving the overall latency.

4   Application

The target application is to determine the appropriate action (buy or sell) given the market data. Market information is compiled into images, and then processed by CNN, and finally results in a binary buy or sell decision. The order book data are obtained from an online limit order data tool, LOBSTER [15]. NASDAQ Data of 5 companies are chosen for the test, including Apple (AAPL), Alphabet (GOOG), Amazon (AMZN), Intel (INTC), and Microsoft (MSFT). Each of the stocks would be referred to as a financial instrument.

As the PYNQ board available for the FINN implementation is a small board with limited resources, the CNNs used in this section are simple CNNs with VGG16-like architecture, consisting of a minimum number of convolution, ReLU, max pooling, dropout, and linear layers. The key point for this section is to explore how different structures would affect design choices and provide a design guideline when using FINN, instead of aiming to obtain the most accurate neural network to make trading decisions.

A maximum folded design is used as the base case, with no parallelism applied at all. The latency and resource usage are treated as the base case reference to investigate the effect of parallelism. Each neural network is implemented by FINN separately and compiled into individual IPs. The IPs are then combined and connected to form the ensemble.

Table 1. Test case set up

Input Size	7x7
Height	7 levels of the order book
Width	7 features
Channel	N/A
Remarks	Each image represents a particular time instance of the order book data

(a) Details of the dimension

Input
7(H)x7(W)x1(C)
conv3-16
conv3-32
2x2 max pool
conv3-64
2x2 max pool
FC-15
FC-1

(b) CNN structure

4.1 Test Case Set Up

A test case is set up to investigate the behavior of the optimal configuration under different input sizes. The details of each case are shown in Table 1a, and the corresponding CNN structure is shown in Table 1b. Due to the constraint of FINN, the height and width of the image must be equal.

4.2 Software Testing

In this section, the accuracy of the neural networks is compared for different bit widths used. The results of different test cases would also be explored to identify the best potential candidate for data and network structure.

All neural networks are trained with 50 images and 100 epochs using brevitas to investigate the effect of varying bit width on accuracy. Input data, weights, and activation of neural networks are set to have the same bit width to reduce complexity and design space. 32-bit floating point number is used as the full precision counterpart, providing a reference for the quantized CNN to compare against. The data set is split into 80% for training and 20% for testing.

Figure 2a shows the accuracy of the test case. As expected, the float point implementation achieved the highest accuracy slightly over 92%. With 8 or more bits used, the accuracy of the quantized CNN is similar to the floating point accuracy. There is a slight drop in accuracy when 3 and 6 bits are used, giving an accuracy of around 90%.

A similar trend can be found for training loss, as shown in Fig. 2b. CNNs with 8 or more bits used have a performance comparable to the floating point representation, achieving around 0.27 training loss. CNN with 3 and 6 bits has slightly worse performance, with a training loss of around 0.35 and 0.3.

When fewer than 3 bits are used, the accuracy fluctuates around 50%, indicating insufficient bits are used for the neural network to learn from the data.

4.3 Hardware Testing

In this section, the relation between bit width and resource usage is explored to determine the best available configuration of the network.

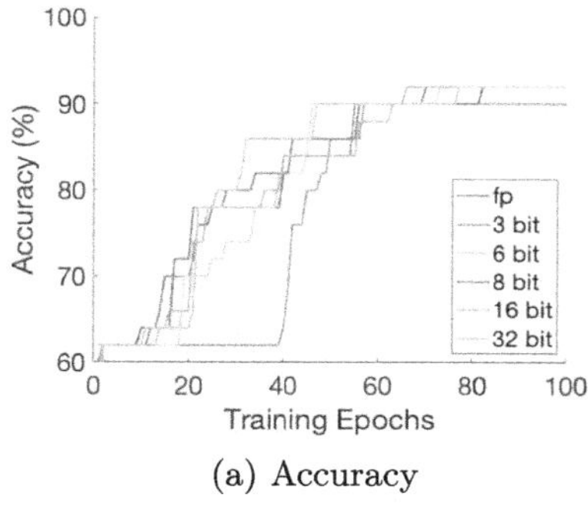

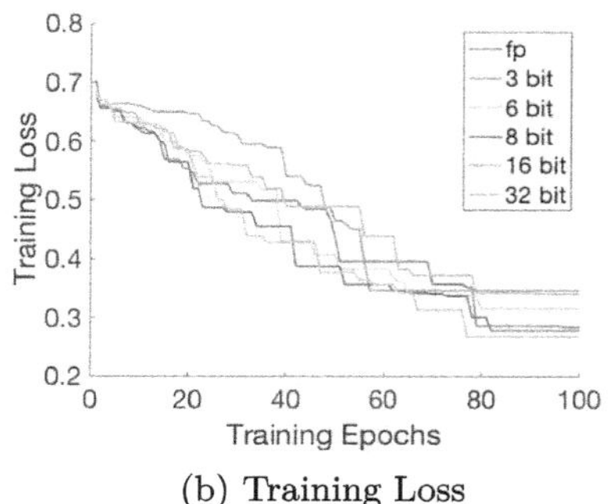

(a) Accuracy   (b) Training Loss

Fig. 2. Software testing result of the test case.

Table 2. Hardware testing result for the test case

	3-bit	6-bit	8bit
Normalized Latency	0.95	0.96	1
Normalized LUT	1	2.44	3.23
Normalized BRAM	1	1.48	1.40

The FINN implementation workflow [7,8] is used in this paper. The network is first transformed into an ONNX image, then FINN compiler builds the hardware based on the image. The hardware is implemented on the PYNQ Z1 board (Zynq 7000 SoC XC7Z020) due to its compatibility with FINN.

From the software testing results, using more than 8 bits does not significantly improve accuracy. Further increasing the bit width would only lead to an increase in resource usage and latency, with no extra benefit. Hardware build would only be done for 3-bit, 6-bit, and 8-bit implementation.

Table 2 shows the normalized latency and resource usage for the case. Latency is normalized with 8-bit to show the speed up, while LUT and BRAM are normalized with 3-bit to show the increase in resource usage.

As FINN imposes a size limit on individual components, with higher bit width and larger systems, it is more likely to reach the limit and restrict the available parallelism. Since the test case is small, only a few components come close to the size limit. Most of the layer can still be fully unfolded for the 3 implementations, leading to only a small reduction in normalized latency of about 4% and 5% for the 6-bit and 8-bit implementations.

As no DSP is used for convolutions and multiplications for 3-bit, 6-bit, and 8-bit implementations, LUT and BRAM are the major resources used.

For LUT, 6-bit design on average used around twice the resource compared to the 3-bit design, while the 8-bit design used triple the resources. This goes roughly in line with the ratio of the number of bits used.

For BRAM, the 8-bit implementation used around 40% more BRAM than the 3-bit implementation. This falls in line with the expectation that 3-bit data does not utilize all the space in BRAM, while 8-bit data fits perfectly in the standard BRAM structure. Also, comparatively less unfolding is done on 8-bit design toward the later layers when size increases, there is less of a growth in BRAM usage for the 8-bit implementation. The 6-bit implementation uses even more BRAM than the 8-bit design. This can be explained by the inefficiency in storing 6-bit data while having more unfolding.

4.4   Ensemble Configuration Determination

To determine the configuration of the ensemble, the network structure and its precision are the first design choices to make. According to the software testing result, the 8-bit implementation is already as good as the full precision counterpart. Selecting a precision of more than 8 bits would only increase resource usage without improving accuracy.

The next design choice to be made is the ensemble structure, i.e. determining having a heterogeneous or homogeneous ensemble, and the number of members. Upon further testing, an ensemble of 3 3-bit and an ensemble of 3 6-bit both restored the accuracy to around 92%, which is comparable to the full precision. As the 3-bit design would use much fewer resources while allowing a high unfolding factor, the 3-bit implementation is chosen over the 6-bit design. A homogeneous ensemble design is chosen over a heterogeneous ensemble, as for the target application, the 3-bit implementation shows the best accuracy and latency-to-resource ratio.

The last step is to determine the unfolding factor of each layer, which is done using the proposed algorithm with the baseline latency and resource usage obtained by the compilation of the 3-bit implementation with maximum folding.

The optimal configuration of the network yields a latency of 127720ns, with 51 BRAM and 15149 LUT used. With the three optimal networks, the integrated ensemble uses around 60% of BRAM, and 90% of LUT available on the PYNQ Z1 board, achieving 33 times speed up compared to the base case with no unfolding. The ensemble achieved 10% improvement in accuracy over its members.

5   Discussion

5.1   Limitation and Adaptability of the Algorithms

This method serves as a good estimate of the parallelism to be applied to the ensemble. However, the actual performance for implementation may differ slightly, as the scaling of resource usage in actual deployment is not always strictly linear to the parallelism applied. When resource utilization is high, the theoretically feasible configuration might not be implementable due to the difficulty in place and route. A simple workaround would be to slightly reduce the available resources to reserve some buffer.

One way to further improve the estimation of the algorithms is by applying a more sophisticated algorithm than simply latency-to-resource ratio in deciding

Table 3. Comparison of ensemble learning methods

Design	[10]	[11]	This paper
Key Idea	Determining the optimal number of members and their respective structures	Determining the optimal structure used for individual members	Determining the optimal configuration of the members given their structure
Targeted device	Virtex-7 XC7V2000tflg1925-1	Zynq 7000 SoC XC7Z7045	Zynq 7000 SoC XC7Z020
Test case	11 benchmarks from Polybench, CHStone and MachSuite	CIFAR-10	Test case in section IV
Base case structure	1. Linear Model 2. 1 decision tree model (1-avg)	ResNet 110	1. A fully unfolded 8-bit network 2. A fully unfolded 32-bit network
Ensemble member	Decision Tree models	ResNet 20, ResNet 32, ResNet 44, ResNet 56	3-bit CNN
Number of member network used	21-53	3-4	3
Improvement over base case			
-Accuracy	Linear case, MAE reduced from 10.75%-19.83% to 2.56%-4.51%, i.e. 58.5% to 83.5% MAE reduction	Improved accuracy by 1.25 - 1.5%	Improve accuracy by 2% Reduced loss by 9.03%
-Latency	No latency information provided	5 ensembles tested, 4 ensembles are slower than the base case, with the worst case being 1.67% slower 1 ensemble is 28.8% faster than base case	For 8-bit case, latency reduced by 4.88% For 32-bit case, latency reduced by 15.1%
-Resource Usage	No information provided for base case resource usage, however, resource usage scales linearly with increasing number of member network used	LUT increased by 79% - 137% Register increased by 68% -124% BRAM increased by 19% - 59% DSP reduced by 0% - 25%	For 8-bit case, LUT reduced by 7.36% For 32-bit case, LUT reduced by 76.8% BRAM reduced by 10%

the next unfolding. As the proposed algorithm reduces the ensemble optimization problem to single neural network optimization, other existing approaches for neural network optimization, such as design space exploration framework [16], Pareto Optimal Design Space Exploration [17], and Mixed-Integer Linear Programming (MILP) [18] can be integrated into the proposed algorithm.

For homogeneous ensembles, the exact design space exploration tool can be used with reduced resources available being considered in the algorithm. For heterogeneous ensembles, lines 3 to 8 for Algorithm 2 can be replaced by other design space exploration tools, as long as that tool can return a neural network configuration achieving latency with minimal resources used. Using different optimization strategies would affect the final configuration, however, the key idea of optimizing the homogeneous and heterogeneous ensemble remains the same.

5.2   Comparison to Other Ensemble Learning Methods

The comparison among the existing ensemble learning methods and this work is shown in Table 3. The improvement is compared with the respective base case chosen in the papers. The base case chosen for this paper is the fully unfolded 8-bit implementation, as it is the best-performing neural network, with the highest accuracy and lowest latency. The ensemble design used is a homogeneous ensemble with 3 3-bit neural networks, each with different weights and bias obtained from the training process. A comparison with the fully unfolded 32-bit design is also shown to illustrate the comparison with the full precision.

The homogeneous ensemble of this paper increases accuracy by 2% and reduces loss by 9% compared to the single precision floating-point implementation. The FPGA implementation yields a latency of 127720ns with clock frequency 100MHz, which is 3.13 times and 23.49 times faster than the floating-point and 3-bit implementation on 6-Core Intel Core i7. The FPGA implementation is fully pipelined with high throughput, producing one output per cycle.

This paper provides the ensemble configuration optimization method to achieve the best improvement over the base case by considering the latency of individual networks and allocating resources to speed up accordingly. More resources would be used to accelerate the slower networks, thus improving the overall latency of the ensemble, while existing methods either have no speed up for individual networks ([10,12]), or apply the same unfolding to every individual network ([11]). Using the proposed optimization method, every network would have a similar latency, reducing the control required to synchronize the results due to different arrival times. As our proposed ensemble consists of several significantly smaller networks compared to the base cases, the ensemble is smaller, faster, and more accurate than both base cases.

The major difference is that this paper focuses more on obtaining the optimal **configuration**, i.e. unfolding and precision used, to speed up given a particular structure and target hardware, while [10,11] focuses more on getting the **structure** and **parameter** of the ensemble, i.e. the number of members used and what member to use. [12] focuses its discussion on the iterative implementation of members when the entire ensemble cannot be fitted onto the hardware at the same time. The best way to make use of this paper is to first apply other ensemble learning methods to determine the best possible structure, and then apply this work to utilize the target hardware to speed up the ensemble execution.

5.3 Comparison to Partial Reconfiguration Methods

As demonstrated in [12–14], partial reconfiguration is applied to swap out undesirable networks and bring in other networks when needed, reducing the requirement in size of the FPGA and keeping all resources on the board active.

However, having to swap the networks means that the networks would be working sequentially with the overhead incurred by partial reconfiguration, delaying the overall result. This becomes an even more serious problem when the input is coming as a data stream and a high throughput decision is required. As shown in Sect. 3, the order of the company from the orderbook is constantly coming in, and a buy/sell decision has to be made as soon as possible. Any delay in decision making would be costly, as the market might have been different and the decision could no longer be relevant. Processing the input data in batches would effectively reduce the frequency of reconfiguration needed, however, that would impose more delay in processing the data and producing the decision.

One of the key ideas for applying reconfiguration is to minimize the chance of resources being idle. The method proposed in this paper achieves this by allocating resources to the slowest member of the ensemble, ensuring that the overall result can be produced as soon as possible. When the input data comes in as a stream, all the allocated resources would be active. Compared to partial reconfiguration, one clear advantage of using the proposed method is that no overhead of reconfiguration is incurred, and its implementation fits much better when being used as a dataflow engine to process input data streams.

6 Conclusion

This paper introduced three algorithms to estimate the optimal parallelism configuration for homogeneous and heterogeneous ensembles. Different data and structures are being tested for the trade off between bit width, accuracy, latency, and resource usage. In general, with 8 bits used, the accuracy of the neural network can be preserved. 3-bit implementations are about 5% faster than 8-bit implementations while using around one-third of the resources, making it a desirable candidate for the network used in the ensemble. The design flow of the ensemble is illustrated using the financial trading application with input being a data stream, utilizing 60% BRAM and 90% LUT on the available PYNQ Z1 board for a 33 times speed up compared to the maximum folded design with 10% increase in accuracy over its members, and 5% improvement in speed and 2% in accuracy compared to best performing single network. The FPGA design is 23.49 times faster than the CPU implementation. Future work includes automating design with IP reuse, extending the framework to other neural networks, and supporting implementation on multiple FPGAs.

Acknowledgement. The support of the United Kingdom EPSRC (grant number UKRI256, EP/V028251/1, EP/S030069/1, and EP/X036006/1), KIAT, AMD and the Croucher Foundation is gratefully acknowledged.

References

1. OpenAI, Gpt-4 Technical report (2023)
2. Vondrick, C., Pirsiavash, H., Torralba, A.: Generating videos with scene dynamics (2016). https://arxiv.org/abs/1609.02612
3. e. a, W.J.W.W.S.W.C.G.X.S., Chen, Z.: Intern VL: scaling up vision foundation models and aligning for generic visual-linguistic tasks. In: CVF conference on computer vision and pattern recognition (2023)
4. e. a. Xu, Z.: A fragmented neural network ensemble method and its application to image classification, vol. 14, 1, p. 2291 (2024)
5. Imrie, F., Denner, S., Brunschwig, L.S., Maier-Hein, K., van der Schaar, M.: Automated ensemble multimodal machine learning for healthcare, IEEE J. Biomed. Health Inform. **29**(6), 4213–4226 (2025). http://dx.doi.org/10.1109/JBHI.2025.3530156
6. Khotimah, B.K., Setiawan, E., Anamisa, D., Puspitarini, O.: Using ensemble neural network based on sampling for multiclass classification, BIO Web of Conferences, vol. 146 (2024)
7. Umuroglu, Y., Fraser, N.J., Gambardella, G., Blott, M., Leong, P., Jahre, M., Vissers, K.: Finn: a framework for fast, scalable binarized neural network inference, In: Proceedings of the 2017 ACM/SIGDA International Symposium on Field Programmable Gate Arrays, ser. FPGA '2017, pp. 65–74. ACM (2017)
8. Blott, M., et al.: FINN-R: An End-to-end Deep-learning Framework for Fast Exploration of Quantized Neural Networks, ACM Trans. Reconfig. Technol. Syst. (TRETS), **11**(3), 1–23 (2018)
9. Wang, H., Li, J., He, K., Cai, W.: Work-in-progress: hierarchical ensemble learning for resource-aware FPGA computing, In: 2018 International Conference on Hardware/Software Codesign and System Synthesis (CODES+ISSS) (2018)
10. Lin, Z., Sinha, S., Zhang, W.: An ensemble learning approach for in-situ monitoring of FPGA dynamic power, IEEE Trans. Comput.-Aided Design Integrated Circ. Syst. **38**(9), 1661–1674 (2019)
11. Gao, Z., et al.: Soft error tolerant convolutional neural networks on FPGAs with ensemble learning, IEEE Trans. Very Large Scale Integration (VLSI) Syst. **30**(3), 291–302 (2022)
12. Cardarilli, G.C., et al.: Efficient ensemble machine learning implementation on FPGA using partial reconfiguration, In: Applications in Electronics Pervading Industry, Environment and Society, Saponara, S., De Gloria, A. Eds. (2019)
13. Cilardo, A., Maisto, V., Mazzocca, N., Rocco di Torrepadula, F.: A proposal for FPGA-accelerated deep learning ensembles in MPSOC platforms applied to malware detection, In: Quality of Information and Communications Technology, Vallecillo, A., Visser, J., Pérez-Castillo, R., Eds., pp. 239–249 Springer International Publishing (2022)
14. Farhadi, M., Ghasemi, M., Yang, Y.: A novel design of adaptive and hierarchical convolutional neural networks using partial reconfiguration on FPGA, In: 2019 IEEE High Performance Extreme Computing Conference (HPEC), pp. 1–7 (2019)

15. LOBSTER: high-frequency, easy-to-use and latest limit order book data for your research, https://lobsterdata.com. Accessed: 24-June-2022
16. Rahman, A., Oh, S., Lee, J., Choi, K.: Design space exploration of FPGA accelerators for convolutional neural networks, In: Design, Automation & Test in Europe Conference & Exhibition (DATE), 2017, pp. 1147–1152 (2017)
17. Reggiani, E., Rabozzi, M., Nestorov, A.M., Scolari, A., Stornaiuolo, L., Santambrogio, M.: Pareto optimal design space exploration for accelerated CNN on FPGA, In: 2019 IEEE International Parallel and Distributed Processing Symposium Workshops (IPDPSW), pp. 107–114 (2019)
18. Seyoum, B., Pagani, M., Biondi, A., Balleri, S., Buttazzo, G.: Spatio-temporal optimization of deep neural networks for reconfigurable FPGA socs, IEEE Trans. Comput. **70**(11), 1988–2000 (2021)

AI-Guided DSE of GEMM Kernels for Vision Transformers on FPGA-Based Edge Platforms

Fabio Cabeccia[1]([⊠]), Luigi Raffo[1], Francesca Palumbo[1], and Claudio Rubattu[2]

[1] University of Cagliari, 09123 Cagliari, Italy
`{fabio.cabeccia,raffo,francesca.palumbo}@unica.it`
[2] University of Sassari, 07100 Sassari, Italy
`crubattu@uniss.it`

Abstract. Vision Transformers (ViTs) have recently demonstrated superior accuracy compared to Convolutional Neural Networks (CNNs) in several computer vision tasks. Nevertheless, their deployment on resource-constrained edge devices remains challenging due to their high computational and memory demands. This work investigates the feasibility of Field Programmable Gate Array (FPGA)-based acceleration of General Matrix Multiplication (GEMM) layers in ViTs, where they represent the dominant computational workload, by means of a structured and parametric Design Space Exploration (DSE) methodology. These kernels are implemented using AMD Vitis HLS and optimized by varying key parameters (e.g., unrolling, pipelining, data precision, etc.). In parallel, the feasibility of representative ViT-related GEMM workloads, each defined by different matrix sizes and layer composition, is evaluated in terms of estimated FPGA resource usage and latency. The resulting hardware configurations are evaluated on two target FPGA platforms with different resource profiles: the AMD Kria KV260, representative of edge-oriented devices, and the more resource-rich AMD ZCU102. The proposed DSE aims to untangle the large number of possible configurations and their complex trade-offs among resource usage, latency, and numerical precision. To address this challenge, an Artificial Intelligence (AI)-based predictive search method is proposed to identify the most suitable implementation that minimizes latency while meeting target precision settings and resource constraints. The proposed approach achieves prediction errors comparable to state-of-the-art methods and shows the feasibility limits of deploying ViT-related GEMM workloads on FPGA-based edge devices.

Keywords: Vision Transformers · FPGA · AMD Vitis HLS · Design Space Exploration · GEMM

© The Author(s), under exclusive license to Springer Nature Switzerland AG 2026
G. Leone et al. (Eds.): ARC 2026, LNCS 16514, pp. 189–200, 2026.
https://doi.org/10.1007/978-3-032-29365-7_12

1   Introduction

In recent years, the rapid proliferation of edge computing has significantly reshaped the landscape of computer vision applications. Modern edge scenarios, such as smart cameras, autonomous robots, industrial inspection systems, and intelligent sensing platforms, increasingly require the execution of complex vision pipelines directly on embedded devices, close to where data are generated [30]. This paradigm shift is mainly driven by stringent constraints on latency, bandwidth, privacy, and reliability, which often make cloud-based processing impractical or undesirable. As a consequence, AI techniques for computer vision are progressively migrating from centralized data centers to the edge, where inference must be performed under tight power, memory, and computational constraints typical of embedded systems [27]. Achieving high inference accuracy while maintaining low latency and energy efficiency thus represents a fundamental challenge for edge-oriented AI systems [9].

From an algorithmic perspective, the evolution of computer vision models has moved beyond traditional CNNs, which have long dominated the field. Although CNNs remain widely adopted due to their favorable trade-off between accuracy and computational cost, recent advances have introduced alternative architectures capable of capturing richer global dependencies in visual data. Among these, ViTs have emerged as a particularly promising solution, demonstrating superior accuracy and remarkable flexibility across a wide range of vision tasks [22]. By relying on self-attention mechanisms rather than convolutional operations, ViTs are able to model long-range interactions more effectively and to scale more naturally with model size and data complexity. However, these advantages come at the cost of significantly increased computational and memory demands, which pose substantial obstacles to their deployment on resource-constrained edge devices. On the hardware side, only a limited set of edge platforms is currently capable of supporting the inference of such computationally intensive models. State-of-the-art edge systems are often built around heterogeneous architectures that combine general-purpose processing units, such as Central Processing Units (CPUs), with specialized accelerators tailored for high-throughput and energy-efficient execution of AI workloads [25]. CPUs are essential for running operating systems, managing system-level tasks, and orchestrating applications, often through virtualization or container-based frameworks [23]. At the same time, acceleration platforms such as Graphics Processing Units (GPUs) and FPGAs are employed to offload and speed up computationally demanding kernels, including neural network inference. Representative examples include GPU-based platforms like the NVIDIA Jetson Orin family [20], and FPGA-based solutions such as the AMD Zynq Ultrascale+ (ZU+) family [1], which integrate programmable logic with embedded processors in a single System on a Chip (SoC).

Despite the growing interest in ViTs, their adoption on edge platforms remains limited, especially when compared to CNN-based solutions [24]. Most existing deployments of ViTs are still confined to high-end GPUs or cloud infrastructures, where computational resources and memory bandwidth are abundant.

FPGA-based edge platforms, while offering compelling advantages in terms of energy efficiency, parallelism, and hardware-level customization, have seen only a small number of ViT implementations to date [6,28]. This is mainly due to the intrinsic complexity of ViT architectures, which involve large matrix multiplications, attention mechanisms, and substantial memory traffic, all of which complicate efficient mapping onto FPGA fabrics. As a result, an open question remains as to whether ViTs can be effectively implemented on edge-class FPGAs, and whether FPGA-optimized ViT implementations can retain the accuracy benefits that make these models attractive in the first place, or whether more conventional CNN-based approaches remain the preferable choice in such constrained environments, even in the presence of flexible functionalities [16].

Motivated by these research questions, this work aims to investigate the feasibility of GEMM-centric ViT acceleration on FPGA-based edge platforms by analyzing the design trade-offs involved in mapping the GEMM layers, which dominate the execution time of modern ViTs [14], onto FPGAs. Non-GEMM operations, such as *Softmax*, *GELU*, *LayerNorm*, and *tensor reshaping* are left for future work and may introduce additional latency or resources overhead in a full, end-to-end implementation. Therefore, the central question addressed in this study is whether it is possible to automatically identify hardware configurations for representative ViT GEMM workloads that are resource-efficient and capable of meeting the latency requirements of edge applications under limited FPGA resources. To this end, a set of configurations derived from real ViT architectures is evaluated on two representative devices from the AMD ZU+ family: the AMD Kria KV260 [3], which targets edge-oriented applications with relatively constrained FPGA resources, and the AMD ZCU102 [2], which is used as a higher-capacity reference platform within the same family. By considering these two targets, the proposed GEMM-oriented exploration methodology can be assessed across different FPGA resource budgets. The contributions of this paper are as follows.

1. First, two datasets are introduced for the exploration of GEMM-centric ViT acceleration on FPGAs. The first one covers GEMM kernels, synthetized on AMD Vitis HLS with different optimizations, such as loop unrolling, pipelining, tiling, and bit-width selection. The second captures representative ViT-related GEMM workloads derived from real architectures, varying in terms of matrix sizes, layer compositions, and attention-related configurations.
2. Second, two predictors built on the aforementioned datasets have been trained to estimate the key metrics of the hardware configurations before hardware synthesis: one targeting latency and the other FPGA resource usage.
3. Third, a systematic feasibility analysis has been conducted to select the optimal hardware configuration for representative ViT GEMM workloads that minimize latency while satisfying platform resource constraints. This analysis is required to verify whether a given workload can be successfully mapped onto the target FPGA devices while satisfying platform resource constraints under the selected precision settings.

The remainder of this paper is organized as follows. Section 2 describes the proposed methodology, including dataset generation, hardware synthesis process, and the AI-driven search strategy. Finally, Sect. 4 summarizes the main findings of this work, and outlines limitations and future work.

2 Methodology

This section presents a modular AI-based search methodology capable of predicting not only performance metrics but also the physical implementability of High-Level Synthesis (HLS) designs prior to synthesis. As illustrated in Fig. 1, the proposed methodology comprises three stages, which are discussed in details in the following sections.

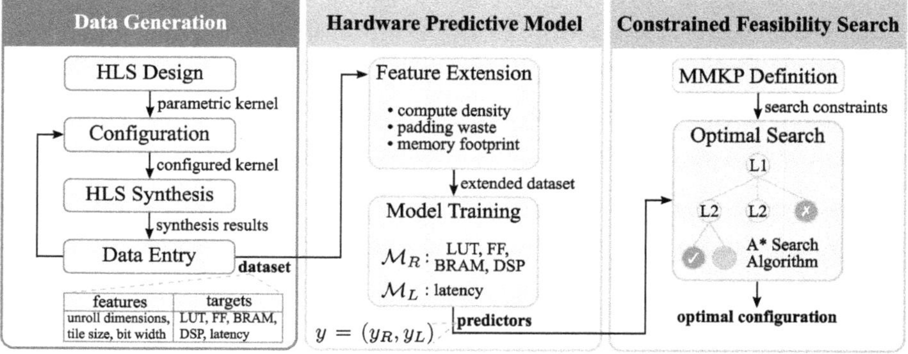

Fig. 1. Overview of the three-stage AI-based methodology.

2.1 Data Generation

Table 1. GEMM kernel parameters.

Parameter	Values	Description
m	$64 - 2048$	rows of first matrix
k	$64 - 2048$	shared matrices dimension
n	$64 - 2048$	columns of second matrix
T_m, T_n, T_k	32, 64, 128	tile size
U_m	4, 8, 16, 32	unroll factor over m loop
Bit Width	4, 8, 16	precision level (bits)

The prediction of hardware performance metrics from HLS-derived data is performed by a Machine Learning (ML) model, thus the data generation procedure is critical for achieving reasonable performance. Datasets have been based on the analysis of HLS implementations of both general GEMM kernels and ViT-specific GEMM workloads. To this aim, the proposed methodology starts from the *HLS design* of a kernel parameterized by matrix sizes, tiling and unroll factors, and bit-width. The loop unroll across the n dimension is not reported since it depends chosen bit width and it is not directly set by a targeted parameter. Table 1 lists the parameters paired with their respective domain. Once the kernel has been configured, the next step consists of a *HLS synthesis* with Vitis HLS. This tool provides an estimation of resource usage and latency, which serve as the targets of the dataset generated through multiple kernel configurations and the corresponding synthesis processes, enabling efficient *data entry.*

2.2 Hardware Predictive Model

In the proposed methodology, each hardware configuration, corresponding to a row of the dataset, is a vector $h \in \mathbb{R}^f$, with f number of features. Specifically, the set of features is a combination of implementation parameters, as defined in Sect. 2.1, and derived domain-aware features capturing tile geometry, loop structure, memory footprint, and parallelism characteristics has been added. Notably, compute density and padding waste are also included. The former is defined as the ratio of arithmetic operations to data volume per tile, and serves as a measure for arithmetic intensity in the Roofline model [29], indicating whether a configuration is compute-bound or memory-bound. The latter arises from partial tiles at matrix boundaries when dimensions are not evenly divisible by tile sizes, a well-known overhead in tiled computations [13,26].

The extended dataset is used for training predictive models of latency (in clock cycles) and hardware resource usage, including Look-Up Tables (LUTs), Flip Flops (FFs), Block Random Access Memories (BRAMs), and Digital Signal Processors (DSPs) Formally, given the set of possible hardware configurations $\mathcal{H}$, the goal is to build a predictor $\mathcal{M} : \mathcal{H} \rightarrow (\mathbb{N}^k, \mathbb{N})$ that maps a hardware configuration $h \in \mathcal{H}$ to a pair resources-latency $y = (y_R, y_L)$, where $y_R \in \mathbb{N}^k$ is the resource vector of size $k = 4$, while $y_l \in \mathbb{N}$ is the scalar latency. Furthermore, ablation studies and model-selection experiments comparing linear models and tree-based ensembles have been conducted, leading to to the adoption of gradient-boosted decision trees [8], a non-linear ensemble method offering several advantages for the prediction task: (1) it naturally captures complex, non-additive interactions among heterogeneous design parameters without requiring explicit feature engineering; (2) it is robust to mixed feature types (continuous, discrete, categorical) and varying scales, eliminating the need for extensive normalization; (3) it delivers strong out-of-the-box performance with modest hyperparameter tuning; and (4) it provides interpretable feature-importance diagnostics that offer insights into which design parameters most influence resource utilization and latency.

In conclusion, considering that resource counts (LUTs, FFs, BRAMs, and DSPs) and latency cycles exhibit distinct statistical distributions and serve different roles in the downstream optimization, two specialized predictors need to be trained: one for the resource vector $y_R \in \mathbb{N}^k$, called $\mathcal{M}_R$, and one for the latency scalar $y_L \in \mathbb{N}$, called $\mathcal{M}_L$. This separation enables target-specific pre-processing and regularization, improving prediction error and interpretability compared to a single multi-output model [5].

2.3 Resource-Constrained Feasibility Search

Given the two trained predictors, $\mathcal{M}_L$ for the latency and $\mathcal{M}_R$ for the resources, the final stage determines an optimal configuration that minimizes latency while strictly respecting hardware resource constraints. The optimization is formulated as a *Multidimensional Multiple-Choice Knapsack Problem (MMKP)* [18] as follows. Consider a neural network with L layers, each corresponding to a matrix multiplication. For each layer i, a set of configurations $\mathcal{H}_i = \{h_{i,1}, \ldots, h_{i,|\mathcal{H}_i|}\}$, with $\mathcal{H}_i \subseteq \mathcal{H}$, is generated, where each candidate $h_{i,j}$ is characterized by a predicted latency $y_L(h_{i,j}) \in \mathbb{N}$ and a resource vector $y_R(h_{i,j}) \in \mathbb{N}^4$, representing LUT, FF, BRAM, and DSP usage. The objective is to select exactly one configuration per layer such that total latency is minimized and the aggregate resource usage does not exceed the platform capacity $\mathbf{R}_{\max}$, or more formally: $\min_{h_i} \sum_{i=1}^{N} lat(h_i)$ s.t. $\sum_{i=1}^{N} \mathbf{r}(h_i) \leq \mathbf{R}_{\max}$, $h_i \in \mathcal{H}_i$. Note that the solver will always prefer the solution with higher bit width.

Although MMKP is NP-hard in general, the sequential structure of neural network layers enables efficient solving via A* search [10]. The *optimal search* tree is constructed such that each depth corresponds to a layer, and the heuristic estimates the minimum achievable latency for remaining layers. This approach guarantees feasibility, since every returned solution satisfies all resource constraints.

3   Assessment

The proposed methodology is evaluated on two aspects: (1) the prediction error of the resource and latency models across the hardware configuration search space, and (2) the effectiveness of the feasibility solver in identifying deployable configurations under strict resource constraints.

3.1 Experimental Setup

Predictors Evaluation. The resource predictor $\mathcal{M}_R$ and latency predictor $\mathcal{M}_L$ are assessed using the dataset described in Sect. 2.1, comprising 2000 synthesis-based samples. Configurations defined by specific parameter values are randomly drawn from the bounded search space in Table 1. This sampling strategy ensures broad coverage across matrix sizes, tiling/unrolling choices and data precision levels. Therefore, the resulting matrix multiplication dataset contains diverse implementation configurations with their synthesis outcomes: resource usage, latency and related metrics. In particular, the dataset is partitioned into training (70%), validation (15%), and test (15%) splits. Prediction error is evaluated using complementary metrics on the held-out test set. The Coefficient of Determination (R^2) measures the proportion of variance explained by the model, indicating overall predictive power (the higher the better). Mean Absolute Percentage Error (MAPE) quantifies the average relative deviation, enabling comparison across targets with different scales. Normalized Root Mean Squared Error (NRMSE) provides a scale-independent measure of absolute error magnitude, with sensitivity to outliers. Together, these metrics characterize both the correlation strength and the error distribution of the predictors [4,11,19].

Feasibility Solver Evaluation. The feasibility solver is evaluated on various matrix multiplication configurations, either single executions or stacked. Additionally, some real-world workloads, extracted from real ViT attention mechanism, are used. Table 2 gives a quick-view of each tested configuration. Note that for the real case the focus the evaluation are the four projection layers (Q, K, V, $Output$) of the attention block, which dominate computational cost for typical ViT configurations where embedding dimension exceeds sequence length ($D > S$) [12]. To demonstrate the solver's generality across resource budgets, two AMD ZU+ FPGA platforms are targeted. The former is the AMD Kria KV260, considered as an edge-oriented platform with constrained resources (117,120 LUTs, 234,240 FFs, 144 BRAM, 1248 DSPs), representing a case where feasibility is the primary challenge. The latter is the ZCU102, which has been considered as a high-performance evaluation platform (274,080 LUTs, 548,160 FFs, 912 BRAM, 2520 DSPs), representing a case where the solver must exploit available parallelism to minimize latency.

Table 2. Benchmarks for feasibility solver evaluation.

Benchmark	Layers	($m \times k \times n$)	Objective
`Scale_4096`	1	$4096 \times 4096 \times 4096$	Max single-layer size
`Depth_L`	2–6	$256 \times 256 \times 256$	Layer count limits
`MobileViT-XS` [17]	3	$256 \times 96 \times 96$ $256 \times 96 \times 384$ $256 \times 384 \times 96$	MobileViT attention
`ViT-Huge` [12]	4	$197 \times 1280 \times 1280$ ($\times 4$)	ViT-Huge attention

3.2 Predictors Accuracy

Table 3 reports the prediction accuracy of the resource model $\mathcal{M}_R$ and latency model $\mathcal{M}_L$ on the held-out test set. Considering the small amount of data available, both models shows good prediction capacities. The resource predictor $\mathcal{M}_R$

achieves strong performance across all targets, with $R^2 \geq 0.93$ indicating that the model explains the vast majority of variance in resource usage. MAPE values remain below 2.3% for all resource types, confirming low relative error suitable for constraint checking. BRAM prediction achieves perfect accuracy, reflecting the deterministic relationship between tile dimensions and local buffer allocation. DSP exhibits the highest NRMSE (23.34%) despite low MAPE (1.12%), indicating the presence of occasional larger absolute errors; however, since MAPE remains small, these deviations are concentrated among low-usage configurations where absolute error has minimal impact on feasibility decisions. LUT and FF predictions show balanced metrics, indicating both strong correlation and well-bounded error distributions. The latency predictor $\mathcal{M}_L$ achieves $R^2 = 0.99$, indicating strong correlation with actual synthesis results. The higher MAPE (10.43%) and NRMSE (17.85%) compared to resource targets are expected: latency spans three orders of magnitude and is influenced by scheduling decisions within the HLS tool that are not fully captured by the input feature. These results demonstrate that the proposed predictors provide sufficient accuracy for the downstream feasibility solver. Prior work on HLS quality-of-results prediction has established that MAPE below $10-15\%$ enables effective design space exploration [5], while $R^2 > 0.90$ is considered strong predictive performance for FPGA accelerator modeling [7]. The latency predictor's MAPE of 10.4% is also consistent with prior works [15].

Table 3. Final Predictor Performance on Held-Out Test Set.

Predictor	Target	R^2	MAPE [%]	NRMSE [%]
$\mathcal{M}_R$	LUT Usage	0.95	2.23	13.28
	FF Usage	0.97	1.58	10.50
	BRAM Usage	1.00	0.00	0.00
	DSP Usage	0.93	1.12	23.34
$\mathcal{M}_L$	Latency	0.99	10.43	17.85

3.3 Feasibility Solver Evaluation

The efficacy of the MMKP-based solver is evaluated on the benchmarks described in Table 2. Figure 2 illustrates how the solver adapts the generated configurations to the resource constraints of both target platforms. Importantly, with this specific hardware design, the solver is able to understand that the boundary depends on the number of concurrent layers rather than their individual dimensions: a single $4096 \times 4096 \times 4096$ multiplication is feasible, while six $256 \times 256 \times 256$ layers are not. The solver does not attempt to force infeasible designs; instead, it mathematically proves that no parameter combination satisfies the resource constraints. On the higher-capacity ZCU102, the solver founds that even six layers are not enough to saturate it, but DSPs start to behave like the bottleneck resource that may prevent deeper designs to be deployed.

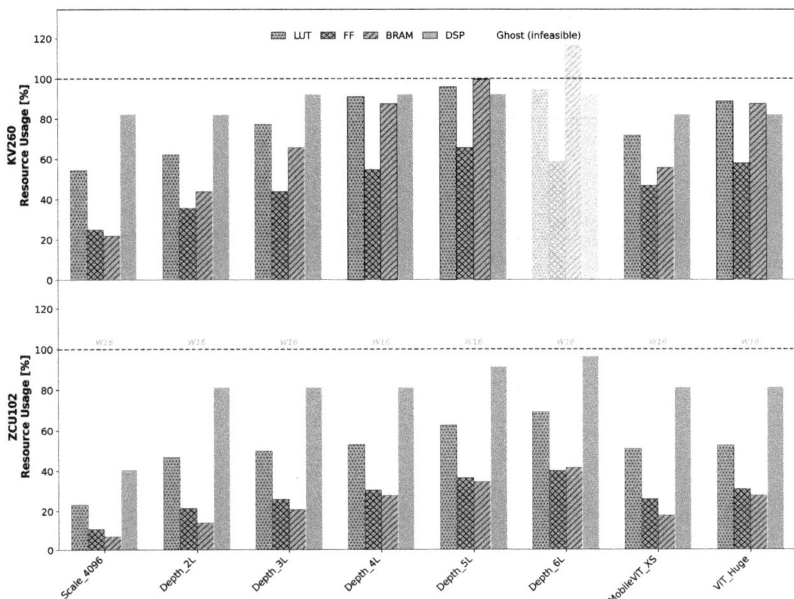

Fig. 2. Resource usage for each benchmark on both platforms.

Configuration Analysis. Table 4 reports salient examples of the chosen configurations. For Depth_5L, the solver throttles unrolling on KV260 ($U=32\rightarrow16$) and reduces the tile sizes as the depth increases in order to respect BRAM limits; on the other hand, the ZCU102 sustains higher parallelism ($U=64$) and only shows a lower unroll in the last layer. In compute-bound tasks like Scale_4096 and ViT-Huge, the algorithm consistently converges to maximal tile dimensions (128^3) to exploit more DSP resources. MobileViT demonstrates the handling of irregular layer shapes with heterogeneous tiling, more evident on the smaller board. On the latency side, the difference between KV260 and ZCU102 is modest, and in the Scale_4096 case the reported latency, in cycles, is identical but this is expected: the two boards share the same architectural family and the chosen kernel configuration is also equal, causing the latency to be the same. A richer kernel library and a wider parameter range are expected to expose a larger board-dependent performance gap.

Data Precision. The explored design space includes bit-widths from 4 to 16 bits, but only the configurations of the latter are showed since they are the most resource-demanding. Consequently, feasibility at 16 bits implies feasibility for the lower-precision configurations as well. While state-of-the-art FPGA accelerators often adopt aggressive 8-bit [31] or 16-bit [21] quantization to meet resource constraints, current results show that even 16-bit precision fits within the target edge platforms.

Table 4. Latency is the total number of clock cycles (cc). Configuration: $T_m \times T_n \times T_k \,|\, U_m \,|\, \times l$ repeats layer.

Board	Benchmark	Latency[cc]	Search Time[ms]	Configuration
KV260	Depth_5L	1.1×10^6	2520	$128\times128\times128\,|\,U{=}32$ $64\times64\times128\,|\,U{=}32\,|\,\times3$ $64\times64\times128\,|\,U{=}16$
	Scale_4096	3.7×10^8	270	$128\times128\times128\,|\,U{=}128$
	MobileViT	3.7×10^5	500	$64\times64\times64\,|\,U{=}32$ $128\times64\times64\,|\,U{=}64$ $64\times64\times128\,|\,U{=}16$
	ViT-Huge	1.1×10^7	970	$128\times128\times128\,|\,U{=}32\,|\,\times4$
ZCU102	Depth_5L	8.8×10^5	1990	$128\times128\times128\,|\,U{=}64\,|\,\times4$ $128\times128\times128\,|\,U{=}32$
	Depth_6L	1.1×10^6	2730	$128\times128\times128\,|\,U{=}64\,|\,\times4$ $128\times128\times128\,|\,U{=}32\,|\,\times2$
	Scale_4096	3.7×10^8	300	$128\times128\times128\,|\,U{=}128$
	MobileViT	3.4×10^5	590	$128\times64\times64\,|\,U{=}64\,|\,\times2$ $128\times64\times128\,|\,U{=}128$
	ViT-Huge	9.4×10^6	820	$128\times128\times128\,|\,U{=}64\,|\,\times4$

4 Conclusions

This work has explored the feasibility of ViT-based inference on FPGA-based edge platforms through a structured and parametric DSE. The results highlight the importance of DSE in understanding the feasibility limits of GEMM-centric ViT acceleration at the edge, where FPGA resource constraints and inference latency are strongly interdependent. By modeling and exploring matrix multiplication kernels derived from multiple ViT structural configurations, the proposed approach enables a systematic analysis of trade-offs across heterogeneous platforms. The findings indicate that predictive AI-based exploration can identify viable configurations. Future work includes extending the proposed framework toward a more comprehensive DSE flow for FPGA-based edge platforms, by incorporating additional ViT operators beyond GEMM, validating selected configurations through implementation on physical devices, and leveraging a library of optimized parametric kernels together with a runtime decision mechanism to dynamically select the most suitable configuration based on device conditions, environmental requirements, or user demands.

Acknowledgments. This work was supported by MYRTUS project, funded by the European Union by grant No. 101135183. Views and opinions expressed are however those of the author(s) only and do not necessarily reflect those of the European Union. Neither the European Union nor the granting authority can be held responsible for them.

References

1. AMD: AMD Zynq UltraScale+ MPSoCs (2026). https://www.amd.com/en/produ cts/adaptive-socs-and-fpgas/soc/zynq-ultrascale-plus-mpsoc.html. Accessed 20 Jan 2026
2. AMD: AMD Zynq UltraScale+™ MPSoC ZCU102 Evaluation Kit (2026). https:// www.amd.com/en/products/adaptive-socs-and-fpgas/evaluation-boards/ek-u1-zcu102-g.html. Accessed 20 Jan 2026
3. AMD: Kria KV260 Vision AI Starter Kit (2026). https://www.amd.com/en/ products/system-on-modules/kria/k26/kv260-vision-starter-kit.html. Accessed 20 Jan 2026
4. Chai, T., Draxler, R.R.: Root mean square error (RMSE) or mean absolute error (MAE)? – arguments against avoiding RMSE in the literature. Geosci. Model Dev. **7**(3), 1247–1250 (2014). https://doi.org/10.5194/gmd-7-1247-2014, https://gmd.copernicus.org/articles/7/1247/2014/
5. Dai, S., Zhou, Y., Zhang, H., et al.: Fast and accurate estimation of quality of results in high-level synthesis with machine learning. In: IEEE International Symposium on Field-Programmable Custom Computing Machines (FCCM), pp. 129–132 (2018)
6. Du, C., Ko, S.B., Zhang, H.: Energy efficient FPGA-based binary transformer accelerator for edge devices. In: 2024 IEEE International Symposium on Circuits and Systems (ISCAS), pp. 1–5 (2024). https://doi.org/10.1109/ISCAS58744.2024.10558631
7. Ferianc, M., Fan, H., Sherborne, T., et al.: Improving performance estimation for FPGA-based accelerators for convolutional neural networks. In: International Symposium on Applied Reconfigurable Computing (ARC), pp. 3–13 (2021)
8. Friedman, J.H.: Greedy function approximation: a gradient boosting machine. Ann. Stat. **29**(5), 1189–1232 (2001)
9. Gauttam, H., Nain, G., Pattanaik, K., Mendes, P.: Edge-AI: a systematic review on architectures, applications, and challenges. J. Netw. Comput. Appl. **245**, 104375 (2026). https://doi.org/10.1016/j.jnca.2025.104375
10. Hart, P.E., Nilsson, N.J., Raphael, B.: A formal basis for the heuristic determination of minimum cost paths. IEEE Trans. Syst. Sci. Cybern. **4**(2), 100–107 (1968). https://doi.org/10.1109/TSSC.1968.300136
11. James, G., Witten, D., Hastie, T., Tibshirani, R.: An Introduction to Statistical Learning: with Applications in R. Springer, Cham (2013). https://faculty.marshall.usc.edu/gareth-james/ISL/
12. Kolesnikov, A., et al.: An image is worth 16x16 words: transformers for image recognition at scale (2021)
13. Lam, M.S., Rothberg, E.E., Wolf, M.E.: The cache performance and optimizations of blocked algorithms. In: ASPLOS IV Proceedings, pp. 63–74 (1991)
14. Li, Z., et al.: Quasar-ViT: hardware-oriented quantization-aware architecture search for vision transformers. In: Proceedings of the 38th ACM International Conference on Supercomputing, pp. 324–337 (2024). https://doi.org/10.1145/3650200.3656622
15. Makrani, H.M., Sayadi, H., et al.: Xppe: cross-platform performance estimation of hardware accelerators using machine learning. In: Asia and South Pacific Design Automation Conference (ASP-DAC), pp. 727–732 (2019)
16. Manca, F., Ratto, F., Rubattu, C., Raffo, L., Palumbo, F.: Adaptive CNN acceleration on FPGAs: closing the gap with state-of-the-art solutions. IEEE Embed. Syst. Lett. 1–1 (2025). https://doi.org/10.1109/LES.2025.3599237

17. Mehta, S., Rastegari, M.: MobileViT: light-weight, general-purpose, and mobile-friendly vision transformer. ArXiv **abs/2110.02178** (2021). https://api.semanticscholar.org/CorpusID:238354201

18. Moser, M., Jokanovic, D.P., Shiratori, N.: An algorithm for the multidimensional multiple-choice knapsack problem. IEICE Trans. Fundam. **E80-A**(3), 582–589 (1997)

19. de Myttenaere, A., Golden, B., Le Grand, B., Rossi, F.: Mean absolute percentage error for regression models. Neurocomputing **192**, 38–48 (2016). https://doi.org/10.1016/j.neucom.2015.12.114

20. NVIDIA: Nvidia jetson orin series (including jetson orin nano) (2026). https://www.nvidia.com/en-us/autonomous-machines/embedded-systems/jetson-orin/. Accessed 20 Jan 2026

21. Parikh, D., Li, S., Zhang, B., Kannan, R., Busart, C., Prasanna, V.: Accelerating ViT inference on FPGA through static and dynamic pruning. In: 2024 IEEE 32nd Annual International Symposium on Field-Programmable Custom Computing Machines (FCCM), pp. 78–89 (2024). https://doi.org/10.1109/FCCM60383.2024.00018

22. Rosy, N.A., Balasubadra, K., Deepa, K.: Are vision transformers replacing convolutional neural networks in scene interpretation?: A review. Discov. Appl. Sci. **7**(9), 932 (2025). https://doi.org/10.1007/s42452-025-07574-1

23. Rubattu, C., Ledda, A., Ratto, F., Jugade, C., Goswami, D., Palumbo, F.: Integrating FPGA-based acceleration in industrial motion control system. IEEE Open J. Ind. Electron. Soc. **6**, 898–914 (2025). https://doi.org/10.1109/OJIES.2025.3571218

24. Saha, S., Xu, L.: Vision transformers on the edge: a comprehensive survey of model compression and acceleration strategies. Neurocomputing **643**(C), 130417 (2025). https://doi.org/10.1016/j.neucom.2025.130417

25. Samanta, A., Hatai, I., Mal, A.K.: A survey on hardware accelerator design of deep learning for edge devices. Wirel. Pers. Commun. **137**(3), 1715–1760 (2024). https://doi.org/10.1007/s11277-024-11443-2

26. Wang, J., Guo, L., Cong, J.: AutoSA: a polyhedral compiler for high-performance systolic arrays on FPGA. In: The 2021 ACM/SIGDA International Symposium on Field-Programmable Gate Arrays, pp. 93–104 (2021). https://doi.org/10.1145/3431920.3439292

27. Wang, X., et al.: Empowering edge intelligence: a comprehensive survey on on-device AI models. ACM Comput. Surv. **57**(9) (2025). https://doi.org/10.1145/3724420

28. Wang, Y., Mao, W., Shi, H., Sha, J., Wang, Z.: An energy-efficient FPGA accelerator for swin transformer. IEEE Trans. Very Large Scale Integr. (VLSI) Syst. **33**(6), 1774–1778 (2025). https://doi.org/10.1109/TVLSI.2025.3540844

29. Williams, S., Waterman, A., Patterson, D.: Roofline: an insightful visual performance model for multicore architectures. Commun. ACM **52**, 65–76 (2009). https://doi.org/10.1145/1498765.1498785

30. Xu, Y., Khan, T.M., Song, Y., Meijering, E.: Edge deep learning in computer vision and medical diagnostics: a comprehensive survey. Artif. Intell. Rev. **58**(3), 93 (2025). https://doi.org/10.1007/s10462-024-11033-5

31. Zhang, Y., Feng, L., Shan, H., Zhu, Z.: A 109-GOPs/W FPGA-based vision transformer accelerator with weight-loop dataflow featuring data reusing and resource saving. IEEE Trans. Circuits Syst. Video Technol. **34**(12), 13596–13610 (2024)

Arrhythmia Classification at the Edge Using a Weightless Neural Network Hardware Accelerator

Anshul Jha[1]([✉]) [iD], Shashank Nag[2] [iD], Igor D. S. Miranda[3] [iD],
Felipe M. G. Franca[4] [iD], Lizy K. John[2] [iD], Priscila M. V. Lima[5] [iD],
and Eugene B. John[6] [iD]

[1] University of The Pacific, Stockton, California, USA
ajha@pacific.edu
[2] The University of Texas at Austin, Austin, Texas, USA
shashanknag@utexas.edu, ljohn@ece.utexas.edu
[3] Federal University of Reconcavo da Bahia (UFRB), Cruz das Almas, Brazil
igordantas@ufrb.edu.br
[4] Instituto de Telecomunicações, Portugal (now at Google LLC), Lisbon, Portugal
felipe@ieee.org
[5] Federal University of Rio de Janeiro, Rio de Janeiro, Brazil
priscilamvl@cos.ufrj.br
[6] The University of Texas at San Antonio, San Antonio, USA
Eugene.John@utsa.edu

Abstract. Recent advances in hardware architectures enable real-time, low-latency, and energy-efficient computation capabilities that are essential in medical applications where timely and reliable decisions can directly affect patient outcomes. While traditional Artificial Intelligence (AI) approaches such as Convolutional Neural Networks (CNNs) and Deep Neural Networks (DNNs) have shown strong performance in biomedical signal analysis, their reliance on computationally intensive operations often limits deployment in low-power, resource-constrained medical devices. This paper presents a lightweight hardware accelerator for real-time detection and classification of cardiac arrhythmias from electrocardiogram (ECG) signals using Weightless Neural Networks (WNNs). The proposed architecture leverages an ensemble of Wilkie–Stonham–Aleksander Recognition Device (WiSARD)-based classifiers, replacing conventional weight-based computation with RAM-based storage. Multi-threshold binarization is used to extract discriminative ECG features across multiple intensity levels, while a tie-breaking mechanism improves robustness during ensemble decision-making. The complete design is implemented in synthesizable SystemVerilog and validated through functional simulation. The proposed model achieves 92.57% accuracy on the MIT-BIH dataset across five Association for the Advancement of Medical Instrumentation (AAMI) standard heartbeat classes. ASIC synthesis in 45 nm and 90 nm technology nodes further demonstrates the accelerator's energy efficiency, with the 45 nm implementation consuming 30.18 mW at 100 MHz, underscoring its suitability for low-power, real-time point-of-care medical inference.

G. Leone et al. (Eds.): ARC 2026, LNCS 16514, pp. 201–216, 2026.
https://doi.org/10.1007/978-3-032-29365-7_13

Keywords: Arrhythmia classification · Weightless Neural Network · Low-power hardware accelerator

1   Introduction

Improvements in semiconductor technology and hardware accelerator architectures have substantially enhanced the ability to execute complex algorithms in real time while maintaining low power consumption. These developments are particularly critical in medical applications, where millisecond-level delays or inaccurate predictions can directly impact patient outcomes. With the growing adoption of point-of-care and wearable medical devices, there is an increasing demand for on-device intelligence capable of real-time signal processing, classification, and decision-making. Consequently, the design of energy-efficient hardware accelerators has emerged as a key enabler for next-generation medical systems.

AI techniques have demonstrated strong capability in biomedical signal and image analysis, supporting automated diagnosis and continuous patient monitoring. Deep learning (DL) models such as CNNs and DNNs have been widely deployed for tasks including medical image classification and physiological signal analysis. However, these models rely heavily on floating-point arithmetic and large-scale matrix multiplications, which result in significant computational complexity and energy consumption. Therefore, these limitations make the deployment of DL models on low-power, real-time medical hardware accelerators particularly challenging. To address this issue, an alternative AI model is explored, which is inherently more hardware-efficient.

WNNs offer an essentially different learning and inference approach as compared to conventional weight-based models. Instead of performing weighted summations, WNNs store learned patterns directly in Random Access Memory (RAM), and the inference is performed through simple memory access operations. Hence, the memory-centric architecture enables fast, deterministic inference with minimal computational resources. The WiSARD WNN architecture is especially attractive due to its single-pass training, deterministic classification, and suitability for lightweight, low-power hardware implementations.

To further enhance performance, the Ensemble WiSARD architecture employs multiple WiSARD classifiers, each trained on different subsets or distinct input mappings of the data [4]. The WiSARD outputs are combined using majority voting to yield the final classification. This approach reduces overfitting associated with single models and improves robustness and generalization.

The requirement for efficient and reliable AI-driven hardware accelerators is recognizable for cardiovascular health monitoring. Cardiac disorders are among the most prevalent health conditions globally. According to the World Health Organization (WHO) [12], cardiovascular diseases (CVDs) remain the leading cause of death worldwide, accounting for 17.9 million deaths annually. A major subset of these conditions is cardiac arrhythmia, which results from abnormalities in the heart's electrical activation sequence and leads to irregular heart rhythms. While preliminary indications of arrhythmia may be observed through pulse assessment or auscultation during routine examinations, accurate diagnosis requires signal-based and imaging techniques. Among available diagnostic modalities, including electrocardiography (ECG), cardiac magnetic resonance imaging (MRI), and computed tomography (CT), ECG remains the most widely used and clinically practical tool for arrhythmia detection. ECG is a non-invasive technique that records the heart's electrical activity during each contraction and relaxation cycle using surface electrodes placed on the chest and, in some cases, on the limbs. The resulting electrical signals are transmitted via leads to a recording device, which generates characteristic waveforms for clinical interpretation and treatment monitoring.

Building upon these observations, this paper focuses on the design and hardware realization of an ensemble of WiSARD-based WNN accelerator for real-time cardiac arrhythmia detection using ECG signals. Cardiac arrhythmias are characterized by irregular electrical patterns; if not detected promptly, can lead to severe or life-threatening conditions. Under normal conditions, ECG signals exhibit repetitive and structured waveforms, making them well-suited for pattern-based classification. The proposed model is evaluated at the algorithmic level using the MIT-BIH dataset and is subsequently translated into a fully synthesizable ASIC design and evaluated on ECG signals. Hardware implementations across multiple technology nodes are explored to assess power consumption and area efficiency.

The remainder of this paper is organized as follows. Section 2 provides background information and reviews related work on WNN-based approaches for arrhythmia classification and detection. Section 3 details the methodology and implementation of the proposed WNN-based hardware architecture. Section 4 presents the experimental results and hardware evaluation, followed by concluding remarks in Sect. 5.

2   Literature Review

The integration of AI into medical diagnostics has significantly reformed disease detection by enabling faster, more accurate, and scalable solutions that support clinical decision-making. In recent years, the global healthcare community has faced growing challenges in diagnosing and managing life-threatening conditions such as cardiac arrhythmias. These challenges highlight the need for intelligent and automated diagnostic systems that can deliver real-time, reliable results, particularly in resource-constrained and point-of-care settings.

Under normal conditions, the heart transmits electrical impulses through specialized conduction pathways that transmit signals from the atria (upper chambers) to the ventricles (lower chambers). This rhythmic electrical activity regulates cardiac contractions and is controlled by the sinoatrial and atrioventricular nodes, which ensure the timely excitation of myocardial tissues [6]. ECGs are a non-invasive test that captures these electrical signals using surface electrodes placed on the skin. The acquired ECG signal is typically filtered to remove noise and artifacts before being digitized using an analog-to-digital converter. A healthy ECG waveform exhibits periodic and consistent morphology, characterized by the P wave, PR interval, QRS complex, ST segment, T wave, and the subsequent resting phase.

To enable efficient detection of arrhythmias on edge and wearable platforms, WNN-based hardware accelerators have gained increasing attention. Unlike conventional DL models, WNN accelerators leverage lightweight operations and avoid computationally expensive multiply-accumulate (MAC) units. Large WNN arrays can be implemented as RAM-based neurons, which helps to achieve throughput with substantially lower energy consumption. Due to the lower hardware utilization, WNN accelerators are inherently well-suited for deployment in energy and area-constrained edge devices. Compared to weight-based neural networks such as CNNs and DNNs, which rely heavily on high-precision arithmetic operations, WNN-based hardware offers a powerful replacement for low-power medical inference.

Pillai et al. [10] proposed arrWNN, a two-class WNN architecture designed for normal and arrhythmia classification. The proposed architecture converts arriving serial ECG bit streams into 8-bit parallel words and instantiates 741 logic minterms derived using the Combinational Intelligent Networks (COIN) training methodology [8]. During inference, a multiplier selects the appropriate minterm group corresponding to each input tuple, while up-down counters accumulate class-wise votes. The final prediction is determined using an argmax operation. The arrWNN model was evaluated using a 50-iteration Monte Carlo cross-validation framework on the MIT-BIH arrhythmia database, achieving a mean classification accuracy of 88.27%. The trained model was synthesized in a 0.6-μm indium–gallium–zinc–oxide (IGZO)–based flexible integrated circuit (FlexIC) technology, resulting in a 24-mm^2 core with 5,706 NAND2-equivalent gates. Operating at 100 kHz and 3 V, the design consumed 9.4 mW, demonstrating its feasibility for low-power medical applications.

In subsequent work, Pillai et al. [11] proposed arrDWNN, an edge-optimized arrhythmia detection model inspired by LogicWiSARD [9] and COIN [8] architectures. ECG signals from the MIT-BIH database were preprocessed, unary-encoded, and mapped to 8-bit addresses as inputs to the WNN. The architecture employs 741 minterms, a serial-to-parallel converter, and up-down counters, with final classification performed via an argmax unit. The arrDWNN model achieved an accuracy of 88.27%, sensitivity of 68.62%, specificity of 99.83%, and an area under the curve (AUC) of 0.8422. Implemented in a 45-nm CMOS technology, the hardware consumed 4.24 mW of power, occupied 12.4 mm^2, and operated at 500 MHz, highlighting its suitability for low-power, real-time wearable ECG monitoring systems.

3   Methodology and Implementation

The paper proposes an algorithm-hardware co-design methodology. The proposed methodology utilizes a WiSARD-based WNN ensemble with an integrated tie-breaking mechanism to improve robustness under overlapping feature distributions. The WNN algorithm is translated to an application-specific hardware accelerator and synthesized on ASIC technology nodes to analyze area and power efficiency for edge medical applications.

3.1   Arrhythmia Dataset

The proposed implementation and evaluation of the ensembled WiSARD-based WNN are conducted using the MIT-BIH Arrhythmia Database, which is a widely accepted benchmark for cardiac signal analysis. The dataset consists of 48 ECG recordings obtained from 47 distinct subjects, with each record containing a 30-minute segment selected from continuous 24-hour ambulatory monitoring. The signals were acquired using a two-channel Holter monitor and digitized at a sampling frequency of 360 Hz, offering sufficient temporal resolution to capture the morphological characteristics of individual heartbeats. Fig. 1 represents the annotated beats of record 101.

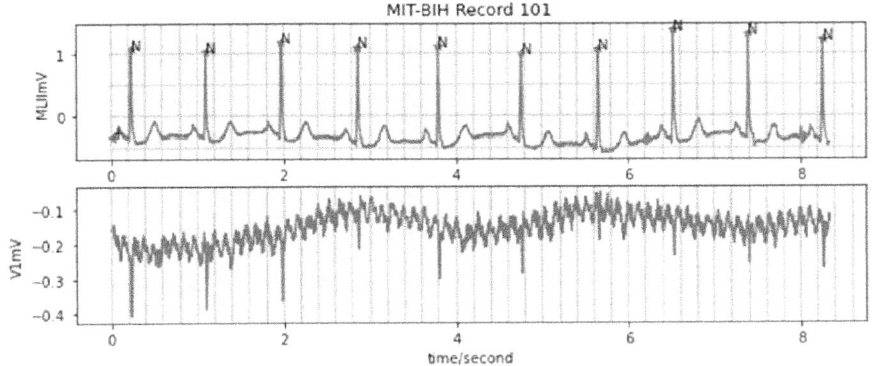

Fig. 1. Annotated beat of record 101 from the MIT-BIH Database. [5]

In this research, heartbeat annotations follow the Association for the Advancement of Medical Instrumentation (AAMI) standard [3], which consists of five primary beat types: normal (N), supraventricular (S), ventricular (V), fusion (F), and unknown (Q). Table 1 summarizes the subsequent MIT-BIH arrhythmia categories based on the AAMI standard. The data is first converted to grayscale images. Each heartbeat is segmented using a fixed window size of 179×179 images [2], ensuring preservation of local waveform morphology. The segmented beats are subsequently normalized and transformed into grayscale images to represent the temporal features of each heartbeat, as illustrated in Fig. 2.

To evaluate the model performance, the dataset is partitioned into 80%training samples and 20%testing samples. The distribution of heartbeats across different classes is reported in Table 2. This partitioning uncovers the class imbalance across different classes. Therefore, to mitigate the challenge of learning parameters from classes with an imbalanced dataset, robust modeling strategies are adopted, such as ensemble learning and multi-threshold processing.

Table 1. MIT-BIH arrhythmia dataset according to AAMI standards. [3]

AAMI Class	Content Description	Subclass Description
N	Non-Ectopic Beats	N: Left bundle branch block
		L: Normal ECG beat
		R: Right bundle branch block
		e: Atrial escape beat
		j: Borderline escape beat
S	Supraventricular Ectopic Beats	A: Atrial premature beats
		a: Abnormal atrial premature beats
		J: Borderline premature beats
		S: Supraventricular premature beats
V	Ventricular Ectopic Beats	V: Ventricular premature beats
		E: Ventricular escape beat
F	Fusion Beats	F: Ventricular fusion heartbeat
Q	Unknown Beats	/: Paced beat
		f: Pacing and normal fusion heartbeat
		Q: Unclassifiable beat
		?: Beat not classified during learning

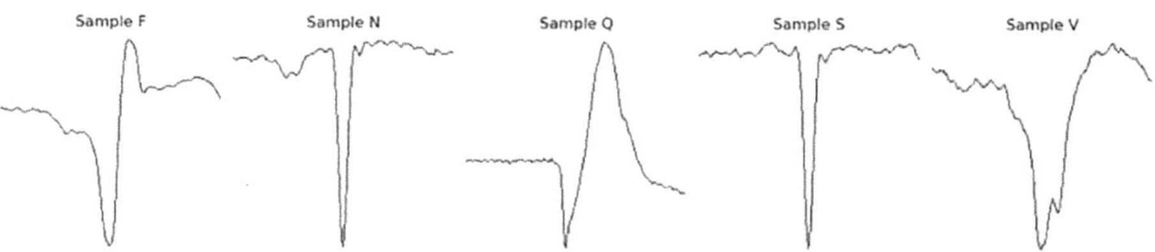

Fig. 2. Images of the segmented beats from each class of the MIT-BIH database.

3.2 Data Preprocessing and Multi-threshold Binarization

Single-threshold binarization is often insufficient for capturing subtle variations in ECG signals, as clinical information can be impacted from small change in the waveform. In WiSARD-based WNNs, binarization is an essential requirement, as the model operates directly on binary inputs, with each bit corresponding to

Table 2. MIT-BIH arrhythmia dataset classification for training and testing of the proposed model

MIT-BIH Arrhythmia Classes	Total Heartbeats	Training Heartbeats	Testing Heartbeats
N	3195	2556	639
S	1382	1105	277
V	992	793	199
F	373	298	75
Q	2084	1667	417

a unique address in the RAM-based architecture. Therefore, an effective binarization method is critical to preserve ECG signal characteristics. To address the information loss associated with single-threshold binarization, this paper employs a multi-threshold binarization system that enhances feature representation without complex preprocessing. Three binary maps are generated for each input sample using different intensity thresholds of low (≥ 0.3), mid (≥ 0.5), and high (≥ 0.7). This approach enables the model to capture corresponding signal features across multiple intensity levels. Thus, improving sensitivity to subtle morphological variations associated with different arrhythmia classes.

The resulting binary maps are combined to form a three-channel binary representation of each input. This representation is flattened into a one-dimensional binary vector for compatibility with the tuple-mapping process in the WiSARD model. The threshold-encoded input provides a prolific and more discriminative binary representation.

3.3 Proposed Model Architecture

The proposed model adopts a WNN based on the WiSARD architecture [1], which replaces weight-based learning and backpropagation with a RAM-centric pattern storage mechanism. The output of each class is represented by a dedicated discriminator composed of multiple RAM nodes, where each RAM observes a fixed-length tuple of size n from the binary input vector. For an input length I, each discriminator contains $N \triangleq \frac{I}{n}$ RAMs. Pseudo-random but consistent input-to-RAM mappings are applied across all discriminators to ensure uniform feature interpretation among various classes.

Training of the model follows a single-pass learning paradigm in which only the discriminator corresponding to the true class is updated. Each RAM writes a binary value at the address generated by its input tuple, directly storing observed patterns. During inference, the input is simultaneously evaluated by all discriminators, and each RAM contributes a vote based on whether its addressed memory location is active. The discriminator response is processed as a pop count of activated RAMs, and the class with the highest response is the prediction. If the pattern matches precisely, it results in full activation, while partial matches results into generalization to unobserved but similar inputs. This characteristic makes WiSARD well-suited for ECG-based arrhythmia classification.

The tuple size n controls the trade-off between generalization and capacity to learn intricate input patterns. The larger tuple values capture more complex patterns at the risk of overfitting. This paper selected a tuple size n = 12, resulting in 4096 memory locations per RAM, with each class discriminator consisting of 120 RAM nodes. To improve robustness and reduce bias, an ensemble of five independently trained WiSARD models is employed to leverage the variety in random mappings. A tie-breaker mechanism is integrated to resolve tied predictions by gradually increasing the activation threshold until a single class standout as a winner. The resulting ensemble WiSARD architecture is interpretable, memory-efficient, and hardware-friendly, making it well-suited for low-power edge deployment in ECG arrhythmia classification. Fig 3 illustrates the implemented ensemble WiSARD architecture with a tie-breaker, tailored for this classification task

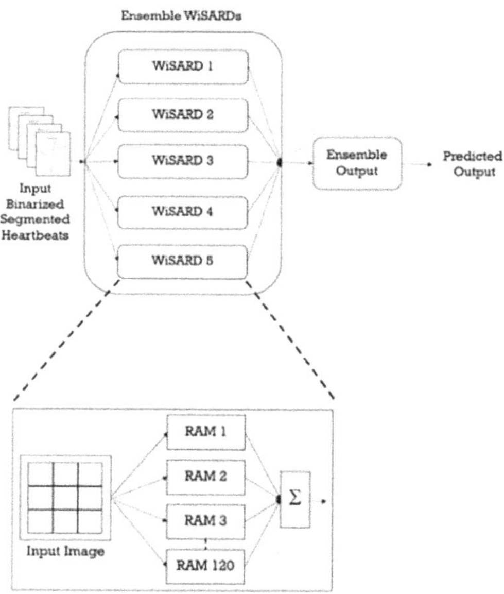

Fig. 3. Overview of the proposed Multi-threshold Ensemble WiSARD Architecture

3.4 Proposed Model training

The WiSARD model employs a one-pass learning strategy that trades iterative weight updates with direct pattern storage in RAM. During training, each input is turned into fixed-size tuples, where each tuple forms an address to a RAM node in a class-specific discriminator. Only the discriminator corresponding to the correct class is updated. The addressed memory locations are written once with a binary value of '1'. Therefore, this non-iterative learning approach enables rapid training and deterministic behavior, making it well-suited for resource-constrained applications such as real-time ECG-based arrhythmia classification.

During inference, the model operates in read-only mode, evaluating all class discriminators concurrently. Each RAM node contributes a vote if its addressed memory location is active, and class-wise responses are computed by aggregating these votes. This process is independently performed across all ensemble components is combined k response vector element-wise, to produce an ensemble-level response vector.

$$R_{\text{ensemble}}(c) = \sum_{i=1}^{k} R_i(c) \tag{1}$$

where $R_i(c)$ is the count for model i for the class c.

The final prediction c^* is achieved by summing class responses and selecting the maximum.

$$c^* = \arg\max_c R_{\text{ensemble}}(c) \tag{2}$$

Further to improve reliability for overlapping or uncertain patterns, a tie-breaker mechanism is incorporated to resolve tied predictions by gradually increasing a confidence threshold, allowing only strongly activated RAMs to participate. The resulting ensemble WiSARD framework is interpretable, memory-efficient, and hardware-friendly, making it suitable for low-power edge deployment without reliance on gradient-based optimization.

3.5   HDL-Based Implementation of the Ensemble WiSARD

The HDL-based implementation of the ensemble WiSARD accelerator is generated using the Mako [7] template, which enables SystemVerilog code generation through Python-based templates. This approach allows complex hardware structures to be expressed compactly and flexibly ahead of the restrictions of SystemVerilog preprocessing. A Python script retrieves the trained model checkpoints and extracts multi-threshold binarization patterns aligned with the address mappings of individual WiSARD discriminators. These patterns are implanted directly into RAM structures via Mako templates, presenting synthesizable RTL that instantiates local pattern memory. Unlike conventional neural networks that rely on floating-point weights and external memory access, the proposed architecture employs logic-based memory, reducing memory access latency and energy consumption.

The hardware realization of the ensemble WiSARD focuses on efficiently mapping memory-based pattern recognition instead of arithmetic-intensive computation. Each trained RAM node is implemented as a synthesizable lookup structure indexed by input tuples. The proposed architecture supports parallel address generation, concurrent RAM access across class discriminators, and aggregation of ensemble responses using pipelined summation to enhance the throughput and reduce inference latency of the accelerator. The functional verification is accomplished by utilizing binarized test vectors, which are generated by using the same preprocessing pipeline as the software model. The RTL design predicted class outputs are compared against software outcomes. This step is used to verify the behavioral functionality between the trained model and hardware realization before synthesis.

3.6 Evaluation Criteria

Model performance is evaluated using standard classification metrics, including accuracy, precision, recall, F1-score, and the confusion matrix. Collectively, these metrics provide a thorough assessment of classification efficiency, whereas the confusion matrix offers complete insight into class-wise misclassifications. The model performance analysis is very crucial for arrhythmia detection, where errors within specific classes may result in different clinical consequences.

Precision, recall, F1-score, and accuracy are computed using the counts of true positives, true negatives, false positives, and false negatives. Precision reflects the correctness of positive predictions.

$$\text{Precision} = \frac{TP}{TP + FP} \tag{3}$$

Recall or sensitivity measures the model's ability to correctly identify positive cases.

$$\text{Recall} = \frac{TP}{TP + FN} \tag{4}$$

The F1-score captures the balance between precision and recall.

$$F1\text{-}score = 2 \cdot \frac{TP}{TP + FP + FN} \tag{5}$$

Accuracy represents the ratio of correctly classified samples to the total number of samples.

$$\text{Accuracy} = \frac{TP + TN}{TP + TN + FP + FN} \tag{6}$$

where
TP (True Positive): correctly identified positive samples.
TN (True Negative): correctly identified negative samples.
FP (False Positive): negative samples are incorrectly classified as positive.
FN (False Negative): positive samples incorrectly classified as negative.

These metrics are critical for medical diagnostic systems, where minimizing missed detections and false alarms is essential. The resulting performance comparison enables an objective evaluation of model reliability and suitability for clinical deployment.

To evaluate hardware accelerator efficiency, the SystemVerilog-HDL design is synthesized using Synopsys Design Compiler targeting 90 nm and 45 nm ASIC technology nodes under operating conditions: 1.2 V power supply, 100 MHz clock frequency, 12.5% switching activity, and 25 °C temperature. The synthesis process yields area and power reports, facilitating comparative analysis among technology nodes. Cadence Innovus is utilized for physical design exploration to synthesis, floorplanning, placement, routing, and the production of the final layout in GDS II format. Together, these results provide insight into the scalability, energy efficiency, and suitability of the ensemble WiSARD architecture for low-power ASIC-based edge deployment.

4   Results

An ensemble of five WiSARD-based WNNs was developed and evaluated for arrhythmia classification using the MIT-BIH database as per AAMI standards. The model classifies heartbeats into five clinically relevant classes: normal (N), supraventricular ectopic (S), ventricular ectopic (V), fusion (F), and unknown (Q). The dataset is split using an 80:20 training-testing ratio, and performance is evaluated using accuracy and cross-entropy loss, along with macro and weighted accuracy to account for class imbalance. The macro accuracy gives equal weight to all classes regardless of their sample sizes. In contrast, weighted accuracy considers the relative size of each class and is determined by dividing the total number of correctly identified samples by the total number of samples.

$$\text{Macro Accuracy} = \frac{1}{N} \sum_{i=1}^{N} \frac{TP_i}{\text{Total samples of class } i} \tag{7}$$

$$\text{Weighted (Overall) Accuracy} = \frac{\text{Total correct predictions}}{\text{Total number of samples}} \tag{8}$$

On the algorithmic-level the ensemble achieved a training accuracy of 92.7% and a validation accuracy of 93.3%, with training and validation losses of 0.5159 and 0.5425, respectively. The Table 3 presents the class-wise macro accuracy, which shows strong performance across most arrhythmia types, with particularly high accuracy for N, Q, and S classes, while, due to limited data availability, the F class shows expected prediction.

The Table 4 represents the precision, recall, and F1-score results, which further prove that the ensemble WiSARD model efficiently adapts to class imbalance, maintaining high recall for minority classes.

As shown in Fig. 4, the confusion matrix confirms the model's reliability across all classes, including the recognition of fusion beats. The results highlight the benefit of ensemble learning for clinically relevant minority patterns.

Algorithm-level evaluation confirms that the proposed WiSARD ensemble model can be efficiently translated from PyTorch to synthesize HDL without loss of classification accuracy. For HDL functional verification, 1,607 inference vectors are utilized, which shows the same behavior between software and hardware

Table 3. Macro Accuracy for each arrhythmia class

Class	Macro-Accuracy
F	47%
N	97%
Q	98%
S	95%
V	85%

Table 4. Classification report of Ensemble-WiSARD on the MIT-BIH arrhythmia dataset

Classes	Precision	Recall	F1-score
F	0.95	0.47	0.62
N	0.96	0.97	0.96
Q	0.87	0.98	0.93
S	0.96	0.95	0.96
V	0.96	0.85	0.90

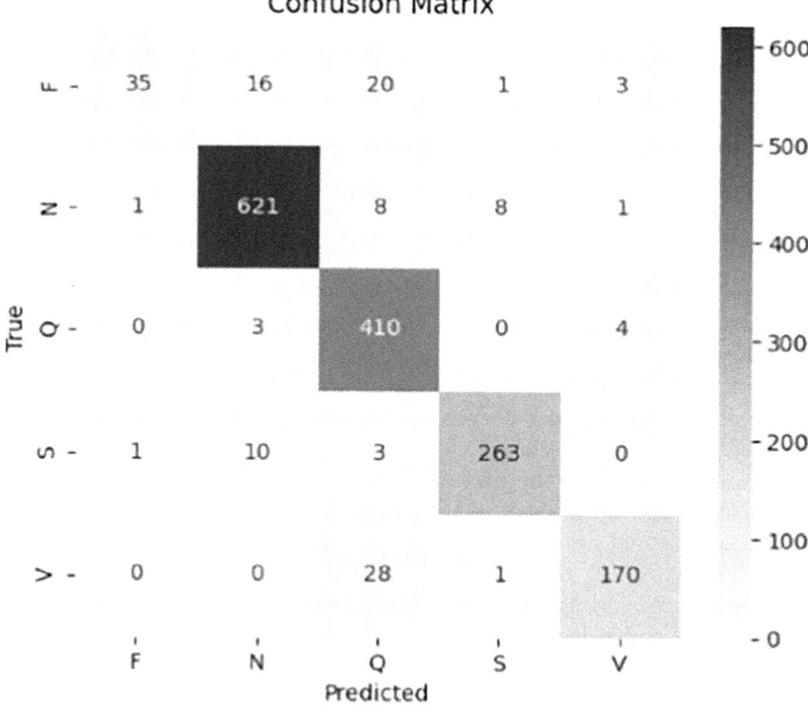

Fig. 4. Confusion matrix of Ensemble-WiSARD on the MIT-BIH dataset.

output, achieving a hardware accelerator accuracy of 92.57%. Table 5 presents a comparison of the test accuracy of each standalone model, along with the ensemble implementation. Each WiSARD model utilizes 1-bit precision per input, 12 inputs per filter, 4096 memory entries per filter, 120 RAMs, and a memory size of 500 KiB per WiSARD, leading to 2500 KiB for the entire ensemble model. The results clearly demonstrate the improvement in classification performance achieved through ensemble learning.

Table 5. Performance of Individual WiSARD Models and Ensemble

Model / Submodels	Test Acc. (%)
WiSARD1	86.02
WiSARD2	88.18
WiSARD3	79.06
WiSARD4	81.34
WiSARD5	82.18
Ensemble (5 models)	**92.57**

An ASIC synthesized using Synopsys Design Compiler demonstrates scaling across 90 nm and 45 nm technology nodes under identical operating conditions. Table 6 represents the total, dynamic, switching, and internal power consumption on the 45 nm and 90 nm technology nodes. Table 7 represents the chip area consumption on 45 nm and 90 nm technology nodes.

Table 6. Power consumption of the ensemble WiSARD model on 45 nm and 90 nm technology nodes

Technology Node	Dynamic Power (mW)	Switching Power (mW)	Leakage Power (mW)	Total Power (mW)
45 nm	26.4433	0.528927	3.7429	30.181
90 nm	47.2034	1.77099	7.8228	55.026

Table 7. Chip area of the ensemble WiSARD model on 45 nm and 90 nm technology nodes

Technology Node	Area (μm^2)
45 nm	5,009,366.59
90 nm	13,982,588.92

The 45 nm implementation achieves significant reductions in both area and total power consumption. Fig. 5 presents the physical design placement results obtained using Cadence Innovus, validating the feasibility of a full place-and-route implementation, showing well-distributed logic, robust power delivery, and compliance with timing and design-rule constraints. Together these results demonstrate that the ensemble WiSARD architecture provides an effective balance between classification accuracy and hardware efficiency, making it suitable for low-power, real-time arrhythmia detection in edge medical devices.

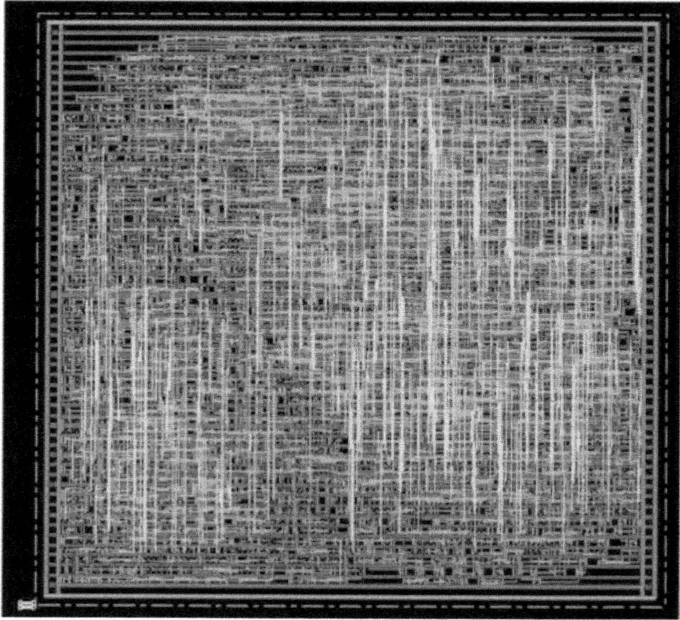

Fig. 5. Placement of the ensemble WiSARD model using Cadence Innovus.

At the system level, the proposed ensemble WiSARD model is synthesized and physically realized using Cadence Innovus with TSMC 0.18 μm CMOS technology, resulting in a complete GDS II layout. The design achieves an arrhythmia classification accuracy of approximately 92.57% on the MIT-BIH dataset. Power and area characteristics are evaluated using Synopsys Design Compiler across 45 nm and 90 nm technology nodes. At 45 nm, the implementation consumes 30.18 mW of total power and occupies 5009366.59 μm^2 of silicon area, demonstrating efficiency for resource-constrained biomedical edge applications. While Pillai et al. [10] and Pillai et al. [11] reported arrWNN and arrDWNN models based on LogicWiSARD and COIN-based WNN architectures with accuracies of 88.27% and 89%, respectively, the proposed ensemble of five WiSARD networks achieves a competitive accuracy of 92.57%.

5 Conclusion

This paper presents an ensemble-based WiSARD weightless neural network (WNN) for real-time arrhythmia classification. The hardware design is evaluated on the MIT-BIH dataset under AAMI standards. While WNNs have previously been explored for arrhythmia detection, to the best of our knowledge this is the first work to apply a WNN-based approach to multi-class arrhythmia classification. An ensemble of five WiSARD models delivers strong system-level performance, achieving 92.57% accuracy with consistently high precision, recall, and F1-scores across all arrhythmia classes. These results highlight the effectiveness of ensemble learning in addressing class imbalance and reducing classification ambiguity. The proposed model is implemented in synthesizable SystemVerilog HDL and validated through a complete ASIC design flow, with hardware results matching software accuracy. ASIC synthesis in 45 nm technology achieves 30.18 mW power consumption and a compact area of 5.01 mm^2 at 100 MHz. Overall, the results demonstrate the practicality of the ensemble WiSARD architecture as an energy-efficient, hardware-friendly solution for deployable, edge-level medical diagnostics.

Acknowledgments. This research was supported in part by NSF Grants 2326894 and 2425655. Any opinions, findings, conclusions, or recommendations are those of the authors and not of the funding agencies.

Disclosure of Interests. Authors have no competing interests.

References

1. Aleksander, I., Thomas, W., Bowden, P.: Wisard· a radical step forward in image recognition. Sens. Rev. **4**(3), 120–124 (1984)
2. Aphale, S., Jha, A., John, E.: High accuracy arrhythmia classification using transfer learning with fine-tuning. In: 2022 IEEE 13th Annual Ubiquitous Computing, Electronics & Mobile Communication Conference (UEMCON), pp. 0480–0487. IEEE (2022)
3. Aphale, S.S., John, E., Banerjee, T.: Arrhynet: a high accuracy arrhythmia classification convolutional neural network. In: 2021 IEEE International Midwest Symposium on Circuits and Systems (MWSCAS), pp. 453–457. IEEE (2021)
4. Filho, L.L., França, F.M., Lima, P.M.: Wisard-based ensemble learning. In: ESANN 2023 Proceedings, European Symposium on Artificial Neural Networks, Computational Intelligence and Machine Learning. i6doc.com, Bruges, Belgium (2023)
5. Goldberger, A.L., et al.: Physiobank, physiotoolkit, and physionet: components of a new research resource for complex physiologic signals. circulation **101**(23), e215–e220 (2000)
6. Haddad, S.A., Serdijn, W.A.: The evolution of pacemakers: an electronics perspective. In: Ultra Low-Power Biomedical Signal Processing: An Analog Wavelet Filter Approach for Pacemakers, pp. 13–31. Springer (2009)
7. Mako Templates: Welcome to mako! https://www.makotemplates.org/ Accessed: Jan 2026

8. Miranda, I.D., et al.: Coin: combinational intelligent networks. In: 2023 IEEE 34th International Conference on Application specific Systems, Architectures and Processors (ASAP), pp. 27–28. IEEE (2023)
9. Miranda, I.D., et al.: Logicwisard: memoryless synthesis of weightless neural networks. In: 2022 IEEE 33rd International Conference on Application-specific Systems, Architectures and Processors (ASAP), pp. 19–26. IEEE (2022)
10. Pillai, V., et al.: arrwnn: Arrhythmia-detecting weightless neural network flexic. In: 2024 IEEE International Flexible Electronics Technology Conference (IFETC), pp. 1–4. IEEE (2024)
11. Pillai, V., et al.: Edge-optimized weightless neural network for low-power wearable arrhythmia detection. In: 2025 IEEE 18th Dallas Circuits and Systems Conference (DCAS), pp. 1–6. IEEE (2025)
12. World Health Organization: Cardiovascular diseases. World Health Organization: CVD (2025). https://www.who.int/health-topics/cardiovascular-diseases. Accessed: Jan 2026

Design Tools

Learning Based Presilicon Estimation of Design Area from Early EDA Metrics

Tarun Kholay[1]([✉])(iD), Anup Ashok Kedilaya[1](iD), Aman Arora[2](iD),
Jaydeep P. Kulkarni[1](iD), and Lizy K. John[1](iD)

[1] The University of Texas at Austin, Austin, TX, USA
{tarunkholay,anup027,jaydeep,ljohn}@utexas.edu
[2] Arizona State University, Phoenix, AZ, USA
aman.kbm@asu.edu

Abstract. In early stages of prototyping and acceleration, designers rely on vendor-specific and architecture-specific resource metrics (e.g., LUTs, ALMs, DSP blocks), which prevent direct cross-platform comparison and complicate design space exploration. We present MARU (Machine Learning-based Approaches for Resource-to-Area Estimation), a framework that predicts ASIC-like physical area directly from FPGA resource utilization estimates (e.g., post-HLS or synthesis reports). MARU achieves an average of 4% Mean Absolute Percentage Error (MAPE) in cross-FPGA experiments using the PolyBench suite, while reducing estimation time from the order of 2.5 days of full ASIC synthesis and place-and-route to just 5 min per design. The framework enables three key capabilities: (1) unified area-based comparison across heterogeneous FPGA platforms, (2) real-time area prediction for accelerated HLS design space exploration, and (3) ASIC migration feasibility analysis through technology-aware predictive area modeling. MARU bridges the FPGA–ASIC methodology gap, serving both as a comparative research tool and as a practical framework for cost-driven hardware co-design decisions.

Keywords: Area Estimation · Machine Learning for EDA · FPGA-to-ASIC Mapping · High-Level Synthesis

1 Introduction

Field-Programmable Gate Arrays (FPGAs) have become a dominant platform for rapid prototyping, and accelerating applications in machine learning, communications, and embedded systems [2,3,19]. Their reconfigurable nature enables rapid prototyping, hardware/software co-design, and workload-specific optimization. In both academia and industry, FPGAs are increasingly used as a first step in the hardware design lifecycle—allowing designers to validate architectures, explore microarchitectural trade-offs, and evaluate performance before committing to fabrication. However, design tradeoff evaluation is complicated by vendor-specific and architecture-specific resource metrics (e.g., Look Up Tables

(LUTs) [2,3], adaptive Logic Modules (ALMs) [19], Digital Signal Processing (DSP) blocks) [1,4], which prevent direct cross-platform comparison.

The FPGA design ecosystem reports resource usage using heterogeneous, architecture-specific primitives such as LUTs, FFs, DSPs, BRAMs [2,3,6,35] and ALMs [19]. These primitives differ not only across vendors (e.g., LUTs vs. ALMs) but also across FPGA generations (e.g., DSP48 [1] vs. DSP58 [4] blocks).

This heterogeneity creates two fundamental barriers - First, even within the FPGA domain, fair comparison between designs is challenging. For example, one accelerator implementation may consume more BRAMs but fewer LUTs, while another exhibits the opposite trade-off [35]. Without a common abstraction layer, determining which design is more area-efficient, or more ASIC-ready, is ambiguous. This ambiguity becomes even more pronounced across vendors, where architectural primitives differ substantially in granularity and functionality.

Second, and more critically, there is no direct mapping from FPGA resource utilization to ASIC area. Unlike ASIC flows, where Electronic Design Automation (EDA) tools report area in standardized physical units (e.g., mm^2) derived from technology libraries, FPGA flows lack a unified, technology-aware area metric. As a result, designers cannot easily estimate whether an FPGA prototype will translate into a feasible or cost-effective ASIC implementation. This limits FPGA's effectiveness as a prototyping vehicle for silicon-bound designs.

The challenge is amplified in High-Level Synthesis (HLS)-based flows. HLS [32] is widely adopted for rapid design space exploration, where numerous variants are generated and compared. However, HLS-reported resource estimates are often inaccurate, and obtaining precise post-place-and-route results requires time-consuming compilation flows. When exploring large design spaces, this can require days per design point. Moreover, even when resource estimates are available, whether from HLS or from machine learning-based predictors, the outputs remain disaggregated (LUTs, FFs, DSPs, BRAMs), providing no direct insight into ASIC-equivalent area or migration feasibility.

In this paper, we argue that area can become a unifying abstraction layer for comparison of different FPGA designs and for migrating between FPGA prototyping and ASIC realization. Area is a reasonable proxy for power and cost, making accurate area estimation critical for feasibility. We propose MARU (Machine Learning-based Approaches for Resource-to-Area Estimation), a framework that predicts ASIC-equivalent area directly from FPGA resource utilization statistics. By learning the relationship between FPGA primitives and synthesized ASIC area, MARU enables technology-aware area estimation without requiring full ASIC synthesis and place-and-route.

A naive approach is to estimate design area from resource counts using area weights for each resource, as explored in prior works [7–9]. We applied a similar methodology utilizing area ratios of various FPGA building blocks from VTR's [31] flagship FPGA architecture to estimate an equivalent area. Since the ASIC area depends on specific technology nodes, we used linear regression to scale it. We ran this experiment for all Polybench designs from HLSDataset [36] - atax, bicg, gemm, gesummv, k2mm, k3mm, mvt, syrk, and syr2k. Across these designs, the MAPE between the area obtained from ASIC synthesis and the area obtained by using area weights from the VTR architecture was 57%, with the worst MAPE being 66.97% for k3mm and least MAPE being 46.67% for k3mm. The large errors observed here provides a solid motivation for our framework.

To realize our objective, we train machine learning models to estimate the area required for a given FPGA design. We use utilization statistics reported by commercial HLS EDA tools like Vitis [5] as input features, and extract an area estimate from open-source ASIC synthesis tools like Yosys [40] as labels.

The use of ML is critical because the relationship between high-level FPGA resource metrics (such as LUTs, FFs, and DSPs) and area is highly complex and not amenable to analytical modeling or linear regression. This complexity arises from complex architectural patterns—such as variations in DSP block structures or logic cluster configurations—which are difficult to capture analytically, or different circuits having different wiring complexities. For example, across Polybench designs from HLSDataset [36], gemm benchmarks exhibit greater area variance than atax across different FPGA families, highlighting the need for circuit-architecture-aware prediction. ML-based prediction not only captures these complexities but also offers fast inference times and high accuracy. In this way, our approach offers a fast and generalizable abstraction layer for resource estimation across circuit types and FPGA architectures. Our prediction framework can operate at the HLS or RTL levels.

The proposed MARU framework correlates HLS-derived features with gate-level implementation metrics extracted from both commercial and open-source synthesis flows. MARU is trained on datasets that include multi-FPGA implementation statistics for standard benchmark suites such as PolyBench [36]. It incorporates high-level utilization features (e.g., LUT, FF, DSP, and BRAM counts) and maps them to an area estimate derived using both proprietary and open-source backend flows.

While traditional flows involve running multiple tools across synthesis, place and route, our ML-based MARU flow predicts metrics available at lower design abstraction levels much earlier using reports from higher abstraction levels. Thanks to recent advances in ML, particularly tree-based ensemble models such as XGBoost and Random Forest, MARU captures nonlinear relationships between resource features and area, achieving average percentage errors as low as 1–4% across unseen circuit configurations. While a traditional flow running Vitis for HLS and Vivado/Yosys for synthesis, place and route per circuit requires around 2.5 days to report area on large datasets like HLSDataset [36], the trained MARU model itself requires sub-millisecond inference time per design, with lightweight transfer adaptation completing in under one second on average. As summarized in Table 1, MARU provides key advantages over traditional flows: it offers predictive modeling without re-running the backend flow, supports transfer learning to enable generalization across circuits and FPGAs, and produces results in real-time during early-stage design. Cross-circuit or cross-FPGA analysis using traditional flows to explore new design spaces typically requires a full rerun of the toolchain. In contrast, MARU allows circuit knowledge to be reused across architectures, enabling efficient estimation through direct prediction or

Table 1. Comparison of traditional FPGA flow and MARU metric and workflow.

Metric	Traditional Flow	MARU Flow (Ours)
Flow steps	HLS → Synthesis, place and route	HLS → ML inference
Comparison metrics	No	Yes
Dev. cost	None	Requires large dataset
User cost	Vivado or similar tools	(1) Inference only (no effort)
		(2) Transfer learning + inference
Time (user)	Minutes–hours	(1) < 0.12 ms (inference)
		(2) < 1 s (transfer + inference)
Average Error	0%	4%

[1] Model trained on user's circuit/FPGA.
[2] Dataset excludes user's circuit/FPGA.

lightweight transfer learning (<10 min), even for incremental design updates. In this work, we explore specific cases based on circuit varieties and cross-platform FPGA varieties.

In this work, we evaluate these capabilities across multiple circuit benchmarks and FPGA platforms to demonstrate scalability and generalization.

Our contributions extend prior research in following key directions:

- We build a systematic machine learning-based framework, MARU, to predict ASIC area from FPGA resource utilization data. MARU achieves accuracy in the range of 94%-99% for circuits from PolyBench from HLSDataset.
- We explore different machine-learning algorithms: linear models like regression, decision trees to complex models like multi-layer perceptrons, neural networks, random forest and gradient boosted decision trees (XGB) accounting for nonlinearities in predictions.
- Intra-circuit and cross-FPGA analysis to test model robustness and generalization capabilities are evaluated as part of MARU. We evaluate direct and transfer-learning protocols to fine-tune predictions.

2   Related Work

The Need for a Single Comparison Metric: Many prior works on FPGA hardware design focus on optimizing metrics like area or performance per unit resource. These are often reported in terms of Configuration Logic Blocks (CLBs) [7,8] plus DSP slices and BRAMs. Some studies exploring FPGA versus ASIC efficiency gaps [9] convert resource utilization into Adaptive Logic Modules (ALMs), using the number of ALMs to represent area, where various building blocks are converted to an equivalent ALM. However, such vendor-specific representations limit the generalizability of results across different architectures. This is because the number and structure of logic elements—such as LUTs, flip-flops (FFs), and multiplexers (MUXs)—within a CLB or ALM can vary widely between FPGA vendors and even across different generations from the same vendor. For example, a CLB in a Xilinx and Zynq UltraScale+ FPGA [2,3] may contain 6-input LUTs, while a Lattice ECP5 and iCE40 FPGA [24,25] may use 4-input LUTs, and Intel's ALMs follow their own logic structure. A unit ALM contains one LUT and one Flip-Flop. This would correspond to 1/10 of a CLB in Altera FPGAs. A unit DSP and BRAM area corresponds to 40 and 30 ALMs respectively [34]. Such an architecture-specific metric makes it difficult to compare area or performance fairly between designs implemented on different hardware. To solve this, some works report the usage of raw components like LUTs, FFs, BRAMs, and DSPs across designs. For example, [35] evaluated custom FPGA accelerators on neural networks by comparing these components. However, because these metrics depend heavily on the FPGA architecture, toolchain, and synthesis settings, the results are often not transferable or comparable across platforms. This motivates the need for a common comparison metric, such as an area estimate, which can abstract over architecture-specific implementations and enable cross-platform comparisons for area, performance, and resource efficiency.

HLS Based Design: High-level synthesis (HLS) has become increasingly widespread in the FPGA design landscape, indicating a significant shift from traditional register-transfer level (RTL) methodologies. As indicated in [10,32], HLS has moved from a prototyping tool to production with broader accessibility. HLS offers several advantages over RTL-based design, including faster development cycles [23], higher abstraction levels [42], and the ability to leverage software engineering practices, which collectively reduce the time-to-market [18] and lower the barrier for hardware acceleration [22]. HLS facilitates rapid design space exploration and easier integration of complex algorithms, making it more adaptable to evolving application requirements [15,21]. Furthermore, HLS also enables code optimizations leveraging software engineering practices to simplify hardware acceleration [26].

Machine Learning for Early HLS Metric Prediction: High-Level Synthesis (HLS), which converts C/C++ code into RTL, is widely used in modern FPGA workflows [10,17,18,21–23,42]. However, the process of evaluating tradeoffs—like resource usage, power, and timing—is slow, since full synthesis and implementation tools can take hours to days per design iteration. This slows down rapid exploration of design alternatives. To address this, many recent works use Machine Learning (ML) models to predict post-synthesis metrics such as LUT counts, FF counts, and critical path delays. Techniques like convolutional neural networks (CNNs), graph neural networks (GNNs), and tree-based models (e.g., XGBoost) have been applied to predict key HLS metrics, including resource usage [12], power consumption [27,28,37], and timing performance [41]. Dai et al. [13], for example, showed that using synthesis report features can reduce HLS estimation errors by up to 138%. Similarly, Wu et al. [41] used GNNs on abstract syntax trees to predict post-implementation timing. Large datasets like HLSDataset [36], which includes over 9,000 design variants across multiple FPGA families, have enabled these models to be trained effectively at scale. Still, challenges remain in making predictions that generalize well across different FPGAs, toolchains, and designs.

Cross-Platform Prediction and Transfer Learning: Recent works have explored the challenge of predicting design metrics across different FPGA platforms [29,33,38,39]. ATAPP [38] and XPNet [39] predict the power consumption on unseen FPGAs using machine learning. HLSPredict [33] applies ML models to predict performance for new FPGA targets without running the full toolchain. Similarly, XPPE [29] estimates kernel-level performance for unseen hardware types using CPU execution traces. These methods aim to reduce the time and compute resources needed for evaluating new designs or migrating designs across devices. In the context of HLS, machine learning models trained on one FPGA architecture often perform poorly when applied to another, due to differences in logic block configurations, synthesis behavior, and implementation tools. To address this, transfer learning has emerged as a powerful method. Transfer learning allows a model trained on one dataset to be adapted to a new target using a small amount of labeled data—greatly reducing the need for full retraining and large-scale data collection. For HLS-based flows, where generating post-implementation metrics like area, power, and timing typically requires a full synthesis and place-and-route run, transfer learning enables fast reuse of existing knowledge. This makes it particularly useful for design space exploration (DSE) under resource constraints. Previous works such as [14,20] demonstrate that transfer learning can speed up DSE across different circuits or FPGAs, reducing latency while maintaining high prediction accuracy.

3   Methodology

The data set used in MARU is based on a HLS dataset [36] that could be used for rapid development of machine learning platforms with end-to-end integration. HLS enables the translation of high-level descriptions (e.g., C/C++) into hardware implementations while exposing design trade-offs through resource utilization reports [11]. It consists of 9 different benchmarks, each containing atleast 500 different configurations parametrized by applying pragmas to each kernel in the Polybench benchmark suites - array partitioning, loop unrolling, and pipelining factors. This results in a net **total of 4,500+ circuits available for training and inference.** Since the HLS dataset contains proprietary Xilinx modules for implementing optimized floating point addition and multiplication operations, custom modules needed to be added to replicate this in ASIC gate-level synthesis.

3.1   MARU Data Generation Framework

The flow for data generation is as shown in Fig. 1. The Polybench benchmark consists of C++ benchmark with pragma statements for loop unrolling, array partitioning and pipelining. These are used to run HLS in Xilinx Vitis FPGA to generate Verilog files and utilization reports. The utilization reports contain features such as BRAMs, DSPs, FFs, and LUT counts used in FPGA design. We use Vitis HLS [5] to generate these HLS resource utilization reports.

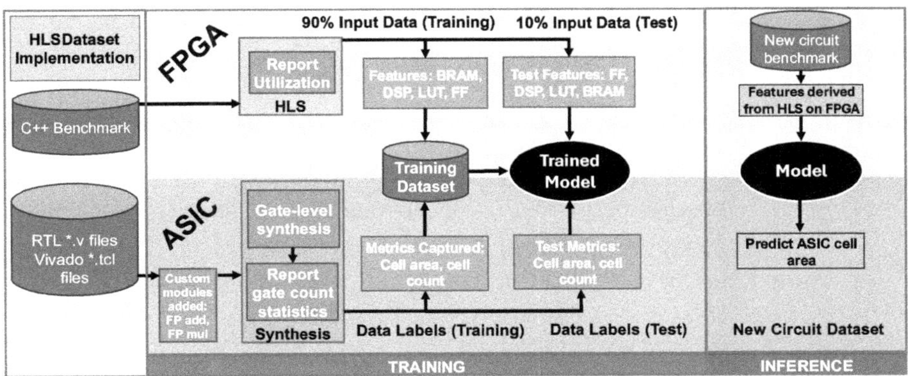

Fig. 1. MARU training and inference frameworks using Vitis HLS for FPGA and Yosys for ASIC gate-level synthesis implementations.

For building output data label set containing standard cell area estimates for an equivalent ASIC implementation using Yosys and which are to be predicted by a machine-learning model, we process HLS Verilog files containing circuit implementations and any other Vivado TCL files as input to the ML model. Since the design from HLSDataset contains binary files with Xilinx proprietary modules, we designed custom modules like floating-point addition and multiplication. ASIC gate-level synthesis is done in Yosys [40] using a basic synthesis recipe with no tool specific parametric optimizations. FPGA resource utilization from HLSDataset and ASIC post-implementation area summary reports from Yosys are parsed and merged to create a single comma-separated values (CSV) file with training data and labels. Model training is done using training and test datasets. Trained model is validated using inference dataset.

Table 2 shows a snippet of FPGA input data and generated equivalent ASIC area per benchmark. Here area is the output that needs to be predicted. Along with total cell area and cell count, Yosys also provides cell counts for different types of cells used in ASIC design. We use Skywater130 PDK [16] for implementation. During implementation, unit area per cell for a given technology is known. Thus, estimating cell area and cell count per cell-type provides an accurate picture of total chip/silicon area needed for implementing a given circuit in ASIC. At an abstract-level we do see a correlation between LUT, FF and DSP counts with total cell area. Further, the number of registers/ flip-flops and block RAMs influences the various D-type flip-flop counts after gate-level synthesis.

3.2   MARU Learning Framework

In this section, we describe a systematic machine learning-based framework, MARU to evaluate various ML models across multiple performance metrics, including R^2, Root Mean-Square Error (RMSE), and MAPE. The learning pipeline begins with simple models such as linear regression and multi-layer perceptrons, and progressively explores more expressive models like neural networks and ensemble learners (e.g., Random Forest and XGBoost) to capture underlying nonlinear relationships.

Table 2. Training data summary. Input features from Vitis HLS, while area labels are extracted from Yosys gate-level synthesis.

Benchmark	LUT	FF	DSP	BRAM	CellArea (μm^2)
ATAX	1054	680	5	11	2,396,601
BICG	1103	781	13	5	2,466,626
GEMM	4091	4649	32	5	12,106,403
GESUMMV	1212	739	20	5	4,677,871
K2MM	3827	2505	56	10	18,734,007
K3MM	2096	1164	56	5	15,763,217
MVT	1074	679	12	5	2,432,109
SYRK	1412	829	32	5	9,025,421
SYR2K	5069	3276	56	14	19,554,186

A part of this motivation stems from early observations that raw utilization metrics alone do not map linearly to estimated area. For example, although the overall resource usage (LUTs, FFs, DSPs, BRAMs) for benchmarks such as `atax` and `syrk` falls within a similar range, the synthesized area estimate differs significantly. As shown in Table 2, `syrk` uses only moderately more total resources than `atax`, but exhibits nearly 4× higher cell area, largely due to increased DSP utilization. This highlights that differences in resource composition—not just total counts—can lead to substantial variation in resulting area.

Table 3. List of features used for gate count prediction.

Feature Name	Description/Formula
LUT	Number of Look-Up Tables used
FF	Number of Flip-Flops used
DSP	Number of DSP slices used
BRAM	Number of Block RAMs used
LUT_FF_ratio	LUT ÷ (FF + 1)
total_resources	LUT + FF + DSP + BRAM
DSP_LUT_ratio	DSP ÷ (LUT + 1)
log_LUT	$\log(1 + LUT)$
log_FF	$\log(1 + FF)$

To address these discrepancies while preserving generalization, we deliberately kept feature engineering minimal and interpretable in early experiments.

The goal was to isolate model performance without relying on complex or highly domain-specific transformations. Only a small number of features—primarily the raw utilization metrics—were used initially, and later experiments introduced modest extensions such as resource ratios (e.g., LUT/FF), log transformations, and simple aggregations. Table 3 lists the complete set of nine features used in the final models, including both raw inputs and engineered variants. These were selected for their simplicity, interpretability, and relevance across FPGAs.

Feature scaling (via MinMax or RobustScaler) and log transformations (on target values) were applied where needed to normalize feature ranges and improve regression stability. The training data was used to fit four representative models: Multi-Layer Perceptron (MLP), Keras-based neural network, Random Forest, and XGBoost. These models were evaluated using R^2, RMSE, and MAPE metrics, and the best model was chosen based on highest R^2 and lowest error. This is shown in Fig. 2.

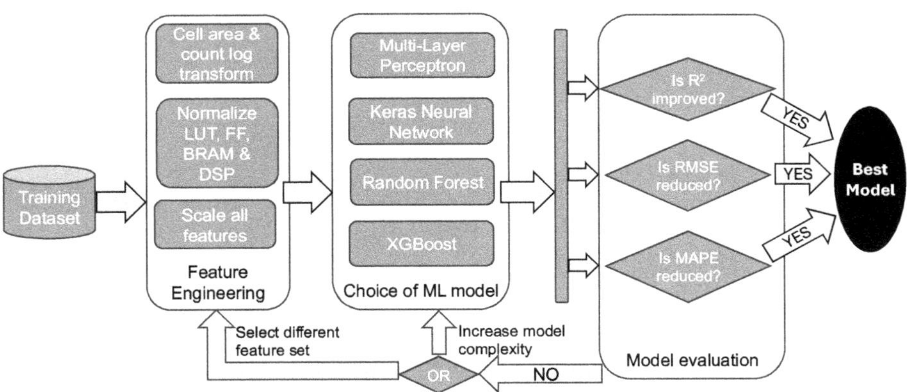

Fig. 2. Feature engineering, model choice and evaluation metrics used in MARU learning framework.

Figure 3 shows implementing an ensemble based machine learning model (e.g., Random Forest) as part of our framework. The input data and data labels that needs to be predicted is merged together to form a training dataset. We apply bootstrap sampling and K-Fold cross validation [30] methods to help reduce variance, add more robustness to predicted models, avoid over-fitting, explore more diverse feature combinations compared to naive weighted coefficient based predictions in linear regression.

To support cross-FPGA generalization, MARU incorporates transfer learning through fine-tuning and residual-based adaptation. Fine-tuning is performed by warm-starting the pretrained XGBoost model and continuing training on a small subset of labeled designs from the target FPGA (e.g., tens to a few hundred samples), rather than retraining from scratch. In residual-based adaptation, the pretrained model is kept fixed and a lightweight model is trained to predict residual errors on the target domain. Fine-tuning is required only when adapting to a new FPGA family and does not require re-running the synthesis flow for each new design. After this one-time step, inference on new designs requires only FPGA resource utilization features and incurs sub-millisecond latency, with no additional synthesis or place-and-route steps.

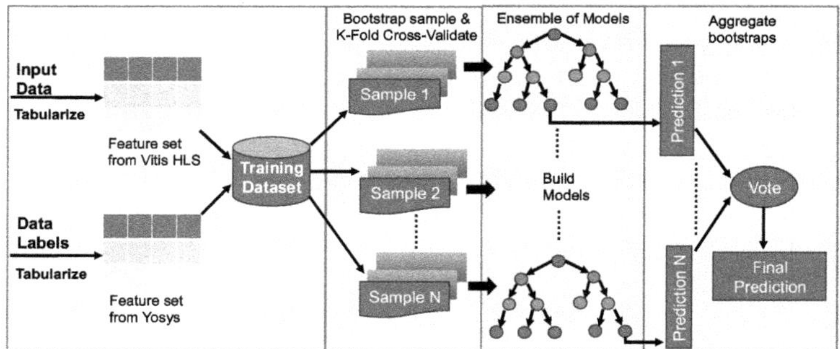

Fig. 3. Implementing area estimate prediction with random forest based predictors, bootstrap sampling and K-Fold cross-validation.

3.3 Experimental Setup Overview

To systematically evaluate the predictive capabilities of the MARU framework, we designed five distinct experiments that vary along benchmarks and prediction settings. Each experiment explores a different generalization axis—ranging from evaluation within the same benchmark and FPGA to multiple benchmarks modeling across different FPGA versions—and informs the design of the training and test splits.

Table 4 summarizes the experimental setup. It outlines the specific scenario explored in each experiment, the number of benchmarks involved, and the nature of the modeling case (e.g., direct prediction vs. transfer learning). This structured evaluation enables a comprehensive assessment of model robustness and portability across diverse circuit configurations.

Circuits are synthesized in FPGA using HLS and ASIC using Yosys with a fixed 10ns clock period. This enables timing-aware resource utilization across both tools. We also used liberty files from open-source Skywater130 PDK [16] to capture standard area estimates.

4 Results

In this section, we evaluate MARU for ASIC area prediction under progressively more challenging generalization settings: (i) across benchmarks and (ii) across FPGA architectures as in Table 4. Performance is reported using the coefficient of determination (R^2), RMSE, and MAPE.

4.1   Experiment 1: Intra-Benchmark Prediction

This experiment corresponds to setting #1 (Same FPGA, Same Benchmark) in Table 4. We establish a baseline by training models on variants of a single benchmark, `atax`, synthesized for the Xilinx `xc7v` FPGA, and evaluating on unseen variants from the same benchmark. The goal is to identify effective model classes for area estimation, and to assess whether accurate prediction is achievable within a relatively homogeneous setting before extending to cross-benchmark and cross-FPGA scenarios.

Table 4. Summary of experimental scenarios and cases for training and inference for each experiment and their corresponding modeling configurations.

Exp	Training Benchmarks	Inference Benchmarks	Methods evaluated
1 (Sec 4.1)	FPGA V (80% of A)	FPGA V (20% of A)	Baseline
2 (Sec 4.2)	FPGA V (80% of A)	FPGA V (B, G, M, K, S)	Direct, Fine-tuned
3 (Sec 4.3)	FPGA V (each benchmark 80%)	FPGA Z (same benchmark 20%)	Direct, Fine-tuned
4 (Sec 4.4)	FPGA V (8 benchmarks)	FPGA V (1 benchmark)	Leave-one-out, Fine-tuned
5 (Sec 4.5)	FPGA V (9 benchmarks)	FPGA Z (1 benchmark)	Direct, Fine-tuned

Benchmarks: A=atax, B=bicg, G=gemm/gesummv, M=mvt, K=k2mm/k3mm, S=syrk/syr2k. FPGA: V=xc7v585tffg1157-3, Z=xczu9eg-ffvb1156-2.

Linear models fail to capture the underlying complexity of the data due to nonlinear interactions between resource features (e.g., LUT, FF, BRAM). As a result, we evaluate nonlinear models, including tree-based ensemble methods (Random Forest, XGBoost) and neural networks (MLP, Keras). Among these, XGBoost achieves the best performance, and is therefore used in all experiments.

Table 5. Comparison of models for ASIC area prediction on unseen circuit variants.

ML Model	MLP	Keras NN	Random Forest	XGBoost
R^2	−11.42	0.0033	0.9912	0.9942
RMSE (%)	104.30	29.54	2.77	2.26
MAPE (%)	99.99	25.05	1.44	1.47

As shown in Table 5, XGBoost achieves the highest accuracy ($R^2 = 0.9942$, RMSE = 2.26%, MAPE = 1.47%), closely followed by Random Forest ($R^2 = 0.9912$, RMSE = 2.77%, MAPE = 1.44%). In contrast, neural networks perform poorly, with unstable or near-zero R^2 values and significantly higher errors.

4.2 Experiment 2: Inter-Benchmark Prediction

This experiment corresponds to setting #2 (same FPGA, different benchmark) in Table 4. We evaluate how the baseline model trained on `atax` benchmark generalizes to unseen benchmarks (e.g., `bicg`, `gemm`) on the same FPGA. We consider direct prediction, where the trained model is applied to unseen benchmarks without modification, and transfer learning, where the model is fine-tuned using 20% of the target benchmark and evaluated on the remaining 80%.

Table 6. Cross-benchmark transfer from a model trained on `atax`.

Benchmark	R^2		RMSE		MAPE (%)	
	Direct	Transfer	Direct	Transfer	Direct	Transfer
BICG	0.47	0.99	1.36e6	1.32e5	4.49	1.77
GEMM	−10.99	0.93	8.15e6	6.04e5	71.13	3.09
MVT	0.32	0.99	2.13e6	2.59e5	11.22	4.45
GESUMMV	−0.38	1.00	4.24e6	9.14e4	41.48	0.80
K2MM	−23.15	0.89	1.54e7	1.03e6	81.70	3.44
K3MM	−44.55	0.78	1.45e7	1.01e6	82.58	3.34
SYR2K	−17.44	0.94	1.55e7	8.59e5	81.30	2.39
SYRK	−9.43	0.95	7.88e6	5.64e5	70.43	2.53
Average	**−13.52**	**0.94**	**8.28e6**	**6.63e5**	**45.54**	**2.73**

Case 1: Direct Prediction. As shown in Table 6, direct prediction performs inconsistently across benchmarks. While simpler benchmarks such as `bicg` achieve moderate accuracy ($R^2 = 0.465$), most benchmarks exhibit poor generalization, with several cases yielding large negative R^2 values (e.g., `k3mm`: −44.55). This indicates that a model trained on a single benchmark does not capture cross-benchmark variability in resource–area relationships.

Case 2: Transfer Learning. Applying transfer learning (via fine-tuning on a small subset of target-benchmark data) significantly improves performance across all benchmarks. For example, R^2 improves from −10.99 to 0.934 for `gemm`, from −23.15 to 0.893 for `k2mm`, and from −44.55 to 0.780 for `k3mm`. Even benchmarks with moderate baseline performance (e.g., `bicg`, `mvt`) improve to near-perfect accuracy ($R^2 > 0.99$). As shown in Fig. 4, predictions after transfer learning align closely with the ideal diagonal. These results demonstrate that while direct prediction provides limited generalization across benchmarks, lightweight transfer learning enables accurate and robust area estimation.

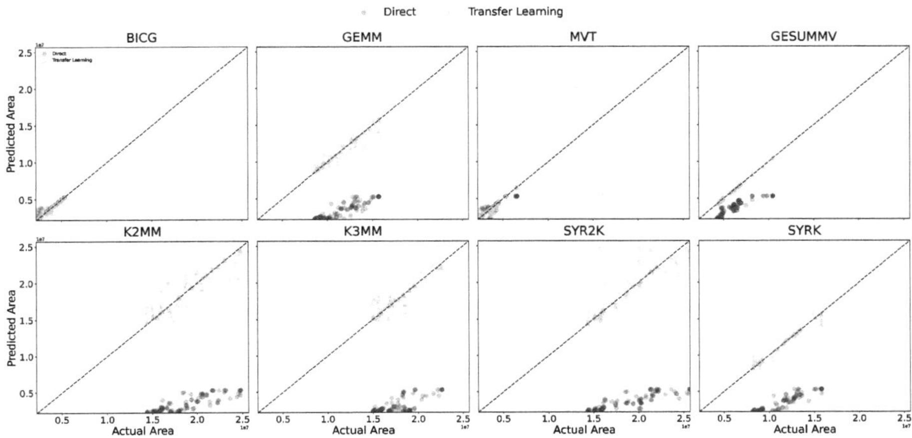

Fig. 4. Transfer learning and prediction of **atax** ML model on different benchmarks. Blue is direct prediction and green is transfer learning.

4.3   Experiment 3: Testing Cross-FPGA Generalization

A frequent question is, if a model is trained using a particular FPGA, will the model work even if features are collected on a different FPGA. This experiment corresponds to the setting #3 (same benchmark, different FPGA) in Table 4. We evaluate how a model trained using the **xc7v** FPGA generalizes even if the inference features are obtained from a different FPGA (**xczu9**), while still predicting ASIC-equivalent area metric from FPGA-derived features. We consider direct prediction across FPGA architectures, and residual-based transfer learning, where the model is lightly adapted using target-FPGA data.

Table 7. Cross-FPGA prediction accuracy across Polybench (Experiment 3).

Benchmark	R^2		RMSE		MAPE (%)	
	Direct	Transfer	Direct	Transfer	Direct	Transfer
ATAX	1.0000	1.0000	10120	9633	0.20%	0.21%
BICG	0.9991	0.9992	58685	55556	0.82%	0.82%
GEMM	0.9618	0.9635	452905	442636	2.24%	2.34%
MVT	0.9878	0.9881	241168	237592	2.82%	3.10%
GESUMMV	0.9679	0.9720	652365	608872	1.21%	0.83%
K2MM	0.9682	0.9738	583385	529027	1.57%	1.49%
K3MM	0.9494	0.9560	581696	542479	1.74%	1.86%
SYR2K	0.9869	0.9901	405690	353009	1.04%	1.08%
SYRK	0.9916	0.9921	228287	221292	0.68%	0.72%
Average	**0.9792**	**0.9816**	**357144**	**333344**	**1.37**	**1.38**

Case 1: Direct Prediction. As shown in Table 7, direct cross-FPGA prediction achieves strong baseline performance, with an average R^2 of 0.979, indicating that the learned resource–area relationships transfer well across FPGA architectures. This is further supported by low prediction error, with an average RMSE of 357,144 and MAPE of 1.37%, demonstrating accurate absolute and relative estimation across benchmarks.

Case 2: Transfer Learning. Applying residual-based transfer learning further improves performance, increasing the average R^2 to 0.9816 while reducing RMSE to 333,344 and maintaining low MAPE (1.38%). Direct prediction already produces close estimates, but residual-based transfer learning reduces outliers and improves consistency. Across all benchmarks, transfer learning yields consistent improvements (average $\Delta R^2 \approx +0.0043$), with larger gains observed in compute-intensive benchmarks such as k3mm (+0.0066) and k2mm (+0.0057), where FPGA-specific DSP and BRAM mappings differ more significantly. These results indicate that cross-FPGA generalization is inherently strong, and lightweight transfer learning enhances robustness.

4.4   Experiment 4: Multi-Benchmark Prediction

This experiment corresponds to setting #4 (different benchmark, same FPGA) in Table 4. We train a unified model across multiple benchmarks and evaluate generalization using a leave-one-benchmark-out strategy. In each iteration, one benchmark is held out for testing, while the model is trained on the remaining benchmarks. We then apply transfer learning by fine-tuning on 50% of the held-out benchmark.

Case 1: Direct Prediction. As shown in Table 8, direct prediction gives mixed results across benchmarks. Memory-bound benchmarks such as bicg ($R^2 = 0.795$) and mvt ($R^2 = 0.831$) achieve reasonable accuracy, showing that learned patterns can be partially transferred. In contrast, compute-intensive designs such as k2mm ($R^2 = -0.805$) and k3mm ($R^2 = -3.205$) perform poorly, reflecting differences in DSP/BRAM-driven scaling behavior. This variability is also reflected in the error metrics, with a high average RMSE of 2,608,956 and MAPE of 20.15%, indicating poor generalization to unseen resource distributions. Overall, direct multi-benchmark prediction is inconsistent, with several benchmarks exhibiting negative R^2 values.

Table 8. Multi-benchmark leave-one-out validation results (Experiment 4).

Benchmark	R^2		RMSE		MAPE (%)	
	Direct	Transfer	Direct	Transfer	Direct	Transfer
ATAX	0.42	0.99	1532263	217783	24.20%	1.28%
BICG	0.80	1.00	909064	128045	11.94%	1.19%
GEMM	0.21	0.95	2073505	538106	11.15%	2.30%
GESUMMV	-1.00	1.00	5075980	210338	67.98%	0.76%
K2MM	-0.80	0.94	4286101	779003	13.24%	1.90%
K3MM	-3.21	0.93	4942444	635418	16.85%	1.58%
MVT	0.83	0.99	1066137	256862	16.59%	3.22%
SYR2K	-0.12	0.95	3889193	857838	13.98%	1.74%
SYRK	0.67	0.97	1405916	448094	7.41%	1.37%
Average	**−0.24**	**0.97**	**2608956**	**452832**	**20.15**	**1.71**

Case 2: Transfer Learning. Applying transfer learning significantly improves performance across all benchmarks. As shown in Table 8, the largest gains occur for benchmarks with poor baseline performance—for example, gesummv improves from −0.997 to 0.997, and k3mm from −3.205 to 0.930. Even benchmarks with moderate baseline accuracy (e.g., bicg, mvt) improve performance ($R^2 > 0.99$).

In addition to the R^2 improvement, transfer learning substantially reduces prediction error, lowering the average RMSE from 2,608,956 to 452,832 and MAPE from 20.15% to 1.71%. The results in Table 8 show that while direct prediction is unreliable (mean $R^2 = -0.2449$), transfer learning produces consistently accurate estimates (mean $R^2 = 0.97$). A multi-benchmark model provides a strong starting point, but accurate area estimation across different benchmarks requires lightweight transfer learning to adapt to each benchmark.

4.5   Experiment 5: Multi-Benchmark Cross-FPGA Generalization.

This experiment evaluates whether a multi-benchmark model trained on xc7v data can generalize to xczu9 while still predicting a unified ASIC-equivalent area metric from FPGA-derived features, and corresponds to setting #5 in Table 4. We report both direct cross-FPGA prediction and residual-based transfer learning for adaptation.

Case 1: Direct Prediction. Table 9 summarizes direct prediction results using a multi-benchmark model trained on xc7v. Direct transfer achieves a strong baseline (average $R^2 = 0.8948$), but performance varies across benchmarks, with the largest degradation observed for compute-intensive benchmarks such as k3mm. This variability is also reflected in the error metrics, with an average RMSE of 2.82M and MAPE of 4.96%, indicating that cross-FPGA transfer becomes more challenging when training across diverse benchmarks.

Table 9. Multi-benchmark model Cross-FPGA prediction accuracy (Experiment 5).

Benchmark	R^2		RMSE		MAPE (%)	
	Direct	Transfer	Direct	Transfer	Direct	Transfer
ATAX	0.99	0.99	0.15M	0.14M	2.63	2.73
BICG	0.99	0.99	0.17M	0.14M	3.47	3.11
GEMM	0.84	0.88	0.92M	0.81M	4.64	4.20
MVT	0.96	0.98	0.42M	0.31M	7.28	5.85
GESUMMV	0.92	0.96	1.05M	0.72M	10.89	5.60
K2MM	0.89	0.92	1.11M	0.95M	3.78	3.31
K3MM	0.66	0.78	1.51M	1.20M	4.65	4.20
SYR2K	0.87	0.88	1.28M	1.23M	3.92	4.16
SYRK	0.93	0.94	0.64M	0.60M	3.34	2.95
Average	**0.89**	**0.93**	**2.82M**	**1.08M**	**4.96**	**4.01**

Case 2: Residual-Based Transfer Learning. Residual-based transfer learning (adapted using 20% of the target `xczu9` data) improves robustness and increases average performance to $R^2 = 0.9252$ (Table 9). In addition to the R^2 improvement, transfer learning reduces prediction error, lowering the average RMSE from 2.82M to 1.08M and MAPE from 4.96% to 4.01%. Gains are most pronounced for benchmarks that exhibit larger cross-FPGA mismatch under direct prediction (e.g., `k3mm` and `gesummv`), indicating that residual adaptation helps correct FPGA-specific implementation differences. Overall, these results show that a unified multi-benchmark model transfers effectively across FPGA generations, and lightweight residual adaptation further improves consistency and reduces large errors, particularly for benchmarks with distinct DSP/BRAM-driven scaling behavior.

5   Conclusion

In this work, we built a learning-based framework, MARU, to predict ASIC area estimates from Vitis HLS resource utilization statistics. Across multiple carefully designed experiments, the MARU framework demonstrated strong predictive performance and generalization across circuits and FPGAs. MARU achieves an average MAPE of around 4% in cross-FPGA, multi-benchmark scenarios, with R^2 values up to 0.99. While per-benchmark models achieve near-perfect accuracy, generalization across benchmarks and platforms benefits significantly from transfer learning. Inference requires less than 0.12 ms per design on average, while lightweight transfer adaptation completes in under one second.

Acknowledgments. This research was supported in part by NSF Grants 2326894, 2425655, and 2417658. Any opinions, findings, conclusions, or recommendations are those of the authors and not of the funding agencies.

Disclosure of Interests. Authors have no competing interests.

References

1. AMD Xilinx: 7 series dsp48e1 slice user guide (ug479) (2018). https://www.xilinx. com/support/documentation/user_guides/ug479_7Series_D-SP48E1.pdf
2. AMD Xilinx: 7 series fpgas data sheet: Overview (virtex-7, kintex-7, artix-7) (2018). https://www.xilinx.com/support/documentation/data_sheets/ds180_ 7Series_O-verview.pdf
3. AMD Xilinx: Ultrascale architecture and product data sheet (2019). https://www. xilinx.com/support/documentation/data_sheets/ds890-ultrascale-overview.pdf
4. AMD Xilinx: Versal dsp58 architecture (2023). https://docs.amd.com/r/en-US/ am004-versal-dsp-engine/DSP58-Architecture
5. AMD Xilinx: Vitis high-level synthesis (hls) (2023). https://www.xilinx.com/ products/design-tools/vitis/vitis-hls.html
6. Bacellar, A.T.L., et al.: Differentiable weightless neural networks. In: Salakhutdinov, R., et al. (eds.) Proceedings of the 41st International Conference on Machine Learning. Proceedings of Machine Learning Research, vol. 235, pp. 2277–2295. PMLR (2024). https://proceedings.mlr.press/v235/bacellar24a.html
7. Boutros, A., Nurvitadhi, E., Betz, V.: Specializing for efficiency: Customizing ai inference processors on fpgas. In: 2021 International Conference on Microelectronics (ICM), pp. 62–65 (2021). https://doi.org/10.1109/ICM52667.2021.9664938
8. Boutros, A., Yazdanshenas, S., Betz, V.: Embracing diversity: Enhanced dsp blocks for low-precision deep learning on fpgas. In: 2018 28th International Conference on Field Programmable Logic and Applications (FPL), pp. 35–357 (2018). https:// doi.org/10.1109/FPL.2018.00014
9. Boutros, A., Yazdanshenas, S., Betz, V.: You cannot improve what you do not measure: Fpga vs. asic efficiency gaps for convolutional neural network inference **11**(3) (2018). https://doi.org/10.1145/3242898
10. Cong, J., et al.: Fpga hls today: Successes, challenges, and opportunities. ACM Trans. Reconfigurable Technol. Syst. **15**(4), 1–42 (2022)
11. Cong, J., Liu, B., Neuendorffer, S., Noguera, J., Vissers, K., Zhang, Z.: High-level synthesis for fpgas: From prototyping to deployment. IEEE Trans. Comput. Aided Des. Integr. Circuits Syst. **30**(4), 473–491 (2011). https://doi.org/10.1109/TCAD. 2011.2110592
12. Dai, S., Zhou, Y., Zhang, H., Ustun, E., Young, E.F., Zhang, Z.: Fast and accurate estimation of quality of results in high-level synthesis with machine learning. In: 2018 IEEE 26th Annual International Symposium on Field-Programmable Custom Computing Machines (FCCM), pp. 129–132 (2018). https://doi.org/10.1109/ FCCM.2018.00029
13. Dai, S., Zhou, Y., Zhang, H., Ustun, E., Young, E.F., Zhang, Z.: Fast and accurate estimation of quality of results in high-level synthesis with machine learning. In: 2018 IEEE 26th Annual International Symposium on Field-Programmable Custom Computing Machines (FCCM), pp. 129–132 (2018). https://doi.org/10.1109/ FCCM.2018.00029

14. Ding, Z., Sohrabizadeh, A., Li, W., Qin, Z., Sun, Y., Cong, J.: Efficient Task Transfer for HLS DSE. Association for Computing Machinery, New York, NY, USA (2025). https://doi.org/10.1145/3676536.3676723
15. Du, Y., Hu, Y., Zhou, Z., Zhang, Z.: High-performance sparse linear algebra on hbm-equipped fpgas using hls: A case study on spmv. Association for Computing Machinery, New York, NY, USA (2022). https://doi.org/10.1145/3490422.3502368
16. Google, SkyWater Technology Foundry: SkyWater Open Source PDK. https://github.com/google/skywater-pdk, Accessed 30 Sep 2025
17. Goswami, P., Shahshahani, M., Bhatia, D.: Mlsbench: A benchmark set for machine learning based fpga hls design flows. In: 2022 IEEE 13th Latin America Symposium on Circuits and System (LASCAS), pp. 1–4 (2022). https://doi.org/10.1109/LASCAS53948.2022.9789084
18. Guo, L., et al.: Rapidstream: Parallel physical implementation of fpga hls designs. Association for Computing Machinery, New York, NY, USA (2022). https://doi.org/10.1145/3490422.3502361
19. Intel: Stratix v device handbook (2018). https://www.intel.com/content/www/us/en/docs/programmable/683665
20. Kwon, J., Carloni, L.P.: Transfer learning for design-space exploration with high-level synthesis. In: 2020 ACM/IEEE 2nd Workshop on Machine Learning for CAD (MLCAD), pp. 163–168 (2020). https://doi.org/10.1145/3380446.3430636
21. Lahti, S., Hämäläinen, T.D.: High-level synthesis for fpgas—a hardware engineer's perspective. IEEE Access **13**, 28574–28593 (2025). https://doi.org/10.1109/ACCESS.2025.3540320
22. Lahti, S., Sjövall, P., Vanne, J., Hämäläinen, T.D.: Are we there yet? a study on the state of high-level synthesis. IEEE Trans. Comput. Aided Des. Integr. Circuits Syst. **38**(5), 898–911 (2019). https://doi.org/10.1109/TCAD.2018.2834439
23. Lai, Y.H., et al.: Susy: A programming model for productive construction of high-performance systolic arrays on fpgas. In: 2020 IEEE/ACM International Conference On Computer Aided Design (ICCAD), pp. 1–9 (2020)
24. Lattice Semiconductor: ice40 ultraplus family data sheet (2019). https://www.latticesemi.com/-/media/LatticeSemi/Documents/DataSheets/iCE/iCE40-UltraPlus-Family-Data-Sheet.pdf
25. Lattice Semiconductor: Lattice ecp5 family data sheet (2020). https://www.latticesemi.com/-/media/LatticeSemi/Documents/DataSheets/ECP-5/FPGA-DS-02012.pdf
26. Lau, J., Sivaraman, A., Zhang, Q., Gulzar, M.A., Cong, J., Kim, M.: Heterorefactor: refactoring for heterogeneous computing with fpga. Association for Computing Machinery, New York, NY, USA (2020). https://doi.org/10.1145/3377811.3380340
27. Lin, Z., Yuan, Z., Zhao, J., Zhang, W., Wang, H., Tian, Y.: Powergear: Early-stage power estimation in FPGA HLS via heterogeneous edge-centric gnns. CoRR (2022)
28. Lin, Z., Zhao, J., Sinha, S., Zhang, W.: Hl-pow: A learning-based power modeling framework for high-level synthesis. In: 2020 25th Asia and South Pacific Design Automation Conference (ASP-DAC), pp. 574–580 (2020). https://doi.org/10.1109/ASP-DAC47756.2020.9045442
29. Makrani, H.M., Sayadi, H., Mohsenin, T., Rafatirad, S., Sasan, A., Homayoun, H.: Xppe: cross-platform performance estimation of hardware accelerators using machine learning. Association for Computing Machinery, New York, NY, USA (2019). https://doi.org/10.1145/3287624.3288756
30. Marcot, B.G., Hanea, A.M.: What is an optimal value of k in k-fold cross-validation in discrete Bayesian network analysis? Comput. Stat. **36**(3), 2009–2031 (2020). https://doi.org/10.1007/s00180-020-00999-9

31. Murray, K.E., et al.: Vtr 8: High-performance cad and customizable fpga architecture modelling **13**(2) (2020). https://doi-org.ezproxy1.lib.asu.edu/10.1145/3388617
32. Nane, R., et al.: A survey and evaluation of fpga high-level synthesis tools **35**(10) (2016). https://doi.org/10.1109/TCAD.2015.2513673
33. O'Neal, K., Liu, M., Tang, H., Kalantar, A., DeRenard, K., Brisk, P.: Hlspredict: Cross platform performance prediction for fpga high-level synthesis. In: 2018 IEEE/ACM International Conference on Computer-Aided Design (ICCAD), pp. 1–8 (2018). https://doi.org/10.1145/3240765.3240816
34. Rashid, R., Steffan, J.G., Betz, V.: Comparing performance, productivity and scalability of the tilt overlay processor to opencl hls. In: 2014 International Conference on Field-Programmable Technology (FPT), pp. 20–27 (2014). https://doi.org/10.1109/FPT.2014.7082748
35. Susskind, Z., et al.: Weightless neural networks for efficient edge inference. Association for Computing Machinery, New York, NY, USA (2023). https://doi.org/10.1145/3559009.3569680
36. Wei, Z., Arora, A., Li, R., John, L.: Hlsdataset: Open-source dataset for ml-assisted fpga design using high level synthesis. In: 2023 IEEE 34th International Conference on Application-specific Systems, Architectures and Processors (ASAP), pp. 197–204 (2023). https://doi.org/10.1109/ASAP57973.2023.00040
37. Wei, Z., Arora, A., Shriver, E., John, L.: Cross-fpga power estimation from high level synthesis via transfer-learning. Association for Computing Machinery, New York, NY, USA (2024). https://doi.org/10.1145/3626202.3637621
38. Wei, Z., Arora, A., Shriver, E., John, L.: Atapp: Architecture and technology aware power predictor for unseen fpgas (2025)
39. Wei, Z., Seigler, A., Lowe, S., Shriver, E., Arora, A., John, L.K.: Xpnet: Cross-fpga power prediction from high level language code. IEEE Trans. Comput.-Aided Des. Integr. Circ. Syst. (2025)
40. Wolf, C.: Yosys open synthesis suite. https://yosyshq.net/yosys/
41. Wu, N., Yang, H., Xie, Y., Li, P., Hao, C.: High-level synthesis performance prediction using gnns: benchmarking, modeling, and advancing. Association for Computing Machinery, New York, NY, USA (2022). https://doi.org/10.1145/3489517.3530408
42. Xiang, S., et al.: Heteroflow: An accelerator programming model with decoupled data placement for software-defined fpgas. Association for Computing Machinery, New York, NY, USA (2022). https://doi.org/10.1145/3490422.3502369

Revisiting Priority Cuts for Technology Mapping of LUT-Based FPGAs

Christoph Flothow[✉][iD] and Christian Hochberger[iD]

Department of Electrical Engineering and Information Technology, Computer
Systems Group, TU Darmstadt, Darmstadt, Germany
`{flothow,hochberger}@rs.tu-darmstadt.de`

Abstract. Traditionally, a primary goal of technology mapping for K-input lookup-tables (LUTs) is depth minimization. A typical approach is to make cuts in a Boolean network such that the logic of each cut fits into a single LUT, and thus cover the entire graph. Many different cuts can potentially be mapped into a LUT and finding the optimal cut has a very high complexity. The widely used priority cuts algorithm only stores a small fixed number of cuts per node during the mapping, the so-called priority cuts, yet produces very good results at a comparatively low runtime.

In this work, the priority cuts algorithm is examined using the well-known EPFL benchmark set. A number of these benchmarks are significantly larger than those used in the original paper, enabling an analysis of the mapping quality that better represents modern requirements. In particular, the performance is compared to exhaustive cut enumeration, while focusing on the achieved depth.

The insights obtained are applied to a recent extension of the priority cuts algorithm that uses the Ashenhurst-Curtis decomposition to effectively utilize larger cuts, which can not be directly implemented by a single LUT, during mapping. As a result, three new records are set in terms of depth in the ongoing EPFL competition. To alleviate the increased runtime from storing more cuts per node, a method of sorting the cuts before attempting the decomposition is introduced. This procedure roughly halves the runtime for a given number of cuts stored per node while maintaining the result quality.

Keywords: Technology Mapping · LUT Mapping · Priority Cuts · Ashenhurst-Curtis Decomposition

1 Introduction

Most modern field programmable gate arrays (FPGAs) use lookup-tables (LUTs) to implement logic. This means that functions realized by one LUT can only have a small, limited number of input variables. Technology mapping for LUT-based FPGAs went through many steps of evolution. The first approaches used classical library binding, but produced inefficient mappings. Later, algebraic division was

© The Author(s), under exclusive license to Springer Nature Switzerland AG 2026
G. Leone et al. (Eds.): ARC 2026, LNCS 16514, pp. 238–254, 2026.
https://doi.org/10.1007/978-3-032-29365-7_15

used to decompose large functions into feasible functions. The primary goal here was to minimize the number of LUTs required for the mapping as the FPGAs of that generation provided a very limited number of LUTs. Another step in this evolution was the functional decomposition, for example with the Roth-Karp method [18]. The goal was still to use as few LUTs as possible. Many FPGA vendors today work with the next evolutionary step, structural mapping, with FlowMap [8] being one of the prominent early examples. Here, the optimization goal is typically no longer the number of LUTs, but rather the depth of the mapped network, that is how many LUTs are cascaded in the longest path, as this defines the maximum clock frequency that can be achieved. The LUT size evolved from 3/4 inputs in the early years to 6/8 inputs nowadays, but the number of LUTs is continuously increasing. Thus, it becomes more and more important to optimize the delay of the mapped network. A CTO of a major FPGA vendor once said: "You can always buy larger FPGAs, you can never buy faster FPGAs".

Today's most successful technology mapping approaches are cut based. They start from Boolean networks, typically in the form of And-Inverter-Graphs (AIGs), and search for cuts that create subgraphs that each fit into a single LUT. In general, it is infeasible to explore all possible cuts, in particular for larger input networks and LUT sizes. Instead, a small, limited number of cuts is kept with every node.

In this paper, we revisit such cut-based technology mapping approaches and investigate what influence the number of cuts per node has. It turns out that with growing LUT size, this influence becomes quite noticeable. We will then show an approach that reduces the computational cost by applying an optimized sorting strategy at each node. In this way our approach reaches three new record breaking mapping depths for the well known and widely used EPFL benchmark set [1].

The remainder of this paper is structured as follows: The next section explains some background information and the related work. Section 3 explains how the state-of-the-art algorithm uses only a small number of cuts per node. It shows, by exhaustive enumeration of all cuts, that for larger LUTs the optimal result is not reached in a considerable number of cases. Section 4 then shows that this situation becomes even more critical if a more advanced mapping method is used. The evaluation of our proposed method is then shown in Sect. 5. It is followed by a conclusion and an outlook onto possible next steps.

2 Background and Related Work

With the introduction of the first FPGAs in 1985, the question of how to efficiently map logic onto them in order to fully utilize their capabilities quickly gained interest. It became clear very early on that library binding was not an appropriate approach, as even a single 4-input LUT could implement $2^{2^4} = 65536$ different functions when including input permutations, too many for efficient matching to be possible.

An early approach that achieved significant improvements in terms of runtime and the number of LUTs required for a mapping was Chortle [11]. This worked on a directed acyclic graph (DAG) by first converting it into a forest of fanout-free trees, and then mapping each of these trees in an area optimal way. Naturally, the initially required transformation into the forest of trees represented a drawback, and as such the overall mapping was not guaranteed to be area optimal.

A very well-known approach that did not have this drawback was later introduced with FlowMap [8]. This approach promised to be *an optimal technology mapping algorithm for delay optimization*. Indeed, for a given input network, it produced mappings that were demonstrably depth-optimal. It achieved this by computing minimum height K-feasible cuts in the network based on the maximal flow through the network.

A cut for a given node, N, is defined as a set of nodes such that any path from a primary input to N has to pass through at least one of the nodes within the cut. A cut is said to be K-feasible if it has at most K nodes in its cut set. K-feasibility is important in the context of LUT mapping, as it describes how many signals enter into the cut from outside. Thus, the logic represented by all of the internal nodes covered by a K-feasible cut can always be completely implemented by a K-input LUT, regardless of the amount of internal nodes. An example of a network covered by 3- and 4-feasible cuts, is shown in Fig. 1.

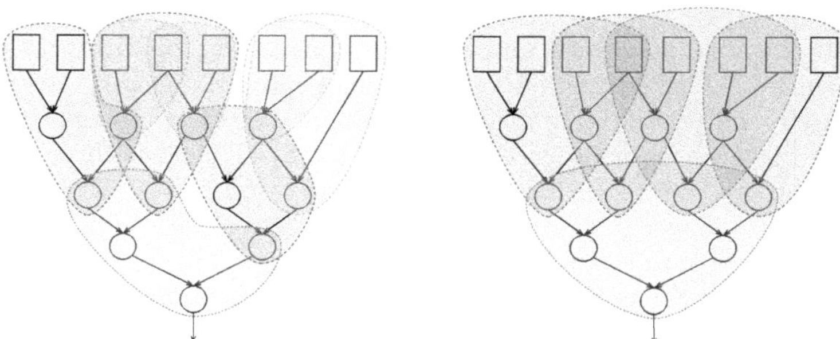

Fig. 1. A generic Boolean network covered by 3-feasible and 4-feasible cuts on the left and right respectively. The rectangles represent inputs to the network, and the circles represent inner nodes with an arbitrary 2-input function associated with them. The colour of the cut represents the depth at which is it is implemented, counting from the output node, with red, blue and green each indicating a depth of 1, 2 and 3 respectively.

After FlowMap, further demonstrably depth-optimal mapping approaches were introduced such as CutMap [9] which aimed to improve the number of LUTs required and DAOmap [7] which further improved both the LUT count as well as the runtime. On the other hand, the priority cuts algorithm [17] no longer guaranteed depth optimality, but in practice it showed very good results and significantly improved runtime, which led to its widespread use even today. Its spread was further aided by its implementation in the open source logic synthesis tool ABC [4], which was also used and extended in this work.

Although depth optimality had been achieved, this was only true for a given input network, not for the underlying Boolean function. This dependency on the initial network structure is known as *structual bias* and it has resulted in a large amount of literature dedicated to the problem of logic optimization, where the initial network is transformed such that the later mapping is improved. An example of this is the use of structural choices [6], where multiple representations of the same logic are included in the graph, allowing the mapper to choose whichever is more beneficial. Another is the so-called lazy man's synthesis [20] where the network is modified by replacing small sections of it with functionally identical versions from a pre-computed library, in such a way as to reduce the overall depth.

A recent development has been the application of reinforcement learning to the problem of technology mapping in [21] and the use of GPUs [12] to greatly speed up the mapping time of large networks. The priority cuts algorithm itself was recently extended to reduce structural bias in [5], which will be covered in more detail in Sect. 4.

3   Priority Cuts

The priority cuts algorithm, introduced in [17], takes a Boolean network as an input, typically in the form of an AIG, and computes a covering for the entire graph in two main stages. First a number of passes over all the nodes in the graph are performed, going from the inputs to the outputs, in order to select a single representative K-feasible cut for each node. This representative cut is then used in the second stage, where the cover is computed by going from the outputs to the inputs. Initially all outputs are added to a queue of nodes to be handled. Each time that a node from the queue is handled, the nodes in its representative cut are placed into the queue, provided that they have not been placed into the queue before, and the logic that this cut represents is mapped onto a single LUT. This continues until there are no more nodes in the queue, and thus the graph has been effectively covered. This process of first computing cuts and then computing the covering was quite common. The novelty was the way in which the cuts were computed.

A simple method of computing the cuts for a node, provided that the cuts of the predecessor nodes have already been computed, is as follows: Take the set of all cuts of each predecessor node, add the respective predecessor node itself to each set as a so-called trivial cut, and then form all possible pair-wise combinations. The union of each of these pairs of cuts is a valid cut of the successor node, as this node can only be reached from the primary outputs through one of the predecessor nodes. If all possible cuts of the predecessors are used, this also results in all possible cuts of the successor node being computed. This number can grow very large very quickly for larger LUTs, and so in general such an exhaustive enumeration is not feasible.

The priority cuts algorithm limits the number of cuts stored at each node during mapping to a small number of so-called priority cuts. When computing the cuts for a certain node, the K-feasible cuts are sorted by a certain criterion, and only the C best cuts are stored and then further used when computing the cuts of the following successor node(s). As the two trivial cuts of the predecessors are also included, this means that in each step at most $(C + 1)^2$ different cuts have to be computed. For the default value of $C = 8$ that is used, this results in a significant reduction in the computational cost. In order to optimize for depth while also reducing the required area, a number of passes are performed using different sorting criteria, initially focusing on depth and then focusing on area recovery on the non-critical paths. According to the original publication:

> Experiments indicate that such prioritization gives a depth-optimum mapping for 95% of all benchmarks and LUT sizes, even if only one cut is stored at each node! Increasing the number of priority cuts to 8 allows the algorithm to avoid area penalty due to not enumerating all cuts, while still offering dramatic improvements in memory and runtime, compared to exhaustive cut enumeration.[17]

In order to analyze the performance on a more modern set of benchmarks, mappings were performed on the EPFL benchmark set [2] in three different ways: using only a single cut, using the default 8 cuts and finally exhaustively enumerating all of the cuts. As in [17], the LUT sizes $K = 4, 6, 8$ and 10 were considered. As some AIG optimization will typically be done before mapping, in this case the two light-weight AIG optimization scripts **resyn** and **resyn2** were applied. These perform multiple rounds of balancing, rewriting and refactoring [14] to reduce both the number of levels and the number of nodes in the AIG. These scripts were also used in [17] in tests with sequential mapping of some industrial benchmarks. The results are shown in Table 1.

The entries in the table are sorted by the number of nodes in the AIG directly before mapping. As expected, most of the improvements that are achieved through the use of more cuts occur in larger graphs towards the bottom of the table. The evaluation in [17] used the 20 largest MCNC benchmarks [19], as was also done in [15]. Here it can be seen that the AIGs had between 1700 and 13000 nodes, with an average of around 5000 nodes. This highlights the benefit of this new evaluation on a very diverse benchmark set where the AIG sizes in terms of nodes span multiple orders of magnitude, with multiple benchmarks that are significantly larger than the largest benchmark in the previous set.

Looking more closely at the results, it can be seen that for smaller LUTs with up to 6 inputs, using the default of 8 cuts always achieved the best possible depth. Indeed, even just storing a single cut in these cases resulted in mappings that were depth-optimal in the vast majority of cases, and very close to depth-optimal in the rest. It should be reiterated that *depth-optimal* in this case refers to mapping via cuts on a given AIG without any further transformations. Due to structural bias, the actual *depth-optimal* mapping with respect to the underlying Boolean function may be far better!

Table 1. Comparison of the depths achieved when mapping for different LUT sizes with different numbers of cuts. Nodes means the number of nodes in the AIG before mapping. Light green indicates that the mapping improved in comparison to the single-cut mapping. Dark green indicates that the mapping improved in comparison to the default 8-cut mapping. Gray indicates a trivial mapping where only a single level of LUTs is needed to implement the mapping. k following a number means thousands.

	K	4			6			8			10		
	C	1	8	Exh.	1	8	Exh.	1	8	Exh.	1	8	Exh.
	Nodes												
ctrl	109	3	3	3	2	2	2	1	1	1	1	1	1
router	190	9	9	9	6	6	6	5	4	4	4	4	4
int2float	215	6	6	6	3	3	3	3	3	3	2	2	2
dec	304	2	2	2	2	2	2	1	1	1	1	1	1
cavlc	655	6	6	6	4	4	4	2	2	2	1	1	1
priority	660	51	51	51	26	26	26	18	18	18	13	13	13
adder	1019	85	85	85	51	51	51	37	37	37	29	29	29
i2c	1131	6	6	6	4	4	4	3	3	3	3	3	3
max	2832	65	65	65	39	39	39	28	28	28	22	22	22
bar	3141	6	6	6	4	4	4	4	4	4	3	3	3
sin	5035	59	59	59	37	36	36	27	27	25	22	20	19
voter	9767	19	19	19	13	13	13	11	11	10	9	9	9
arbiter	12k	30	30	30	18	18	18	13	13	13	11	11	11
square	17k	83	83	83	50	50	50	36	35	35	28	28	28
sqrt	19k	1995	1995	1995	1017	1017	1017	696	687	687	523	522	515
multiplier	25k	87	87	87	53	53	53	40	40	40	31	31	31
log2	29k	114	114	114	71	71	71	49	49	49	39	39	39
div	41k	1429	1428	1428	858	856	856	617	613	613	483	482	476
mem_ctrl	45k	38	38	38	25	25	25	19	19	19	15	14	14
hyp	211k	8256	8256	8256	4192	4191	4191	2818	2818	2817	2132	2117	2104

The picture changes when dealing with larger LUTs with 8 or 10 inputs. Using a single cut more frequently does not result in an optimal mapping, and perhaps more importantly, at times neither does using 8 cuts! For $K = 10$, 4 out of 17 non-trivial mappings were not depth-optimal when using the default 8 cuts. The reason for this becomes quite evident when looking at Table 2, which shows the maximum number of cuts stored at a single node during mapping with exhaustive cut enumeration for the 4 circuits that showed improvement.

Table 2. The maximum number of cuts, for each LUT size respectively, stored at a single node during the exhaustive cut enumeration for the four circuits where the mapping was improved in terms of depth for $K = 10$. k following a number means thousands.

K	4	6	8	10
div	17	176	1915	22k
hyp	20	227	3652	58k
sin	25	287	4379	62k
sqrt	18	177	1990	26k

With each increase in LUT sizes, the maximum number of cuts stored for each circuit increases by an order of magnitude. Thus, storing only 8 cuts makes up an increasingly smaller amount of the total number of possible cuts for a given node, thereby making it increasingly unlikely that the optimal cut, or one of the optimal cuts, is found. It is rather remarkable how good the results are in terms of depth when considering the tiny proportion of cuts computed. This efficiency is highlighted when considering the runtimes. During exhaustive enumeration for $K = 10$, a single depth-focused pass for the hyp benchmark took just under 87 hours, whereas the entire mapping with 8 cuts took under 4 seconds! To better understand how the number of cuts stored during mapping affects the achieved depth, a sweep with a varying number of cuts was performed for the same 4 circuits. The results are shown in Fig. 2.

Clearly, each case initially benefits from an increase in the number of cuts stored during mapping. However, the behaviour after the initial improvement differs. sin quickly reaches its optimal value and then remains stable. div reaches its optimal depth of 476 fairly quickly, but then continues fluctuating and only seems to reach a stable state at the optimal depth towards the end of the sweep. hyp and sqrt on the other hand never reach the respective optimal depths of 2104 and 515 during the entire sweep, with the results for sqrt actually slightly deteriorating in the latter half of the sweep.

As continuously increasing the number of cuts stored during a mapping is not feasible in terms of runtime and memory requirements, these results suggest that when mapping for larger LUTs an adjustment of the sorting heuristics could be beneficial to further improve the mapping quality. Even so, modern FPGAs do not have LUTs with 10 inputs, and as such the relevance of these findings may be questioned. The relevance is that it is possible to reduce the structural bias by allowing the use of larger cuts during the mapping, and then performing a Boolean decomposition on these cuts in such a way that the depth of the resulting mapping is reduced, as shown in [5].

4   Ashenhurst-Curtis Decomposition

Boolean decomposition refers to the process of expressing a given Boolean function, $F(x_1, x_2, ..., x_n)$, as a combination of multiple smaller Boolean functions,

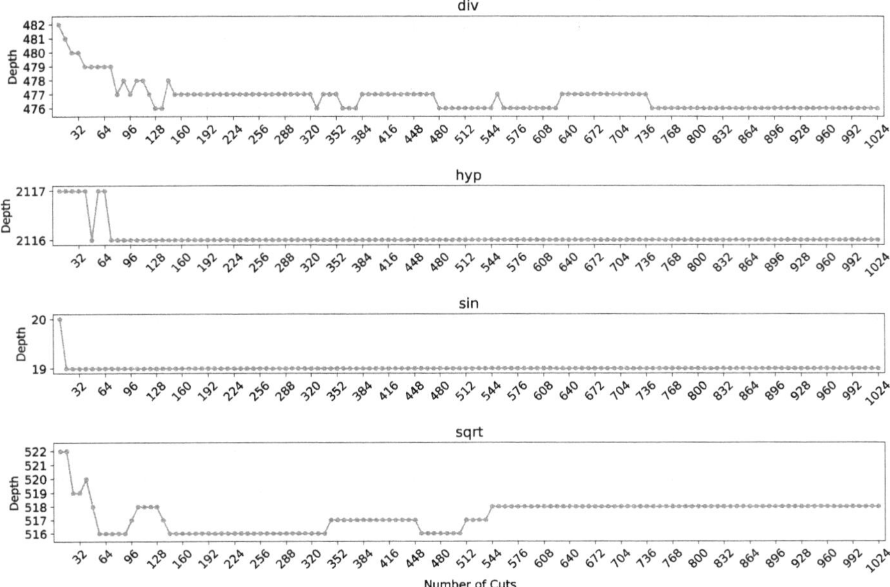

Fig. 2. A sweep of the 4 circuits where the mapping improved in terms of depth with the exhaustive cut enumeration for $K = 10$. The achieved depth is shown while varying the maximum number of cuts stored at a given node.

that are each dependent on fewer variables than the original function. This may be done in many different ways, and the previously described priority cuts approach is also evidently a decomposition. Such approaches that are applied to Boolean networks are typically referred to as *structural decomposition*. Though they are often able to handle very large functions, in terms of the number of inputs, they also suffer from so-called *structural bias*. That is, the quality of the decomposition is strongly dependent on the initial structure of the network. As a given Boolean function can be represented by a myriad of different Boolean networks, a large part of the effort often goes into first transforming the input network in such a way that benefits the goals of the later decomposition, such as reducing the number of nodes in the longest path of the network.

On the other hand, *functional decomposition* is done directly on a Boolean representation of the function, such as a truth table. Following the seminal work of Ashenhurst [3] and Curtis [10], this is typically described in terms of splitting the input variables of F into a so-called *free set*, x_{fs}, *bound set*, x_{bs}, and optionally a *shared set*, x_{ss}. One or more *subfunctions*, $S(x_{bs}, x_{ss})$, are defined that only depend on variables in the bound set and shared set. The objective then is to find a *composition function*, $G(y_1, y_2, ..., y_m)$, with $m < n$, such that

$$F(x_1, x_2, ..., x_n) = G(S_1(x_{bs}, x_{ss}), S_2(x_{bs}, x_{ss}), ..., S_p(x_{bs}, x_{ss}), x_{fs}, x_{ss}).$$

Thus, the variables in the free set are only used directly in the composition function, the variables in the bound set are only used in the subfunctions, and the variables in the shared set may be used in both.

As the decomposition is done directly on a Boolean representation, there is no structural bias. However, a drawback is that in general such decompositions are only feasible for functions with a fairly low number of variables. As such, the combination of a structural decomposition approach with a functional decomposition approach could result in a hybrid approach that can be applied to large functions, but is less sensitive to structural bias. This is exactly what was done in [5], where the priority cuts algorithm was extended by making use of the Ashenhurst-Curtis decomposition (ACD) during the cut computation, thereby improving the mappings in terms of depth, in some cases quite dramatically.

The combination of the two approaches is achieved as follows: during the first depth-mapping pass, rather than only allowing K-feasible cuts, somewhat larger cuts are also allowed as candidates. Thus, for example, when mapping for 6 input LUTs, 8- or 10-feasible cuts might also be examined. When such a cut is selected as a candidate, the existence of a depth-minimizing decomposition is checked. This is done by going through all the different combinations of variable assignments such that the variables that are depth-critical remain in the free set, and then attempting a decomposition. This reduces the resulting depth as the critical variables will be directly used as inputs of the LUT that implements the composition function, whereas the less critical variables are used as inputs of the LUT(s) implementing the subfunction(s). If such a decomposition is found, the cut is sorted into the list of priority cuts, and if not, the cut is discarded. For more details on the exact implementation of the decomposition, the reader is referred to the original publication [5].

As such the performance of the priority cuts algorithm when using larger cuts becomes very relevant. To examine this, another set of tests was run comparing the performance of the standard priority cuts algorithm with the enhanced algorithm using ACD when mapping to 6-input LUTs, performing one run with the default 8 cuts per node and one run with a significantly larger number of cuts per node, in this case arbitrarily set to 100 cuts. Mapping with ACD takes significantly longer, as many decompositions need to be checked during a single run, and as such performing an exhaustive search in this case was not an option. As mentioned previously, for mappers based on structural decomposition, the structure of the initial network has a large effect on the resulting mapping. Thus to examine the behaviour on a network optimized for depth, these tests were formulated as a resynthesis of an existing mapping. That is, the best available mappings for depth [1] were used as the starting point, these were then strashed to create an AIG and this resulting network was then mapped with the mapping flow also used in [5] when mapping for the EPFL synthesis competition. In particular, this means that first structural choices were computed for the network with `dch -f` and then the mapping was done. The results are shown in Table 3.

Table 3. Comparison of different mappings starting from the current best available depth mapping. In each case, the network is strashed and structural choices are computed with `dch -f` before the mapping is done. `if -K 6` means that the mapping was done for 6-input LUTs with the priority cuts algorithm. ACD means that the mapping was done with `if -Z 6 -K 10`, which means that 10-feasible cuts were considered for decomposition during the first mapping pass. `-C 100` means that 100 cuts were stored per node, otherwise the default 8 cuts were used. Light green indicates that the depth is improved by increasing the number of cuts. Blue indicates that the depth is improved and even beats the best known depth in the EPFL competition. Red indicates that this depth was not achieved. `k` following a number means thousands.

	if -K 6		if -K 6 -C 100		ACD		ACD -C 100		EPFL Best	
	Depth	LUTs	Depth	LUTs	Depth	LUTs	Depth	LUTs	Depth	LUTs
adder	5	356	5	358	5	377	5	364	5	343
arbiter	5	383	5	383	5	383	5	383	5	370
bar	4	512	4	512	4	512	4	512	4	512
cavlc	3	60	3	60	3	60	3	60	3	60
ctrl	2	25	2	25	2	25	2	25	2	25
dec	2	264	2	264	2	264	2	264	2	264
div	189	24k	188	23k	174	32k	171	30k	173	22k
i2c	3	195	3	194	3	195	3	194	3	193
int2float	2	24	2	24	2	24	2	24	2	24
log2	56	9475	54	9248	52	11k	51	11k	51	9613
max	6	1020	6	1023	6	1030	6	1027	6	1008
mem_ctrl	5	1821	5	1818	5	1835	5	1818	5	1764
multiplier	26	6775	26	6691	25	6862	25	6682	25	6488
priority	4	123	4	125	4	127	4	127	4	119
router	3	25	3	25	3	25	3	25	3	25
sin	11	773k	11	758k	11	788k	—	—	10	676k
sqrt	179	34k	178	32k	152	48k	150	49k	153	34k
square	11	4065	11	4055	10	4163	10	4169	10	3700
voter	13	1407	12	1362	13	1406	12	1368	11	1329
hyp	581	135k	580	130k	488	173k	482	171k	473	153k
hyp*	485	149k	484	144k	464	178k	458	176k	473	153k

It can be seen that for both mapping approaches using more cuts results in improvements in terms of depth a number of times, highlighted in green or blue. Green indicates that the depth was improved with more cuts, whereas blue indicates that the depth was improved and even beat the best known depth in the EPFL competition. Furthermore, by increasing the number of cuts the LUT count can also be decreased by a considerable margin in some of the cases. In the few cases where the LUT count increases, the difference is around 10 LUTs or less, and as such is simply due to the heuristic nature of the mapping. The only exception to this is the ACD mapping of the `sqrt` circuit, but here the improved depth is likely the cause of the increase in LUT count.

It must be emphasized that in these tests, even though the standard priority cuts mapping was done with $K = 6$, it still showed an improvement when using more cuts. In the exhaustive tests in Sect. 3, improvements over the default 8 cuts were only found for $K = 8$ and $K = 10$, suggesting that the degree of optimization of the initial network also plays a role in how many cuts are required per node to find the depth-optimal mapping. To rule out that this behaviour was only due to the use of structural choices, the mapping was repeated without structural choices for the 5 circuits that showed an improved depth with more cuts. In each case the depth could be improved by using more cuts, suggesting that the difference was indeed due to the structure of the network itself, rather than the inclusion of structural choices.

The three cases highlighted in red indicate that this depth was not achieved by any of the four mappings. For `voter`, simply running the mapping again with even more cuts per node allowed both of the mappings to match the previously achieved depth of 11. The standard priority cuts mapper achieved it with 200 cuts, whereas ACD could achieve it with 150 cuts. For `sin` on the other hand, the ACD mapping with 100 cuts could not complete as it ran out of memory. The issue here is that the mapping that achieved the best depth required extensive logic duplication, and a resynthesis with so many and such large cuts becomes infeasible. The extent of this logic duplication is evident when comparing the required $676k$ LUTs for the mapping to the 5035 AIG nodes that represent the same functionality, listed in Table 1. Looking at the rest of the table, the only other circuit where there were fewer AIG nodes than LUTs in the best mapping is `sqrt`, with $19k$ AIG nodes and $24k$ LUTs. Of course, a one-to-one comparison between the different circuits is not necessarily meaningful, but the stark contrast is noteworthy. The significant increase in depth seen in the standard priority cuts mapping of `hyp` prompted a further test, which will be covered in Sect. 5.

Finally, it seems worth commenting on the LUT counts compared to the best known results. Although the differences for the smaller circuits are often negligible, the differences for the bigger circuits are at times quite significant, even when the depth achieved is worse than the original depth. An example of this is the behavior of `square`, which required roughly 10% more LUTs even when a worse depth was achieved, and again slightly more in those cases where the depth of 10 was matched. This seems to be caused by the generation of an AIG from an already mapped network resulting in a certain amount of duplication compared to the original AIG which the mapping was based on. For example, if parts of the network in the original AIG were partially covered by multiple LUTs during mapping, these would then be duplicated when the individual LUTs are transformed back into an AIG. Thus, it seems likely that depth improvements could be achieved with fewer additional LUTs if resynthesis isn't employed. Nevertheless, the results clearly show the benefit of using a greater number of cuts per node during the mapping of a given network.

5   Performance Analysis

Although some notable improvements could be achieved through the use of more cuts, it is also computationally expensive, in particular when thousands or even millions of decompositions are attempted during the first pass. As such, finding a way to retain the improvement in mapping depth while reducing the required runtime was a logical next step.

As the decompositions are so expensive, a method of minimizing how many decompositions are required was sought. In the first mapping pass, the primary criteria by which the cuts are sorted are the *delay* and the *number of leaves*. The delay of a cut for a given node effectively means the maximum length of the LUT-cascade between the primary inputs and this node, if the selected cut is implemented. Thus if depth-optimization is the goal, then preferring cuts with a smaller delay when implementing a given node is reasonable. Furthermore, if a cut is created through the union of two cuts, then its delay will be as large as the greater of the two delays. The number of leaves of a cut simply means how many nodes make up the actual cut set. Reducing this also makes sense for two reasons: On the one hand, later on in the mapping, when the cuts for the successor node(s) are computed, if the predecessors both have a selection of cuts with fewer leaves, then it becomes more likely that combinations of these cuts are also K-feasible, and can thus be accepted. On the other hand, using cuts with fewer leaves might help to reduce the total number of LUTs required, as it may result in less logic being implemented during the covering stage later on.

Thus, in order to minimize the number of decompositions required, a presorting of the cuts is done as follows: assuming up to C cuts can be stored at a node, first all $(C + 1)^2$ cut combinations are formed and their feasibility is checked. Assuming that the final mapping is done onto 6-input LUTs and 10-feasible cuts should be used when checking decompositions, the cuts are divided into groups based on their feasibility: a 6-feasible group which also includes all smaller cuts, a 7-feasible group, an 8-feasible group, a 9-feasible group and finally a 10-feasible group. Then, to select the priority cuts for this node, first of all the cuts in the 6-feasible group are considered and sorted into the C available positions.

At this point, the decision of whether or not further cuts must be handled, and hence decompositions have to be checked, is made. As the priority cuts of the two predecessor nodes have already been computed, it is also known what the delay of the respective best cuts is. Thus for the current node, we can define a target delay which is equal to the greater of the two delays of the predecessor nodes. If this delay is reached by a cut, then no extra LUT-level will be required to implement this node. However, rather than only achieving this delay with a single cut, it is beneficial to have as many cuts as possible with this delay, as this then further increases the likelihood of later on finding a combination of one of these cuts with another cut that is still 6-feasible or at least decomposable.

Thus, the termination criterion is whether or not the *Cth* priority cut has the target delay or not. If it has the target delay, then no more cuts need to be checked for this node and the next node is handled. If it does not have the target delay, then further cuts are considered, starting from the 7-feasible group and continuing to the 8-, 9- and finally the 10-feasible group. Each time that a new priority cut is added, the termination criterion is rechecked.

This has a two-fold benefit: firstly, checking if a smaller cut can be decomposed is quicker than checking if a bigger cut can be decomposed. Secondly, as previously mentioned, the second sorting criterion is the number of leaves of the cut. As such, if at any point the priority cuts list is filled with cuts that have the target depth, then all larger cuts would not have been chosen anyway and hence these decompositions would have been superfluous. Algorithm 1 summarizes how this preliminary sorting is performed. Note that when C cuts are already stored, then `insert_into_priority_cuts(cut)` only inserts the cut if it is at least better than the current worst cut.

Algorithm 1: Compute Priority Cuts Modified

---

1 **Input:** Node N, LUT Size K, Max Cut Size M, Max Cut Number C;
2 *target_depth* $\leftarrow$ get_max_depth_of_predecessors(N);
3 *candidate_cuts* $\leftarrow$ enumerate_predecessor_cut_pairs(N);
4 **for** *cut in candidate_cuts* **do**
5     $f \leftarrow$ compute_feasibility(cut);
6   **if** $f \leq K$ **then**
7   **add** *cut* to $k\_feasible\_cuts$;
8   **else if** $f \leq M$ **then**
9   add_to_appropriate_feasibility_class(cut);
10 **for** *cut in k_feasible_cuts* **do**
11   insert_into_priority_cuts(cut)
12 *highest_depth* $\leftarrow$ get_depth_of_last_priority_cut(N);
13 **for** *class* **in** *ascending feasibility_classes* **do**
14   **while** *number_of_cuts* $< C \lor highest\_depth > target\_depth$ **do**
15   *cut* $\leftarrow$ get_next_cut($class$);
16   insert_into_priority_cuts(cut);
17   *highest_depth* $\leftarrow$ get_depth_of_last_priority_cut(N);

To evaluate this modified approach[1] and to compare its performance with the unmodified code when using different amounts of cuts, sweeps were performed on the three circuits in Table 3 where the depth was improved by multiple levels with the ACD approach. The results are shown in Fig. 3.

---

[1] Modified code available at https://gitlab.rs.e-technik.tu-darmstadt.de/flothow/ 2026_arc_abc_changes.

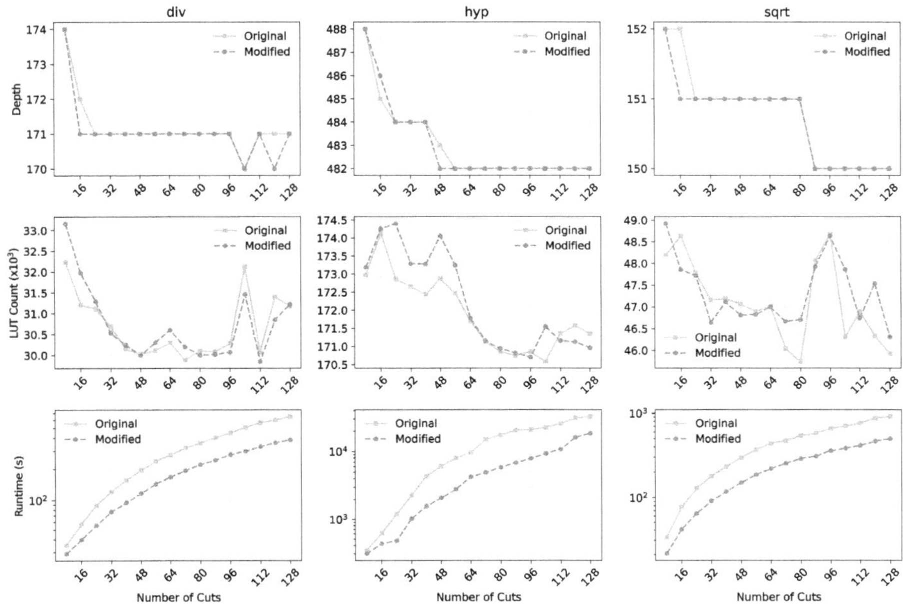

Fig. 3. A sweep of the three circuits that showed improvements of greater than 1 level when using 100 cuts with the Ashenhurst-Curtis decomposition, using the same setup as in Table 3. For each run the maximum number of cuts stored at a given node is varied, and from top to bottom the graphs show the achieved depth, the number of LUTs required, and the runtime. Modified refers to the runs which use a preliminary sorting to reduce the number of total decompositions performed.

The figure is divided into three parts for each circuit, showing the achieved depth, the number of LUTs and finally the runtime. Looking at the depth, we see that both approaches perform very similarly, with the modified code achieving a slightly better depth in 4 of the runs, and a slightly worse depth in 1 run. When considering the number of LUTs on the other hand, the new approach tends to perform slightly worse for a given number of cuts. The third sorting criterion during the first pass, the so-called *area flow*, appears to be useful to reduce the area. To remedy this, the cuts could be sorted by their area flow within the respective feasibility groups, but as the main focus has been depth, and here the new approach performed slightly better, this was not further considered.

However the real benefit of the presorting is clear when looking at the runtime graphs. The runtime for a given number of cuts is greatly reduced, in some cases it is even halved compared to the original code, thus facilitating the use of more cuts while keeping the runtime more manageable.

Another notable point is that compared to the results in Table 3, the depth of `div` could actually be reduced even further to 170, and for `sqrt` the number of LUTs required could also be reduced while maintaining the achieved depth.

Finally, as mentioned in Sect. 4, the surprisingly poor performance of the `hyp` benchmark in the resynthesis test, particularly with the standard priority cuts algorithm, prompted another set of runs for this circuit to see if the mapping quality could be brought more in line with that of the best published mapping. Thus, after generating the AIG, the same set of AIG optimization scripts used in [5] when generating the baselines, was applied once. The following series of commands was used: `dfraig; resyn; resyn2; resyn2rs; if -y -K 6; resyn2rs`. Along with the previously mentioned balancing, rewriting and refactoring, these further optimize the AIG through fraiging [16], resubstitution [13] and the so-called lazy man's synthesis [20]. The results of the mappings after this optimization are shown in Table 3 as `hyp*`. The priority cuts runs were considerably better than they were previously, and with ACD the previous record for depth was even beaten! A summary of the records is shown in Table 4.

Table 4. A summary of the new records in terms of depth compared to the best known results.

	EPFL Best Depth 2025		New Depth Record		
	Depth	LUTs	Depth	LUTs	Δ Depth
div	173	22258	170	30849	-1.73%
hyp	473	152793	458	176274	-3.17%
sqrt	153	34421	150	45934	-1.96%

6   Conclusion

In this contribution, we have shown that it can be beneficial to store more cuts in one node than the typical approach of priority cuts does. First, we studied exhaustive enumeration to show the effect of keeping more cuts at every node. However, exhaustive enumeration is certainly not possible for larger problems, in particular when using the Ashenhurst-Curtis decomposition to reduce structural bias. Thus, we improved the priority cuts approach by introducing a new sorting order, yet keeping only a small, limited number of cuts in every node. In this way we could already reach two new record breaking depth results in the EPFL competition, while maintaining the same quality in most of the other cases. Only in three cases a slight degredation of the results was found. In the case of the `hyp` benchmark, we added a special pass to reduce structural bias in the AIG and after that pass, we were able to find one more record breaking depth result.

The results with the Ashenhurst-Curtis decomposition point us to some future work. We believe that better heuristics for sorting the cuts in each node exist and we are planing to search for them. This applies to both the achievable depth as well as the the number of LUTs required, as reducing this is also an important goal. Furthermore, the current version uses cut sizes of at most 10 before applying Boolean decomposition.[2] We believe that this size can be increased by using a slightly different method for the Boolean decomposition. We are convinced that in this way, even better mappings can be found.

References

1. EPFL Synthesis Competition Best Results (2025). https://github.com/lsils/benchmarks/tree/v2025.1/best_results
2. The EPFL Combinational Benchmark Suite. https://github.com/lsils/benchmarks
3. Ashenhurst, R.L.: The Decomposition of Switching Functions. In: Proceedings of an International Symposium on the Theory of Switching, pp. 74–116 (1959)
4. Brayton, R., Mishchenko, A.: ABC: An Academic Industrial-Strength Verification Tool. In: Touili, T., Cook, B., Jackson, P. (eds.) CAV 2010. LNCS, vol. 6174, pp. 24–40. Springer, Heidelberg (2010). https://doi.org/10.1007/978-3-642-14295-6_5
5. Calvino, A.T., De Micheli, G., Mishchenko, A., Brayton, R.: Enhancing delay-driven LUT mapping with boolean decomposition. IEEE Trans. Comput. Aided Des. Integr. Circuits Syst. **44**(3), 1017–1030 (2025)
6. Chatterjee, S., Mishchenko, A., Brayton, R.K., Wang, X., Kam, T.: Reducing structural bias in technology mapping. IEEE Trans. Comput. Aided Des. Integr. Circuits Syst. **25**(12), 2894–2903 (2006)
7. Chen, D., Cong, J.: DAOmap: A depth-optimal area optimization mapping algorithm for FPGA designs. In: IEEE/ACM International Conference on Computer Aided Design, ICCAD-2004, pp. 752–759. IEEE (2004)
8. Cong, J., Ding, Y.: FlowMap: an optimal technology mapping algorithm for delay optimization in lookup-table based FPGA designs. IEEE Trans. Comput. Aided Des. Integr. Circuits Syst. **13**(1), 1–12 (1994)
9. Cong, J., Hwang, Y.Y.: Simultaneous depth and area minimization in LUT-based FPGA mapping. In: Third International ACM Symposium on Field-Programmable Gate Arrays, pp. 68–74 (1995)
10. Curtis, H.A.: A New Approach to the Design of Switching Circuits. Van Nostrand, Princeton, NJ (1962)
11. Francis, R.J., Rose, J., Chung, K.: Chortle: A technology mapping program for lookup table-based field programmable gate arrays. In: Proceedings of the 27th ACM/IEEE Design Automation Conference, pp. 613–619 (1990)
12. Liu, T., Chen, L., Li, X., Yuan, M., Young, E.F.: FineMap: A fine-grained GPU-parallel LUT mapping engine. In: 2024 29th Asia and South Pacific Design Automation Conference (ASP-DAC), pp. 392–397. IEEE (2024)
13. Mishchenko, A., Brayton, R.: Scalable logic synthesis using a simple circuit structure. In: Proceedings of IWLS (2006)
14. Mishchenko, A., Chatterjee, S., Brayton, R.: DAG-aware AIG rewriting: a fresh look at combinational logic synthesis. In: Proceedings of the 43rd Annual Design Automation Conference, pp. 532–535 (2006)
15. Mishchenko, A., Chatterjee, S., Brayton, R.K.: Improvements to technology mapping for LUT-based FPGAs. IEEE Trans. Comput. Aided Des. Integr. Circuits Syst. **26**(2), 240–253 (2007)
16. Mishchenko, A., Chatterjee, S., Jiang, R., Brayton, R.: FRAIGs: A Unifying Representation for Logic Synthesis and Verification. Tech. rep, ERL Technical Report (2005)

---

[2] In [5] the use of 11 variables is also mentioned, but only 10 are used for the evaluation.

17. Mishchenko, A., Cho, S., Chatterjee, S., Brayton, R.: Combinational and sequential mapping with priority cuts. In: 2007 IEEE/ACM International Conference on Computer-Aided Design, pp. 354–361. IEEE (2007)
18. Roth, J.P., Karp, R.M.: Minimization over boolean graphs. IBM J. Res. Dev. **6**(2), 227–238 (1962)
19. Yang, S.: Logic Synthesis and Optimization Benchmarks User Guide: Version 3.0. Tech. rep., Microelectronics Center of North Carolina (1991)
20. Yang, W., Wang, L., Mishchenko, A.: Lazy man's logic synthesis. In: 2012 IEEE/ACM International Conference on Computer-Aided Design (ICCAD), pp. 597–604. IEEE (2012)
21. Yuan, J., Wang, P., Ye, J., Yuan, M., Hao, J., Yan, J.: EasySO: Exploration-enhanced Reinforcement Learning for Logic Synthesis Sequence Optimization and a Comprehensive RL Environment. In: 2023 IEEE/ACM International Conference on Computer Aided Design (ICCAD), pp. 1–9. IEEE (2023)

CLAS: A C̲ross-L̲ayer A̲pproximate S̲ynthesis Framework for LUT-Based DNN Accelerators

Atousa Jafari[1], Amir Hossein Hadipour[1(✉)], Muhammad Awais[1], Mohammadparsa Rostamzadehkhameneh[1], Hassan Ghasemzadeh Mohammadi[2], and Marco Platzner[1]

[1] Paderborn University, 33098 Paderborn, Germany
{atousa,ahh,mawais,paros,platzner}@mail.upb.com
[2] Reneo Group GmbH, Hamburg, Germany
ghasemzadeh@reneo.de

Abstract. LUT-based DNN accelerators offer ultra-low latency FPGA inference, but their adoption is severely constrained by excessive resource consumption. This paper introduces CLAS, a cross-layer approximation framework for LUT-based DNNs that redefines approximation in fully unrolled networks by (i) treating neurons as substitutable RTL components and (ii) jointly exploring combinations of approximated layers at the RTL across the network. The proposed framework effectively combines algorithmic-level approximations, including sensitivity-driven pruning and quantization, with a library-based RTL approximation strategy to enable cross-layer optimization.

Key stages of CLAS, including neuron library construction and two-level design space exploration (DSE), are fully parallelized, enabling scalable exploration of large approximation spaces that would otherwise be computationally impractical. Our combined layer- and network-level DSE strategy effectively evaluates a diverse range of approximate layer combinations, globally optimizing accuracy–area trade-offs under strict constraints. CLAS achieves substantial LUT reductions with a small accuracy loss, outperforming algorithmic-level approximation baselines by delivering an additional 32.6% area savings with only a 4.4% drop in classification accuracy on the MNIST dataset. Moreover, it provides a diverse set of solutions, enabling flexible trade-offs between accuracy and area. These results demonstrate that neuron-level, library-based approximation unlocks a powerful and previously unexplored dimension of the FPGA DNN design space.

Keywords: Approximate computing · Design Space Exploration · Direct logic implementation · DNN · FPGA

1 Introduction

Ultra-low latency applications such as particle physics experiments [13], structure-borne noise monitoring, wireless communication systems [29], and

A. Jafari and A. H. Hadipour—These authors contributed equally.

© The Author(s), under exclusive license to Springer Nature Switzerland AG 2026
G. Leone et al. (Eds.): ARC 2026, LNCS 16514, pp. 255–272, 2026.
https://doi.org/10.1007/978-3-032-29365-7_16

high-frequency oscillation analysis impose strict requirements on data acquisition and processing, including MHz-level sampling rates and nanosecond-scale latency [21]. Efficient deployment on edge platforms, in particular FPGAs, is therefore essential to meet the throughput and timing requirements.

Among various approaches to DNN inference on FPGAs, the lookup table (LUT)-based approach [2,16,24,33] meets the rigid criteria in terms of throughput and latency, making it particularly well-suited for extreme throughput and ultra-low latency applications. In these architectures, the computation of each neuron across all network layers is fully unrolled, and the complete neuron functionality, including multiply–accumulate operations (MACs) and nonlinear activation functions, is entirely absorbed into lookup tables and later implemented using the FPGA's physical LUTs. LUT-based designs eliminate the need for memory accesses to store and load weights, biases, and intermediate results by embedding weights, biases, and the activation function directly into logic. Furthermore, additional gains in latency and throughput can be achieved through architectural optimization such as pipelining. Representative examples of LUT-based methods include LogicNets [33], PolyLUT [2], NullaNet [24] and, NeuraLUT [3].

Despite the performance advantages, a key challenge regarding the deployment of the LUT-based approach is scalability given the limited available physical LUTs on the target FPGA device. However, this also opens up new opportunities for optimizations. Emerging paradigms, such as approximate computing, can be employed to greatly reduce the network size while still withstanding the strict latency requirements. Recent works have already considered approximations of DNNs, albeit mostly at higher abstraction levels. Generally, approximation opportunities available for DNNs shown target two main levels: i) Algorithmic-level, and ii) Register transfer level (RTL). Common examples of algorithmic level approximations are quantization and pruning, among others, targeting reduced bit-width for parameters and redundant network connections, respectively [5].

At the RTL, approximation can offer a significant reduction in circuit parameters such as resource utilization, power consumption, etc., at the cost of marginal accuracy degradation on top of the algorithmic approximation. Combining RTL approximations with algorithmic approximations has been greatly overlooked by the research community. Most prior works, specifically those targeting LUT-based implementation, focus on only algorithmic-level optimizations [2,4,24], disregarding potential additional gains at lower levels. Completely motivated by this potential, we propose a cross-layer approach by leveraging the joint impact of both algorithmic and RTL approximations for FPGA-based accelerators. To this end, we propose a framework equipped with statistical sensitivity profiling, joint cross-layer approximation, and hierarchical design space exploration, resulting in an end-to-end framework for ultra-low latency DNN deployment on FPGAs. Key contributions of this paper are illustrated in Fig. 1 and summarized as follows:

- We propose a systematic framework to profile a quantized DNN for approximation resilience using efficient statistical techniques.

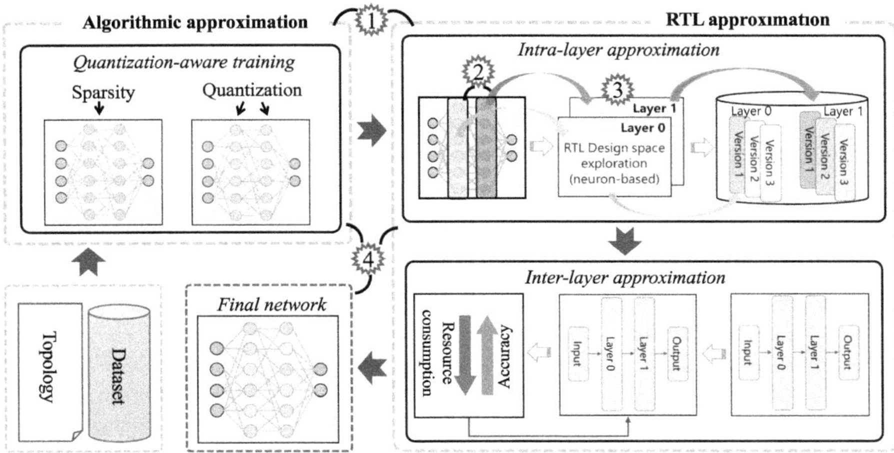

Fig. 1. High-level overview of the contributions in this paper. The key contributions are numbered. (1) A cross-layer approximation strategy that systematically combines algorithmic-level and RTL approximations. (2) A sensitivity profiling methodology to assess approximation resilience per neuron. (3) A novel library-based approach enabling neuron-level RTL approximations. (4) An end-to-end framework for cross-layer approximation for LUT-based DNNs.

- We introduce library-based approximation at RTL for individual layers in a network, which, unlike prior approaches that rely on predefined arithmetic components, enables approximations directly at the neuron level. To the best of our knowledge, this is the first approach that supports RTL approximation at this granularity.
- We introduce a cross-layer approximation strategy effectively combining algorithmic and RTL approximations for network layers (intra-layer), followed by an inter-layer design space exploration at the network level to selectively optimize the DNN while preserving critical features.
- Based on our key steps, we develop a fully automated, end-to-end framework for cross-layer approximation techniques for area-efficient FPGA implementation, and we demonstrate competitive area reduction on contemporary FPGA devices with a small accuracy loss compared to the baseline. The framework is available as an open-source contribution (https://git.uni-paderborn.de/ceg_upb/clas) to support reproducibility and adoption.

The paper is organized as follows: Related work is discussed in Sect. 2, the proposed framework details are elaborated in Sect. 3, and the evaluation is presented in Sect. 4. Finally, Sect. 5 concludes the paper.

2   Related Work

This section reviews prior work on FPGA-based DNN implementations, with a particular focus on the intersection of approximation techniques and DNN deployment on FPGAs. It also discusses existing sensitivity analysis approaches used to identify neurons that can be approximated with minimal impact on overall performance.

2.1 Mapping DNN on FPGA

Hardware co-design strategies for DNN deployment onto FPGAs have been considerably explored in prior work [20]. Broadly, these can be classified into two categories: time-sequential execution of DNN layers and streamlined dataflow architectures. In a time-sequential manner, layers are processed one after another, with data passed through a systolic array of processing elements (PEs), whereas a streamlined dataflow approach emphasizes low latency and high throughput by allocating dedicated functional units to each layer. The latter enables the entire network to be realized as a pipelined architecture, where layers operate concurrently without requiring intermediate data buffering in memory. A notable example of this methodology is the FINN framework [9, 20].

A specific and highly efficient instance of the streamlined dataflow is a LUT-based deployment strategy [33] that employs LUTs as the sole functional blocks at the RTL, effectively hardwiring the entire neuron behavior directly into so-called L-LUTs [2, 3, 24, 33]. Later, FPGA synthesis tools can decompose these high-level L-LUTs into physical LUTs on the FPGA fabric. Notably, the number of LUTs scales exponentially in the number of input bitwidths, affecting scalability and thus limiting the application domain to inference of only small and medium-sized models. Typically, these approaches require extensive quantization, sparsity, and hardware optimization to fit neurons or sub-networks into the available physical LUTs that exhibit rather small fan-in. Consequently, approximation techniques are essential in this setup to enable feasible and efficient deployment.

2.2 Approximate DNN on FPGA

Efficient hardware implementation of DNNs primarily aims to mitigate high computational complexity, large memory footprints, and significant energy consumption [13]. Such requirements impose major challenges for resource-constrained platforms such as FPGA accelerators. Approximate computing has emerged as a promising approach to address these challenges by reducing the requirement for exact numerical computation in exchange for performance gains. Several approximation strategies have been explored to enable efficient DNN acceleration on FPGAs. At the algorithmic level, widely adopted techniques such as quantization and pruning reduce numerical precision and exploit model redundancy, respectively [5]. The majority of works have only considered this level for approximations and proceeded with the deployment of the model. However, beyond algorithmic-level optimizations, approximation techniques can also be applied at the RTL to further improve the efficiency of FPGA-based DNN accelerators. It is important to note that in most cases, off-the-shelf approximation techniques [17,28,36] from contemporary works can be equally applicable and suitable for DNN accelerators as they are for other accelerators.

RTL offers an enormous design space for approximation opportunities, including approximate arithmetic units substitution [6,22], precision scaling [36], and logic simplifications [7,17], among others. While some previous works have considered applying approximations for simplifying arithmetic components inside DNNs [11,23], the potential for RTL approximations has not been fully explored since (i) the arithmetic components were required to be identified before approximation, and (ii) the techniques only explored high-level modeling of approximations, and deployment was not targeted for FPGAs.

Adopting RTL-level approximation leads to an enlarged design space, as the impact of specific approximation techniques can be amplified depending on whether and how they are combined with algorithmic-level approximations, as well as on the chosen target hardware mapping paradigm. While algorithmic approximations such as quantization typically derive MAC-based architectures built around multiplier–adder datapaths, RTL-level approximations are largely architecture-agnostic and can be applied to a broader range of circuits, including LUT-based architectures. Specifically, Boolean Matrix Factorization (BMF) [17] is particularly suitable for LUT-based networks, as it treats LUT-defined functions as matrices, more specifically, as truth tables in the case of Boolean networks, and applies matrix transformations to derive approximate variants. This contrasts with prior LUT-based approaches that largely restrict LUT transformations to higher (algorithmic) levels [2–4].

Based on the above discussion, we believe that although RTL-level approximations offer significant potential for DNN approximation, their adoption, especially in combination with higher-level approximation techniques to exploit cross-layer approximation opportunities for FPGA-based DNN deployment, remains limited so far.

2.3 Sensitivity Profiling for DNN Approximation

A crucial prerequisite for effective and systematic approximation of a DNN is the identification of network components that can be safely approximated while preserving the overall accuracy. Prior works focus a lot on identifying the most critical network components, primarily neurons, that have the highest impact on the network output [1,11,23]. Consequently, these neurons can be preserved, while the remaining can be treated as candidates for approximation. Regardless of the underlying approximation technique, such as pruning [18], precision scaling [15,39], or arithmetic simplifications [27,39], the sensitivity profiling step directly impacts the quality of design space exploration for approximate DNN.

Many recent works have leveraged sensitivity profiling for applying high-level approximations with a reliability-aware approach [10,31]. A recent survey [1], has identified two main categories of sensitivity profiling: analytical and hybrid approaches. The key distinction between these approaches lies in whether explicit fault injection mechanisms are employed during analysis. Although reliability analysis is outside the scope of this work, we observe that many DNN approximation approaches leverage known techniques originally developed for reliability analysis to identify critical neurons. Armeniakos et al. [5] categorize DNN approximation techniques based on whether they are applied at the software or hardware level. They further argue that many of these techniques are orthogonal and can therefore be combined.

Many initial efforts preferred to apply a uniform bit-width quantization for all layers to reduce model complexity. Subsequent work, such as [38], applied feature ranking to compute neuron importance scores at the output layer and propagated them backward to guide structured pruning. More recent work [30] demonstrates that mixed-precision optimization can yield near-optimal complexity reductions while incurring minimal accuracy loss.

3   CLAS: The Cross-Layer DNN Approximation Framework

In this section, we present our cross-layer approximation framework for efficient FPGA-based DNN implementation. We first introduce the overall end-to-end design flow and then provide a detailed description of its key stages.

Figure 2 illustrates the complete design flow of the proposed CLAS framework. The process begins with a configuration file specifying the architectural and quantization parameters of the target neural network. Based on these configurations and the selected dataset, a quantized network is instantiated and trained using *quantization-aware training* (QAT).

To maximize the impact of high-level approximations, we jointly apply quantization and structured sparsity, reducing both numerical precision and network connectivity (cf. Fig. 2, Stage ①). At this stage, we extend the LogicNets framework [33] to support fully unrolled DNNs with configurable quantization and sparsity. The trained network is then evaluated on a test set to establish a baseline accuracy that serves as a reference for all subsequent approximation stages.

The second stage performs sensitivity profiling to identify neurons that are sensitive to approximation. This analysis ranks network components based on their contribution to the final prediction and guides the selection of approximation candidates.

In the third stage, RTL-level approximation is introduced using an automated design space exploration (DSE) framework. For each layer, multiple approximate implementations are generated under predefined accuracy constraints, producing a set of Pareto points for each layer.

Finally, the framework performs inter-layer approximation by combining per-layer variants to identify a complete network configuration that maximizes hardware efficiency (measured primarily in FPGA LUT reduction) while preserving accuracy as close as possible to the baseline.

The following subsections describe the three core stages of the flow in detail: sensitivity profiling, RTL approximation, and inter-layer accuracy validation.

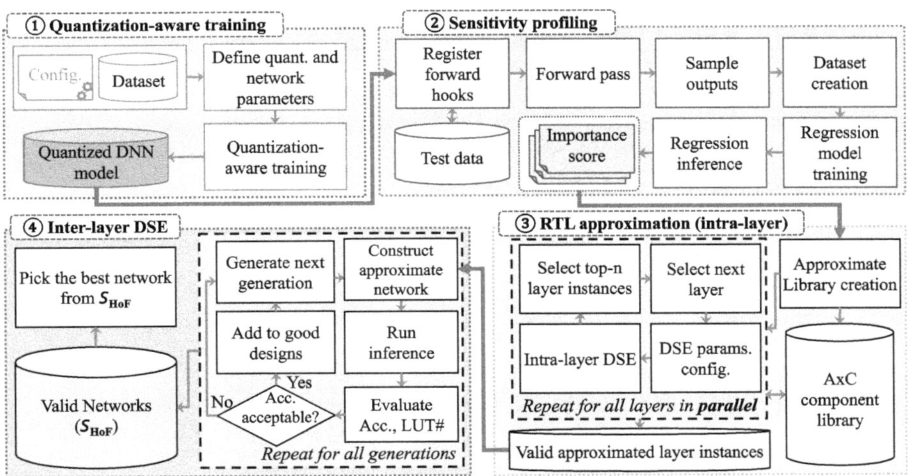

Fig. 2. The overall flow for the CLAS framework.

3.1 Sensitivity Profiling

Sensitivity profiling operates on the quantized network obtained from the first stage. We perform a forward inference pass over the test dataset while registering layer activations via hooks in the PyTorch framework. For each neuron, the output activations across all test samples are collected and paired with the corresponding class labels, forming a regression dataset.

To quantify relative importance, we apply feature ranking using the *Least Absolute Shrinkage and Selection Operator* (LASSO) [32]. LASSO employs L_1 regularization, which drives the coefficients of less informative features to zero, enabling explicit identification of neurons whose outputs have the strongest influence on the network's predictions. Neurons with nonzero coefficients are therefore considered sensitive and are targeted for conservative approximation in later stages. The choice of LASSO is deliberate. Alternative methods such as Ridge regression [19] and HSIC LASSO [37] have been explored in prior work [14]. Ridge regression relies on L_2 regularization and distributes importance across all features. This is less suitable for our setting, where the number of neurons is large and a clear separation between sensitive and non-critical components is required. HSIC LASSO can capture nonlinear dependencies and also enforces sparsity; however, it incurs significantly higher computational overhead and often results in more aggressive pruning.

In a comparative study, we observe substantial overlap between the sensitive neurons identified by LASSO and HSIC LASSO, indicating that both methods capture similar structural importance. Given its runtime efficiency, scalability, and sufficient discriminative power, we adopt LASSO for sensitivity profiling in this work. It may be noted that a detailed comparative analysis of various feature ranking methods and their impact on output accuracy is a compelling and insightful study, yet out of the scope of this work.

Algorithm 1: Intra-layer Design Space Exploration with NSGA-II

Input: Set of network layers $\mathcal{L}$ with Verilog descriptions;
For each layer $L_i \in \mathcal{L}$: candidate neuron set C_{L_i};
Local error threshold ϵ_{local} as mean Hamming distance percentage (MHD%)
Output: For each layer L_i: set of valid approximate configurations
$$\mathcal{V}_{L_i} = \{(S, \text{Acc}(S), \text{LUT}\#(S))\}$$

1 **foreach** *layer $L_i \in \mathcal{L}$ **in parallel*** **do**
2   Initialize initial NSGA-II population $\mathcal{P}_0$ using C_{L_i};
3   Initialize valid configuration set $\mathcal{V}_{L_i} \leftarrow \emptyset$;
4 $g \leftarrow 0$;
5   **while** $g < G_{\max}$ *and* $\mathcal{P}_g \neq \emptyset$;   // G_{max} = No. of generations
6   **do**
7   **foreach** $S \in \mathcal{P}_g$ **do**
8 $(valid, MHD\%, LUT) \leftarrow$ **runRTLFlow**$(L_i, S, \epsilon_{\text{local}})$;
9   Compute fitness $f(S)$ using objectives (MHD% $\uparrow$, LUT $\downarrow$);
10   **if** *valid* **then**
11   Add $(S, MHD\%, LUT\#)$ to $\mathcal{V}_{L_i}$;
12   Select best designs from $\mathcal{P}_g$ based on $f(S)$;
13   Generate next population $\mathcal{P}_{g+1}$ via selection and variation;
14 $g \leftarrow g + 1$;
15 **return** $\{\mathcal{V}_{L_i}\}_{L_i \in \mathcal{L}}$;

3.2   RTL Approximation

Based on the sensitivity scores, neurons are sorted in ascending order of importance and used to identify candidates for RTL-level approximation, and the importance scores are normalized in the range $[0, 1]$. A fixed fraction of neurons per layer is then selected from this ordered list. To determine this fraction, we evaluate three candidate ratios (10.0%, 20.0%, and 30.0%) on a representative benchmark (JSC-S). Across these experiments, a 20.0% selection ratio consistently provided the best trade-off between accuracy degradation and hardware savings and is therefore used throughout this work.

For each selected neuron, we generate a large set of RTL-level approximate implementations and evaluate them to construct Pareto frontiers capturing accuracy–hardware trade-offs (measured in LUT count). For this work, we apply *Boolean Matrix Factorization* (BMF) [17] as a representative RTL approximation technique. Nevertheless, the framework is independent of the specific approximation method and can incorporate any Verilog-level RTL approximation approach, e.g., AIG-rewriting [7, 36] or even precision-scaling [36]. To the best of our knowledge, this represents a novel contribution: unlike prior DNN approximation approaches that primarily target arithmetic operators such as adders and multipliers, our method treats neurons as atomic, substitutable components. This abstraction enables the approximation of a broader class of networks, including those not explicitly structured around arithmetic primitives (e.g., LUT-based networks), and substantially expands the available design space.

Algorithm 2: Inter-layer Design Space Exploration with NSGA-II

Input: Original network $\mathcal{N}$; For each layer L_i in $\mathcal{N}$: Selected n valid configurations $\mathcal{V}_{L_i}$ (including the original); Global accuracy constraint ϵ_{global}

Output: Set of approximate networks $\mathcal{S}_{HoF}$

1 Initialize population $\mathcal{P}_0$ by randomly selecting one configuration from $\mathcal{V}_{L_i}$ for each layer L_i

2 $\mathcal{S}_{HoF} \leftarrow \emptyset$

3 $g \leftarrow 0$

4 $\mathcal{P}_g \leftarrow \mathcal{P}_0$

5 **while** $g < G_{\max}$ **and** $\mathcal{P}_g \neq \emptyset$ **do**

6   **foreach** $\mathcal{N} \in \mathcal{P}_g$ **do**

7       $(acc, LUT) \leftarrow \texttt{EvaluateNetwork}(\mathcal{N})$

8    $\mathcal{P}_g \leftarrow \{\mathcal{N} \in \mathcal{P}_g \mid acc(\mathcal{N}) \geq (1 - \epsilon_{\text{global}})\}$

9   **if** $\mathcal{P}_g = \emptyset$ **then**

10   **break**

11   Update $\mathcal{S}_{\text{HoF}}$ if a solution in $\mathcal{P}_g$ has lower LUT

12   Fitness computation on $\mathcal{P}_g$ using objectives (LUT $\downarrow$, accuracy $\uparrow$)

13   Apply crossover and mutation to generate offspring $\mathcal{Q}_g$

14    $\mathcal{P}_{g+1} \leftarrow \mathcal{Q}_g$

15    $g \leftarrow g + 1$

16 **return** $\mathcal{S}_{\text{HoF}}$

The neuron library characterization is a one-time, fully parallelizable process. Although it incurs an upfront computational cost, this step scales systematically with increasing lookup table (LUT) bitwidth and can be tailored to the desired characterization granularity. Once completed, the resulting library enables rapid substitution of pre-characterized neuron variants, thereby substantially accelerating subsequent design space exploration (DSE) phases. To ensure a compact yet diverse solution set, we partition this Pareto set into a user-specified number of equal-sized groups and select one representative from each group. This yields a set of neuron variants that cover distinct accuracy–area operating points. Preserving this diversity is important for the subsequent DSE because it increases the likelihood of finding combinations that meet a given resource budget while controlling accuracy loss. Figure 3 illustrates the Pareto front spread of tradeoffs in the constructed library for a candidate neuron from our datasets.

Following library construction, an intra-layer approximation is performed independently for each layer. Initially, a preparation step identifies layer-specific approximation candidates, configures local error thresholds, and initializes DSE parameters. NSGA-II [12] has been widely used in multi-objective optimization problems [34], and particularly in the field of Approximate Computing [8, 25, 26]. Leveraging this, we employ NSGA-II as the intra-layer DSE engine, generating approximate layer variants by substituting candidate neurons with implementations drawn from our approximate neuron library (Fig. 2, Stage ③). Each variant is evaluated for accuracy and hardware cost (in terms of LUT count). Algorithm 1 provides detailed steps of the intra-layer DSE process. Since each intra-layer task is independent of the others, this exploration is executed fully in parallel across all layers. Layer-wise accuracy (Algorithm 1, Line 8) is assessed by measuring the Mean Hamming Distance (MHD) at the bit level between the approximated outputs and the golden reference of the corresponding layer across the full output vector. This metric directly quantifies how much a layer's output deviates from its pre-approximation reference at the bit level, thereby enforcing an explicit bound on the output perturbation introduced by neuron-level approximations (ϵ_{local}). To obtain the required golden layer-wise outputs, we employ the Icarus Verilog [35] simulator to sample the inputs and outputs of each individual DNN layer based on the test inputs of the respective dataset. Specifically, the test input is applied to the unmodified version of the first layer, and the resulting output serves as the input to the subsequent layer, continuing sequentially until the final layer. Each approximate layer instance that passes the accuracy test is then added to the set of valid layer instances $\mathcal{V}_{L_i}$ (Algorithm 1, Line 11). The internal while loop terminates either after a predefined number of generations or when further exploration is constrained by the specified accuracy limits (Algorithm 2, Line 6–14). Once the inner while loop has finished for all layers, a pool of approximate implementations per-layer is collected ($\mathcal{V}_{L_i} : L_i \in \mathcal{L}$), concluding the intra-layer DSE process. To reduce redundancy while preserving diversity for the subsequent inter-layer exploration, we partition $\{\mathcal{V}_{L_i}\}$ into n evenly spaced groups along the Pareto frontier and select one representative from each group. This sampling strategy ensures that the retained variants span a broad range of accuracy–area trade-offs, thereby providing a compact yet diverse candidate set for the inter-layer DSE.

3.3   Inter-layer Design Space Exploration

The final stage identifies the most effective approximate network configuration that minimizes hardware cost while incurring minimal accuracy loss. This stage operates on the pool of per-layer Pareto-front variants generated during intra-layer DSE within RTL approximation phase.

As multiple implementations exist for each layer, the problem is formulated as a second-level library substitution–based approximation task at the network level. We again employ NSGA-II to explore an inter-layer design space (see Algorithm 2). Each candidate solution selects one approximate variant per layer, forming a complete network configuration. Accuracy is evaluated via inference on the test set with a hardware simulation using icarus Verilog, while hardware cost is estimated using Vivado post-synthesis LUT utilization for the target FPGA device. The fitness of each individual solution is determined by comparing the network's predictions with ground-truth labels from the test dataset. A maximum allowable network accuracy degradation threshold (ϵ_{global}) filters the solution space. Configurations that violate the accuracy constraint are pruned, while feasible designs are promoted to subsequent generations (Algorithm 2,

Table 1. Model architecture used for selected datasets and algorithmic-level phase results. The accuracy and LUTs shown in the table for each dataset represents the baseline accuracy and resource consumption before RTL-level approximation step.

Dataset Name	Neurons per Layer	β, F^*	Alg. Level Acc. (%)	LUTs (#)
JSC-S	[64, 32, 32, 32, 5]	2, 3	63.5	245
MNIST 8×8	[256, 100, 100, 100, 100, 10]	2, 6	90.0	42083
MNIST 16×16	[256, 100, 100, 100, 100, 10]	2, 6	90.9	42877

* β and F denote bit-width and fan-in for each neuron in the network layers, respectively.

Line 7–15). All valid configurations encountered during the search are accumulated in a candidate set $\mathcal{S}_{HoF}$. The optimization terminates after a fixed number of generations or when convergence is observed. Finally, $\mathcal{S}_{HoF}$ is queried to select the network that maximizes area savings while maintaining accuracy as close as possible to the baseline (cf. Fig. 2, Stage ④).

4 Experiments and Results

In this section, we present the results. We organize this section based on the key approximation and DSE stages as highlighted in our framework (cf. Fig. 2). The experimental setup and parameters are also explained in the corresponding subsections. To evaluate the effectiveness of our framework, we conducted experiments on two benchmark datasets: the Jet Substructure Classification (JSC) (small version) and the MNIST datasets (8 × 8 and 16 × 16 versions).

4.1 Algorithmic Level Phase

Setup: For the first stage of approximation, we design a total of three configurations following the prior LUT-based methodologies, in particular the Logic-Nets [33] framework. Table 1 provides a summary of the architectures and training hyperparameters used for the selected datasets, with training conducted using a batch size of 1024 over 100 and 1000 epochs for MNIST and JSC-S, respectively. For each configuration, the generated Verilog description was synthesized using Vivado 2022.2 and implemented targeting the FPGA with part number `xcvu9p-flgb2104-2-i` to ensure consistency with the LogicNets framework [33].

Results: Following this stage of approximation, LUT utilization and the corresponding inference accuracy are measured and reported as baseline metrics for each benchmark in Table 1. These baselines are subsequently used as reference points for the proposed RTL-level approximation stage.

4.2   Library Building Phase

Setup: In the library-building step, we use the open-source BLASYS framework [17] to generate a set of approximate implementations for each selected candidate neuron. To accelerate the BLASYS library construction, we partition the full candidate-neuron list into three disjoint groups and execute them concurrently on three separate nodes on a high-performance cluster. Within each compute node, BLASYS jobs are further parallelized by running up to five neurons simultaneously. For each of these runs, BLASYS is configured to use Mean Absolute Error (MAE) as the error metric with a 50.0% error threshold, exhaustive input sample generation per neuron in the corresponding testbench, an exploration track parameter of 3, and the parallel mode enabled. All experiments in this phase and the subsequent phase are conducted on a compute cluster with 990 compute nodes, each equipped with 128 AMD Milan 7763 (2.45 GHz) cores and 256 GiB of main memory.

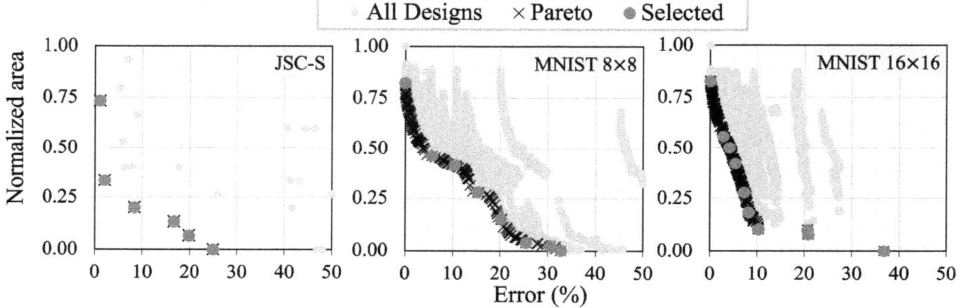

Fig. 3. Neuron library characterization results for JSC-S and MNIST datasets.

Results: Figure 3 summarizes the outcome of this step for representative neurons from our datasets, illustrating the accuracy–area tradeoff space produced by the library construction process. Each gray point corresponds to an explored design alternative, while the black colored points mark the Pareto-optimal subset that is not dominated in terms of error and normalized area cost. Since the Pareto set can contain many closely spaced solutions, we retain a compact yet diverse subset (selected points in Fig. 3) by selecting representatives that span different operating points along the front, ranging from low-error/high-area to higher-error/lower-area implementations. While further optimization of each individual candidate neuron is possible by adjusting the BLASYS parameters, we found our setup sufficient for our work. Naturally, longer runtimes are to be expected for more aggressive configurations.

4.3   Intra-layer and Inter-layer Design Space Exploration

Setup: Table 2 reports the genetic algorithm parameters and evaluation methodology adopted for both Intra-layer and Inter-layer DSE. The $\mu + \lambda$ evolution-

Table 2. Genetic algorithm configuration and evaluation parameters for Intra- and Inter-layer DSE.

Category	Parameter	Value
Genetic Algorithm	Evolution Strategy	$\mu + \lambda$
	Initial Population ($\mathcal{P}_0$)	100
	Max. Generations ($G_{\max}$)	50
	Crossover Type	Uniform
	Crossover Probability (p_c)	0.7
	Mutation Type	Uniform Integer
	Mutation Probability (p_m)	0.3
	Per-gene Probability (p_g)	0.1

ary strategy with uniform crossover and uniform integer mutation is employed within the DEAP framework as a strict elitist mechanism where the survival of the fittest solution is determined from a pool of parents and offspring.

In generation g, where $g \leq G_{\max}$, a parent population $\mathcal{P}_g$ of size $\mu = 100$ generates an offspring population $\mathcal{Q}_g$ of size $\lambda = 100$ via crossover and mutation. These populations are then combined into a unified mating pool $\mathcal{R}_g = \mathcal{P}_g \cup \mathcal{Q}_g$ of size $\mu + \lambda$. Unlike other evolution strategies that discard parents, this strategy ensures that the fittest solutions are preserved indefinitely, as the selection for the next generation $\mathcal{P}_{g+1}$ is performed on the entirety of $\mathcal{R}_g$, guaranteeing that the best individuals are retained regardless of whether they are parents or children.

To select μ individuals for $\mathcal{P}_{g+1}$, the NSGA-II selection strategy with a bi-objective fitness evaluation is utilized. The combined population $\mathcal{R}_g$ is partitioned into a hierarchy of non-dominated fronts $\mathcal{F}_1, \mathcal{F}_2, \ldots, \mathcal{F}_k$, where $\mathcal{F}_1$ contains all non-dominated solutions in $\mathcal{R}_g$, and each subsequent front $\mathcal{F}_j$ contains solutions dominated only by those in preceding fronts. The new population $\mathcal{P}_{g+1}$ is constructed by sequentially filling it with complete fronts ($\mathcal{F}_1, \mathcal{F}_2, \ldots$) until the addition of the critical front $\mathcal{F}_i$ would cause the population size to exceed μ. At this juncture, all individuals from fronts $\mathcal{F}_1$ to $\mathcal{F}_{i-1}$ are accepted, and the remaining slots are filled by selecting the best individuals exclusively from the critical front $\mathcal{F}_i$.

To discriminate between solutions within the critical front $\mathcal{F}_i$, the NSGA-II selection strategy utilizes the *Crowding Distance* metric operating within the defined bi-objective optimization space. Since the problem is formulated as a two-dimensional minimization task ($M = 2$) aiming to jointly minimize LUT count and accuracy degradation, the crowding distance d_I for a specific individual I is calculated by measuring the Euclidean proximity of adjacent solutions along these two dimensions. For each objective $m \in \{1, 2\}$, the solutions in $\mathcal{F}_i$ are sorted, and the distance is computed as the normalized difference between the objective values of the two adjacent neighbors:

$$d_I = \sum_{m=1}^{M=2} \frac{f_m(I+1) - f_m(I-1)}{f_m^{\max} - f_m^{\min}}$$

where $f_m(I+1)$ and $f_m(I-1)$ are the objective values of the neighboring individuals. It then sorts the members of $\mathcal{F}_i$ in descending order of d_I and selects those with the largest values, thereby favoring solutions located in less populated regions of the Pareto front.

In the intra-layer DSE, each layer is first processed independently on a separate compute node. This is possible because of our prior extraction of per-layer input–output traces from a single simulation of the non-approximated network interface, which decouples the layer evaluations from the rest of the model during exploration. For all intra-layer DSE runs, we enforced an error threshold of a maximum of 10.0% Mean Hamming Distance between the layer outputs produced by an approximated layer and the corresponding golden outputs.

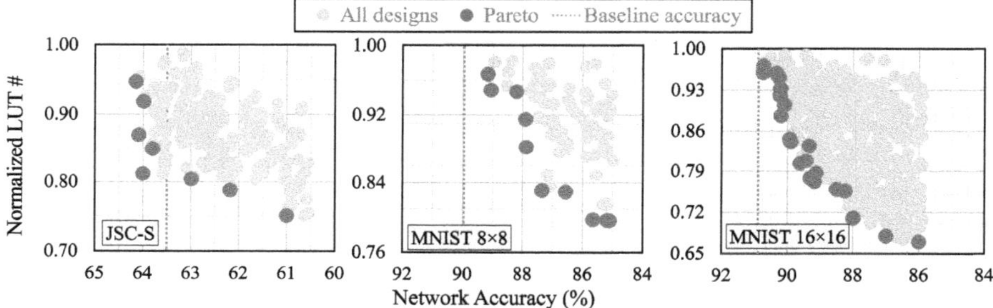

Fig. 4. Results of inter-layer DSE for JSC and MNIST datasets.

Once completed, the selected approximated-layer sets for all layers are integrated with the (non-approximated) output layer to form a complete network, which is then evaluated in an inter-layer DSE step on a single compute node. In contrast to the intra-layer stage, this inter-layer evaluation computes the end-to-end inference accuracy of the assembled DNN via full simulation of the network interface using Icarus Verilog [35]. We enforce a strict global constraint on accuracy degradation, allowing at most a 3.0% and 5.0% accuracy drop relative to the non-approximated baseline, for JSC-S and MNIST (both versions), respectively. For example, for MNIST 8×8, whose baseline accuracy is 90.0%, candidate networks are required to achieve an accuracy of at least 85.0%.

Results: Figure 4 illustrates the results of inter-layer DSE for all selected benchmarks. For the JSC-S benchmark, the results are shown in Fig. 4(left). The explored design space yields a diverse set of solutions, with classification accuracy ranging from 60.6% to 64.2%, while achieving LUT savings of up to 24.9% relative to the baseline design. Interestingly, in the case of JSC-S, some configurations surpass the baseline accuracy while simultaneously reducing LUT count. This indicates that optimization gains introduced in earlier layers can be

Table 3. Runtime breakdown of the proposed flow across benchmarks

Stage	Detail	JSC-S	MNIST 8×8	MNIST 16×16
Library building		0:20:00	480:28:48	568:44:24
Intra-layer DSE	L0	**18:50:37**	**92:12:25**	**94:52:28**
	L1	8:18:12	51:23:53	49:38:05
	L2	10:14:04	49:56:40	48:02:04
	L3	11:47:21	49:42:17	50:39:10
	L4	–	50:04:27	48:46:21
Inter-layer DSE		3:26:17	27:55:20	33:46:36
Total		**22:36:54**	**600:36:33**	**697:23:28**

Note: All runtimes are reported in *hh:mm:ss* format. Intra-layer DSE is executed independently and in parallel for each layer, enabling scalable exploration. For example, in case of JSC-S dataset, our parallel strategy reduces execution from 84h to 18h50min, yielding a 4.5×speedup that scales further to larger datasets. Library construction is performed once per benchmark; its runtime scales with the input bit-width and can be fully configured to trade off quality and execution time.

preserved or sometimes even amplified through approximations applied at lower levels of abstraction.

The results for the MNIST 8×8 benchmark are presented in Fig. 4(middle). The DSE achieves network accuracy ranging from 85.0% to 89.2%, with LUT reductions reaching up to 20.3% compared to the baseline implementation. The Pareto-front reveals several solutions that maintain near-baseline accuracy while delivering noticeable hardware savings. For the MNIST 16×16 benchmark, shown in Fig. 4(right), the exploration yields a notably larger solution set spanning accuracy values from 85.9% to 90.8%. The increased number of Pareto-optimal solutions stems directly from the expanded design space. With more candidate neurons per layer compared to the 8×8 variant, the optimization framework has access to a wider variety of approximated layer versions. This expanded design space allows deeper exploration of the accuracy-hardware trade-off. Additionally, as reflected in Table 3, configurations with more approximated neurons benefit from reduced synthesis and simulation times, which allows more evaluations to be completed within the same time frame. The results demonstrate LUT savings of up to 32.6% while maintaining accuracy above 86.5%, with several solutions achieving over 87.0% accuracy at a minimum of 17.0% LUT reduction.

Across all three benchmarks, the results validate the effectiveness of the proposed framework. The inter-layer optimization successfully identifies diverse design points that balance the DNN inference performance with resource efficiency and provides designers with a range of implementation options tailored to specific application requirements.

5 Conclusion and Future Work

LUT-based DNN accelerators offer the promise of ultra-low-latency inference on FPGAs, but their deployment has been limited by resource costs. In this work, we present a CLAS framework that rethinks how approximation is applied in fully unrolled LUT-based DNNs. By treating neurons in each layer of DNNs to RTL components, we enable the approximation of the neurons extracted by sensitivity profiling. Experimental results across multiple benchmarks on FPGA demonstrate significant LUT savings with negligible impact on accuracy.

As future work, we aim to extend this framework toward exploring tighter interactions across multiple approximation levels by investigating a broader range of combinations between algorithmic and RTL approximations and by identifying which combinations are best suited to specific network types and datasets. This would enable a more effective exploitation of the hierarchical nature of the design space exploration. In addition, we plan to extend the approach beyond LUT-based networks to architectures based on streamlined dataflow implementations.

Acknowledgments. This research is funded by the German Federal Ministry for the Environment, Nature Conservation, Nuclear Safety, and Consumer Protection under grant no. 67KI32004A, and the German Research Foundation (DFG) under grant number PL 471/9-1.

References

1. Ahmadilivani, M.H., Taheri, M., Raik, J., Daneshtalab, M., Jenihhin, M.: A systematic literature review on hardware reliability assessment methods for deep neural networks. ACM Comput. Surv. **56**(6), 1–39 (2024)
2. Andronic, M., Constantinides, G.A.: PolyLUT: learning piecewise polynomials for ultra-low latency FPGA LUT-based inference. In: 2023 International Conference on Field Programmable Technology (ICFPT), pp. 60–68 (2023). https://doi.org/10.1109/ICFPT59805.2023.00012
3. Andronic, M., Constantinides, G.A.: NeuraLUT: hiding neural network density in Boolean synthesizable functions. In: 2024 34th International Conference on Field-Programmable Logic and Applications (FPL), pp. 140–148. IEEE (2024)
4. Andronic, M., Constantinides, G.A.: NeuraLUT-assemble: hardware-aware assembling of sub-neural networks for efficient LUT inference. In: 2025 IEEE 33rd Annual International Symposium on Field-Programmable Custom Computing Machines (FCCM), pp. 208–216. IEEE (2025)
5. Armeniakos, G., Zervakis, G., Soudris, D., Henkel, J.: Hardware approximate techniques for deep neural network accelerators: a survey. ACM Comput. Surv. **55**(4), 1–36 (2022)
6. Awais, M., Mohammadi, H.G., Platzner, M.: Design space exploration for approximate circuits via checkpointing and DNN-based estimators. IEEE Trans. Very Large Scale Integr. (VLSI) Syst. (2025)
7. Barbareschi, M., Barone, S., Mazzocca, N., Moriconi, A.: A catalog-based AIG-rewriting approach to the design of approximate components. IEEE Trans. Emerg. Top. Comput. **11**(1), 70–81 (2022)

8. Barone, S., Traiola, M., Barbareschi, M., Bosio, A.: Multi-objective application-driven approximate design method. IEEE Access **9**, 86975–86993 (2021)
9. Blott, M., et al.: FINN-R: an end-to-end deep-learning framework for fast exploration of quantized neural networks. ACM Trans. Reconfigurable Technol. Syst. (TRETS) **11**, 1–23 (2018)
10. Bosio, A., Deveautour, B., O'Connor, I.: Exploiting approximate computing for efficient and reliable convolutional neural networks. In: 2022 IEEE Computer Society Annual Symposium on VLSI (ISVLSI), pp. 326–326. IEEE (2022)
11. Danopoulos, D., Zervakis, G., Siozios, K., Soudris, D., Henkel, J.: AdaPT: fast emulation of approximate DNN accelerators in PyTorch. IEEE Trans. Comput. Aided Des. Integr. Circuits Syst. **42**(6), 2074–2078 (2022)
12. Deb, K., Pratap, A., Agarwal, S., Meyarivan, T.: A fast and elitist multiobjective genetic algorithm: NSGA-II. IEEE Trans. Evol. Comput. **6**(2), 182–197 (2002)
13. Duarte, J., et al.: Fast inference of deep neural networks in FPGAs for particle physics. J. Instrum. **13**(07), P07027 (2018)
14. Ghasemzadeh Mohammadi, H., Gaillardon, P.E., De Micheli, G.: Efficient statistical parameter selection for nonlinear modeling of process/performance variation. IEEE Trans. Comput. Aided Des. Integr. Circuits Syst. **35**(12), 1995–2007 (2016)
15. Gysel, P., Pimentel, J., Motamedi, M., Ghiasi, S.: Ristretto: a framework for empirical study of resource-efficient inference in convolutional neural networks. IEEE Trans. Neural Netw. Learn. Syst. **29**(11), 5784–5789 (2018)
16. Hadipour, A.H., Jafari, A., Awais, M., Platzner, M.: A two-stage approximation methodology for efficient DNN hardware implementation. In: 2025 IEEE 28th International Symposium on Design and Diagnostics of Electronic Circuits and Systems (DDECS), pp. 119–122. IEEE (2025)
17. Hashemi, S., Tann, H., Reda, S.: BLASYS: approximate logic synthesis using Boolean matrix factorization. In: Proceedings of the 55th Annual Design Automation Conference, pp. 1–6 (2018)
18. He, Y., Xiao, L.: Structured pruning for deep convolutional neural networks: a survey. IEEE Trans. Pattern Anal. Mach. Intell. **46**(5), 2900–2919 (2023)
19. Hoerl, A.E., Kennard, R.W.: Ridge regression: biased estimation for nonorthogonal problems. Technometrics **12**(1), 55–67 (1970)
20. Jafari, A., Platzner, M.: Ultra-low latency and extreme-throughput echo state neural networks on FPGA. In: International Symposium on Applied Reconfigurable Computing, pp. 179–195. Springer (2025)
21. Legl, F.C., Kantic, J.: Fully automated implementation of reservoir computing models on FPGAs for nanosecond inference times. In: 2024 IEEE Nordic Circuits and Systems Conference (NorCAS), pp. 1–7. IEEE (2024)
22. Mrazek, V., Hrbacek, R., Vasicek, Z., Sekanina, L.: EvoApprox8b: library of approximate adders and multipliers for circuit design and benchmarking of approximation methods. In: Design, Automation & Test in Europe Conference & Exhibition (DATE), 2017, pp. 258–261. IEEE (2017)
23. Mrazek, V., Vasícek, Z., Sekanina, L., Hanif, M.A., Shafique, M.: ALWANN: automatic layer-wise approximation of deep neural network accelerators without retraining. In: 2019 IEEE/ACM International Conference on Computer-Aided Design (ICCAD), pp. 1–8. IEEE (2019)
24. Nazemi, M., Pasandi, G., Pedram, M.: NullaNet: training deep neural networks for reduced-memory-access inference. arXiv preprint: arXiv:1807.08716 (2018)
25. Nepal, K., Hashemi, S., Tann, H., Bahar, R.I., Reda, S.: Automated high-level generation of low-power approximate computing circuits. IEEE Trans. Emerg. Top. Comput. **7**(1), 18–30 (2016)

26. Nepal, K., Li, Y., Bahar, R.I., Reda, S.: Abacus: a technique for automated behavioral synthesis of approximate computing circuits. In: 2014 Design, Automation & Test in Europe Conference & Exhibition (DATE), pp. 1–6. IEEE (2014)
27. Sarwar, S.S., Venkataramani, S., Ankit, A., Raghunathan, A., Roy, K.: Energy-efficient neural computing with approximate multipliers. ACM J. Emerg. Technol. Comput. Syst. (JETC) **14**(2), 1–23 (2018)
28. Scarabottolo, I., Ansaloni, G., Constantinides, G.A., Pozzi, L., Reda, S.: Approximate logic synthesis: a survey. Proc. IEEE **108**(12), 2195–2213 (2020)
29. Shi, Y., Davaslioglu, K., Sagduyu, Y.E., Headley, W.C., Fowler, M., Green, G.: Deep learning for RF signal classification in unknown and dynamic spectrum environments. In: 2019 IEEE International Symposium on Dynamic Spectrum Access Networks (DySPAN), pp. 1–10. IEEE (2019)
30. Shinde, T.: Adaptive quantization and pruning of deep neural networks via layer importance estimation. In: Workshop on Machine Learning and Compression, NeurIPS 2024 (2024)
31. Taheri, M., et al.: DeepAxe: a framework for exploration of approximation and reliability trade-offs in DNN accelerators. In: 2023 24th International Symposium on Quality Electronic Design (ISQED), pp. 1–8. IEEE (2023)
32. Tibshirani, R.: Regression shrinkage and selection via the lasso. J. R. Stat. Soc. Ser. B Stat Methodol. **58**(1), 267–288 (1996)
33. Umuroglu, Y., Akhauri, Y., Fraser, N.J., Blott, M.: LogicNets: co-designed neural networks and circuits for extreme-throughput applications. In: 2020 30th International Conference on Field-Programmable Logic and Applications (FPL), pp. 291–297 (2020). https://doi.org/10.1109/FPL50879.2020.00055
34. Verma, S., Pant, M., Snasel, V.: A comprehensive review on NSGA-II for multi-objective combinatorial optimization problems. IEEE Access **9**, 57757–57791 (2021)
35. Williams, S., Baxter, M.: Icarus Verilog: open-source Verilog more than a year later. Linux J. **2002**(99), 3 (2002)
36. Witschen, L., Awais, M., Mohammadi, H.G., Wiersema, T., Platzner, M.: CIRCA: towards a modular and extensible framework for approximate circuit generation. Microelectron. Reliab. **99**, 277–290 (2019)
37. Yamada, M., Jitkrittum, W., Sigal, L., Xing, E.P., Sugiyama, M.: High-dimensional feature selection by feature-wise kernelized lasso. Neural Comput. **26**(1), 185–207 (2014)
38. Yu, R., et al.: NISP: pruning networks using neuron importance score propagation. In: Proceedings of the IEEE Conference on Computer Vision and Pattern Recognition, pp. 9194–9203 (2018)
39. Zhang, Q., Wang, T., Tian, Y., Yuan, F., Xu, Q.: ApproxANN: an approximate computing framework for artificial neural network. In: 2015 Design, Automation & Test in Europe Conference & Exhibition (DATE), pp. 701–706. IEEE (2015)

Applications

Exploiting Sum-Product Networks to Offload Database Query Cardinality Estimation to FPGA-Based Smart Storage Devices

Lukas Weber[1]([✉]) [ID], Yannick Lavan[1] [ID], Johannes Wehrstein[2] [ID],
Torben Kalkhof[1] [ID], Carsten Heinz[1] [ID], Carsten Binnig[2] [ID],
and Andreas Koch[1] [ID]

[1] Embedded Systems and Applications Group, TU Darmstadt, Darmstadt, Germany
{weber,lavan,kalkhof,heinz,koch}@esa.tu-darmstadt.de
[2] Systems Group, TU Darmstadt, Darmstadt, Germany
{johannes.wehrstein,carsten.binnig}@cs.tu-darmstadt.de

Abstract. Cardinality estimation is crucial for optimizing query performance in database systems. This study explores the application of Sum-Product Networks for estimating the cardinalities of database queries across various architectures. We analyze the capability of SPNs to handle different query types, highlighting their strengths and limitations.

Building upon existing research, we have developed a framework that creates both offload and smart storage hardware accelerators tailored for cardinality estimation. Compared to prior work, these accelerators utilize simplified fixed-point arithmetic to enhance resource efficiency. Our framework enables the generation of variants optimized for latency and throughput adaptable to diverse system architectures. Our approach now supports marginal and range-based queries essential for accurate cardinality estimation by extending prior functionality.

We applied our framework to generate accelerators and integrated them into two distinct architectures: a PCIe-based accelerator card for offloading tasks in large-scale general-purpose databases and a Near-Data Processing system within the COSMOS+ OpenSSD smart storage SSD. Our evaluation indicates that the PCIe-based architecture achieves over 165 million inferences per second, with latencies as low as 6.62 microseconds, and the Smart Storage device achieves latencies under 2 microseconds. Additionally, we analyzed the impact of our simplified fixed-point number system on resource efficiency and error margins, enabling a different trade-off between the different resources in a typical FPGA to make the existing framework more adaptable to different environments and applications.

Keywords: Sum-Product Networks · Probabilistic Models · Machine Learning · Cardinality Estimation · FPGA

G. Leone et al. (Eds.): ARC 2026, LNCS 16514, pp. 275–291, 2026.
https://doi.org/10.1007/978-3-032-29365-7_17

1   Introduction

In recent years, machine learning and big data have become active research fields within computer science. With the development of models such as ChatGPT by OpenAI, interest in AI has increased significantly. More recently, companies like Google and Anthropic have started creating and training their respective models, and even more open alternatives like DeepSeek have become public, virtually sparking an AI race with researchers and corporations delivering improved models regularly. These models deal with an ever-increasing amount of data produced and stored daily, making data storage and management equally important. However, while there have been efforts to improve storage systems, they are much less in the public eye, and there is still significant potential for optimization. New GPUs and CPUs often come with specific optimizations for AI, with AI permeating into all sections of the hardware market, starting at data-center GPUs and desktop and mobile CPUs and GPUs.

While consumer storage devices have advanced in capacity, latency, and throughput, most of these advances are not specific to machine learning. One potential improvement to storage devices for machine learning applications is the use of Near-Data Processing (NDP), which offloads computational load from the CPU to the storage device. NDP is especially interesting in applications where the stored data can be pre-processed on the storage device using data-reductive operations such as selections. By performing these operations on the storage device, bandwidth on the PCIe bus can be freed up, and the transported data is more relevant to the application. For example, consider training a model on a vast dataset containing functionally dependent data (e.g., age and birth date). Removing such redundancies using NDP projection avoids inefficient data transfers and could increase performance if data movement is a bottleneck.

To implement NDP, smart storage devices such as the Samsung SmartSSD [3] or the Zynq-7000-based COSMOS+ OpenSSD [16] are employed. The COSMOS+ OpenSSD is a regular NVMe-based SSD, but its flash controllers are implemented in the programmable logic (PL) of the Zynq-7000 SoC, and the Cortex A9 cores are used to run firmware. To enable NDP, the hardware on the PL and firmware of the COSMOS+ can be extended with user-defined functionality. Thanks to the FPGA-based SoC, simple NDP operations can be realized in hardware or software, as shown in [20]. For more complex NDP operations, result handling becomes an important problem [17], as intermediary results must be materialized. Efficient materialization is only possible for results that fit into block RAM (BRAM) or dynamic RAM (DRAM), making the prediction of result sizes a relevant issue to determine the best result-handling strategy. Predicting result sizes is generally called Cardinality Estimation (CE).

In addition to NDP, CE is also relevant in more traditional database systems. Specifically, it is used in query optimization, translating complex database queries into a sequence of subqueries called an execution plan. Optimally, data-reductive selections and projections are performed *early* in an execution plan since this will reduce the runtime of more complex later operations like joins.

One relatively novel approach to CE is using Sum-Product Networks (SPNs), as demonstrated in DeepDB [8]. While this work provides an interesting proof of concept for using SPNs in CE, it lacks detail on how queries are estimated using SPNs. Instead, the paper focuses on additional applications of SPNs in database and storage systems. SPNs are a probabilistic graphical model used for various tasks, including classification, regression, and density estimation. In the context of CE, SPNs can be trained to estimate the cardinality of data sets, potentially improving performance and accuracy over traditional methods. However, further research is needed beyond DeepDB to explore the feasibility and effectiveness of this approach in practical applications.

This paper has three specific contributions. First, we further elaborate the advantages and drawbacks of using SPNs for CE, explicitly focusing on the types of queries required for estimating the materialization within smart storage systems. While the underlying approach is similar to the prior work, we precisely define the types of queries and evaluate their suitability for usability in smart storage. Second, we implement an accelerator generation framework to allow for more complex queries by replacing the naive histogram probability lookup with a module capable of computing a multitude of sub-operations on the histogram. Lastly, we use a set of typical SPNs to generate several accelerator examples and drop them into multiple different architectures, evaluating the suitability of the approach in smart storage as well as general-purpose database systems. To this end, we evaluate the approach in detail on two specific platforms (COSMOS+ & AMD Alveo U280) while also providing a forward-looking What-If analysis using the Avnet Ultra96 as a stand-in for a potential UltraScale+ -based update of the limited COSMOS+ platform. We also include the Xilinx VC709 to allow a more direct comparison to prior work, which already employed that platform. Ultimately, our work provides new insights into the feasibility and effectiveness of using SPNs for CE in the context of practical NDP and general-purpose database applications on a wide range of different potential application spaces.

2 Background

2.1 Sum-Product Networks

SPNs [12] are probabilistic circuits represented as directed acyclic graphs (DAGs) that encode joint distributions over random variables. SPNs consist of three types of nodes: weighted sums, products, and leaves, which encode univariate or multivariate distributions over random variables. By performing a bottom-up pass through the DAG, joint and marginal inference can be efficiently performed on complete or partial evidence. Figure 1a provides an example of joint and marginal inference in an SPN.

SPNs can be constructed by hand for a specific purpose, or automatically trained on a given dataset. Different training approaches can be classified as structure learning, weight learning, or a combination of both. Random generation of SPNs with subsequent weight learning has also been shown to be a practical approach [11]. For example, an SPN can be learned from scratch by

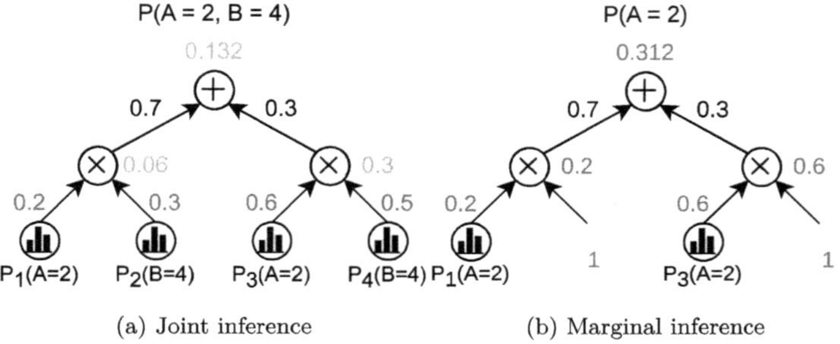

(a) Joint inference   (b) Marginal inference

Fig. 1. Inference example in an SPN, representing the joint probability distribution $P(A, B)$. In joint inference, all histograms output a corresponding value (a), while in marginal inference some histograms are marginalized and always output the value 1.0 (b).

performing structure learning to identify the relevant independent variables and their relationships, or refined by adjusting the weights of an existing SPN to improve accuracy. Relevant for this work, there is also research on learning SPNs from relational databases [8], with the goals of performing CE and Approximate Query Processing (AQP) in database and storage systems. This involves learning the underlying structure of the database schema and using that information to construct an SPN that accurately estimates the number of distinct values in a given query. The ability to automatically learn SPNs from data makes them a powerful tool for a wide range of applications in machine learning and artificial intelligence.

2.2 Cardinality Estimation

CE is a key operation in database and storage systems and used to predict the size (cardinality) of query results. In relational databases, CE specifically estimates the number of rows in a table or in an intermediary result. CE is often used in query optimization to rearrange subqueries for improved performance. Most databases use simple approaches for CE based on approximating data distributions using histograms and/or cost models. However, recent work suggests that machine learning and learned models are also a valid approach for CE [8]. SPNs are a promising approach for CE because they can perform very precise estimations of probabilities. Since CE does not require high precision, we are able to trade lower arithmetic for space efficiency.

3 Related Work

Cardinality Estimation. The core idea of this work is derived from [8], which uses SPNs to perform CE, as well as AQP. In their work, Hilprecht et al. define Relational SPNs (RSPNs), which are an extension of regular SPNs aimed towards relational databases. Specifically, RSPNs typically come in sets or ensembles which represent multiple datasets or database tables. Additionally, RSPNs support typical database-specifics like NULL values, handling of functional dependencies, and incremental training to keep the RSPN in sync with updates of the dataset. The authors show that CE and AQP using RSPNs is feasible. While there is prior work on CE for relational databases, most of those works do not use SPNs as model. The relatively extensive survey by Harmouch et al. discusses typical approaches for CE [5].

Near-Data Processing. While first experiments towards NDP took place as early as the 1970s, most of these early approaches (like database machines [2] and ActiveDisk [1]) were rather unsuccessful, due to I/O and general bandwidth limitations. More recently, there has been work with Smart SSDs that exploit the higher bandwidth of typical flash memories [3].

Also, *bump-in-the-wire* processing has become more relevant, with a number of publications by Vincon et al. [20], which introduced the concept of cross-layer data formats in NDP-based key-value stores. By giving the storage device knowledge about the structure of the stored data, typical key-value store operations like GET and SCAN could be performed on a COSMOS+ OpenSSD. They describe corresponding implementations in [20], proving that more complex operations like SCAN can profit from software- and FPGA-based NDP. Furthermore, the work was later extended by an approach to generate the FPGA-based NDP operators *automatically* from annotated code [19]. Lastly, the authors have shown the importance of result-set handling and suggest possible solutions in [17].

Sum-Product Networks. The first relevant paper considering the generation of specific hardware modules for SPN inference was published in 2018 by Sommer et al. [14]. It originally employed a compiler-like approach to read SPNs from a textual representation and generate corresponding accelerators using FloPoCo 64-bit floating point operators. In later works, this approach was extended to different custom data types like a logarithmic number system [18], as well as posit numbers and a custom floating point number system [15]. In more recent works, the SPN accelerators were integrated in different architectures enabling inference in 100G networks [6] and using fast on-chip HBM [21].

In parallel, Shah et al. developed a custom architecture for executing inference on probabilistic circuits [4,13]. Their approach also features improvements to the learning process that ensure that intermediary results are as precise as possible given different configuration parameters of the overall architecture.

4 SPNs and Cardinality Estimation

Prior to discussing the hardware implementation of probabilistic cardinality estimation as FPGA accelerators, we present a brief overview of key concepts driving the implementation approach. For a comprehensive discussion on incorporating SPNs into database systems, we refer the reader to Hilprecht et al. [8]. In this study, we focus on applying FPGA-based cardinality estimation for data distributions represented as SPNs over histogram leaf nodes. We assume *normalized* histograms, where each bucket signifies a probability rather than a density.

4.1   Estimating Query Cardinalities

In this section, we describe the probabilistic operations executed for corresponding database queries. Throughout this section, we represent the learned probability distribution for a database table T by $P(\mathbf{X})$, where $\mathbf{X}$ is the vector of random variables corresponding to each column in T. Generally, the estimated cardinality c of a query result is calculated as an expectation over the learned data distribution by determining the probability of the provided evidence vector $\mathbf{E}$ and multiplying it by the number of rows n in the table, as follows:

$$c = \mathbb{E}_{x \sim P(\mathbf{X}|\mathbf{E})}(\mathbf{X}) \approx n \cdot P(\mathbf{E}). \tag{1}$$

Next, we explain how to obtain $P(\mathbf{E})$ for various types of database queries.

Single-Column Equality Queries. In the most trivial filtering case, we aim to estimate the outcome of filtering a table for a provided value in a specific column. The evidence provided to the SPN consists of a single random variable X_i corresponding to the column i of interest, resulting in the computation

$$c \approx P(X_i = x) \cdot n, \tag{2}$$

effectively marginalizing every other column. In SPNs, the marginalization is achieved by outputting the value 1.0 for leaf nodes of marginalized variables.

Range Queries. In many applications, we are interested not only in single values for columns but also in ranges of data, such as "determine the number of scientists who have published *less* than five papers". Formally, we aim to evaluate the probability that the value of a random variable X_i falls within the range $[x_l, x_m]$ with $l < m$. Calculating the probability involves determining the probability of the or-event of several mutually exclusive events:

$$P(x_l \leq X_i \leq x_m) = \sum_{j=l}^{m} P(X_i = x_j). \tag{3}$$

Since non-leaf operations in SPNs remain constant w.r.t. j in Eq. 3, the sum propagates into the histogram leaves corresponding to X_i. This property enables us to compute the probability of single-column range queries without evaluating the entire SPN multiple times. Modifying the comparison operators within the query only changes the start and end indices for the sum operation.

AND Queries. While the previous paragraphs focused on single-column queries, we can also combine queries. In this work, we restrict our scope to queries of the form `A <= 42 AND B = 123`, excluding queries like `A <= 42 OR B >= 10`, as the latter would require multiple SPN passes, since SPNs encode joint probabilities. To compute the corresponding query, at least three passes are required: One to determine `A <= 42`, and a second one for `B >= 10`. Since both subqueries might overlap on the underlying dataset, the overlap has to be determined as well (`A <= 42 AND B >= 10`), to ensure that the overlap is not included twice. Furthermore, we limit the range queries to one predicate over a range and any number of equality predicates, as we cannot propagate the sum over all outcomes as before. Formally, we assess the probability $P(x_l \leq X_i \leq x_m, \mathbf{E} = \mathbf{e})$, with X_i corresponding to the column for the range computation and $\mathbf{e}$ representing evidence for other columns of interest $\mathbf{E}$. This probability is obtained by computing the sum inside X_i's histogram nodes, setting all other histograms for relevant columns to the corresponding evidence, and outputting *one* for all histogram nodes of marginalized columns. For practical purposes, we later empirically evaluate the effect of approximating cardinalities by applying the histogram summing of single range queries to multiple columns.

4.2   Hardware-Specific Model Optimization

While histograms with few buckets can be realized easily on FPGA through BRAM, histograms with a growing number of buckets, e.g. for 32-bit integers would either require LUTs with an unfeasible number of entries or merging of histogram buckets which may result in loss of representation accuracy. Due to the nature of SPNs to learn distributions over arbitrary data, we can make use of the underlying probabilistic semantics and simplify the resulting hardware.

Let X^n denote some n bit wide random variable. Then $P_L(X^n = x)$ denotes the probability output by a histogram leaf L for X^n taking the value x. Let us now assume w.l.o.g. that we slice X^n evenly into four bit chunks. Then we can view $P_L(X^n = x)$ as the joint probability
$\hat{P}_L(X^4_{\lfloor n/4 \rfloor - 1} = x_{n-1:4 \cdot (\lfloor n/4 \rfloor - 1)}, ..., X^4_1 = x_{7:4}, X^4_0 = x_{3:0})$, with X^4_i denoting the random variable corresponding to the i-th nibble of X^n and $x_{m:n}$ corresponding to the concrete assignments of bits m through n of x.

Leveraging this insight, we can either retrain the entire SPN by pre-processing the training data and bit-slicing each data point to the desired BRAM size or by learning SPNs representing each histogram node and replacing the histogram nodes with the corresponding SPN.

4.3   Empirical Analysis

To evaluate the feasibility of SPNs for CE, we developed a software simulation that executes queries both exactly—by filtering the dataset—and approximately—via inference on a trained SPN. Our preliminary evaluation uses the NIPS dataset, which represents word frequencies in ML publications as a large table. Its many columns with small value ranges allow systematic query enumeration. While the approach can be applied to other datasets (see Sect. 4.2), the NIPS dataset offers variants with increasing column counts, which is particularly useful for later performance and hardware utilization analysis (Sect. 6).

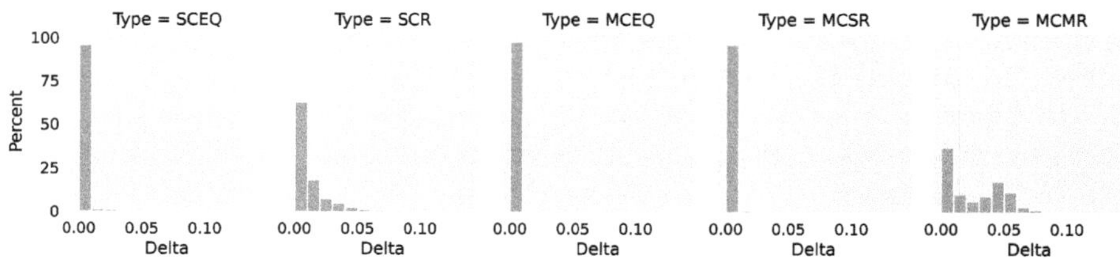

Fig. 2. Observed estimation error for range queries on all NIPS datasets.

Since SPN inference outputs query selectivity, we base our analysis on selectivity and derive cardinality by multiplying it with the dataset size. Queries are generated through range analysis per column, enabling enumeration of all single-column (SC) queries and their combination into multi-column (MC) queries. SC queries are classified as equality (SCEQ) or range-based (SCR), while MC queries are grouped into equality-only (MCEQ), single-range (MCSR), or multi-range (MCMR) queries.

We restrict MC queries to at most three columns, as larger queries would typically be decomposed by query optimization. Additionally, we exclude queries with zero true results, since SPN inference yields near-zero selectivities with negligible absolute error in these cases, making them irrelevant for typical CE use cases. Table 1 summarizes the datasets and query counts used in our analysis.

Table 1. Datasets and the corresponding number of benchmark queries

Dataset	SC		MC			
	EQ	R	EQ	SR	MR	Overall
NIPS5	111	710	9,782	134,682	200,000	345,285
NIPS10	227	1,426	92,548	200,000	200,000	494,201
NIPS20	480	2,882	129,092	200,000	200,000	532,454
NIPS30	740	4,400	165,960	200,000	200,000	571,100
NIPS40	1,027	5,980	200,000	200,000	200,000	607,007
NIPS50	1,255	7,626	200,000	200,000	200,000	608,881
NIPS60	1,573	9,308	200,000	200,000	200,000	610,880

Single-Column Equality (SCEQ). First, we enumerate all SCEQ queries yielding at least one result. For each query, we then execute the query and the corresponding SPN inference to compute the actual and estimated selectivity. The leftmost subplot of Fig. 2 shows the distribution of the estimation error. It shows that the estimation error is below 0.05 for almost all queries over all datasets. The maximum estimation error is 0.075.

Single-Column Range (SCR). For single-column range queries, we take a similar approach. As we can see in Fig. 2, the distribution of estimation errors changes. While most estimation errors are still relatively small, there are less cases with an estimation error of less than 0.01. This is the case, since the histograms of the trained SPNs sometimes do not sum up to exactly one due to the used double-precision floating point numbers.

Multi-Column Equality (MCEQ). As discussed in Sect. 4, the error of this class of queries should not significantly increase over SCEQ, as the inference does not introduce any mathematical issues apart from potential precision errors due to the digital arithmetic. Accordingly, the estimation error behaves relatively similar to SCEQ. Additionally, the errors are also typically less than for the SCR queries, since they compute over more histogram buckets.

Multi-Column Single Range (MCSR). For these queries, the estimation error also behaves as expected. Interestingly enough, the impact of the range-based subquery is not as prevalent as in SCR. While the range-based subquery will introduce an estimation error, its impact is not as high, as the rest of the computation is still relatively precise.

Multi-Column Multiple Ranges (MCMR). This class is the most interesting. As discussed in Sect. 4, the estimation error in this class should be relatively high, since summing up multiple histograms actually violates the mathematical precedence. As expected, the violation of precedence leads to more queries yielding higher estimation errors. But while more queries have higher estimation errors, the worst-case error still remains below 0.1, and is thus still in the same magnitude as for the other classes. So empirically, it is possible to perform CE for the given queries on the given dataset.

5   SPN Accelerators

Although SPNs are a relatively new ML model, substantial prior work explores FPGA acceleration for SPN inference. We build a separate framework inspired by [14], but simplify the numeric encoding by using fixed-point arithmetic instead of the more complex schemes in prior work. Since SPN values are probabilities in the range $[0, 1]$, a single integer bit suffices, and the number of fractional bits is configurable in Chisel3 to trade precision for resource usage. Unlike prior work targeting very low relative errors 10^{-6} [15], CE tolerates larger errors, as SPN estimation errors are already small in practice [8]. This allows a simpler encoding and reduced hardware cost.

SPN inference requires three hardware modules: FxAdder, FxMultiplier, and FxHistogram. The FxAdder performs saturated fixed-point addition, while the FxMultiplier uses a parameterized tiling approach to map onto FPGA DSP resources. All modules are implemented as parameterized Chisel3 generators and instantiated by traversing the SPN DAG, yielding a fully spatial, pipelined accelerator with AXI Stream interfaces.

The accelerator supports both low-latency single inference via AXI4-Lite and high-throughput batch inference via AXI4, enabling use in smart storage and PCIe-based database accelerators.

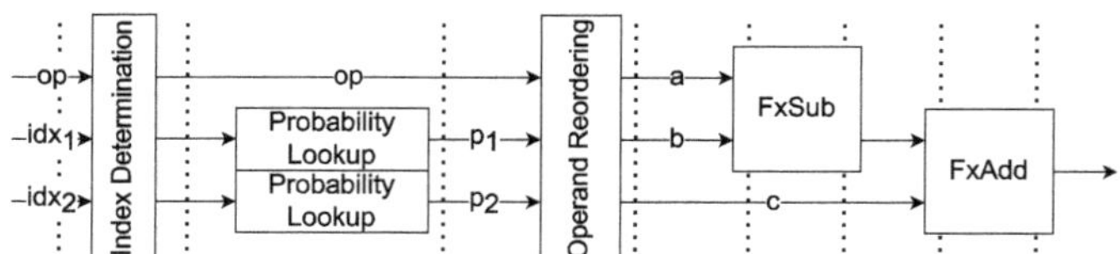

Fig. 3. FxHistogram Module. Dotted Lines indicate pipeline stages. The number of pipeline stages for FxSub and FxAdder depends on the used encoding.

FxHistogram Module. The FxHistogram module is novel over prior work, which exclusively focused on *equality*-based bottom-up inference. It enables other compare operations $(\neq, <, \leq, >, \geq)$, as well as a range- and a marginalization-operations.

Table 2. Functionality of FxHistogram and its submodules. b denotes the memory storing the accumulated histogram buckets.

Op	Calculation	Probabilities		Operands		
		p_1	p_2	a	$-b$	$+c$
$=$	$(b[i] - b[i-1])$	$b[id_1]$	$b[id_2]$	p_1	p_2	0
$\neq$	$1 - (b[i] - b[i-1])$	$b[id_1]$	$b[id_2]$	1	p_1	p_2
$<$	$(b[i-1] - 0)$	$b[id_1]$		p_1	0	0
$\leq$	$(b[i] - 0)$	$b[id_1]$		p_1	0	0
$>$	$1 - (b[i] - 0)$	$b[id_1]$		1	p_1	0
$\geq$	$1 - (b[i-1] - 0)$	$b[id_1]$		1	p_1	0
R	$(b[j] - b[i])$	$b[id_1]$	$b[id_2]$	p_2	p_1	0
M				1	0	0

The new module (cf. Fig. 3) enables additional operators, while the implementations from prior work could only compute equality-based inference. The first step in enabling the additional operations was the introduction of accumulated probabilities. In prior work, the probability lookup was limited to equality, so the value of each bucket could simply be stored in read-only memory using the index of the bucket as address. To enable the computation of ranges of buckets, we instead compute the accumulated probability. For each bucket, all probabilities up to and including the current one are summed and stored. By using this approach, the calculation for each of the corresponding operations can be done using two probability lookups. The corresponding addresses (idx_1 and idx_2) are determined in the Index Determination stage. Depending on the operation, up to two lookups happen concurrently, yielding the probabilities p_1 and p_2. The required calculations can be computed using three operands (a, b and c), where up to two operands are set to either zero or one, depending on the operation.

The Operand Reordering stage will reorder the incoming probabilities and add zeroes or ones accordingly, so that the correct final result can be computed using the normalized computation $a - b + c$. The exact mathematical calculations, the required lookups and the final operands are shown in Table 2.

5.1 System Integration

As detailed earlier, the main accelerator can be integrated using the two provided wrappers. Additionally, it could also be used standalone in a more complex accelerator or in a network-attached use-case. Both provided wrappers use an AXI4Lite interface to expose control registers, as well as an interrupt signal to enable asynchronous execution. The throughput-optimized variant also provides an AXI4 interface for batch processing. Using the latency-optimized variant, we tested the accelerator on five setups for the NIPS40 dataset, achieving end-to-end execution times shown in Table 3. The software interface runs on the ARM cores in SoC-based platforms and on the host CPU in PCIe-based platforms.

Setup (a) integrates the accelerator in a *Near-Data Processing* (NDP) scenario on the COSMOS+ smart (computational) SSD. Execution of SPN inference takes 6.85 µs, when controlling the accelerator from a baremetal firmware running on the Cortex A9 of the Zynq 7000 SoC. Polling is used to determine whether the execution has finished. As the Zynq-7000 in the COSMOS+ has been superseded by more recent FPGAs, Setup (b) evaluates the accelerator on more recent hardware (Ultra96), but retains the rest of the COSMOS+ architecture, achieving a latency of just 1.6 µs.

Setups (c), (d), and (e) employ the accelerator in *offload* mode, instead of the baremetal NDP approach of (a) and (b). They use the TaPaSCo framework [7,9] for system integration and as runtime API. Setup (c) uses TaPaSCo on an Ultra96, running an embedded Linux on the PS of the Zynq UltraScale+. Setups (d) and (e) both use PCIe-based accelerator cards (VC709 and Alveo U280). These are connected to their respective host via PCIe Gen3 x8 and x16 respectively. While inference is still relatively fast, the added overheads of operating systems and interrupts increases latency significantly. This is especially visible for the Ultra96 with a latency of 26.7 µs. This is due to the OS running on the rather limited embedded CPUs. For the PCIe-based platforms, the impact of OSs and interrupts is less significant, due to the much higher performance of the host CPUs. Thus, the resulting latencies are better here than for setup (c), even though the latency includes PCIe transfers. While the U280 is more recent compared to the VC709, the VC709 still reaches a lower latency. This shows the impact of the employed host machine: The VC709 is connected to a workstation, while the U280 resides in a server with a more complex PCIe subsystem, which increases latency. We report the value based on the server-setup as it is more representative of real-world usage of a data-center FPGA card.

Table 3. Tested Architectures

Test Setup	(a)	(b)	(c)	(d)	(e)
Platform	COSMOS+	Ultra96	Ultra96	VC709	U280
Arch	Zynq 7000	Zynq US+	Zynq US+	PCIe	PCIe
Fabric	Kintex 7	UltraScale+	UltraScale+	Virtex 7	UltraScale+
Driver	none	none	TaPaSCo	TaPaSCo	TaPaSCo
Control	Polling	Polling	Interrupt	Interrupt	Interrupt
Freq.	200 MHz	440 MHz	440 MHz	200 MHz	420 MHz
Latency	6.85 µs	1.6 µs	26.7 µs	16.1 µs	21.3 µs

6 Evaluation

To evaluate our framework, we use the different variations of the NIPS dataset
as benchmarks. Each variation comes with a trained SPN, which was trained
using the *SPFlow* library [10]. As queries we use the enumerated and combined
queries we generated for the empirical analysis of SPN-based CE. In addition
to the different SPNs, we also want to evaluate the two accelerator objectives
(latency- vs. throughput-optimized). Finally, we also want to evaluate the error
margins of the fixed-point encoding depending on the number of bits. Thus,
we generate the accelerators using different encodings, resulting in 56 different
accelerators (7 SPNs $\times$ 2 variants $\times$ 4 encodings).

6.1 Benchmarks

For our evaluation, we rely on the NIPS dataset. While not being a traditional
database or cardinality estimation benchmark, it is advantageous for our study
due to its scalability. The number of each benchmark indicates the size of the
underlying entries in bytes. For example, a NIPS60 entry is comprised of 60
separate values that are encoded with a single byte each. Accordingly, the NIPS
dataset is useful for showing increasing error margins, and decreasing throughput
and latency, depending on the entry-sizes of the underlying data. It also makes
our results comparable to prior art, such as the acceleration of key-value stores
in smart storage devices [19,20], which employed the same dataset. As discussed
in Sect. 4.2, our results are applicable to more traditional database benchmarks.

6.2 Fixed-Point Encoding

In a first step, we evaluate the arithmetic error introduced by the encoding.
Since it is based on fixed-point numbers, the maximum error can be derived
depending on the encoding and the SPN. Additionally, we use the enumerated
and generated queries to gain an empirical perspective shown in Fig. 4. The plot
shows the maximum theoretical error in light color and the empirical maximum
error in darker color for all datasets and four configurations of the fixed-point

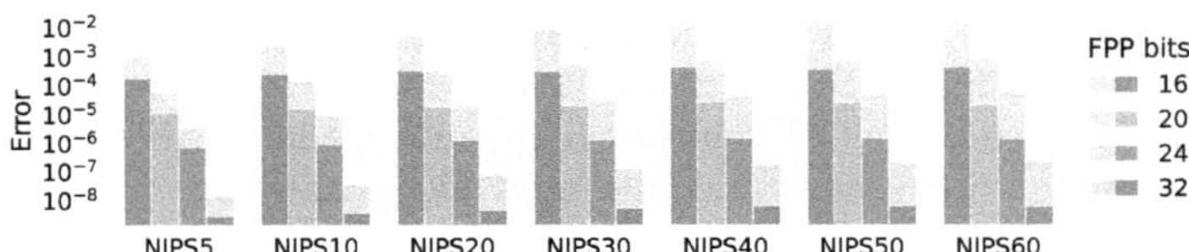

Fig. 4. Arithmetic errors of the encoding depending on the combination of SPN and encoding. The darker bar in front is the maximum measured error, while the lighter bar behind is the theoretical maximum error.

encoding. We observe that theoretical and empirical maximum error always differ by at least a factor of 5. The worst case occurs if each column is queried using a range query. Additionally, it is clear that increasing the number of bits in the encoding will reduce the maximum error, since numbers can be represented more accurately.

Lastly, we observe an increased error towards the more complex versions of the NIPS dataset like NIPS50 and NIPS60. This is the case, because the corresponding SPNs are more complex with more histograms and more operations. While more histograms also add more potential for conversion errors during accelerator generation, additional operations introduce more potential for accumulating or multiplying conversion errors. Most importantly, the empirical error of the arithmetic is relatively small compared to the error introduced by CE (cf. Sect. 4.3). Thus, fixed-point encodings with 16 or 20 bits will most likely be enough for most CE use-cases.

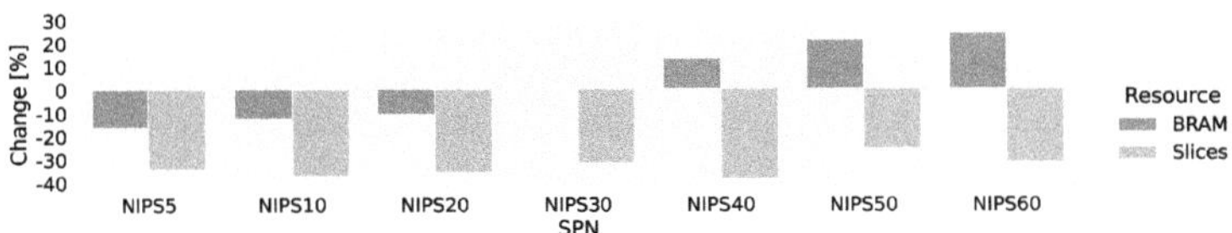

Fig. 5. Changes in resource utilization of a 24 bit fixed-point encoding compared against the closest matching CFP encoding from [15]. DSP utilization is identical for both encodings.

Resource Utilization. To gauge the resource efficiency of our design, we used the 24 bit fixed-point accelerators and compared them against the Custom Floating Point (CFP) variants from [15]. We synthesize for the VC709 to achieve comparable results. The changes in resource utilization from [15] to our work are shown in Fig. 5. The diagram shows that there are no changes in DSP utilization. This is the case, since the multiplications in both variants are similar in size and can both be done using 2 DSP slices per multiplication. The BRAM utilization for smaller SPNs is slightly reduced, but will increase for bigger SPNs. This change is the result of three factors: 1) In our work, we need two BRAM lookups to enable the more complex operations in the FxHistogram, which doubles the required memory. 2) The encoding used in our work is more compact, as no exponent is stored. This reduces the required BRAM by about 30%. 3) The use of accumulated histograms and the Index Determination stage allows us to store the buckets without replication. Since 1) and 2) are more or less constant, the changes show mostly 3), which is SPN-dependant. Lastly, we see a reduction in Slice utilization. Overall, our accelerators are more resource efficient. While BRAM utilization is increased, this is not as problematic, as overall BRAM utilization is below 5% for all SPNs. The reduced resource footprint is paramount for enabling the apporach on the COSMOS+ due to reduced size compared to data-center FPGAs used in prior work.

6.3   Performance

For brevity, we focus our performance evaluation on accelerators using a 24 bit fixed-point encoding, as the encoding has no relevant impact on performance.

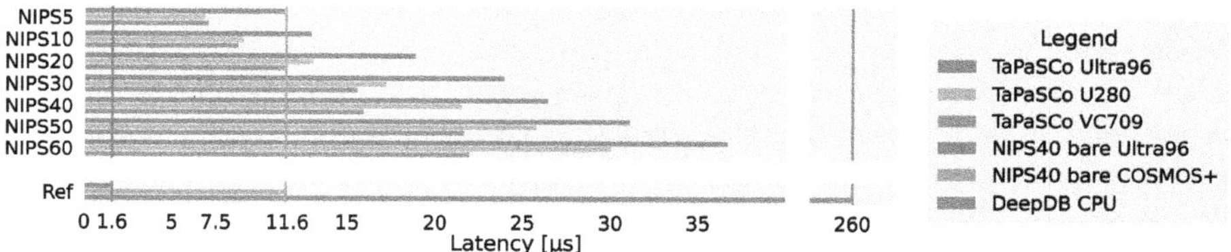

Fig. 6. End-to-End inference latencies (less is better) of TaPaSCo-based architectures in comparison against baremetal NIPS40-accelerators on Ultra96 and COSMOS+ and a RSPN CPU implementation from prior work [8].

Latency. First, we want to look at end-to-end latency. For this, we rely on latency measurements that are comparable to real-world implementations, including necessary data movement. We achieve this by using the TaPaSCo-based system integrations (cf. test setups (c)–(e)). The corresponding measurements are shown in Fig. 6. The figure shows that bigger SPNs have higher latencies, which can be attributed to increased data-transfers, as the actual computation takes less than 1 µs. Interestingly, this impact is similar for PCIe-based and SoC-based platforms. While there is no overhead for data-transfers via PCIe in SoC-based systems, the latter are much slower due to the slow ARM cores of the Ultra96. While the latencies seem high compared to the baremetal implementations from Table 3, we still outperform prior CPU-only work [8] by up to 40x. Even for the biggest SPN (NIPS60), our achieved speed-up is still more than 10x. Note that the result reported in prior work is not based on the NIPS dataset. To keep the comparison fair, we thus always compare against their *overall best* reported result of 260 µs. Reproducing the numbers of the original work for the well-known Job-Light benchmark even yields a latency of 910 µs on an Intel

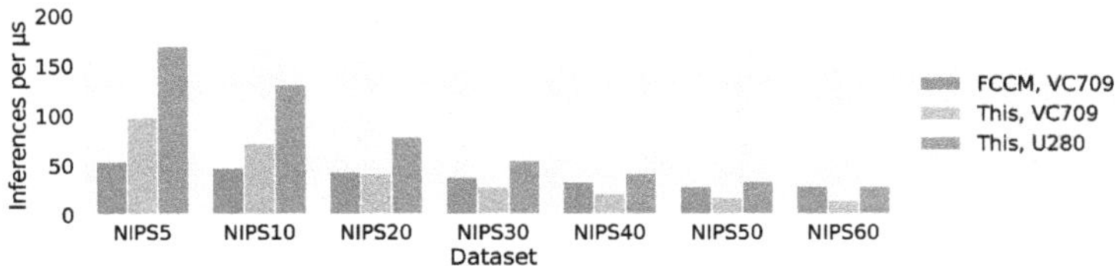

Fig. 7. Throughput of the throughput-optimized accelerator variants on VC709 and Alveo U280 in comparison to single-core prior work published at FCCM [15].

Xeon Platinum 8268, showing that the FPGA-based approach can significantly improve the latency.

Throughput. Prior CPU-based work does not report throughput, so we compare against existing SPN implementations. Although [15] was later improved via replication, HBM, and 100G networking [6,21], these effects are hard to isolate. We therefore restrict the comparison to a single accelerator on PCIe platforms, excluding the Ultra96 due to limited memory bandwidth.

Results (Fig. 7) show that, despite 4x larger inputs per inference (1→4 bytes) due to range-supporting histograms, throughput does not drop proportionally. Instead, improved TaPaSCo and SoC design—using optimized vendor IP over custom AXI-Stream interconnects—enable higher throughput for smaller SPNs. On a PCIe Gen3 x16 U280, this yields up to 3x speedup (NIPS5). While gains decrease for larger models, performance remains competitive up to NIPS60.

7   Conclusion

In this work, we extend the use of SPNs for CE [8] and evaluate FPGA-based acceleration. Our framework generates accelerator variants for diverse architectures, including smart storage devices and FPGA cards in database systems, achieving up to 40x latency speedup over prior CPU-based work. On COSMOS+, CE is accelerated by 100x, with newer hardware enabling up to 400x for latency-optimized designs. Compared to prior throughput-oriented approaches, we achieve competitive or better performance despite supporting more complex queries: similar worst-case performance and up to 2x higher throughput, reaching 165 million inferences per second.

Overall, our work shows the overall applicability of the approach in very different system architectures and shows the potential not only in theory, but also in practice on a multitude of different target platforms, including mainstream datacenter cards like the Alveo U280, as well as the more niche architectures such as smart storage, here in the form of the COSMOS+ Smart SSD.

Acknowledgments. AI tools were used for language refinement. This work was partially funded by the Hessian Center for Artificial Intelligence, Germany.

Disclosure of Interests. The authors have no competing interests to declare that are relevant to the content of this article.

References

1. Acharya, A., Uysal, M., Saltz, J.: Active disks: programming model, algorithms and evaluation. In: Proceedings of ASPLOS 1998 (1998)
2. Boral, H., DeWitt, D.J.: Parallel architectures for database systems. In: Database Machines, chap. Database Machines: An Idea Whose Time Has Passed? A Critique of the Future of Database Machines, pp. 11–28. Springer (1989)
3. Do, J., Patel, J., DeWitt, D., et al.: Query processing on smart SSDs: opportunities and challenges. In: Proceedings of SIGMOD 2013 (2013)
4. Galindez Olascoaga, L.I., Meert, W., Shah, N., Verhelst, M., Van den Broeck, G.: Towards hardware-aware tractable learning of probabilistic models. In: Wallach, H., Larochelle, H., Beygelzimer, A., d'Alché-Buc, F., Fox, E., Garnett, R. (eds.) Advances in Neural Information Processing Systems, vol. 32. Curran Associates, Inc. (2019)
5. Harmouch, H., Naumann, F.: Cardinality estimation: an experimental survey. Proc. VLDB Endow. **11**(4), 499–512 (2017). https://doi.org/10.1145/3186728.3164145
6. Hartmann, M., Weber, L., Wirth, J., Sommer, L., Koch, A.: Optimizing a hardware network stack to realize an in-network ml inference application. In: 2021 IEEE/ACM International Workshop on Heterogeneous High-Performance Reconfigurable Computing (H2RC) (2021)
7. Heinz, C., Hofmann, J., Korinth, J., Sommer, L., Weber, L., Koch, A.: The TaPaSCo open-source toolflow. J. Signal Process. Syst. **93**(5), 545–563 (2021). https://doi.org/10.1007/s11265-021-01640-8
8. Hilprecht, B., Schmidt, A., Kulessa, M., Molina, A., Kersting, K., Binnig, C.: Deepdb: learn from data, not from queries! Proc. VLDB Endow. **13**(7), 992–1005 (2020). https://doi.org/10.14778/3384345.3384349
9. Korinth, J., Hofmann, J., Heinz, C., Koch, A.: The TaPaSCo open-source toolflow for the automated composition of task-based parallel reconfigurable computing systems. In: Applied Reconfigurable Computing (2019)
10. Molina, A., et al.: Spflow: an easy and extensible library for deep probabilistic learning using sum-product networks (2019)
11. Peharz, R., et al.: Random sum-product networks: a simple but effective approach to probabilistic deep learning. In: Proceedings of the Thirty-Fifth Conference on Uncertainty in Artificial Intelligence (UAI) (2019)
12. Poon, H., Domingos, P.: Sum-product networks: a new deep architecture. In: Proceedings of UAI (2011)
13. Shah, N., Galindez Olascoaga, L.I., Meert, W., Verhelst, M.: Acceleration of probabilistic reasoning through custom processor architecture. In: 2020 Design, Automation & Test in Europe Conference & Exhibition (DATE), pp. 322–325 (2020). https://doi.org/10.23919/DATE48585.2020.9116326
14. Sommer, L., Oppermann, J., Molina, A., Binnig, C., Kersting, K., Koch, A.: Automatic mapping of the sum-product network inference problem to FPGA-based accelerators. In: 36th International Conference on Computer Design (ICCD) (2018)
15. Sommer, L., Weber, L., Kumm, M., Koch, A.: Comparison of arithmetic number formats for inference in sum-product networks on FPGAs. In: International Symposium on Field-Programmable Custom Computing Machines (FCCM) (2020)
16. Song, Y.H., Jung, S., Lee, S.W., Kim, J.S.: Cosmos+ OpenSSD: a NVME-based open source SSD platform. Flash Memory Summit (2016)
17. Vinçon, T., et al.: Result-set management for NDP operations on smart storage. In: 18th International Workshop on Data Management on New Hardware (DaMoN) (2022). https://doi.org/10.1145/3533737.3535097

18. Weber, L., Sommer, L., Oppermann, J., Molina, A., Kersting, K., Koch, A.: Resource-efficient logarithmic number scale arithmetic for SPN inference on FPGAs. In: International Conference on Field-Programmable Technology (FPT) (2019)
19. Weber, L., et al.: A framework for the automatic generation of FPGA-based near-data processing accelerators in smart storage systems. In: 2021 IEEE International Parallel and Distributed Processing Symposium Workshops (IPDPSW), pp. 136–143 (2021). https://doi.org/10.1109/IPDPSW52791.2021.00028
20. Weber, L., et al.: On the necessity of explicit cross-layer data formats in near-data processing systems. Distrib. Parallel Databases (2021). https://doi.org/10.1007/s10619-021-07328-z
21. Weber, L., Wirth, J., Sommer, L., Koch, A.: Exploiting high-bandwidth memory for FPGA- acceleration of inference on sum-product networks. In: 2022 IEEE International Parallel and Distributed Processing Symposium Workshops (IPDPSW) (2022)

FPGA-SORT: Complete Hardware Pipeline for Real-Time Multi-Object Tracking

Lu Jiang[1]([✉]) [iD], Aswanth Thayyil[1] [iD], Jin Yuan[1,2] [iD], and Diana Goehringer[1,2] [iD]

[1] Technische Universität Dresden, Dresden, Germany
`{lu.jiang1,aswanth.thayyil}@mailbox.tu-dresden.de,`
`{jin.yuan,diana.goehringer}@tu-dresden.de`
[2] Center for Scalable Data Analytics and Artificial Intelligence (ScaDS.AI)
Dresden/Leipzig, Dresden/Leipzig, Germany

Abstract. In real-time applications such as obstacle avoidance in mobile robots, environmental perception systems need to continuously provide reliable object state information in dynamic scenarios. Multi-object tracking (MOT) lies on the critical path between perception and decision-making, and its processing latency directly impacts system responsiveness, particularly in scenes with dense targets or rapid motion. Compared with software implementations on general-purpose processors, Field Programmable Gate Arrays (FPGAs) provide architectural support for parallel processing and predictable timing behavior. This paper presents a hardware-oriented analysis and implementation of the classical Simple Online and Realtime Tracking (SORT) algorithm. The key computational components are restructured to improve hardware efficiency, and a complete tracking pipeline is subsequently implemented for FPGAs. The proposed design aims to enhance both computational efficiency and timing determinism in the MOT stage, enabling low-latency and predictable execution for downstream decision-making modules. Experimental results show that the proposed FPGA solution achieves up to $100\times$ speedup over the embedded software implementation under identical input conditions. Moreover, across different scenarios and object counts, the FPGA design maintains a significantly narrower latency distribution than the software baseline. These results confirm that the proposed approach delivers both high computational performance and stable timing behavior.

Keywords: Robotics · Multi-object tracking · FPGA · Real-time

1 Introduction

Multi-object tracking (MOT) is a fundamental task in computer vision and plays a key role in real-time systems such as autonomous driving, drone navigation, and mobile robotics [11,14]. By associating detections across video frames, MOT

G. Leone et al. (Eds.): ARC 2026, LNCS 16514, pp. 292–308, 2026.
https://doi.org/10.1007/978-3-032-29365-7_18

maintains object identities and trajectories over time. In latency-sensitive vision systems, the tracking module lies on the critical path of the perception pipeline and must operate within strict timing constraints while maintaining association accuracy. As object density increases or scene complexity grows, the computational demand of tracking algorithms rises substantially, posing challenges to real-time execution.

Traditional software implementations offer flexibility but are constrained by sequential execution and operating system scheduling, which introduce timing variability and make it difficult to guarantee bounded execution latency. Deterministic latency refers to execution time that remains either fixed or confined within a predictable range, enabling downstream decision modules to rely on explicit timing assumptions for stable control behavior. Field Programmable Gate Arrays (FPGAs) offer an alternative computing paradigm that emphasizes spatial parallelism and predictable execution. By mapping algorithms directly onto dedicated hardware structures, FPGAs mitigate timing variability inherent in software-based execution environments. These properties make FPGA-based implementations particularly attractive for real-time tracking systems that demand not only speed but also stable latency.

Recent research on FPGA-based acceleration for real-time perception systems has primarily focused on object detection, covering both neural network inference and post-processing stages. Numerous works have optimized deep learning detection models through quantization and pruning, enabling efficient inference with widely used architectures such as You Only Look Once (YOLO) [2,7,17] and Single Shot MultiBox Detector (SSD) [6]. In addition, Non-Maximum Suppression (NMS) has been implemented in hardware using parallel architectures, serving as a key post-processing step in detection pipelines [3,9]. These efforts cover the complete acceleration path from image input to detection output.

However, hardware-oriented research on MOT algorithms beyond detection remains relatively limited. Existing efforts typically accelerate individual computational modules, such as Kalman filtering [4] or data association [12], rather than addressing the tracking pipeline as an integrated system. Because MOT stages are interdependent and coupled through dataflow and control, module-level optimization alone cannot guarantee improved end-to-end efficiency or predictable execution. Therefore, a pipeline-level hardware implementation is needed to enable coordinated parallelism and consistent system-level behavior.

Simple Online and Realtime Tracking (SORT) is widely adopted as a baseline framework in modern MOT research, and its core principles have been integrated into numerous advanced tracking algorithms [5,16]. In this work, it is selected as the target algorithm to explore systematic FPGA-based hardware design for object tracking. We present a complete end-to-end implementation and analyze the overall hardware architecture to investigate design methodologies for FPGA-based tracking systems. The proposed approach aims to improve timing stability while maintaining computational efficiency, providing a foundation for extending hardware acceleration to more complex tracking frameworks. The main contributions of this paper are summarized as follows:

- **Unified FPGA-based pipeline architecture for SORT:** We propose an integrated hardware architecture that transforms the sequential SORT workflow into a fully coordinated FPGA-based pipeline, enabling stage-by-stage processing across prediction, association, and update.
- **FPGA Realization of Data Association:** We present a structured hardware implementation of Hungarian-based data association using a Jonker-Volgenant (JV) formulation. Compared to the conventional approach, the JV-based design reduces redundant full-matrix operations and exhibits a more localized execution pattern, thereby improving suitability to efficient hardware realization.
- **Experimental characterization of performance and timing behavior:** We provide a comprehensive functional validation of the complete SORT pipeline and report its end-to-end latency. Furthermore, the data association module is systematically evaluated across diverse tracking scenarios and object scales, demonstrating stable latency scaling and consistent execution behavior under varying problem sizes.

Section 2 reviews the background of MOT and related FPGA-based acceleration work in perception systems. Section 3 introduces the SORT algorithm and analyzes its hardware adaptability. Section 4 details the proposed FPGA architecture and module-level implementations. Section 5 presents the end-to-end latency of the complete hardware pipeline and a quantitative latency analysis of the data association module under varying tracking complexities. Section 6 concludes this work.

2   Background and Related Work

2.1   MOT Background and SORT Family

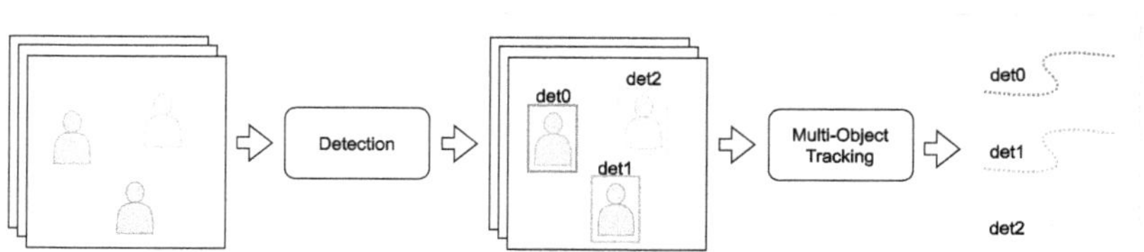

Fig. 1. Two-stage workflow of the tracking-by-detection framework. Det0, det1, and det2 denote detection results.

MOT aims to consistently identify and track multiple objects over time in a video sequence. Among the widely used approaches for MOT, tracking-bydetection

(TBD) follows a two-stage "detect-then-associate" paradigm [11,14], as illustrated in Fig. 1. First, an object detector processes each frame independently and produces a set of detections, typically represented as bounding boxes. These detections are then passed to the MOT module, which links corresponding detections across frames to produce continuous trajectories and maintain object identities.

SORT is a foundational algorithm for TBD methods [5]. Building on the SORT framework, numerous improved algorithms have been proposed. Deep-SORT [16] and StrongSORT [8] incorporate appearance features into the association stage to improve identity preservation. ByteTrack [18] enhances tracking continuity in unstable detection scenarios by utilizing detections across multiple confidence levels for matching. BoT-SORT [1] further integrates motion information, appearance features, and refined association strategies to systematically optimize the data association process.

While current research has significantly improved identity consistency, tracking accuracy, and robustness to occlusion, these improvements often come at the cost of increased computational complexity. In applications involving many objects or strict real-time requirements, execution latency and stability become critical factors limiting system performance. Moreover, relatively little work has focused on developing efficient MOT solutions suitable for resource-constrained platforms or environments with deterministic timing requirements.

2.2 FPGA-Based Acceleration for Perception

Due to the high computational cost and strict real-time requirements of detection, many studies have explored FPGA-based acceleration for perception tasks, particularly object detection. Cai et al. [6] developed an SSD object detection accelerator on a heterogeneous FPGA-based platform. The SSD network is partitioned into an FPGA subgraph, which handles most convolutional operations, and a CPU subgraph responsible for post-processing tasks such as NMS. The hardware adopts a single-engine architecture integrating a Processing Element (PE) array, a feature map buffer, and various operator modules. Optimization techniques, including FP16/FP11 quantization and batch normalization fusion, are applied to accelerate SSD inference. As a result, the system achieves approximately a 4.5× speedup over a CPU implementation when running SSD-MobileNetV2.

Zhai et al. [17] implemented a vehicle detection accelerator based on YOLOv3 and YOLOv3-Tiny, reducing the model size by 85% / 98.2% through structured pruning and INT16 fixed-point quantization. The hardware architecture was developed using High-Level Synthesis (HLS), with overall efficiency improved through optimizations such as inter-layer memory reuse and parameter rearrangement. This dual-module parallel acceleration achieves a detection throughput of 168.72 fps at 16-bit fixed-point precision and supports simultaneous processing of six video streams. Similarly, Amin et al. [2] deployed an 8-bit quantized YOLOv3-Tiny detector on an FPGA using the Vitis Artificial Intelligence (AI) toolchain, which quantizes the model and maps it to a Data Processing Unit

(DPU) for acceleration. Post-processing tasks such as NMS are executed on the Processing System (PS), enabling real-time detection at 15 fps for HD video streams. In the latest work, Danilowicz et al. [7] implemented a 4-bit quantized YOLOv8-nano detector using the FINN framework [15]. They extended FINN to support the Split and Concat operators required by YOLOv8 and utilized external RAM to store model parameters. Experimental results show that the hardware detector achieves a throughput of 195.3 fps, while the complete multi-object tracking system runs at 24 fps because the SORT tracking algorithm executes on the PS side.

The post-processing module follows detection and lies on the critical path between perception and decision-making. Due to its computational complexity and limited inherent parallelism, it often becomes a performance bottleneck in FPGA-accelerated systems. Hence, recent research has focused on improving end-to-end detection efficiency by optimizing this post-processing stage. Guo et al. [9] proposed a hardware-accelerated post-processing framework for object detection, implementing a pipelined data path that fuses scanning, decoding, class identification, and NMS operations. Their design achieves low latency and high throughput through this deeply pipelined architecture and 48 parallel Intersection-over-Union (IoU) PEs for NMS acceleration. Anupreetham et al. [3] further addressed system-level hardware implementation of the detection pipeline. By introducing hardware-based NMS with pipelining and multithreading, they enabled seamless integration with a Convolutional Neural Networks (CNN) accelerator. This design significantly improves end-to-end throughput and reduces total latency for the SSD-MobileNetV1 detection system. Experimental results demonstrate that the multi-threaded NMS module fully matches the throughput of the CNN accelerator, eliminating pipeline stalls and achieving the system's performance upper bound.

In contrast, research on hardware acceleration in the tracking stage has primarily focused on optimizing individual algorithmic components. Babu et al. [4] implemented an Multi-dimensional Kalman Filter (MDKF) on an FPGA, expressing the filter equations in matrix form to accelerate computation and deploying the design on a Zynq board. Their implementation achieves higher tracking speed compared with a software approach. Ribas-Xirgo [12] mapped the Hungarian algorithm to an extended Finite State Machine (FSM) model and reduced execution cycles using a multi-memory architecture. Although this work demonstrates the feasibility of hardware implementation of the Hungarian algorithm, it targets general task allocation problems and does not extend to the full tracking pipeline. Shen et al. [13] proposed NeuroSORT, which replaces the iterative optimization process of the traditional Hungarian algorithm with a neural network-based learning approach. They jointly implemented a Kalman filter and a Spiking Neural Network (SNN) inference engine in hardware, achieving a highly power-efficient complete MOT system. However, the learning-based linear assignment strategy sacrifices a degree of algorithmic determinism, and its Application-Specific Integrated Circuit (ASIC)-oriented architecture is not easily transferable to FPGA platforms.

FPGA acceleration has been widely studied for perception, including detection and post-processing. In contrast, tracking-stage acceleration remains fragmented, with most works addressing only isolated modules rather than the complete workflow. As a result, a fully integrated SORT pipeline on FPGA, together with a systematic analysis of its timing stability and real-time capability under varying object scales, remains underexplored.

3   Algorithm-Hardware Compatibility Analysis

SORT was proposed by Bewley et al. [5] in 2016 and is widely used due to its simple structure, competitive accuracy, and real-time performance. As shown in Fig. 2, the algorithm operates in a recursive manner across consecutive frames. At each time step t, the states of existing tracks from $Frame_{t-1}$ are propagated via the Kalman filter prediction step, yielding predicted bounding boxes ($Prediction_t$). Once the detections at time t become available, data association is performed to obtain the optimal matching between predicted tracks and current detections. Specifically, an IoU-based cost matrix is constructed, and the Hungarian algorithm is applied to compute the optimal assignment. After the matching process concludes, associated tracks are updated using the Kalman filter update step. Unmatched detections are used to initialize new tracks, while unmatched tracks are either retained or removed according to a predefined management strategy.

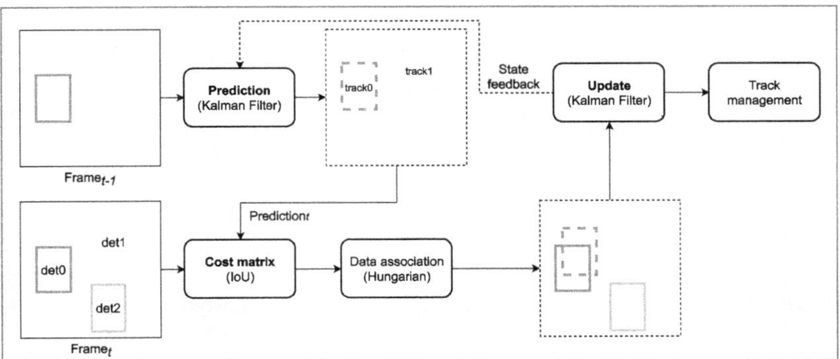

Fig. 2. Overview of the SORT algorithm. Colored dashed boxes represent predicted bounding boxes, and colored solid boxes indicate current detections. The state feedback arrow indicates that updated track states are carried forward to the next frame.

The above procedure is executed iteratively on consecutive video frames, thereby achieving continuous online tracking. This section further analyzes the computational patterns, parallelism, control complexity, and data storage requirements of each module from a hardware implementation perspective, considering the operational mechanisms of the core components. The analysis aims to evaluate their structural compatibility with FPGA and to provide a foundation for the subsequent hardware design.

3.1 Kalman Filter-Based State Estimation

Based on the defined state model, the Kalman filter performs state estimation recursively in two stages: prediction and update.

State model characterizes the motion and geometric properties of an object at a given moment, and is the core representation form throughout the prediction and update process. In this model, each tracked object is described by a state vector $\mathbf{x}_k$ at time step k, which encompasses the bounding box parameters and their corresponding velocity components. For 2D bounding box tracking, the state is modeled as an 8-dimensional vector as shown in Eq. (1):

$$\mathbf{x}_k = \left[u, v, s, r, \dot{u}, \dot{v}, \dot{s}, \dot{r}\right]^T \tag{1}$$

where: u and v represent the horizontal and vertical pixel coordinates of the bounding box center; s denotes the scale (area) of the bounding box; r represents the aspect ratio, typically assumed constant $(\dot{r} = 0)$; $\dot{u}, \dot{v}, \dot{s}, \dot{r}$ are their corresponding velocities.

Prediction stage propagates the state of the previous frame to the current frame, as shown in Eq. (2) and Eq. (3), the state estimate $\hat{\mathbf{x}}_{k-1|k-1}$ and the error covariance matrix $\mathbf{P}_{k-1|k-1}$ from the previous time step are propagated to the current time step k through state transitions. The state transition matrix $\mathbf{F}$ is constructed under the assumption of a constant velocity model. The process noise covariance matrix $\mathbf{Q}$ is introduced to characterize the uncertainty of the motion model [x].

$$\hat{\mathbf{x}}_{k|k-1} = \mathbf{F}\hat{\mathbf{x}}_{k-1|k-1} \tag{2}$$

$$\mathbf{P}_{k|k-1} = \mathbf{F}\mathbf{P}_{k-1|k-1}\mathbf{F}^T + \mathbf{Q} \tag{3}$$

Update stage corrects the predicted state estimate using the optimal Kalman Gain $\mathbf{K}_k$, when receiving new observation information from detection. $\mathbf{H}$ is the measurement matrix, used to establish a linear mapping between the state space and the measurement space, and $\mathbf{R}$ is the measurement noise covariance matrix, used to characterize the detection error. As shown in Eq. (4), its value is jointly determined by the prediction error covariance matrix $\mathbf{P}_{k|k-1}$ and the noise covariance, reflecting the relative trade-off between prediction and observation uncertainty.

$$\mathbf{K}_k = \mathbf{P}_{k|k-1}\mathbf{H}^T(\mathbf{H}\mathbf{P}_{k|k-1}\mathbf{H}^T + \mathbf{R})^{-1} \tag{4}$$

The state estimate $\hat{\mathbf{x}}_{k|k}$, and its corresponding error covariance $\mathbf{P}_{k|k}$ are updated as following Eq. (5) and Eq. (6) shows. $\mathbf{z}_k$ corresponds to the observable components of the state vector $\mathbf{x}_k$ in Eq. (1).

$$\hat{\mathbf{x}}_{k|k} = \hat{\mathbf{x}}_{k|k-1} + \mathbf{K}_k(\mathbf{z}_k - \mathbf{H}\hat{\mathbf{x}}_{k|k-1}) \tag{5}$$

$$\mathbf{P}_{k|k} = (\mathbf{I} - \mathbf{K}_k\mathbf{H})\mathbf{P}_{k|k-1} \tag{6}$$

Through its prediction-update mechanism, the Kalman filter can continuously estimate the object state and provide predicted bounding boxes for subsequent data association.

Compatibility. The Kalman filter module in SORT exhibits strong hardware affinity due to its fixed-dimensional linear algebra structure. Both prediction and update stages consist primarily of small-scale matrix multiplications and additions, with no dynamic data structures or irregular control flow. The state and covariance matrices have constant dimensions, enabling static resource allocation. These characteristics make the Kalman filter particularly suitable for FPGA-based implementation.

3.2 Data Association

The data association stage matches predicted trajectories with current detections via IoU calculation, cost matrix construction, and Hungarian algorithm assignment.

IoU measures the spatial overlap between the predicted bounding box $\mathbf{b}_i$ and the current detection result $\mathbf{b}_j$, and serves as a similarity metric in the data association stage. IoU is converted into a cost form to construct a ***cost matrix*** c_{ij} as shown in Eq. (8), which is then used to solve for the optimal trajectory assignment.

$$\mathrm{IoU}(\mathbf{b}_i, \mathbf{b}_j) = \frac{\mathbf{b}_i \cap \mathbf{b}_j}{\mathbf{b}_i \cup \mathbf{b}_j} \tag{7}$$

$$c_{ij} = 1 - \mathrm{IoU}(\mathbf{b}_i, \mathbf{b}_j) \tag{8}$$

Hungarian algorithm addresses the assignment problem, which seeks an optimal matching in a cost matrix. The objective is to find a permutation of assignments $\mathcal{A}$ that minimizes the total cost such that each row (track) is assigned to exactly one column (detection), and vice versa:

$$\min_{\mathcal{A}} \sum_{(i,j)\in\mathcal{A}} c_{ij} \tag{9}$$

Compatibility. The IoU cost matrix computation involves simple element-wise arithmetic with no data dependencies between elements, making it well-suited for parallel hardware implementation.

In contrast to the Kalman filter and cost matrix computation, which exhibit regular dataflow patterns, the classical Hungarian algorithm relies on iterative reductions and augmenting path searches over the full matrix. Its iterative row and column reductions, zero-covering, and augmenting path searches result in $\mathcal{O}(n^3)$ complexity with irregular memory access patterns and heavy control dependencies. To address this, the JV algorithm [10] is adopted in this work, which reformulates the assignment problem using shortest augmenting paths and achieves better practical performance. In typical SORT deployments the number of tracked objects remains moderate, keeping the matrix dimension small.

3.3 Datasize and Memory

The memory footprint of SORT is modest due to its low-dimensional state representation and limited number of objects. Given a conservative assumption of 64 concurrent objects and 32-bit precision, the total storage requirement for state vectors, covariance matrices, detection boxes, and the IoU cost matrix remains on the order of tens of kilobytes. Such a data scale can be entirely accommodated within on-chip Block RAM (BRAM) resource, eliminating the need for frequent off-chip memory access and enabling low-latency dataflow-oriented architectures.

4 System Architecture and Implementation

This section presents the architecture and implementation of the proposed SORT hardware accelerator. Each subsection addresses one processing stage, from a top-level overview through the implementation of each pipeline component.

4.1 Architecture Overview

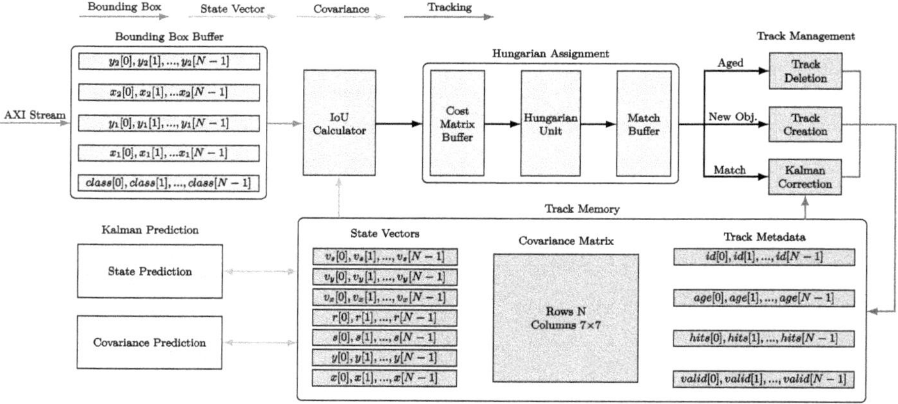

Fig. 3. Overall architecture of the proposed SORT hardware unit. The system comprises three main components: bounding box buffer for detection input, track memory for storing Kalman filter states, and SORT computation pipeline for performing prediction, data association, and track management.

Figure 3 illustrates the overall architecture of the proposed SORT hardware design. The system consists of three main components: a bounding box buffer that receives detection results from an external object detector, a track memory module that stores Kalman filter parameters for all active tracks including state vectors and covariance matrices, and a SORT computation pipeline that performs the core tracking operations.

The system receives detection bounding boxes through a 128-bit Advanced eXtensible Interface (AXI)-Stream interface. Each bounding box is encoded using the coordinates of its two diagonal vertices along with a class Identity (ID), where the vertex coordinates are represented as 16-bit unsigned integers and the class ID as an 8-bit unsigned integer, occupying 72 bits of the available 128-bit data width. The remaining 56 bits are reserved for future use.

The tracking process follows a fixed pipeline executed once per frame, as illustrated in Fig. 3. Upon receiving all detections for the current frame, the system sequentially invokes four processing stages: Kalman prediction estimates the current-frame states of all existing tracks; IoU computation constructs a cost matrix by calculating the overlap between each detection and each predicted track; Hungarian assignment solves the optimal detection-to-track matching problem; and track management updates matched tracks, removes stale tracks, and initializes new ones. After all updates are committed to track memory, the system waits for the next frame's detections. The following sections describe each stage in detail.

4.2 Kalman Prediction

The Kalman prediction unit implements the prediction step of the Kalman filter, projecting the state of each active track from the previous frame to the current frame. The unit is composed of an HLS computation core, a controller, and data buffers for interfacing with track memory.

The prediction is based on a constant velocity motion model. Each track state is represented as a 7-element vector $[x, y, s, r, v_x, v_y, v_s]$, where (x, y) denotes the bounding box center, s the scale, r the aspect ratio, and v_x, v_y, v_s their respective velocities. The state prediction applies the transition $x' = x + v_x$, $y' = y + v_y$, $s' = s + v_s$, with r and all velocity components remaining unchanged. The covariance matrix is updated according to $P' = F \cdot P \cdot F^T + Q$, where F is the state transition matrix and Q is the process noise covariance. Both F and Q are constant matrices stored in the HLS core's internal buffers.

The HLS core implements these two operations in parallel. The state prediction is fully unrolled for single-cycle execution, while the covariance update is implemented as a pipelined matrix operation to balance resource usage and latency.

The controller manages the prediction workflow through a multi-state FSM. For each active track, it reads the state vector and covariance matrix from track memory, configures the HLS core via AXI-Lite interface and triggers execution, polls for completion, and writes the predicted state and error covariance matrix back to track memory. This process repeats until all active tracks have been processed, after which control is passed to the IoU computation unit.

4.3 IoU Computation

The IoU computation unit constructs the association cost matrix by calculating pairwise IoU values between all predicted tracks and incoming detections. The unit interfaces with the bounding box buffer through a random-access read port and with the Kalman prediction unit via a request–grant handshake to obtain predicted track states. Computed costs are written to an on-chip BRAM that stores the complete $N_{det} \times N_{trk}$ cost matrix prior to Hungarian assignment.

IoU computation is implemented as a four-stage pipeline. The first stage computes the intersection rectangle via coordinate max/min operations. The second stage calculates the intersection area, detection area, and track area using integer multipliers. The third stage performs the IoU division using an integer divider IP, with internal sub-stages handling operand preparation, divider handshaking, and result latching. Scaled integer arithmetic is employed, computing the IoU as $iou_{q8} = (inter\_area << 8)/union\_area$, which produces an 8-bit representation in Q8 format with a range of 0–255. The multi-cycle latency introduced by the integer divider is fully absorbed by surrounding pipeline registers and the control FSM, ensuring that throughput is unaffected once the pipeline is filled. The fourth stage converts the IoU value to an association cost as $cost = 255 - iou_{q8}$, where a cost of 0 represents a perfect match and a cost of 255 represents no overlap. This formulation naturally suppresses weak associations without requiring an explicit threshold.

A control FSM coordinates the nested iteration over detection and track indices. For each detection, the FSM retrieves the detection bounding box, issues a track state request, waits for the predictor response, and feeds the detection–track pair into the pipeline. After an initial fill latency of approximately 7–8 cycles, the unit produces one cost entry per clock cycle, ensuring the complete cost matrix is available before the Hungarian assignment stage begins.

4.4 Hungarian Assignment

The Hungarian assignment unit solves the optimal detection-to-track matching problem by minimizing the total association cost. The HLS core receives the cost matrix via a BRAM interface and the matrix dimensions via AXI-Lite, and supports matrices up to HUNGARIAN_MAX_SIZE × HUNGARIAN_MAX_SIZE, where HUNGARIAN_MAX_SIZE is set to 32, accommodating up to 32 simultaneous detections and active tracks per frame. Upon completion, matched detection-track index pairs are written to an output BRAM and the match count is returned via AXI-Lite.

The assignment problem is solved using the JV algorithm, which operates on dual variables to maintain optimality throughout the augmentation process. The implementation consists of three phases: row reduction to establish initial dual feasibility, greedy zero matching to construct an initial assignment, and Dijkstra-based shortest augmenting path search to resolve unmatched rows. To improve memory throughput, the cost matrix, dual variable array, and assignment arrays are partitioned with a cyclic factor of 4, enabling parallel column access per cycle. Inner loops of the augmenting path search are pipelined with $II = 1$, and the path traceback loop is pipelined with $II = 2$. The resulting match pairs are forwarded to the track management unit to initiate track updates.

4.5   Track Management

The track management unit handles three types of track operations based on the Hungarian assignment results: updating matched tracks with Kalman correction, incrementing age for unmatched tracks and deleting stale ones, and initializing new tracks from unmatched detections.

The Kalman correction module receives matched detection-track pairs from the Hungarian unit. For each match, it reads the detection bounding box, converts it to measurement space $[x, y, s, r]$, and invokes Kalman unit in correction mode. The Kalman unit performs the correction step by reading the track's predicted state and covariance, computing the Kalman gain and innovation, updating the state and covariance, and writing the corrected values back to track memory. The track's hit counter is incremented and age is reset to zero, indicating successful observation.

The track deletion module precesses tracks that were not matched with any detection. It reads each unmatched track's metadata from track memory and increments its age counter, representing the number of consecutive frames without observation. Tracks with age exceeding a threshold are marked for deletion by issuing delete commands to track memory, which compacts the track memory and updates the active track count.

The track creation module handles unmatched detections by initializing new tracks. For each unmatched detection, it reads the bounding box, converts it to state space $[x, y, s, r, 0, 0, 0]$ with zero velocities, initializing the covariance matrix with diagonal values, assigns a unique track ID from a global counter, and writes the new track to the next available slot in track memory with age $= 0$, and hits $= 1$. This allows new objects entering the scene to be tracked in subsequent frames.

5   Evaluation

The hardware design is implemented and synthesized in Vivado 2022.2, targeting a clock frequency of 100 MHz. Post-implementation timing analysis confirms timing closure at up to 166 MHz, indicating sufficient timing margin at the selected operating frequency. In this implementation, the Hungarian algorithm and Kalman filter modules are synthesized using Vitis HLS 2022.2, while the remaining logic is implemented using custom Verilog and Xilinx Intellectual Property (IP) cores. The software baseline is executed on an Xilinx ZCU104 board equipped with a 1.2 GHz quad-core ARM Cortex-A53 processor. It implements the open-source SORT tracking algorithm[1], with performance-critical modules such as the Hungarian algorithm optimized in C/C++, and the entire program is executed in the embedded Linux environment (Ubuntu 22.04). Latency is measured consistently across both platforms. For hardware, latency is obtained from cycle-accurate functional simulation. The measured cycle counts are converted to time units based on the verified 100 MHz target frequency.

---

[1] https://github.com/abewley/sort.

Software latency is recorded using a Python-based timing interface. All experiments use identical input data and operating scenarios to ensure fairness and reproducibility. Each configuration is evaluated over multiple independent runs to capture runtime variability: the full SORT pipeline is repeated 30 times due to longer simulation duration, whereas the Hungarian algorithm module is evaluated over 50 runs.

5.1 End-to-End Latency (Complete SORT)

End-to-end evaluation measures the latency of the complete SORT hardware pipeline under two representative tracking scenarios. The matched scenario models successful associations between consecutive frames, following the standard predict–associate–update sequence. The unmatched scenario introduces spatial displacement beyond the matching threshold, resulting in new track initialization. Together, these cases cover the primary execution paths of SORT.

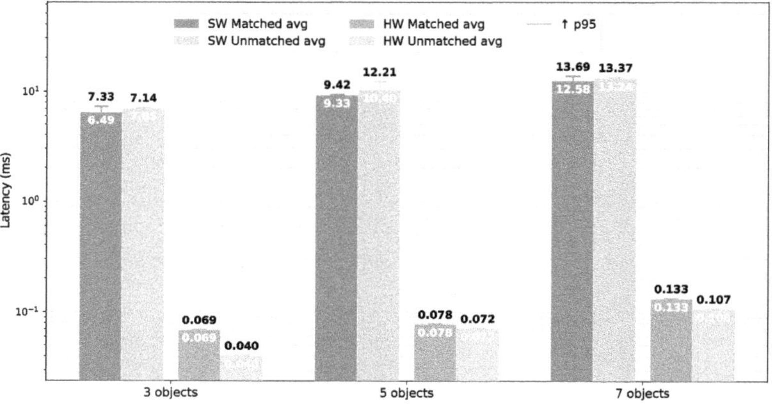

Fig. 4. Average matching latency (*ms*) of software (SW) and hardware (HW) implementations under matched and unmatched conditions for different object counts (3, 5, and 7), with p95 error bars.

Experiments are conducted with up to eight concurrent targets per frame, specifically evaluating object counts of 3, 5, and 7 objects. Detection inputs are synthetically generated with fixed spatial patterns to ensure reproducibility. Latency is defined as the total cycle count required to process two consecutive frames. The mean and 95th percentile (*p*95) latencies are reported to characterize average performance and tail latency behavior.

As shown in Fig. 4, hardware implementation is approximately 100× faster than the software baseline across all conditions. This difference reflects the efficiency of dedicated hardware execution compared to a general-purpose processor. Interestingly, the two implementations show opposite trends between matched and unmatched scenarios. In software, unmatched cases are consistently slower, as the search must evaluate all candidates before failure is determined. In hardware, successful matches incur additional cost due to the full Kalman filter update, while unmatched cases bypass these computations and therefore complete more quickly. Software latency exhibits noticeable variability, as reflected in the $p95$ error bars, due to execution on a general-purpose processor subject to OS scheduling and memory access effects, among other factors. In contrast, hardware latency remains tightly bounded and nearly jitter-free, as its fixed execution path provides deterministic timing largely independent of object count and match outcome.

5.2 Hungarian Data Association Module Evaluation

To evaluate scalability and latency variability, the Hungarian module is tested independently across increasing object densities and representative association patterns. The number of targets N is varied from 4 to 32 in increments of 4 using square cost matrices. Mean, minimum, and maximum latencies are reported to characterize performance scaling and latency bounds. Three association scenarios are considered. The normal tracking case produces a diagonally dominant cost matrix representing ideal one-to-one matches. The drift scenario shifts each row's optimal assignment within ± 2 positions, forming a banded structure that models bounded prediction error. The crowding scenario introduces near-tie costs among adjacent entries, generating ambiguous local minima while preserving the diagonal as the global optimum. Cost matrices are constructed according to predefined structural rules. Controlled random perturbations are applied across repeated trials to simulate realistic IoU noise while maintaining each scenario's structural characteristics and optimal assignment.

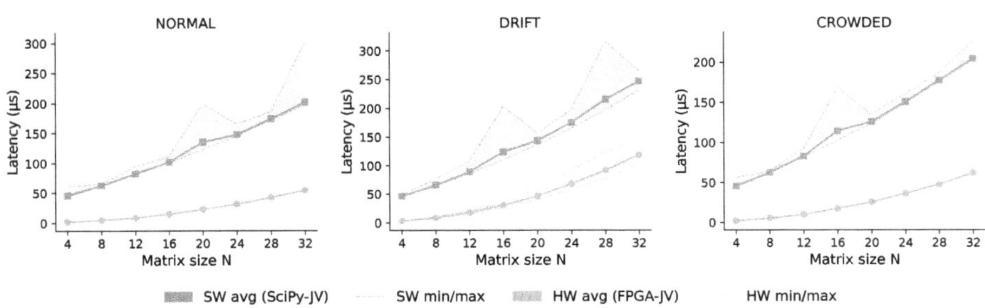

Fig. 5. Average latency (µs) of SW (SciPy JV, optimized compiled) and HW (FPGA JV) implementations of the JV assignment algorithm across matrix sizes N, evaluated under three scenarios: Normal, Drift, and Crowded. Shaded regions indicate min/max bounds.

As Fig. 5 shows, across all three scenarios, hardware consistently outperforms software by a significant margin, with hardware latency remaining below 120 µs even at N is equal to 32, while software latency reaches up to 250 μs at the same size. Both implementations scale with matrix size, but the software grows slightly faster. Software variance is large and irregular across all scenarios, with occasional spikes in the min/max bounds that lack a clear pattern tied to scenario type or matrix size. Hardware variance, by contrast, remains negligible throughout, except for a slight spread observed under the Drift scenario, suggesting that certain cost matrix structures may occasionally trigger longer internal iteration paths within the FPGA implementation.

5.3 Resource Utilization

Table 1 summarizes the post-implementation resource utilization of the proposed hardware design. The Kalman filter dominates resource utilization, accounting for the majority of LUT and DSP consumption due to its computation-intensive floating-point prediction and update operations. In contrast, the Hungarian algorithm and the cost matrix builder impose relatively modest hardware overheads, as they primarily handle optimal assignment and cost calculations, respectively. The remaining resource usage is attributed to memory requirements shared by different modules and other control logic.

Table 1. Post-implementation resource utilization

Module	LUT	FF	BRAM	DSP
Kalman Filter	31187	25636	12	67
Hungarian Algorithm	1508	1067	2	1
Cost Matrix Builder	528	931	0	8
Other Logic	8960	18131	4.5	2
Total	**42198**	**45798**	**18.5**	**78**

6 Conclusion

This work presents a complete FPGA implementation of the SORT algorithm. Based on an analysis of its computational characteristics, the key components, including Kalman filtering, IoU based cost matrix construction, and Hungarian data association, are redesigned into a pipelined hardware architecture with explicit timing control. The proposed design achieves lower and more predictable end-to-end latency than the software baseline operating at a significantly higher clock frequency. Multiple scenario evaluations further confirm the latency stability of the Hungarian module under increasing object scales and structured perturbations. Overall, the implementation maintains stable execution behavior while integrating the complete SORT workflow within a unified hardware architecture. Future work will focus on optimizing data association and state estimation to further reduce resource usage and improve scalability.

Acknowledgments. This work gratefully acknowledges funding from the China Scholarship Council program (Project ID: 202208510013); Further, the authors acknowledge the financial support by the Federal Ministry of Education and Research of Germany and by Sächsische Staatsministerium für Wissenschaft, Kultur und Tourismus in the programme Center of Excellence for AI-research "Center for Scalable Data Analytics and Artificial Intelligence Dresden/Leipzig", project identification number: ScaDS.AI.

References

1. Aharon, N., Orfaig, R., Bobrovsky, B.Z.: Bot-sort: robust associations multi-pedestrian tracking. arXiv preprint arXiv:2206.14651 (2022)
2. Al Amin, R., Hasan, M., Wiese, V., Obermaisser, R.: FPGA-based real-time object detection and classification system using yolo for edge computing. IEEE Access **12**, 73268–73278 (2024)
3. Anupreetham, A., et al.: High throughput FPGA-based object detection via algorithm-hardware co-design. ACM Trans. Reconfig. Technol. Syst. **17**(1), 1–20 (2024)
4. Babu, P., Parthasarathy, E.: FPGA implementation of multi-dimensional Kalman filter for object tracking and motion detection. Eng. Sci. Technol. Int. J. **33**, 101084 (2022)
5. Bewley, A., Ge, Z., Ott, L., Ramos, F., Upcroft, B.: Simple online and realtime tracking. In: 2016 IEEE International Conference on Image Processing (ICIP), pp. 3464–3468. IEEE (2016)
6. Cai, L., Dong, F., Chen, K., Yu, K., Qu, W., Jiang, J.: An FPGA based heterogeneous accelerator for single shot multibox detector (SSD). In: 2020 IEEE 15th International Conference on Solid-State & Integrated Circuit Technology (ICSICT), pp. 1–3. IEEE (2020)
7. Danilowicz, M., Kryjak, T.: Real-time multi-object tracking using yolov8 and sort on a soc FPGA. In: International Symposium on Applied Reconfigurable Computing, pp. 214–230. Springer (2025)
8. Du, Y., et al.: Strongsort: make deepsort great again. IEEE Trans. Multimedia **25**, 8725–8737 (2023)
9. Guo, Z., Liu, K., Liu, W., Li, S.: Efficient FPGA-based accelerator for post-processing in object detection. In: 2023 International Conference on Field Programmable Technology (ICFPT), pp. 125–131. IEEE (2023)
10. Jonker, R., Volgenant, A.: A shortest augmenting path algorithm for dense and sparse linear assignment problems. Computing **38**(4), 325–340 (1987)
11. Luo, W., Xing, J., Milan, A., Zhang, X., Liu, W., Kim, T.K.: Multiple object tracking: a literature review. Artif. Intell. **293**, 103448 (2021)
12. Ribas-Xirgo, L.: Hardware implementation of the Hungarian algorithm for optimum task assignments. In: 2025 40th Conference on Design of Circuits and Integrated Systems (DCIS), pp. 205–210. IEEE (2025)
13. Shen, Z., et al.: Neurosort: a neuromorphic accelerator for spike-based online and real-time tracking. In: 2024 IEEE 6th International Conference on AI Circuits and Systems (AICAS), pp. 312–316. IEEE (2024)
14. Sun, Z., Chen, J., Chao, L., Ruan, W., Mukherjee, M.: A survey of multiple pedestrian tracking based on tracking-by-detection framework. IEEE Trans. Circuits Syst. Video Technol. **31**(5), 1819–1833 (2020)

15. Umuroglu, Y., Fraser, N.J.: Finn: a framework for fast, scalable binarized neural network inference. In: Proceedings of the 2017 ACM/SIGDA International Symposium on Field-Programmable Gate Arrays, pp. 65–74 (2017)
16. Wojke, N., Bewley, A., Paulus, D.: Simple online and realtime tracking with a deep association metric. In: 2017 IEEE International Conference on Image Processing (ICIP), pp. 3645–3649. IEEE (2017)
17. Zhai, J., Li, B., Lv, S., Zhou, Q.: FPGA-based vehicle detection and tracking accelerator. Sensors **23**(4), 2208 (2023)
18. Zhang, Y., et al.: Bytetrack: multi-object tracking by associating every detection box. In: European Conference on Computer Vision, pp. 1–21. Springer (2022)

FPGA-Based Hardware Architecture for Contrast Maximization in Event-Based Vision

Michał Filipkowski[(✉)], Marcin Kowalczyk, and Tomasz Kryjak

AGH University of Krakow, Krakow, Poland
mfilipkowski@student.agh.edu.pl, {kowalczyk,kryjak}@agh.edu.pl

Abstract. This paper presents a hardware architecture that implements the Contrast Maximization (CM) algorithm on Field-Programmable Gate Array (FPGA) resources for event-based vision systems. CM estimates motion parameters by maximizing the contrast of an Image of Warped Events (IWE) reconstructed from asynchronous event streams. Event-based vision sensors generate sparse, high-temporal-resolution data with low spatial redundancy, making them well-suited for hardware processing. The deterministic and massively parallel nature of FPGA devices is leveraged to design a deeply pipelined architecture that delivers high-throughput, energy-efficient processing suitable for real-time embedded applications. This paper describes the hardware modules responsible for event warping, contrast computation, and iterative optimization, discusses key implementation decisions, and presents the hardware-aware optimization method used in the design. Experimental results demonstrate substantial speed and efficiency improvements over CPU-based implementations. The acceleration factor depends on the number of input events and the region of interest (ROI) resolution, ranging from $1.6\times$ to $20\times$ across the evaluated settings. To the best of our knowledge, at the time of writing, this is the first hardware architecture that accelerates the CM algorithm in FPGA hardware. Performance is evaluated in terms of processing speed, energy efficiency, and hardware resource utilization. The proposed design is validated using an event-based object tracking example application. The results confirm that the proposed architecture provides a solid foundation for real-time motion estimation in high-speed, low-power embedded systems.

Keywords: FPGA · Contrast Maximization · Event-based camera · Object tracking · Neuromorphic vision

1 Introduction

The rapid development of sensing technologies has made event-based cameras, also known as dynamic vision sensors (DVS), an increasingly prominent topic in computer vision and robotics. Event cameras are bio-inspired sensors that

G. Leone et al. (Eds.): ARC 2026, LNCS 16514, pp. 309–325, 2026.
https://doi.org/10.1007/978-3-032-29365-7_19

offer several advantages over conventional frame-based cameras, including independent (asynchronous) pixel operation, high temporal resolution, high dynamic range, reduced motion blur, and microsecond-scale latency [2,5]. Instead of capturing full images at fixed intervals, they report per-pixel brightness changes as a sparse stream of events. This sparse output makes event cameras well suited for real-time, high-speed applications such as advanced driver assistance systems, autonomous vehicles, and drone navigation [2,11].

However, processing data from event cameras typically requires specialized algorithms that can handle high temporal resolution and irregular input patterns, or it requires converting the data to a dense representation. One technique for processing such data is the Contrast Maximization (CM) algorithm, which estimates motion parameters. This method can serve as a foundation for tasks such as visual odometry, optical flow, and depth estimation in event-based vision [4,6]. However, CM relies on iterative optimization to maximize an objective function that measures the sharpness of a warped event frame. As a result, it is computationally demanding, leading to high power consumption and making real-time operation challenging even on desktop-grade hardware. For this reason, we designed a dedicated hardware architecture implemented using Field-Programmable Gate Array (FPGA) resources.

The high performance of FPGAs stems from their flexibility and fine-grained parallelism, which enables the design of a highly optimized circuit for a given application [1]. As a result, complex operations, such as event warping and the computation of the Image of Warped Events (IWE) and its gradients, can be executed concurrently, with the architecture tailored to maximize throughput for the target algorithm. For complete vision pipelines, FPGAs often outperform Graphics Processing Units (GPUs) and Central Processing Units (CPUs), and their advantage increases as pipeline complexity grows [15]. However, developing FPGA applications also comes with constraints. First, the design process typically requires more effort than implementing the same algorithm on a CPU or GPU. Second, on-chip memory resources in FPGAs are limited, which prevents storing large amounts of data and necessitates careful architectural design.

In this work, we use an object-tracking application to assess the CM algorithm under practical conditions. The model estimates the target translation by fitting motion parameters, which are then used to update the region of interest (ROI). In particular, the application estimates the horizontal and vertical velocity components of the tracked object, enabling accurate motion estimation from event-based data.

The main contribution of this paper is the design of an FPGA architecture that accelerates the Contrast Maximization algorithm. The design includes event preprocessing, event warping, gradient computation, an optimization loop for estimating motion parameters, and ROI updates based on the CM output. We compare the obtained results against CPU implementations of the same CM algorithm. Experiments conducted on a variety of parameters revealed that the proposed architecture processes data 1.6 to 20 times faster while consuming less than 1 W of on-chip power.

The remainder of this paper is organized as follows. Section 2 reviews related work. Section 3 presents the CM methodology and its mathematical model. Section 4 describes the proposed FPGA architecture. Section 5 reports the experimental results. Finally, Sect. 6 concludes the paper and discusses directions for future research.

2   Related Work

The CM algorithm is a popular approach for event-data processing. It enables the estimation of motion, depth, and optical flow by warping events and maximizing the IWE variance [4]. CM has also been applied to event-based visual odometry for real-time camera-trajectory estimation, for example in methods based on IWE and geometric optimization with contrast maximization in the volumetric ray field [21]. A review of commonly used cost functions for CM-based methods is provided in [18]. In addition, several extensions of the classical CM framework have been proposed to improve performance, including multi-scale warping to enhance convergence and avoid local minima, as well as geometric regularizers to prevent event collapse [16,17]. Most work to date relies on CPU implementations of CM, which typically do not operate fully in real time [10,14]. This limitation stems directly from the high computational complexity of event warping and the heavily iterative nature of the algorithm.

However, real-time CPU implementations have also been reported. Using globally aligned event data can reduce drift and improve IWE contrast over longer time windows [8]. Despite the relatively high computational complexity, stable performance can be maintained with well-organized event buffers and optimized strategies for combining them.

The literature also reports GPU-accelerated CM implementations using the Compute Unified Device Architecture (CUDA). Integrating CM with sequential learning methods and optical-flow estimation techniques is also becoming increasingly common. Running these algorithms on GPUs enables very high inference speeds and near real-time operation [7,13].

Prior work has also explored hardware acceleration for event-based vision processing. A hardware architecture implemented in an SoC FPGA system that enables real-time optical flow estimation is presented in [19]. Furthermore, in [22] the authors propose a bio-inspired, FPGA-based architecture that employs an attention-guided mechanism to filter salient regions in event data. A comprehensive overview of hardware solutions for event vision is provided in [9], which surveys research combining SoC FPGA platforms with neuromorphic sensors across applications such as event filtering, optical flow estimation, stereo vision, object detection, recognition and tracking, and AI-based methods.

Although the above works demonstrate effective hardware acceleration for event-data processing, at the time of writing and initial submission of this manuscript, our review of the scientific literature found no examples of architectures implementing the CM algorithm on an FPGA platform. In particular, the survey of hardware implementations for event vision in [9] does not report any

FPGA-based implementation of contrast maximization. During the review process of this paper, a concurrent work [20] was published, introducing an FPGA implementation of CM that supports rotational motion model. Nevertheless, our results confirm the feasibility of accelerating event processing with the CM algorithm, demonstrating that the translational approach presented in this paper achieves this goal efficiently in practice. It should be emphasized that using the proposed architecture for object tracking serves only as a test case. The main focus is the FPGA implementation of the contrast maximization algorithm itself and demonstrating the benefits of its acceleration, particularly in terms of computational efficiency and hardware performance.

3   Methodology

This section presents the methodology used in the CM algorithm.

3.1   Events Representation and Warping

Event cameras consist of independent pixels that operate continuously and generate events when a change in brightness is detected. Each event $e_k = (t_k, x_k, y_k, p_k)$ includes the event timestamp, pixel coordinates (x_k, y_k), and the polarity of the change $p_k \in \{-1, 1\}$. In most datasets, the polarity is encoded as $p_k = 0$ for brightness decreases and $p_k = 1$ for increases. The event rate is scene dependent and varies with the observed dynamics. In the CM algorithm, events are processed in successive batches and warped to a selected reference time using a motion model so that edges and textures in the observed scene become maximally aligned. Several strategies for choosing the reference time exist. In our experiments we use the midpoint of the batch, defined in (1).

$$t_{\text{ref}} = t_1 + \left(\frac{t_{N_e} - t_1}{2} \right) \tag{1}$$

where t_1 and t_{N_e} are the minimum and maximum timestamps in the event batch, respectively, and N_e denotes the number of events in the batch.

Each event in the batch is then warped to the reference time according to the adopted motion model and its parameters. The event coordinates are propagated forward or backward in time based on the model-predicted displacement. In this study, we use a two-dimensional motion model with constant translational velocities along the x and y axes. For each event, we compute the time difference between the reference time (t_{ref}) and the event timestamp (t_k), as defined in (2).

$$dt = t_k - t_{ref} \tag{2}$$

The warped event position is then computed according to (3) and (4) using the time difference and the motion parameters (v_x, v_y).

$$e_k = (t_k, x_k, y_k, p_k) \rightarrow e_k' = (dt_k, x_k', y_k', p_k) \tag{3}$$

$$x'_k = x_k - dt_k \cdot v_x \qquad y'_k = y_k - dt_k \cdot v_y \tag{4}$$

This warping step compensates for edge motion in the scene, so that events originating from the same physical edge converge to consistent spatial locations at time t_{ref}. The quality of the result depends directly on the accuracy of the assumed motion model.

3.2 Image of Warped Events

Once all events have been transformed to the reference time, the next step is to construct the Image of Warped Events (IWE). This is done by accumulating the warped events on a two-dimensional pixel grid, resulting in an image that represents event density after motion compensation.

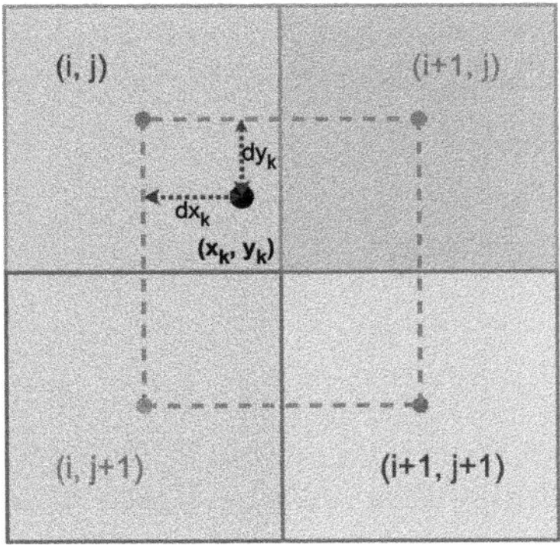

Fig. 1. Visualization of bilinear voting operation.

After warping, event locations often fall between discrete pixel coordinates. Assigning each event to the nearest pixel can introduce significant quantization artifacts in the reconstructed IWE. To mitigate this, we use bilinear voting, in which the four neighboring pixels receive contributions proportional to their distances from the warped event. In practice, we extract the fractional parts of the warped coordinates (x'_k, y'_k) and use them to compute the weights that distribute each event among the surrounding pixels, as in (5).

$$w_{k,i,j} = \begin{cases} (1 - dx_k) \cdot (1 - dy_k) & \text{for pixel } (i_k, j_k) \\ dx_k \cdot (1 - dy_k) & \text{for pixel } (i_k + 1, j_k) \\ (1 - dx_k) \cdot dy_k & \text{for pixel } (i_k, j_k + 1) \\ dx_k \cdot dy_k & \text{for pixel } (i_k + 1, j_k + 1) \end{cases} \tag{5}$$

where $w_{k,i,j}$ denotes the weights assigned to the neighboring pixels of the warped event e'_k, and dx_k and dy_k represent the fractional offsets from the integer pixel coordinate (i_k, j_k) along the x and y axes, respectively: $dx_k = x'_k - i_k$, $dy_k = y'_k - j_k$. This operation is visualized in Fig. 1.

Summing the coefficients $w_{k,i,j}$ over all events yields the Image of Warped Events (IWE), described by (6).

$$I_W(i,j) = \sum_{k=1}^{N_e} w_{k,i,j} \tag{6}$$

3.3 Objective Function

The resulting image serves as the basis for computing the contrast function, which acts as the objective in the optimization process. Contrast can be defined in several ways; these alternatives are discussed and compared in [3]. In this work, we use the variance of pixel intensities in the reconstructed image. Intuitively, when the motion parameters are closer to their true values, events corresponding to the same physical edge are better aligned, producing a sharper and more concentrated IWE and, consequently, a higher variance. The objective function is given by (7).

$$C = Var(I_w) = \frac{1}{N_p} \sum_{(i,j) \in \Omega} (I_w(i,j) - \mu)^2 \qquad \mu = \frac{1}{N_p} \sum_{(i,j) \in \Omega} I_w(i,j) \tag{7}$$

where N_p is the number of pixels and Ω is the set of all pixels; thus, $N_p = |\Omega|$.

Hence, the value of the contrast function reflects the accuracy of the current motion model: the higher the value, the better the parameters v_x and v_y compensate for the apparent edge motion in the scene. The optimization algorithm uses this value to update the motion parameters, iteratively seeking an optimal estimate.

3.4 Gradient Calculation

To maximize the contrast function efficiently, we employ a gradient-based optimization method, which uses derivatives of the objective function to determine the direction of steepest ascent. This requires computing the gradient of the contrast function with respect to the motion parameters, given by (8).

$$\nabla C = \left[\frac{\partial C}{\partial v_x}, \frac{\partial C}{\partial v_y}\right]^T \tag{8}$$

Changes in event positions affect the pixel values of the warped image and, consequently, the contrast function. The gradient can be derived using the chain rule; for the x-axis it is expressed by (9).

$$\frac{\partial C}{\partial v_x} = \frac{\partial C}{\partial I_w} \cdot \frac{\partial I_w}{\partial x'} \cdot \frac{\partial x'}{\partial v_x} \tag{9}$$

This yields (10).

$$\frac{\partial C}{\partial v_x} = \frac{2}{N_p} \sum_{(i,j)\in\Omega} (I_w(i,j;v_x) - \mu(v_x)) \left(\frac{\partial I_w(i,j;v_x)}{\partial v_x} - \frac{\partial \mu(v_x)}{\partial v_x} \right) \tag{10}$$

The derivative of the mean intensity can be expressed as (11).

$$\frac{\partial \mu(v_x)}{\partial v_x} = \frac{1}{N_p} \sum_{(i,j)\in\Omega} \frac{\partial I_w(i,j;v_x)}{\partial v_x} \tag{11}$$

This term is simply the average of $\partial I_w / \partial v_x$ over all pixels. Using (6), we compute the derivative of I_w with respect to velocity, obtaining (12).

$$\frac{\partial I_w(i,j)}{\partial v_x} = \sum_{k=1}^{N_e} \frac{\partial w_{k,i,j}}{\partial dx_k} \cdot \frac{\partial dx_k}{\partial x'_k} \cdot \frac{\partial x'_k}{\partial v_x} \tag{12}$$

From the previous expressions, the remaining terms can be obtained as (13) and (14).

$$\frac{\partial w_{k,i,j}}{\partial dx_k} = \begin{cases} -(1 - dy_k) & \text{pixel } (i,j) \\ (1 - dy_k) & \text{pixel } (i+1,j) \\ -dy_k & \text{pixel } (i,j+1) \\ dy_k & \text{pixel } (i+1,j+1) \end{cases} \tag{13}$$

$$\frac{\partial dx_k}{\partial x'_k} = 1 \qquad \frac{\partial x'_k}{\partial v_x} = -dt_k \tag{14}$$

Analogous expressions can be derived for the y-axis. Overall, computing the gradient requires three images: the IWE from (6) and two derivative images with respect to v_x and v_y obtained using (12). These images are formed by accumulating contributions from successive events. Finally, following (10), we subtract the corresponding means, multiply the terms, and sum over all pixels.

3.5   Optimization Loop

With the gradient of the objective function determined, the gradient ascent method was chosen to find the motion parameters that maximize the objective function. In each iteration of the optimization loop, a new estimate of the parameters v_x and v_y is computed according to (15).

$$\begin{bmatrix} v_x^{(n+1)} \\ v_y^{(n+1)} \end{bmatrix} = \begin{bmatrix} v_x^{(n)} \\ v_y^{(n)} \end{bmatrix} + \eta \cdot \nabla C^{(n)} \tag{15}$$

where η denotes the learning rate of the gradient ascent algorithm and n is the iteration index.

When the maximum number of iterations T is reached, the coordinates of the ROI (x_{roi}, y_{roi}) are updated based on the calculated motion parameters in the example object tracking application. This is shown in (16). Then, processing of the next batch of events begins.

$$\begin{bmatrix} x_{roi}^{(N_b+1)} \\ y_{roi}^{(N_b+1)} \end{bmatrix} = \begin{bmatrix} x_{roi}^{(N_b)} \\ y_{roi}^{(N_b)} \end{bmatrix} + \begin{bmatrix} v_x^{(T)} \\ v_y^{(T)} \end{bmatrix} \tag{16}$$

where N_b denotes the batch index.

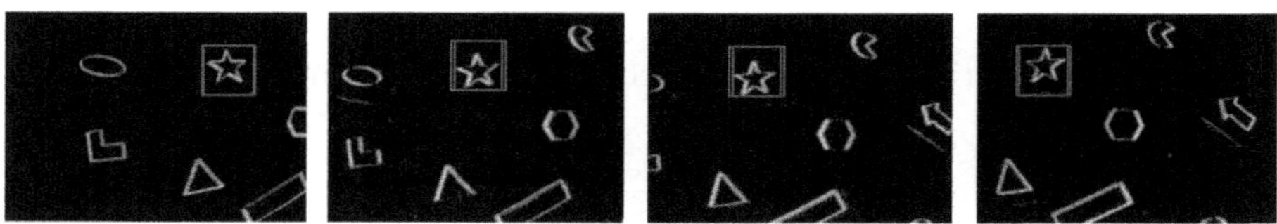

Fig. 2. Sequence of event frames from DAVIS 240C datasets [12] demonstrating the CM-based tracking and ROI update process.

Figure 2 visualizes the ROI update process between successive event batches. Accumulated events are shown as white dots, while the red frame indicates the current position of the ROI window.

4 FPGA Architecture Design

4.1 Filtering Events with ROI

We designed a hardware architecture implementing the CM algorithm at the Register Transfer Level (RTL) using Verilog HDL. Its block diagram is shown in Fig. 3. The first pipeline stage performs preprocessing of the input events. Processing of batch n starts once the previous batch has been finished. Filtering begins when the completion signal from the previous computation is asserted, which is also an input to the first module. Each event is represented as a 54-bit vector, where the timestamp t_k is encoded on 32 bits, indicating the time of the event's occurrence in microseconds, matching the native output of the event camera. During evaluation, the system was tested on datasets recorded with a DAVIS 240C camera [12], with a resolution of 240×180 pixels. Znaczniki czasowe wystąpienia zdarzeń rejestronwanych przez kamerę zdarzeniową są 32-bitowe jednostkach mikrosekund. To allow scalability to higher resolutions (e.g., 1280×720), the coordinate widths were set to 11 bits for x_k and 10 bits for y_k. The brightness-change polarity p_k is a 1-bit signal (datasets typically encode a decrease in brightness as $p_k = 0$). Each event is checked to determine whether it lies within the ROI. Events that satisfy this condition are stored in BRAM configured as single-port RAM. Since each stored entry is 54 bits wide, it contains the full event information. The BRAM depth is sized for the selected batch size,

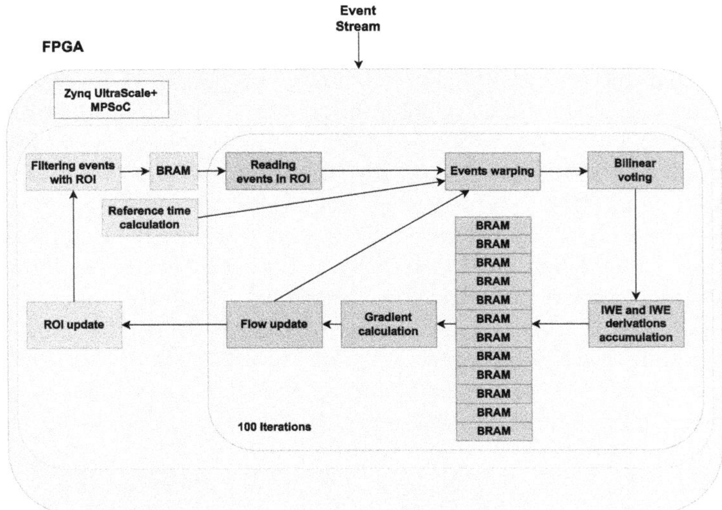

Fig. 3. Hardware architecture diagram of an application for object tracking using CM.

corresponding to the worst case where all input events fall within the ROI. The write address increments for each accepted event, and the number of stored events is counted for subsequent gradient computation. In parallel with event selection, the reference time is computed according to (1), and the timestamp differences are scaled to the range $[-1, 1]$.

4.2   Events Warping

Once preprocessing is complete, events are read back from BRAM and forwarded to the warping module. This initiates the stream-processing phase, in which events from the current batch are processed across 100 optimization iterations to estimate the motion. The iteration count was selected empirically: it was sufficient for the optimization to converge in our experiments, and it can be adjusted in the architecture if needed. The 54-bit vectors stored in memory are unpacked into the event representation $e_k = (t_k, x_k, y_k, p_k)$. BRAM readout introduces a latency of two clock cycles, after which the filtered-event stream is generated and delivered to the event-warping module.

The first stage of the warping module computes the timestamp difference $dt_k = t_k - t_{ref}$ according to (2). This subtraction is implemented using DSP resources; it takes two 32-bit inputs and produces a 33-bit result. Next, dt_k is normalized by multiplying it by the inverse of the time interval between the first and last events in the current packet. A DSP multiplier multiplies the 33-bit dt_k value by a 32-bit inverse of the interval length with an 8-cycle latency, producing a 65-bit normalized value. This value is then truncated to 33 bits (sign, 1 integer bit, and 31 fractional bits).

The next step computes the event coordinate shift according to (4). Two DSP multipliers evaluate the shifts for both coordinates using the normalized dt_k and the motion parameters (v_x, v_y). Each velocity component is represented on 40 bits (1 sign bit, 7 integer bits, and 32 fractional bits). The multiplier outputs are 72-bit displacement values, which are reduced to 44 bits for the x-shift (1 sign, 11 integer, 32 fractional) and 43 bits for the y-shift (with a 10-bit integer part, by design). The multiplier latency is 8 clock cycles.

Finally, the warped coordinates (x'_k, y'_k) are computed by subtracting the displacement from the original coordinates using two DSP-based subtractors. The x'_k subtractor takes the original x_k (extended to 43 bits) and subtracts the 44-bit x-shift; the y'_k subtractor takes y_k (extended to 42 bits) and subtracts the 43-bit y-shift. Each subtraction completes in two clock cycles. The resulting warped coordinates are 43 bits wide for x'_k and 42 bits wide for y'_k. Together with the normalized timestamp difference dt_k, they are streamed at the output of the event-warping module on an event-by-event basis.

4.3   Bilinear Voting and IWE Accumulation

Warped events are then forwarded to the bilinear voting module. In this stage, each warped event is distributed among the four neighboring pixels using bilinear weights. Weight computation requires extracting the fractional parts of the warped coordinates, and the arithmetic follows (5) and (13). Next, the terms $1 - dx_k$ and $1 - dy_k$ are computed using a DSP-based subtractor with a latency of two clock cycles, producing 33-bit results. The subsequent multiplications are also mapped to DSP resources, with a latency of six clock cycles. As a result, after this stage the weights and their derivatives are available at the module output.

The final weights are represented on 33 bits; the sign bit is dropped because bilinear weights are constrained to the range $[0, 1]$. The derivative values are likewise reduced to 33 bits (1 sign bit and 32 fractional bits). This specific 33-bit width was chosen to preserve the full 32-bit fractional precision from the coordinate warping stage.

Another module is responsible for accumulating the weights to construct the IWE and its derivatives (6). Outputs from the bilinear voting stage are written to 12 independent BRAM instances: four store I_w, four accumulate the partial derivatives with respect to v_x, and the remaining four accumulate the derivatives with respect to v_y. Within each group, the four banks correspond to ROI pixels partitioned by the parity of their coordinates. The parity and the corresponding target addresses are computed relative to the ROI origin. This 12-bank organization enables all contributions from a single event to be written in the same clock cycle. The complete memory management and addressing scheme is illustrated in Fig. 4.

The architecture includes combinational logic for address generation and bank selection, determining which BRAM instance receives a given bilinear weight contribution. To avoid overflow during accumulation in the IWE pixels (and in the corresponding derivative images), the weights and their deriva-

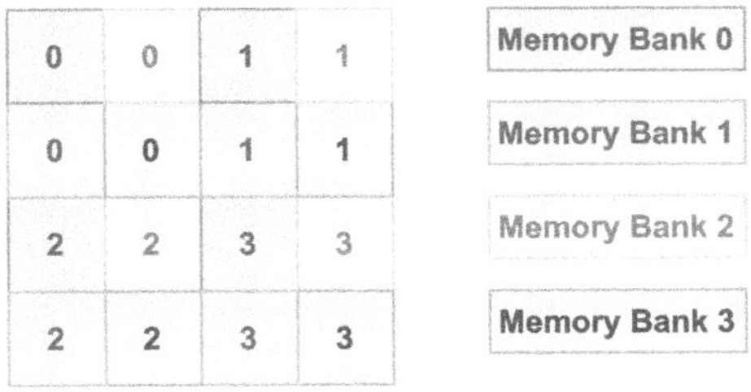

Fig. 4. Visualization of memory management for bilinear voting weights.

tives are extended by seven additional integer bits, yielding 40-bit fixed-point signals. The image memories are implemented using BRAM configured as dual-port RAM. The design uses 12 BRAM instances, each supporting read and write access to 40-bit words. The depth of each memory depends on the selected ROI resolution. With this configuration, both read and write operations have a one-cycle latency.

Pixel-value accumulation is implemented as a three-stage pipeline. In the first cycle, the target address for the incoming weight is presented to the module and the current value at this location is read from BRAM. In the second cycle, the read value is added to the incoming weight. In the third cycle, the updated value is written back to the corresponding BRAM cell. This pipeline can lead to write hazards: if two events target the same address within a few clock cycles, the second event may read a stale value because the update from the first event has not yet been committed to BRAM. To eliminate this hazard, we add a small register-based bypass buffer that stores the addresses and accumulated values of the three most recently updated entries. If the address of a new event matches a buffered address, the accumulator uses the buffered value instead of the BRAM output. The incoming weight is then added to this value, preserving correctness until the updated result is written back. The same accumulation mechanism is used for both derivative images.

4.4 Gradient Calculation

Once accumulation in all memory blocks is complete, the next module computes the gradient according to (10). The first required quantity is the IWE mean μ. Since the sum of I_w over all pixels equals the number of ROI events, μ can be obtained by multiplying this count by the inverse of the number of pixels. The DSP-multiplier latency does not affect the overall batch processing time because the ROI-event count is already available from the filter stage and the inverse of the ROI size is a constant. In our implementation, two unsigned 32-bit values are multiplied, producing a 65-bit result, which is then reduced to 40 bits (8 integer bits and 32 fractional bits).

Reading from the 12 BRAM instances has a one-cycle latency. An important implementation detail is that BRAM cannot be truly reset in hardware. Therefore, one cycle after reading a value for gradient evaluation at a given address, a zero is written back to the same location. This ensures that, before the current iteration finishes, all BRAM instances have already been cleared and are ready to accumulate new bilinear weights in the next iteration.

To compute the gradient, the difference between each pixel value and the IWE mean must be evaluated. This is implemented using four DSP-based subtractors. Each subtractor operates on 40-bit signed inputs (with the most significant bit as the sign bit), enabling the differences for four pixels to be computed per clock cycle. This step highlights the close relationship between packet-processing time and ROI size. For a 64×64 window, computing all differences takes 1026 clock cycles (1024 pixel differences plus two cycles of module latency).

Next, the computed difference is multiplied by the corresponding IWE-derivative value at the same pixel. This stage uses eight DSP multipliers operating in parallel. Each multiplier takes two 40-bit inputs and produces a 79-bit product; the multiplier pipeline introduces a latency of nine clock cycles. The products are then truncated to 40 bits before accumulation. Accumulation is performed by eight dedicated DSP-based accumulator modules, one per multiplier output. Each accumulator produces a 48-bit partial sum with a latency of two clock cycles. The partial sums are then combined using an adder tree. For each gradient component, four partial sums must be added, which takes four clock cycles in total (a single DSP adder has a latency of two clock cycles). Finally, the per-pixel products must be accumulated over the entire image. Since the gradient is a two-element vector and the IWE data are distributed across four memory banks, the overall summation is performed incrementally.

Once the final sum is obtained, it is scaled by a factor of two and normalized by the ROI size. For simplicity, we implement the factor $2/N$ as a precomputed constant, so this step reduces to a multiplication carried out by two DSP multipliers with an eight-cycle latency. Both gradient components are represented as 40-bit fixed-point values (1 sign bit, 7 integer bits, and 32 fractional bits).

4.5 Flow and ROI Update

Each optimization iteration concludes by updating the horizontal and vertical motion components according to (15). This step is performed by the flow-update module. The computation of the updated motion parameters begins with evaluating their change. In hardware, two DSP multipliers (one per component) multiply the 4-bit learning rate by the 40-bit gradient component, with a latency of four clock cycles. The products are 44-bit values and are reduced to 40 bits for subsequent processing. Next, the updated velocities are obtained by combining the previous-iteration velocities with the computed increments. This operation is implemented using two DSP subtractors, each with a latency of two clock cycles. The module operates on 40-bit inputs and produces 40-bit outputs corresponding to the updated velocity components. Once both updated velocities are available, the next optimization iteration begins and events are warped again using the new motion estimates. After the maximum number of iterations is reached, the module outputs the flow values from the final iteration. These motion estimates are then used to update the ROI according to (16).

5   Experimental Results

The proposed architecture was implemented on the *Kria KV260 Vision AI Starter Kit* and verified against a floating-point C++ reference model. Intermediate results were inspected using the *Integrated Logic Analyzer (ILA)*. Based on an analysis of the design, (17) was derived to estimate the number of clock cycles required to process a single batch of events.

$$C_{batch}(N, T, n, P) = N + T \cdot (n + L_r + \frac{P}{4} + L_v) \tag{17}$$

where N is the total number of events in a batch, T is the number of optimization iterations, n is the number of events within the ROI, L_r is the latency associated with processing readouts from the ROI (32 cycles), P is the total number of ROI pixels, and L_v is the latency of the bilinear voting stage (35 cycles).

Therefore, the total processing time for a single batch can be estimated as C_{batch}/f_{clk}, where f_{clk} is the clock frequency of the architecture. The architecture achieved a maximum clock frequency of 210 MHz. A comparison was then performed for the batch-processing time under different input batch sizes and ROI resolutions. Processing time was evaluated for 100 optimization iterations. Although implementing an adaptive convergence check is generally highly beneficial, a fixed count was chosen here to provide a reliable, data-independent baseline for throughput evaluation. The reference model was executed on an *Intel Core i5-11300H 3.10 GHz CPU*. The results are summarized in Table 1. Processing times were measured for a single batch containing a specific number of events. The results demonstrate a substantial speedup of the proposed FPGA architecture over the C++ CPU reference implementation. Depending on the number of input events and the ROI resolution, the speedup ranges from less than 1.6× to 20× in terms of reduced batch-processing time. The lowest acceleration (approximately 1.6×) was observed with an ROI size of 200 × 140, whereas the highest acceleration (20×) was achieved for a batch size of 1 000 and an ROI resolution of 32 × 32. This improvement stems from exploiting spatial parallelism and tailored on-chip memory management within the FPGA architecture. The achievable clock frequency is also critical to meeting real-time constraints. Accurately estimating the exact CPU-FPGA tradeoff point is difficult. Once the increasing ROI size exceeds the CPU's cache capacity, sudden memory bottlenecks will cause a non-linear degradation in software performance.

These results can also be compared with the computation times reported in [8], which presents an optimized CPU implementation of the contrast maximization algorithm. However, that work uses a different motion model, which makes a direct comparison difficult. The authors report processing times of approximately 30–60 ms for 90 optimization iterations, 5 000 events, and a resolution of 240 × 180 on an *Intel Core i7-7500U@2.7 GHz* CPU. For the same parameters (resolution, number of events, and number of iterations), the processing time of the proposed architecture operating at 200 MHz can be estimated from (17) as 7.2 ms, whereas the reference C++ model requires approximately

Table 1. Comparison of processing time t_{batch} for 100 optimization iterations for different ROI resolutions and input batch sizes.

ROI	Input batch	Events in ROI	CPU [ms]	FPGA [ms]
32×32	1000	159	4.64	0.23
	3000	484	4.70	0.40
	5000	795	5.18	0.56
	10000	1589	5.70	0.96
64×64	1000	160	4.49	0.60
	3000	487	4.58	0.75
	5000	800	4.90	0.92
	10000	1604	5.82	1.33
128×128	1000	377	4.72	2.17
	3000	1185	5.32	2.56
	5000	2028	5.94	2.97
	10000	4133	7.80	4.00
200×140	1000	824	5.44	3.76
	3000	2481	7.13	4.56
	5000	4181	7.78	5.38
	10000	8351	11.86	7.39

8.67 ms. Note, however, that supporting a 240×180 ROI with the presented architecture would require an FPGA with more BRAM resources than the device used in this work or usage of external RAM.

Table 2. Resource utilization summary for the CM algorithm on FPGA.

CLB LUTs	CLB Registers	CLB	Block RAM	DSPs	CARRY8
3655 (3.12%)	7857 (3.35%)	1218 (8.32%)	25.5 (17.70%)	151 (12.10%)	274 (1.87%)

Table 2 summarizes the FPGA resource utilization of the proposed architecture. The percentage of the total available on-chip resources are given in parentheses. The CM implementation uses only a small fraction of the available logic on the *Kria KV260 Vision AI Starter Kit*—less than 4% of LUTs and registers. Higher utilization is observed for DSP resources (12.1%) and BRAM (17.7%), reflecting the extensive use of arithmetic operations and parallel buffering. These results also indicate that a larger ROI (e.g., 128×128) could be supported, at the cost of an approximately fourfold increase in BRAM utilization.

According to power estimates obtained with the Vivado Power tool, the FPGA consumes approximately 0.813 W of on-chip power, including both dynamic and static components. This represents a relatively low power demand given the achieved performance and efficiency. For comparison, wattmeter measurements of the baseline CPU implementation revealed an active power overhead of roughly 11 W above the system's idle state. Considering this alongside the significant reduction in processing time, the proposed hardware architecture offers orders of magnitude lower total energy consumption per optimization step, clearly demonstrating its suitability for power-constrained edge applications.

6   Conclusions

In this paper, we present a hardware architecture implementing the CM algorithm on FPGA resources. Experimental results show that the FPGA processing time is reduced from $1.6\times$ to $20\times$ compared to a CPU implementation, depending on the number of input events and the ROI resolution. This confirms the benefits of a hardware implementation, as FPGA devices exploit spatial parallelism and deep pipelining to process event streams efficiently. To the best of our knowledge, at the time of writing, this is the first FPGA-based hardware architecture that accelerates the Contrast Maximization algorithm[1]. The system operates at up to 210 MHz while maintaining low FPGA resource utilization and low power consumption, demonstrating the high speed and efficiency of the proposed solution.

Future work includes optimizing the architecture to increase the maximum operating frequency, reducing resource utilization, and extending the design to support more advanced motion models. Another important direction is to increase the maximum ROI size, for example by using external RAM as an additional accumulation buffer. It may also be beneficial to introduce double buffering, enabling continuous event acquisition during optimization. Finally, the architecture could be extended with more advanced optimization methods than simple gradient ascent, as well as mechanisms such as early stopping to terminate the computation once the objective no longer improves. While this work primarily demonstrates CM acceleration in the context of object tracking, the proposed architecture could also be applied to other event-based vision tasks, such as estimating optical flow. To adapt the system for optical flow estimation, a larger number of processing windows would need to be deployed to cover the entire image space.

Acknowledgments. The work presented in this paper was supported by the programme "Excellence initiative - research university" for the AGH University of Krakow (first author), the National Science Centre project no. 2021/41/N/ST6/03915 entitled "Acceleration of processing event-based visual data with the use of heterogeneous, reprogrammable computing devices" (second author), and the research subsidy (funds from the Ministry of Science and Higher Education) (third author).

---

[1] During the review process, a concurrent work [20] was published introducing an FPGA implementation of CM that supports a rotational motion model.

References

1. Asano, S., Maruyama, T., Yamaguchi, Y.: Performance comparison of FPGA, GPU and CPU in image processing. In: 2009 International Conference on Field Programmable Logic and Applications, pp. 126–131. IEEE (2009)
2. Gallego, G., et al.: Event-based vision: a survey. IEEE Trans. Pattern Anal. Mach. Intell. **44**(1), 154–180 (2020)
3. Gallego, G., Gehrig, M., Scaramuzza, D.: Focus is all you need: loss functions for event-based vision. In: Proceedings of the IEEE/CVF Conference on Computer Vision and Pattern Recognition, pp. 12280–12289 (2019)
4. Gallego, G., Rebecq, H., Scaramuzza, D.: A unifying contrast maximization framework for event cameras, with applications to motion, depth, and optical flow estimation. In: Proceedings of the IEEE Conference on Computer Vision and Pattern Recognition, pp. 3867–3876 (2018)
5. Gehrig, D., Rebecq, H., Gallego, G., Scaramuzza, D.: Asynchronous, photometric feature tracking using events and frames. In: Proceedings of the European Conference on Computer Vision (ECCV), pp. 750–765 (2018)
6. Guo, S., Gallego, G.: CMax-SLAM: event-based rotational-motion bundle adjustment and SLAM system using contrast maximization. IEEE Trans. Rob. **40**, 2442–2461 (2024)
7. Hamann, F., Wang, Z., Asmanis, I., Chaney, K., Gallego, G., Daniilidis, K.: Motion-prior contrast maximization for dense continuous-time motion estimation. In: Leonardis, A., Ricci, E., Roth, S., Russakovsky, O., Sattler, T., Varol, G. (eds.) ECCV 2024. LNCS, vol. 15061, pp. 18–37. Springer, Cham (2024). https://doi.org/10.1007/978-3-031-72646-0_2
8. Kim, H., Kim, H.J.: Real-time rotational motion estimation with contrast maximization over globally aligned events. IEEE Robot. Autom. Lett. **6**(3), 6016–6023 (2021)
9. Kryjak, T.: Event-based vision on FPGAs-a survey. In: 2024 27th Euromicro conference on digital system Design (DSD), pp. 541–550. IEEE (2024)
10. Liu, D., Parra, A., Chin, T.J.: Globally optimal contrast maximisation for event-based motion estimation. In: Proceedings of the IEEE/CVF Conference on Computer Vision and Pattern Recognition, pp. 6349–6358 (2020)
11. Maqueda, A.I., Loquercio, A., Gallego, G., García, N., Scaramuzza, D.: Event-based vision meets deep learning on steering prediction for self-driving cars. In: Proceedings of the IEEE Conference on Computer Vision and Pattern Recognition, pp. 5419–5427 (2018)
12. Mueggler, E., Rebecq, H., Gallego, G., Delbruck, T., Scaramuzza, D.: The event-camera dataset and simulator: event-based data for pose estimation, visual odometry, and slam. Int. J. Robot. Res. **36**(2), 142–149 (2017)
13. Paredes-Vallés, F., Scheper, K.Y., De Wagter, C., De Croon, G.C.: Taming contrast maximization for learning sequential, low-latency, event-based optical flow. In: Proceedings of the IEEE/CVF International Conference on Computer Vision, pp. 9695–9705 (2023)
14. Peng, X., Gao, L., Wang, Y., Kneip, L.: Globally-optimal contrast maximisation for event cameras. IEEE Trans. Pattern Anal. Mach. Intell. **44**(7), 3479–3495 (2021)
15. Qasaimeh, M., Denolf, K., Lo, J., Vissers, K., Zambreno, J., Jones, P.H.: Comparing energy efficiency of CPU, GPU and FPGA implementations for vision kernels. In: 2019 IEEE International Conference on Embedded Software and Systems (ICESS), pp. 1–8. IEEE (2019)

16. Shiba, S., Aoki, Y., Gallego, G.: Event collapse in contrast maximization frameworks. Sensors **22**(14), 5190 (2022)
17. Shiba, S., Klose, Y., Aoki, Y., Gallego, G.: Secrets of event-based optical flow, depth and ego-motion estimation by contrast maximization. IEEE Trans. Pattern Anal. Mach. Intell. **46**(12), 7742–7759 (2024)
18. Stoffregen, T., Kleeman, L.: Event cameras, contrast maximization and reward functions: an analysis. In: Proceedings of the IEEE/CVF Conference on Computer Vision and Pattern Recognition, pp. 12300–12308 (2019)
19. Stumpp, D.C., Akolkar, H., George, A.D., Benosman, R.B.: Harms: a hardware acceleration architecture for real-time event-based optical flow. IEEE Access **10**, 58181–58198 (2022)
20. Wang, R., et al.: FRME: an FPGA-accelerated event-based real-time rotational motion estimator for SLAM. In: 2025 International Conference on Field Programmable Technology (ICFPT), pp. 128–136. IEEE (2025)
21. Wang, Y., et al.: Visual odometry with an event camera using continuous ray warping and volumetric contrast maximization. Sensors **22**(15), 5687 (2022)
22. Wang, Z., Fortney, W.A., Bobda, C.: Bio-inspired event cameras for robust edge system in challenging environments. In: 2025 IEEE 36th International Conference on Application-specific Systems, Architectures and Processors (ASAP), pp. 131–138. IEEE (2025)

Multiplier-Free Robust Adaptive Beamforming for UAV Radars: A Double-Shift PoT Approach

Siming Chen[1,2], Xin Zhang[1,2(✉)], and Weibo Deng[1,2]

[1] Harbin Institute of Technology, Harbin 150001, China
chsmhit@stu.hit.edu.cn, {zhangxinhit,dengweibo}@hit.edu.cn
[2] The Key Laboratory of Marine Environmental Monitoring and Information Processing, Ministry of Industry and Information Technology, Beijing, China

Abstract. Deploying robust adaptive beamforming (RABF) algorithms on Unmanned Aerial Vehicle (UAV) swarm radars presents a severe conflict between anti-jamming performance and hardware efficiency. Traditional RABF algorithms demand high-precision continuous floating-point weights, necessitating numerous power-hungry hardware multipliers (e.g., DSP slices on FPGAs) during the high-speed real-time spatial filtering stage. This is highly detrimental to the stringent Size, Weight, and Power (SWaP) constraints of edge UAVs. While naive single-shift Power-of-Two (PoT) quantization mitigates multiplier usage, it inevitably suffers from severe null-shallowing effects, failing to suppress strong active jammers. In this paper, we propose a multiplier-free hardware/algorithm co-design: the Double-Shift PoT RABF. By mapping the complex weights to a meticulously designed double-shift discrete dictionary, our approach entirely eradicates multipliers in the data path, substituting them with energy-efficient programmable bit-shifters and adders. We formulate the discrete optimization problem using the Alternating Direction Method of Multipliers (ADMM) framework to guarantee deep jamming nulls. Extensive simulations demonstrate that under UAV position perturbations, the proposed multiplier-free method exhibits nearly zero performance degradation (less than 0.1 dB SINR loss) compared to the traditional 32-bit floating-point baseline, offering a highly hardware-efficient solution for next-generation UAV edge computing.

Keywords: Robust Adaptive Beamforming · UAV Swarm Radar · Multiplier-Free · Power-of-Two (PoT) · Hardware-Algorithm Co-Design · ADMM

1 Introduction

Distributed Unmanned Aerial Vehicle (UAV) swarm radars have emerged as a transformative technology in modern electronic warfare, offering enhanced spatial coverage, survivability, and flexible array configurations [10,11]. In distributed array radar scenarios, suppressing strong main-lobe/side-lobe jamming through adaptive spatial filtering is a central capability [12].

G. Leone et al. (Eds.): ARC 2026, LNCS 16514, pp. 326–337, 2026.
https://doi.org/10.1007/978-3-032-29365-7_20

To survive in severely contested electromagnetic environments, UAV swarms must employ robust adaptive beamforming (RABF) to actively synthesize deep nulls toward powerful jamming sources while maintaining a distortionless response toward the target of interest [1–4, 6, 9, 13].

However, translating advanced RABF algorithms into operational UAV platforms is heavily bottlenecked by the stringent Size, Weight, and Power (SWaP) constraints of edge computing hardware. Conventional RABF solutions, such as the Diagonal Loading Sample Matrix Inversion (DL-SMI), generate optimal weights as high-precision continuous floating-point numbers [2, 5]. In digital phased array receivers, executing the real-time spatial filtering $y(k) = \mathbf{w}^H \mathbf{x}(k)$ at sampling rates of hundreds of megahertz demands massive concurrent complex multiplications. On Field-Programmable Gate Arrays (FPGAs), these operations exhaust power-hungry Digital Signal Processing (DSP) slices, causing significant thermal dissipation and drastically reducing the mission endurance of battery-powered UAVs [14, 16, 17, 20].

To alleviate the hardware computational burden, low-bit quantization techniques have been investigated [18]. Among them, Power-of-Two (PoT)/multiplierless coefficient representations replace multipliers with shift-and-add structures, which is widely used in multiplierless DSP implementations [15, 16, 19]. Unfortunately, applying coarse single-shift PoT quantization directly to adaptive beamforming disrupts the delicate phase and amplitude relationships across the array elements. This phenomenon, known as the null-shallowing effect, allows strong active jammers to leak through the degraded nulls, catastrophically deteriorating the output Signal-to-Interference-plus-Noise Ratio (SINR).

To bridge the critical gap between radar anti-jamming accuracy and hardware efficiency, we propose a multiplier-free Double-Shift PoT RABF approach. By exploiting the Alternating Direction Method of Multipliers (ADMM), we seamlessly integrate a hardware-friendly discrete constraint into the robust optimization framework [7, 8]. The main contributions of this paper are summarized as follows:

- We design a novel Double-Shift PoT discrete dictionary for complex weight mapping. This architecture elegantly eradicates all multipliers in the high-speed spatial filtering stage, relying strictly on bit-shifters and adders, thereby enabling a multiplier-free datapath with potential dynamic-power savings on FPGA platforms.
- We develop an ADMM-based solver equipped with a warm-start strategy to decouple the continuous target response constraint from the discrete hardware constraints, ensuring stable convergence despite the non-convex nature of the PoT grid.
- Through theoretical complexity analysis and extensive numerical simulations, we prove that the proposed multiplier-free algorithm completely overcomes the null-shallowing effect, achieving a deep jamming suppression capability virtually identical to the power-intensive 32-bit floating-point baseline.

Unlike prior multiplierless DSP implementations that mainly focus on generic coefficient quantization, this work targets robust adaptive beamforming under

UAV-induced steering mismatch and strong jamming. The novelty lies in combining a double-shift discrete dictionary with an ADMM-based constrained optimization framework, so that multiplier-free implementation is achieved without the severe null-shallowing typically caused by coarse PoT quantization.

The remainder of this paper is organized as follows. Section 2 introduces the UAV radar signal model and formulates the hardware-constrained problem. Section 3 details the Double-Shift PoT ADMM algorithm. Section 4 provides a comprehensive computational complexity analysis. Section 5 presents the simulation results, and Sect. 6 concludes the paper.

2   System Model and Problem Formulation

2.1   Signal Model of UAV Swarm Radar

Consider a distributed UAV swarm acting as an airborne Uniform Linear Array (ULA) radar receiver [10, 11]. The swarm consists of N UAV nodes hovering in formation, with a nominal inter-element spacing of $d = \lambda/2$, where λ is the radar operating wavelength. Assume the array receives a narrowband target signal from direction θ_s, along with J active jamming signals from directions θ_j $(j = 1, 2, \ldots, J)$. The complex baseband snapshot received by the array at time index k can be modeled as:

$$\mathbf{x}(k) = \mathbf{a}(\theta_s)s(k) + \sum_{j=1}^{J} \mathbf{a}(\theta_j)j_j(k) + \mathbf{n}(k), \tag{1}$$

where $s(k)$ and $j_j(k)$ denote the waveforms of the target and the j-th jammer, respectively. The vector $\mathbf{n}(k) \in \mathbb{C}^{N \times 1}$ represents the additive white Gaussian noise (AWGN) with variance σ_n^2. $\mathbf{a}(\theta)$ is the array steering vector.

Due to the high-mobility and hovering inaccuracies of the UAV swarm, inevitable position perturbations occur. Let Δp_n denote the position error of the n-th UAV node. The actual steering vector with mismatch, denoted by $\tilde{\mathbf{a}}(\theta) \in \mathbb{C}^{N \times 1}$, is given by:

$$[\tilde{\mathbf{a}}(\theta)]_n = \frac{1}{\sqrt{N}} e^{j \frac{2\pi}{\lambda} (nd + \Delta p_n) \sin \theta}, \quad n = 0, 1, \ldots, N - 1. \tag{2}$$

2.2   Robust Adaptive Beamforming Formulation

The objective of adaptive beamforming is to design a complex weight vector $\mathbf{w} \in \mathbb{C}^{N \times 1}$ to linearly combine the array spatial observations, i.e., $y(k) = \mathbf{w}^H \mathbf{x}(k)$, such that the jamming signals and noise are minimized while preserving the target signal. The classic Minimum Variance Distortionless Response (MVDR) beamformer is formulated as [1]:

$$\min_{\mathbf{w}} \ \mathbf{w}^H \mathbf{R} \mathbf{w} \quad \text{s.t.} \quad \mathbf{w}^H \mathbf{a}(\theta_s) = 1, \tag{3}$$

where $\mathbf{R} = \mathbb{E}[\mathbf{x}(k)\mathbf{x}^H(k)]$ is the theoretical covariance matrix.

In practice, $\mathbf{R}$ is estimated by the Sample Matrix Inversion (SMI) method using K snapshots. Under UAV-induced steering mismatch, robust formulations are typically required to maintain stable nulling performance [3,6]. In this work, Diagonal Loading (DL) is adopted due to its simplicity and effectiveness [2,5]. The classic DL-SMI robust beamforming problem is formulated as:

$$\min_{\mathbf{w}} \ \mathbf{w}^H \mathbf{R}_{dl} \mathbf{w} \quad \text{s.t.} \quad \mathbf{w}^H \mathbf{a}_0 = 1, \tag{4}$$

where $\mathbf{R}_{dl} = \hat{\mathbf{R}} + \alpha \mathbf{I}$ with α being the loading factor, and $\mathbf{a}_0$ is the nominal target steering vector without position errors.

2.3 Hardware-Constrained Problem Formulation

Solving (4) yields an optimal continuous weight vector $\mathbf{w}_{opt} = \frac{\mathbf{R}_{dl}^{-1} \mathbf{a}_0}{\mathbf{a}_0^H \mathbf{R}_{dl}^{-1} \mathbf{a}_0}$. However, mapping these high-precision floating-point weights to resource-constrained UAV hardware poses a significant challenge. The real-time filtering process $y(k) = \mathbf{w}^H \mathbf{x}(k)$ requires N complex multipliers, which aggressively consume power-hungry DSP slices on modern FPGAs [14,20].

To achieve multiplier-free beamforming on the edge, we constrain the real and imaginary parts of the weights to a hardware-friendly discrete dictionary $\mathbb{P}$. Multiplierless (shift/add) coefficient representations are widely used in low-power DSP designs [15,16]. Thus, the hardware-oriented RABF problem is reformulated as:

$$\min_{\mathbf{w}} \ \mathbf{w}^H \mathbf{R}_{dl} \mathbf{w}$$
$$\text{s.t.} \ \ \mathbf{w}^H \mathbf{a}_0 = 1, \tag{5}$$
$$\Re\{w_n\}, \Im\{w_n\} \in \mathbb{P}, \ \forall n.$$

Traditional single-shift Power-of-Two (PoT) quantization defines $\mathbb{P} = \{0, \pm 2^{-b}\}$. However, coarse quantization can significantly distort array responses and degrade suppression performance under strong interference [18]. In Sect. 3, we propose a *Double-Shift* PoT dictionary and an ADMM-based solver to address (5) efficiently [7,8].

3 Proposed Double-Shift PoT Beamforming

To overcome the catastrophic null-shallowing effect caused by coarse quantization while strictly maintaining a multiplier-free hardware architecture, we propose a Double-Shift PoT RABF algorithm optimized via the Alternating Direction Method of Multipliers (ADMM) [7,8].

3.1 Hardware-Efficient Double-Shift Dictionary

In standard FPGA implementations, substituting a continuous weight w with a single-shift PoT value, i.e., $w \in \{0, \pm 2^{-b}\}$, allows the complex multiplication

$w \times x$ to be executed purely by bit-wise right-shift operations. However, single-shift quantization suffers from a low dynamic range ceiling (max value $2^{-1} = 0.5$) and a sparse quantization grid, which severely degrades the nulling depth against strong jammers.

To bridge the performance gap without introducing DSP multipliers, we propose the Double-Shift PoT dictionary, denoted as $\mathbb{P}_{ds}$. We construct the dictionary by allowing each real and imaginary component of the weight to be represented by the sum or difference of two PoT values:

$$\mathbb{P}_{ds} = \left\{ s_1 2^{-b_1} + s_2 2^{-b_2} \mid b_1, b_2 \in \{0, 1, \ldots, B\}, \; s_1, s_2 \in \{-1, 0, 1\} \right\}, \qquad (6)$$

where B is the maximum hardware shift bit-width (e.g., $B = 8$).

Crucially, the inclusion of $2^0 = 1$ resolves the ceiling clipping issue, ensuring the mainlobe response constraint $\mathbf{w}^H \mathbf{a}_0 = 1$ is mathematically feasible. In hardware, multiplying a signal by a coefficient from $\mathbb{P}_{ds}$ requires exactly zero multipliers; it is strictly implemented using two programmable bit-shifters and one adder.

3.2   ADMM-Based Robust Optimization

Directly solving (5) with the discrete constraint $\mathbb{P}_{ds}$ is a non-convex NP-hard problem. We reformulate it by introducing an auxiliary variable $\mathbf{z} \in \mathbb{C}^{N \times 1}$ to decouple the continuous target constraint from the discrete hardware constraint:

$$\min_{\mathbf{w}, \mathbf{z}} \quad \mathbf{w}^H \mathbf{R}_{dl} \mathbf{w}$$

$$\text{s.t.} \quad \mathbf{w}^H \mathbf{a}_0 = 1, \quad \mathbf{w} = \mathbf{z}, \qquad (7)$$

$$\Re\{z_n\}, \Im\{z_n\} \in \mathbb{P}_{ds}, \; \forall n.$$

The augmented Lagrangian for (7) is formulated as:

$$\mathcal{L}_\rho(\mathbf{w}, \mathbf{z}, \mathbf{u}) = \mathbf{w}^H \mathbf{R}_{dl} \mathbf{w} + \frac{\rho}{2} \|\mathbf{w} - \mathbf{z} + \mathbf{u}\|_2^2, \qquad (8)$$

where $\mathbf{u} \in \mathbb{C}^{N \times 1}$ is the scaled dual variable, and $\rho > 0$ is the adaptive penalty parameter defined as $\rho = \text{Tr}(\mathbf{R}_{dl})/N$ to balance the convergence speed and the scale of the covariance matrix.

The ADMM framework iteratively updates $\mathbf{w}$, $\mathbf{z}$, and $\mathbf{u}$ until convergence. At the $(k+1)$-th iteration, the subproblems are solved as follows:

Continuous Weight Update (w-Update). The variable $\mathbf{w}$ is updated by minimizing (8) subject to the distortionless constraint. This forms an equality-constrained quadratic programming problem:

$$\mathbf{w}^{(k+1)} = \arg \min_{\mathbf{w}^H \mathbf{a}_0 = 1} \mathbf{w}^H \mathbf{A} \mathbf{w} - \rho \mathbf{w}^H (\mathbf{z}^{(k)} - \mathbf{u}^{(k)}), \qquad (9)$$

where $\mathbf{A} = 2\mathbf{R}_{dl} + \rho \mathbf{I}$. Since $\mathbf{A}$ is a Hermitian positive-definite matrix, it remains constant across iterations. By applying the method of Lagrange multipliers, the closed-form update is derived as:

$$\mathbf{w}^{(k+1)} = \tilde{\mathbf{w}} + \frac{1 - \mathbf{a}_0^H \tilde{\mathbf{w}}}{\mathbf{a}_0^H \mathbf{A}^{-1} \mathbf{a}_0} \mathbf{A}^{-1} \mathbf{a}_0, \tag{10}$$

where $\tilde{\mathbf{w}} = \rho \mathbf{A}^{-1}(\mathbf{z}^{(k)} - \mathbf{u}^{(k)})$ is the unconstrained minimizer. To avoid repeated matrix inversions, $\mathbf{A}^{-1}$ is implemented via Cholesky factorization $\mathbf{A} = \mathbf{L}\mathbf{L}^H$ computed strictly once prior to the iterations.

Discrete Dictionary Projection (z-Update). The auxiliary variable $\mathbf{z}$ absorbs the discrete hardware constraints. The update is a Euclidean projection onto the Double-Shift dictionary $\mathbb{P}_{ds}$:

$$\mathbf{z}^{(k+1)} = \Pi_{\mathbb{P}_{ds}}\left(\mathbf{w}^{(k+1)} + \mathbf{u}^{(k)}\right). \tag{11}$$

Since $\mathbb{P}_{ds}$ is independently applied to the real and imaginary parts, the projection $\Pi_{\mathbb{P}_{ds}}(\cdot)$ simply performs an element-wise nearest-neighbor mapping from the continuous values to the pre-generated $\mathbb{P}_{ds}$ grid.

Dual Variable Update (u-Update). Finally, the scaled dual variable is updated via gradient ascent:

$$\mathbf{u}^{(k+1)} = \mathbf{u}^{(k)} + \mathbf{w}^{(k+1)} - \mathbf{z}^{(k+1)}. \tag{12}$$

3.3   Warm Start Initialization

Due to the non-convexity introduced by the discrete constraint $\mathbb{P}_{ds}$, random initialization often traps the ADMM solver in undesirable local minima, resulting in shifted nulls. To guarantee reliable jamming suppression, we employ a *warm start* strategy. The continuous optimal solution from the conventional DL-SMI algorithm, i.e., $\mathbf{w}_{init} = \frac{\mathbf{R}_{dl}^{-1} \mathbf{a}_0}{\mathbf{a}_0^H \mathbf{R}_{dl}^{-1} \mathbf{a}_0}$, is utilized to initialize $\mathbf{w}^{(0)}$. This strategy accelerates convergence and bounds the quantization loss within negligible margins.

4   Computational Complexity and Hardware Implications

The primary motivation of the proposed Double-Shift PoT RABF is to enable real-time, low-power interference suppression on SWaP-constrained UAV platforms. The computation of adaptive beamforming is inherently decoupled into two distinct stages: the high-speed real-time filtering stage and the slow-time weight update stage.

4.1   Complexity of Real-Time Beamforming

In a digital phased array radar, the real-time spatial filtering $y(k) = \mathbf{w}^H \mathbf{x}(k)$ is executed at the baseband sampling rate (often on the order of hundreds of

---

Algorithm 1. Double-Shift PoT Robust Adaptive Beamforming via ADMM

Require: $\hat{\mathbf{R}}$, $\mathbf{a}_0$, DL factor α, max shift B, tol ϵ, max iters $K_{\max}$
Ensure: $\mathbf{w}_{\mathrm{PoT}} \in \mathbb{P}_{ds}^N$
1: Build $\mathbb{P}_{ds}$ by (6); $\mathbf{R}_{dl} = \hat{\mathbf{R}} + \alpha\mathbf{I}$; $\rho = \mathrm{Tr}(\mathbf{R}_{dl})/N$
2: Warm start: $\mathbf{w}^{(0)} = \dfrac{\mathbf{R}_{dl}^{-1}\mathbf{a}_0}{\mathbf{a}_0^H \mathbf{R}_{dl}^{-1}\mathbf{a}_0}$; $\mathbf{z}^{(0)} = \Pi_{\mathbb{P}_{ds}}(\mathbf{w}^{(0)})$; $\mathbf{u}^{(0)} = \mathbf{0}$
3: Precompute: $\mathbf{A} = 2\mathbf{R}_{dl} + \rho\mathbf{I}$; Cholesky $\mathbf{A} = \mathbf{L}\mathbf{L}^H$; solve $\mathbf{g} = \mathbf{A}^{-1}\mathbf{a}_0$; $d = \mathbf{a}_0^H\mathbf{g}$
4: **for** $t = 0, 1, \ldots, K_{\max} - 1$ **do**
5:     Solve $\mathbf{v} = \rho\mathbf{A}^{-1}(\mathbf{z}^{(t)} - \mathbf{u}^{(t)})$ using $\mathbf{L}$
6:     $\mathbf{w}^{(t+1)} = \mathbf{v} + \dfrac{1 - \mathbf{a}_0^H\mathbf{v}}{d}\mathbf{g}$
7:     $\mathbf{z}^{(t+1)} = \Pi_{\mathbb{P}_{ds}}(\mathbf{w}^{(t+1)} + \mathbf{u}^{(t)})$
8:     $\mathbf{u}^{(t+1)} = \mathbf{u}^{(t)} + \mathbf{w}^{(t+1)} - \mathbf{z}^{(t+1)}$
9:     **if** $\|\mathbf{w}^{(t+1)} - \mathbf{z}^{(t+1)}\|_2 \leq \epsilon$ **and** $\rho\|\mathbf{z}^{(t+1)} - \mathbf{z}^{(t)}\|_2 \leq \epsilon$ **then**
10:          **break**
11:     **end if**
12: **end for**
13: **return** $\mathbf{w}_{\mathrm{PoT}} = \mathbf{z}^{(t+1)}$

MHz). Consequently, this stage dictates the dynamic power consumption of the receiver frontend [17,20].

Let the received signal at the n-th antenna be $x_n = x_{n,R} + jx_{n,I}$, and the corresponding complex weight be $w_n = w_{n,R} + jw_{n,I}$. A standard complex multiplication requires 4 real multipliers and 2 real adders. For an N-element array, generating one output sample requires $4N$ real multipliers and $4N-2$ real adders.

In contrast, the proposed Double-Shift PoT method constrains the weights such that $w_{n,R}, w_{n,I} \in \mathbb{P}_{ds}$. Multiplying x_n by a Double-Shift PoT coefficient completely eliminates the need for hardware multipliers. Instead, it is executed via programmable bit-shifts ($\gg$) and additions/subtractions. Specifically, the operation $x_{n,R} \times w_{n,R} = x_{n,R} \times (\pm 2^{-b_1} \pm 2^{-b_2})$ is implemented as $\pm(x_{n,R} \gg b_1) \pm (x_{n,R} \gg b_2)$. Therefore, the proposed algorithm requires exactly **zero** multipliers, replacing them with bit-shifts and adders.

4.2   Complexity of Weight Update

The optimal weights are updated periodically (e.g., per Coherent Processing Interval, CPI) to adapt to the dynamic jamming environment. For the traditional DL-SMI algorithm, solving $\mathbf{w} = \mathbf{R}_{dl}^{-1}\mathbf{a}_0$ via Cholesky factorization requires $\mathcal{O}(N^3/3)$ complex multiplications.

For the proposed ADMM-based solver (Algorithm 1), the $\mathcal{O}(N^3)$ Cholesky factorization of the constant matrix $\mathbf{A}$ is strictly performed only *once* prior to the iterations. Within the $K_{\max}$ ADMM iterations, the dominant operations are the forward and backward substitutions to solve the linear system, which require $\mathcal{O}(N^2)$ complex multiplications per iteration. The projection operation $\Pi_{\mathbb{P}_{ds}}(\cdot)$ is merely a hardware-friendly look-up table (LUT) mapping or a set of simple comparators, introducing negligible arithmetic overhead.

Table 1. Computational Complexity Comparison (in real-valued operations)

Operation Stage	Standard DL-SMI (Floating-Point)	Proposed Double-Shift PoT
Real-Time Spatial Filtering (Executed at MHz Sampling Rate)		
Real Multipliers	$4N$	**0**
Real Adders	$4N - 2$	$12N - 2$
Bit-Shifts	0	$8N$
Slow-Time Weight Update (Executed per CPI)		
Complex Multipliers	$\approx \frac{1}{3}N^3 + \frac{1}{2}N^2$	$\approx \frac{1}{3}N^3 + K_{\max}(N^2 + N)$
Matrix Inversion	Required (Implicitly via Cholesky)	Avoided in loop
Dictionary Mapping	N/A	$2NK_{\max}$ (Comparisons)

4.3 Hardware Resource Implications

Table 1 summarizes the arithmetic operation counts. In modern FPGA architectures (e.g., Xilinx Zynq Ultrascale+ commonly used in UAVs), multipliers are mapped to scarce and power-hungry DSP48 slices, whereas adders and bit-shifts are efficiently mapped to abundant Look-Up Tables (LUTs) and routing resources. By completely eradicating multipliers in the high-speed data path, the proposed Double-Shift PoT architecture significantly alleviates thermal dissipation and extends the mission endurance of the UAV swarm, making it highly amenable to edge-computing environments.

5 Simulation Results

In this section, we evaluate the performance of the proposed Double-Shift PoT RABF algorithm. To simulate a realistic SWaP-constrained UAV swarm radar, we consider a uniform linear array with $N = 16$ hovering nodes. The inter-element spacing is $d = 0.5\lambda$. The position perturbation of each UAV is modeled as an independent Gaussian random variable with zero mean and standard deviation $\sigma_{pos} = 0.02\lambda$. The target signal impinges from $\theta_s = 10°$. Three powerful active jammers are located at $\theta_j \in \{-30°, 40°, 60°\}$, each with a Jamming-to-Noise Ratio (JNR) of 35 dB. The hardware shift bit-width for the proposed method is set to $B = 8$.

We benchmark the proposed hardware-efficient algorithm against two continuous floating-point baselines: the ideal MVDR (assuming perfect knowledge of the true covariance matrix and steering vector, providing the theoretical upper bound) and the conventional DL-SMI robust beamformer (employing continuous weights).

334   S. Chen et al.

5.1 Spatial Beampattern Analysis

Figure 1 illustrates the normalized beampatterns evaluated at an input Signal-to-Noise Ratio (SNR) of 0 dB. As expected, the ideal MVDR forms exact nulls at the jammer directions. The conventional DL-SMI algorithm successfully maintains a distortionless response at the target direction ($\theta_s = 10°$) and suppresses the jammers by forming deep nulls ranging from -50 dB to -80 dB, despite the presence of UAV position errors. A slight deviation is observed near the angular boundary, but it has negligible impact on the target response and jammer suppression performance.

Crucially, the proposed Double-Shift PoT-ADMM algorithm (yellow dashed line) almost perfectly aligns with the floating-point DL-SMI algorithm. Even though the weights are rigidly constrained to a discrete multiplier-free dictionary $\mathbb{P}_{ds}$, the algorithm exhibits no noticeable null-shallowing effect. It forms sharp and deep nulls precisely at $-30°$, $40°$, and $60°$. This visually validates that the proposed double-shift quantization grid possesses sufficient resolution to counteract strong active interference without requiring high-precision hardware multipliers.

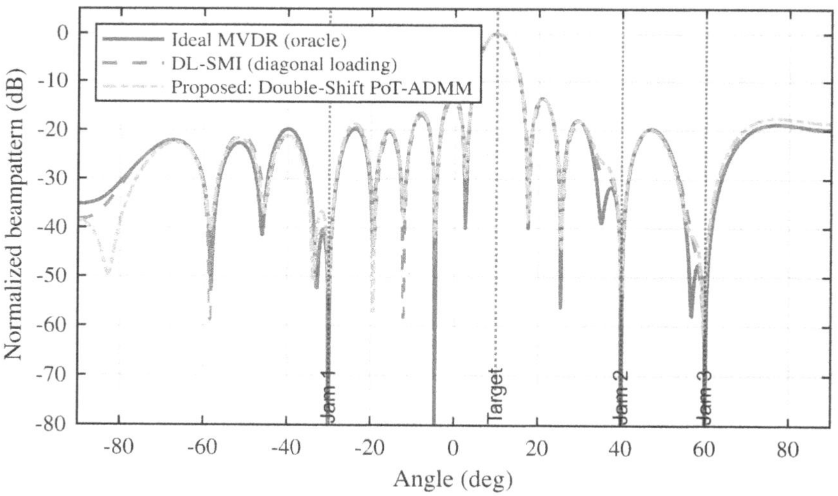

Fig. 1. Normalized beampattern comparison at input SNR = 0 dB. The proposed multiplier-free method successfully forms deep nulls at all three jammer directions, closely tracking the floating-point baseline.

5.2 Output SINR Performance

To rigorously quantify the interference suppression capability, Fig. 2 presents the average output Signal-to-Interference-plus-Noise Ratio (SINR) versus the input SNR, sweeping from -10 dB to 20 dB over 50 Monte-Carlo trials.

As observed, the proposed Double-Shift PoT method strictly tracks the performance curve of the conventional DL-SMI algorithm across the entire SNR regime. The performance penalty incurred by mapping the continuous optimal weights to the discrete double-shift hardware grid is negligibly small (typically less than 0.1 dB).

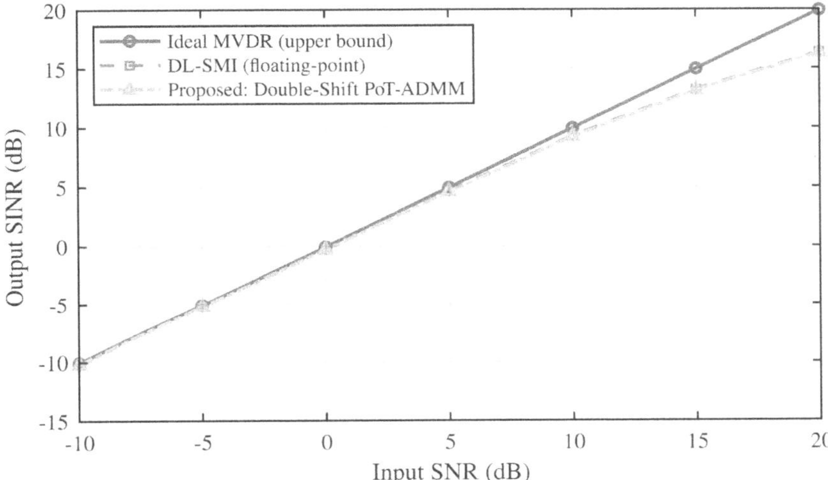

Fig. 2. Output SINR versus input SNR. The proposed discrete algorithm achieves near-identical performance to the continuous floating-point DL-SMI algorithm across the entire evaluated range.

Correlating these simulation results with the complexity analysis in Sect. 4, we conclude that the proposed method achieves an optimal algorithm-hardware co-design. It eradicates the $4N$ complex multipliers required in the high-speed real-time filtering datapath while maintaining a radar anti-jamming accuracy that is virtually indistinguishable from power-hungry 32-bit floating-point processing architectures.

6   Conclusion

In this paper, we addressed the critical challenge of deploying power-intensive robust adaptive beamforming algorithms on SWaP-constrained UAV swarm radars. To bridge the gap between algorithmic performance and hardware efficiency, we proposed a multiplier-free Double-Shift Power-of-Two (PoT) RABF algorithm optimized via the Alternating Direction Method of Multipliers (ADMM). By constraining the complex weights to a meticulously designed double-shift discrete dictionary, our method completely eliminates the need for expensive hardware multipliers in the high-speed real-time spatial filtering stage, replacing them exclusively with energy-efficient programmable bit-shifters and adders.

Extensive simulations demonstrate that the proposed algorithm preserves near-identical SINR performance under discrete coefficient constraints and UAV position perturbations. The main practical benefit established in this work is the elimination of multipliers in the high-speed filtering datapath; quantitative evaluation of FPGA resource usage, timing, and power will be carried out in future hardware implementation.

Disclosure of Interests. The authors declare that they have no competing interests.

References

1. Capon, J.: High-resolution frequency-wavenumber spectrum analysis. Proc. IEEE **57**(8), 1408–1418 (1969). https://doi.org/10.1109/PROC.1969.7278
2. Li, J., Stoica, P., Wang, Z.: On robust Capon beamforming and diagonal loading. IEEE Trans. Signal Process. **51**(7), 1702–1715 (2003). https://doi.org/10.1109/TSP.2003.812831
3. Vorobyov, S.A., Gershman, A.B., Luo, Z.-Q.: Robust adaptive beamforming using worst-case performance optimization: a solution to the signal mismatch problem. IEEE Trans. Signal Process. **51**(2), 313–324 (2003). https://doi.org/10.1109/TSP.2002.806865
4. Lorenz, R.G., Boyd, S.P.: Robust minimum variance beamforming. IEEE Trans. Signal Process. **53**(5), 1684–1696 (2005). https://doi.org/10.1109/TSP.2005.845436
5. Du, L., Li, J., Stoica, P.: Fully automatic computation of diagonal loading levels for robust adaptive beamforming. IEEE Trans. Aerosp. Electron. Syst. **46**(1), 449–458 (2010). https://doi.org/10.1109/TAES.2010.5417174
6. Gu, Y.J., Leshem, A.: Robust adaptive beamforming based on interference covariance matrix reconstruction and steering vector estimation. IEEE Trans. Signal Process. **60**(7), 3881–3885 (2012). https://doi.org/10.1109/TSP.2012.2194289
7. Boyd, S., Parikh, N., Chu, E., Peleato, B., Eckstein, J.: Distributed optimization and statistical learning via the alternating direction method of multipliers. Found. Trends Mach. Learn. **3**(1), 1–122 (2011). https://doi.org/10.1561/2200000016
8. Huang, H., So, H.C., Zoubir, A.M.: Sparse array beamformer design via ADMM. IEEE Trans. Signal Process. **71**, 3357–3372 (2023). https://doi.org/10.1109/TSP.2023.3315448
9. Yang, Y., Xu, X., Yang, H., Li, W.: Robust adaptive beamforming via covariance matrix reconstruction with diagonal loading on interference sources covariance matrix. Digit. Signal Process. **136**, 103977 (2023). https://doi.org/10.1016/j.dsp.2023.103977
10. Yang, Z., et al.: Beamforming for unmanned aerial vehicle swarm-based distributed radar array: theoretical analysis and engineering demonstration. IEEE Trans. Aerosp. Electron. Syst. **60**(6), 8976–8991 (2024). https://doi.org/10.1109/TAES.2024.3436546
11. Zhang, Y., Wang, G., Peng, S., Leng, Y., Wang, B.: Near-field beamforming method based on motion model analysis for UAVs communication. Digit. Signal Process. **149**, 104478 (2024). https://doi.org/10.1016/j.dsp.2024.104478

12. Ma, X., Jiang, S., Zhang, S., Zhang, R., Sheng, W.: Joint wideband beamforming algorithm for main lobe jamming suppression in distributed array radar. Remote Sens. **16**(13), 2402 (2024). https://doi.org/10.3390/rs16132402
13. Lim, J., Yoo, H., Lee, E., Oh, S., Lee, J.: Robust anti-jamming method for large-array radar systems using deep learning based null-space beamforming. IEEE Access **13**, 103599–103612 (2025). https://doi.org/10.1109/ACCESS.2025.3579422
14. Wang, Y., Zhu, L., Wu, T., Ma, S.: A reconfigurable digital beamformer implemented on a field-programmable gate array for real-time and resource-efficient direction-of-arrival estimation. Sensors **25**(8), 2497 (2025). https://doi.org/10.3390/s25082497
15. Kumm, M., Volkova, A., Filip, S.I.: Design of optimal multiplierless FIR filters with minimal number of adders. IEEE Trans. Comput. Aided Des. Integr. Circuits Syst. **42**(2), 658–671 (2023). https://doi.org/10.1109/TCAD.2022.3179221
16. Ariyarathna, V., et al.: A multibeam digital array receiver using a 16-point multiplierless DFT approximation. IEEE Trans. Antennas Propag. **67**(2), 925–933 (2019). https://doi.org/10.1109/TAP.2018.2882629
17. Madanayake, A., et al.: Towards a low-SWaP 1024-beam digital array: a 32-beam subsystem at 5.8 GHz. IEEE Trans. Antennas Propag. **68**(2), 900–912 (2020). https://doi.org/10.1109/TAP.2019.2938704
18. Mo, J., Heath, R.W.: Capacity analysis of one-bit quantized MIMO systems with transmitter channel state information. IEEE Trans. Signal Process. **63**(20), 5498–5512 (2015). https://doi.org/10.1109/TSP.2015.2455527
19. Portella, L., Bayer, F.M., Cintra, R.J.: Multiplierless DFT approximation based on the prime factor algorithm. IEEE Trans. Signal Process. **73**, 5273–5285 (2025). https://doi.org/10.1109/TSP.2025.3634427
20. AMD: UltraScale Architecture DSP Slice User Guide (UG579), version 1.11 (2021). https://docs.amd.com/v/u/en-US/ug579-ultrascale-dsp. Accessed 19 Mar 2026

Accelerating Physical AI
with Event-driven Reconfigurable
Hardware for Neuromorphic Perception

Neuromorphic Robot Controller on FPGA for Supporting SNN-Based Smooth Trajectories

Alejandro Linares-Barranco[✉][iD], Daniel Casanueva-Morato[iD],
Diogenes Trejos-Hernandez[iD], Daniel Cascado Caballero[iD],
Juan Pedro Domínguez Morales[iD], and Angel Jiménez-Fernández[iD]

Neuromorphic Engineering Group, Smart Computer Systems Research and
Engineering Lab (SCORE), I3US, EPS-ETSII, Universidad de Sevilla, Sevilla, Spain
alinares@atc.us.es

Abstract. This paper presents the development and implementation of a neuromorphic robot controller on a Field-Programmable Gate Array (FPGA) designed to support smooth, spiking neural network (SNN)-based trajectories. Utilizing the ED-Scorbot framework, the system controls a Scorbot ER-VII robotic arm with six degrees of freedom through an event-driven proportional-integral-derivative (SPID) architecture. Unlike traditional robotic control, this approach employs Pulse Frequency Modulation (PFM) to drive DC motors, mimicking biological motor neuron activation. The controller is synthesized within the Programmable Logic (PL) of a Xilinx Zynq 7100, while the Processing System (PS) manages configuration via MQTT protocols and remote connectivity. Our results demonstrate that the spike-based processing architecture is highly efficient, consuming only 4.8% of Slice LUTs and 2.0% of Slice Registers. With a total estimated on-chip power consumption of 2.045 W, the system proves to be a low-power, scalable solution for real-time neuro-inspired motor control in robots with multiple degrees of freedom.

Keywords: FPGA · MPSoC · Spiking PID control · DC-motors · neuromorphic engineering

1 Introduction

Neuromorphic robotics research is primarily conducted at the intersection of computer science, engineering, and neuroscience. The area is also referred to by several related terms, including biologically inspired robots, event-driven robots, brain-based devices, cognitive robots, neuromorphic engineering, and neurorobotics, among others. A commonly cited origin of this field is William Grey Walter's turtle robots from the 1950s [29,30], whose surprisingly complex actions emerged from a simple analog electronic "nervous system." Another key milestone was Braitenberg's Vehicles [2] that motivated many researchers to

G. Leone et al. (Eds.): ARC 2026, LNCS 16514, pp. 341–351, 2026.
https://doi.org/10.1007/978-3-032-29365-7_21

adopt what he called a "synthetic methodology" to investigate the integrated system of brain, body, and behavior. The synthetic methodology can be interpreted as "understanding by building," a particularly fitting guiding principle for neuromorphic and brain-based robotics.

The term robot was first introduced in 1921 in Karel Čapek's play R.U.R. (Rossum's Universal Robots) [5], during the Industrial Revolution, to describe machines intended to take over human tasks. The field of robotics advanced substantially over the twentieth century, particularly in industry, although the detailed imitation of human capabilities received comparatively little attention. In the present century, expectations for technological progress are even higher. Robots are now deployed in commercial, industrial, military, medical, and entertainment domains (e.g., robotic vacuum cleaners, robot soccer players, ground and aerial autonomous vehicles, and robotic surgical systems), significantly enhancing productivity.

However, despite improvements in powerful embedded processors, edge-AI devices, and low-power techniques, the behavior, intelligence, and energy efficiency of robots still fall far short of those of humans, animals, or even insects with nervous systems. Biological organisms thrive in dynamic environments, exhibiting flexibility, adaptability, and robust survival strategies unmatched by artificial systems. Neuromorphic robotics aims to investigate the foundations of biological intelligence by embedding models of neural systems into robotic platforms. Neuromorphic robots are physical devices whose control system has been modelled mimicking some key aspect of the biological neural system, such as its anthropomorphic architecture, its neuro-inspired motor control, its neuromorphic set of sensors, etc.

Neuromorphic robotics is grounded in embodied cognition, positing that intelligent behavior emerges from the dynamic interplay between the central nervous system, the physical body, and the environment [20]. While traditional neuroscience employs analytic techniques to study brain function, neuromorphic engineering utilizes a synthetic methodology. By constructing neurobiologically inspired robots, researchers establish empirical heuristics to understand how neural networks process sensations to govern motion and generate complex, adaptive behavior.

Reaching movements represent a primary focus within this domain [27]. In biological systems, the central nervous system (CNS) coordinates these actions via spike-based neuronal communication. The cerebral cortex processes sensorimotor information through a hierarchically organized architecture—comprising primary, secondary, and tertiary areas—that translates external stimuli into precise motor execution. This continuous sensorimotor loop operates across the spinal cord, brainstem, and motor cortex via a massively interconnected, feedback-driven network [13]. Current literature demonstrates the efficacy of neuro-inspired motor controllers in bridging biological adaptability and computational efficiency [1,15]. Implementations range from VLSI emulations of closed-loop spinal circuitry for antagonistic muscle control [22], to mobile robots leveraging quarter-million-neuron models for low-power sensorimotor learning

[9]. Further successful models include insect-inspired locomotion driven by Spiking Neural Network (SNN) Central Pattern Generators on SpiNNaker hardware [12], and maze navigation executed via organic neuromorphic circuits [19].

As the third generation of artificial intelligence, neuromorphic architectures provide a critical cognitive layer for modern robotics [26]. Nevertheless, optimizing spiking motor controllers to further reduce latency and power consumption remains an open research challenge. Over the past decade, several biologically inspired controllers, such as SECLOC [10], SPID [18], VITE-FLETE [3], and SVITE [24], have been successfully deployed.

This paper focuses on the FPGA implementation of the SPID for event-driven robotic arm control. Initially, the ED-Biorob [21] infrastructure demonstrated the application of the SPID to control multiple robotic joints via a neuromorphic approach, utilizing two Spartan FPGAs alongside a host computer for controller configuration and command generation. Subsequently, the SPID architecture was ported to the ED-Scorbot framework [11] utilizing a Zynq MPSoC [4]. In this integrated system, the requisite motor controllers were synthesized within the Programmable Logic (PL), while the configuration and remote connectivity protocols were executed on the Processing System (PS). The ED-Scorbot infrastructure has since been expanded to support interfacing with Spiking Neural Network (SNN) hardware accelerators, including SpiNNaker [6] and Dynap-SE [7]. The subsequent sections detail the FPGA logic architecture and present a comprehensive analysis of system latency and power consumption.

2   FPGA Architecture

The ED-Scorbot is a neuromorphic robotic arm composed of an FPGA-based board for spiking motor control, an electrical power stage that supports Pulse-Frequency-Modulation (PFM) to drive DC-motors, a Scorbot ER-VII (Fig. 1) with six degrees of freedom (DOF), six 12 V DC motors that, through transmissions, produce motion in the axes of its five rotary-type joints and open and close a gripper (sixth joint) [28]. Each motor is driven by an event-driven PID (SPID) controller [18], which uses PFM to supply power to the motors. Unlike Pulse Width Modulation (PWM), which is traditionally used in robotics, PFM replicates the operation of biological systems, in which muscles are activated by pulse bursts generated by motor neurons [4].

The predecessor implementation was done in the ED-BioRob [21], where the SPIDs were replicated and spread among two Spartan boards for controlling the robotic arms. The Spartan-6 1500 of the AER-Node board [14] had enough capacity for most of the logic, and a second board, based on a Spartan-3 400, and called AER-Scorbot [11] was connected to the AER-Node through two AER bus interfaces to expand the output spikes of the integrative plus derivative part of the controller, and to convert into spikes the output of the optical encoders. Therefore, the AER-Scorbot was directly connected to the DC-motors.

For the ED-Scorbot, that logic was integrated and improved into the PL of a Xilinx Mini-Module Plus 7Z100 module (Zynq) [25]. Since this robot did not include proprioceptive sensors, the only way to know the actual position of the joints is through the optical encoders. Therefore, to read the joint positions, the ED-Scorbot uses a 16-bit register for each joint. These registers are implemented in the PL of the Zynq, and their values increment or decrement (thus functioning as counters) depending on the signal coming from the incremental optical encoder of each joint. This information is transferred to the processing system (PS) of the Zynq via the AXI (Advanced eXtensible Interface) bus. The counters provide a feedback method, via the MQTT (Message Queuing Telemetry Transport) protocol running on the PS. The counter values are then published in an MQTT topic. A second MQTT topic is used to receive target positions for the joints. For further details, see the Py-EDScorbotTool website[1].

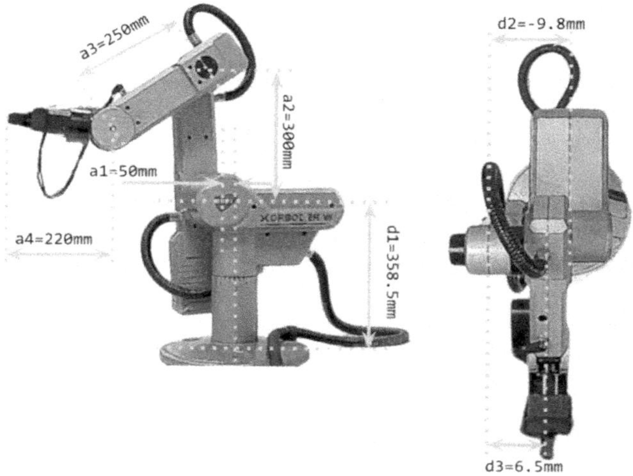

Fig. 1. Diagram of the Scorbot ER-VII. Top view (right). Side view (left). Adapted from [23].

2.1   Motor Controllers

Utilizing Pulse Frequency Modulation (PFM), the SPID processes sensory information and drives actuators entirely in the spike domain. While an earlier iteration was used to control the speed of mobile wheeled robots [17], this version is adapted to control the precise joint positions of an articulated robotic arm [21]. The system mirrors the classical S-domain PID formulation through specialized hardware modules known as Spike-Signal-Processing (SSP) blocks [16]. The foundational module is the Spike-Generator, which converts digital control

---

[1] https://py-edscorbottool.readthedocs.io/en/latest/index.html (Accessed on June 19, 2026).

values into PFM spike streams. Designed for efficient FPGA implementation, it uses an internal clock-driven counter and comparator to trigger spikes whenever the reverse-order bit value of the counter falls below the input. This algorithmic approach computationally guarantees a regularly spaced, near-uniform temporal distribution of spikes with a very low resource cost. The integrative term (K_i) of the PID is handled by the Integrate-And-Generate (I&G) Motor Neuron Model. It features an integrator counter that increments or decrements based on the polarity of incoming spikes, acting as a digital analog to a biological neuron's membrane potential. A connected generator then emits spikes proportional to this accumulated potential, producing the fast-firing rates typical of biological motoneurons. The integration constant (K_i) is mathematically defined by the counter size, the clock frequency, and a frequency divider. To calculate differences between spike streams, the system utilizes a Hold-And-Fire (H&F) block. This module waits for a spike, temporarily holding it until a second input arrives. If the two spikes share the same polarity, one is propagated; if they have opposite polarities, they cancel each other out, effectively yielding an output frequency that is the difference of the inputs. By establishing a closed loop between an H&F block and an I&G block, the system forms the Spike-Derivative module. This configuration outputs a rate representing the derivative of the input rate, fulfilling the K_d requirement of the PID equation. Lastly, the Spike-Expander functions as the proportional (K_p) component and serves as the final physical interface to the hardware. Because standard DC motors possess inherent inertia and act as low-pass filters, the single-clock-cycle spikes used for internal FPGA processing would be filtered out without generating any physical movement. The Spike-Expander stretches the duration of these narrow spikes, allowing them to exert actual mechanical force. The K_p gain is directly tied to the newly expanded spike width, the system's clock period, and the 12V motor power supply. Together, these interconnected SSP blocks form the full SPID speed controller. DC-motors are required to have an attached optical encoder, whose output is converted to spikes for every change in the output signal, to be used to calculate the error through an H&F block. To adapt an SPID to be used as a position controller for an articulated robotic arm, a second I&G block is added in the loop to convert the spiking signal obtained from the optical encoders from joint speed to joint position. By utilizing spike timing and frequency to power the arm's joints, it closely mimics how biological nervous systems actuate muscles, effectively translating sensorimotor spikes into 3D Cartesian coordinates for the robot's end-effector.

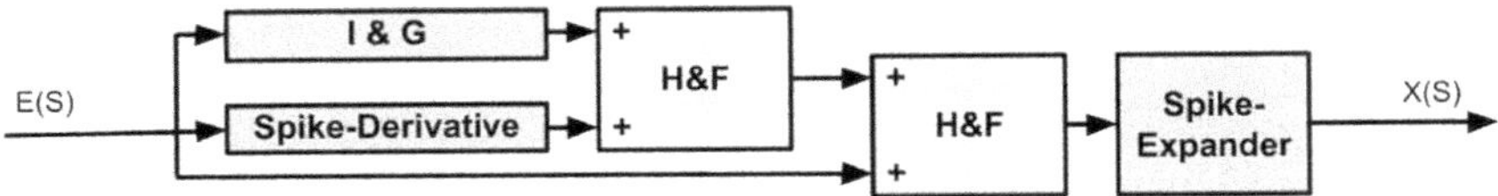

Fig. 2. Spiking PID controller.

Figure 2 shows the block diagram of the spiking PID controller with the described blocks. As it can be seen, the main difference with respect to the classic PID controller is that the proportional part (Spike-Expander) is not processed in parallel to the integrative and the derivative parts, but at the end of the process.

2.2 Zynq 7100 ED-Scorbot Controller

Figure 3 represents the architecture. The PS is running Petalinux 2016.4, which supports USB, UART, and Ethernet. The file system is stored on the external SD card. Through SSH, a user can access the system and deploy their own scripts to interact with the PL through the AXI bus. The functionality of each block is described next:

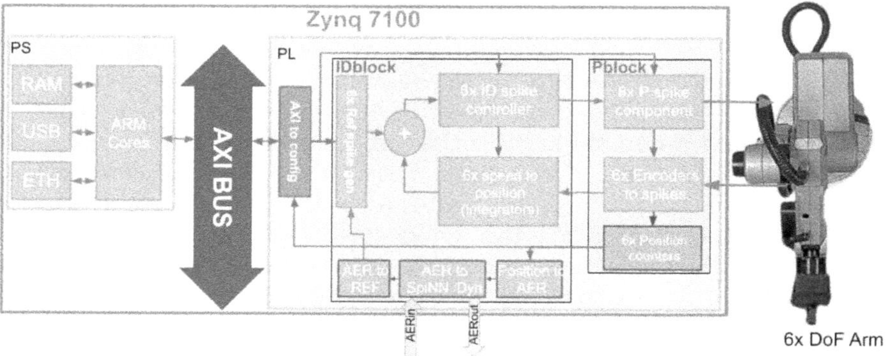

Fig. 3. Diagram of the SPID controllers for the Scorbot ER-VII on the Zynq FPGA.

a. AXI to Config. The different parameters to configure the functionality of the system are mapped in the memory of the PS. An AXI transfer is configured for the same memory address, 0x4000000 for a 32-bit data word. From this value, the LSB 24-bit are taken and sent to the two main internal blocks as an 8-bit address and a 16-bit data bus, together with a strobe signal, to write any of the 256 possible configuration registers spread into the system. This internal configuration bus (strobe, address and data) is represented in the figure with a green bus that reaches all the internal blocks.

b. Integrative-Derivative Block. This block ('IDblock' in the figure) not only implements the integrative and derivative part of the controllers, but it is also integrates other important functionalities: (1) the H&F block of the close-loop, (2) the I&G for converting the speed spiking signal into a position spiking signal to close the loop, (3) the generation/adaptation of the input spiking reference signal for each joint SPID, and (4) the interface for SpiNNaker and/or Dynap-SE chips.

The H&F block is represented in the figure with the '+' connector, while the I&G blocks for the speed to position conversion is represented with a square box connected to the '+' connector. The 'Ref spike gen' block is a spike generator that obtains a spiking signal from a digital number. This number can come from the AXI bus or it can come from the external neuromorphic chip through the 'AER to SpiNN/Dyn' block. Regarding the (4) functionality, its implementation depends on the external neuromorphic chip. The VHDL code for this block must translate the event's format of such external chip into plain AER with the classic handshake protocol, based on REQ and ACK signals. This AER protocol is also used internally to connect the 'IDblock' to the 'Pblock'. Depending on the meaning of the events coming from the neuromorphic chip, the 'AER to REF' block could be adapted to translate those events into the right reference for the 'Ref spike gen'. In the same way, the 'Position to AER' block translates the current position counters of the joints into events to be sent to the neuromorphic chip.

For example, for the control of a smooth trajectory implemented in SpiN-Naker with several SNNs working in that chip [8], it was required to provide the current status of the joints as a spiking signal whenever the position of each joint surpassed a configured degree angle step. Each joint operational workspace was divided into 16 sections; therefore, a new event was sent to SpiNNaker when the joint crossed from one section to the next. In the same way, when the SNN running at SpiNNaker decides that a particular joint has to move from its current position to the next one, an event is received from SpiNNaker that is converted into the corresponding spiking reference to move that joint to the next target angle.

Each 'ID spike controller' block represents the integrative and derivative part of the PID. The proportional part ('P spike component') is delegated to the 'Pblock' where the communication is based on AER buses.

c. Proportional Block. This block ('Pblock' in the figure) prepares the AER spiking Integrative-Derivative output signal, to be sent to the DC-motors, using the 'Spike-Expander' circuit. For each input event, a pulse with a configurable width is sent to the motor drivers. This configured width was provided through the 'AXI to config' block (green bus in the figure). Additionally, this 'Pblock' manages the optical encoders' output to be used in the control loop. For each change on the A or B channels of the encoder, an AER event is generated and sent to the 'IDblock' for the feedback control. These events provide a polarity that indicates whether the joint movement is clockwise or counterclockwise. Finally, with these events, a set of 16-bit counters are fed to provide a global position of the joints. These counters can be read, through the AXI bus, from the PS scripts using addresses from `0x4000001:6`, or converted to AER for the external neuromorphic chip by the 'IDblock' as mentioned in the previous paragraph.

3   Results

The system described in the previous section is coded in VHDL and synthesized and implemented on the AvNet MMP platform, based on the Zynq 7100, using Vivado 2022.1. Table 1 summarizes the required resources. The spike-based processing basically requires up-down counters and comparators of different resolutions. Since the configuration parameters are mapped into registers, there is no requirement for DSPs or block RAM memory unless an ILA is inserted into the design for debugging purposes. This low necessity of resources makes this neuromorphic controller viable for robots with many degrees of freedom, or multiple robots control with the same device.

Table 1. Resource consumption on Zynq 7100.

Resource	Max available	Consumed	Consumed (%)
Slice LUT	277,400	13,483	4.8
Slice Registers	554,800	11,190	2.0
LUT as Logic	277,400	12,821	4.6
LUT as Memory	108,200	662	0.6
Block RAM	755	0	0.0

Table 2 presents a list of internal parameters of our implementation in Vivado. After the implementation with PL clock frequency of 50 MHz, the Worst Negative Slack parameter was 1.47 ns. Regarding the power consumption, a total on-chip estimation of 2.04 W is estimated by Vivado with a switching rate of 50% and a junction temperature of 28.6 °C. This total power is divided into 1.8 W as dynamic power and 245 mW as static. From the dynamic power, 1.57 W are consumed by the PS and 232 mW by the PL, being 106 mW for the PLL, 63 mW for the clocks, 22 mW for I/Os and 39 mW for the logic and routing.

Table 2. Zynq implementation parameters.

Parameter	Value (units)
PS input F_{clk}	33.33 (MHz)
ARM F_{clk}	667 (MHz)
DDR3 F_{clk}	533.33 (MHz)
PL F_{clk}	50 (MHz)
WNS	1.46 (ns)
Max PL F_{clk}	53.95 (MHz)
Synthesis settings	Vivado defaults
Implementation settings	Vivado defaults

4   Conclusions

The implementation of the SPID controller on the Zynq 7100 platform demonstrates the viability of using synthetic methodologies to bridge the gap between biological adaptability and computational efficiency in robotics. By processing sensory information and driving actuators entirely in the spike domain, the system successfully emulates the sensorimotor loops found in biological organisms. The architecture proves to be highly resource-efficient, relying primarily on up-down counters and comparators with no requirement for DSPs or block RAM, which facilitates the control of multiple robots on a single device. Furthermore, the system exhibits a low-power profile, with the PL consuming only 232 mW of dynamic power, making it suitable for edge-AI applications. The framework's successful integration with advanced SNN hardware accelerators like SpiNNaker and Dynap-SE confirms its capacity for complex, closed-loop trajectory control. Future research will continue to optimize spiking motor controllers to further reduce latency and power consumption, addressing the remaining challenges in the field of neuromorphic robotics.

Acknowledgments. The Spanish Ministry partially supported this research for Digital Transformation and Public Function through grant USECHIP (TSI-069100-2023-001) of PERTE Chip Chair program, funded by European Union – Next Generation EU, by NEKOR (PID2023-149071NB-C54/AEI/10.13039/501100011033) and by PAIDI 2020 complementary action (QUAL21 008 USE) from Andalusian Council. D.E.T.-H. is supported by a SENACYT grant to study a PhD at the University of Seville.

Disclosure of Interests. The authors have no competing interests to declare that are relevant to the content of this article.

References

1. Bartolozzi, C., Indiveri, G., Donati, E.: Embodied neuromorphic intelligence. Nat. Commun. **13**(1024) (2022). https://doi.org/10.1038/s41467-022-28487-2
2. Braitenberg, V.: Vehicles: Experiments in Synthetic Psychology. MIT Press, Cambridge (1984)
3. Bullock, D., Grossberg, S.: Neural dynamics of planned arm movements: emergent invariants and speed-accuracy properties during trajectory formation. Psychol. Rev. **95**(1), 49 (1988)
4. Canas-Moreno, S., Piñero-Fuentes, E., Rios-Navarro, A., Cascado-Caballero, D., Perez-Peña, F., Linares-Barranco, A.: Towards neuromorphic FPGA-based infrastructures for a robotic arm. Auton. Robot. **47**(7), 947–961 (2023)
5. Čapek, K.: R.U.R. (Rossum's Universal Robots). Aventinum, Prague (1920)
6. Casanueva-Morato, D., et al.: Integrating a hippocampus memory model into a neuromorphic robotic-arm for trajectory navigation. In: 2024 IEEE International Symposium on Circuits and Systems (ISCAS), pp. 1–5. IEEE (2024)
7. Casanueva-Morato, D., Wu, C., Indiveri, G., Dominguez-Morales, J.P., Linares-Barranco, A.: Space-time smooth control of closed-loop neuromorphic robotic arms

using spiking neural networks. In: 2025 International Joint Conference on Neural Networks (IJCNN), pp. 1–9 (2025). https://doi.org/10.1109/IJCNN64981.2025.11228735

8. Casanueva-Morato, D., Wu, C., Indiveri, G., Linares-Barranco, A., Dominguez-Morales, J.P.: Toward a dynamic closed-loop neuromorphic trajectory interpolation model: hardware emulation and software simulation. IEEE Trans. Circuits Syst. II Express Briefs **72**(12), 1892–1896 (2025)

9. Conradt, J., Galluppi, F., Stewart, T.C.: Trainable sensorimotor mapping in a neuromorphic robot. Robot. Auton. Syst. **71**, 60–68 (2015). https://doi.org/10.1016/j.robot.2014.11.004. emerging Spatial Competences: From Machine Perception to Sensorimotor Intelligence

10. Daye, P., Ieng, S.H., Benosman, R.: A theory for sparse event-based closed loop control. Front. Neurosci. **13** (2019). https://doi.org/10.3389/fnins.2019.00827

11. Gomez-Rodriguez, F., et al.: ED-Scorbot: a robotic test-bed framework for FPGA-based neuromorphic systems. In: Proceedings of the IEEE RAS and EMBS International Conference on Biomedical Robotics and Biomechatronics, vol. 2016-July (2016). https://doi.org/10.1109/BIOROB.2016.7523630

12. Gutierrez-Galan, D., Dominguez-Morales, J.P., Perez-Peña, F., Jimenez-Fernandez, A., Linares-Barranco, A.: NeuroPod: a real-time neuromorphic spiking CPG applied to robotics. Neurocomputing **381**, 10–19 (2020). https://doi.org/10.1016/j.neucom.2019.11.007

13. Guyton, A.C., Hall, J.E., et al.: Textbook of Medical Physiology, vol. 548. Saunders Philadelphia (1986)

14. Iakymchuk, T., et al.: An AER handshake-less modular infrastructure PCB with x8 2.5Gbps LVDS serial links. In: 2014 IEEE International Symposium on Circuits and Systems (ISCAS), pp. 1556–1559 (2014). https://doi.org/10.1109/ISCAS.2014.6865445

15. Indiveri, G., Douglas, R.: Neuromorphic vision sensors. Science **288**(5469), 1189–1190 (2000). https://doi.org/10.1126/science.288.5469.1189

16. Jimenez-Fernandez, A., Linares-Barranco, A., Paz-Vicente, R., Jiménez, G., Civit, A.: Building blocks for spikes signals processing. In: The 2010 International Joint Conference on Neural Networks (IJCNN), pp. 1–8 (2010). https://doi.org/10.1109/IJCNN.2010.5596845

17. Jimenez-Fernandez, A., Paz-Vicente, R., Rivas, M., Linares-Barranco, A., Jimenez, G., Civit, A.: Aer-based robotic closed-loop control system. In: 2008 IEEE International Symposium on Circuits and Systems (ISCAS), pp. 1044–1047. IEEE (2008)

18. Jimenez-Fernandez, A., Jimenez-Moreno, G., Linares-Barranco, A., Dominguez-Morales, M.J., Paz-Vicente, R., Civit-Balcells, A.: A neuro-inspired spike-based PID motor controller for multi-motor robots with low cost FPGAs. Sensors **12**(4), 3831–3856 (2012). https://doi.org/10.3390/s120403831

19. Krauhausen, I., et al.: Organic neuromorphic electronics for sensorimotor integration and learning in robotics. Sci. Adv. **7**(50), eabl5068 (2021). https://doi.org/10.1126/sciadv.abl5068

20. Krichmar, J., Wagatsuma, H.: Neuromorphic and Brain-Based Robots. Cambridge University Press, Cambridge (2011)

21. Linares-Barranco, A., Perez-Peña, F., Jimenez-Fernandez, A., Chicca, E.: ED-BioRob: a neuromorphic robotic arm with FPGA-based infrastructure for bio-inspired spiking motor controllers. Front. Neurorobot. **14**, 590163 (2020)

22. Niu, C.M., Jalaleddini, K., Sohn, W.J., Rocamora, J., Sanger, T.D., Valero-Cuevas, F.J.: Neuromorphic meets neuromechanics, part i: the methodology and implementation. J. Neural Eng. **14**(2), 025001 (2017). https://doi.org/10.1088/1741-2552/aa593c
23. Ortner, T., et al.: Rapid learning with phase-change memory-based in-memory computing through learning-to-learn. Nat. Commun. **16**(1), 1243 (2025). https://doi.org/10.1038/s41467-025-56345-4
24. Perez-Peña, F., et al.: Neuro-inspired spike-based motion: rom dynamic vision sensor to robot motor open-loop control through Spike-VITE. Sensors **13**(11), 15805–15832 (2013). https://doi.org/10.3390/s131115805
25. Piñero-Fuentes, E., et al.: A hybrid neuromorphic robotic-arm lemniscate trajectories dataset for learning-based applications. In: 2024 31st IEEE International Conference on Electronics, Circuits and Systems (ICECS), pp. 1–4 (2024). https://doi.org/10.1109/ICECS61496.2024.10849213
26. Rast, A.D., et al.: Behavioral learning in a cognitive neuromorphic robot: An integrative approach. IEEE Trans. Neural Netw. Learn. Syst. **29**(12), 6132–6144 (2018). https://doi.org/10.1109/TNNLS.2018.2816518
27. Sherrington, C.: The Integrative Action of the Nervous System. CUP Archive (1952)
28. Trejos-Hernández, D., Cerezuela-Escudero, E., Linares-Barranco, A.: On the simulation of a neuromorphic robotic arm with dynamic control for rapid trajectories evaluation. In: Lecture Notes of the Institute for Computer Sciences, Social-Informatics and Telecommunications Engineering, LNICST 603 LNICST, pp. 221–238 (2025)
29. Walter, W.G.: An imitation of life. Sci. Am. **182**(5), 42–45 (1950)
30. Walter, W.G.: The Living Brain. W. W. Norton & Company (1953)

Collaborative Projects

Hierarchical Reconfiguration Across the Edge–Cloud Continuum: An Architectural Perspective from H2TRAIN

Paolo Azzoni[1], Marco Ottella[2], and Juan Antonio Montiel-Nelson[3]([✉])

[1] European Technology Program, Eurotech Group, Amaro, Italy
`paolo.azzoni@eurotech.com`
[2] Research and Innovation, Xtremion Technology, Velden, Austria
`marco.ottella@xtremion.com`
[3] Institute for Applied Microelectronics, University of Las Palmas de Gran Canaria, Las Palmas de Gran Canaria, Spain
`j.montiel-nelson@ulpgc.es`

Abstract. Applied Reconfigurable Computing (ARC) is evolving from kernel-level hardware acceleration toward distributed adaptability across heterogeneous infrastructures. Contemporary edge-centric systems operate under dynamic constraints of latency, energy variability, security, and scalability, requiring coordinated structural adaptation across sensing nodes, edge gateways, and cloud platforms. This paper presents the architectural framework developed within the H2TRAIN collaborative project as an implementation of hierarchical reconfiguration across the edge–cloud continuum. Although deployed in health-oriented scenarios, the architectural contribution is domain-agnostic and generalizable. The proposed architecture distributes configurable signal processing, adaptive AI execution, service-level redeployment, secure remote management, and multi-cloud orchestration across sensing subsystems, a programmable edge gateway, and cloud services. Reconfiguration occurs at hardware, runtime, and infrastructure levels, illustrating how reconfigurable computing extends beyond accelerator design and becomes a systemic property of distributed intelligent systems.

Keywords: Applied Reconfigurable Computing · Edge–Cloud Continuum · Edge AI · System-of-Systems · Distributed Reconfiguration

1 Introduction

Reconfigurable computing has traditionally focused on accelerating computational kernels through programmable logic and hardware specialization [1,2]. FPGA-based architectures have demonstrated substantial gains in throughput and energy efficiency for signal processing and machine learning workloads [4]. However, the decentralization of computation into edge environments introduces systemic requirements beyond the acceleration level of the device.

G. Leone et al. (Eds.): ARC 2026, LNCS 16514, pp. 355–364, 2026.
https://doi.org/10.1007/978-3-032-29365-7_22

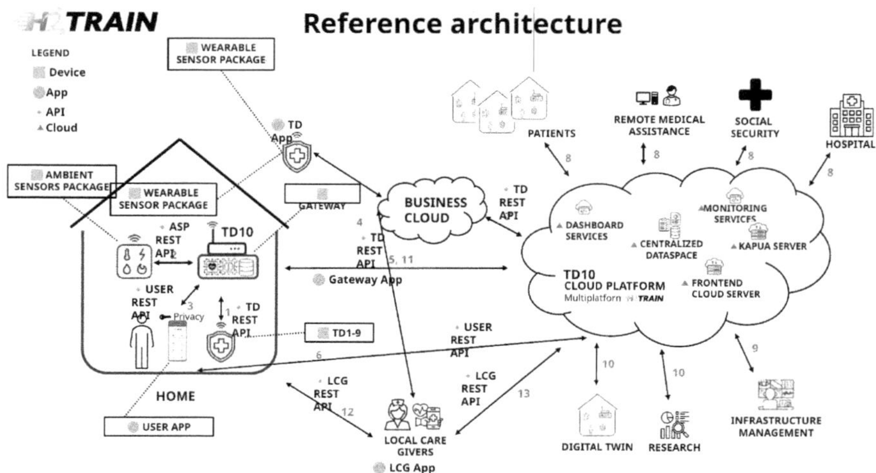

Fig. 1. Top-level H2TRAIN edge-to-cloud architecture, showing sensing packages, the edge multiservice gateway, and cloud-level services. The figure illustrates hierarchical reconfiguration across hardware, runtime, and orchestration domains.

Modern distributed systems must adapt dynamically to workload variability, fluctuating energy conditions, heterogeneous platforms, and evolving security requirements. Edge computing paradigms formalize this migration of intelligence towards distributed infrastructures [6,7]. Simultaneously, semiconductor initiatives such as the European Chips Act highlight the strategic relevance of advanced heterogeneous and reconfigurable architectures in critical infrastructures [10].

The H2TRAIN reference architecture defines a computational hierarchy composed of sensing subsystems, an edge multiservice gateway, and a multi-platform cloud infrastructure. Rather than forming a static processing chain, these layers operate as a coordinated reconfiguration topology. This work interprets such hierarchical adaptability as a continuum-oriented extension of Applied Reconfigurable Computing (Fig. 1).

2   Hierarchical Reconfiguration Across the Continuum

The architecture distributes computational, orchestration, and security capabilities across an edge-to-cloud hierarchy. Reconfiguration manifests itself at three levels: hardware adaptation, runtime service orchestration, and infrastructure coordination.

At the sensing layer, subsystems incorporate hardware abstraction modules and local processing units capable of selective activation of filtering, feature extraction, and lightweight inference tasks. Hardware/software partitioning allows latency-critical kernels to be migrated to configurable resources when necessary [2]. Event-driven execution reduces communication overhead and energy consumption.

The edge multiservice gateway functions as a programmable runtime fabric. It integrates message brokering, local databases, AI modules, secure services, and remote management clients. Services can be dynamically deployed, updated, suspended, or isolated. Runtime frameworks enable adaptive workload partitioning and precision scaling.

At the cloud layer, distributed storage and orchestration services close the adaptive loop. Model retraining, configuration updates, and workload redistribution strategies are propagated across the hierarchy [6]. Reconfiguration therefore extends vertically from logic resources to distributed policy enforcement mechanisms.

3   Energy-Aware Structural Adaptation

Energy variability at sensing and edge layers introduces dynamic power constraints. Energy-aware computing techniques emphasize adapting computational intensity to available power budgets [8]. Within the proposed architecture, selective deactivation of AI modules, reduction of inference precision, suspension of non-critical services, and frequency scaling are applied under constrained energy states.

4   Secure Distributed Reconfiguration

Security is embedded within the reconfiguration hierarchy. Hardware-assisted cryptographic primitives reduce computational overhead associated with encryption and authentication [9]. Dynamic service isolation and secure redeployment enable modification of execution topologies in response to policy updates or anomalies.

5   Architectural Generality

Although deployed in health-oriented scenarios, the structural properties of the architecture are independent of sensing modality or application semantics. The coordinated interaction between sensing subsystems, programmable edge gateways, and cloud orchestration services establishes a reusable framework for hierarchical distributed reconfiguration.

6   Use-Case-Driven Architectural Reconfiguration

The proposed architecture supports dynamic reconfiguration across the edge–cloud continuum, enabling adaptation to diverse operational scenarios. Rather than defining a fixed processing pipeline, the system allows the redistribution of computation, sensing, and communication functions according to application requirements and resource availability.

In low-latency monitoring scenarios, such as real-time physiological signal tracking, processing is shifted toward the sensing and edge layers. Lightweight inference models and event-driven processing are deployed locally to minimize communication delays and ensure timely response. In this configuration, cloud interaction is limited to periodic synchronization and metadata aggregation.

Conversely, in data-intensive or long-term analytics scenarios, computational workloads are migrated toward the cloud layer. High-capacity processing resources enable complex model execution, large-scale data aggregation, and cross-user analysis. The sensing and edge layers operate primarily as data acquisition and pre-processing units, reducing local computational load.

Energy-constrained deployments introduce an additional dimension of reconfiguration. Under limited energy availability, the system dynamically reduces sampling rates, simplifies inference models, and selectively activates sensing modalities. Edge services are minimized, and communication is restricted to essential data. When energy availability increases, dormant processing modules and sensing channels are reactivated, restoring full system functionality.

Infrastructure-rich environments enable the full activation of the architectural stack. In such configurations, sensing, edge, and cloud layers operate concurrently with high-resolution data acquisition, distributed inference, and continuous synchronization. Advanced services, including real-time analytics and remote orchestration, can be maintained without resource constraints.

These configuration profiles demonstrate that the architecture does not operate as a static deployment but as a dynamically adaptable system. From an Applied Reconfigurable Computing perspective, this behavior extends reconfiguration beyond hardware-level adaptation to coordinated system-level reconfiguration across heterogeneous and distributed computing layers.

6.1 Remote Assisted Living

In remote assisted living scenarios, the architecture is instantiated as a distributed system-of-systems integrating patients, local caregivers, healthcare institutions, and external service providers. The system combines wearable and ambient sensing packages with rehabilitation and monitoring devices, generating heterogeneous physiological and environmental data streams (Fig. 2).

At the sensing layer, embedded edge algorithms (e.g., TD10 modules) perform data interpretation, validation, and extraction of clinically relevant metrics directly at the device level. This local processing reduces communication overhead and supports early detection of relevant events. Data security is enforced through AES-256 encryption, ensuring secure transmission and compliance with healthcare data requirements. Notification mechanisms are also implemented at this level to support real-time feedback and alerting.

The edge multiservice gateway operates as a central coordination node, integrating sensing data and managing communication with local and remote enti-

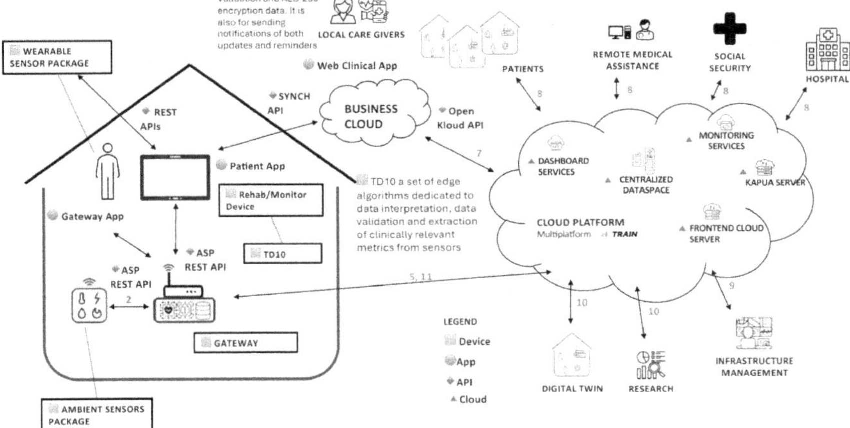

Fig. 2. UC1 Remote Assisted Living instantiation of the H2TRAIN architecture, illustrating system-of-systems integration across sensing, edge, and cloud layers, including external domains such as hospital, social security, and research services.

ties. It supports message brokering, local storage, and execution of intermediate analytics, while enabling interaction with local caregivers and remote medical assistance services. The gateway is managed through a dedicated platform layer, enabling remote configuration, service deployment, and lifecycle management of edge components.

At the cloud layer, the architecture extends into a multi-domain service ecosystem. Cloud services include centralized data spaces, monitoring services, digital twin representations, and dashboard-based visualization tools. These services enable healthcare professionals to access patient information in near real time and support decision-making processes. The system also interfaces with external domains, including hospital infrastructures, social security systems, research platforms, and business-oriented cloud services, forming a broader system-of-systems environment.

Interoperability across the architecture is achieved through standardized APIs, including REST-based interfaces and cloud integration layers, enabling synchronization between sensing, edge, and cloud components. This API-driven design supports flexible integration of services and dynamic reconfiguration of system functionality.

From an Applied Reconfigurable Computing perspective, this use case demonstrates multi-layer and multi-domain reconfiguration. Processing is distributed across sensing, edge, and cloud layers according to latency, energy, and application requirements. In addition, system-level reconfiguration extends across organizational domains, enabling dynamic adaptation of services, data flows, and orchestration policies. This configuration illustrates how the same

Table 1. Example configuration profiles across deployment scenarios

Scenario	Sensing	Edge	Cloud	Energy
Low-latency monitoring	High	High	Low	Medium
Long-term analytics	Medium	Low	High	High
Energy-constrained	Low	Low	Low	Low
Infrastructure-rich	High	High	High	High

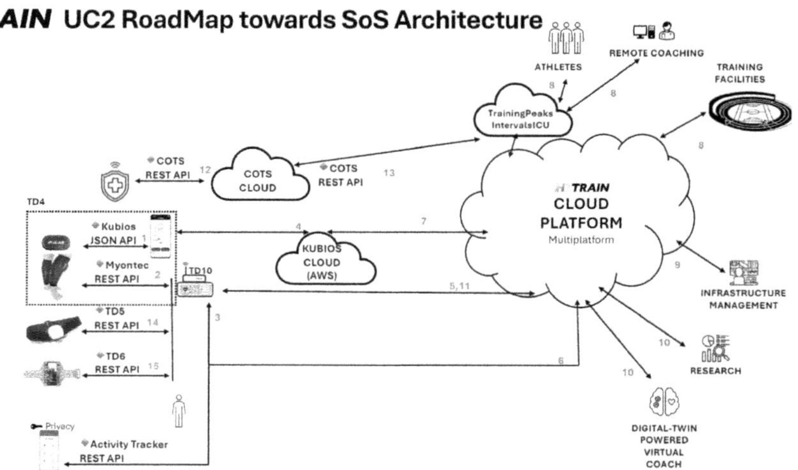

Fig. 3. UC2 Intelligent Sport Coaching instantiation of the H2TRAIN architecture, illustrating integration of wearable sensing, edge processing, cloud orchestration, and external coaching platforms within a system-of-systems environment.

architectural framework supports continuous, secure, and scalable monitoring through coordinated reconfiguration across both computational layers and system-of-systems boundaries (Table 1).

6.2 Intelligent Sport Coaching

In intelligent sport coaching scenarios, the architecture is configured to support real-time performance monitoring, adaptive training, and interaction between athletes, coaches, and cloud-based services. As illustrated in the UC2 system-of-systems architecture (Fig. 3), the system integrates multiple wearable sensing technologies, including inertial measurement units, heart rate and HRV sensors, electromyography, and biochemical sensing devices.

At the sensing layer, wearable devices perform continuous data acquisition and local pre-processing. Edge-level intelligence enables real-time feedback, including technique correction and workload estimation during training sessions, minimizing latency and dependence on remote infrastructure.

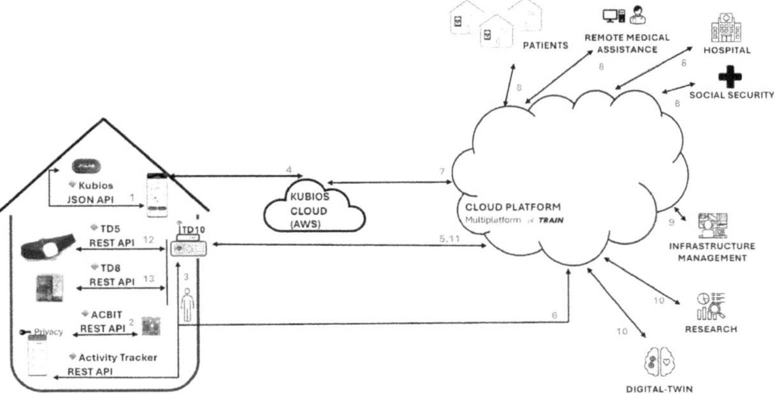

Fig. 4. UC3 Clinical Monitoring instantiation of the H2TRAIN architecture, illustrating integration of wearable sensing, edge–cloud processing, hospital systems, and healthcare ecosystem services within a system-of-systems environment.

The edge layer aggregates multi-sensor data streams and ensures synchronization across heterogeneous devices. Communication with higher layers is enabled through REST and JSON APIs, supporting interoperability and scalable integration. Edge services perform initial data fusion and filtering before transmission.

At the cloud layer, the H2TRAIN platform provides large-scale data aggregation, AI-driven analytics, and orchestration services. Models estimate performance, predict fatigue, and support adaptive training planning. Digital twin and virtual coaching services enable personalized recommendations and longitudinal tracking.

The system integrates training facilities, remote coaching environments, and research infrastructures into a unified system-of-systems framework. External platforms such as TrainingPeaks and IntervalsICU are connected via APIs, enabling extended functionality.

From an Applied Reconfigurable Computing perspective, this use case emphasizes edge-centric reconfiguration driven by real-time constraints. Tasks are dynamically distributed between sensing, edge, and cloud layers. The architecture adapts to variations in training conditions, sensor availability, and user requirements by reconfiguring processing pipelines, AI deployment, and communication patterns.

6.3   Clinical Monitoring

In clinical monitoring scenarios, the architecture is instantiated to support remote post-surgery supervision and rehabilitation monitoring, with strong requirements in terms of reliability, security, and regulatory compliance. As illustrated in the UC3 system-of-systems architecture (Fig. 4), the system integrates wearable sensing devices, healthcare infrastructure, and cloud-based clinical services into a unified and interoperable ecosystem.

At the sensing layer, wearable devices capture multimodal physiological and biochemical signals, including cardiovascular activity, motion, and disease-specific biomarkers. These devices are designed to operate in clinical and semi-controlled environments, ensuring high accuracy and robustness. Initial processing is performed locally to guarantee data integrity and enable early anomaly detection.

At the edge layer, processing units aggregate sensor data and perform intermediate analytics, including signal conditioning, feature extraction, and event detection. Edge nodes also enforce security mechanisms, such as data encryption and authentication, ensuring compliance with healthcare data protection requirements. Communication with higher layers is implemented through standardized REST and JSON APIs, enabling interoperability with medical platforms.

At the cloud layer, the H2TRAIN platform integrates advanced analytics, clinical dashboards, and digital twin services to support healthcare professionals. The architecture connects to hospital systems, social security infrastructures, and research platforms, enabling data sharing and coordinated care pathways. Cloud-based AI models support predictive monitoring, rehabilitation assessment, and clinical decision support.

The system extends across multiple domains, including hospitals, remote medical assistance services, and public healthcare infrastructures, forming a complex system-of-systems. Integration with external platforms such as Kubios Cloud and infrastructure management services enables scalable deployment and interoperability across healthcare ecosystems.

From an Applied Reconfigurable Computing perspective, this use case emphasizes reliability-aware and security-driven reconfiguration. Computational workloads are dynamically distributed across sensing, edge, and cloud layers, balancing latency, accuracy, and energy constraints. The architecture adapts to clinical conditions, patient-specific requirements, and regulatory constraints by reconfiguring data flows, AI models, and system interfaces. This results in a highly robust and compliant computational continuum tailored to healthcare applications.

6.4   Cross-Use-Case Reconfiguration Analysis

The three use cases demonstrate how the proposed architecture supports distinct reconfiguration profiles across application domains while preserving a common structural framework. In remote assisted living, computation is balanced across sensing, edge, and cloud layers, emphasizing continuous monitoring and system-of-systems integration. In intelligent sport coaching, the architecture shifts toward an edge-dominant configuration, prioritizing real-time feedback and low-latency processing directly at the sensing and edge layers. In clinical monitoring, reconfiguration is driven by reliability, security, and regulatory constraints, resulting in a more controlled distribution of computation and stricter data handling policies.

Across all scenarios, reconfiguration is not limited to hardware adaptation but extends to dynamic redistribution of computational workloads, activation of sensing and processing modules, and orchestration of services across heterogeneous domains. These variations illustrate that the same architectural framework can be instantiated into multiple operational configurations by adapting processing placement, communication patterns, and system interfaces.

From an Applied Reconfigurable Computing perspective, this cross-use-case analysis highlights reconfiguration as a system-level property of the edge–cloud continuum. The architecture enables coordinated adaptation across layers and domains, supporting diverse requirements ranging from real-time responsiveness to clinical reliability. This demonstrates that reconfigurable computing can be effectively extended beyond device-level mechanisms toward distributed and application-driven system reconfiguration.

7   Conclusion

This paper presented the H2TRAIN architectural framework as a concrete realization of hierarchical reconfiguration across the edge–cloud continuum. Moving beyond traditional interpretations of Applied Reconfigurable Computing centered on device-level acceleration, the proposed approach demonstrates how reconfiguration can be elevated to a coordinated, system-level capability spanning sensing subsystems, programmable edge gateways, and cloud orchestration infrastructures.

The proposed framework highlights a key shift in the role of reconfigurable computing within modern distributed systems. Rather than optimizing isolated computational kernels, reconfiguration becomes a mechanism for orchestrating system behavior across heterogeneous and geographically distributed resources. This enables the realization of scalable, energy-aware, and secure intelligent systems capable of continuous operation in dynamic environments.

Furthermore, the architecture demonstrates strong generality and transferability beyond the health domain. Its system-of-systems structure, API-driven interoperability, and layered reconfiguration model provide a reusable blueprint for a wide range of edge-centric applications, including smart environments, industrial monitoring, and cyber-physical systems. This reinforces the relevance of the approach in the context of emerging edge AI ecosystems and large-scale distributed infrastructures.

From a technological perspective, the integration of edge intelligence, secure communication, and cloud-based orchestration establishes a foundation for future adaptive systems capable of self-optimization. The ability to dynamically reconfigure sensing modalities, processing pipelines, and service deployment strategies opens the door to autonomous and context-aware operation.

Future work will focus on the formalization of reconfiguration policies and decision mechanisms, enabling automated adaptation based on system state and environmental conditions. In addition, the integration of learning-based optimization techniques and digital twin representations will be explored to enhance predictive capabilities and system robustness. Alignment with emerging interoperability standards and European initiatives in data spaces and semiconductor technologies will also be pursued to support large-scale deployment and ecosystem integration.

Overall, this work contributes to the evolution of Applied Reconfigurable Computing toward a holistic paradigm in which adaptability is not confined to hardware, but is embedded across the entire edge–cloud computing continuum as a fundamental property of distributed intelligent systems.

Acknowledgments. This work was funded by the H2TRAIN project, supported by the Chips Joint Undertaking (Grant Agreement No. 101140052) and its members, including top-up funding by the National Funding Agency for Austria, Business Finland, the Bundesministerium für Bildung und Forschung (Germany), the Ministry of Universities and Research (Italy), the Ministry of Enterprises and Made in Italy, the National Centre for Research and Innovation (Poland), the Ministry for Digital Transformation and the Civil Service (Spain), and the State Research Agency (Spain).

References

1. Compton, K., Hauck, S.: Reconfigurable computing: a survey of systems and software. ACM Comput. Surv. **34**(2), 171–210 (2002)
2. Tessier, R., Pocek, K., DeHon, A.: Reconfigurable computing architectures. Proc. IEEE **103**(3), 332–354 (2015)
3. DeHon, A.: The density advantage of configurable computing. Computer **33**(4), 41–49 (2000)
4. Cong, J., Xiao, B.: Minimizing computation in convolutional neural networks using FPGA-based acceleration. In: Proceedings of the ACM/SIGDA International Symposium on Field-Programmable Gate Arrays (FPGA), pp. 83–92 (2014)
5. Vaishnav, A., Pham, K.D., Koch, D.: A survey on FPGA virtualization. IEEE Access **6**, 64573–64594 (2018)
6. Shi, W., Cao, J., Zhang, Q., Li, Y., Xu, L.: Edge computing: vision and challenges. IEEE Internet Things J. **3**(5), 637–646 (2016)
7. Satyanarayanan, M.: The emergence of edge computing. Computer **50**(1), 30–39 (2017)
8. Mittal, S.: A survey of techniques for improving energy efficiency in embedded computing systems. Int. J. Comput. Aided Eng. Technol. **6**(4), 440–459 (2014)
9. Tehranipoor, M., Wang, C.: Introduction to Hardware Security and Trust. Springer, New York (2012)
10. European commission: proposal for a Regulation establishing a framework of measures for strengthening Europe's semiconductor ecosystem (European Chips Act). COM 46 Final (2022)

MYRTUS: A Preliminary Assessment of The Heterogeneous Computing Continuum Infrastructure

Juan Encinas[1], Francesco Ratto[2], Marco Fois[2], Alfonso Rodríguez[1], Veena Rao[3], Luca Castello[4], Maria Katiuscia Zedda[5], Claudio Rubattu[6(✉)], Andrés Otero[1], and Francesca Palumbo[2]

[1] Centro de Electrónica Industrial, Universidad Politécnica de Madrid, Madrid, Spain
{juan.encinas,alfonso.rodriguezm,joseandres.otero}@upm.es
[2] University of Cagliari, via Marengo 2, 09123 Cagliari, Italy
{marco.fois3,francesco.ratto,francesca.palumbo}@unica.it
[3] HIRO-MicroDataCenters B.V., Prinses Marijkekade 11, 2273AB Voorburg, The Netherlands
veena.rao@hiro-microdatacenters.nl
[4] ArubaKube Srl, C.so Francia 2 bis, 10143 Torino, Italy
luca.castello@staff.aruba.it
[5] Abinsula Srl, Viale Umberto I 28, 07100 Sassari, Italy
katiuscia.zedda@abinsula.com
[6] University of Sassari, Via Vienna 2, 07100 Sassari, Italy
crubattu@uniss.it

Abstract. The increasing diffusion of cyber-physical systems and Internet of Things applications demands computing infrastructures capable of handling large data volumes under strict latency, scalability, and energy constraints. Traditional cloud-centric approaches are often inadequate for such requirements, motivating the adoption of the computing continuum paradigm, which integrates edge, fog, and cloud resources. This paper presents a preliminary assessment of the MYRTUS project, a Horizon Europe initiative aimed at enabling seamless orchestration across heterogeneous computing infrastructures. The MYRTUS architecture combines a distributed infrastructure, an AI-driven orchestration engine, and a dedicated development environment to support adaptive applications. A demonstrator based on UAV navigation in GPS-denied environments is introduced to evaluate the infrastructure. The application distributes processing tasks across continuum layers, leveraging edge devices for real-time operations and cloud resources for intensive computation. Results highlight the potential of MYRTUS to support efficient, scalable, and energy-aware execution of complex distributed applications.

Keywords: Computing Continuum · Edge Computing · UAV Navigation · Container Orchestration · FPGA

G. Leone et al. (Eds.): ARC 2026, LNCS 16514, pp. 365–370, 2026.
https://doi.org/10.1007/978-3-032-29365-7_23

1   The MYRTUS Project

The growing deployment of cyber-physical systems (CPS) and Internet-of-Things (IoT) systems generates large volumes of data that require continuous processing with strict constraints on latency, scalability, energy efficiency, and privacy. Traditional centralized cloud computing often fails to meet these requirements, especially for real-time applications. As a result, research has moved toward the *computing continuum*, which integrates edge, fog, and cloud resources to dynamically distribute workloads. However, orchestrating such heterogeneous infrastructures remains challenging due to fragmentation, interoperability limitations, and diverse hardware and software platforms.

The MYRTUS project[1] (Multi-layer 360° dYnamic orchestration and interopeRable design environmenT for compute-continUum Systems) is a Horizon Europe initiative that aims to address these challenges by developing technologies that enable the seamless integration, orchestration, and design of distributed systems across the computing continuum [2]. The project aligns with the objectives of the European EUCloudEdgeIoT (EU-CEI) initiative, which promotes the development of interoperable and sovereign digital infrastructures that combine cloud, edge, and IoT technologies.

Beyond the integration of distributed computing resources, MYRTUS envisions the evolution of cyber-physical systems toward a *living dimension*, where digital and physical components continuously interact, adapt, and cooperate with human users. In such systems, distributed components are capable of learning from their environment, dynamically adapting their behavior, and coordinating with other agents in a decentralized manner. This vision requires infrastructures capable of supporting highly distributed, heterogeneous, and adaptive computing environments.

To realize this vision, the MYRTUS architecture is structured around three main technological pillars:

- *Computing Continuum Infrastructure*, which provides the underlying distributed infrastructure integrating heterogeneous computing resources across the edge–fog–cloud continuum.
- *MIRTO Cognitive Engine*, an AI-driven runtime orchestration framework responsible for dynamic workload distribution and system adaptation across infrastructure layers.
- *Design and Programming Environment (DPE)*, a development environment that supports the modeling, analysis, and deployment of distributed applications targeting heterogeneous continuum infrastructures.

Together, these pillars provide a comprehensive framework for the design, deployment, and management of distributed applications across heterogeneous infrastructures [1]. The project is currently in Month 27, midway through its second implementation phase.

---

[1] https://myrtus-project.eu/.

This presentation focuses on the MYRTUS reference architecture and introduces a preliminary demonstrator designed to assess the capabilities and potential of the infrastructure developed within the project.

2   Computing Continuum Infrastructure in MYRTUS

The MYRTUS infrastructure is organized as a layered architecture that integrates heterogeneous computing resources across three main levels: edge, fog, and cloud. These layers collectively form an *onion-like* computing continuum in which resources are composable and interconnected, enabling seamless execution of distributed computational workflows.

A key feature of the MYRTUS infrastructure is its ability to integrate heterogeneous computing resources. The system is designed to support a wide range of hardware platforms, including general-purpose processors, hardware accelerators, reconfigurable architectures, and specialized computing units. This heterogeneity enables the infrastructure to adapt to different performance and energy requirements. For instance, computationally intensive tasks can be assigned to high-performance cloud resources, while latency-sensitive operations can be executed at the edge. Additionally, hardware specialization allows certain workloads, such as artificial intelligence inference, to be executed efficiently using dedicated accelerators.

The infrastructure also supports a composable resource model, where computing nodes from different providers can be federated and orchestrated as part of a unified system. This approach improves flexibility and scalability while reducing dependency on specific vendors.

3   A Preliminary Demonstrator: Vision-Based Navigation in GPS-Denied Environments

This section describes an application developed to demonstrate how a realistic industrial scenario can exploit the capabilities of the MYRTUS cloudâĂŞedge computing continuum infrastructure. The selected use case focuses on the navigation of Unmanned Aerial Vehicles (UAVs) in GPS-denied environments.

Small UAV often need precise position updates in places with a lack of GPS satellite signals (i.e., along narrow streets with tall buildings, across valleys, or in areas with deliberate interference). In these scenarios, the ground becomes the only reliable reference: roads, roofs, and field boundaries form a stable visual aid that does not depend on external infrastructure. The challenge is to read that information quickly and reliably from a moving device with limited energy budgets and strict latency requirements.

A common approach to solving this problem relies on a downward-facing camera to provide a continuous stream of visual information, and feature extraction and matching algorithms to process that stream, identifying specific structures in the image that can be used to infer the UAV's position. The method is deliberately simple: convert each frame into a set of distinctive indicators (i.e., features),

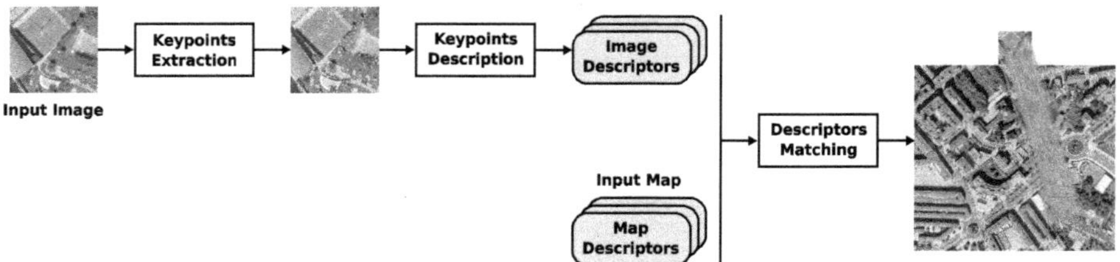

Fig. 1. UAV image-to-map matching pipeline (images from the real application).

search for those indicators on a prepared map, and deduce the position when a consistent set of correlations is detected. This approach, shown in Fig. 1, is both low-cost and scalable.

The processing pipeline associated with visual navigation typically includes three main stages: feature extraction, feature description, and feature matching. Feature extraction identifies distinctive keypoints in the captured image, such as corners or textured patterns. Feature description then generates compact numerical representations of these keypoints that capture the structure of their surrounding regions. Finally, feature matching compares descriptors between images to identify corresponding points and estimate the geometric relationship between them. Once a sufficient number of correspondences is identified, algorithms such as RANSAC can estimate the transformation between the images, allowing the UAV to determine its relative position within the environment.

This application represents an ideal candidate for deployment across the MYRTUS computing continuum. Certain stages of the processing pipeline, such as feature extraction and initial filtering, can be performed directly on edge devices integrated within the UAV platform. These edge implementations can leverage energy-efficient hardware accelerators such as FPGA-based architectures to achieve real-time performance while minimizing power consumption. Intermediate processing tasks can be offloaded to nearby fog nodes when additional computational resources are required, enabling collaborative processing across multiple nodes. Meanwhile, cloud resources can be used for large-scale data storage, map generation, and model training tasks that require significant computational power.

To do so, a feature-extraction and matching pipeline has been developed and evaluated using the two-cluster architecture developed according to the MYRTUS principles, and shown in Fig. 2. The experimental setup consists of two Kubernetes clusters connected via Liqo. Each cluster contains nodes corresponding to the three layers of the continuum: one cloud-layer node featuring a vast resource FPGA, one fog-layer node with moderate resources, and four edge-level nodes optimized for low-power operation.

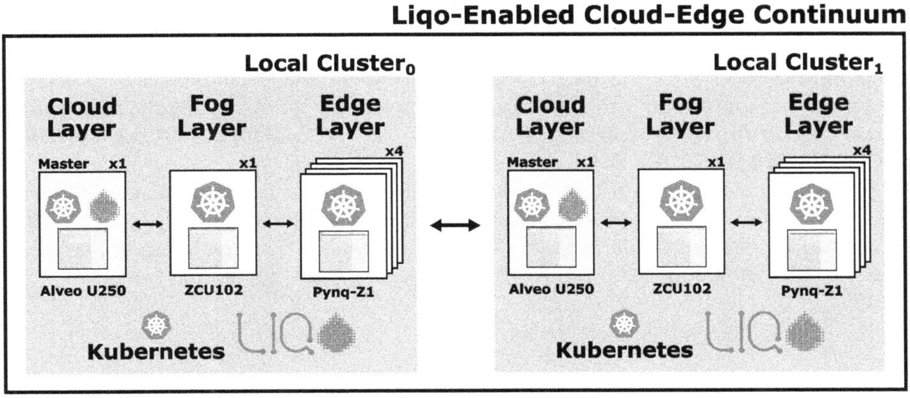

Liqo-Enabled Cloud-Edge Continuum

Local Cluster$_0$ **Local Cluster$_1$**

Cloud Layer   Fog Layer   Edge Layer   Cloud Layer   Fog Layer   Edge Layer

Master x1   x1   x4   Master x1   x1   x4

Alveo U250   ZCU102   Pynq-Z1   Alveo U250   ZCU102   Pynq-Z1

Kubernetes   LIQ   Kubernetes   LIQ

Fig. 2. Representation of the two-cluster architecture used for validation. The master nodes that run the Liqo processes are highlighted in green. (Color figure online)

4 Conclusions

By distributing computation across multiple layers of the infrastructure, MYRTUS enables efficient execution while respecting constraints related to latency, bandwidth, and energy consumption. The UAV use case illustrates how heterogeneous resources across the continuum can cooperate to support complex real-time applications. More broadly, this approach demonstrates how computing continuum infrastructures can support emerging intelligent systems that must operate across highly dynamic and resource-constrained environments.

The MYRTUS project represents an important step toward realizing a unified computing cohigh-capacity FPGA, one fog-layer node with moderate resources, and four edge-layerng heterogeneous hardware platforms, intelligent orchestration mechanisms, and advanced development tools, MYRTUS enables the deployment of distributed applications capable of adapting to changing conditions and resource availability. The vision-based UAV navigation use case highlights the practical benefits of this approach, illustrating how complex workloads can be distributed across multiple infrastructure layers to achieve both high performance and energy efficiency. The results of this work contribute to the broader European effort to build interoperable digital infrastructures capable of supporting next-generation cyber-physical systems and data-driven services.

Acknowledgments. The work has been conducted within the MYRTUS project, funded by the European Union, by grant No. 101135183. Views and opinions expressed are however those of the author(s) only and do not necessarily reflect those of the European Union. Neither the European Union nor the granting authority can be held responsible for them.

References

1. Palumbo, F., et al.: Multi-partner project: key enabling technologies for cognitive computing continuum - myrtus project perspective. In: 2025 Design, Automation and Test in Europe Conference (DATE), pp. 1–7 (2025). https://doi.org/10.23919/DATE64628.2025.10992704
2. Palumbo, F., et al.: MYRTUS: multi-layer 360°dYnamic orchestration and interoperable design environmentfor compute-continuum systems: invited Paper. In: 21st ACM International Conference on Computing Frontiers Workshops and Special Sessions (CF '24 Companion) (2024). https://doi.org/10.1145/3637543.36546

SIMON: Intelligent System for Automatic Selection of Machine Learning Algorithms in Social Sciences

Dijana Oreski[✉] [iD], Marija Pokos Lukinec [iD], and Dino Vlahek [iD]

Faculty of Organization and Informatics, University of Zagreb, Varazdin, Croatia
`dijana.oreski@foi.hr`

1 Introduction

The integration of machine learning (ML) within the social sciences has emerged as a transformative force, enabling researchers to uncover complex patterns and insights from vast datasets. However, the effectiveness of machine learning applications in this domain is heavily dependent on the selection of appropriate algorithms, a process that can be intricate due to the diversity of available algorithms and their varying performance across different contexts. This highlights the critical importance of algorithm selection, which can significantly influence the outcomes of social science research. In response to this challenge, we present idea of SIMON (Intelligent System for Automatic Selection of Machine Learning Algorithms), a novel system designed to streamline the algorithm selection process tailored specifically for social science applications. By leveraging advanced methodologies, SIMON aims to empower researchers to make informed decisions regarding algorithm choice, thereby enhancing the robustness and relevance of their findings. This paper explores the design and implications of the SIMON system, alongside a literature review that contextualizes existing methods and identifies the challenges faced in current algorithm selection approaches. Through this exploration, we aim to contribute to the ongoing research surrounding the intersection of machine learning and social sciences.

This paper is organized as follows. Section 2 presents literature review. Section 3 explains research methodology. Section 4 discusses SIMON project research results.

2 Related Work

The challenge of selecting the most appropriate machine learning algorithm for a given problem instance, known as the Algorithm Selection Problem (ASP), has gained increasing attention due to the vast variety of available algorithms and their varying performance across different datasets. Traditional manual trial-and-error approaches are costly and inefficient, prompting the development of automated, data-driven methods. Meta-learning has emerged as a prominent strategy, leveraging historical performance data and dataset characterizations- termed meta-features - to predict algorithm suitability without exhaustive experimentation [1, 2]. Meta-learning frameworks operate on two levels: the

G. Leone et al. (Eds.): ARC 2026, LNCS 16514, pp. 371–377, 2026.
https://doi.org/10.1007/978-3-032-29365-7_24

base level, where algorithms are trained on datasets, and the meta level, which learns the relationships between dataset properties and algorithm performance. Early approaches focused on simple statistical meta-features such as dataset size and class distribution, providing a basic but often insufficient characterization [3, 4]. Recent advancements have introduced sophisticated meta-feature designs that include topological landscape analysis and deep learning methods [5–7]. These approaches have expanded applicability to complex scenarios including mixed-variable and multi-objective optimization [8, 9]. Additionally, domain-specific meta-features have been developed for tasks like clustering, materials science, and time series classification, enhancing algorithm recommendation accuracy in specialized contexts [10, 11]. The choice of meta-model architecture critically influences selection performance. Traditional regression models like Random Forests and Support Vector Machines remain prevalent, but deep learning models, particularly convolutional neural networks trained directly on raw data, have shown promising results by eliminating the need for manual feature engineering [12].

Algorithm performance prediction often benefits from ranking formulations rather than direct regression, yielding higher correlation with true algorithm efficacy [13, 14]. Practical recommendation systems balance prediction accuracy with computational cost [25]. Real-world deployments in different fields exemplify the utility of meta-learning in reducing computational overhead and democratizing algorithm selection for non-expert users [15, 16]. Despite significant progress, challenges endure. Generalization beyond training distributions remains difficult, and the computational expense of meta-feature extraction can offset gains from algorithm selection [17–19]. Methodological issues in evaluation practices have been identified, underscoring the need for rigorous validation [20]. In conclusion, meta-models based on meta-features constitute a mature yet evolving approach to algorithm selection. Continued efforts to enhance meta-feature robustness, improve computational efficiency, and translate advances into accessible tools will be vital for advancing automated machine learning systems capable of broad and reliable application.

3   Research Methodology

SIMON project develops an intelligent system that recommends suitable machine learning algorithms for given datasets by leveraging a meta-learning framework grounded in explainable meta-models. The methodology consists of several key stages: dataset collection, meta-feature extraction and processing, meta-model development, and interpretability analysis.

3.1   Meta-feature Extraction and Transformation

A diverse repository of datasets compiled from two social science domains (education and business analytics). These datasets represent a variety of data characteristics, including size, feature types, and complexity, to ensure broad applicability of the recommendation system. Each dataset is preprocessed as necessary to standardize formats and handle missing values. From each dataset, a comprehensive set of meta-features is extracted to quantitatively describe its structural, statistical, and informational properties. These meta-features include:

- General characteristics (e.g., number of instances, number of features, ratio of categorical to numerical attributes)
- Statistical measures (e.g., mean, variance, skewness, kurtosis of features)
- Information-theoretic metrics (e.g., entropy, mutual information)
- Complexity indicators (e.g., feature correlations, class separability)
- Model-based descriptors (e.g., landmarking performance of simple classifiers)

To enhance interpretability and comparability across datasets, continuous meta-feature values will be discretized into ordered categories using quantile-based binning, creating ordinal bins that capture relative magnitudes while reducing scale effects.

To identify the most relevant dataset characteristics for algorithm recommendation, various feature selection methods will be explored. This includes evaluating mutual information scores to understand the dependency between meta-features and algorithm performance, as well as using rank correlation metrics like Kendall's tau to capture monotonic relationships with target outcomes. The goal is to select a robust subset of meta-features that balances informativeness with computational efficiency. This process will be iteratively refined based on the performance of different meta-model variants.

SIMON research results regarding meta-features have been published in [21–23].

3.2 Meta-model Development, Evaluation and Interpretation

Multiple meta-model architectures will be examined to develop diverse variants of the intelligent recommendation system, referred to as SIMON. These will include traditional machine learning algorithms (such as decision trees, support vector machines, and ensemble methods), decision-making frameworks (including multi-criteria decision analysis), and potentially hybrid approaches that combine interpretable scoring with data-driven learning. Each meta-model will utilize the selected meta-features as inputs to estimate the suitability of candidate machine learning algorithms for a given dataset. The system will compare the predictive performance, interpretability, and computational demands of these variants, aiming to identify configurations that optimally balance accuracy with transparency. This comparative approach will enable the development of SIMON versions tailored to different use cases, user expertise levels, and domain requirements, offering flexibility in how recommendations are generated and explained.

To ensure the interpretability of the meta-models, sensitivity analysis techniques will be applied to assess how changes in input meta-features impact recommendation outcomes. This includes systematically varying or removing individual meta-features and observing the resulting effect on model predictions and performance metrics.Such analyses provide insight into which dataset characteristics most strongly influence algorithm selection decisions across different meta-model variants. By understanding the dependencies and robustness of the recommendation system, the approach enhances transparency and supports user trust. In addition, explanations will be generated to communicate these influences in an accessible manner, helping users grasp the rationale behind recommendations regardless of their technical background.

SIMON research results regarding meta-features have been published in [24–26].

4   SIMON Project Results

4.1   Project Goals

The SIMON project aims to address this challenge by developing an adaptive intelligent system for ML algorithm selection based on meta-learning. The central idea is to leverage knowledge derived from previously analysed datasets in order to recommend suitable algorithms for new analytical tasks. The project achieved following objectives. First, it constructed a large repository of datasets originating from educational and business systems, representing diverse real-world scenarios from social sciences. Second, the meta-features that describe structural and statistical characteristics of datasets were extracted (116 meta-features for each dataset). Third, the project developed meta-learning models capable of predicting suitable ML algorithms based on these dataset characteristics. Finally, the project implemented a recommender system that provides interpretable algorithm recommendations to support analysts who work with data but may not possess deep expertise in ML.

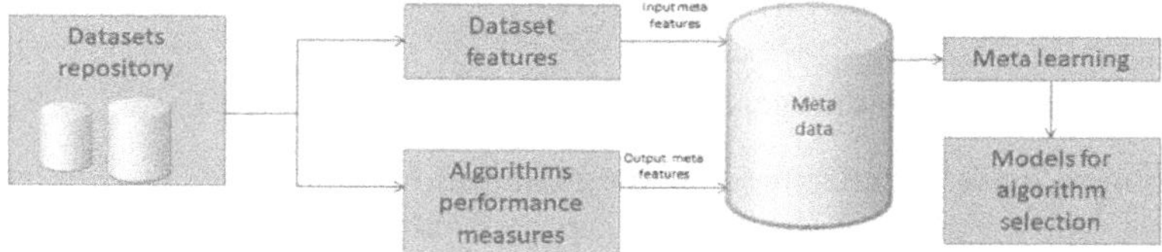

Fig. 1. Architecture of the SIMON intelligent system

Figure 1 shows SIMON system architecture. Instead of manually selecting algorithms, the system leverages accumulated knowledge from previous experiments to recommend suitable algorithm configurations for new datasets.

4.2   Recent Achievements

First SIMON achievement refers to structured dataset repository containing more than 100 datasets collected from educational and business domains. These datasets represent a variety of analytical tasks and provide a valuable empirical basis for studying algorithm performance across different problem contexts. For each dataset, a comprehensive set of meta-features has been computed. Based on this repository, the project developed meta-models that recommend suitable ML algorithms for new datasets. The resulting system functions as an adaptive recommender system for data analysis, suggesting algorithms that are expected to achieve strong predictive performance given the characteristics of the dataset.

The project also explored the potential role of recent advances in generative AI. Since the rapid development of large language models (LLMs) occurred after the initial project proposal, the research team conducted experiments comparing traditional meta-learning approaches with LLM-based reasoning strategies for algorithm recommendation based on dataset descriptions.

Another important research direction within the project focuses on explainable artificial intelligence (XAI). Because algorithm recommendations influence analytical decisions, interpretability and transparency are essential. The project therefore investigates interpretable meta-models and explanation mechanisms that allow users to understand the reasoning behind algorithm recommendations.

In parallel, the project has produced research contributions related to AI literacy, recognising that effective adoption of AI tools requires users to understand their capabilities and limitations.

4.3 Lessons Learned

The research conducted within SIMON has produced several important insights: (i) dataset characteristics play a decisive role in algorithm performance, (ii) interpretability is essential for recommendation systems used in analytical workflows, (iii) emergence of generative AI technologies introduces new possibilities for supporting data analysis tasks. Initial experiments suggest that LLM-based approaches can assist in reasoning about algorithm suitability, although data-driven meta-learning models remain important for capturing empirical performance patterns.

The SIMON project started in 2021 and finishes in April 2026. The project is funded by Croatian Science Foundation and conducted at the University of Zagreb, Faculty of Organization and Informatics integrating expertise in AI, ML and social sciences.

Acknowledgments. This work has been fully supported by the Croatian Science Foundation under the project UIP-2020-02-6312.

References

1. Palumbo, G., Carneiro, D., Guimarães, M., Alves, V., Novais, P.: Algorithm recommendation and performance prediction using meta-learning. Int. J. Neural Syst. (2022)
2. Kerschke, P., Trautmann, H.: Automated algorithm selection on continuous black-box problems by combining exploratory landscape analysis and machine learning. Evol. Comput. (2017)
3. Cenikj, G., Nikolikj., Petelin, G., van Stein, N., Doerr, C., Eftimov, T.: A survey of meta-features used for automated selection of algorithms for black-box single-objective continuous optimization. arXiv.org (2024)
4. Pimentel, B.A., Carvalho, A.: Statistical versus distance-based meta-features for clustering algorithm recommendation using meta-learning. In: IEEE International Joint Conference on Neural Network (2018)
5. Petelin, G., Cenikj, G., Eftimov, T.: TLA: topological landscape analysis for single-objective continuous optimization problem instances. In: IEEE Symposium Series on Computational Intelligence (2022)
6. van Stein, N., Long, F.X., Frenzel, M., Krause, P., Gitterle, M., Bäck, T.H.W.: DoE2Vec: deep-learning based features for exploratory landscape analysis. In: GECCO Companion (2023)
7. Seiler, M., Kerschke, P., Trautmann, H.: Deep-ELA: deep exploratory landscape analysis with self-supervised pretrained transformers for single- and multi-objective continuous optimization problems. Evol. Comput. (2024)

8. Dietrich, K., Prager, R.P., Doerr, C., Trautmann, H.: Hybridizing target- and SHAP-encoded features for algorithm selection in mixed-variable black-box optimization. In: Parallel Problem Solving from Nature (2024)
9. Preuß, O., Rook, J.G., Bossek, J., Trautmann, H.: MO-ELA: rigorously expanding exploratory landscape features for automated algorithm selection in continuous multi-objective optimisation. arXiv.org (2026)
10. Pimentel, B.A., Carvalho, A.: A new data characterization for selecting clustering algorithms using meta-learning. Inf. Sci. (2019)
11. Mu, T., et al.: TSC-AutoML: meta-learning for automatic time series classification algorithm selection. In: IEEE International Conference on Data Engineering (2023)
12. Maldonado, S., Vairetti, C., Figueroa, I.: One-step learning algorithm selection for classification via convolutional neural networks. Inf. Sci. (2023)
13. Corona, J., Teixeira, R.G., Antunes, M., Aguiar, R.L.: Modeling and predicting machine learning performance. In: IEEE International Conference on Tools with Artificial Intelligence (2025)
14. Wegmeth, L., Vente, T., Beel, J.: Recommender systems algorithm selection for ranking prediction on implicit feedback datasets. In: ACM Conference on Recommender Systems (2024)
15. Liu, Y., Wang, S., Yang, Z., Avdeev, M., Shi, S.: Auto-MatRegressor: liberating machine learning alchemists. Sci. Bull. (2023)
16. Smetanin, A., Dukhanov, A., Gerasimchuk, M., Gudov, E.: Development of an algorithm for formulating recommendations for the selection of object detection models based on data meta-features and an experimental knowledge base. Sci. Tech. J. Inf. Technol., Mech. Opt. (2026)
17. Petelin, G., Cenikj, G.: How far out of distribution can we go with ELA features and still be able to rank algorithms? In: IEEE Symposium Series on Computational Intelligence (2023)
18. Cenikj, G., Petelin, G., Seiler, M., Cenikj, N., Eftimov, T.: Landscape features in single-objective continuous optimization: have we hit a wall in algorithm selection generalization? Swarm Evol. Comput. (2025)
19. Nikolikj, A., Trajanov, R., Cenikj, G., Korošec, P., Eftimov, T.: Identifying minimal set of exploratory landscape analysis features for reliable algorithm performance prediction. In: IEEE Congress on Evolutionary Computation (2022)
20. Petelin, G., Cenikj, G.: The pitfalls of benchmarking in algorithm selection: what we are getting wrong. In: Annual Conference on Genetic and Evolutionary Computation (2025)
21. Oreški, D., Pihir, I.: Data understanding and preparation in business domain: importance of meta-features characterization. In: AIP Conference Proceedings, vol. 2919, no. 1, p. 090012 (2024)
22. Oreški, D., Višnjić, D., Kadoić, N.: Unlocking automated machine learning efficiency: meta-learning dynamics in social sciences for education and business data. In: UIKTEN - Association for Information Communication Technology Education and Science
23. Oreški, D., Višnjić, D., Kadoić, N.: Discretization of numerical meta-features into categorical: analysis of educational and business data sets. In: 2022 45th Jubilee International Convention on Information, Communication and Electronic Technology (MIPRO), Opatija, Croatia, pp. 1179–1184 (2022). https://doi.org/10.23919/MIPRO55190.2022.9803574
24. Oreški, D., Pihir, I., Višnjiů, D.: Comparative analysis of machine learning algorithms on data sets of different characteristics for digital transformation. In: 2023 46th MIPRO ICT and Electronics Convention (MIPRO), Opatija, Croatia, pp. 1428–1433 (2023). https://doi.org/10.23919/MIPRO57284.2023.10159910

25. Pilosta, B., Oreški, D., Kadoić, N.: Comparison of artificial neural networks algorithms on datasets with different characteristics. In: Arai, K. (ed.) Intelligent Systems and Applications, Lecture Notes in Networks and Systems, vol. 822. Springer, Cham (2024). https://doi.org/10.1007/978-3-031-47721-8_25
26. Oreški, D., Pokos Lukinec, M., Vlahek, D.: Meta-model for recommendation of machine learning algorithm in education. Int. J.Cross-Disc. Subj. Educ. **16**(2) (2025)

Author Index

GPSR Compliance
The European Union's (EU) General Product Safety Regulation (GPSR) is a set
of rules that requires consumer products to be safe and our obligations to
ensure this.

If you have any concerns about our products, you can contact us on

ProductSafety@springernature.com

In case Publisher is established outside the EU, the EU authorized
representative is:

Springer Nature Customer Service Center GmbH
Europaplatz 3
69115 Heidelberg, Germany